CW00348808

Navigating Cyber Threats and Cybersecurity in the Logistics Industry

Noor Zaman Jhanjhi
School of Computing Science, Taylor's University, Malaysia

Imdad Ali Shah
School of Computing Science, Taylor's University, Malaysia

A volume in the Advances in Information Security, Privacy, and Ethics (AISPE) Book Series

Published in the United States of America by
IGI Global
Information Science Reference (an imprint of IGI Global)
701 E. Chocolate Avenue
Hershey PA, USA 17033
Tel: 717-533-8845
Fax: 717-533-8661
E-mail: cust@igi-global.com
Web site: http://www.igi-global.com

Library of Congress Cataloging-in-Publication Data

CIP Data in progress

Title: Navigating Cyber Threats and Cybersecurity in the Logistics Industry

ISBN: 9798369338162

British Cataloguing in Publication Data
A Cataloguing in Publication record for this book is available from the British Library.

For electronic access to this publication, please contact: eresources@igi-global.com.

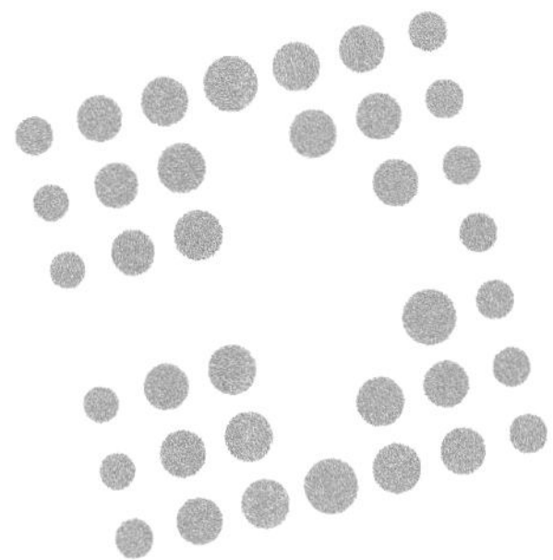

Advances in Information Security, Privacy, and Ethics (AISPE) Book Series

ISSN:1948-9730
EISSN:1948-9749

Editor-in-Chief: Manish Gupta, State University of New York, USA

MISSION

As digital technologies become more pervasive in everyday life and the Internet is utilized in ever increasing ways by both private and public entities, concern over digital threats becomes more prevalent.

The **Advances in Information Security, Privacy, & Ethics (AISPE) Book Series** provides cutting-edge research on the protection and misuse of information and technology across various industries and settings. Comprised of scholarly research on topics such as identity management, cryptography, system security, authentication, and data protection, this book series is ideal for reference by IT professionals, academicians, and upper-level students.

COVERAGE

- Security Information Management
- Computer ethics
- Information Security Standards
- Telecommunications Regulations
- Risk Management
- Electronic Mail Security
- Data Storage of Minors
- Network Security Services
- Access Control
- Global Privacy Concerns

IGI Global is currently accepting manuscripts for publication within this series. To submit a proposal for a volume in this series, please contact our Acquisition Editors at Acquisitions@igi-global.com or visit: http://www.igi-global.com/publish/.

The Advances in Information Security, Privacy, and Ethics (AISPE) Book Series (ISSN 1948-9730) is published by IGI Global, 701 E. Chocolate Avenue, Hershey, PA 17033-1240, USA, www.igi-global.com. This series is composed of titles available for purchase individually; each title is edited to be contextually exclusive from any other title within the series. For pricing and ordering information please visit http://www.igi-global.com/book-series/advances-information-security-privacy-ethics/37157. Postmaster: Send all address changes to above address.

Titles in this Series

For a list of additional titles in this series, please visit:
http://www.igi-global.com/book-series/advances-information-security-privacy-ethics/37157

Cybersecurity Issues and Challenges in the Drone Industry
Imdad Ali Shah (School of Computing Science and Engineering, Taylor's University, Malaysia) and Noor Zaman Jhanjhi (School of Computing Science and Engineering SCE, Taylor's University, Malaysia)
Information Science Reference • copyright 2024 • 300pp • H/C (ISBN: 9798369307748) • US $275.00 (our price)

Analyzing and Mitigating Security Risks in Cloud Computing
Pawan Kumar Goel (Raj Kumar Goel Institute of Technology, India) Hari Mohan Pandey (Bournemouth University, UK) Amit Singhal (Raj Kumar Goel Institute of Technology, India) and Sanyam Agarwal (ACE Group of Colleges, India)
Engineering Science Reference • copyright 2024 • 320pp • H/C (ISBN: 9798369332498) • US $290.00 (our price)

Emerging Technologies and Security in Cloud Computing
D. Lakshmi (VIT Bhopal University, India) and Amit Kumar Tyagi (National Institute of Fashion Technology, New Delhi, India)
Information Science Reference • copyright 2024 • 400pp • H/C (ISBN: 9798369320815) • US $315.00 (our price)

Risk Detection and Cyber Security for the Success of Contemporary Computing
Raghvendra Kumar (GIET University, India) and Prasant Kumar Pattnaik (KIIT Univeristy, India)
Information Science Reference • copyright 2023 • 480pp • H/C (ISBN: 9781668493175) • US $225.00 (our price)

Privacy Preservation and Secured Data Storage in Cloud Computing
Lakshmi D. (VIT Bhopal University, India) and Amit Kumar Tyagi (National Institute of Fashion Technology, New Delhi, India)

For an entire list of titles in this series, please visit:
http://www.igi-global.com/book-series/advances-information-security-privacy-ethics/37157

701 East Chocolate Avenue, Hershey, PA 17033, USA
Tel: 717-533-8845 x100 • Fax: 717-533-8661
E-Mail: cust@igi-global.com • www.igi-global.com

Table of Contents

Preface xiv

Chapter 1
Cybersecurity Measures for Logistics Industry 1
Siva Raja Sindiramutty, Taylor's University, Malaysia
Noor Zaman Jhanjhi, Taylor's University, Malaysia
Chong Eng Tan, Universiti Malaysia Sarawak, Malaysia
Navid Ali Khan, Taylor's University, Malaysia
Bhavin Shah, Lok Jagruti University, India
Amaranadha Reddy Manchuri, Kyungpook National University, South Korea

Chapter 2
Supply Chain Management Security Issues and Challenges in the Context of AI Applications 59
Imdad Ali Shah, School of Computing Science, Taylor's University, Malaysia
Raja Kumar Murugesan, School of Computer Science, Taylor's University, Malaysia
Samina Rajper, Shah Abdul Latif University, Khairpur, Pakistan

Chapter 3
Sustainable Computing-Based Simulation of Intelligent Border Surveillance Using Mobile WSN 90
Rana Muhammad Amir Latif, Center for Modern Chinese City Studies, Institute of Urban Development, East China Normal University, Shanghai, China
Muhammad Farhan, Department of Computer Science, COMSATS University Islamabad, Sahiwal, Pakistan
Navid Ali Khan, Taylor's University, Malaysia
R. Sujatha, School of Information Technology and Engineering, Vellore Institute of Technology, India

Chapter 4
The Internet of Things (IoT) Is Revolutionizing Inventory Management..........123
Imdad Ali Shah, School of Computing Science, Taylor's University, Malaysia
Areesha Sial, Mehran University of Engineering and Technology, Pakistan
Sarfraz Brohi, University of the West of England, UK

Chapter 5
Perspectives, Applications, Challenges, and Future Trends of IoT-Based Logistics..........148
Kassim Kalinaki, Islamic University in Uganda, Uganda
Wasswa Shafik, Ndejje University, Uganda
Sarah Namuwaya, Public Procurement and Disposal of Public Assets, Uganda
Sumaya Namuwaya, Absa Bank Uganda Limited, Uganda

Chapter 6
Logistics With the Internet of Things: Challenges, Perspectives, and Applications..........172
Imdad Ali Shah, School of Computing Science, Taylor's University, Malaysia
N. Z. Jhanjhi, School of Computing Science, Taylor's University, Malaysia
Humaira Ashraf, School of Computing Science, Taylor's University, Malaysia

Chapter 7
Blockchain-Based Authentication for the Internet of Vehicles (BBA-IoV) 196
Rida Zehra, University of the West of England, UK

Chapter 8
Logistics Industry in the Context of the Blockchain Technology......................214
Imdad Ali Shah, School of Computing Science, Taylor's University, Malaysia
Areeba Laraib, Mehran University of Engineering and Technology, Pakistan
Fida Hussain, Shaheed Benazir Bhutto Dewan University, Pakistan

Chapter 9
A Comprehensive Exploration of DDoS Attacks and Cybersecurity Imperatives in the Digital Age..........236
Humaira Ashraf, Taylor's University, Malaysia
Noor Zaman Jhanjhi, Taylor's University, Malaysia
Sarfraz Brohi, University of the West of England, UK
Saira Muzafar, King Faisal University, Saudi Arabia

Chapter 10
Digital Safeguards: Navigating Cyber Threats in the Logistics Industry Framework 258
Muhammad Tayyab, Taylor's University, Malaysia
Khizar Hameed, University of Tasmania, Australia
Noor Zaman Jhanjhi, Taylor's University, Malaysia
Amer Zaheer, Shifa Tameer-e-Millat University, Islamabad, Pakistan
Faizan Qamar, Universiti Kebangsaan Malaysia, Malaysia

Chapter 11
Securing the Supply Chain: Cybersecurity Strategies for Logistics Resilience 300
Siva Raja Sindiramutty, Taylor's University, Malaysia
Chong Eng Tan, Universiti Malaysia Sarawak, Malaysia
Wei Wei Goh, Taylor's University, Malaysia
Sumathi Balakrishnan, Taylor's University, Malaysia
Norhidayah Hamzah, Taylor's University, Malaysia
Rehan Akbar, Florida International University, USA

Compilation of References 366

About the Contributors 442

Index 447

Detailed Table of Contents

The logistics sector plays a crucial role in the worldwide economy by facilitating the efficient and punctual transportation of commodities and services. Nevertheless, the growing reliance on technological and digital infrastructure has highlighted the significance of implementing resilient cybersecurity protocols within the logistics industry. The occurrence of cybersecurity threats within the logistics industry may result in notable ramifications such as financial losses, impairment of reputation, and disturbances to the supply chain. The chapter investigates the various categories of cybersecurity threats confronting the logistics sector while furnishing instances of recent cybersecurity assaults perpetrated against companies within this industry. Furthermore, this chapter delves into several cybersecurity frameworks and strategies that can be adopted to forestall or alleviate these threats. By implementing these measures, logistics companies can secure their operations, clients, and affiliates from cyber threats.

Logistics generally relates to the careful preparation and performance strenuous activity. To meet the needs of customers or enterprises, logistics is broadly defined as managing the flow of items from their point of production to their location of consumption. According to studies, up to 90% of a company's sustainability consequences are attributable to its supply chain. These crucial supply chain flaws have been made public by the COVID-19 pandemic. Additionally, businesses are making many sustainability pledges because of legislative and consumer pressure for climate action. Current procedures have the potential to be streamlined with artificial intelligence (AI) innovation in logistics. Numerous developments are pushing automation to the top of the logistics CEO's agenda. The first step toward extensive optimization is automation, which many businesses have already adopted to maintain competitiveness.

This chapter has simulated and designed the intrusion detection and border surveillance system using mobile WSN technology. Due to increased terrorism globally, border protection has become a crucial issue in every country. Conventionally in border protection, a troop cannot provide security all over time. The authors have simulated the design of border protection by using mobile WSN technology on a CupCarbon simulator tool. They have analyzed the scenario of the smart city. So, a troop can be intimated with intrusions occurring on the border. They have created the authentication protocol for the better security of the application. The security protocol is necessary because the soldier's mobile device can be stolen during the war. It can be going into the hands of the enemy in the situation when troops expire. The Android app can guide the troop in the time of emergency and what the next step should be followed. The authors can check the status of the sensors deployed on the border. They have analyzed these applications based on the application's rating with machine learning techniques.

Every part of the supply chain has been affected by the rise of Industry 4.0 technologies. Many businesses have been trying out this modern technology to see if it can help them make more money. IoT devices make it simple for companies to keep track of an item's specific location, which helps inventory management (IM). The time it takes to find inventory is shortened as a result. The abundance of real-time data makes it possible to offer insightful information that supports strategic and tactical business decisions. Developing a supply chain into a fully integrated supply chain has several benefits. The differences between fourth-generation technology and earlier generations make it seem like traditional ways of restocking inventory don't adapt well enough to new technologies and can't handle IoT systems. Thanks to technological advancements, supply chains are undergoing rapid transformation.

The emergence of the internet of things (IoT) has revolutionized many sectors of the economy, including logistics and supply chain management. By seamlessly integrating IoT into logistics operations, real-time tracking and monitoring of shipments becomes a reality, and optimizing routes and equipment performance becomes a breeze. Accordingly, supply chain operations have become streamlined like never before. This study delves into the various perspectives, applications, and challenges of deploying IoT in the logistics industry, offering a comprehensive overview for stakeholders, researchers, and students alike. With the potential for improved efficiency, effectiveness, and sustainability, the benefits of IoT in logistics are undeniable. The authors highlight future directions of this exciting field and learn how IoT shapes how we do business.

The objective of logistics is to meet client demands in a timely and economical manner. The internet of things (IoT) vision allows numerous embedded, resource-constrained devices, things, and people to connect via the Internet protocol for constant data exchange. In this vision, logistics is a crucial player positioned to achieve complete visibility and transparency by utilizing pervasive interconnectivity to gather reliable and secure real-time data. It is essential for all retailers and logistics companies who want to preserve their leading positions to stay on top of logistical challenges and trends. A global supply chain disruption resulted from COVID-19's imbalance in the supply and demand for goods. 2020 saw a decrease in global productivity because of the pandemic and the lockdown. Due to this, the idea of digital transformation has gained traction during the past two years.

IoV has become an appealing application that can provide a wide range of mobile services for drivers. In order to mitigate traffic congestion and reduce the occurrence of accidents, vehicles can be provided with up-to-date information regarding the location, trajectory, speed, and other relevant details of adjacent vehicles. Such an open environment leaves a lot of room for malicious nodes to pass falsified and tampered information. Due to the potential relevance and sensitivity of the information, IoV must address the security and privacy concerns in the network. In this chapter, they propose an efficient IoV-based decentralised authentication mechanism based on the blockchain named BBA- IoV to ensure secure node communication. This method requires the exchange of keys to encrypt communication. From performance analysis, they show that this approach protects communication against several attacks such as Sybil, GPS spoofing, tampering, and fabrication attacks.

Blockchain technology has garnered considerable interest from academics and businesses. One of the primary reasons to keep track of customer satisfaction and adoption is that customers don't use the product or service enough. Identifying the factors that influence the use and adoption of blockchain technologies will help solve the adoption problems effectively. Many significant firms, like Google, Amazon, and others, will embrace blockchain technology. It will indeed be found in the future and revolutionise logistics and transportation. Even though the advantages of blockchain technology have been well studied in the financial sector, using blockchain technology can help decrease significant logistical challenges such as border delays, product damage, errors, and multiple data entry.

This study emphasizes the critical role of cybersecurity in safeguarding digital infrastructure, ensuring passenger safety, and maintaining operational integrity. By highlighting the multifaceted challenges of DDoS attacks, the document advocates for a comprehensive and forward-thinking approach. The imperative need for robust security measures, a cybersecurity-aware culture, and continuous vigilance against emerging threats is underscored. This proactive stance is vital for fortifying the transportation sector against the evolving landscape of digital threats, ensuring uninterrupted and secure operations.

The rapid integration of internet and technological advancements over the past two decades has reshaped the global landscape, leading to transformative changes in various sectors.The emergence of Industry 4.0, conceptualized in 2011, has particularly revolutionized manufacturing and logistics by advocating for systematic digitalization technology integration to enhance efficiency and reduce costs. However, this technological evolution, while fostering efficiency and process optimization, also introduces vulnerabilities to cyber threats. The logistics sector, heavily reliant on interconnected systems like internet of things, faces potential risks from cyberattacks that target sensitive data across the interconnected supply chain. This chapter aims to address the intricate relationship between digitalization and the logistics sector, emphasizing the crucial role of digital safeguards in navigating cyber dangers. Furthermore, the chapter delves into the significance of visibility in supply-chain operations and explores technologies and practices for enhancing supply-chain visibility.

Chapter 11
Securing the Supply Chain: Cybersecurity Strategies for Logistics Resilience 300
Siva Raja Sindiramutty, Taylor's University, Malaysia
Chong Eng Tan, Universiti Malaysia Sarawak, Malaysia
Wei Wei Goh, Taylor's University, Malaysia
Sumathi Balakrishnan, Taylor's University, Malaysia
Norhidayah Hamzah, Taylor's University, Malaysia
Rehan Akbar, Florida International University, USA

The exponential growth of digital connectivity in the logistics landscape has heightened the significance of cybersecurity. This chapter delves into the intricate fabric of securing supply chains against evolving cyber threats, aiming to equip logistics professionals with actionable strategies for resilience. Beginning with analysing the prevailing cyber threat landscape, it illuminates common vulnerabilities and highlights recent impactful attacks targeting supply chains. Understanding the nexus between cybersecurity and logistics resilience becomes pivotal, emphasizing the need for continuous operations amidst adversities. To fortify this resilience, the chapter meticulously navigates through risk assessment methodologies, mitigation strategies, and the imperative role of supply chain visibility. It elaborates on vendor and partner management protocols, advocating for stringent cybersecurity considerations within contractual agreements. Moreover, it outlines robust incident response plans and recovery strategies essential for mitigating cyber incidents' ramifications.

Compilation of References 366

About the Contributors 442

Index 447

Preface

Dear Readers,

It is with great pleasure and enthusiasm that we present the revised edition of *Navigating Cyber Threats and Cybersecurity in the Logistics Industry*, edited by Prof. Noor Zaman Jhanjhi and Imdad Ali Shah. In an era where global supply chains are evolving to be more customer-centric and sustainable, the significance of cybersecurity in the logistics industry cannot be overstated.

This reference book delves into the intricate landscape of next-generation logistics management technologies that are reshaping the industry. As we witness the automation of logistics procedures, the productivity and efficiency of workflows are soaring. The creation of flexible and dynamic relationships among stakeholders is becoming paramount, while the transparency and traceability of the supply chain must be continually improved.

In our quest for comprehensive insights, we conducted an in-depth study, evaluating 901 startups and scale-ups globally. The result is a detailed exploration of the Top Logistics Industry Trends & Startups, shedding light on the challenges and opportunities that lie ahead.

The past two years have seen unprecedented challenges in supply chains, from the impact of the pandemic on health and travel to its implications on the global economy. From shortages of used vehicle parts to a shortage of manpower, every sector has felt the repercussions. In response, a significant shift toward digitization is underway, connecting people globally and streamlining operations. However, as highlighted by Mike Wilson in Forbes, this digital transformation brings forth new security concerns that demand our attention.

The main objective of this publication is to provide a comprehensive environment for the logistics industry in the context of new technologies. This book serves as a generic roadmap, catering to academics, employees, businessmen, and citizens alike.

The chapters within this book cover a wide array of topics, from the challenges and perspectives of Logistics with the Internet of Things to the application of Blockchain Technology in the Supply Chain. Each chapter offers a nuanced exploration, providing valuable insights into the evolving landscape of the logistics industry.

We extend our gratitude to the authors, Noor Zaman Jhanjhi and Imdad Ali Shah, for their invaluable contributions, and we hope that this edited reference book becomes a valuable resource for all those navigating the complex intersection of cybersecurity and logistics.

ORGANIZATION OF THE BOOK

Chapter 1: Cybersecurity Measures for Logistics Industry

Authored by Siva Raja Sindiramutty, Noor Zaman Jhanjhi, Chong Eng Tan, Navid Ali Khan, Bhavin Shah, and Amaranadha Reddy Manchuri, this chapter delves into the critical role played by the logistics sector in the global economy. As technology becomes integral to logistics, the need for resilient cybersecurity protocols is emphasized. The chapter explores various cybersecurity threats confronting the industry, providing instances of recent assaults. It also discusses cybersecurity frameworks and strategies to prevent or mitigate these threats, offering insights to secure operations, clients, and affiliates from potential cyber threats.

Chapter 2: Supply Chain Management Security Issues and Challenges in the Context of AI Applications

Authored by Imdad Ali Shah, Raja Murugesan, and Samina Rajper, this chapter explores the intersection of logistics and supply chain management with artificial intelligence (AI) applications. It highlights the significance of sustainability in the supply chain and how AI innovation can streamline procedures, pushing automation to the forefront of logistics CEOs' agendas. The chapter explores how AI can be the first step toward extensive optimization, crucial for maintaining competitiveness in the industry.

Chapter 3: Sustainable Computing-Based Simulation of Intelligent Border Surveillance Using Mobile WSN

Authored by Rana Muhammad Amir Latif, Muhammad Farhan, Navid Ali Khan, and R Sujatha, this chapter addresses the critical issue of border protection using mobile Wireless Sensor Network (WSN) technology. The simulation and design of intrusion detection and border surveillance systems are explored, providing insights into securing borders through technology. The chapter discusses authentication protocols, ensuring better security even in challenging situations, and employs machine learning techniques for analyzing applications based on their ratings.

Chapter 4: The Internet of Things (IoT) is Revolutionizing Inventory Management

Authored by Imdad Ali Shah, Areesha Sial, and Sarfraz Brohi, this chapter explores the impact of the Internet of Things (IoT) on inventory management within the supply chain. It highlights how Industry 4.0 technologies, including IoT devices, are transforming every part of the supply chain. The chapter discusses how real-time data from IoT devices facilitates insightful information, supporting strategic and tactical business decisions and contributing to the rapid transformation of supply chains.

Chapter 5: Perspectives, Applications, Challenges, and Future Trend of IoT-Based Logistics

Authored by Kassim Kalinaki, Wasswa Shafik, Sarah Namuwaya, and Sumaya Namuwaya, this chapter provides a comprehensive exploration of the Internet of Things (IoT) in logistics. It discusses the perspectives, applications, and challenges of deploying IoT in the logistics industry, emphasizing real-time tracking, monitoring of shipments, and optimization of routes. The chapter highlights the undeniable benefits of IoT in logistics and offers insights into future directions in this dynamic field.

Chapter 6: Logistics with the Internet of Things Challenges, Perspectives, and Applications

Authored by Imdad Ali Shah, NZ Jhanjhi, and Humaira Ashraf, this chapter focuses on the role of the Internet of Things (IoT) in logistics. It explores the vision of complete visibility and transparency achieved through pervasive interconnectivity, emphasizing the importance for retailers and logistics companies to stay ahead of challenges and trends. The chapter also addresses the global supply chain disruption caused by the COVID-19 pandemic, leading to increased traction for digital transformation in the past two years.

Chapter 7: Blockchain-Based Authentication for the Internet of Vehicles (BBA-IoV)

Authored by Rida Zehra, this chapter introduces a blockchain-based authentication mechanism for the Internet of Vehicles (IoV). It addresses security and privacy concerns in IoV by proposing an efficient decentralized authentication mechanism using blockchain technology. The chapter emphasizes the protection of communication against various attacks, showcasing the effectiveness of this approach through performance analysis.

Chapter 8: Blockchain Technology in the Context of the Logistics Industry: The Role Blockchain in the Logistics Industry

Authored by Imdad Ali Shah, Areeba Laraib, and Fida Hussain, this chapter explores the considerable interest in blockchain technology from academics and businesses. It discusses the potential of blockchain to revolutionize logistics and transportation, highlighting its ability to address significant challenges such as border delays, product damage, errors, and multiple data entry. The chapter anticipates widespread adoption of blockchain technology by major firms.

Chapter 9: A Comprehensive Exploration of DDoS Attacks and Cybersecurity Imperatives in the Digital Age: "DDoS and Transportation Cybersecurity"

Authored by Humaira Ashraf, Noor Jhanjhi, Sarfraz Brohi, and Saira Muzafar, this chapter addresses the disruptive threat of Distributed Denial of Service (DDoS) attacks in the transportation industry. It emphasizes proactive cybersecurity strategies for DDoS resilience, underlining the critical role of cybersecurity in safeguarding digital infrastructure, ensuring passenger safety, and maintaining operational integrity.

Chapter 10: Digital Safeguards Navigating Cyber Threats in the Logistics Industry Framework: Digital Safeguards

Authored by Muhammad Tayyab, Khizar Hameed, Noor Jhanjhi, Amer Zaheer, and Faizan Qamar, this chapter explores the transformative changes brought about by the rapid integration of the internet and technological advancements. Focused on the logistics sector, the chapter addresses the intricate relationship between digitalization and cyber threats, emphasizing the crucial role of digital safeguards. It also explores technologies and practices for enhancing supply-chain visibility in the face of cyber dangers.

Chapter 11: Securing the Supply Chain - Cybersecurity Strategies for Logistics Resilience

Authored by Siva Raja Sindiramutty, Chong Eng Tan, Wei Wei Goh, Sumathi Balakrishnan, Norhidayah Hamzah, and Rehan Akbar, this chapter delves into the heightened significance of cybersecurity in the logistics landscape. It provides actionable strategies for securing supply chains against evolving cyber threats, emphasizing continuous operations amidst adversities. The chapter navigates through risk assessment methodologies, mitigation strategies, and the imperative role of supply chain visibility, outlining robust incident response plans and recovery strategies.

IN SUMMARY

As we conclude this edited reference book on *Navigating Cyber Threats and Cybersecurity in the Logistics Industry,* we reflect on the depth and breadth of insights shared by the distinguished authors. This comprehensive compilation explores the intricate intersection of cybersecurity and the logistics sector, providing a panoramic view of the challenges, applications, and strategies that shape this dynamic landscape.

From the fundamental importance of resilient cybersecurity protocols in the logistics industry, as discussed in Chapter 1, to the transformative potential of artificial intelligence (AI) applications in supply chain management highlighted in Chapter 2, each chapter unfolds a unique facet of the evolving logistics ecosystem. The integration of sustainable computing and intelligent border surveillance in Chapter 3 further exemplifies the innovative approaches employed to address crucial issues like border protection.

Chapters 4 and 5 shed light on the revolutionizing impact of the Internet of Things (IoT) on inventory management and logistics operations, emphasizing real-time tracking, monitoring, and optimization. Chapter 6 takes a closer look at the challenges, perspectives, and applications of logistics with the Internet of Things, underlining the urgency for companies to adapt to pervasive interconnectivity.

Blockchain technology's role in authentication (Chapter 7) and its broader implications in the logistics industry (Chapter 8) open new avenues for secure and efficient operations. Chapter 9 delves into the critical realm of cybersecurity imperatives, focusing on Distributed Denial of Service (DDoS) attacks and strategies for resilience in the transportation industry.

The transformative changes brought by the rapid integration of technology, as discussed in Chapter 10, underline the need for digital safeguards in navigating cyber threats within the logistics industry framework. Finally, Chapter 11 provides invaluable strategies for securing the supply chain against evolving cyber threats, emphasizing the need for continuous operations amidst adversities.

As editors, we are grateful to the esteemed authors for their insightful contributions, which collectively form a rich tapestry of knowledge. We believe that this edited reference book will serve as a valuable resource for academics, professionals, researchers, and students navigating the complex terrain of cybersecurity in the logistics industry.

In a world where digitalization and technological advancements continually reshape industries, the insights presented in these chapters offer a compass for those seeking to understand, adapt, and fortify their positions in the logistics landscape. We hope that readers find inspiration, knowledge, and practical guidance within these pages as they embark on their journey of navigating cyber threats and ensuring resilient cybersecurity in the logistics industry.

Noor Zaman Jhanjhi
School of Computing Science, Taylor's University, Malaysia

Imdad Ali Shah
School of Computing Science, Taylor's University, Malaysia

Chapter 1
Cybersecurity Measures for Logistics Industry

Siva Raja Sindiramutty
Taylor's University, Malaysia

Noor Zaman Jhanjhi
https://orcid.org/0000-0001-8116-4733
Taylor's University, Malaysia

Chong Eng Tan
https://orcid.org/0000-0002-3990-3501
Universiti Malaysia Sarawak, Malaysia

Navid Ali Khan
Taylor's University, Malaysia

Bhavin Shah
Lok Jagruti University, India

Amaranadha Reddy Manchuri
https://orcid.org/0000-0002-3873-0469
Kyungpook National University, South Korea

ABSTRACT

The logistics sector plays a crucial role in the worldwide economy by facilitating the efficient and punctual transportation of commodities and services. Nevertheless, the growing reliance on technological and digital infrastructure has highlighted the significance of implementing resilient cybersecurity protocols within the logistics industry. The occurrence of cybersecurity threats within the logistics industry may result in notable ramifications such as financial losses, impairment of reputation, and disturbances to the supply chain. The chapter investigates the various categories of cybersecurity threats confronting the logistics sector while furnishing instances of recent cybersecurity assaults perpetrated against companies within this industry. Furthermore, this chapter delves into several cybersecurity frameworks and strategies that can be adopted to forestall or alleviate these threats. By implementing these measures, logistics companies can secure their operations, clients, and affiliates from cyber threats.

DOI: 10.4018/979-8-3693-3816-2.ch001

INTRODUCTION

As per a report by Transparency Market Research, the logistics industry is one of the swiftest growing sectors worldwide. The global logistics market was appraised at USD 8,186.2 billion in 2019, and it is anticipated to reach USD 12,975.64 billion by 2027, registering a CAGR of 5.7% from 2020 to 2027 (Choudhury, 2020). The logistics industry's expansion is primarily fueled by the upsurge in e-commerce and international trade (Singh, 2016; Priyadarshini et al., 2021). As more enterprises shift their operations online, the demand for logistics services to transport products to customers is escalating (Andrejić, 2019). The logistics industry assumes a pivotal role in fostering international trade (Suki et al., 2021). It enables enterprises to gain access to global markets and furnishes them with the requisite infrastructure for transporting commodities and services across borders. The logistics industry is fundamental to the advancement of international trade, which, in turn, is crucial for economic progress (Mangan et al., 2008). The logistics sector is responsible for administering enterprises' supply chains (Christopher, 2016; Gaur et al., 2022). The logistics industry entails harmonizing the transportation of commodities and services from suppliers to manufacturers, and eventually to retailers and customers. It assists enterprises in minimizing costs by streamlining the movement of goods and services (Y. Yu et al., 2016; Taj & Zaman, 2022). Logistics companies can curtail the expense of transporting commodities from one location to another by employing efficient transportation routes, warehousing, and inventory management techniques. This cost reduction can enable enterprises to sustain their competitiveness in the worldwide market (Ali et al., 2008; Humayun et al., 2021b). The logistics industry assumes a pivotal role in guaranteeing customer satisfaction (Chow et al., 1994). By delivering products punctually and in proper condition, logistics companies can aid enterprises in constructing a favourable reputation and retaining customers. The logistics industry has experienced significant transformations over time, propelled by technological advancements, alterations in consumer behaviour, and globalization. One such transformation is the introduction of containerization, which has revolutionized the transportation of commodities by making it faster and more effective. Another significant impact on the logistics industry is the advent of e-commerce, which has led to the emergence of novel technologies such as warehouse automation, last-mile delivery solutions, and real-time tracking systems (Bowersox, Closs & Cooper, 2019; Humayun et al., 2020).

Although the logistics industry is of paramount importance, it faces a plethora of challenges that can potentially disrupt its operations and undermine its ability to sustain international trade. Among the most significant challenges is the mounting intricacy of global supply chains, which has been amplified by the COVID-19 pandemic. In addition to the mounting complexity of global supply chains, the logistics industry confronts a myriad of other obstacles that can adversely affect its operations and its ability to maintain international trade. These include escalating transportation costs, shortages of skilled labour, and the challenge of balancing the speed and cost of goods delivery (Deloitte, 2021; Ponnusamy et al., 2020; R. Sujatha et al., 2022). In summary, the logistics industry is a vital component of the global economy, serving as a backbone for international trade and commerce. It is a dynamic and intricate system of interconnected entities that collaborate to transport goods and services from producers to consumers. Although the logistics industry has undergone significant changes due to technological advancements and shifting consumer behavior, it still confronts several obstacles that may impede its operations. Despite these challenges, the logistics industry is poised to continue driving economic growth and employment in the future. Figure 1 shows the overview of the picture of the logistics industry.

Figure 1. Overview of the logistic industry
(Admin, 2022)

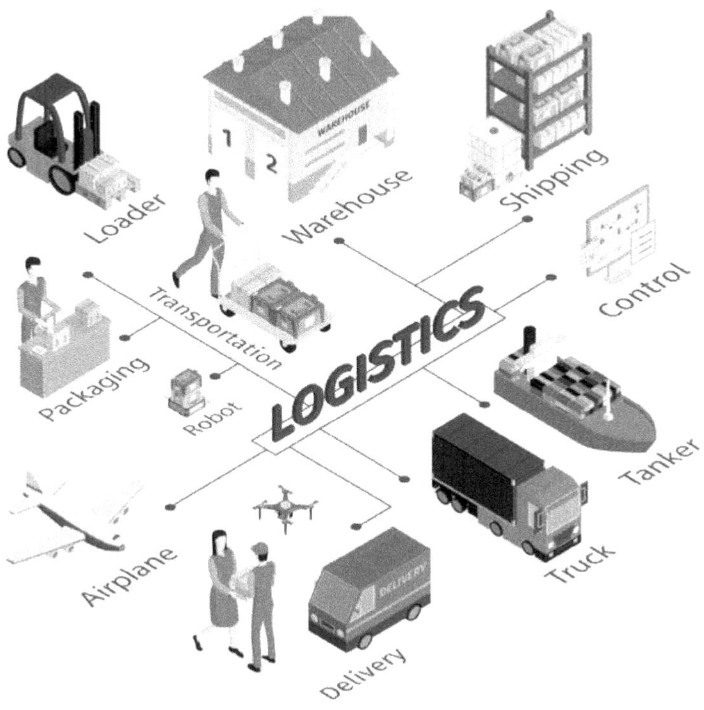

The Increasing Need for Cybersecurity in Logistics

The significance of cybersecurity has become increasingly crucial in light of the advancements in logistics technology and the growth of digitalization, as noted by Cheung et al. (2021) in their research. The requirement for cybersecurity in logistics is imperative to protect vital data, thwart cyber-attacks, and reduce the possibility of disruptions in supply chain activities, as noted by Kron (2019). This report aims to examine the growing demand for cybersecurity in logistics by outlining the potential hazards linked to cyber-attacks and emphasizing the significance of a robust cybersecurity structure to secure logistics operations. This report offers a comprehensive evaluation of logistics cybersecurity issues and presents practical suggestions to organizations for minimizing these risks. The transportation of goods and services from one location to another is a multifaceted procedure referred to as logistics. This industry is a critical player in worldwide commerce, making a substantial contribution to economic progress and expansion. In recent times, the logistics sector has undergone significant transformations due to the rise of digitalization. The integration of cutting-edge technologies like the Internet of Things (IoT), blockchain, and cloud computing has enhanced the swiftness and productivity of logistics activities, as highlighted by Nagy et al. (2018). Despite the benefits of adopting advanced technologies in logistics, the likelihood of cyber-attacks has escalated. The logistics industry is particularly vulnerable to cyber-attacks due to the extensive data associated with supply chain activities. These attacks can potentially interrupt supply chain operations, resulting in substantial financial loss and harm to reputation. Thus, the necessity for cybersecurity in logistics has become more paramount than ever, as emphasized by Managers (2022).

The logistics sector is exposed to several cyber-attacks, such as phishing, malware, ransomware, and distributed Denial of Service (DDoS) attacks, which can jeopardize the confidentiality, integrity, and accessibility of crucial data, potentially resulting in severe financial losses and harm to reputation, as noted by Viveros, Chao, & Kline (2020). For instance, the 2017 NotPetya ransomware attack caused major disruptions in the operations of Maersk, the leading container shipping firm globally. The attack inflicted substantial financial damage, forcing the company to replace over 45,000 infected computers and reinstall software on its complete network. Additionally, the attack caused significant disruptions to the company's supply chain operations, leading to delayed shipments and lost revenue, as reported by McKevitt (2017).

To safeguard logistics operations from cyber-attacks, a robust cybersecurity framework is fundamental. A cybersecurity framework encompasses a collection of guidelines, protocols, and technologies devised to safeguard essential information from unauthorized access, disclosure, use, modification, disruption, or destruction, as outlined by Fedele and Roner (2021). The cybersecurity framework should incorporate measures to recognize, evaluate, and control the risks linked to cyber threats. Additionally, the framework should offer guidance on incident response and recovery procedures in case of a cyber-attack. To lessen cybersecurity risks in logistics, enterprises should consider implementing the following practical recommendations:

1. Regular risk assessments should be conducted by organizations to identify potential vulnerabilities in their systems and networks (Chandra et al., 2020).
2. Cybersecurity awareness and best practices should be taught to employees to prevent cyber-attacks (Rohan et al., 2023).
3. Access controls ought to be implemented to limit access to critical information only to authorized personnel (Bozhilov, 2023).
4. Encryption is necessary to safeguard sensitive data during transmission and storage (Chung & Lee, 2021).
5. Multi-factor authentication is an essential measure that should be implemented to provide an additional layer of security to user accounts (Kayapinar & Lorcu, 2020).
6. Regular updates of software and security patches are necessary to ensure that systems are protected against known vulnerabilities (Nayyar et al., 2019).
7. Regular backups of critical data are essential to ensure that they can be recovered in the event of a cyber-attack or system failure (Rejeb et al., 2021).

Conclusively, the assimilation of sophisticated technologies in logistics has enhanced the efficiency and rapidity of operations. Nevertheless, the incorporation of such technologies has concurrently escalated the susceptibility to cyber-attacks. The logistics sector, owing to the massive volume of data implicated in the supply chain, is exceedingly vulnerable to cyber-attacks. The disruption caused by cyber-attacks in supply chain operations can result in substantial financial losses and tarnish the reputation of the logistics organization. Hence, the significance of cybersecurity in the logistics domain has become more crucial than ever. To alleviate the cybersecurity risks involved in logistics operations, organizations must espouse a sturdy cybersecurity framework and put into practice practical recommendations. Figure 2 shows the main elements involved in the logistics industry.

Figure 2. Main elements in the logistic industry
(Kozma et al., 2019)

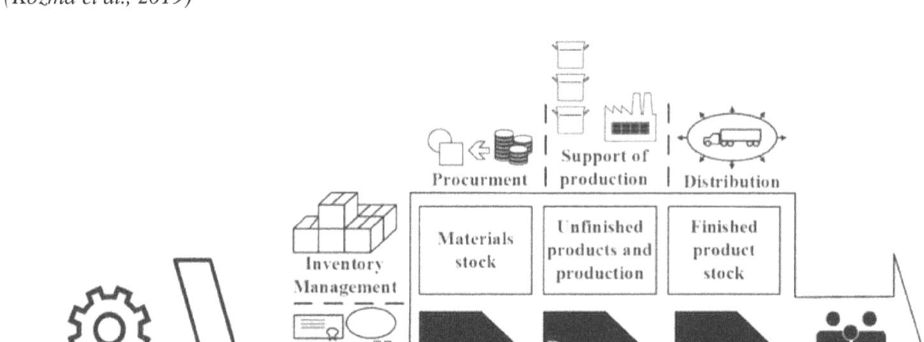

CYBERSECURITY THREATS IN THE LOGISTICS INDUSTRY

Overview of the Different Types of Cybersecurity Threats Faced by the Logistics Industry

The pivotal role of the logistics industry in the global economy lies in its ability to facilitate the transportation of goods across borders, oceans, and continents. With digital technology now being an indispensable component of logistics operations, the industry has become more susceptible to cybersecurity risks. The adverse impact of cybersecurity threats on logistics operations cannot be overlooked, as they can cause significant disruptions, resulting in financial losses, reputational harm, and even safety hazards (Hamid et al., 2019). This report aims to present a comprehensive overview of the various categories of cybersecurity threats that the logistics industry is confronted with. The logistics industry faces a diverse range of cybersecurity threats that pose significant risks to its operations. These threats include:

1. Phishing Attacks and Ransomware

The logistics industry encounters phishing attacks as one of the most prevalent types of cybersecurity threats. Social engineering techniques are utilized by cybercriminals in phishing attacks to deceive individuals into disclosing confidential information, including login credentials, bank account particulars, and credit card details. In the transportation industry, phishing attacks contributed to 22% of all security incidents, as per a report published by Verizon in 2020. The logistics industry is confronted with another substantial cybersecurity threat in the form of ransomware. During a ransomware attack, cybercriminals encrypt an organization's data and demand payment in exchange for the decryption key (Saeed et al., 2023; Khan et al., 2022). The occurrence of ransomware attacks may result in significant disruption to logistics operations, leading to delivery delays of goods and potential financial losses. As per a report published by Coveware in 2021, the average ransom payment rose by 43% to $220,298 in Q1 2021.

2. DDoS and Insider Threats

Organizations face a cybersecurity threat called DDoS attacks, which aim at their network infrastructure. During a DDoS attack, cybercriminals inundate an organization's network with traffic to make it inundated and prevent legitimate users from accessing it. The occurrence of DDoS attacks may cause significant disruption to logistics operations, leading to delivery delays of goods and potential financial losses. In Q1 2020, the transportation and logistics industry was the most targeted industry for DDoS attacks, accounting for 35% of all attacks, according to a report published by Neustar in 2020. An organization may face a type of cybersecurity threat called insider threats, which originates from within the organization. Insider threats, which can be either intentional or unintentional, have the potential to lead to sensitive data theft or logistics operations disruption. As per a report published by IBM in 2020, insider-related incidents in the transportation industry resulted in an average cost of $4.47 million.

3. Advanced Persistent Threats (APTs) and Malware

A targeted type of cybersecurity threat called APTs aims at particular individuals or organizations. The design of APTs is to remain hidden for extended periods, which enables cybercriminals to engage in sensitive data theft or operations disruption. As per a report published by Mandiant (2021), the transportation and logistics industry ranked fifth among the most targeted industries for APTs in 2020. Malware is a type of cybersecurity threat that is designed to harm an organization's network or devices. Malware can be leveraged to engage in sensitive data theft, logistics operations disruption, or unauthorized access to an organization's network. A report published by AV-TEST in 2021 indicates that the transportation and logistics industry represented 6% of all malware infections in Q1 2021.

4. Supply Chain Attacks and Social Engineering Attacks

Supply chain attacks, which target an organization's third-party vendors or suppliers, may facilitate unauthorized access to its network or sensitive data theft. Symantec's (2021) report revealed that supply chain attacks rose by 42% in 2020. Individuals within an organization can be the target of social engineering attacks, a type of cybersecurity threat that can manifest in various forms such as phishing, pretexting, and baiting attacks. Social engineering attacks are often used to extract sensitive information from individuals or to deploy malware on their devices. In the transportation industry, social engineering attacks represented 11% of all security incidents, according to IBM (2021).

5. IoT-Based Attacks and Cloud-Based Attacks

Cybercriminals can target an organization's IoT devices through IoT-based attacks. These attacks can affect IoT devices such as sensors, cameras, and other connected devices. IoT-based attacks can cause severe disruption to logistics operations and result in the theft of sensitive data. Per the F5 Labs report (2021), attacks leveraging the IoT have the potential to exfiltrate confidential information, impede logistics operations, or illicitly penetrate organizational networks (Alferidah & Zaman, 2020b; Chaurasiya et al., 2023). In the first quarter of 2021, the transportation and logistics sector constituted 9% of the total number of IoT attacks, as stated in the aforementioned report. As per the McAfee report (2020), cybersecurity threats in the form of cloud-based attacks pose a significant risk to an organization's cloud infrastructure, which could lead to the compromise of confidential data or impairment of logistics operations. In the first quarter of 2020, the transportation and logistics sector constituted 14% of the total number of cloud-based attacks, as reported by McAfee.

6. Identity Theft and Cyber Espionage

As reported by Javelin (2021), cybersecurity threats in the form of identity theft pose a serious risk to individuals as it involves the pilferage of their personal information, which can be utilized to gain unauthorized access to an organization's network or filch confidential data. In the year 2020, the transportation and logistics industry accounted for 1.5% of the overall number of identity theft incidents, as per the Javelin report. Per the CrowdStrike report (2021), cyber espionage is a form of cybersecurity threat perpetrated by nation-states or other entities sponsored by states. Cyber espionage activities can result in the theft of confidential information or disturbance of logistics operations. In 2020, the transportation and logistics sector was ranked sixth among the most targeted industries for cyber espionage, as stated in the aforementioned report by CrowdStrike.

7. Insider Trading and Physical Security Breaches

As per the Accenture report (2020), insider trading is a form of cybersecurity threat that involves the unauthorized appropriation of sensitive financial information. This threat can be utilized to secure an inequitable advantage in the stock market or to sabotage logistics operations. In the year 2020, the transportation and logistics industry accounted for 1% of the total number of insider trading incidents, according to the aforementioned report by Accenture. Per the Verkada report (2021), physical security breaches are a type of cybersecurity threat that involves the illicit appropriation or destruction of physical assets, which can be used to disrupt logistics operations or pilfer confidential data. In the year 2020, the transportation and logistics industry constituted 5% of the total number of physical security breaches, as reported by Verkada.

8. Cyber-Physical Attacks

As per the Gartner report (2021), cybersecurity threats in the form of cyber-physical attacks pose a risk to physical systems as they involve the manipulation of digital means to tamper with physical systems, which can lead to the disruption of logistics operations or cause harm to individuals. In the year 2020, the transportation and logistics industry accounted for 4% of the total number of cyber-physical attacks, as reported by Gartner.

The logistics sector encounters an extensive array of cybersecurity threats, which span from phishing attacks to cyber-physical attacks. The aforementioned cybersecurity threats can severely hamper logistics operations, resulting in substantial financial losses, impairment of reputation, and increased safety risks. To shield against the said threats, logistics organizations must adopt a proactive cybersecurity approach, which entails implementing resilient security measures, educating employees about cybersecurity best practices, and keeping themselves informed of the current cybersecurity trends and threats. By following the aforementioned measures, organizations operating in the logistics sector can bolster their defense against cybersecurity threats and, as a result, ensure the smooth, secure, and efficient transportation of goods worldwide. Figure 3 shows supply chain attacks on the rise.

Figure 3. Supply chain attack
(ENISA, n.d.)

Examples Of Recent Cybersecurity Attacks on Logistics Companies

The upsurge in cyber attacks targeting logistics companies can be attributed to the handling of sensitive information, including but not limited to customer data, financial records, and transaction details. A successful cybersecurity breach on logistics companies may lead to disruption in supply chain operations, significant financial losses, and harm to their reputation. In this report, recent instances of cybersecurity attacks on logistics companies are discussed, and various protective measures that these companies can adopt are highlighted. The 2017 WannaCry ransomware attack, which had a global impact on multiple organizations, is among the most prominent cyber attacks on logistics companies. By exploiting a vulnerability in Microsoft Windows operating systems, the attack encrypted user data and demanded payment in Bitcoin for decryption. It had a widespread impact on various organizations, including logistics companies like Maersk and FedEx, both of which suffered losses of up to $300 million (Novet, 2017). In 2018, Cosco Shipping Lines experienced a network security incident that led to disruptions in the company's email system and data center. The security breach had significant consequences for operations at ports across the United States, Europe, and Asia, leading to delays in the delivery of cargo. Moreover, the company's website and customer service hotline were inaccessible during the attack (Cosco, 2018). In 2017, Maersk, which is the largest container shipping company globally, experienced a cyber attack that caused significant disruptions in its worldwide operations that lasted for several days. The cyber attack had a severe impact on the company's IT systems, telephone and email communications, leading to delays in cargo deliveries and loss of revenue. The company estimated losses of around $300 million due to the attack (Maersk, 2017). Another significant cyber attack that impacted logistics companies is the 2017 NotPetya malware attack, which targeted organizations worldwide. The malware was distributed through a software update for a Ukrainian accounting program and encrypted the hard drives of infected computers, rendering them inoperable. The attack had a severe impact on logistics companies like Maersk, FedEx, and TNT Express, leading to significant disruptions in their operations. Maersk reported losses of up to $1.2 billion as a result of the attack (CBS News, 2017). To safeguard themselves from cyber attacks, logistics companies can adopt various preventive measures, such as:

Employee Education and Training: To mitigate cyber attacks, logistics companies should educate and train their employees regularly on how to identify and avoid phishing emails and other social engineering tactics. This can involve simulated phishing exercises to aid employees in recognizing and responding to such attacks more efficiently. Implement Security Measures: Logistics companies should implement strong security measures such as firewalls, IDS, and antivirus software to safeguard their networks and systems from cyber threats. Additionally, companies should ensure that their software and systems are regularly updated with the latest security patches and updates. Third-Party Risk Management: To reduce the risk of cyber attacks, logistics companies should evaluate the cybersecurity risks of their third-party suppliers and partners and implement suitable measures to mitigate those risks. This can involve conducting periodic security assessments, mandating suppliers to comply with specific security standards, and implementing contractual agreements that include cybersecurity provisions. Incident Response Planning Logistics companies should have a comprehensive incident response plan in place, which outlines the necessary steps to be taken in the event of a cyber attack. This plan should include procedures for containing the attack, evaluating the damage caused, informing affected parties, and recovering from the attack. Insurance: To protect themselves against the financial losses associated with cyber attacks, logistics companies should consider purchasing cyber insurance coverage. Cyber insurance policies can provide coverage for various expenses such as business interruption losses, legal fees, and data recovery costs (National Institute of Standards and Technology, 2020; Humayun, Niazi, et al., 2020).

Cybersecurity attacks on logistics companies can cause significant harm to their operations and reputation. Recent examples like the WannaCry, NotPetya, and Cosco attacks emphasize the necessity for logistics companies to be proactive in protecting themselves from cyber threats. Logistics companies can improve their cybersecurity posture and lower the risk of cyber attacks by adopting security measures, providing employee education and training, conducting third-party risk assessments, having an incident response plan in place, and considering cyber insurance coverage.

The Potential Impact of a Cybersecurity Breach on the Logistics Industry

The financial repercussions of a cybersecurity breach on a logistics company can be substantial, as it can lead to various expenses such as investigating and containing the breach, loss of productivity, loss of revenue, and reputational damage. In the event of a cybersecurity breach, the initial course of action is to conduct an investigation and promptly implement measures to contain the incident. This necessitates enlisting a cadre of cybersecurity professionals to evaluate the extent of the harm and identify the root cause of the breach. Retaining a cybersecurity team can result in substantial expenses, which may fluctuate based on the magnitude of the breach. Based on a report by IBM, the typical expenditure incurred for investigating and mitigating a breach in 2020 was $3.86 million, with an average expenditure of $13 for each record compromised (IBM, 2020). The cumulative expenses can escalate rapidly, particularly for smaller logistics enterprises that may lack the economic wherewithal to invest in cybersecurity. Moreover, cybersecurity breaches can lead to decreased productivity for logistics firms. In the aftermath of a breach, the organization's IT infrastructure may be immobilized or impeded, impinging on its activities. As a result, the delivery of goods may be delayed, leading to reduced productivity. As per Accenture's report, the typical expenditure incurred as a result of diminished productivity due to a cyberattack was $1.4 million in 2020b (Accenture, 2020b). Additionally, cybersecurity breaches may lead to reduced revenue for logistics enterprises. A cybersecurity breach can also result in the loss of customer confidence, potentially leading them to transfer their business to other entities. This can ultimately cause a revenue decline for the organization. Based on IBM's report, the typical expenditure incurred due to lost revenue resulting from a breach in 2020 was $3.86 million, with an average expenditure of $146 for each record compromised (IBM, 2020). Lastly, cybersecurity breaches can inflict reputational harm on logistics firms. In the event of a breach, customers may lose faith in the organization and perceive it as being unreliable or untrustworthy. This can have a long-lasting impact on the reputation of the company, leading to decreased revenue and customer retention. As per Kaspersky's report, almost half (49%) of consumers would cease doing business with an enterprise that experienced a data breach, with 41% choosing not to return (Kaspersky, 2019). Rehabilitating a tarnished reputation can be an expensive and time-consuming process for logistics companies.

The reputational repercussions of cybersecurity breaches on logistics firms can be severe. A primary consequence of a cybersecurity breach is the erosion of customer trust, which can prove detrimental for logistics companies. Customers rely on logistics companies to securely and proficiently transport their goods and services. A cybersecurity breach can result in the compromise of sensitive information, including customer data, shipping details, and payment information, thereby undermining customer trust and confidence in the organization (Kshetri, 2018). Moreover, cybersecurity breaches in the logistics industry can lead to legal ramifications. Logistics companies are subject to numerous regulations, including data protection laws, and a cybersecurity breach can lead to legal consequences and fines. Additionally, logistics firms may be subjected to lawsuits from customers and associates affected by the breach, further exacerbating the damage to the company's reputation (D. N. Burrell et al., 2020). A company that experiences a cybersecurity breach may be viewed as careless, negligent, or inept, potentially resulting in negative media coverage, social media backlash, and customer attrition. The repercussions of reputational damage can be long-lasting and may require years to recover, as demonstrated in the case of Equifax, a credit reporting agency that experienced a data breach in 2017, which impacted approximately 143 million customers. The breach resulted in a congressional hearing, a deluge of lawsuits, and a $575 million settlement, and caused a substantial decline in the organization's stock price and customer loyalty (Yaffe-Bellany, 2019). The consequences of cybersecurity breaches can be significant and far-reaching, impacting not only the logistics industry but also the wider economy and society. One of the immediate impacts of a cybersecurity breach is the disruption of operations, which can result in supply chain delays, cancellations, and backlogs. For instance, suppose the systems of a shipping company are compromised. In that case, it may not be able to monitor and manage its vessels, containers, and cargo, which can result in lost or misplaced shipments and dissatisfied customers. The disruption caused by a cybersecurity breach can also have ripple effects throughout the entire supply chain, affecting the suppliers, manufacturers, and retailers who rely on the logistics provider's services (Editor, 2022). Figure 4 shows statistics of cyber-attacks from 2011 to 2020 in the maritime and logistics industry.

Figure 4. Cyber-attacks in maritime and logistics
(Cyberstar, 2021)

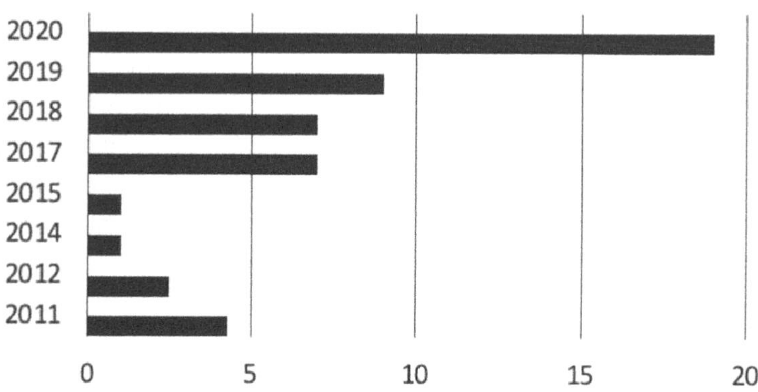

CYBERSECURITY FRAMEWORKS FOR THE LOGISTICS INDUSTRY

Overview of the Different Cybersecurity Frameworks That Can Be Used in the Logistics Industry

The logistics industry faces numerous challenges in ensuring cybersecurity. To address these challenges comprehensively, cybersecurity frameworks offer a valuable approach. The objective of this report is to present a summary of various cybersecurity frameworks that can be implemented within the logistics industry

NIST Cybersecurity Framework and ISO/IEC 27001

Recognized widely for its effectiveness in improving cybersecurity risk management, the NIST Cybersecurity Framework (CSF) provides a voluntary framework comprising guidelines, standards, and best practices that enable organizations to manage and mitigate cybersecurity risks. Built upon five fundamental functions, namely Identify, Protect, Detect, Respond, and Recover, as specified by the National Institute of Standards and Technology (NIST) in 2018, the NIST Cybersecurity Framework (CSF) serves as a highly utilized framework within the logistics industry for managing cybersecurity risks. The International Organization for Standardization (ISO) and International Electrotechnical Commission (IEC) 27001 is a globally recognized standard for managing information security. This standard offers a comprehensive framework for safeguarding sensitive information by utilizing a risk management approach that emphasizes information confidentiality, integrity, and availability. ISO/IEC 27001 provides a systematic method for managing information security risks by creating policies, procedures, and controls to mitigate potential threats. Within the logistics industry, ISO/IEC 27001 is widely implemented to manage information security risks effectively. (International Organization for Standardization, 2020a). Figure 5 shows rising cyber-attacks on logistics and transport.

1. CIS Controls and NIST SP 800-53

The Center for Internet Security (CIS) Controls a set of guidelines that aim to secure computer systems and networks. By prioritizing the most critical security controls, the CIS Controls offer a pragmatic approach to cybersecurity. The framework is based on 20 security controls, which are organized into three categories: Basic, Foundational, and Organizational. The CIS Controls framework offers a practical and effective way to implement cybersecurity measures within the logistics industry. (Center for Internet Security, 2021). The NIST has developed the NIST SP 800-53 framework for managing information security risks. This framework provides a comprehensive set of guidelines, standards, and best practices to help federal agencies and organizations effectively manage and secure their information systems. With a focus on risk management, the NIST SP 800-53 framework is a valuable resource for improving information security posture and protecting against a wide range of cybersecurity threats. The NIST SP 800-53 framework is composed of 18 families of security controls that encompass various facets of information security, including access control, audit and accountability, and system and communications protection (National Institute of Standards and Technology, 2021). These families of security controls serve as a foundation for developing and implementing comprehensive information security programs that can help organizations safeguard their information systems against cyber threats. The logistics industry frequently implements the NIST SP 800-53 framework to manage information security risks effectively. By utilizing the comprehensive set of guidelines, standards, and best practices provided by the NIST SP 800-53 framework, organizations within the logistics industry can establish a robust information security program that helps to protect against a variety of cyber threats.

2. COBIT and IEC 62443

The COBIT framework presents a structured approach to the governance and management of information technology. This framework offers a comprehensive strategy for managing and controlling IT processes and services. Five fundamental principles and seven enablers that aid organizations in aligning their IT objectives with their business objectives underpin COBIT. This framework adopts a comprehensive approach to IT management by formulating policies, procedures, and controls to guarantee the confidentiality, integrity, and availability of information (ISACA, 2019). In the logistics industry, the COBIT framework is widely utilized to mitigate IT risks. For industrial automation and control systems (IACS) cybersecurity, the IEC has developed a series of standards known as IEC 62443. These standards provide an all-encompassing framework for managing cybersecurity risks in IACS environments. This framework employs a risk management methodology that concentrates on upholding the confidentiality, integrity, and availability of IACS data and systems. As such, the IEC 62443 framework presents a comprehensive approach to cybersecurity risk management in the logistics sector (International Electrotechnical Commission, 2020).

FAIR and HITRUST CSF

The Factor Analysis of Information Risk (FAIR) framework is designed to evaluate and quantify information risk. This framework provides a structured methodology for assessing information risks by analyzing the frequency and magnitude of potential losses. FAIR is based on four core factors: assets, threats, vulnerabilities, and impact. This framework offers a comprehensive approach to managing information risks by identifying critical risks and prioritizing resource allocation accordingly (The Open Group, 2019). A FAIR framework is a useful tool for managing information risks in the logistics industry. The HITRUST CSF, created by the Health Information Trust Alliance (HITRUST), is a comprehensive framework for managing cybersecurity risks in the healthcare sector. This framework integrates multiple standards and regulations, such as HIPAA, PCI, and NIST, into a unified framework. By providing a holistic approach to cybersecurity risk management, the HITRUST CSF enables healthcare organizations to manage their cybersecurity risks more efficiently and effectively (Health Information Trust Alliance, 2021). The HITRUST CSF adopts a risk management approach that emphasizes the confidentiality, integrity, and availability of healthcare data. This comprehensive framework can also be tailored to address cybersecurity risks in the logistics industry. By utilizing the HITRUST CSF framework, logistics companies can proactively manage their cybersecurity risks in a structured manner, while ensuring the confidentiality, integrity, and availability of their critical data and systems (Health Information Trust Alliance, 2021).

Figure 5. Rising cyber-attacks on logistics and transport

3. CMMC and CSA Top Threats

The Cybersecurity Maturity Model Certification (CMMC) is a framework devised by the Department of Defense (DoD) aimed at augmenting the cybersecurity stance of its supply chain. The framework entails a holistic strategy to govern cybersecurity risks by mandating that contractors satisfy distinct cybersecurity prerequisites contingent on their degree of engagement in DoD contracts. The CMMC model is structured around five tiers of cybersecurity maturity, which range from rudimentary cybersecurity practices to advanced cybersecurity measures (Department of Defense, 2020). By implementing the CMMC framework, the logistics industry can bolster its cybersecurity posture. In addition, the Cloud Security Alliance (CSA) Top Threats framework is a set of recommendations and best practices for mitigating the foremost cybersecurity threats in cloud environments. This model is built on a risk management methodology that spotlights the most critical threats to cloud infrastructures, such as insider threats, data breaches, and DoS. In this way, the CSA Top Threats framework presents a pragmatic strategy to manage cybersecurity risks in the logistics sector (Cloud Security Alliance, 2020).

ISO/IEC 15408 and CSA Cloud Controls Matrix

ISO/IEC 15408 is a globally acknowledged international standard for assessing information technology security. The standard presents a comprehensive structure for certifying and assessing the security of information technology products and systems. The ISO/IEC 15408 framework is founded on a standard set of criteria and assurance levels that are employed to appraise the security of information technology products and systems (International Organization for Standardization, 2022). The ISO/IEC 15408 model can be applied in the logistics sector to gauge the security of information technology products and systems. The Cloud Security Alliance (CSA) Cloud Controls Matrix (CCM) is a model that offers a set of guidelines and best practices to address security and compliance risks in cloud environments. The CCM framework adopts a risk management strategy that emphasizes the most crucial security and compliance controls in cloud environments. This framework provides a holistic approach to managing security and compliance risks in the logistics industry by recognizing and regulating the most significant security and compliance risks (Cloud Security Alliance, 2020).

4. CSA STAR and SANS Top 20

The Cloud Security Alliance (CSA) has developed the CSA Security, Trust, and Assurance Registry (STAR) program to provide cloud service providers with a structured approach to evaluate their security and compliance posture. The program comprises three assurance levels, namely self-assessment, third-party assessment, and continuous monitoring, and offers a comprehensive framework of guidelines and best practices for managing security and compliance risks. As per Cloud Security Alliance (2021), the CSA STAR program presents a holistic approach to addressing security and compliance concerns in the logistics industry. In managing cybersecurity risks, the SANS Institute has devised the SANS Top 20 framework, which offers practical guidelines and best practices for organizations to manage the most critical cybersecurity risks such as phishing, password attacks, and malware. This framework adopts a risk management approach that emphasizes the most critical cybersecurity risks and proposes practical measures to manage them. As per Kim (2023), the SANS Top 20 framework presents an effective solution to address cybersecurity risks in the logistics industry.

In summary, the logistics industry is confronted with significant cybersecurity risks that can result in data breaches, financial losses, and reputational harm. To mitigate these risks, companies in this industry can adopt various cybersecurity frameworks that offer a comprehensive strategy for managing cybersecurity risks. The cybersecurity frameworks mentioned in this paper, including NIST CSF, ISO/IEC 27001, COBIT, FedRAMP, IEC 62443, HITRUST CSF, FAIR, CMMC, CSA Top Threats, ISO/IEC 15408, CSA Cloud Controls Matrix, SANS Top 20, and CIS Controls, provide a range of guidelines and best practices for addressing cybersecurity risks in organizations. Organizations in the logistics sector can select a cybersecurity framework that aligns with their specific needs, risk tolerance, and regulatory obligations. By implementing a cybersecurity framework, businesses can identify and address cybersecurity risks, improve their cybersecurity posture, and meet regulatory requirements. Adopting a comprehensive approach to managing cybersecurity risks can enable organizations in the logistics industry to safeguard their data, systems, and reputation against cybersecurity threats.

Comparison of Different Frameworks and Their Applicability to the Logistics Industry

The management of logistics has emerged as a crucial aspect of business operations, particularly in the current era of globalization, where firms operate in a highly competitive and fast-paced environment. The integration of technology has played a vital role in optimizing logistics operations, and multiple frameworks have been developed to improve efficiency and effectiveness in logistics management. This report comprehensively analyses different frameworks and their relevance to the logistics industry. The frameworks discussed include Six Sigma, Lean, Agile, and the Theory of Constraints. The report delves into the principles, concepts, and methodologies underpinning each framework and highlights their respective strengths and weaknesses in the logistics sector. Based on the findings, it is evident that different frameworks have varying levels of applicability to logistics management, depending on the nature and complexity of the logistics operations. A combination of frameworks may be necessary to address diverse aspects of logistics management, including transportation, inventory management, warehousing, and supply chain management. This report aims to provide readers with an in-depth understanding of the different frameworks available for optimizing logistics management and their relevance to the logistics industry. Figure 6 shows based NIST cybersecurity framework.

1. Six Sigma Framework

The Six Sigma quality management framework concentrates on diminishing defects in both processes and products. By utilizing a data-driven approach, the framework recognizes and eradicates variations in processes that lead to defects. Based on the DMAIC methodology, which provides a structured approach to problem-solving, Six Sigma is widely implemented in the manufacturing industry to enhance quality, reduce costs, and augment customer satisfaction (Hoerl & Snee, 2012). In the logistics industry, Six Sigma can be applied to improve various aspects of logistics management, such as transportation, inventory management, and supply chain management. By identifying and eliminating inefficiencies in transportation, including delays, errors, and breakdowns, Six Sigma can enhance transportation optimization. It can also optimize inventory management by reducing inventory levels, improving accuracy, and minimizing lead times. Moreover, in supply chain management, Six Sigma can enhance supplier quality, minimize process defects, and boost collaboration between supply chain partners (Zhang et al., 2016; Tampubolon, S., & Purba, H. H. 2021). However, the application of Six Sigma to logistics management may be restricted by the complexity of logistics operations. Logistics operations include various stakeholders, such as suppliers, manufacturers, distributors, and retailers, and coordinating these stakeholders can be challenging. Although Six Sigma may be effective in enhancing specific aspects of logistics management, it may not be suitable for addressing the complexity and uncertainty of logistics operations.

2. Lean Framework

The Lean framework is a well-established approach that concentrates on minimizing wasteful practices in processes and maximizing customer value. Its core principles are continuous improvement, respect for people, and a focus on delivering value to customers, as stated by Womack and Jones (1997). This framework is predominantly employed in the manufacturing sector to minimize waste, enhance quality, and augment customer satisfaction. In logistics management, Lean can be leveraged to enhance various aspects, such as transportation, inventory

Figure 6. NIST cybersecurity framework
(Global, 2020)

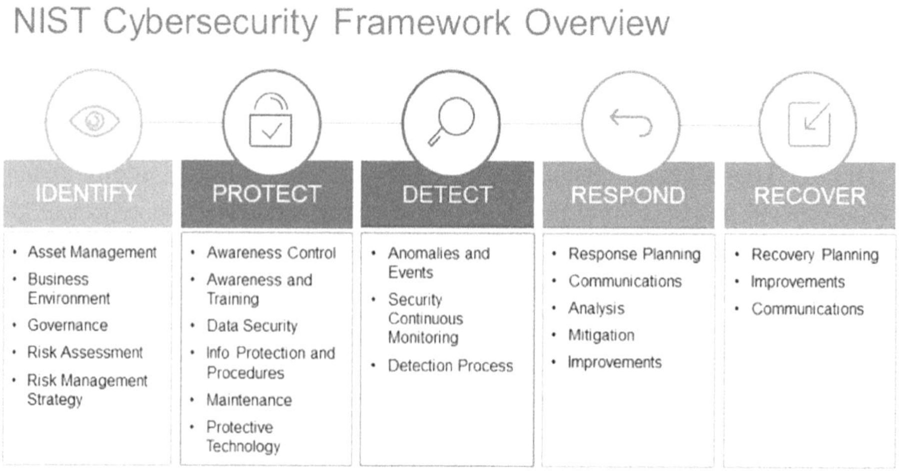

management, and warehousing. By minimizing lead times, eliminating delays, and boosting delivery reliability, Lean can optimize transportation operations. Additionally, Lean can minimize inventory levels, enhance accuracy, and eliminate process waste in inventory management. For warehousing, Lean can improve layout and design, minimize handling time, and maximize space utilization (Waters, 2016). The Lean framework is widely applied in logistics operations, particularly in e-commerce and last-mile delivery, due to its emphasis on reducing waste and improving customer value, which aligns with the goals of these operations. However, the applicability of Lean in logistics operations may be constrained by their complexity and uncertainty. Logistics operations involve various stakeholders, such as suppliers, manufacturers, distributors, and retailers, making stakeholder coordination challenging. While Lean may be effective in enhancing specific logistics management aspects, it may not be suitable for addressing the intricate and unpredictable nature of logistics operations.

3. Agile Framework

The Agile framework is a renowned approach that emphasizes flexibility and responsiveness in both processes and products. The core principles of Agile are customer collaboration, iterative development, and adaptive planning, as proposed by Beck et al. (2001). Agile is widely implemented in software development to boost flexibility, responsiveness, and customer satisfaction. Similarly, in logistics management, Agile can be leveraged to enhance various aspects, including transportation, inventory management, and supply chain management. By providing real-time visibility and tracking of shipments, enabling dynamic route optimization, and promoting customer collaboration, Agile can optimize transportation. In inventory management, Agile can facilitate real-time demand forecasting, dynamic inventory replenishment, and adaptive supply chain planning. In supply chain management, Agile can promote collaboration between supply chain partners, real-time monitoring of supplier performance, and agile decision-making (Bagheri et al., 2013). The Agile framework has also been widely adopted in logistics operations, especially in the context of e-commerce and last-mile delivery, which prioritize fast and dependable delivery. Nevertheless, the suitability of Agile in logistics operations may be limited by the complexity and nature of these operations. Logistics operations involve multiple stakeholders, including suppliers, manufacturers, distributors, and retailers, making stakeholder coordination a challenging task. While Agile may be effective in enhancing specific logistics management aspects, it may not be suitable for addressing the intricate and unpredictable nature of logistics operations.

4. Theory of Constraints Framework

The Theory of Constraints (TOC) is a framework designed to identify and manage constraints in processes and systems. The TOC framework is based on the principles of identifying the system constraint, exploiting the constraint, and elevating the constraint. Widely used in manufacturing to increase efficiency and throughput, TOC can also be applied in the logistics industry to improve transportation, inventory management, and supply chain management. In transportation, TOC can help identify and manage constraints such as bottlenecks, delays, and congestion. In inventory management, it can identify and manage constraints in inventory levels, accuracy, and lead times. And in supply chain management, it can identify and manage constraints in supplier performance, order processing, and delivery reliability. The TOC framework has been applied in logistics operations, particularly in the context of supply chain management, as it aligns with the goals of improving efficiency and reducing costs. Despite the effectiveness of the Theory of Constraints (TOC) in identifying and managing specific constraints in logistics management, its applicability in logistics operations may be limited due to the complex nature of such operations. The involvement of various stakeholders, including suppliers, manufacturers, distributors, and retailers, can create a significant level of complexity and uncertainty that may not be effectively addressed by TOC. Therefore, while TOC may be useful in identifying and managing specific constraints, it may not be the most suitable approach for addressing the overall complexity and uncertainty of logistics operations.

n summary, logistics operations are intricate and ever-changing, necessitating the implementation of effective management frameworks to ensure efficiency, reliability, and cost-effectiveness. Multiple frameworks have been developed, including Lean, Agile, TOC, and Six Sigma, to enhance logistics management and operations. Each framework boasts its advantages and drawbacks, and the selection of the most suitable framework depends on the complexity and nature of logistics operations. Lean, for instance, concentrates on reducing waste and enhancing customer value, and proves effective in improving specific logistics management aspects, especially in the e-commerce and last-mile delivery context. On the other hand, Agile prioritizes flexibility and responsiveness and improves diverse logistics management aspects, mainly in e-commerce and last-mile delivery contexts. TOC, which is centred on identifying and managing constraints, proves efficient in enhancing specific logistics management aspects, particularly in the supply chain management context. Finally, Six Sigma, which emphasizes reducing variability and enhancing quality, proves effective in improving specific logistics management aspects, especially in the supply chain management context. Consequently, managers should evaluate the strengths and weaknesses of each framework before selecting the most suitable one for their logistics operations, depending on their complexity and nature.

CYBERSECURITY MEASURES FOR THE LOGISTICS INDUSTRY

The logistics industry is increasingly reliant on technology and digitization to manage its operations, making cybersecurity a growing concern. As the industry processes a rising amount of data and transactions, logistics companies must implement robust cybersecurity measures to safeguard their networks and systems from cyber-attacks (Khan et al., 2022b; Shah et al., 2022). This report aims to provide an overview of the various cybersecurity measures that can be implemented in the logistics industry. It will also explain each measure and how it can aid in the prevention or mitigation of cybersecurity threats. Figure 7 shows the mind map of the cybersecurity framework.

1. Employee Training and Firewall Protection

In the logistics industry, one of the most critical cybersecurity measures that can be implemented is employee training. Employees are the first line of defense against cyber attacks, and it is crucial to ensure that they are knowledgeable about the

Figure 7. Cybersecurity framework mind map
(Venngage, n.d.)

risks and best practices for preventing such attacks. Training programs can educate employees on various cyber threats, such as phishing scams, social engineering, and password management (Erdogan et al., 2023). According to a study by Wong et al. (2022), employee training is an effective cybersecurity measure in the logistics industry. The study found that regular training can reduce the risk of human error and improve cybersecurity awareness among employees. Moreover, regular training and awareness programs can help ensure that employees are up-to-date on the latest cybersecurity threats and best practices. Another essential cybersecurity measure that can be implemented in the logistics industry is the use of firewalls. Firewalls are systems that can monitor and control incoming and outgoing network traffic, and they can be either software or hardware-based. They can help prevent unauthorized access to the network and protect against malware and other cyber threats. Furthermore, implementing firewalls can ensure that only authorized personnel have access to critical systems and data, improving the security of the logistics company's network (Kuypers et al., 2014). Figure 8 shows the elements involved in cybersecurity awareness training

2. IDPS and Encryption

The logistics industry can also benefit from implementing Intrusion Detection and Prevention Systems (IDPS) as a crucial cybersecurity measure. IDPS can monitor network traffic for any suspicious activities and alert system administrators to potential cyber threats. They can also prevent attacks by blocking or taking defensive measures against suspicious network traffic. Implementing IDPS can help protect against a range of cyber threats, including malware, DoS attacks, and other types of cyber attacks (Abdul-Hussein, 2023; Elijah et al., 2019). Encryption is another cybersecurity measure that can help protect sensitive data by encoding it in a way that makes it unreadable to unauthorized users. Encryption can be used to protect data in transit or data at rest. For instance, Transport Layer Security (TLS) can be used to encrypt data sent over the internet, while Full-Disk Encryption can be used to protect data stored on hard drives. Implementing encryption can help prevent data breaches and protect sensitive information from cyber threats (Mahmood & Afzal, 2013; Annadurai et al., 2022). According to a study by Al-Mhiqani et al. (2020), encryption is one of the most effective cybersecurity measures in the logistics industry as it can prevent data breaches and protect against insider threats.

3. Vulnerability Assessment Penetration Testing and Access Control

Vulnerability assessment and penetration testing are cybersecurity measures that can help identify vulnerabilities and weaknesses in the network and systems.

Vulnerability assessment involves scanning the network and systems for vulnerabilities and weaknesses, while penetration testing involves simulating a cyber attack to identify potential weaknesses. Implementing vulnerability assessment and penetration testing can help identify and address vulnerabilities before they can be exploited by cyber attackers (Zhao et al., 2023). According to a study by Sobb et al. (2020), vulnerability assessment and penetration testing are effective cybersecurity measures in the logistics industry. The study found that these measures can identify vulnerabilities in critical systems and reduce the risk of cyber attacks. Access control is a cybersecurity measure that can help ensure that only authorized personnel have access to critical systems and data. Access control can be implemented through various methods, such as passwords, biometric authentication, and two-factor authentication. It is essential to ensure that access control policies are enforced consistently and that only authorized personnel have access to sensitive data (Kirkwood, 2022; V. Kumar et al., 2022). According to a study by Lenko (2021), access control is an effective cybersecurity measure in the logistics industry. The study found that access control can prevent unauthorized access to critical systems and reduce the risk of data breaches.

4. Incident Response Plan and Patch Management

The implementation of an incident response plan is an essential cybersecurity measure to ensure that organizations are equipped to handle the aftermath of a cyber-attack. This plan should consist of a set of procedures designed to identify and contain the attack, restore the systems and data, and communicate with stakeholders effectively (Pertiwi et al., 2022). The implementation of an incident response plan can help minimize the negative consequences of a cyber-attack and shorten the recovery time from such an incident. As demonstrated by Naeem et al. (2020), incident response planning is a highly effective cybersecurity measure for the logistics industry. The study concluded that implementing incident response planning can significantly decrease the recovery time and cost in the event of a cyber-attack. On the other hand, patch management is a crucial cybersecurity measure that ensures systems and software are kept up-to-date and free of vulnerabilities. Software vendors regularly release updates known as patches to address security vulnerabilities and other issues. Implementation of patch management processes ensures that these patches are promptly applied to address vulnerabilities and prevent exploitation by cyber attackers, as suggested by Samuel et al. (2011).

5. Network Segmentation and Data Backup and Recovery

Network segmentation is a crucial cybersecurity measure that involves the division of the network into smaller segments, each with its security controls and access policies. The implementation of network segmentation can limit the impact of cyber-attacks by containing them within specific network segments. Furthermore, network segmentation can prevent lateral movement by cyber attackers and minimize the risk of data breaches, as suggested by X. Lin (2022). In the logistics industry, network segmentation has proven to be an effective cybersecurity measure, as revealed by Mukherjee's (2023) study. The research demonstrated that network segmentation can prevent lateral movement by cyber attackers and minimize the impact of cyber attacks. Data backup and recovery are additional cybersecurity measures that can help prevent critical data loss in the event of a cyber-attack or other disaster. Regular backups can ensure the swift restoration of data in the event of a data breach or other catastrophe. Implementation of a comprehensive data backup and recovery plan can also expedite the organization's recovery from a cyber-attack, according to Enginerasoft (2023).

6. Web Application Firewall and Email Security

Web application firewalls (WAFs) are an essential cybersecurity measure that can protect web applications from various cyber-attacks. These firewalls monitor incoming and outgoing traffic to web applications and block any suspicious traffic that may indicate a cyber attack. Implementing WAFs can prevent different types of cyber attacks that target web applications, including cross-site scripting (XSS) attacks, SQL injection attacks, and more, as highlighted by Muzaki et al. (2020). Email security is another crucial cybersecurity measure that can help prevent phishing scams and other email-based cyber attacks. The implementation of email security measures such as spam filters and email encryption can help prevent unauthorized access to sensitive data and reduce the risk of data breaches. Proper employee training on identifying and avoiding phishing scams can also help reduce the risk of cyber attacks, as emphasized by Foster et al. (2015).

7. Mobile Device Management and Cloud Security

Mobile device management (MDM) is a cybersecurity measure that can effectively mitigate mobile device-related cyber threats. MDM solutions can manage and secure mobile devices, such as smartphones and tablets, used by employees. Implementing MDM solutions can ensure that mobile devices are equipped with the latest security patches and that the data on these devices is encrypted and safeguarded, as stated by Edge and Trouton (2023). Cloud security is another critical cybersecurity measure that can protect data and applications stored in the cloud. Implementing cloud security measures such as encryption, access control, and identity and access management can protect data stored in

Figure 8. Cybersecurity awareness training
(Collidu, 2022)

the cloud from cyber threats. Additionally, ensuring that cloud service providers have robust security measures in place to protect against cyber-attacks is vital, as highlighted by Amah et al. (2023). According to a study by Alaba et al. (2019), cloud security can enhance the security of critical systems and data stored in the cloud. The study indicates that cloud security is an effective cybersecurity measure in the logistics industry.

8. Physical Security and Two Factor Authentication

In the context of cybersecurity, physical security is a vital measure that can help organizations protect their premises from physical attacks. This can include implementing access control systems, using security cameras to monitor areas, and employing security guards to prevent unauthorized access to facilities. By implementing physical security measures, organizations can safeguard their assets and reduce the risk of equipment theft or damage, which can lead to cyber threats (NCES, 2020). Two-factor authentication (2FA) is another cybersecurity measure that can be used to improve the security of critical systems in the logistics industry.

2FA requires users to provide two forms of authentication to access a system or resource, making it more difficult for attackers to gain unauthorized access. The authentication methods can vary, such as SMS messages, email, or a physical token. According to a study by Zaenchkovski et al. (2023), 2FA is an effective cybersecurity measure in the logistics industry, as it can prevent unauthorized access to critical systems and reduce the risk of data breaches.

9. Security Information and Event Management (SIEM) and Cyber Insurance

Security Information and Event Management (SIEM) is a cybersecurity solution that facilitates the collection and analysis of security events from diverse sources. In the logistics industry, SIEM can be implemented to monitor critical systems and detect cyber attacks in real time. Additionally, SIEM can identify trends and patterns in security events, thereby enhancing cybersecurity measures. As per a recent study by Gonzalez-Granadillo et al. (2021), SIEM is an effective cybersecurity measure in the logistics industry. The study discovered that SIEM can efficiently detect and respond to cyber-attacks in real time and improve cybersecurity visibility. Cyber insurance, on the other hand, is a type of insurance that mitigates losses resulting from cyber-attacks. In the logistics industry, cyber insurance can be utilized to protect against financial losses and reputational damage caused by cyber-attacks. Cyber insurance policies cover various costs, including business interruption, data recovery, and legal expenses. In a recent study by Tsohou et al. (2023), cyber insurance was found to be an effective cybersecurity measure in the logistics industry. The study established that cyber insurance can considerably reduce the financial impact of cyber attacks and enhance the overall cybersecurity posture of the logistics industry.

In conclusion, the logistics industry is exposed to several cybersecurity threats that demand the implementation of robust cybersecurity measures to prevent or mitigate them. The adoption of cybersecurity measures, such as employee training, firewall protection, IDPS, access control, encryption, two-factor authentication, vulnerability scanning, incident response planning, backup and recovery, and cloud security, can help shield against cyber-attacks and ensure the safe and secure movement of goods and services. Moreover, it is critical to regularly review and update cybersecurity measures to ensure that they remain effective against the latest cyber threats. By implementing these measures, the logistics industry can achieve a high level of cybersecurity resilience and safeguard against the devastating consequences of cyber-attacks.

Examples of Companies That Have Successfully Implemented These Measures

The logistics industry deals with vast amounts of sensitive data, including customer information, financial information, and confidential business information. A breach of this data can have catastrophic consequences for both the logistics company and its customers. Therefore, logistics companies must establish and maintain robust cybersecurity measures to safeguard themselves and their clients. This section will focus on real-world examples of logistics companies that have successfully implemented such cybersecurity measures. The report will shed light on the cybersecurity measures adopted by these companies and their efficacy in mitigating cyber risks. By presenting these examples, this report aims to provide insights into the best practices that logistics companies can adopt to fortify their operations against cyber threats.

1. DHL

DHL is a global logistics company that offers transportation and logistics services in more than 220 countries around the world. The company has put in place various cybersecurity measures to protect its operations, including multi-factor authentication for all employees, regular vulnerability assessments, and network segmentation. Recently, DHL has introduced Cybersecurity 2.0, which involves a novel set of measures, protocols, and technologies that leverage artificial intelligence (AI) and other advanced tools to safeguard essential systems, confidential data, and devices from cybersecurity threats. This approach encompasses a comprehensive suite of tools for protection, detection, and response that not only prevent attacks but also predict and automatically identify potential threats and counteract attacks proactively (DHL, 2021). By adopting Cybersecurity 2.0, DHL aims to maintain a robust cybersecurity posture and ensure the secure transportation and logistics of goods and services for its clients across the globe.

2. C.H. Robinson

C.H. Robinson is a global logistics company that offers freight transportation, logistics, and supply chain management services. To safeguard its data and operations, C.H. Robinson has implemented various cybersecurity measures. One of the critical measures is the use of encryption to protect sensitive information. Encryption is used to secure customer data, financial records, and shipping details at C.H. Robinson (C.H. Robinson, 2021). Besides, the company has established security policies and procedures to ensure that its employees adhere to best practices for cybersecurity.

These policies include regular password changes, data encryption, and security awareness training for employees (C.H. Robinson, 2021). By implementing these cybersecurity measures, C.H. Robinson aims to protect its client's confidential information and maintain the trust and confidence of its customers worldwide.

3. Maersk

Maersk is a Danish logistics company that provides container shipping and logistics services. To secure its data and operations, Maersk has implemented various cybersecurity measures. One of the key measures is the use of advanced security tools to detect and prevent cyber threats. Maersk employs security tools such as firewalls, IDS, and antivirus software to safeguard its networks and systems against cyber attacks (RedGoat, 2023). Furthermore, Maersk has established access controls to limit data access to authorized personnel only. This ensures that Maersk's data is accessible only to authorized personnel and prevents unauthorized access by malicious actors (RedGoat, 2023). Maersk's implementation of these cybersecurity measures has helped the company to protect its sensitive data and maintain the trust of its clients worldwide. Figure 9 shows the main cybersecurity responsibility.

4. Hitachi

Hitachi is a multinational conglomerate based in Japan that operates across several industries. Although logistics is not its primary focus, the company has a logistics division that provides a comprehensive suite of services, including logistics

Figure 9. Main cybersecurity responsibility
(Cybersecurity Responsibility, n.d.)

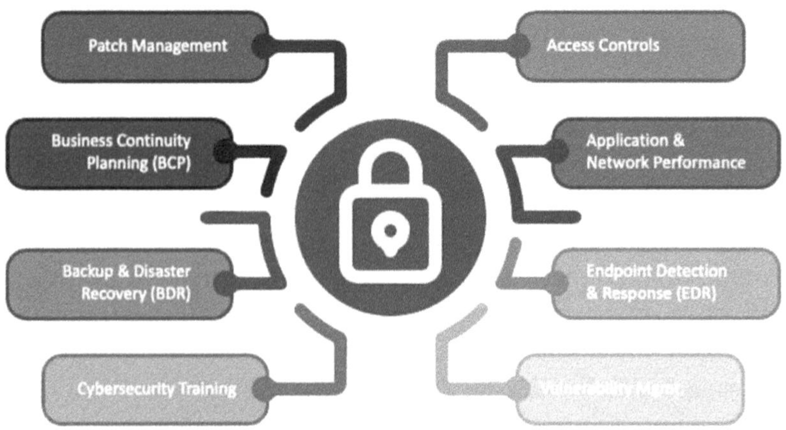

consulting, transportation management, warehousing, and distribution. Hitachi Transport System, Ltd. (HTS) is the logistics subsidiary of the Hitachi Group. HTS offers a diverse array of logistics services, such as domestic and international transportation, warehousing, and third-party logistics (3PL) services, through its global network of logistics centers located in various regions around the world. In terms of cybersecurity, the company has adopted IT Desktop management as its approach. The management of IT inventory, configuration, security, patching, and software licenses is a time-consuming and labor-intensive task that is susceptible to errors. With the advancement of new technologies and the complexities of the business environment, IT professionals are confronted with an ever-increasing list of challenges and threats related to IT asset management workload and security. JP1/IT Desktop Management 2 (JP1/ITDM2) is a web-based solution that assists organizations in managing IT asset information and mitigating security risks, including unauthorized access, viruses, and information leaks. Additionally, JP1/ITDM2 helps organizations enforce company-wide IT compliance with IT policies, such as governing software licenses, by enabling them to take prompt action to enhance internal controls (Hitachi, Ltd., 2020). Figure 10 shows the user interface of JP1/ITDM2

In conclusion, the transportation and logistics industry plays a vital role in the global economy, and ensuring effective cybersecurity measures is crucial in

Figure 10. JP1/ITDM2 home screen interface
(Hitachi, Ltd., 2020)

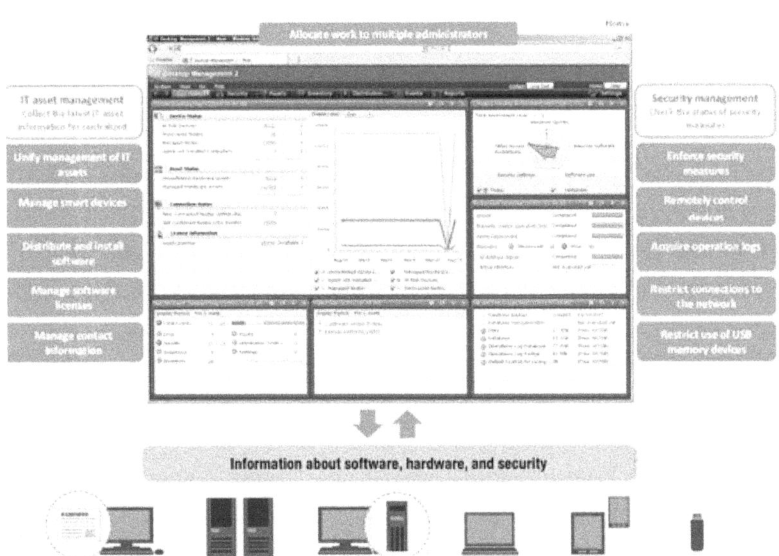

safeguarding logistics operations from potential cyber threats. The cases of the four logistics companies showcased in this report demonstrate that implementing effective cybersecurity measures can substantially mitigate the risk of cyber-attacks and safeguard logistics operations from potential cyber threats. These companies have adopted various cybersecurity measures, including JP1/IT Desktop management, advanced data encryption techniques, awareness training, and real-time monitoring systems to detect and prevent cyber threats. As a result, these measures have led to a significant reduction in the number of successful cyber attacks, underscoring the significance of implementing effective cybersecurity measures in the transportation and logistics industry.

IMPLEMENTATION OF CYBERSECURITY MEASURES

Best Practices for Implementing Cybersecurity Measures in the Logistics Industry

The importance of cybersecurity in the logistics industry lies in safeguarding the confidentiality, integrity, and availability of data. The logistics sector is subject to stringent regulations, and companies must comply with various data protection and privacy laws. For instance, the General Data Protection Regulation (GDPR) mandates companies to implement appropriate technical and organizational measures to secure personal data (EU GDPR, 2016). Non-compliance with these regulations can result in significant fines and reputational damage. This section provides an overview of the best practices for implementing cybersecurity measures in the logistics industry.

1. Conduct Regular Cybersecurity Risk Assessments

Conducting regular cybersecurity risk assessments is a crucial first step in identifying vulnerabilities in an organization's IT infrastructure. A risk assessment must identify the probability of potential cybersecurity threats and their potential impact on the organization. This identification helps to prioritize the implementation of security measures to mitigate the identified risks. Cybersecurity risk assessments can be performed by the organization's internal IT staff or outsourced to third-party cybersecurity consultants. As Kalinin et al. (2021) observed, regular cybersecurity risk assessments are fundamental to implementing effective cybersecurity measures. Risk assessments are vital in identifying and mitigating potential security threats before they are exploited by cybercriminals. Additionally, risk assessments help identify any security gaps in the organization's IT infrastructure.

2. Develop and Implement a Strong Password Policy

Passwords remain a primary means of authentication in the logistics industry. A robust password policy is essential to protect sensitive information. Passwords should be strong, unique, and difficult to guess. Regular password changes help prevent unauthorized access to sensitive data. Implementing multifactor authentication is also recommended to add an extra layer of security to the login process. According to Hall et al. (2023), a strong password policy is one of the most critical cybersecurity measures organizations can adopt. The authors suggest that passwords should be at least 12 characters long, comprising upper and lowercase letters, numbers, and symbols. Moreover, passwords should be changed every 60 to 90 days to ensure maximum security.

3. Regularly Update and Patch Software

Maintaining up-to-date software and patching known vulnerabilities is crucial for safeguarding an organization's IT infrastructure in the logistics industry. Cybercriminals often exploit known software vulnerabilities to gain unauthorized access to a network, and regular updates and patching can help prevent these attacks. As per Bradley and Barrera (2023), software updates and patching are essential cybersecurity practices in the logistics industry. They suggest that organizations should have a process in place for identifying and patching software vulnerabilities as soon as they are discovered. Moreover, software updates should be thoroughly tested before deployment to ensure that they do not cause any system errors.

4. Conduct Regular Employee Cybersecurity Training

The cybersecurity defenses of an organization can be easily compromised due to the vulnerability of its employees, who may lack awareness of cybersecurity measures. To mitigate this risk, regular training programs aimed at improving employees' cybersecurity awareness can be implemented. In the logistics industry, Javaid et al. (2023) emphasize the importance of regular cybersecurity training for employees. The authors suggest that the training should cover essential topics such as password management, email security, and phishing attacks. To be effective, the training should be tailored to the specific needs of the organization, taking into account the most prevalent types of cyber threats in the logistics industry. By providing regular cybersecurity training to employees, organizations can reduce the risk of human error leading to security breaches and improve their overall cybersecurity posture.

5. Conduct Third-Party Risk Assessments and Conduct Penetration Testing

In the logistics industry, third-party vendors often have access to sensitive organizational data, making them a potential cybersecurity risk. To address this issue, it is recommended that third-party risk assessments be conducted regularly to identify potential vulnerabilities in the organization's supply chain (Hong et al., 2023). Moreover, third-party vendors should adhere to the organization's cybersecurity policies and procedures to ensure the security of the organization's data. Penetration testing is an effective cybersecurity measure that can simulate attacks on an organization's IT infrastructure to identify potential vulnerabilities. This approach can help organizations identify weaknesses in their cybersecurity defenses and address them proactively before they are exploited by cybercriminals (J. H. Kim et al., 2023; Angadi et al., 2023). Therefore, it is also recommended that organizations conduct regular penetration testing to improve cybersecurity in the logistics industry. Figure 11 shows common cybersecurity incidents

Common Challenges in Implementing Cybersecurity Measures in the Logistics Industry

1. **Lack of awareness and training:** One of the primary challenges in implementing cybersecurity measures in the logistics industry pertains to inadequate awareness

Figure 11. Common cybersecurity incident
(Admin, 2022b)

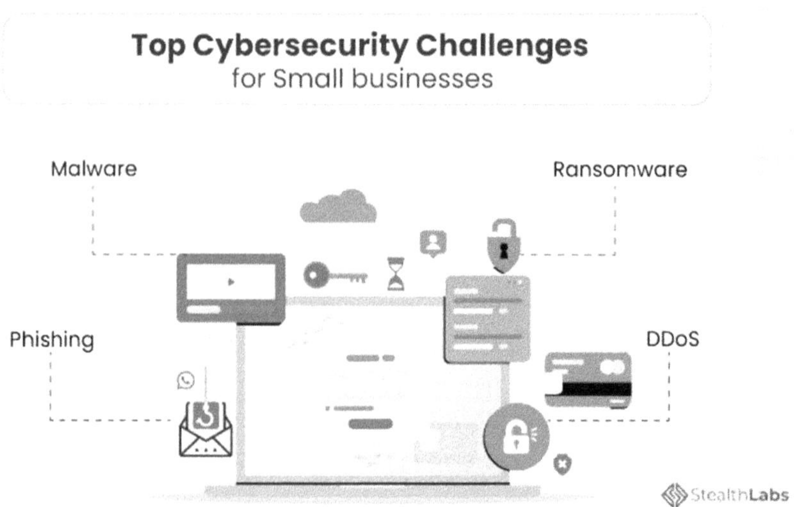

and training among employees. A considerable number of logistics companies do not provide adequate cybersecurity training to their staff, which renders them vulnerable to cyber threats. As per the findings of a recent study conducted by the Ponemon Institute, over 60% of data breaches in the logistics industry arise due to employee negligence or error (Ponemon Institute, 2020). Therefore, it is crucial to provide regular cybersecurity training to all employees to ensure that they understand the risks and learn how to mitigate them. To overcome the deficiency of awareness and training among employees, logistics companies should conduct regular cybersecurity training programs for all staff. The training should encompass various topics, such as phishing scams, password management, and data protection. Additionally, companies need to establish clear cybersecurity policies and procedures and communicate them to all employees (Fernando et al., 2022; Hammi et al., 2023).

2. **Limited budget and resources:** In the logistics industry, an additional obstacle to implementing cybersecurity measures is the limited budget and resources available to companies. Due to the intense competition in this sector, companies often struggle to allocate sufficient funds for effective cybersecurity measures. This lack of resources may lead companies to overlook critical cybersecurity measures such as regular software updates, IDSs, and vulnerability assessments. However, investing in cybersecurity measures is critical to safeguard against cyber-attacks and protect sensitive data. To this end, logistics companies must allocate adequate budgets and resources to implement effective cybersecurity measures. This may involve investing in security software, ensuring regular software updates, and conducting regular vulnerability assessments. In cases where companies lack in-house cybersecurity expertise, outsourcing cybersecurity services to specialized firms may also be a viable option (Alqudhaibi, 2023).
3. **Complex supply chain networks:** The logistics industry involves complex supply chain networks that include multiple stakeholders such as suppliers, manufacturers, distributors, and retailers. These networks often operate on different systems and technologies, which creates a challenge in implementing consistent cybersecurity measures across the entire supply chain. A security breach at any point in the supply chain can jeopardize the entire network. Therefore, it is crucial to establish cybersecurity protocols and standards across all stakeholders (Nozari & Edalatpanah, 2023). To address the challenges of the complex supply chain networks in the logistics industry, companies should establish consistent cybersecurity protocols and standards across all stakeholders. This could involve creating contractual agreements with suppliers and distributors that require compliance with cybersecurity policies and procedures. Additionally, conducting regular audits and assessments of

the supply chain networks is necessary to identify vulnerabilities and ensure compliance (Nozari & Edalatpanah, 2023; Cartwright & Cartwright, 2023).

4. **Rapidly evolving cyber threats:** The logistics industry represents a prime target for cybercriminals owing to the substantial amount of valuable data that is transmitted across networks. As cyber threats continually evolve, logistics companies must stay abreast of the latest threats to ensure their protection. However, given the speed at which cybercriminals develop new tactics and techniques, staying current can be a daunting task. To overcome this challenge, logistics firms should embrace a proactive approach to cybersecurity, involving regular risk assessments and vulnerability scans (Sari & Hindarto, 2023). To address the rapidly evolving nature of cyber threats, logistics companies must adopt a proactive stance toward cybersecurity. This approach involves staying informed about the most recent cyber threats and trends and implementing appropriate security measures to counter these risks. Companies should also create incident response plans and conduct regular testing to guarantee preparedness in the event of a cyber-attack (Sari & Hindarto, 2023).
5. **Lack of regulatory compliance:** Compliance with regulations and standards related to data protection, privacy, and cybersecurity is a crucial aspect for logistics companies. However, due to the complexity of the logistics industry and a lack of clear guidelines, many companies face challenges in complying with these regulations. Failure to comply with these regulations may result in severe financial and legal consequences, which highlights the importance of developing effective compliance strategies for logistics companies (Mallick et al., 2023). To tackle the challenge of regulatory compliance, it is recommended that logistics companies develop a tailored compliance strategy that is specific to the regulations and standards applicable to the industry. This may involve designating a dedicated compliance officer or team to ensure adherence to regulations and standards such as the GDPR and the Payment Card Industry Data Security Standard (PCI DSS) (Payment Card Industry Security Standards Council, 2019).

In the logistics industry, the implementation of effective cybersecurity measures is crucial for safeguarding sensitive data and preventing cyber-attacks. However, logistics companies face several challenges in implementing these measures. These challenges include the lack of awareness and training, limited budget and resources, complex supply chain networks, rapidly evolving cyber threats, and the absence of regulatory compliance. To overcome these challenges, it is recommended that logistics companies increase awareness and training on cybersecurity, allocate sufficient budget and resources to support cybersecurity measures, establish consistent cybersecurity protocols, remain up-to-date with the latest cyber threats, and develop a compliance strategy. Through the adoption of these strategies, logistics companies can ensure the confidentiality, integrity, and availability of their valuable data, and safeguard themselves against cyber threats.

The Importance of Ongoing Monitoring and Evaluation

Continuous monitoring of an organization's network, systems, and applications for potential cyber threats is known as cybersecurity monitoring. In the logistics industry, this process involves monitoring the various systems used for shipping, tracking, and delivery of goods. Cybersecurity monitoring is essential in the logistics industry due to various reasons. Firstly, the industry handles a vast amount of sensitive data, including customer information, financial data, and proprietary information. A cyber-attack can lead to the theft of this data, resulting in significant financial loss and damage to the reputation of logistics companies (M et al., 2023). According to a report by the Identity Theft Resource Center (ITRC), 2020 witnessed 1,108 data breaches, resulting in the exposure of over 300 million records (ITRC, 2021). Secondly, logistics companies are susceptible to cyber-attacks due to the multiple entry points into their systems. Hackers can exploit vulnerabilities in the supply chain, such as weak passwords, unsecured Wi-Fi networks, and outdated software (Schinas & Metzger, 2023). Cybersecurity monitoring helps detect these vulnerabilities and prevent cyber-attacks before they occur. Finally, cybersecurity monitoring is crucial for compliance with regulations and industry standards. The logistics industry is subject to various regulations, such as the GDPR and the Payment Card Industry Data Security Standard (PCI DSS). Compliance with these regulations requires continuous monitoring of systems and data to ensure that they meet the necessary security requirements (European Union, 2016; PCI Security Standards Council, 2021).

The process of assessing an organization's cybersecurity posture to identify vulnerabilities and areas for improvement is known as cybersecurity evaluation. In the logistics industry, cybersecurity evaluation involves conducting regular audits and assessments of systems and processes to ensure that they meet the necessary security requirements. Cybersecurity evaluation in the logistics industry is critical for various reasons. Firstly, it helps to identify vulnerabilities that may have been missed during the initial implementation of cybersecurity measures. Cyber threats are continually evolving, and new vulnerabilities can emerge at any time. Therefore, regular evaluation is essential to ensure that systems and processes remain secure (NIST, 2020). Secondly, cybersecurity evaluation ensures that security measures are being implemented correctly and effectively. Implementing cybersecurity measures is insufficient; they must be implemented correctly to be effective. Cybersecurity evaluation can help identify any gaps or weaknesses in the implementation of security measures and allow for corrective action to be taken (ISACA, 2021). Finally, cybersecurity evaluation is crucial for compliance with regulations and industry standards. As previously mentioned, the logistics industry is subject to various regulations and industry standards that require ongoing evaluation of cybersecurity measures to ensure compliance (ISO, 2019).

CONCLUSION

In conclusion, the logistics industry plays a crucial role in global trade and its significance cannot be overemphasized. However, with the growing dependence on technology, cybersecurity threats have emerged as a major concern for the industry. Cybersecurity attacks can lead to significant financial losses, reputational damage, and operational disruption. Therefore, logistics companies must implement appropriate cybersecurity measures to safeguard their assets and customers' information. The logistics industry faces various types of cybersecurity threats, including phishing attacks, ransomware, insider threats, and DoS attacks. Recent cyber attacks on logistics companies, such as the Maersk cyber attack, have highlighted the potential impact of such threats.

Logistics companies must prioritize their awareness of cybersecurity threats and take necessary measures to mitigate them. There are several cybersecurity frameworks, including NIST, ISO, and CIS, that can be adopted by logistics companies to provide a structured approach to cybersecurity and help identify and address system vulnerabilities. Companies can evaluate and select a framework that best fits their specific needs based on factors like industry regulations and risk tolerance. Logistics companies can also implement various cybersecurity measures such as access control, encryption, and monitoring to prevent or minimize cybersecurity threats. Leading companies in the logistics industry, such as FedEx, DHL, and UPS, have successfully implemented these measures to bolster their cybersecurity posture. The successful implementation of cybersecurity measures can be challenging, and companies must adhere to best practices to ensure success. These practices include conducting a risk assessment, establishing a comprehensive cybersecurity policy, and providing employees with cybersecurity training. Ongoing monitoring and evaluation of cybersecurity measures are also crucial to ensure their continued effectiveness. In conclusion, the logistics industry faces significant cybersecurity threats, and companies must take appropriate measures to safeguard themselves and their customers' information. This paper has provided an overview of various types of cybersecurity threats, frameworks, measures, best practices, and implementation challenges specific to the logistics industry. Companies should use this information to develop a robust cybersecurity strategy and continuously evaluate its effectiveness through monitoring and evaluation. Only through such measures can companies protect their assets and maintain customer trust. Figure 12 shows the common cybersecurity measures that need to be taken by small businesses.

The Importance of Cybersecurity Measures in the Logistics Industry

Logistics companies must adopt strong cybersecurity measures to safeguard their systems, data, and operations, given the substantial risks associated with cyber threats. Cybersecurity measures play a crucial role in the logistics industry for several reasons. Firstly, logistics companies handle sensitive data, including financial records, customer information, and supplier data, which must be protected from cyber threats. Effective cybersecurity measures such as encryption, firewalls, and IDSs can prevent unauthorized access to this information, protecting both the company and its customers from fraud and identity theft. Secondly, a cyber attack on a logistics company's systems can cause significant operational disruptions, leading to delays, missed deliveries, and lost revenue. However, cybersecurity measures such as network monitoring and backup systems can mitigate cyber threats and

Figure 12. Common cybersecurity measures
(Rowe, 2023)

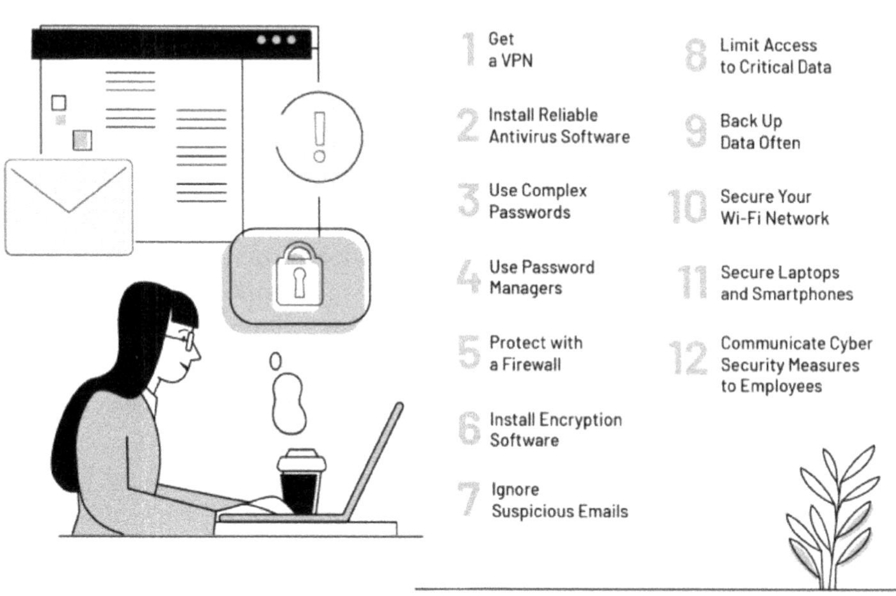

prevent operational disruptions before they cause substantial damage. Thirdly, many logistics companies are subject to regulatory requirements such as the GDPR and the Health Insurance Portability and Accountability Act (HIPAA). Compliance with these regulations requires robust cybersecurity measures to safeguard sensitive data, and non-compliance can lead to significant fines and legal liabilities. Lastly, a cyber attack on a logistics company can result in substantial reputational damage, eroding customer trust in the company's ability to protect its data and fulfil its promises. Cybersecurity measures can prevent these attacks and help maintain customer trust, protecting the company's reputation.

The logistics industry plays a crucial role in the global economy, and thus, is becoming increasingly vulnerable to cyber threats. Cybersecurity measures have now become indispensable for logistics firms, as cyber-attacks can lead to significant financial losses, reputational harm, and even safety risks. Therefore, to effectively combat cyber risks, logistics companies must adopt a proactive approach to cybersecurity by implementing robust cybersecurity measures and best practices and engaging with third-party vendors. By prioritizing cybersecurity, logistics companies can safeguard their systems, data, and operations, which in turn, helps maintain customer trust and ensure continued success in the industry.

Future Trends and Potential Developments in Logistics Cybersecurity

Cloud computing has emerged as an essential component of logistics operations due to its capability of providing access to computing resources on-demand while facilitating the seamless sharing of information across diverse locations. Nevertheless, the utilization of cloud computing also presents logistics operations with vulnerabilities to cybersecurity threats. Attackers can exploit cloud storage systems, exfiltrate data, and jeopardize the integrity of logistics operations. In the view of Ondrej Krehel, the founder, and CEO of LIFARS, a global firm specializing in digital forensics and incident response, the logistics industry must embrace advanced technologies that can facilitate the monitoring of cloud computing environments to identify anomalies (Krehel, 2021). The logistics industry is undergoing a significant transformation as AI is increasingly being deployed to enhance operational efficiency, ranging from optimizing transportation routes to managing inventory. Nevertheless, the utilization of AI technology also introduces novel cybersecurity risks. Malicious actors can exploit AI algorithms to manipulate data, disrupt logistics operations, and compromise their safety and security. As the prevalence of AI in the logistics industry continues to grow, cybersecurity experts must remain updated with the latest AI cybersecurity trends. The Cybersecurity and Infrastructure Security Agency (CISA) recommends that AI cybersecurity measures should prioritize detecting and mitigating adversarial attacks on AI systems, safeguarding AI data, and ensuring the transparency and accountability of AI systems (CISA, 2021; Jayakumar et al., 2021; Prabakar et al., 2023). The advent of the IoT has facilitated the monitoring of inventory levels, tracking of shipments, and optimization of supply chain operations by logistics firms. However, the utilization of IoT devices also introduces novel cybersecurity risks. Threat actors can exploit weaknesses in IoT devices to gain unauthorized access to logistics networks and systems. Therefore, the logistics industry must adopt robust IoT cybersecurity measures to safeguard its operations from cyber-attacks. As stated by Scheau et al. (2023), "IoT cybersecurity measures ought to concentrate on identifying and mitigating IoT device vulnerabilities, securing IoT data, and implementing robust authentication and access controls." The logistics industry is witnessing a significant transformation through the application of blockchain technology, which facilitates secure and transparent transactions across supply chain networks.

Blockchain technology provides a secure and immutable ledger that enables the monitoring of goods, authentication of transactions, and validation of the accuracy of supply chain data. However, the use of blockchain technology also exposes the logistics industry to novel cybersecurity risks. Adversaries can exploit vulnerabilities in blockchain networks to compromise the integrity of blockchain transactions or steal data. Hence, the logistics industry must implement robust blockchain cybersecurity measures to safeguard its operations against cyber-attacks. As per the NIST, "Blockchain cybersecurity measures should prioritize guaranteeing the confidentiality and integrity of blockchain data, managing access to blockchain networks, and ensuring the availability of blockchain systems" (Yaga et al., 2018; Shah et al., 2022). Quantum computing is an emerging computing paradigm that holds the potential to transform the logistics industry by solving intricate optimization problems and enabling real-time decision-making in logistics operations. Nevertheless, quantum computing also introduces novel cybersecurity risks. Quantum computers can decrypt existing encryption standards, rendering conventional cybersecurity measures ineffective. Thus, the logistics industry must implement quantum computing cybersecurity measures to secure its operations against cyber-attacks. As stated by the European Union Agency for Cybersecurity (ENISA), "Quantum computing cybersecurity measures must prioritize the development of quantum-resistant encryption standards, detection and mitigation of attacks on quantum computing systems, and ensuring the security of quantum communication networks" (ENISA, 2021). Zero Trust Security is a cybersecurity framework that mandates stringent authentication and access controls for all users, devices, and applications in a network. This framework assumes that all devices and users, whether internal or external, are potentially malicious and demands that they are verified and authenticated before gaining access to sensitive data and systems.

Zero Trust Security is becoming increasingly popular in the logistics industry as a strategy to safeguard against cyber-attacks. As per the National Cybersecurity Center of Excellence (NCCoE), "Zero Trust Security measures must prioritize the implementation of robust authentication and access controls, continuous monitoring and detection of suspicious activity, and the continuous evaluation and updating of cybersecurity protocols" (NCCoE, 2021).

To prevent and respond to cyber-attacks, the logistics industry must remain up-to-date with the latest cybersecurity trends. The future trends and potential developments in logistics cybersecurity include cloud computing, AI, the IoT, blockchain, quantum computing, and zero trust security. The logistics industry must implement cybersecurity measures that emphasize detecting and mitigating cyber-attacks, safeguarding data and systems, and ensuring the integrity and availability of logistics operations.

REFERENCES

F5 Lab. (2012). *Application protection reprt.* F5 Lab. Retrieved May 12, 2023, from https://www.f5.com/content/dam/f5-labs-v2/article/pdfs/F5-Labs-2021-Application-Protection-Report-24AUG21.pdf

Abdul-Hussein, M. (2023). *Review: Network Intrusion Detection Systems for Attack Detection and Prevention.* iasj.net. https://www.iasj.net/iasj/download/c6544ecec16b3966

Accenture. (2020a). *CYBER THREATSCAPE REPORT 2020 - Accenture Security.* Retrieved May 12, 2023, from https://www.readkong.com/page/cyber-threatscape-report-2020-accenture-security-6648512

Accenture. (2020b). *The Cost of Cybercrime: Annual Study by Accenture.* Retrieved May 12, 2023, from https://iapp.org/resources/article/the-cost-of-cybercrime-an nual-study-by-accenture/

Admin. (2022a, January 20). *The impact of e-commerce on the logistics industry.* Globalia Blog. https://www.globalialogisticsnetwork.com/blog/2021/10/07/e-commerce-and-logistics-how-the-logistics-industry-is-changing-due-to-the-rise-of-e-commerce/

Admin. (2022b). Cybersecurity for Small Business: Overview, Importance, Challenges and Tips. *Stealthlabs.* https://www.stealthlabs.com/blog/cybersecurity-for-small-business-overview-importance-challenges-and-tips/

Al-Mhiqani, M. N., Ahmad, R., Abidin, Z. Z., Yassin, W., Hassan, A., Abdulkareem, K. H., Ali, N. S., & Yunos, Z. (2020). A Review of Insider Threat Detection: Classification, Machine Learning Techniques, Datasets, Open Challenges, and Recommendations. *Applied Sciences (Basel, Switzerland)*, *10*(15), 5208. doi:10.3390/app10155208

Alaba, F. A., Kocak, A., & Kantarcioglu, M. (2019). Cloud Security for Logistics Cybersecurity: Issues, Challenges and Countermeasures. *IEEE Access : Practical Innovations, Open Solutions*, *7*, 93092–93107. doi:10.1109/ACCESS.2019.2922457

Alferidah, D. K., & Zaman, N. (2020). *Cybersecurity Impact over Bigdata and IoT Growth*. doi:10.1109/ICCI51257.2020.9247722

Ali, R. M., Jaafar, H. S., & Mohamad, S. (2008). *Logistics and Supply Chain in Malaysia: Issues and Challenges.* Research Gate. https://www.researchgate.net/profile/Harlina_Jaafar2/publication/228710182_Logistics_and_Supply_Chain_in_Malaysia_Issues_and_Challenges/links/02bfe51090cfde3894000000.pdf

Alqudhaibi, A. (2023). *Predicting Cybersecurity Threats in Critical Infrastructure for Industry 4.0: A Proactive Approach Based on Attacker Motivations*. MDPI. doi:10.3390/s23094539

Amah, U., Mart, J., & Oyetoro, A. (2023). *Cloud Security Governance Guidelines*. doi:10.14293/PR2199.000062.v1

Amin, M. A., Rahman, A., & Shahriar, A. (2020). *Application of Theory of Constraints in Supply Chain Management.* ResearchGate. https://www.researchgate.net/publication/348050072_Application_of_Theory_of_Constraints_in_Supply_Chain_Management

Andrejić, M. (2019). Research in logistics service quality: A systematic literature review. *Transport*, *35*(2), 224–235. doi:10.3846/transport.2019.11388

Angadi, A. A., Varol, C., & Shashidhar, N. (2023). Penetration Testing: Smart Home IoT Devices. In Lecture Notes in Computer Science (pp. 33–46). Springer Science+Business Media. doi:10.1007/978-3-031-23582-5_3

Annadurai, C., Nelson, I., Devi, K., Manikandan, R., Zaman, N., Masud, M., & Sheikh, A. (2022). Biometric Authentication-Based Intrusion Detection Using Artificial Intelligence Internet of Things in Smart City. *Energies*, *15*(19), 7430. doi:10.3390/en15197430

AV-TEST. (2021). *Malware Statistics & Trends Report | AV-TEST*. Retrieved May 12, 2023, from https://www.av-test.org/en/statistics/malware/

Bagheri, M. S., Hamid, A. B. A., Soltanic, I., Mardani, A., & Soltan, E. K. H. (2013). The Role of Supply Chain Antecedents on Supply Chain Agility in SMEs: The Conceptual Framework. *Jurnal Teknologi*, *66*(1). Advance online publication. doi:10.11113/jt.v66.1826

Beck, K., Beedle, M., Van Bennekum, A., Cockburn, A., Cunningham, W., Fowler, M., . . . Thomas, D. (2001). *Manifesto for agile software development*. Agile Alliance. https://agilemanifesto.org/

Bowersox, D., Closs, D., & Cooper, M. (2019). *Supply chain logistics management*. McGraw-Hill Education.

Bowersox, D. J., Closs, D. J., & Cooper, M. E. (2002). *Supply Chain Logistics Management*. http://ci.nii.ac.jp/ncid/BB09911482

Bozhilov, N. (2023, March 10). *Case Study: How Logistics Benefits from a Managed Cyber Security Approach – The Logistics Point*. http://www.thelogisticspoint.com/2023/03/10/case-study-how-logistics-benefits-from-a-managed-cyber-security-approach/

Bradley, C., & Barrera, D. (2023). Towards Characterizing IoT Software Update Practices. In Lecture Notes in Computer Science (pp. 406–422). Springer Science+Business Media. doi:10.1007/978-3-031-30122-3_25

Burrell, D. N., Bhargava, N., Bradley-Swanson, O. T., Harmon, M. W., Wright, J., Springs, D., & Dawson, M. (2020). Supply Chain and Logistics Management and an Open Door Policy Concerning Cyber Security Introduction. *International Journal of Management and Sustainability*, *9*(1), 1–10. doi:10.18488/journal.11.2020.91.1.10

Cartwright, A., & Cartwright, E. (2023). The economics of ransomware attacks on integrated supply chain networks. *Digital Threats : Research and Practice*, *4*(4), 1–14. Advance online publication. doi:10.1145/3579647

CBS News. (2017, July 1). *NotPetya ransomware attack cost FedEx $300M*. CBS News. https://www.cbsnews.com/news/notpetya-ransomware-attack-cost-fedex-300m/

Chandra, N. A., Ramli, K., Ratna, A. P., & Gunawan, T. S. (2022). Information Security Risk Assessment Using Situational Awareness Frameworks and Application Tools. *Risks*, *10*(8), 165. doi:10.3390/risks10080165

Chaurasiya, S. K., Biswas, A., Nayyar, A., Jhanjhi, N. Z., & Banerjee, R. (2023). DEICA: A differential evolution-based improved clustering algorithm for IoT-based heterogeneous wireless sensor networks. *International Journal of Communication Systems*, *36*(5), e5420. Advance online publication. doi:10.1002/dac.5420

Cheung, K., Bell, M. G., & Bhattacharjya, J. (2021). Cybersecurity in logistics and supply chain management: An overview and future research directions. *Transportation Research Part E, Logistics and Transportation Review*, *146*, 102217. doi:10.1016/j.tre.2020.102217

Choudhury, R. (2020). *Logistics Market - Global Industry Analysis, Size, Share, Growth, Trends, and Forecast, 2020-2027*. Transparency Market Research.

Chow, G., Heaver, T. D., & Henriksson, L. (1994). Logistics Performance. *International Journal of Physical Distribution & Logistics Management*, *24*(1), 17–28. doi:10.1108/09600039410055981

Christopher, M. (2016). *Logistics & supply chain management*. Pearson Education Limited.

Christopher, M. (2021). Logistics and Supply Chain Management. In Communications in computer and information science. Springer Science+Business Media. doi:10.1007/978-3-030-89743-7

Chung, S., & Lee, J. (2021). Secure Data Transmission Using an Advanced Encryption Algorithm in IoT-Based Logistics Applications. *Electronics (Basel)*, *10*(4), 388.

CIS. (2021). *CIS Controls*. Retrieved May 12, 2023, from https://www.cisecurity.org/controls

CISA. (2021, May 10). *Home Page | CISA*. Retrieved May 11, 2023, from https://www.cisa.gov/ncas/current-activity/2021/01/14/artificial-intelligence-ai-cybersecurity

Cloud Security Alliance. (2019). *Top Threats to Cloud Computing, Version 4*. https://downloads.cloudsecurityalliance.org/assets/research/top-threats/tc_v4.pdf

Cloud Security Alliance. (2020). *Cloud Controls Matrix*. Retrieved May 12, 2023, from https://cloudsecurityalliance.org/artifacts/cloud-controls-matrix-v3-0-1/

Collidu. (2022, December 7). *Cybersecurity Awareness*. https://www.collidu.com/presentation-cybersecurity-awareness

Committee on National Security Systems. (2016). *CNSS Instruction No. 1253: Security Categorization and Control Selection for National Security Systems. Committee on National Security Systems.* Retrieved May 11, 2023, from https://www.dcsa.mil/portals/91/documents/ctp/nao/CNSSI_No1253.pdf

Cosco. (2018, July 25). *COSCO Shipping Lines Falls Victim to Cyber Attack.* Offshore Energy. Retrieved May 12, 2023, from https://www.offshore-energy.biz/cosco-shipping-lines-falls-victim-to-cyber-attack/

Coveware. (2023, April 28). *Ransomware Quarterly Reports. Coveware: Ransomware Recovery First Responders.* Retrieved May 12, 2023, from https://www.coveware.com/ransomware-quarterly-reports

CrowdStrike. (2022, February 15). *2021 Global Threat Report*. crowdstrike.com. Retrieved May 12, 2023, from https://www.crowdstrike.com/global-threat-report-2021/

Cybersecurity 2.0. (2021). Retrieved May 13, 2023, from https://www.dhl.com/global-en/home/insights-and-innovation/thought-leadership/trend-reports/cybersecurity-supply-chain.html

Cybersecurity Responsibility. (n.d.). https://www.sketchbubble.com/en/presentation-cybersecurity-responsibility.html

Cyberstar. (2021, August 30). *The Maritime Industry is Rethinking Cyber Security resilience. We're Here to Help*. https://www.zkcyberstar.com/2021/08/30/the-maritime-industry-is-rethinking-cyber-security-were-here-to-help/

Deloitte. (2021). *Global supply chain disruption and future strategies survey*. Retrieved from https://www2.deloitte.com/content/dam/Deloitte/us/Documents/strategy/global-supply-chain-disruption-and-future-strategies-survey.pdf

Deloitte. (2021). *Global supply chain disruption and future strategies survey*. Retrieved from https://www2.deloitte.com/content/dam/Deloitte/us/Documents/strategy/global-supply-chain-disruption-and-future-strategies-survey.pdf

Department of Defense. (2020). *Cybersecurity Maturity Model Certification*. Chief Information Officer. Retrieved May 10, 2023, from https://dodcio.defense.gov/CMMC/About/

Edge, C., & Trouton, R. (2023). MDM Internals. In Apress eBooks (pp. 207–279). doi:10.1007/978-1-4842-9156-6_4

Elijah, A. V., Abdullah, A., Zaman, N., Supramaniam, M., & Abdullateef, B. N. (2019). Ensemble and Deep-Learning Methods for Two-Class and Multi-Attack Anomaly Intrusion Detection: An Empirical Study. *International Journal of Advanced Computer Science and Applications, 10*(9). Advance online publication. doi:10.14569/IJACSA.2019.0100969

Enginerasoft. (2023, March 24). *Why is it important to back up data in logistics?* Enginerasoft. Enginerasoft. https://enginerasoft.com/why-is-it-important-to-back-up-data-in-logistics/

ENISA. (2021). *Post-Quantum Cryptography: Anticipating Threats and Preparing the Future*. Retrieved May 10, 2023, from https://www.enisa.europa.eu/news/enisa-news/post-quantum-cryptography-anticipating-threats-and-preparing-the-future

ENISA. (n.d.). *Understanding the increase in Supply Chain Security Attacks*. https://www.enisa.europa.eu/news/enisa-news/understanding-the-increase-in-supply-chain-security-attacks

Erdogan, G., Halvorsrud, R., Boletsis, C., Tverdal, S., & Pickering, J. (2023). *Cybersecurity Awareness and Capacities of SMEs*. doi:10.5220/0011609600003405

European Union. (2016). *General Data Protection Regulation (GDPR)*. https://eur-lex.europa.eu/legal-content/EN/TXT/?uri=CELEX:32016R0679

Factor Analysis of Information Risk. (2021). *What is the FAIR Institute?* FAIR Institute. Retrieved May 11, 2023, from https://www.fairinstitute.org/

Fedele, A., & Roner, C. (2021). Dangerous games: A literature review on cybersecurity investments. *Journal of Economic Surveys, 36*(1), 157–187. doi:10.1111/joes.12456

FedRAMP. (2020). *FedRAMP*. Retrieved May 11, 2023, from https://www.gsa.gov/technology/government-it-initiatives/fedramp

Fernando, Y., Tseng, M., Wahyuni-Td, I. S., De Sousa Jabbour, A. B. L., Jabbour, C. J. C., & Foropon, C. (2022). Cyber supply chain risk management and performance in industry 4.0 era: Information system security practices in Malaysia. *Journal of Industrial and Production Engineering, 40*(2), 102–116. doi:10.1080/21681015.2022.2116495

Foster, I., Larson, J. D., Masich, M., Snoeren, A. C., Savage, S., & Levchenko, K. (2015). *Security by Any Other Name*. doi:10.1145/2810103.2813607

Gartner. (2021). Gartner Top Security Projects for 2020-2021. Gartner. Retrieved May 12, 2023, from https://www.gartner.com/smarterwithgartner/gartner-top-security-projects-for-2020-2021

Gaur, L., Zaman, N., Bakshi, S., & Gupta, P. (2022). Analyzing Consequences of Artificial Intelligence on Jobs using Topic Modeling and Keyword Extraction. In *2022 2nd International Conference on Innovative Practices in Technology and Management (ICIPTM)*. 10.1109/ICIPTM54933.2022.9754064

Global, I. (2020, September 30). A Guide to the NIST Cybersecurity Framework. *Dark Reading*. https://www.darkreading.com/physical-security/a-guide-to-the-nist-cybersecurity-framework

Gnusarev, V. (2019). Logistics in global supply chains. Advances in Economics. *Business and Management Research*, *88*, 177–181. doi:10.2991/978-94-6239-284-6_27

Gonzalez-Granadillo, G., Gonzalez-Zarzosa, S., & Diaz, R. (2021). Security Information and Event Management (SIEM): Analysis, Trends, and Usage in Critical Infrastructures. *Sensors (Basel)*, *21*(14), 4759. doi:10.3390/s21144759 PMID:34300500

Hall, R. C., Hoppa, M. A., & Hu, Y. (2023). An Empirical Study of Password Policy Compliance. *Journal of the Colloquium for Information Systems Security Education*, *10*(1), 8. doi:10.53735/cisse.v10i1.156

Hamid, B., Jhanjhi, N. Z., Humayun, M., Khan, A., & Alsayat, A. (2019, December). Cyber security issues and challenges for smart cities: A survey. In *2019 13th International Conference on Mathematics, Actuarial Science, Computer Science and Statistics (MACS)* (pp. 1-7). IEEE. 10.1109/MACS48846.2019.9024768

Hammi, B., Zeadally, S., & Nebhen, J. (2023). Security threats, countermeasures, and challenges of digital supply chains. *ACM Computing Surveys*, *55*(14s), 1–40. Advance online publication. doi:10.1145/3588999

Health Information Trust Alliance. (2021). *HITRUST CSF*. https://hitrustalliance.net/hitrust-csf/

Hitachi, Ltd. (2020). *JP1 Intelligent Governance: Hitachi ICT Solutions*. Retrieved May 13, 2023, from https://www.hitachi.asia/ict-solutions/solutions/sms/jp1-it-compliance/?gclid=CjwKCAjwx_iBhBGEiwA15gLN3IaGHvkl2SSzzorz10SRC-ZvdlRraeyTFofPf69bsZE O4fB7pgjQshoC7hwQAvD_BwE#assetmgmt

Hoerl, R., & Snee, R. D. (2012). *Statistical Thinking: Improving Business Performance*. http://ci.nii.ac.jp/ncid/BA55971443

Hong, B., Shao, B., Guo, J., Fu, J., Li, C., & Zhu, B. (2023). Dynamic Bayesian network risk probability evolution for third-party damage of natural gas pipelines. *Applied Energy*, *333*, 120620. doi:10.1016/j.apenergy.2022.120620

Humayun, M., Niazi, M., Zaman, N., Alshayeb, M., & Mahmood, S. (2020). Cyber Security Threats and Vulnerabilities: A Systematic Mapping Study. *Arabian Journal for Science and Engineering*, *45*(4), 3171–3189. doi:10.1007/s13369-019-04319-2

Humayun, M., Zaman, N., Hamid, B., & Ahmed, G. (2020). Emerging Smart Logistics and Transportation Using IoT and Blockchain. *IEEE Internet of Things Magazine*, *3*(2), 58–62. doi:10.1109/IOTM.0001.1900097

Humayun, M., Zaman, N., Talib, M. N., Shah, M. H., & Suseendran, G. (2021b). Cybersecurity for Data Science: Issues, Opportunities, and Challenges. In Lecture notes in networks and systems (pp. 435–444). Springer International Publishing. doi:10.1007/978-981-16-3153-5_46

IBM. (2020). *Cost of a data breach 2022*. IBM. Retrieved May 12, 2023, from https://www.ibm.com/reports/data-breach

IBM. (2023). *X-Force Threat Intelligence Index*. IBM Security. Retrieved May 12, 2023, from https://www.cert.hu/sites/default/files/xforce_threat_intelligence_index_2021_90037390usen.pdf

International Electrotechnical Commission. (2018). *An Overview of ISA/IEC 62443 Standards Security of Industrial Automation and Control Systems*. ISA. Retrieved May 10, 2023, from https://gca.isa.org/hubfs/ISAGCA%20Quick%20Start%20Guide%20FINAL.pdf

International Organization for Standardization. (2022, November 29). *ISO/IEC 15408-1:2022 Information security, cybersecurity and privacy protection — Evaluation criteria for IT security — Part 1: Introduction and general model*. ISO. Retrieved May 10, 2023, from https://www.iso.org/standard/72891.html

International Organization for Standardization. (2022a). *ISO/IEC 27001 Information security management systems*. ISO. Retrieved May 10, 2023, from https://www.iso.org/standard/27001

ISACA. (2020). https://www.studocu.com/row/document/islamic-university-of-madinah/system-integration/cobit-2019-framework-introduction-and-methodology-1/24868396

ISACA. (2021). *How Effective Is Your Cybersecurity Audit?* Retrieved May 13, 2023, from https://www.isaca.org/resources/isaca-journal/issues/2022/volume-3/how-effective-is-your-cybersecurity-audit

ISO. (2019). *ISO/IEC 27001:2013 Information technology -- Security techniques -- Information security management systems -- Requirements*. https://www.iso.org/obp/ui/#iso:std:iso-iec:27001:ed-2:v1:en

ITRC. (2022, January 21). *Identity Theft Resource Center's 2021 Annual Data Breach Report Sets New Record for Number of Compromises - ITRC*. Retrieved May 13, 2023, from https://www.idtheftcenter.org/post/identity-theft-resource-center-2021-annual-data-breach-report-sets-new-record-for-number-of-compromises/

Javaid, M., Haleem, A., Singh, R. P., & Suman, R. (2023). Towards insighting Cybersecurity for Healthcare domains: A comprehensive review of recent practices and trends. *Chinese Root Global Impact*, *1*, 100016. doi:10.1016/j.csa.2023.100016

Javelin. (2021). *2021 Identity Fraud Study: Shifting Angles*. Javelin. Retrieved May 12, 2023, from https://javelinstrategy.com/content/2021-identity-fraud-report-shifting-angles-identity-fraud

JayakumarP.BrohiS. N.ZamanN. (2021). Artificial Intelligence and Military Applications: Innovations, Cybersecurity Challenges & Open Research Areas. *Preprint.org*. doi:10.20944/preprints202108.0047.v1

Kalinin, M. O., Krundyshev, V., & Zegzhda, P. D. (2021). Cybersecurity Risk Assessment in Smart City Infrastructures. *Machines*, *9*(4), 78. doi:10.3390/machines9040078

Kaspersky. (2019, May 26). *Brand Reputation Costs $200,000 to Repair*. Retrieved May 12, 2023, from https://www.kaspersky.com/about/press-releases/2015_brand-reputation-costs--200000-to-repair

Kayapinar, Ö., & Lorcu, F. (2020). The Role of Technology Level and Logistics Performance on the Relationship Between Logistics Service Quality and Firm Performance. In *Advances in logistics, operations, and management science book series* (pp. 107–135). Routledge. doi:10.4018/978-1-7998-4601-7.ch006

Khan, A., Jhanjhi, N. Z., & Humayun, M. (2022). The Role of Cybersecurity in Smart Cities. In *Cyber Security Applications for Industry 4.0* (pp. 195–208). Chapman and Hall/CRC. doi:10.1201/9781003203087-9

Khan, A., Jhanjhi, N. Z., & Sujatha, R. (2022b). Emerging Industry Revolution IR 4.0 Issues and Challenges. In Cyber Security Applications for Industry 4.0 (pp. 151-169). Chapman and Hall/CRC.

Kim, A. (2023, March 30). *20 Critical Security Controls | SANS Institute*. https://www.sans.org/webcasts/20-critical-security-controls-96685/

Kim, J. H., Seo, B., Choi, K., & Sung, S. (2023). Ballistic Penetration Test and Simulation of Metallic Aircraft Wing Fuel Tank. *International Journal of Aeronautical and Space Sciences*, *24*(1), 303–314. doi:10.1007/s42405-022-00565-1

Kirkwood, S. (2022). *Cybersecurity in Logistics: How to Protect Your Supply Chain from Cyberattacks*. Evans Distribution Systems. https://www.evansdist.com/cybersecurity-in-logistics/

Kozma, D., Varga, P., & Hegedűs, C. (2019). *Supply Chain Management and Logistics 4.0 - A Study on Arrowhead Framework Integration*. doi:10.1109/ICITM.2019.8710670

Krehel, O. (2021, August 31). *LIFARS Cybersecurity Firm provides Incident Response, Digtial Forensics, Ransomware Solutions*. LIFARS, a SecurityScorecard Company. Retrieved May 13, 2023, from https://www.lifars.com/about/

Kron. (2022). *Cybersecurity in the Logistics Industry*. Kron. Retrieved May 11, 2023, from https://krontech.com/cybersecurity-in-the-logistics-industry

Kshetri, N. (2018). 1 Blockchain's roles in meeting key supply chain management objectives. *International Journal of Information Management*, *39*, 80–89. doi:10.1016/j.ijinfomgt.2017.12.005

Kumar, V., Malik, N., Singla, J., Zaman, N., Amsaad, F., & Razaque, A. (2022). Light Weight Authentication Scheme for Smart Home IoT Devices. *Cryptography*, *6*(3), 37. doi:10.3390/cryptography6030037

Kuypers, M., Heon, G., Martin, P., & Paté-Cornell, M. L. (2014). *Cyber security: The risk of supply chain vulnerabilities in an enterprise firewall*. ResearchGate. https://www.researchgate.net/publication/288365610_Cyber_security_The_risk_of_supply_chain_vulnerabilities_in_an_enterprise_firewall

Lau, L. (2018, February 23). *Cybercrime "pandemic" may have cost the world $600 billion last year*. CNBC. https://www.cnbc.com/2018/02/22/cybercrime-pandemic-may-have-cost-the-world-600-billion-last-year.html

Lenko, F. (2021). Specifics of RFID Based Access Control Systems Used in Logistics Centers. *Transportation Research Procedia*, *55*, 1613–1619. doi:10.1016/j.trpro.2021.07.151

Lin, X. (2022). Network Security Technology of Supply Chain Management Based on Internet of Things and Big Data. *Computational Intelligence and Neuroscience*, *2022*, 1–12. doi:10.1155/2022/7753086 PMID:35774432

Luo, Y., & Zhang, H. (2019). Global logistics management and sustainable economic development. In S. O. Idowu, W. Leal Filho, & S. M. Mifsud (Eds.), Handbook of Research on Global Business Opportunities (pp. 228-240). IGI Global. doi:10.4018/978-1-5225-7180-3.ch011

M, S. S., D, H., & Vallem, R. R. (2023). Cyber Security System Based on Machine Learning Using Logistic Decision Support Vector. *Mesopotamian Journal of Cybersecurity,* 64–72. doi:10.58496/MJCS/2023/011

Maersk. (2017). *Cyber attack update - A.P. Møller - Mærsk A/S. A.P. Møller - Mærsk a/S.* Retrieved May 12, 2023, from https://investor.maersk.com/news-releases/news-release-details/cyber-attack-update

Mahmood, T., & Afzal, U. (2013*). Security Analytics: Big Data Analytics for cybersecurity: A review of trends, techniques and tools*. doi:10.1109/NCIA.2013.6725337

Mallick, P., Salling, K. B., Pigosso, D. C. A., & McAloone, T. C. (2023). Closing the loop: Establishing reverse logistics for a circular economy, a systematic review. *Journal of Environmental Management*, *328*, 117017. doi:10.1016/j.jenvman.2022.117017 PMID:36521223

Managers, S. (2022, February 24). *Role Of Technology In Logistics And Supply Chain Management.* https://genxfreight.co.uk/role-of-information-technology-in-logistics-and-supply-chain-management/

Mandiant. (2021). *M-trends 2021: Insights into Today's Top Cyber Trends and Attacks*. Mandiant. https://www.mandiant.com/resources/reports/m-trends-2021

Mangan, J., Lalwani, C., & Butcher, T. (2008). *Global Logistics and Supply Chain Management.* http://ci.nii.ac.jp/ncid/BA88939934

McAfee. (2020). *Cloud Adoption and Risk Report.* McAfee. Retrieved May 12, 2023, from https://mscdss.ds.unipi.gr/wp-content/uploads/2018/10/Cloud-Adoption-Risk-Report-2019.pdf

McKevitt, J. (2017, June 29). *Maersk, FedEx cases show how cyberattacks can roil global logistics*. Supply Chain Dive. https://www.supplychaindive.com/news/FedEx-TNT-Express-cybersecurity-attack-ransomware/446078/

Mukherjee, D. (2023). *Network Segmentation: Enables enhance security and control access of critical assets.* CXOToday.com. https://www.cxotoday.com/cxo-bytes/network-segmentation-enables-enhance-security-and-control-access-of-critical-assets/

Muzaki, R., Briliyant, O. C., Hasditama, M. A., & Ritchi, H. (2020). *Improving Security of Web-Based Application Using ModSecurity and Reverse Proxy in Web Application Firewall*. doi:10.1109/IWBIS50925.2020.9255601

Naeem, M., Shahbaz, M., & Shafiq, M. (2020). Cyber Security Risks and Challenges in Logistics Industry: Incident Response Planning. *International Journal of Advanced Computer Science and Applications*, *11*(11), 40–47.

Nagy, G., Illés, B., & Bányai, Á. (2018). Impact of Industry 4.0 on production logistics. *IOP Conference Series, 448*, 012013. 10.1088/1757-899X/448/1/012013

Narasimhan, K. (2005). The Goal: A Process of Ongoing Improvement. *Measuring Business Excellence*, *9*(1), 76. Advance online publication. doi:10.1108/13683040510588882

National Institute of Standards and Technology. (2018). *Framework for Improving Critical Infrastructure Cybersecurity, Version 1.1*. doi:10.6028/NIST.CSWP.04162018

National Institute of Standards and Technology. (2021). *NIST Special Publication 800-53: Security and Privacy Controls for Information Systems and Organizations*. https://csrc.nist.gov/publications/detail/sp/800-53/rev-5/final

National Institute of Standards and Technology. (2023, April 17). *Small Business Cybersecurity Corner | NIST*. NIST. Retrieved May 12, 2023, from https://www.nist.gov/itl/smallbusinesscyber

Nayyar, A., Jain, R., Mahapatra, B., & Singh, A. P. (2019). Cyber Security Challenges for Smart Cities. In *Practice, progress, and proficiency in sustainability* (pp. 27–54). IGI Global. doi:10.4018/978-1-5225-8085-0.ch002

NCCoE. (2021, October 21). *National Cybersecurity Center of Excellence (NCCoE) Zero Trust Cybersecurity: Implementing a Zero Trust Architecture.* Federal Register. Retrieved May 10, 2023, from https://www.federalregister.gov/documents/2020/10/21/2020-23292/national-cybersecurity-center-of-excellence-nccoe-zero-trust-cybersecurity-implementing-a-zero-trust

NCES. (2020). *Chapter 5-Protecting Your System: Physical Security, from Safeguarding Your Technology.* NCES Publication 98-297 (National Center for Education Statistics). Retrieved May 13, 2023, from https://nces.ed.gov/pubs98/safetech/chapter5.asp

Neustar. (2020). *Cyber threats and trends: Q1 2020 report.* https://www.home.neustar/resources/research-reports/cyber-threats-and-trends-q1-2020-report

Ng, C. (2018). *The future of logistics: Five technologies that will self-orchestrate the supply chain.* PwC.

NIST. (2020). *Cybersecurity Framework.* https://www.nist.gov/cyberframework

Novet, J. (2017, August 16). *Shipping company Maersk says June cyberattack could cost it up to $300 million.* CNBC. Retrieved May 12, 2023, from https://www.cnbc.com/2017/08/16/maersk-says-notpetya-cyberattack-could-cost-300-million.html

Nozari, H., & Edalatpanah, S. A. (2023). Smart Systems Risk Management in IoT-Based Supply Chain. In *Industrial and applied mathematics* (pp. 251–268). Springer Nature. doi:10.1007/978-981-19-9909-3_11

Payment Card Industry Security Standards Council. (2019). *Payment Card Industry Data Security Standard (PCI DSS) version 3.2.1.* Retrieved from https://www.pcisecuritystandards.org/documents/PCI_DSS_v3-2-1.pdf

PCI Security Standards Council. (2021). *Payment Card Industry (PCI) Data Security Standard (DSS).* https://www.pcisecuritystandards.org/pci-security-standards/pci-dss

Pertiwi, D. A., Yusuf, M., & Efrilianda, D. A. (2022). Operational Supply Chain Risk Management on Apparel Industry Based on Supply Chain Operation Reference (SCOR). *Journal of Information System Exploration and Research, 1*(1), 17–24. doi:10.52465/joiser.v1i1.103

Ponemon Institute. (2020). *Cost of Insider Threats: Global Report 2020.* IBM. Retrieved May 12, 2023, from https://www.ibm.com/downloads/cas/LQZ4RONE

Ponemon Institute. (2020b). *The 2020 state of cybersecurity in small and medium-sized businesses.* Retrieved May 13, 2023, from https://www.ponemon.org/research/ponemon-library/security/security.html

Ponnusamy, V., Zaman, N., & Humayun, M. (2020). Fostering Public-Private Partnership. In *Advances in electronic government, digital divide, and regional development book series* (pp. 237–255). IGI Global. doi:10.4018/978-1-7998-1851-9.ch012

Prabakar, D., Sundarrajan, M., Manikandan, R., Zaman, N., Masud, M., & Alqhatani, A. (2023). Energy Analysis-Based Cyber Attack Detection by IoT with Artificial Intelligence in a Sustainable Smart City. *Sustainability (Basel)*, *15*(7), 6031. doi:10.3390/su15076031

Priyadarshini, I., Chatterjee, J. M., Sujatha, R., Zaman, N., Karime, A., & Masud, M. (2021). Exploring Internet Meme Activity during COVID-19 Lockdown Using Artificial Intelligence Techniques. *Applied Artificial Intelligence*, *36*(1), 2014218. Advance online publication. doi:10.1080/08839514.2021.2014218

RedGoat. (2023, April 18). *Maersk incident response*. Red Goat. https://red-goat.com/why-you-should-test-your-incident-response-a-review-of-the-maersk-incident/

Rejeb, A., Rejeb, K., Simske, S. J., & Treiblmaier, H. (2021). Blockchain Technologies in Logistics and Supply Chain Management: A Bibliometric Review. *Logistics*, *5*(4), 72. doi:10.3390/logistics5040072

Robinson. (2021). *4 Ways to Prepare Your Global Supply Chain for Cyber-Threats*. C.H. Robinson. Retrieved May 13, 2023, from https://www.chrobinson.com/en-us/resources/blog/4-ways-prepare-global-supply-chain-cyber-threats/

Rohan, R., Pal, D., Hautamäki, J., Funilkul, S., Chutimaskul, W., & Thapliyal, H. (2023). A systematic literature review of cybersecurity scales assessing information security awareness. *Heliyon*, *9*(3), e14234. doi:10.1016/j.heliyon.2023.e14234 PMID:36938452

Rowe, A. (2023). 12 Cyber Security Measures That Every Small Business Must Take. *Tech.co*. https://tech.co/vpn/cyber-security-measures

Saeed, S., Almuhaideb, A. M., Kumar, N., Zaman, N., & Zikria, Y. B. (Eds.). (2023). *Handbook of Research on Cybersecurity Issues and Challenges for Business and FinTech Applications*. IGI Global. doi:10.4018/978-1-6684-5284-4

Samuel, K. E., Goury, M., Gunasekaran, A., & Spalanzani, A. (2011). Knowledge management in supply chain: An empirical study from France. *The Journal of Strategic Information Systems*, *20*(3), 283–306. doi:10.1016/j.jsis.2010.11.001

Sari, R. T. K., & Hindarto, D. (2023). Implementation of Cyber-Security Enterprise Architecture Food Industry in Society 5.0 Era. *Sinkron : Jurnal Dan Penelitian Teknik Informatika*, *8*(2), 1074–1084. doi:10.33395/sinkron.v8i2.12377

Şcheau, M. C., Achim, M. V., Găbudeanu, L., Vaidean, V. L., Vilcea, A., & Apetri, L. (2023). Proposals of Processes and Organizational Preventive Measures against Malfunctioning of Drones and User Negligence. *Drones (Basel)*, *7*(1), 64. doi:10.3390/drones7010064

Schinas, O., & Metzger, D. (2023). Cyber-seaworthiness: A critical review of the literature. *Marine Policy*, *151*, 105592. doi:10.1016/j.marpol.2023.105592

Security, H. N. (2021, June 28). *What are the most common cybersecurity challenges SMEs face today? Help Net Security*. Help Net Security. https://www.helpnetsecurity.com/2021/07/07/smes-cybersecurity-challenges/

Shah, I. A., Jhanjhi, N. Z., Amsaad, F., & Razaque, A. (2022). The Role of Cutting-Edge Technologies in Industry 4.0. In *Cyber Security Applications for Industry 4.0* (pp. 97–109). Chapman and Hall/CRC. doi:10.1201/9781003203087-4

Shah, I. A., Zaman, N., & Laraib, A. (2022). Cybersecurity and Blockchain Usage in Contemporary Business. In *Advances in information security, privacy, and ethics book series* (pp. 49–64). IGI Global., doi:10.4018/978-1-6684-5284-4.ch003

Simatupang, T. M., Wright, A. F., & Sridharan, R. (2004). Applying the theory of constraints to supply chain collaboration. *Supply Chain Management*, *9*(1), 57–70. doi:10.1108/13598540410517584

Şimşit, Z. T., Günay, N. S., & Vayvay, O. (2014). Theory of Constraints: A Literature Review. *Procedia: Social and Behavioral Sciences*, *150*, 930–936. doi:10.1016/j.sbspro.2014.09.104

Singh, S. (2016, September 22). Future Of Logistics: Five Technologies That Will Self-Orchestrate The Supply Chain. *Forbes*. https://www.forbes.com/sites/sarwantsingh/2016/09/22/future-of-logistics-5-technologies-that-will-self-orchestrate-the-supply-chain/?sh=5202b1155a63

Sobb, T. M., Turnbull, B., & Moustafa, N. (2020). Supply Chain 4.0: A Survey of Cyber Security Challenges, Solutions and Future Directions. *Electronics (Basel)*, *9*(11), 1864. doi:10.3390/electronics9111864

Srinivasan, M. (2016). The role of logistics in e-commerce. *International Journal of Management and Social Sciences Research*, *5*(4), 52–56.

Stark, J. (2017). Productivity improvements in transport logistics. Journal of Supply Chain Management. *Logistics and Procurement*, *1*(2), 111–119. doi:10.1108/JSCLP-08-2017-0024

Sujatha, R., & Prakash, G. (2022). *Cyber Security Applications for Industry 4.0, Chapman and Hall/CRC Cyber-Physical Systems Series*. CRC Press.

Suki, N. M., Sharif, A., & Afshan, S. (2021). The role of logistics performance for sustainable development in top Asian countries: Evidence from advance panel estimations. *Sustainable Development (Bradford)*, *29*(4), 595–606. doi:10.1002/sd.2160

Symantec. (2021). *Symantec Internet Security Threat Report*. Bradcom. Retrieved May 12, 2023, from https://docs.broadcom.com/doc/istr-03-jan-en

Taj, I., & Zaman, N. (2022). Towards Industrial Revolution 5.0 and Explainable Artificial Intelligence: Challenges and Opportunities. *International Journal of Computing and Digital Systems*, *12*(1), 285–310. doi:10.12785/ijcds/120124

Tampubolon, S., & Purba, H. H. (2021). Lean six sigma implementation, a systematic literature review. *International Journal of Production Management and Engineering*, *9*(2), 125. doi:10.4995/ijpme.2021.14561

Tsohou, A., Diamantopoulou, V., Gritzalis, S., & Lambrinoudakis, C. (2023). Cyber insurance: State of the art, trends and future directions. *International Journal of Information Security*, *22*(3), 737–748. Advance online publication. doi:10.1007/s10207-023-00660-8 PMID:36684688

Venngage. (n.d.). Cyber Security Framework Mind Map. *Venngage*. https://venngage.com/templates/mind-maps/cyber-security-framework-mind-map-4f764669-28f5-411c-aa0b-6119d2c2acce

Verizon Business. (2022). *2022 Data Breach Investigations Report*. Verizon Business. Retrieved May 12, 2023, from https://www.verizon.com/business/resources/reports/dbir/

Verkada. (2021). *State of Physical Security 2021*. Genetec. Retrieved May 12, 2023, from https://resources.genetec.com/en-infographics/state-of-physical-security-2021

Waters, D. (2016). *Supply Chain Risk Management: Vulnerability and Resilience in Logistics*. http://ci.nii.ac.jp/ncid/BB07882667

Womack, J. E., & Jones, D. B. (1997). Lean Thinking—Banish Waste and Create Wealth in your Corporation. *The Journal of the Operational Research Society*, *48*(11), 1148. doi:10.1057/palgrave.jors.2600967

Wong, L., Lee, V., Tan, G. W., Ooi, K., & Sohal, A. S. (2022). The role of cybersecurity and policy awareness in shifting employee compliance attitudes: Building supply chain capabilities. *International Journal of Information Management*, *66*, 102520. doi:10.1016/j.ijinfomgt.2022.102520

Yaffe-Bellany, D. (2019, August 1). Equifax Data-Breach Settlement: Get Up to $20,000 If You Can Prove Harm. *The New York Times*. https://www.nytimes.com/2019/07/22/business/equifax-data-breach-claim.html

Yaga, D. J., Mell, P., Roby, N., & Scarfone, K. A. (2018). *Blockchain technology overview*. doi:10.6028/NIST.IR.8202

Yu, Y., Wang, X., Zhong, R. Y., & Huang, G. Q. (2016). E-commerce Logistics in Supply Chain Management: Practice Perspective. *Procedia CIRP*, *52*, 179–185. doi:10.1016/j.procir.2016.08.002

Zaenchkovski, A., Lazarev, A., & Masyutin, S. (2023). Multi-factor Authentication in Innovative Business Systems of Industrial Clusters. In Lecture notes in electrical engineering (pp. 271–281). Springer Science+Business Media. doi:10.1007/978-3-031-22311-2_27

Zhang, A., Luo, W., Shi, Y., Chia, S. H., & Sim, Z. H. X. (2016). Lean and Six Sigma in logistics: A pilot survey study in Singapore. *International Journal of Operations & Production Management*, *36*(11), 1625–1643. doi:10.1108/IJOPM-02-2015-0093

Zhao, Z., Hao, Y., Chang, R., & Wang, Q. (2023). Assessing the vulnerability of energy supply chains: Influencing factors and countermeasures. *Sustainable Energy Technologies and Assessments*, *56*, 103018. doi:10.1016/j.seta.2023.103018

Zhu, K. J. (2017). A review of literature on the logistics and transportation service quality: A comprehensive analysis. *International Journal of Logistics Management*, *28*(4), 1118–1141. doi:10.1108/IJLM-08-2015-0136

Chapter 2
Supply Chain Management Security Issues and Challenges in the Context of AI Applications

Imdad Ali Shah
School of Computing Science, Taylor's University, Malaysia

Raja Kumar Murugesan
https://orcid.org/0000-0001-9500-1361
School of Computer Science, Taylor's University, Malaysia

Samina Rajper
https://orcid.org/0000-0002-8635-8059
Shah Abdul Latif University, Khairpur, Pakistan

ABSTRACT

Logistics generally relates to the careful preparation and performance strenuous activity. To meet the needs of customers or enterprises, logistics is broadly defined as managing the flow of items from their point of production to their location of consumption. According to studies, up to 90% of a company's sustainability consequences are attributable to its supply chain. These crucial supply chain flaws have been made public by the COVID-19 pandemic. Additionally, businesses are making many sustainability pledges because of legislative and consumer pressure for climate action. Current procedures have the potential to be streamlined with artificial intelligence (AI) innovation in logistics. Numerous developments are pushing automation to the top of the logistics CEO's agenda. The first step toward extensive optimization is automation, which many businesses have already adopted to maintain competitiveness.

DOI: 10.4018/979-8-3693-3816-2.ch002

1. INTRODUCTION

Most likely, artificial intelligence is the most significant project humanity has ever undertaken. Compared to fire or electricity, it is more profound. There will be a new wave of digital disruption caused by AI that will reshape sectors and propel unprecedented levels of innovation. Opportunities to leverage AI's advantages are particularly abundant in the supply chain, which is one of the most data-rich settings within businesses.

A new era of change is upon us, as this saying suggests. The digital revolution is having a tremendous effect on many aspects of our society, much like the agricultural and industrial revolutions did before it (Alexandre & Dmitry, 2021; Entrepreneurship and management, 2021; Krykavskyi et al., 2019; Krykavskyy et al., 2021). Artificial intelligence (AI) is at the heart of this transformation since it has rapidly spread from academic institutions into all facets of society. Business and consumer benefits from AI-driven applications like smart robotics and self-driving cars are already becoming a reality. Organizations should rethink their entire structure considering the data-driven economy and the disruptive effects of technology. The supply chain, considered by many to be the lifeblood of every organisation, is included in this. (Ajaikumar et al., 2021; Dmitry & Alexandre, 2021; Fosso et al., 2021; Krykavskyy et al., 2019; McKibbin & Fernando, 2020) claims that it is one of the business processes where AI can have the greatest impact. SC managers need to be familiar with the variety of applications for AI and their attendant merits and perils if they are to fully capitalise on this promising new field. The work's purpose is to help people grasp this concept by using a pragmatic strategy that involves presenting and evaluating prospective AI applications within the SC framework. The first section of this study is an attempt to define AI by examining its broader setting (Ahmad, 2020; Lallie et al., 2021; Razaque et al., 2019; Rodela et al., 2020; Samtani et al., 2020). The definition, primary subfields, and driving forces of AI will all be investigated. The technology and its possibilities will then be demonstrated through an examination of application cases across a range of industries and businesses. The first section will wrap up with a discussion of the advantages and disadvantages of AI as well as some predictions for the future. Expands on these understandings by analysing the technology in the context of SCs (Hiscox, 2019; Khan, Brohi, & Zaman, 2020; Williams, Chaturvedi, & Chakravarthy, 2020). The analysis of AI applications in SC will build on the definition of generic SC components. In the last section, qualitative expert interviews are used to evaluate the overall effect, advantages, hazards, and future implications of AI on the separate SC components. Using AI to manage the supply chain in fig 1.

Supply chain management and digitization are two areas that firms are focusing on more and more as ways to improve their operations. Supply chain management

Figure 1. Using AI to manage the supply chain

40% 24%	Robotic and Automation	44% 14%	Predictive Analysis	40% 40%	Robotic and Automation
31% 24%	Artificial Intelligence Technologies	41% 13%	Sensors and Automatic Identification	44% 9%	Inventory and Network Optimization
29% 22%	Autonomous Vehicles and Drones	35% 8%	Cloud Computing and Storage	33% 9%	Wearable and Mobile Technology

is becoming increasingly important and significant in terms of value creation, with the help of several technological advancements (Brohi et al., 2020; He et al., 2021; Pranggono & Arabo, 2021; Weil & Murugesan, 2020). This dissertation will explore the historical, contemporary, and prospective perspectives of digitalization in supply chains, as well as the reasons why digitalization plans fail and how they may be handled. In addition, five emerging technologies data analytics, IoT, AI, cloud computing, and blockchain will be dissected in detail. From the perspective of supply chain management, the advantages, difficulties, and potential future developments of each of these technologies are discussed (Carrapico & Farrand, 2020; Ferreira & Cruz-Correia, 2021; Wiggen, 2020; Wijayanto & Prabowo, 2020; World Health Organization, 2020). Five organisations were interviewed for the empirical part; one was a vendor of digital solutions, while the others were either heavy consumers of digital technologies or large companies with extensive supply chains. The interviews were conducted with the goals of comparing the degree of digitalization in supply chain management to that of other departments, discovering the types of digital technologies being used or planned for implementation, and creating a road map of the difficulties and advantages of using such technologies. It was discovered that there is a plethora of ways in which digital technology might boost supply chain operations (Burrell, 2020; Okereafor & Adebola, 2020). Despite this, not all the technologies were being used on a widespread basis by the interviewed companies.

Companies need to find ways to streamline their supply chains and increase productivity in today's highly competitive marketplaces. Additionally, consumer expectations are shifting because of increased individualization; as a result, customers now anticipate a better level of service alongside an increase in the number of purchases that are uniquely tailored to their preferences (Karpenko et al., 2021; Liang et al., 2017; Mensah, 2019). Businesses may boost productivity, decrease expenses, and increase customer satisfaction and loyalty by implementing cutting-edge technology like blockchain and artificial intelligence to create more reliable and efficient supply chains. To top it all off, technology has helped to streamline and increase visibility throughout supply chains, giving C-suite executives more command over their companies' day-to-day activities.

The common thread among these digital technologies is that each presents unique chances to improve supply chain operations (Gupta & Agarwal, 2017; Peng et al., 2017; Saleem et al., 2017; Williams, Chaturvedi, & Chakravarthy, 2020). To give just one example, robotic process automation has led to the digitization of anywhere from 50 to 80% of back-office procedures across a variety of sectors. Profit margins and product quality in manufacturing can both benefit from the use of AI (Khandpur et al., 2017; Luh et al., 2017; Tounsi & Rais, 2018). The banking sector is just one example of an area that might greatly benefit from the use of blockchain technology, which has the potential to change cumbersome and paper-intensive processes. Meanwhile, digital technologies are predicted to cut operational costs by 31% and lost sales and inventories by up to 76% over the next few years. Also, they will make supply networks more flexible.

To compete and provide adequate service to clients in today's complicated digital market, businesses must form and maintain strong partnerships with other organisations and players, and digital technologies are a crucial instrument in doing so (Ding et al., 2018; Huang et al., 2018; Ramadan et al., 2021; Stellios et al., 2018). Moreover, digital technologies are increasingly embedded in products and services, altering the structure of social partnerships from the perspective of both enterprises and their customers. So, it's getting more challenging to separate IT from business operations (Cradduck, 2019; Scarfone et al., 2009). It is safe to say that businesses cannot afford to ignore digital technology if they are to succeed in the future.

While research on the worldwide problem of underutilised digital technology is extensive, no such studies have been conducted in Finland. Many studies have focused on the digitalization of business-to-consumer markets, but the B2B sector has received far less attention (Bhuvana & Vasantha, 2021; Hussain et al., 2021; Ullah et al., n.d.). For these reasons, the businesses involved in B2B markets constitute the primary emphasis of this thesis. Additionally, digital technologies are consistently reshaping business-to-business (Gaur et al., 2021; Humayun, Niazi, Jhanjhi et al, 2020; Lim, Abdullah, & Jhanjhi, 2019; Lim, Abdullah, Jhanjhi et al, 2019; Liu et al., 2020). Businesses selling to other businesses (B2B) that have embraced digital transformation have increased their products' accessibility and quality while simultaneously decreasing their prices.

The term "supply chain management" will be utilised extensively throughout this thesis. Briefly summarised in Supply Chain Resource. To optimise value for customers and maintain a competitive edge over the long term, businesses need to practise supply chain management (SCM). As such, it is indicative of a concerted effort on the part of supply chain companies to design and manage supply chains in the most efficient and effective manner possible (Almusaylim & Jhanjhi, 2020; Amir Latif et al., 2020; Kumar et al., 2021). Everything from brainstorming new products to managing their manufacture, distribution, and storage is part of the supply chain. This thesis aims to investigate the current state of digitalization in supply chain management (SCM), the best practices for overseeing digital transformation, the types of digital technologies that could be applied in SCM, the pros and cons of those applications, and the perspectives of actual businesses on digitalization in their SCM divisions (Khan, Jhanjhi, Humayun et al, 2020). Finally, we hope to investigate how these theoretical frameworks and actual data interact with one another.

2. LITERATURE REVIEW

In today's highly competitive market, where customers have increasingly high expectations for ever-increasing product and service quality at ever-shrinking profit margins and ever-shortening delivery windows, businesses must take advantage of every conceivable advantage to stay ahead of the competition. Improving a company's supply chain efficiency by making it more flexible to absorb any kind of variation in the turbulent business environment is crucial to bolstering the company's commercial competitive excellence in a world in which business is constantly changing (Lee et al., 2021; Najmi et al., 2021; Zong et al., 2019). Modern supply chains have progressed toward increasingly complex frameworks that incorporate a wide range of ship speeds, planning standards, several modes of transport, and constant data exchange among all network nodes. The primary challenge of supply chain management (SCM) is cost-effectively maintaining a continuous flow of goods, information, services, and money. Modern supply chains are characterised by extensive limitations in terms of resources, time, production viability, distribution output, and transport. In addition, organisations must work hard on such problems and developments with a focus on short-term profits (Ahmad, 2019; Humayun, Jhanjhi, Hamid et al, 2020; Korir et al., 2019; Ravi et al., 2021; Singh et al., 2020). The organization's capacity to manage and influence communication has been bolstered by the emergence of cutting-edge information technologies. Nonetheless, there is still some doubt about the reliability of the data, the efficacy of the communication, and the ability to get the right information to the right people. To continue making sound business decisions in an ever-changing market, a growing number of firms are increasing the size and quality of their existing information infrastructure (Alamri et al., 2019; Nosiri & Ndoh, 2018; Sangki, 2018). Decisions in supply chain management can be made under a wide range of conditions and with many limitations. Because of the massive data volume, modern SCM requires increasingly complex software and methods for data analysis (Rajmohan et al., 2020). Therefore, to enhance its procedures, SCM needs to incorporate the intelligence management system. Considering the increasing importance of data to a successful supply chain, managers in charge of these networks are adopting new methods for keeping their data secure while getting the most out of it (Kaur et al., 2018; Liu et al., 2021; NSKT Global, 2021; NSKT Global, 2021; Walden et al., 2020). The Internet of Things (IoT) and artificial intelligence (AI) continue to show promise, but there has been no major advancement in implementing either technology for better supply chain management (SCM). (Le Blond et al., 2017; Sharma, 2021) claim that a company's capacity to trace back via its supply chain is one of several key opportunities that may be used to implement a traceability framework (SC).

There are several benefits, one of which is a network that can trace and follow a path's history in real-time, regardless of how much it changes. In addition, there is increased transparency within organisations, which helps to develop a widespread and functional production flow, and information is broadcast across business shareholders at the appropriate levels of granularity. Furthermore, enhanced wireless data transmission can improve collaboration between manufacturer and storekeeper, leading to more precise requirements (Bhagat et al., 2021; Cowgill & Stevenson, 2020; Dorr et al., 2020). Meanwhile, experts in cyberspace have seen how far mobile wireless communications and related network engineering have come. Multiple high-speed smart appliances actively participated in the development. This bolstered the network with numerous uses, including smart electricity generation, inter-vehicle connectivity, and a database application in the cloud. As a result, more and more buildings and appliances are being outfitted with similar "smart" technology (Arabadzhyiev et al., 2021; Dahwan & Raju, 2021; Mehrotra, 2021; Sadiq et al., 2021). In addition, the system's pervasive nature and the development of the 5G network aim to interconnect all the network nodes. In turn, this encourages SCM's smart appliances to actively participate in the network daily.

Logistics, as described by (Linkov et al., 2018; Muda et al., 2020; Razuleu, 2018) is the study of the dynamic processes of gauging the flow of commodities and information in an organisation, from their origin at the suppliers all the way to the point when the end-users, retail shops, or services acquire the finished goods. There are also major logistics problems in the service industry, which must be mentioned. in the distribution of utilities like water, power, and freight. Focus areas in logistics are often organised in relation to their placement in the production and distribution processes. Supply logistics, in this context, refers to the activities performed in advance of manufacturing facilities and can be broken down into two distinct sub-processes: the management of raw materials and the acquisition of goods and parts (Khatoun & Zeadally, 2017; Malhotra, Bhargava, & Dave, 2017; Soni, Anand, Dey et al, 2017). Internal logistics are carried out at production facilities and include activities such as stocking materials, ordering and receiving raw materials, and switching to processing semi-finished goods. The final step is to box up the finished products and ship them off. The supply chain then moves on to the logistics phase, which occurs after the factories but before the market. They make deliveries to stores or end users. In this diagram, supply chain management and distribution network design are grouped under the umbrella term "external logistics" (Haran, 2016; Ilves, 2016; Soni, Dey, Anand et al, 2017). Logistics tasks ensure that the right quantity of products or services is delivered to the right place at the right time for the right customer at the right price. Until one of these processes breaks down, many customers tend to be oblivious to the substantial or implicit consequences of logistics on practically every aspect of their lives. As the need for a more intricate network grew, the logistics concept was developed to meet it. It's used for things like planning and coordinating the flow of commodities from warehouses to consumers. Present smartness supply chain management in fig 2.

Figure 2. AI smartens supply chain management

Logistics encompasses warehousing, which has close ties to actual motion. Warehouses and commodities stockpiling are typically located at branch stations, in contrast to shipping, which is primarily based on the system core. Nearly twenty per cent of total logistics allocation costs are associated with warehousing and container handling operations, also known as "transportation at zero miles per hour" (Jazri & Jat, 2016; Norris et al., 2015; Oxford Analytica, 2016). The need for stock-keeping in businesses is mandated by the fact that it is difficult to predict the demand for outputs in a timely manner and that commodities cannot be delivered immediately. Companies maintain stock to better manage their customer relationships and reduce their marginal logistical costs by increasing the correlation between supply and demand. This has made warehousing a crucial aspect of many companies' logistical systems, warehouses play a pivotal role in logistics systems, as they guarantee the optimal level of customer relationship performance in conjunction with various logistics procedures (Dubey et al., 2015; Joshi, 2015; Sithole, 2015; Sony, 2015). In a warehouse, many tasks are completed, but they may be broken down into three main categories: material handling, inventory holding, and data transfer. Due to their historical function as places to store commodities for extended periods of time, warehouses have traditionally been viewed as focusing primarily on stock-keeping operations. Despite the best efforts of today's businesses, SC system updates still take time. As a result, modern warehouses place less emphasis on long-term stockpiling and more on their transportation function.

Manufacturing and logistics have grown into decision-making settings using AI. AI has revolutionised semiconductor manufacturing, packaging, and material handling. AI is applied in numerous functional domains to execute things faster and more efficiently without adding time or money (Angelopoulos et al., 2017; Mwangi, 2015; Ramli, 2017). Government and law have been influenced by automation and artificial intelligence ("AI"). According to the OECD, 700 AI policy projects in 60 countries are taking shape. The new Artificial Intelligence Act, due in 2022, will manage high-risk AI systems in the EU (Alguliyev et al., 2018; Meiyanti et al., 2018). Despite many AI legislative attempts from Congress, the US has not embraced the European Commission's complete approach to AI regulation. Instead, the US has prioritised defence and infrastructure expenditures to keep up with AI's rise.

Recent developments in US and European data privacy regulations include a risk-based approach to regulation, a larger emphasis on ethics and "trustworthy" AI, and consumer enforcement channels. The Biden administration announced a "bill of rights regulations include a risk-based approach to regulation, a larger emphasis on ethics and "trustworthy" AI, and consumer enforcement channels. The Biden administration announced a "bill of rights" for AI. The cost of regulating and enforcing will almost certainly rise next year (Abebe, 2019; Dhonju & Shakya, 2019; Yang, Elisa, & Eliot, 2019). The US Federal Trade Commission ("FTC") wants to regulate consumer products and services that use automated technologies and large volumes of data. The new California Privacy Protection Agency is expected to draught AI-related regulations by 2023, which would have substantial repercussions.

3. INFLUENCE OF ARTIFICIAL INTELLIGENCE ON SUPPLY CHAIN MANAGEMENT

The promise of artificial intelligence (AI) in supply chain management has long since passed. Although the rate of adoption may differ among sectors, this technology is having a profound effect on the way businesses function today.

McKinsey's study placed the influence of AI in supply chain management in second and third place, respectively, among the eight business functions analyzed. Overall, 64% of respondents reported increased revenues, while 61% reported decreased expenses. Most likely, the use cases that prompted these changes were found in sales and demand forecasting, spend analytics, and network optimization, all of which are components of supply chain management. According to a recent survey by MHI and Deloitte, only 12% of companies are already using AI in supply chain management. Complementary technologies like the Internet of Things (IoT), robotics, and prescriptive analytics all rank higher than artificial intelligence (AI), which is now ranked ninth in terms of adoption priority (Alharmoodi & Lakulu, 2020; Alqudah & Muradkhanli, 2021; Gouveia, 2020; Sharma et al., 2021). Supply chain planning, warehouse management, fleet management, risk management, inventory management, planning and logistics, and communications are just some of the many places where AI and ML come in handy along the SCM value chain. In this article, we will take a quick look at how these technological advancements can improve the effectiveness, productivity, and overall worth of their many uses (Venkatesh et al., 2016). Modern transportation management solutions are being made possible by AI and ML, which enable them to continuously learn by comparing inputs and outputs. They also include new features, including the ability to monitor a fleet in real-time, increase vehicle usage, and reduce maintenance costs through preventative measures. When it comes to digital supply chains, nothing is more important than having a solid digital supply chain strategy (SCP). In a 2019 research note, Gartner outlined a progressive model for supply chain planning that helps businesses increase the precision and timeliness of their plans while also ensuring that their technological initiatives are in step with the degree to which their supply chain processes have adopted digital transformation. The overview impact of AI on chain management is in fig 3.

More than a third (37%) of the businesses in the sample were found to be operating at the novice level. Even though end-to-end data visibility was very important,

Figure 3. Overview the impact of AI on chain management (Yang & Wibowo, 2020)

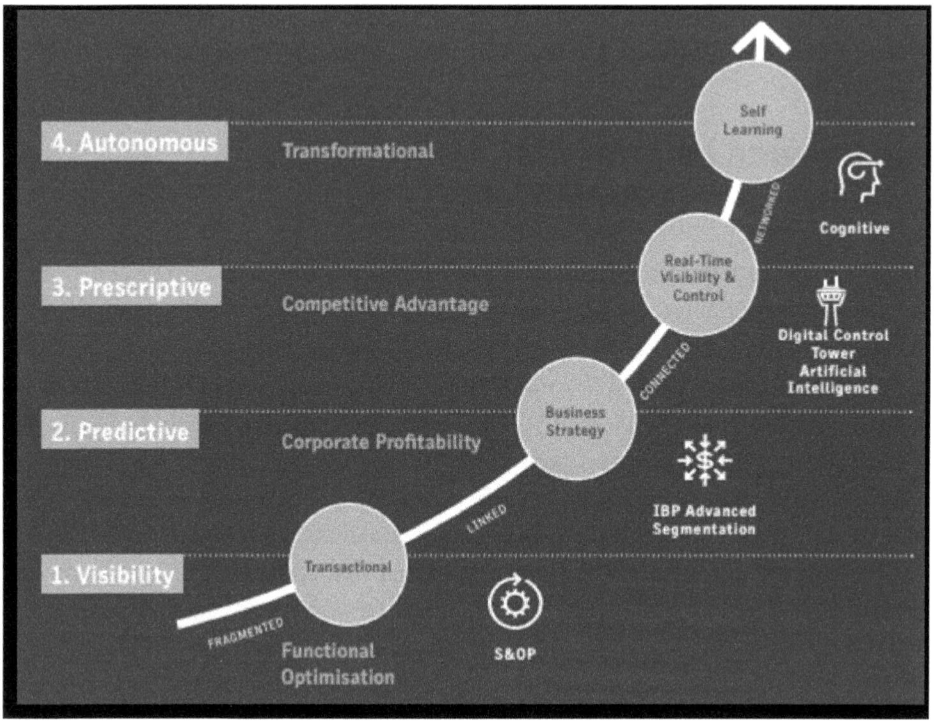

supply chain processes still used simple ERP systems and relied heavily on simple reporting tools like spreadsheets.

4. OVERVIEW SUPPLY CHAIN MANAGEMENT (SCM)

Managing the movement of goods and services, including the transformation of raw materials into finished commodities, is what supply chain management entails. Supply chain management is the process of proactively simplifying a company's supply-side processes to increase customer value and gain a competitive edge.

Essentially, supply chain management (SCM) is the industry's concerted attempt to design and operate more cost-effective and efficient supply chains. Supply chains include everything from making things to designing and putting new products on the market to managing the information systems that go with them (Al-rawahna et al., 2019). An overview of supply chain management is in fig 4.

SCM coordinates and streamlines product manufacturing, transit, and sale. Supply chain management saves money and boosts efficiency. To achieve this purpose, the

Figure 4. Overview of supply chain management (Suleimany, 2021)

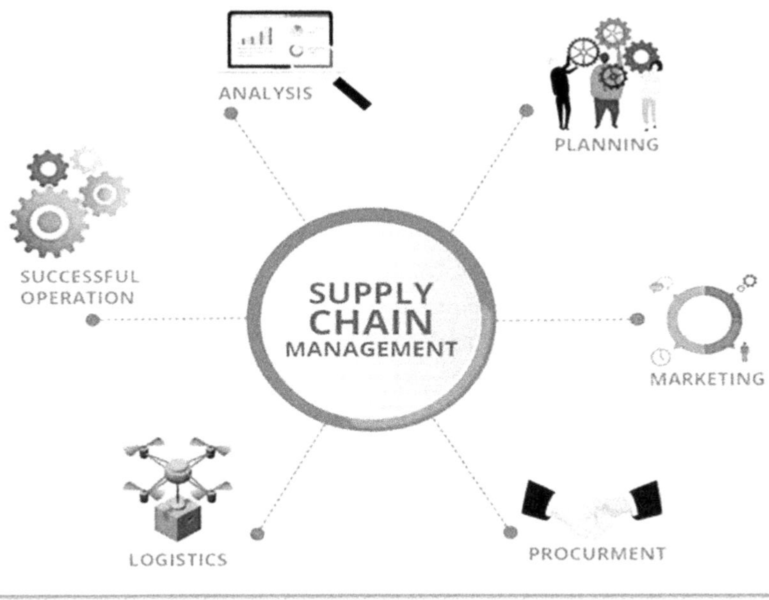

corporation continuously monitors and manages its manufacturing, distribution, and sales operations and supplier stockpiles. Supply chains have been around for a long time, but corporations just recently began to view them as assets.

5. SECURITY ISSUES AND CHALLENGES OF AI APPLICATION IN SCM

Global and international supply chains have made supply chain security an important issue for businesses of all sizes. Our supply chains are especially susceptible to cyberattacks, and while not all attacks on the supply chain are this dramatic and hazardous, ours are. A security flaw in one link of a supply chain might jeopardise the effectiveness of the entire chain (AlMendah, 2021; AlMendah, 2021; Yang, Elisa, & Eliot, 2019). This article discusses seven supply chain security threats that will be important to keep in mind during 2019.

Multiple dangers, both real and virtual, can affect a supply chain at any time. Some places along the supply chain are more vulnerable to physical attacks than others; for example, terrorists could disrupt the oil supply chain by attacking oil facilities. Supply chain terrorism is more prevalent than ever before, with 3.1 terrorist assaults on supply chains each week documented in a recent 10-year study by (Al-Soud, Al-Yaseen, & Al-Jaghoub, 2014; Gorla & Somers, 2014; Waller & Genius, 2015). Physical dangers also include theft, which can occur from within or without the building, and piracy. As well as the ever-present dangers posed by the elements, today's supply chains must contend with a growing range of cyber threats. These dangers exist because modern supply chains rely on a complex web of interconnected software and hardware to track and report on everything from shipments to stock levels to the health of the machines that make the components.

Because of how dependent we are on technology; it has become easier for bad actors to disrupt supply chains and steal money or private information. (Al-Soud, Al-Yaseen, & Al-Jaghoub, 2014; Alhawawsha & Panchenko, 2020; Rana et al., 2013; Waller & Genius, 2015) cyberattack known was particularly damaging, as I described at the outset of this piece. It was aimed at Maersk, the largest container shipping firm in the world, which is based in Denmark. The global IT network of a corporation that controls about a fifth of the world's shipping capacity was immediately and catastrophically brought down because of a ransomware attack.

As the use of technology in supply chains grows, it brings with it a lot of new cyber risks. It's important that, in addition to the traditional security measures put in place to protect against physical risks, steps be taken to protect against the different information security risks. The field of supply chain management has benefited from the rapid development of artificial intelligence in several ways. Key areas where AI has been used successfully are listed in Table 1 below. Warehouse productivity can be improved, costs can be reduced, customer satisfaction can be boosted by ensuring constant availability, and downtime can be reduced through predictive maintenance. How AI can be used to assist with disaster management supply chain activities is an active field of study and application, with a focus on more realistic resource planning and deployment in the case of a disaster (Adjei-Bamfo et al., 2019; Al-Mushayt, 2019; Cheng et al., 2017; Lv et al., 2018; Qi & Wang, 2021). For instance, the Carbon Disclosure Project (CDP) estimates that climate change poses a $1.4 trillion risk to the global supply chain over the next five years. Due to climate change, scientists can only predict with ever-smaller precision when a natural calamity will occur. The increased frequency of extreme weather events, such as prolonged, excessive heat waves, flash floods, and the delayed arrival of the season, has increased the volatility, risk, and resilience testing placed on supply networks. Business operations and strategic planning can be enhanced by incorporating climate-related AI into supply chain models. The AI applications and SCM functions are in fig 5.

Figure 5. The AI applications and SCM functions

SCM Function	AI Usage
Strategy and Operations Planning	Customer Demand Forecast
Sourcing Procurement	Supplier analytics
Production	Preventative maintenance and Defection
Logistics and Distribution	Smart warehousing and Automated
Marketing and Sales	Personalization and Digital Target Marketing

6. DISCUSSION

Customers' top priorities in the transportation and logistics industry include access to data on fuel, maintenance, and vehicle condition across various lifespans, as well as real-time support for customers' journeys, with the goal of proactively anticipating customers' needs through automated processing (Gershon et al., 2018; Shah, Wassan, & Usmani, 2022). The buyer often requests detailed information about the market and its trends, such as the most frequently traded-in automobiles and the current insurance landscape. Artificial intelligence is revolutionising many warehouse processes, including data collection and inventory management. This means that companies may see an increase in their bottom line. The automation of warehouses is being improved with the help of artificial intelligence to better anticipate which products will be in the highest demand. It can be used to adjust orders or have high-demand items shipped to a nearby distribution centre. When demand is predicted and logistics are planned, transportation costs are reduced (Shah, 2022; Shah, Habeeb, Rajper et al, 2022; Shah et al., 2021). As the logistics and freight business becomes more computerised, more information will be collected on customers, supply chains, deliveries, fleets, drivers, and more. The most successful logistics companies in the world are already utilising AI. While more and more businesses are collecting this information, it is largely underutilised.

The transformation to artificial intelligence presents both opportunities and challenges for logistics companies. Currently, there is a huge chasm between the logistics industry's actual needs and the availability of infrastructure supporting intelligent logistics. This includes things like logistics big data and the logistics cloud, but also the reach and precision of the logistics Internet (Shah, Jhanjhi, Amsaad, & Razaque, 2022; Shah, Jhanjhi, Amsaad, & Razaque, 2022; Shah, Jhanjhi, Humayun, & Ghosh, 2022). Talent is the driving force behind technological progress. Data, business scenarios, and real-world challenges abound in the logistics sector. To thrive, it must acquire both cutting-edge tools and top-tier human resources. The development of the logistics business is hindered by the widespread absence of skilled professionals working for logistics companies. Constraints have also emerged from logistical standardisation and a lack of system integrity. Standards and protocols are the backbones of the AI Logistics duo's smooth operation (Kiran et al., 2021; Shah, Jhanjhi, Humayun, & Ghosh, 2022; Umrani et al., 2020). Despite this, there are already substantial differences in data encoding, transmitting media, and bearing units. AI changes the traditional idea of connecting nodes in logistics while keeping many unexpected relationships and making typical market transactions. The digitalization, intelligence, regulation, and integrated management of supply chains and physical logistics will arise from creating a perfect cloud platform. Comprehensive logistics is the foundation upon which cutting-edge AI and logistics technologies may be built to optimise processes, foster collaboration, bring about localised inventory management and distribution, and boost production chain productivity.

Discussion and Chapter Contribution

This chapter aims to assess AI applications and measure security issues and challenges to secure the supply chain network. The recommendations made will clarify research gaps for the new researchers and reveal security challenges for the logistics industry. Supply chain management comprises overseeing the distribution of goods and services, from raw materials to final products. Supply chain management is the process of proactively streamlining a company's supply-side operations to increase customer value and set the company apart from its competitors. Artificial intelligence and data analytics, two of the most promising new technologies, are already popular. While many sectors are still pushing through barriers brought on by the pandemic's aftermath, others have seized the opportunity to implement these cutting-edge technologies on a grand scale. The supply chain sector is just one example. According to recent research, using AI in the supply chain has improved inventory management, smart manufacturing, dynamic logistic systems, and real-time delivery controls. The primary goal of implementing AI in logistics and the supply chain is to boost efficiency and output. As a result of digitalization, supply chain management has become more eco-friendly, prompting companies to question whether a similar digital transformation on their own scale would be beneficial. This post will answer any questions it may have about how artificial intelligence (AI) and analytics might benefit your supply chain. Let's look at the effects that AI has on the supply chain and how modern supply chain management puts people, machines, and software to work.

For AI-based solutions to be used in logistics and supply chain management, smart machines that can solve problems must be used. By automating manufacturing, the Industrial Internet of Things (IIoT) makes it possible for smart industries to make things without having to touch them. Using algorithms and constraint-based modeling, machine learning is applied to supply chain and transportation data to discover influential aspects. In the mathematical method known as constraint-based modelling, the feasibility of each business choice is limited by a set of fixed upper- and lower-bound requirements. Warehouse workers can make better decisions about inventory stocking with the help of this data-rich modelling approach. As an alternative, you can use big data predictive analysis, which provides in-depth insights to help feedback loops improve their own forecasts. Inventory optimization in modern supply chain management is powered by artificial intelligence technologies that keep the warehouse and stock managers apprised of the status of raw materials, components, and finished goods in real-time. As it gets better, artificial intelligence (AI) makes suggestions about what to buy based on what was bought and delivered in the past. The effects of AI on people and the economy have been revolutionary. By 2030, AI has the potential to boost global GDP by $15.8 trillion. From some perspective, that's almost equivalent to the GDP of both China and India right now. Since 2000, the number of AI start-ups has increased dramatically, increasing by a factor of 14. This rapid growth can be attributed to the widespread belief among businesses that AI can raise corporate efficiency by as much as 40%. A wide variety of fields can benefit from AI, from astronomy (observing and cataloguing celestial objects) to medicine (forecasting illnesses), law enforcement (finding novel approaches to combating terrorism), and design (creating products).

Many countries, including India, have instituted severe IT regulations in response to allegations of unethical data collection and usage against tech giants like Google, Facebook, and Apple. Therefore, these businesses now face the challenge of exploiting biassed local data to generate global applications. Labelled data plays a crucial role in teaching machines how to learn and make predictions. It is the goal of certain businesses to develop novel approaches and AI models that can provide reliable findings despite a lack of data. With skewed data, the whole thing might collapse. Big tech firms like Apple and Google have poured billions of dollars into the research and development of AI. Manufacturing, education, retail, and healthcare are just some of the major industries where AI is underutilised. Every day, these companies generate reams of data, although artificial intelligence is rarely employed to sift through these records and extract useful insights about their operations. The big mystery is why this problem is getting so much attention. Why? because of barriers to entry, including a lack of information and the inability to act on it. We are aware of the most pressing issues around AI. We must discover what can solve these AI issues while still allowing businesses to turn a profit.

Unfortunately, most companies lack access to the high-end, costly computing resources necessary for artificial intelligence. In addition, they do not have access to the specialised, highly-priced AI knowledge needed to make good use of these assets. As of the year 2022, 37% of firms have already used AI services and want to keep doing so. By 2025, the artificial intelligence market is expected to generate $126 billion annually. Forbes predicts that by 2030, artificial intelligence will be worth $15.7 trillion and that by 2024, investments will have reached roughly $500 billion. Due to the increasingly interconnected nature of today's global economy, supply chain security has become a critical concern for companies of all kinds. While not all supply chain attacks are as dramatic and dangerous as those targeting us, our supply chains are especially vulnerable to cyberattacks. One vulnerable part of the supply chain can compromise the safety of the whole. A supply chain is vulnerable to numerous real and hypothetical threats at any given time.

Terrorists could potentially disrupt the oil supply chain by attacking oil facilities; however, some points along the supply chain are more at risk from physical attacks than others. A recent 10-year analysis by found that there was an average of 3.1 weekly terrorist attacks on supply chains. Theft, which can occur both inside and outside the facility, and piracy are two more physical threats. Today's supply chains not only face the ever-present risks posed by the elements but also a wide variety of cyber threats. To monitor and report on everything from shipments and stock levels to the condition of the machines that create the components, contemporary supply chains rely on a sophisticated web of interconnected software and hardware.

The increasing reliance on technology has made it simpler for criminals to steal money or access personal data and disrupt supply systems. The cyberattack in question was very destructive. It was meant for Maersk, the Danish company that operates the world's largest container fleet. A ransomware attack swiftly and tragically shut down the global information technology network of a company that manages roughly one-fifth of the world's shipping capacity. The increased integration of technology into supply chains exposes organisations to novel cyber threats. It's crucial to take precautions against the many information security hazards in addition to the more standard security measures in place to guard against physical dangers. The rapid progress of artificial intelligence has improved the field of supply chain management in several ways. Here are some of the most important applications of AI, as listed in Table 1. Predictive maintenance can increase warehouse efficiency, reduce costs, and increase customer satisfaction by minimising downtime and increasing availability. Realistic resource planning and deployment in the event of a disaster is a primary focus of the research and practice surrounding the use of artificial intelligence in disaster management supply chain operations. Climate change, for instance, is predicted to threaten the global supply chain by $1.3 trillion over the next five years, according to the Carbon Disclosure Project (CDP).

Conclusion and Future Work

Logistics, generally relates to the careful preparation and performance of strenuous activity. To meet the needs of customers or enterprises, logistics is broadly defined as managing the flow of items from their point of production to their location of consumption. According to studies, up to 90% of a company's sustainability consequences are attributable to its supply chain. These crucial supply chain flaws have been made public by the COVID-19 epidemic. Additionally, businesses are making many sustainability pledges because of legislative and consumer pressure for climate action. Current procedures have the potential to be streamlined with Artificial Intelligence (AI) innovation in logistics. Numerous developments are pushing automation to the top of the logistics CEO's agenda. The first step toward extensive optimization is automation, which many businesses have already adopted to maintain competitiveness. It is possible to improve current procedures, increasing production and efficiency. Companies are pressured to provide high-quality services at competitive prices, which strains their profit margins and drives them toward labour automation. Due to the complexity of this business, it is challenging to survive without technologies like artificial intelligence (AI), that can handle complicated operations and manage vast volumes of data while providing excellent value to adopters. The process of taking those strategic actions that might assist manufacturers in identifying, analysing, assessing, and ultimately mitigating the risk from supply chain interruption is known as supply chain risk management (SCRM). The complex supply chains of today virtually always experience disruptions. As a result, many multinational corporations are starting to wonder how to evaluate and manage these risks to prepare their supply networks appropriately. It needs to work more the AI applications for supply chain management.

REFERENCES

Abebe, B. (2019). *E-government based land administration framework; trends, challenges and prospects* (Doctoral dissertation). https://ir.bdu.edu.et/handle/123456789/10878

Adjei-Bamfo, P., Maloreh-Nyamekye, T., & Ahenkan, A. (2019). The role of e-government in sustainable public procurement in developing countries: A systematic literature review. *Resources, Conservation and Recycling*, *142*, 189–203. doi:10.1016/j.resconrec.2018.12.001

Ahmad, T. (2019). Technology Convergence and Cybersecurity: A Critical Analysis of Cybercrime Trends in India. *27th Convergence India Pragati Maidan*, 29-31. https://papers.ssrn.com/sol3/papers.cfm?abstract_id=3326232

Ahmad, T. (2020). Corona virus (covid-19) pandemic and work from home: Challenges of cybercrimes and cybersecurity. *SSRN*, *3568830*. doi:10.2139/ssrn.3568830

Ajaikumar, B. K., Varsha, R., & Dey, P. (2021). OVID-19, cytokines, inflammation, and spices: How are they related? *Life Sciences*, *284*, 119–201. doi:10.1016/j.lfs.2021.119201

Al-Mushayt, O. S. (2019). Automating E-government services with artificial intelligence. *IEEE Access : Practical Innovations, Open Solutions*, *7*, 146821–146829. doi:10.1109/ACCESS.2019.2946204

Al-rawahna, A. S. M., Chen, S. C., & Hung, C. W. (2019). The barriers of e-government success: An empirical study from Jordan. *SSRN*, *3498847*. doi:10.2139/ssrn.3498847

Al-Shboul, M., Rababah, O., Ghnemat, R., & Al-Saqqa, S. (2014). Challenges and factors affecting the implementation of e-government in Jordan. *Journal of Software Engineering and Applications*, *7*(13), 1111–1127. doi:10.4236/jsea.2014.713098

Al-Soud, A. R., Al-Yaseen, H., & Al-Jaghoub, S. H. (2014). Jordan's e-Government at the crossroads. *Transforming Government: People, Process and Policy*. https://www.emerald.com/insight/content/doi/10.1108/TG-10-2013-0043/full/html

Alamri, M., Jhanjhi, N. Z., & Humayun, M. (2019). Blockchain for Internet of Things (IoT) research issues challenges & future directions: A review. *Int. J. Comput. Sci. Netw. Secur*, *19*, 244–258. https://seap.taylors.edu.my/file/rems/publication/109566_6018_1.pdf

Alexandre, D., & Dmitry, I. (2021). Ripple Effect and Supply Chain Disruption Management: New Trends and Research Directions. *International Journal of Production Research*, *59*(1), 102–109. doi:10.1080/00207543.2021.1840148

Alguliyev, R., Aliguliyev, R., & Yusifov, F. (2018). Role of Social Networks in E-government: Risks and Security Threats. *Online Journal of Communication and Media Technologies*, *8*(4), 363–376. https://www.ojcmt.net/article/role-of-social-networks-in-e-government-risks-and-security-threats-3957

Alharmoodi, B. Y. R., & Lakulu, M. M. B. (2020). Transition from e-government to m-government: Challenges and opportunities-case study of UAE. *European Journal of Multidisciplinary Studies*, *5*(1), 61–67. doi:10.26417/453fgx96c

Alhawawsha, M., & Panchenko, T. (2020, January). Open Data Platform Architecture and Its Advantages for an Open E-Government. In *International Conference on Computer Science, Engineering and Education Applications* (pp. 631–639). Springer. https://link.springer.com/chapter/10.1007/978-3-030-55506-1_56

AlMendah, O. M. (2021). A Survey of Blockchain and E-governance applications: Security and Privacy issues. *Turkish Journal of Computer and Mathematics Education*, *12*(10), 3117–3125. https://turcomat.org/index.php/turkbilmat/article/view/4964

Almusaylim, Z. A., & Jhanjhi, N. Z. (2020). Comprehensive review: Privacy protection of user in location-aware services of mobile cloud computing. *Wireless Personal Communications*, *111*(1), 541–564. doi:10.1007/s11277-019-06872-3

Alqudah, M. A., & Muradkhanli, L. (2021). Artificial Intelligence in Electric Government; Ethical Challenges and Governance in Jordan. *Electronic Research Journal of Social Sciences and Humanities, 3*, 65-74. https://papers.ssrn.com/sol3/papers.cfm?abstract_id=3806600

Amir Latif, R. M., Hussain, K., Jhanjhi, N. Z., Nayyar, A., & Rizwan, O. (2020). A remix IDE: Smart contract-based framework for the healthcare sector by using Blockchain technology. *Multimedia Tools and Applications*, 1–24. https://link.springer.com/article/10.1007/s11042-020-10087-1

Angelopoulos, K., Diamantopoulou, V., Mouratidis, H., Pavlidis, M., Salnitri, M., Giorgini, P., & Ruiz, J. F. (2017, August). A holistic approach for privacy protection in E-government. In *Proceedings of the 12th International Conference on Availability* (pp. 1–10). Reliability and Security. doi:10.1145/3098954.3098960

Arabadzhyiev, D., Popovych, Y., Lytvynchuk, I., Bakbergen, K., & Kyrychenko, Y. (2021). Digital Society: Regulatory and Institutional Support of Electronic Governance in Modern Realities. In *SHS Web of Conferences* (Vol. 100, p. 03008). EDP Sciences. https://www.shsconferences.org/articles/shsconf/abs/2021/11/shsconf_iscsai2021_03008/shsconf_iscsai2021_03008.html

Bhagat, C., Sharma, B., & Kumar Mishra, A. (2021). *Assessment of E Governance for National Development–A Case Study of Province 1 Nepal*. https://papers.ssrn.com/sol3/papers.cfm?abstract_id=3857194

Bhuvana, M., & Vasantha, S. (2021). The Impact of COVID-19 on Rural Citizens for Accessing E-Governance Services: A Conceptual Model Using the Dimensions of Trust and Technology Acceptance Model. *Recent Advances in Technology Acceptance Models and Theories, 335*, 471. https://www.ncbi.nlm.nih.gov/pmc/articles/PMC7979245/

Brohi, S. N., Jhanjhi, N. Z., Brohi, N. N., & Brohi, M. N. (2020). *Key Applications of State-of-the-Art technologies to mitigate and eliminate COVID-19*. file:///C:/Users/imdad/Downloads/Key%20Applications%20of%20State-of-the-Art%20Technologies%20to%20Mitigate%20and%20Eliminate%20COVID-19%20(1).pdf

Burrell, D. N. (2020). Understanding the talent management intricacies of remote cybersecurity teams in covid-19 induced telework organizational ecosystems. *Land Forces Academy Review, 25*(3), 232-244. https://www.armyacademy.ro/reviste/rev3_2020/Burrell.pdf

Carrapico, H., & Farrand, B. (2020). Discursive continuity and change in the time of Covid-19: The case of EU cybersecurity policy. *Journal of European Integration*, *42*(8), 1111–1126. doi:10.1080/07036337.2020.1853122

Cheng, B., Solmaz, G., Cirillo, F., Kovacs, E., Terasawa, K., & Kitazawa, A. (2017). FogFlow: Easy programming of IoT services over cloud and edges for smart cities. *IEEE Internet of Things Journal*, *5*(2), 696–707. doi:10.1109/JIOT.2017.2747214

Cowgill, B., & Stevenson, M. T. (2020, May). Algorithmic social engineering. In *AEA Papers and Proceedings* (Vol. 110, pp. 96-100). https://www.aeaweb.org/articles?id=10.1257/pandp.20201037

Cradduck, L. (2019). E-conveyancing: a consideration of its risks and rewards. *Property Management*. https://www.emerald.com/insight/content/doi/10.1108/PM-04-2019-0021/full/html

Dahwan, A. A., & Raju, V. (2021). The Infleuence of Online Services and Telecommunication Infrastructure on the Implementation of E-government in Military Institutions in Yemen. *Annals of the Romanian Society for Cell Biology*, 1698–1710. https://www.annalsofrscb.ro/index.php/journal/article/view/2689

Dhonju, G. R., & Shakya, S. (2019). Analyzing Challenges for the Implementation of E-Government in Municipalities within Kathmandu Valley. *Journal of Science and Engineering*, *7*, 70–78. doi:10.3126/jsce.v7i0.26795

Ding, D., Han, Q.-L., Xiang, Y., Ge, X., & Zhang, X.-M. (2018). A survey on security control and attack detection for industrial cyber-physical systems. *Neurocomputing*, *275*, 1674–1683. doi:10.1016/j.neucom.2017.10.009

Dmitry, I., & Alexandre, D. (2021). A digital supply chain twin for managing the disruption risks and resilience in the era of Industry 4.0. *Production Planning and Control*, *32*(9), 775–788. doi:10.1080/09537287.2020.1768450

Dorr, B., Bhatia, A., Dalton, A., Mather, B., Hebenstreit, B., Santhanam, S., . . . Strzalkowski, T. (2020, April). Detecting asks in social engineering attacks: Impact of linguistic and structural knowledge. In *Proceedings of the AAAI Conference on Artificial Intelligence* (Vol. 34, No. 5, pp. 7675-7682). https://ojs.aaai.org/index.php/AAAI/article/view/6269

Dubey, A., Saquib, Z., & Dwivedi, S. (2015). *Electronic authentication for e-Government services-a survey*. https://digital-library.theiet.org/content/conferences/10.1049/cp.2015.0299

Entrepreneurship and management. (2021). http://economicresearch.pl/Books/index.php/eep/catalog/view/85/87/122-1

Ferreira, A., & Cruz-Correia, R. (2021). COVID-19 and cybersecurity: Finally, an opportunity to disrupt? *JMIRx Med*, *2*(2), e21069. doi:10.2196/21069 PMID:34032816

Fosso, J., Wamba, S., Roubaud, D., & Foropon, C. (2021). Empirical investigation of data analytics capability and organizational flexibility as complements to supply chain resilience. *International Journal of Production Research*, *59*(1), 110–128. doi:10.1080/00207543.2019.1582820

Gaur, L., Bhatia, U., Jhanjhi, N. Z., Muhammad, G., & Masud, M. (2021). Medical image-based detection of COVID-19 using Deep Convolution Neural Networks. *Multimedia Systems*, 1–10. https://link.springer.com/article/10.1007/s00530-021-00794-6 PMID:33935377

Gershon, D., Prince, O., & Opoku, A. M. (2018). Promoting Inclusiveness and Participation in Governance: The Directions of Electronic Government in Ghana. *International Journal of Advanced Research*, *7*(3), 397–406. doi:10.21474/IJAR01/7931

Gorla, N., & Somers, T. M. (2014). The impact of IT outsourcing on information systems success. *Information & Management*, *51*(3), 320–335. doi:10.1016/j.im.2013.12.002

Gouveia, L. B. (2020). e-Government and Smart Cities: Contexts and Challenges Taking from Digital Usage and Exploration. *UNU-EGOV| UM DSI PDSI talk*. https://bdigital.ufp.pt/handle/10284/8554

Gupta, R., & Agarwal, S. P. (2017). A Comparative Study of Cyber Threats in Emerging Economies. *Globus: An International Journal of Management & IT*, *8*(2), 24-28. https://globusjournal.com/wp-content/uploads/2018/07/826Ruchika.pdf

Haran, M. H. (2016). Framework Based Approach for the Mitigation of Insider Threats in E-governance IT Infrastructure. *International Journal of Scientific Research*, *3*(4), 5–10. https://citeseerx.ist.psu.edu/viewdoc/download?doi=10.1.1.566.4423&rep=rep1&type=pdf

He, Y., Aliyu, A., Evans, M., & Luo, C. (2021). Health Care Cybersecurity Challenges and Solutions Under the Climate of COVID-19: Scoping Review. *Journal of Medical Internet Research*, *23*(4), e21747. doi:10.2196/21747 PMID:33764885

Herawati, A. R., Warsono, H., Afrizal, T., & Saputra, J. (2021). *The Challenges of Industrial Revolution 4.0: An Evidence from Public Administration Ecology in Indonesia*. http://www.ieomsociety.org/singapore2021/papers/846.pdf

Hiscox. (2019). *The hiscox cyber readiness report 2019*. https://www.sciencedirect.com/science/article/pii/S0167404821000729

Huang, K., Siegel, M., & Madnick, S. (2018). Systematically understanding the cyber attack business: A survey. *ACM Computing Surveys*, *51*(4), 1–36. doi:10.1145/3199674

Humayun, M., Jhanjhi, N. Z., Hamid, B., & Ahmed, G. (2020). Emerging smart logistics and transportation using IoT and blockchain. *IEEE Internet of Things Magazine, 3*(2), 58-62. https://ieeexplore.ieee.org/abstract/document/9125435

Humayun, M., Niazi, M., Jhanjhi, N. Z., Alshayeb, M., & Mahmood, S. (2020). Cyber security threats and vulnerabilities: A systematic mapping study. *Arabian Journal for Science and Engineering*, *45*(4), 3171–3189. doi:10.1007/s13369-019-04319-2

Hussain, S. J., Irfan, M., Jhanjhi, N. Z., Hussain, K., & Humayun, M. (2021). Performance enhancement in wireless body area networks with secure communication. *Wireless Personal Communications*, *116*(1), 1–22. doi:10.1007/s11277-020-07702-7 PMID:33558792

Ilves, T. H. (2016). The consequences of cyber attacks. *Journal of International Affairs*, *70*(1), 175–181.

Jazri, H., & Jat, D. S. (2016, November). A quick cybersecurity wellness evaluation framework for critical organizations. In *2016 International Conference on ICT in Business Industry & Government (ICTBIG)* (pp. 1-5). IEEE. https://ieeexplore.ieee.org/abstract/document/7892725

Joshi, S. (2015). E-Governance in Uttar Pradesh: Challenges and Prospects. *The Indian Journal of Public Administration*, *61*(2), 229–240. doi:10.1177/0019556120150203

Karpenko, O., Kuczabski, A., & Havryliak, V. (2021). Mechanisms for providing cybersecurity during the COVID-19 pandemic: Perspectives for Ukraine. *Security and Defence Quarterly*. http://yadda.icm.edu.pl/yadda/element/bwmeta1.element.doi-10_35467_sdq_133158

Kaur, K., Garg, S., Aujla, G. S., Kumar, N., Rodrigues, J. J., & Guizani, M. (2018). Edge computing in the industrial internet of things environment: Software-defined-networks-based edge-cloud interplay. *IEEE Communications Magazine*, *56*(2), 44–51. doi:10.1109/MCOM.2018.1700622

Khan, A., Jhanjhi, N. Z., Humayun, M., & Ahmad, M. (2020). The Role of IoT in Digital Governance. In *Employing Recent Technologies for Improved Digital Governance* (pp. 128–150). IGI Global. doi:10.4018/978-1-7998-1851-9.ch007

Khan, N. A., Brohi, S. N., & Zaman, N. (2020). *Ten deadly cyber security threats16amid COVID-19 pandemic*. https://www.techrxiv.org/articles/preprint/Ten_Deadly_Cyber_Security_Threats_Amid_COVID-19_Pandemic/12278792/1

Khandpur, R. P., Ji, T., Jan, S., Wang, G., Lu, C. T., & Ramakrishnan, N. (2017, November). Crowdsourcing cybersecurity: Cyber attack detection using social media. In *Proceedings of the 2017 ACM on Conference on Information and Knowledge Management* (pp. 1049-1057). https://dl.acm.org/doi/abs/10.1145/3132847.3132866

Khatoun, R., & Zeadally, S. (2017). Cybersecurity and privacy solutions in smart cities. *IEEE Communications Magazine*, *55*(3), 51–59. doi:10.1109/MCOM.2017.1600297CM

Kiran, S. R. A., Rajper, S., Shaikh, R. A., Shah, I. A., & Danwar, S. H. (2021). Categorization of CVE Based on Vulnerability Software By Using Machine Learning Techniques. *International Journal (Toronto, Ont.)*, *10*(3).

Korir, G., Thiga, M., & Rono, L. (2019). *Implementing the Tool for Assessing Organisation Information Security Preparedness in E-Governance Implementation*. https://www.easpublisher.com/media/features_articles/EASJECS_210_284-299.pdf

Krykavskyi, Ye., Pokhylchenko, O., Fertsch M. (2019). *Lohistyka ta upravlinnia lantsiuhamy postavok* [Logistics and Supply Chain Management]. 848s.

Krykavskyy, Y., Hayvanovych, N., Pokhylchenko, O., Leonova, S., Dovhun, O., & Chornopyska, N. (2021). *Competence determinants of logistics landscape*. Contemporary Issues in Economy.

Krykavskyy, Ye., Pokhylchenko, O., & Hayvanovych, N. (2019) Digitalization of Supply Chains: New Paradigm. *Contemporary Issues in Economy*, 103-112. http://economicresearch.pl/Books/index.php/eep/catalog/view/55/57/86-2

Kumar, M. S., Vimal, S., Jhanjhi, N. Z., Dhanabalan, S. S., & Alhumyani, H. A. (2021). Blockchain based peer to peer communication in autonomous drone operation. *Energy Reports*, *7*, 7925–7939. doi:10.1016/j.egyr.2021.08.073

Lallie, H. S., Shepherd, L. A., Nurse, J. R., Erola, A., Epiphaniou, G., Maple, C., & Bellekens, X. (2021). Cyber security in the age of covid-19: A timeline and analysis of cyber-crime and cyber-attacks during the pandemic. *Computers & Security*, *105*, 102248. doi:10.1016/j.cose.2021.102248 PMID:36540648

Le Blond, S., Gilbert, C., Upadhyay, U., Gomez-Rodriguez, M., & Choffnes, D. R. (2017). A Broad View of the Ecosystem of Socially Engineered Exploit Documents. *NDSS*. https://www.ndss-symposium.org/wp-content/uploads/2017/09/ndss2017_03B-4_LeBlond_paper.pdf

Lee, S., Abdullah, A., Jhanjhi, N., & Kok, S. (2021). Classification of botnet attacks in IoT smart factory using honeypot combined with machine learning. *PeerJ. Computer Science*, *7*, e350. doi:10.7717/peerj-cs.350 PMID:33817000

Liang, Y., Qi, G., Wei, K., & Chen, J. (2017). Exploring the determinant and influence mechanism of e-Government cloud adoption in government agencies in China. *Government Information Quarterly*, *34*(3), 481–495. doi:10.1016/j.giq.2017.06.002

Lim, M., Abdullah, A., & Jhanjhi, N. Z. (2019). Performance optimization of criminal network hidden link prediction model with deep reinforcement learning. *Journal of King Saud University-Computer and Information Sciences*. https://onlinelibrary.wiley.com/doi/abs/10.1002/ett.4171

Lim, M., Abdullah, A., Jhanjhi, N. Z., & Supramaniam, M. (2019). Hidden link prediction in criminal networks using the deep reinforcement learning technique. *Computers, 8*(1), 8. https://www.mdpi.com/2073-431X/8/1/8

Linkov, I., Trump, B. D., Poinsatte-Jones, K., & Florin, M. V. (2018). Governance strategies for a sustainable digital world. *Sustainability (Basel)*, *10*(2), 440. doi:10.3390/su10020440

Liu, J., Wang, C., Li, C., Li, N., Deng, J., & Pan, J. Z. (2021). DTN: Deep triple network for topic specific fake news detection. *Journal of Web Semantics*, *100646*, 100646. doi:10.1016/j.websem.2021.100646

Liu, Z., Wei, W., Wang, L., Ten, C. W., & Rho, Y. (2020). An Actuarial Framework for Power System Reliability Considering Cybersecurity Threats. *IEEE Transactions on Power Systems*. https://dl.acm.org/doi/abs/10.1145/3386723.3387847

Luh, R., Marschalek, S., Kaiser, M., Janicke, H., & Schrittwieser, S. (2017). Semantics-aware detection of targeted attacks: A survey. *Journal of Computer Virology and Hacking Techniques*, *13*(1), 47–85. doi:10.1007/s11416-016-0273-3

Lv, Z., Li, X., Wang, W., Zhang, B., Hu, J., & Feng, S. (2018). Government affairs service platform for smart city. *Future Generation Computer Systems*, *81*, 443–451. doi:10.1016/j.future.2017.08.047

Malhotra, H., Bhargava, R., & Dave, M. (2017). Implementation of E-Governance projects: Development, Threats & Targets. *JIMS8I-International Journal of Information Communication and Computing Technology*, *5*(2), 292-298. https://www.indianjournals.com/ijor.aspx?target=ijor:jims8i&volume=5&issue=2&article=001

Malhotra, H., Bhargava, R., & Dave, M. (2017, November). Challenges related to information security and its implications for evolving e-government structures: A comparative study between India and African countries. In *2017 International Conference on Inventive Computing and Informatics (ICICI)* (pp. 30-35). IEEE. 10.1109/ICICI.2017.8365370

McKibbin, W., & Fernando, R. (2020). The economic impact of COVID-19. *Economics in the Time of COVID-19, 45*. https://www.incae.edu/sites/default/files/covid-19.pdf#page=52

Mehrotra, K. (2021). Data Privacy & Protection. *SSRN*, *3858581*. https://papers.ssrn.com/sol3/papers.cfm?abstract_id=3858581

Meiyanti, R., Utomo, B., Sensuse, D. I., & Wahyuni, R. (2018, August). E-government challenges in developing countries: a literature review. In *2018 6th International Conference on Cyber and IT Service Management (CITSM)* (pp. 1-6). IEEE. 10.1109/CITSM.2018.8674245

Mensah, I. K. (2019). Impact of government capacity and E-government performance on the adoption of E-Government services. *International Journal of Public Administration*. https://www.tandfonline.com/doi/10.1080/01900692.2019.1628059

Muda, J., Tumsa, S., Tuni, A., & Sharma, D. P. (2020). Cloud-Enabled E-Governance Framework for Citizen Centric Services. *Journal of Computer and Communications*, *8*(7), 63–78. doi:10.4236/jcc.2020.87006

Mwangi, N. M. (2015). *E-government adoption by Kenya ministries* (Doctoral dissertation, University of Nairobi). http://erepository.uonbi.ac.ke/handle/11295/94091

Najmi, K. Y., AlZain, M. A., Masud, M., Jhanjhi, N. Z., Al-Amri, J., & Baz, M. (2021). A survey on security threats and countermeasures in IoT to achieve users confidentiality and reliability. *Materials Today: Proceedings*. https://www.sciencedirect.com/science/article/pii/S221478532102469X

Norris, D., Joshi, A., & Finin, T. (2015, June). *Cybersecurity challenges to American state and local governments. In 15th European Conference on eGovernment*. Academic Conferences and Publishing Int. Ltd. https://ebiquity.umbc.edu/paper/abstract/id/774/Cybersecurity-Challenges-to-American-State-and-Local-Governments

Nosiri, U. D., & Ndoh, J. A. (2018). E-Governance. *South East Journal of Political Science, 4*(1). https://journals.aphriapub.com/index.php/SEJPS/article/view/833

NSKT Global. (2021). https://nsktglobal.com/what-are-the-biggest-cybersecurity-threats-in-2021-

Okereafor, K., & Adebola, O. (2020). Tackling the cybersecurity impacts of the coronavirus outbreak as a challenge to internet safety. *Int J IT Eng*, *8*(2). https://papers.ssrn.com/sol3/papers.cfm?abstract_id=3568830

Oxford Analytica. (2016). Estonia's e-governance model may be unique. *Emerald Expert Briefings*. https://www.emerald.com/insight/content/doi/10.1108/OXAN-DB214505/full/html

Peng, C., Xu, M., Xu, S., & Hu, T. (2017). Modeling and predicting extreme cyber attack rates via marked point processes. *Journal of Applied Statistics*, *44*(14), 2534–2563. doi:10.1080/02664763.2016.1257590

Pranggono, B., & Arabo, A. (2021). COVID-19 pandemic cybersecurity issues. *Internet Technology Letters*, *4*(2), e247. doi:10.1002/itl2.247

Qi, M., & Wang, J. (2021). Using the Internet of Things e-government platform to optimize the administrative management mode. *Wireless Communications and Mobile Computing*, *2021*, 1–11. doi:10.1155/2021/2224957

Rajmohan, R., Kumar, T. A., Pavithra, M., Sandhya, S. G., Julie, E. G., Nayahi, J. J. V., & Jhanjhi, N. Z. (2020). Blockchain: Next-generation technology for industry 4.0. *Blockchain Technology*, 177-198. https://www.taylorfrancis.com/chapters/edit/10.1201/9781003004998-11/blockchain-rajmohan-ananth-kumar-pavithra-sandhya

Ramadan, R. A., Aboshosha, B. W., Alshudukhi, J. S., Alzahrani, A. J., El-Sayed, A., & Dessouky, M. M. (2021). Cybersecurity and Countermeasures at the Time of Pandemic. *Journal of Advanced Transportation*, *2021*, 1–19. doi:10.1155/2021/6627264

Ramli, R. M. (2017). Challenges and issues in Malaysian e-government. *Electronic Government, an International Journal, 13*(3), 242-273. https://www.inderscienceonline.com/doi/abs/10.1504/EG.2017.086685

Ramzi, E. H., & Weerakkody, V. (2010). *E-Government implementation Challenges: A Case study*. https://aisel.aisnet.org/cgi/viewcontent.cgi?article=1318&context=amcis2010

Rana, N. P., Dwivedi, Y. K., & Williams, M. D. (2013). Analysing challenges, barriers and CSF of egov adoption. *Transforming Government: People, Process and Policy*. https://www.emerald.com/insight/content/doi/10.1108/17506161311325350/full/html

Ravi, N., Verma, S., Jhanjhi, N. Z., & Talib, M. N. (2021, August). Securing VANET Using Blockchain Technology. In *Journal of Physics: Conference Series* (Vol. 1979, No. 1, p. 012035). IOP Publishing. https://iopscience.iop.org/article/10.1088/1742-6596/1979/1/012035/meta

Razaque, A., Amsaad, F., Khan, M. J., Hariri, S., Chen, S., Siting, C., & Ji, X. (2019). Survey: Cybersecurity vulnerabilities, attacks and solutions in the medical domain. *IEEE Access : Practical Innovations, Open Solutions*, *7*, 168774–168797. doi:10.1109/ACCESS.2019.2950849

Razuleu, L. (2018). *E-Governance and its associated cybersecurity: The challenges and best practices of authentication and authorization among a rapidly growing e-government*. https://scholarworks.calstate.edu/concern/theses/qj72pb20t

RodelaT. T.TasnimS.MazumderH.FaizahF.SultanaA.HossainM. M. (2020). Economic Impacts of Coronavirus Disease (COVID-19) in Developing Countries. doi:10.31235/osf.io/wygpk

Sadiq, A. A. I., Haning, M. T., Nara, N., & Rusdi, M. (2021). Learning Organization on the Implementation of E-Government in the City of Makassar. *Journal Dimensie Management and Public Sector*, *2*(3), 12–21. doi:10.48173/jdmps.v2i3.111

Saleem, J., Adebisi, B., Ande, R., & Hammoudeh, M. (2017, July). A state of the art survey-Impact of cyber attacks on SME's. In *Proceedings of the International Conference on Future Networks and Distributed Systems*. https://dl.acm.org/doi/abs/10.1145/3102304.3109812

Samtani, S., Zhu, H., & Chen, H. (2020). Proactively Identifying Emerging Hacker Threats from the Dark Web: A Diachronic Graph Embedding Framework (D-GEF). *ACM Transactions on Privacy and Security (TOPS), 23*(4), 1-33. https://dl.acm.org/doi/abs/10.1145/3409289

Sangki, J. (2018). Vision of future e-government via new e-government maturity model: Based on Korea's e-government practices. *Telecommunications Policy*, *42*(10), 860–871. doi:10.1016/j.telpol.2017.12.002

Scarfone, K., Hoffman, P., & Souppaya, M. (2009). Guide to enterprise telework and remote access security. *NIST Special Publication, 800*, 46. https://csrc.nist.rip/library/alt-SP800-46r1.pdf

Shah, I. A. (2022). Cybersecurity Issues and Challenges for E-Government During COVID-19: A Review. *Cybersecurity Measures for E-Government Frameworks*, 187-222.

Shah, I. A., Habeeb, R. A. A., Rajper, S., & Laraib, A. (2022). The Influence of Cybersecurity Attacks on E-Governance. In *Cybersecurity Measures for E-Government Frameworks* (pp. 77–95). IGI Global. doi:10.4018/978-1-7998-9624-1.ch005

Shah, I. A., Jhanjhi, N. Z., Amsaad, F., & Razaque, A. (2022). The Role of Cutting-Edge Technologies in Industry 4.0. In *Cyber Security Applications for Industry 4.0* (pp. 97–109). Chapman and Hall/CRC. doi:10.1201/9781003203087-4

Shah, I. A., Jhanjhi, N. Z., Humayun, M., & Ghosh, U. (2022). Health Care Digital Revolution During COVID-19. In *How COVID-19 is Accelerating the Digital Revolution* (pp. 17–30). Springer. doi:10.1007/978-3-030-98167-9_2

Shah, I. A., Jhanjhi, N. Z., Humayun, M., & Ghosh, U. (2022). Impact of COVID-19 on Higher and Post-secondary Education Systems. In *How COVID-19 is Accelerating the Digital Revolution* (pp. 71–83). Springer. doi:10.1007/978-3-030-98167-9_5

Shah, I. A., Rajper, S., & ZamanJhanjhi, N. (2021). Using ML and Data-Mining Techniques in Automatic Vulnerability Software Discovery. *International Journal (Toronto, Ont.)*, *10*(3).

Shah, I. A., Wassan, S., & Usmani, M. H. (2022). E-Government Security and Privacy Issues: Challenges and Preventive Approaches. In Cybersecurity Measures for E-Government Frameworks (pp. 61-76). IGI Global.

Sharma, S. K., Metri, B., Dwivedi, Y. K., & Rana, N. P. (2021). Challenges common service centers (CSCs) face in delivering e-government services in rural India. *Government Information Quarterly*, *38*(2), 101573. doi:10.1016/j.giq.2021.101573

Sharma, T. (2021). *Evolving Phishing Email Prevention Techniques: A Survey to Pin Down Effective Phishing Study Design Concepts*. https://www.ideals.illinois.edu/handle/2142/109179

Singh, A. P., Pradhan, N. R., Luhach, A. K., Agnihotri, S., Jhanjhi, N. Z., Verma, S., Kavita, Ghosh, U., & Roy, D. S. (2020). A novel patient-centric architectural framework for blockchain-enabled healthcare applications. *IEEE Transactions on Industrial Informatics*, *17*(8), 5779–5789. doi:10.1109/TII.2020.3037889

Sithole, V. E. (2015). *An e-governance training model for public managers: The case of selected Free State Provincial departments* (Doctoral dissertation). https://repository.nwu.ac.za/handle/10394/16320

Soni, V., Anand, R., Dey, P. K., Dash, A. P., & Banwet, D. K. (2017). Quantifying e-governance efficacy towards Indian–EU strategic dialogue. *Transforming Government: People, Process and Policy*. https://www.emerald.com/insight/content/doi/10.1108/TG-06-2017-0031/full/html

Soni, V., Dey, P. K., Anand, R., Malhotra, C., & Banwet, D. K. (2017). Digitizing grey portions of e-governance. *Transforming Government: People, Process and Policy*. https://www.emerald.com/insight/content/doi/10.1108/TG-11-2016-0076/full/html

Sony, A. L. (2015). Solving e-Governance Challenges in India through the Incremental Adoption to Cloud Service. *Law: J. Higher Sch. Econ.*, 169. https://heinonline.org/HOL/LandingPage?handle=hein.journals/pravo2015&div=15&id=&page=

Stellios, I., Kotzanikolaou, P., Psarakis, M., Alcaraz, C., & Lopez, J. (2018). A survey of iot-enabled cyberattacks: Assessing attack paths to critical infrastructures and services. *IEEE Communications Surveys and Tutorials*, *20*(4), 3453–3495. doi:10.1109/COMST.2018.2855563

Suleimany, M. (2021, May). Smart Urban Management and IoT; Paradigm of E-Governance and Technologies in Developing Communities. In *2021 5th International Conference on Internet of Things and Applications (IoT)* (pp. 1-6). IEEE. https://ieeexplore.ieee.org/abstract/document/9469713

Tounsi, W., & Rais, H. (2018). A survey on technical threat intelligence in the age of sophisticated cyber attacks. *Computers & Security*, *72*, 212–233. doi:10.1016/j.cose.2017.09.001

Ullah, A., Pinglu, C., Ullah, S., Abbas, H. S. M., & Khan, S. (n.d.). *The Role of E-Governance in Combating COVID-19 and Promoting Sustainable Development: A Comparative Study of China and Pakistan*. https://link.springer.com/article/10.1007/s41111-020-00167-w

Umrani, S., Rajper, S., Talpur, S. H., Shah, I. A., & Shujrah, A. (2020). Games based learning: A case of learning Physics using Angry Birds. *Indian Journal of Science and Technology*, *13*(36), 3778–3784. doi:10.17485/IJST/v13i36.853

Venkatesh, V., Thong, J. Y., Chan, F. K., & Hu, P. J. (2016). Managing citizens' uncertainty in e-government services: The mediating and moderating roles of transparency and trust. *Information Systems Research*, *27*(1), 87–111. doi:10.1287/isre.2015.0612

Walden, A., Cortelyou-Ward, K., Gabriel, M. H., & Noblin, A. (2020). To report or not to report health care data breaches. *The American Journal of Managed Care*, *26*(12), e395–e402. doi:10.37765/ajmc.2020.88546 PMID:33315333

Waller, L., & Genius, A. (2015). Barriers to transforming government in Jamaica: Challenges to implementing initiatives to enhance the efficiency, effectiveness and service delivery of government through ICTs (e-Government). *Transforming Government: People, Process and Policy*. https://www.emerald.com/insight/content/doi/10.1108/TG-12-2014-0067/full/html?fullSc=1

Weil, T., & Murugesan, S. (2020). IT Risk and Resilience-Cybersecurity Response to COVID-19. *IT Professional*, *22*(3), 4–10. doi:10.1109/MITP.2020.2988330

Wiggen, J. (2020). *Impact of COVID-19 on cyber crime and state-sponsored cyber activities*. Konrad Adenauer Stiftung. https://www.jstor.org/stable/pdf/resrep25300.pdf?acceptTC=true&coverpage=false

Wijayanto, H., & Prabowo, I. A. (2020). Cybersecurity Vulnerability Behavior Scale in College During the Covid-19 Pandemic. *Jurnal Sisfokom (Sistem Informasi dan Komputer), 9*(3),395-399. https://www.aimspress.com/article/id/6087e948ba35de2200eea776

Williams, C. M., Chaturvedi, R., & Chakravarthy, K. (2020). Cybersecurity Risks in a Pandemic. *Journal of Medical Internet Research*, *22*(9), e23692. doi:10.2196/23692 PMID:32897869

World Health Organization. (2020). *WHO reports fivefold increase in cyber-attacks, urges vigilance*. WHO.

Yang, L., Elisa, N., & Eliot, N. (2019). Privacy and security aspects of E-government in smart cities. In *Smart cities cybersecurity and privacy* (pp. 89–102). Elsevier. doi:10.1016/B978-0-12-815032-0.00007-X

Yang, R., & Wibowo, S. (2020). *Risks and Uncertainties in Citizens' Trust and Adoption of E-Government: A Proposed Framework*. https://aisel.aisnet.org/cgi/viewcontent.cgi?article=1073&context=acis2020

Zong, S., Ritter, A., Mueller, G., & Wright, E. (2019). Analyzing the perceived severity of cybersecurity threats reported on social media. *arXiv preprint arXiv:1902.10680*. doi:10.18653/v1/N19-1140

Chapter 3
Sustainable Computing-Based Simulation of Intelligent Border Surveillance Using Mobile WSN

Rana Muhammad Amir Latif
Center for Modern Chinese City Studies, Institute of Urban Development, East China Normal University, Shanghai, China

Muhammad Farhan
Department of Computer Science, COMSATS University Islamabad, Sahiwal, Pakistan

Navid Ali Khan
Taylor's University, Malaysia

R. Sujatha
https://orcid.org/0000-0002-1993-7544
School of Information Technology and Engineering, Vellore Institute of Technology, India

ABSTRACT

This chapter has simulated and designed the intrusion detection and border surveillance system using mobile WSN technology. Due to increased terrorism globally, border protection has become a crucial issue in every country. Conventionally in border protection, a troop cannot provide security all over time. The authors have simulated the design of border protection by using mobile WSN technology on a CupCarbon simulator tool. They have analyzed the scenario of the smart city. So, a troop can be intimated with intrusions occurring on the border. They have created the authentication protocol for the better security of the application. The security protocol is necessary because the soldier's mobile device can be stolen during the war. It can be going into the hands of the enemy in the situation when troops expire. The Android app can guide the troop in the time of emergency and what the next step should be followed. The authors can check the status of the sensors deployed on the border. They have analyzed these applications based on the application's rating with machine learning techniques.

DOI: 10.4018/979-8-3693-3816-2.ch003

1. INTRODUCTION

Over the last some decades, on Networked Information and Communication Technologies (ICT), humans have become more dependent than ever before. The latest survey has analyzed that 70% of the world's population transfers into city areas. The cities' population has increased, which causes more dependence on ICT efficient and intelligent management of critical infrastructures like energy, transportation, and addressing development challenges (Soto-Acosta, Del Giudice, & Scuotto, 2018). The concept of smart cities embraces these ICT challenges for achieving the goals. The smart city concept is the idea of the future where every significant portion of the city relates to the different features such as smart governance, smart living, smart people, smart environment, smart mobility, and smart economy (Sharma & Verma, 2022). The Internet of Things (IoT) plays an essential role in the smart city concept. IoT has excellent characteristics to connect with humans, interact with each other, and perform different tasks from the physical world's surroundings (EULAERTS & JOANNY, 2022). In an intelligent smart city setting, the IoT is easy to access to integrate various devices such as smartphones, vehicles, and home appliances (Bhardwaj, Banyal, Sharma, & Al-Numay, 2022). For different application domains, flexible resource management can be achieved in smart cities by integrating the internet of things.

Electricity is the basic need for lighting in public and private residential areas. The limited resources must meet the demand for electricity with the growing population (Mukhtarov, Dieperink, & Driessen, 2018). One major concern is efficient energy management in an IoT smart city environment. The latest report analyzed that 10% of the energy distribution is utilized by public lighting daily (Rao & Deebak, 2022). Significant lighting resources in residential buildings, hospitals, and offices contribute to excessive electricity use. Smart Lighting System, with many IoT technologies, demands efficient management and control of lighting systems in a smart city. The latest technology, the design on a chip (SoC), has been utilized in different IoT devices. A microcontroller is used as a significant component of SoC (Tripathi et al., 2019). A microcontroller (MCU for microcontroller unit (Zhu, 2018), or UC for μ-controller) is a small computer on a single integrated chip (IC) (Papageorge, Freyman, Juskey, & Thome, 1995). In addition to memory and programmable input/output peripherals, microcontrollers can also include several computing cores. A small amount of RAM, NOR flash or OTP ROM is often included on-chip. Microcontrollers are used for general purpose applications and personal computers and are sometimes designed individually for different embedded systems (Deng et al., 2018).

The number of wireless network sensor installations for real-life applications has risen rapidly in recent years. Nevertheless, the energy challenge remains one of the critical challenges to fully exploiting this technology. Sensor nodes usually are powered by batteries of a finite lifespan. They are a limited resource to be safely used while additional energy may be obtained from an outside world, e.g., by solar cells or piezoelectric mechanisms) (Ambika, 2022). Effective energy management is, therefore, an essential prerequisite for a credible wireless sensor network architecture. Wireless sensor networks may regulate radiation levels, control noise emissions, control environmental pollution, track structural stability, and sit in smart cars. The battery-operated devices with minimal battery capacity are all sensors in the wireless sensor network (Almurisi & Tadisetty, 2022). After the introduction of sensor units, any battery on the network cannot be replaced. Energy efficiency must also be taken into consideration. In this paper, we suggested a complicated energy-efficient power management method that can minimize the power consumed by each sensor node by shutting down specific sensor components according to our algorithm that saves and improves the time spent (Khan, Qureshi, & Iqbal, 2015).

One of the major obstacles stopping this technology's total utilization is wireless sensor networks' energy challenge. Batteries usually operate sensor nodes with a finite life. They are also a limited resource that is securely utilized, except through extra energy that may be harvested from the external world (Wu, Wu, Guerrero, & Vasquez, 2022). Therefore, the most critical criterion is adequate energy storage, with most methods believing that data processing requires much fewer resources than data transmission. If this statement is not agreed upon, useful energy efficiency techniques ought to provide measures to utilize energy-hungry sensors effectively (Alippi, Anastasi, Di Francesco, & Roveri, 2009).

Zigbee is a protocol to build a personal area network using limited digital radios and low power. This system is used for small tasks involving wireless connections such as low-power, low-bandwidth standards, data collection from medical devices, and domestic automation. In the future, connected devices will expand and become incredibly high in cities (Patil & Baig, 2018). To this end, in real life, we could use various simulator software to install new networks before they are implemented. These Sustainable Computing Simulation tools will enable us to forecast details such as expense, connectivity, interruption, and location viability. We are presenting a new framework for the CupCarbon network. This platform's fundamental goal is to develop and simulate WSNs for smart cities and IoT (Bounceur et al., 2018).

CupCarbon produces environmental scenarios for mobile, gas, fire control programs, and mobile WSN data collection in education and science projects. This tool provides two distinct simulation worlds. First, a multi-agent environment enables event generation and designs mobility scenarios, including mobile nodes' simulation, for example, gas and fires (Javaid, Haleem, Singh, & Suman, 2022). The concept is focused mainly on the first framework; the second is a different smartphone application of the WSN based on a sustainable computing scenario (Martín, Garrido, Llopis, Rubio, & Díaz, 2022). Interference models are incorporated into the Cup-

Carbon to include a more realistic analysis of WSNs for intelligent city structures focused upon the impulsive existence of noise and external propagation models. These simulations are associated with electromagnetic connections in spatial fields.

It is essential to mention the relationship between ICT, IoT, mobile WSN, and Google play store. ICT is the basic need for computing and communication. IoT is becoming part of daily life, and WSN must communicate among the IoT devices. The use of a smartphone is also a basic need. Smart applications are being developed for Android OS. So, there is a strong relationship between these technologies. Many apps are available for various purposes in the Google Play Store, like IoT, Network commutation, networking, and WSN domain. In this research, we test and review technologies that can promote our software engineers and users, such as intrusion detection troops, troop communication, and many other functionalities appropriate for analysis and artificial intelligence. Table 1 shows the terminology of the different parameters we have used to implement intelligent border surveillance.

Several third-party applications have been uploaded to the Google play store daily, and thousands of users register their personal information on these applications. Also, users install these applications on their tablets and mobile phone. The hundreds and thousands of developers have uploaded millions of applications daily. The play store's content is mostly unchecked, and millions of users download this content (Yang et al., 2014). However, no information about these apps is available on the Google Play Store. The main reason is that there is a lack of scalable tools for analyzing and discovering Android applications. The source code of the application is available to specific third-party developers. Even Google has no access to the source code.

Table 1. Nomenclature of the different parameters of implementation

Parameter	Description
Mc	MicroController
S_e	Sensing the Intruder
I_n	Intruder
Sp	Solar Panel
Ps	Power Source
D_e	Detecting the intruder
A_p	Android Application
A_d	Android device
Zb	ZigBee
S_{mo}	Motion Sensor
Bs	Base Station

Those applications are submitted directly to the google play store as compressed binary packages (Crussell, Gibler, & Chen, 2012).

Google has set many strategies for stopping anyone from crawling; Google is still playing with data storage indexing. For example, the play store's data collection is restricted to only 500 exploration apps in every category or search word through visiting the store web interface. We have crawled details from the play store utilizing crawling and scraping techniques to discover knowledge from Google play store content. We get knowledge from playing every day, focusing even on the material that develops daily. We can then measure and review metadata from Google Play Store, and the index is based on the Google Play Store (Bagnasco et al., 2015). Since millions of apps are retrieved from the play shop, we may get other applications such as paying and free applications. We also have a list of numerous home application types and game applications.

Along with the widespread use of smart devices and software, IoT has undergone meteoric growth in recent years. Many billions of objects or things are now linked to the Internet, and that number will only grow. Furthermore, IDC's most recent research project is that by 2023, there will be 41.6 billion IoT-linked devices (Saleh, Jhanjhi, Abdullah, & Saher, 2022b). Therefore, from an environmental perspective, producing enough power to operate this growing number of devices or other network equipment might result in significant CO_2 emissions. In 2016, Muhammad Ismail presented statistics showing that telecommunications accounted for 2% of the world's carbon dioxide emissions. In 2020, the global carbon footprint of ICT (including Internet of Things devices, cellular phones, and wireless networking) will be three times larger than in 2018. Another significant problem for wireless networks is their high-power consumption. Wireless networks require much more energy than wired networks, releasing heat and pollutants from the associated electronics and power plants. Some research has previously shown that the cost of energy constitutes roughly 18% in the developed European market to 32% in the Indian market and that for those off-the-grid activities, the cost of energy may constitute 50% of the overall OPEX. The lifetime of the rechargeable batteries of mobile devices is expected to be two to three years. However, every year the disposition of batteries is 25000 tons, which is a significant amount considering the number of mobile devices in use (Saleh, Jhanjhi, Abdullah, & Saher, 2022a).

Accordingly, scientists and researchers have shifted the focus of their research and studies to provide optimum performance of a device while making that gadget consume the smallest amount of energy to address these power-consuming and wasting challenges and concerns. Overprovisioning and redundancy are two features extensively employed in conventional network design that may be used to improve the quality of the network in the present-day business. However, the phrase "green networking" has fundamental flaws with these two characteristics. Energy-efficient and environmentally friendly communication technology is poised for future use at standard stations and control systems. According to the paper, this issue has recently gained significant visibility throughout Europe. Some initiatives from the Seventh Research Framework (FP7) (2007-2013) were EARTH, OPERA-Net, ECONET, and TREND (a network of excellence) (Saleh et al., 2022b). These initiatives facilitate networking and communication that consume less power. Smart Energy Systems and Green ICT is a concept developed by the European Institute of Innovation and Technology (EIT ICT Lab) (Information and Communication Technology).

With these projections of energy use and CO_2 emissions in mind, it is clear that the rapid advancement and expanding use of IoT technology will bring about many positive outcomes and major environmental challenges (Latif, Naeem, Rizwan, & Farhan, 2021). Overconsumption of energy, the creation of unnecessary technological trash, carbon emissions, and climate shifts are all examples of such issues. The notion of green computing or green IT must be presented and explored if we are to maintain a balance between environmental concerns and IoT progress. As a result, research has shifted to how to make IoT development less harmful to the environment. This chapter's objective is to provide various paths for resolving this conundrum (Shafiq et al., 2021). As a first step, let us review the fundamentals of the Internet of Things.

One of the most significant uses of environmental science, green computing, provides cost-effective ways to protect the planet's natural wonders. Green computing focuses on reducing the environmental impact of computing in all its forms, from product development to end-of-life recycling. Power and energy efficiency management prefer environmentally friendly hardware and software devices and using recyclable material to lengthen the lifespan of products are all important to the green computing ethos. Green computing may ease the mind by decreasing monthly electricity costs, and it can also help the environment. These days, energy waste is minimized with the use of stellar management strategies and techniques (Zanella, Bui, Castellani, Vangelista, & Zorzi, 2014).

Computing techniques with little to no environmental impact are the focus of research and practice under the umbrella term "virtually green computing," also known as "environmentally sustainable computing." There are several factors to consider when aiming for "green computing," from the initial concept to the final disposal of hardware and software components (Latif et al., 2020).

Here are some guidelines for creating eco-friendly computer systems:

- Using computers and other information systems sustainably, or "green," reduces their environmental impact.
- Reusing obsolete computers and recycling electronics is an examples of environmentally responsible waste management.

- The term "green design" refers to the practice of creating products that are both environmentally friendly and efficient in their use of resources.
- To reduce their environmental impact, manufacturers are adopting "green manufacturing," which involves the creation of eco-friendly electronic parts, computers, and associated subsystems.

Green computing focuses on making more effective use of all available computer and information technology resources. Today, one of the most pressing challenges facing humanity is how to reduce energy use without sacrificing the quality of life. The sustainability of computing and IT is analyzed using green computing and green IT. In order to meet the goals of green computing, it is necessary to lessen reliance on potentially dangerous hardware, boost energy efficiency, and encourage the reuse of old computers and other IT equipment. It is only via environmentally friendly computing that future regulations may be made that will be of any use comprised of environmental sustainability, the commercialization of energy efficiency, and the economic calculation of the disposal and recycling of computer and IT systems (Ullah et al., 2021). The most important focus of research and practice is on minimizing the waste of computational resources. The primary characteristics of environmentally friendly IT are consolidation and cloud computing.

2. LITERATURE REVIEW

A distributed border monitoring device (DBS) with shadowing effects is suggested for a rectangular region-of-interest wireless sensor network. The DBS device evaluates and conserves electricity and the number of obstacles necessary to control the area. The paper states that in the simulator NS-2.35, the proposed device would be 75% faster than current model-based DBS binary sensing range systems. Researchers of the Massachusetts Institute of Technology have reported the study in the journal "Sensors, Security and the Internet of Things." (Amutha, Nagar, & Sharma, 2020).

Sustainable delay-tolerant sensor networks (DTSNs) should be studied to minimize energy usage, satisfy relaxed latency criteria, encourage accessibility, and cope with traffic loads. Efficient MAC protocols are essential for energy saving. They introduce a Traffic-adaptive MAC Protocol (TREEM) to obtain improved transmitting data and energy performance. Regarding energy consumption and adaptability, the simulation results of TREEM show improved efficiency (Boukerche & Zhou, 2020).

Swarm Intelligence (SI) is a philosophy that investigates collaboration in solving complex problems among autonomous groups, such as mobile agents. The usage of the Wireless Sensor Network (WSN) SI solution is exciting since it is a linked network of individual nodes that link together on a network. Increasing sensor usage has attracted the testing community to combine SI in environmental control and health care (Sethi, 2020).

Explosive detection was an active field of study in the aftermath of explosive explosions worldwide triggered by terrorist attacks. Government departments are supplied with explosives observable equipment in multiple nations. Traditional devices used to detect explosives require human effort to make them operate. The researchers have said that it is time for a clear and powerful network to track certain anti-social elements' behavior. It has been known to operate with the algorithm Explosive Detection Algorithm (EDA) (Rejeti, Murali, & Kumar, 2019).

Data Prioritization (DP) is a technique that produces condensed form in original data through analysis of its material. We suggest an energy-efficient DP platform through smart convergence of the Internet of Things, artificial intelligence, and comprehensive data analytics. Real-world monitoring evidence theoretical assessment tests the feasibility of this environment and its applicability in green smart cities. The major issues for DP, their potential criteria, and suggestions for incorporation into green smart cities are outlined in this report. It also recommends a detailed review of DP's latest methods and developments in data of various forms (Muhammad, Lloret, & Baik, 2019).

Multi-hop connectivity in a network of wireless sensors may contribute to unequalled energy usage. According to the poll, it produces "hot spots" around the sensor nodes. Researchers are suggesting two various mobile data processing systems. These aim to reduce energy usage and data loss and optimize data collection and network life. The suggested algorithms are tested using the C programming language through simulation studies. The research was conducted in Cellular Networks (Koley & Samanta, 2019).

The suggested scheme focuses on using compact routes of low-emission small vehicles. The consumer would need to ride a mobile app that gives them a spot. A Wi-Fi Sensor Network captures real-time traffic and environmental details to construct informative and statistical models. The paper has been produced in the sense of the NETCHIP research project submitted to the Italian NR 2015-2020, Call n. From 13 July 2017, 1735 (Ullo et al., 2018).

Air-conditioning (AT), Piped Natural Gas (PNG), and sewage pipelines in significant buildings are the most successful and secure maintenance issues. This article is suggested refining sensors and simple stations' locations linearly to track the different pipelines. The pipeline duration is medium, the proposed scheme is optimized for energy-sensitive buildings, and the network lives are considerably increased using the proposed solution. The most striking characteristic of the plan is its performance. In the end-to-end wait, the duration of the pipeline is more significant (Varshney et al., 2018).

We research the mutual WSN model of cloud-based mass data processing. WSN output is measured using the computational approach of simulation. The authors add that both network survival period and overall time slot of data collection, both Reduce paths achieve good performance. WSN and cloud storage infrastructure were extensively explored and used on the wireless sensor network (Ren, 2018).

Drowsiness is a state of mind until the driver rests, ensuring that the driver cannot adequately execute its acts, such as car stops and vehicle motion control. If drivers are asleep, a warning alarm will be sent to any car drivers near the sleeping driver. In the future, wireless sensor networks are likely to be an essential part of our lives, more so than today's personal computers. The analysis was conducted on Google Play with 550 applications from each group (Ramzan et al., 2019).

This project has been planned to build a robot that uses Android to operate the wireless camera remotely. Camera tracking will help the soldier's team build plans on a runtime basis. This form of the robot may be of use in warfare espionage. The protection framework accepts these instructions and addresses the customer. With the wireless standard 802.11, ZigBee, and Bluetooth protocol, the monitor and motion detector are linked to the remote monitoring device (Imran, Farhan, Latif, & Rafiq, 2018).

The CGV is a routing protocol to increase the network's operation existence. CGV uses the cluster head selection technique to answer the conglomerate gravity value. Network Simulator conducted the CGV efficiency evaluation with findings compared to ER2PR, VBF, and UFCA. According to experts, the protocol would conserve resources and extend the network's lifespan. It uses only those areas that are the best way to pick the relay node and, where necessary, the answer packet transmitting area. It is based on an ER2 PR and VBF-like network simulator for performance evaluation (Shah, Manzoor, Latif, Farhan, & Ashiq, 2019).

High energy usage often implies an unnecessary thermal discharge, which raises cooling costs and allows servers more likely to malfunction. At each stage of the hierarchy, we maximize power & output (performance/watt) while retaining scalability. Compared to conventional methods, our interactive technology decreases energy use by 65% (min-min heuristic). We also present uncertain game theory usage outcomes to maximize performance/watt at the data center cluster stage (Khargharia et al., 2007).

With more processing and storage power, high outputs are thriving. Superior electricity use is absorbed by large-scale networks such as computer grids. These devices also have heating and cooling costs equivalent to procurement costs over a year. We will address the allotment and programming of algorithms, processes, and applications for power reduction and energy dissipation of workflows for single processors (Sheikh, Tan, Ahmad, Ranka, & Bv, 2012).

The algorithm suggested involves problem-specific solution encoding, which specifies the original solution space population. Different schedules have a set of values for span, power usage, and maximum temperature. The suggested algorithm is beneficial since it decreases energy and temperature instead of insulation. The authors state that the difficult duration of the scheme is slightly more significant than the analogous algorithms. The algorithm for preparing node optimization activities can be applied three-way, with a short turnaround time (Sheikh, Ahmad, Fan, & Systems, 2015).

The Two-Volume Series is one of the first manuals to account for recent energy consciousness and green computing studies fully. It also addresses up-to-date studies on several facets of component, software, and machine power-enabled computing. It is innovative computer science and engineering research publication (Sheikh, Ahmad, Wang, Ranka, & Systems, 2012).

In this research, work authors create a graph-based model for network topology. The authors used the Vienna Development Method-Specification Language (VDM-SL) method to verify this topology (Afzaal & Zafar, 2017b). This method is used to find the correctness of this algorithm, examined with appropriate procedure, and the proper specification is clarified, as shown in Figure 1.

2.1 Purpose of Green Computing

Many believe rising global temperatures and environmental change are the planet's biggest threats. The information and communications technology innovation

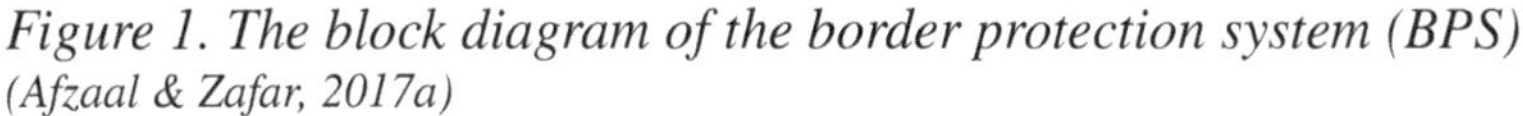

Figure 1. The block diagram of the border protection system (BPS)
(Afzaal & Zafar, 2017a)

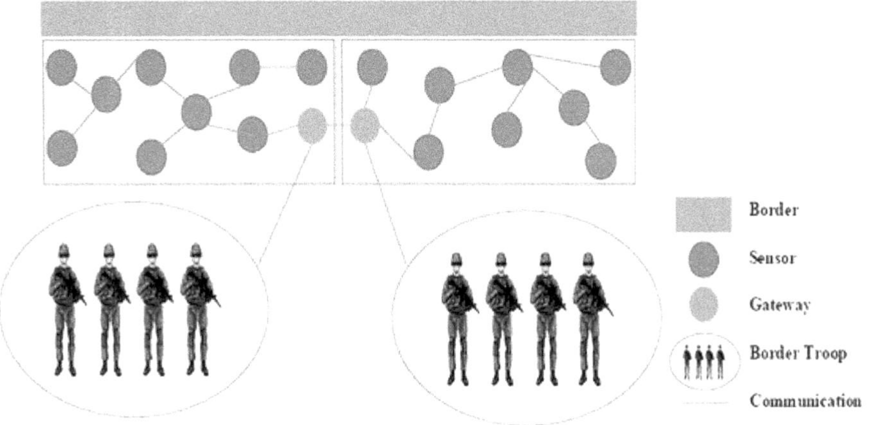

network are working to solve these problems via green IT and, more particularly, green figuring. Its energy consumption and scalability impacts are expected to grow greatly due to the unpredictable growth of Internet-enabled distributed computing and high-quality processing centers. However, efforts are being made to solve this problem by both businesses and academics as shown in Figure 2.

As the demand for computation and transmission of data is expanding day by day, servers, systems, and servers will waste more vitality than ever. Information technology (IT) assets account for over 1.5% of total electricity use in the United States. In 2006, data centers in the United States used 1.5% of the nation's total energy at over $4.5 billion.

The primary focus of modern green correspondences is the development of energy-efficient correspondence techniques for networking systems. Three primary approaches are offered to reduce the board's power consumption in networking systems. These include doing less work, slowing down the rate of work, and turning off unused components. Reducing energy consumption may be achieved by improving processes such that the system performs activities. Diminishing activity speed might forecast recurring asset usage from the crisscrossed pace of sub-forms. Turning down unused nodes and links in a networked system is a simple but effective way to save energy. There has been a steady increase in the total energy consumption

Figure 2. Introduction of eco-friendly computer systems

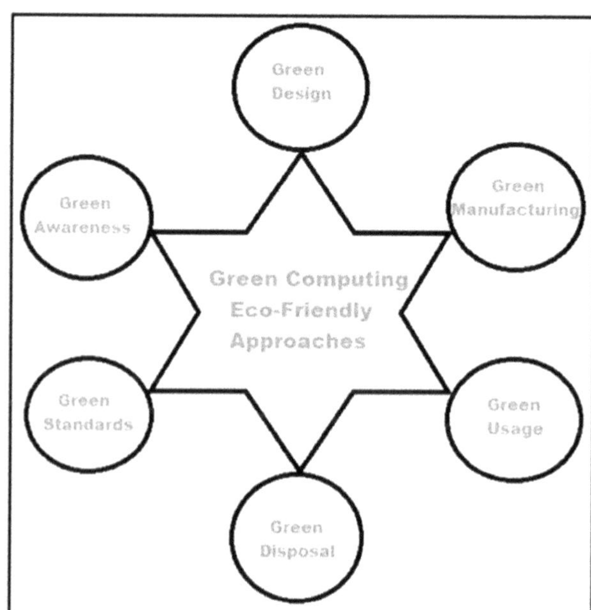

of server farms due to the rising number of servers, personal computers, displays, data transmission needs, and cooling systems (Almusaylim, Zaman, & Jung, 2018).

As energy use rises, so do the ozone-depleting substances released into the atmosphere. Every single computer constantly emits a significant quantity of carbon dioxide. As the vitality emergency grows and the assets drain, we must seriously contemplate rolling out liberal adjustments in our way of life for vitality preservation. One solution to the energy crisis is green registration. This strategy can reduce carbon emissions, save energy, and protect the planet. To "go green" in the context of computing is to use computers and associated technology responsibly. In order to reduce the environmental damage produced by computers, it advocates making substantial changes to how we approach processing, using electronic devices, and adhering to stringent vitality protection standards (A Almusaylim & Jhanjhi, 2020). This move is not only about cutting down on energy use but also about promoting environmentally friendly computer use. One of its facets is the development of original and environment-aware strategies for aging vitality. The following are some of the most often encountered issues with Green Computing today, according to experts:

- Limits on power and temperature may be set for equipment.
- Data centers' energy needs are growing, and the associated costs are rising along with them.
- Limit the ever-increasing need for heat-ejecting devices, which has grown in response to the ever-increasing use of electricity by IT devices of all types.
- The Cradle to Grave Equipment Life Cycle for Top Management.
- Elimination of Electronic Garbage.

2.2 Cloud Computing Status With Green Computing

Computers in a distributed network work together to complete tasks based on requests from other users. The approach allows instant access to a shared pool of adjustable figuring assets such as personal computers, networks, servers, storage, software, and management tools. The cloud platform provides on-demand services available anytime and from any location. The public, businesses, nonprofits, and governmental agencies may all utilize the cloud's computing services. Everything from the underlying architecture and platform to the application and network resources is included in the supplier vendors' ready-made administrations. Each service is referred to by its acronym: IaaS, PaaS, and SaaS. Since cloud resources are sensitive to incalculable carbon dioxide emissions, rising demand has prompted service providers to rethink their energy strategies (Humayun et al., 2020). Cloud computing uses 2.5%-3% of all energy produced globally and 2.7%-3% in the United

States. According to Pike's research, by 2020, cloud services would use roughly 150 TWh of electricity as shown in Figure 3.

Focusing efforts at the base of physical center points and switching seats out of rigging centers off is a crucial strategy connected with using debilitates. It is possible to turn off unused components (including the central processing unit, cache memory, and network interfaces) and to switch the system's approach control center to the "off" position. After the initial setup of a server, the system switches are dynamically modified to accommodate the new dynamic architecture. When the internal server is set to power-saving mode, less energy is used (e.g., rest, sleep). Astoundingly, green distributed computing has been accomplished via the economic approach, exploitation of the figure foundation, and reducing energy consumption. The cloud's asset tagging system is also a major sticking point. Asset management will be aided by more precise, up-to-date estimates, particularly for the virtual machine (VM) and cloudlet components (Latif et al., 2019). The goal of the ruleset is to allocate resources to jobs so that physical system CPU consumption is minimized. It is generally accepted that, in a perfect system, the CPU would be used directly for roughly 70% of the time. Those materials and machinery need to be destroyed or put to sleep. Operators keep an eye out for jobs that are likely to increase shortly, then schedule the various tasks that will be performed on their host computers.

Moreover, allocating resources should provide constant, permanent quality, and flexible execution of tasks in the cloud. Avoiding both over- and under-utilization of resources is linked to the stack-changing strategy, which may be used to improve execution. It is preferable to move tasks across already operating virtual machines rather than launching a new virtual machine, considering the CPU utilization threshold estimates for each physical system. Using the suggested framework, we may reduce

Figure 3. Cloud computing and its management

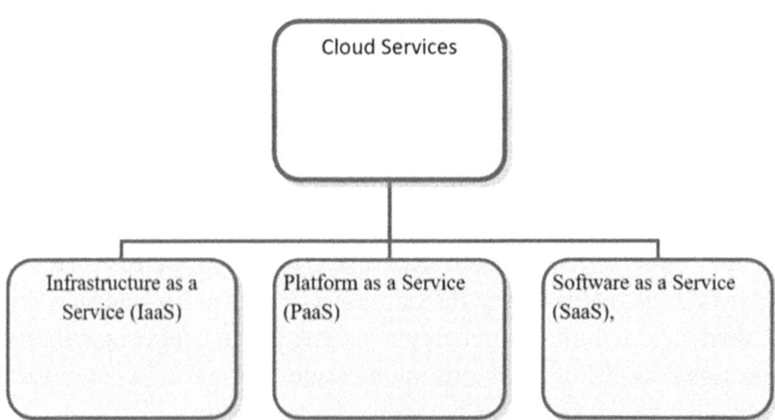

the total amount of power used based on the number of active hosts at any time. In addition, the VM allocation process, which is employed as a parameter, such as the number of components, reduces power consumption in an alternative approach, making this method particularly attractive. Storage space, bandwidth, data centers, and servers. By installing each OS in its virtual machine (VM), VMware allows you to utilize the same hardware to run several unmodified PC operating systems simultaneously. A "guest OS" is an operating system run as a software application on top of VMware. The "host OS" system is designed to operate on physical hardware.

2.3 Green Cloud Environment

Whereas Para denotes the presence of a resource in the physical world, VRA stands for the presence of that resource. A company's PRAtn is the total number of available physical assets at any moment. The availability of virtual resources in real-time is measured in terms of the Vern. The method used to calculate how much of a given resource should be allotted to each endeavor is shown by an asset classification. Assigns the assets created to carry out the processing limit. Maximum utilization predicts how a firm's process assets may be used to free up time for more productive pursuit's asset utilization during assignment estimation in explicit labor in a particular process asset arrangement. The term "assets usage" refers to the time and effort spent preparing or maintaining assets or the value of work provided by assets; the $74,000 figure varies depending on the amount and kind of calculation trip to manage. In contrast to other assignments, which need less time spent using resources due to their focus on employment and availability, bound assignments demand a substantial amount of time spent using resources.

Which CRU is being registered and used, CRU presents an opportunity to capitalize on, and so does the volume of customer solicitation work required to disperse process assets. The CRE is cloud plus energy, it calculates the percentage of energy used on each journey, and it might be a great opportunity to increase energy usage across the whole process and the actual execution of the activity. There may be a drag on the combined total of registering assets after they have been assigned to a job. That might be split among several uses of assets. In order to maintain an appropriate distribution of assets across various vocations in a space with a high volume of customers, such limits are often imposed by the dispersed assets themselves. The efficiency of green cloud resources is measured by the gap between traditional infrastructure and cloud computing in terms of primary energy consumption as shown in Eq. 1.

$$CDCEE = ITU \times ITE / PUE \tag{1}$$

IT utilization (ITU) is the ratio of typical IT usage to maximum IT capacity in the cloud data center, and IT efficiency (ITE) is the amount of useful IT work accomplished per joule of energy.

CRE Cloud Resource Energy, CRU Cloud Resource Utilization, CREE Cloud Resource Energy Efficiency. By taking into account both the static and dynamic parts of resource allocation and resource utilization, the solution for the green cloud environment may reduce its environmental effect and energy consumption under the new model. Several health issues are linked to prolonged exposure to high quantities of carbon dioxide. The Occupational Safety and Health Administration has set a limit of 6,000 parts per million of carbon dioxide (ppmv) for an 8-hour work shift. Extremely high carbon monoxide (CO_2) concentrations, between 40,000 and 60,000 parts per million by volume (ppmv), may lead to dizziness, nausea, and an increase in heart rate and breathing rate due to oxygen deprivation. At a concentration of 200,000 ppmv, unconsciousness and death may result as shown in Figure 4.

2.4 Energy-Efficient Cloud Environment

A distributed computing environment is a massive cyber-physical system that includes electrical, mechanical, and IT systems performing various tasks across many server pools and capacity devices linked by a complex aggregate, switch and switch chain. In the framework of material flow and the most widespread form, the use of vitality is of primary importance. With a yearly growth rate of 12%, the global energy consumption of data centers is predicted to reach 46 GW or around 3.4% of global electrical energy consumption. The yearly energy expenditure for the 2.2 MV used by the Barcelona medium-sized Supercomputing Center (a data center) is roughly £1 million, the same as the electricity used by 1,400 average homes. It considers the $6.5 billion price tag and 2.5% of all U.S. electricity used by data centers, as detailed in a U.S. Environmental Protection Agency (EPA) report to Congress.

U.S. data centers, which house exactly 40% of all cloud datacenters servers, had a 40% rise in their electrical usage during the financial breakdown, with servers, cooling, communication, storage, and power distribution equipment (PDU) accounting for between 1.7% and 2.2% of that total. The percentage of energy produced in the United States rose from 0.8% in 2000 to 1.5% in 2005. In 2006, it was projected that cloud datacenters were responsible for 116.2 million metric tons of CO_2 emissions. In 2010, Google's data center used roughly 2.26 million MW hours of electricity, leaving behind 1.46 million metric tons of carbon dioxide as a byproduct of its operations. According to the Intergovernmental Panel on Climate Change, a complete decrease of 60–80% is needed by 2050 to prevent digital–physical environmental harm as shown in Figure 5.

Figure 4. Structured components of a cloud computing system

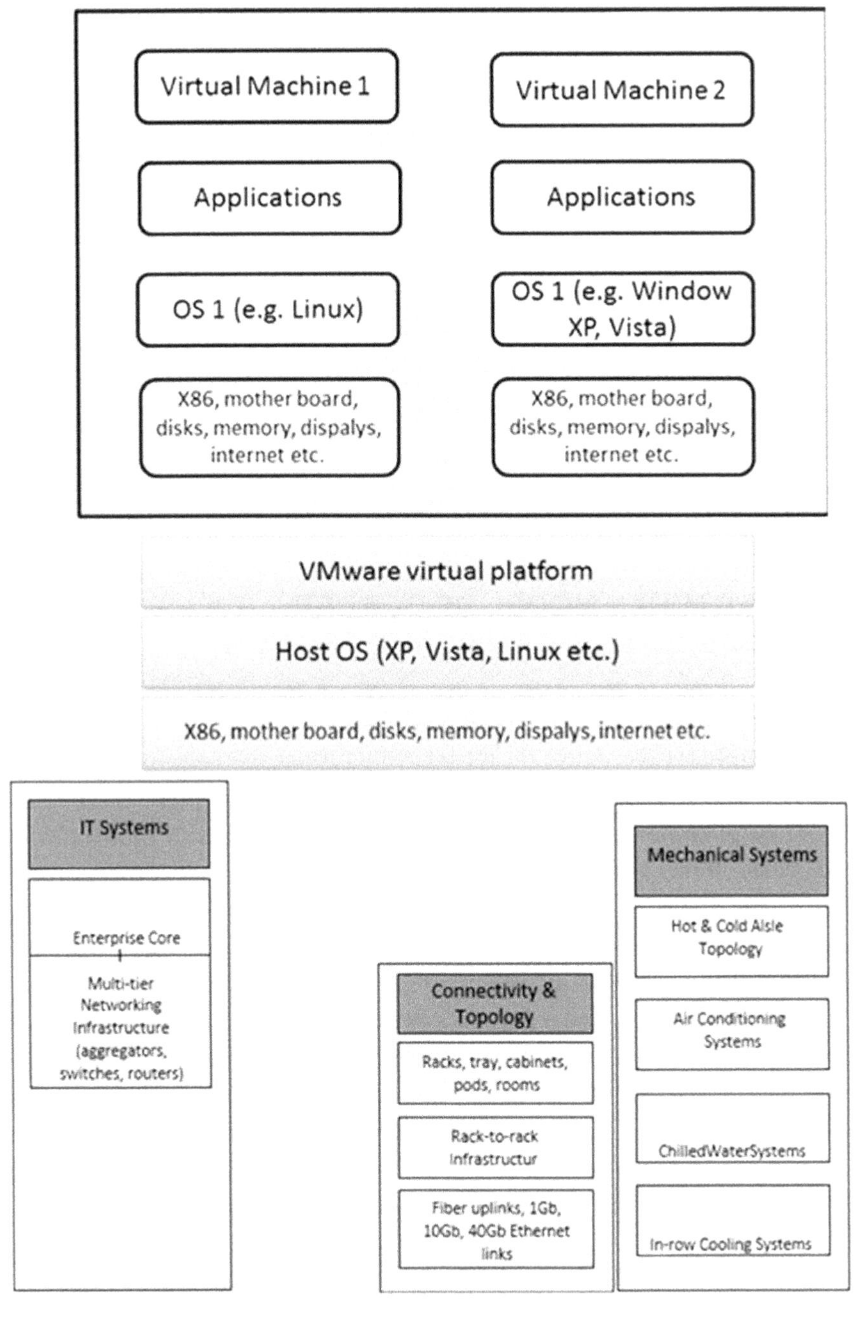

Figure 5. Cloud computing characteristics and their environmental impact

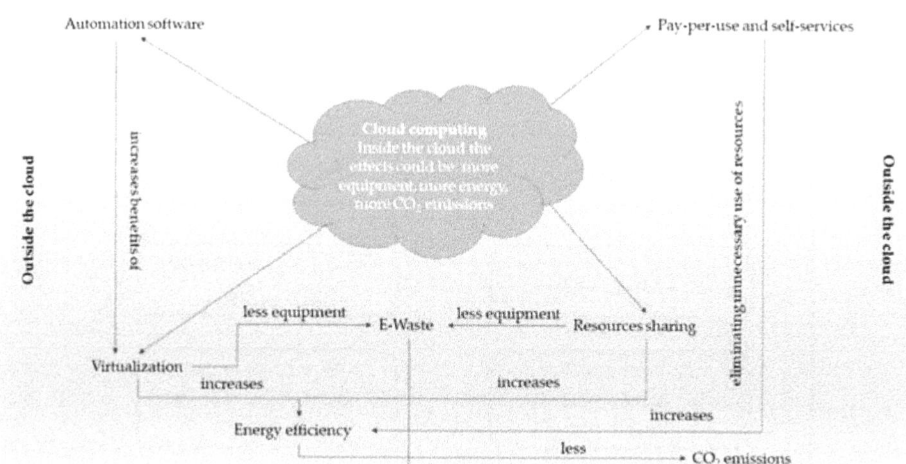

3. ARCHITECTURAL MODEL OF BORDER SURVEILLANCE AND INTRUSION DETECTION

The block diagram of our system is shown. We have wireless sensors attached to our microcontroller; these detect the intruder and further share the information with other sensors and base stations. Further, we have an Android application attached to the microcontroller through which the soldier gets the information of intruders and other information on mobile. The ZigBee device is attached to the microcontroller to send information to the base station. The base station then sends the information to the cloud, which is displayed on the website. The essential factor of wireless technology is the battery life, so we have attached the solar panel with the battery. Our system contains active and passive states to improve the battery life. When there is no intruder or anything, our system turns into a sleep state, but if an intruder and other sensors sense some information regarding the active state, as shown in Figure 6. The attachment of the Android application is with a microcontroller, shown in Eq 2. The sensors are connected to a microcontroller, powered by a solar panel and power source, as shown in Eq 3.

$$\sum_{a-1}^{n} H_a = \left(A_p + M_c\right) \rightarrow ZB \rightarrow A_d \tag{2}$$

Figure 6. Block Diagram of the BPS in the form of Architectural Model

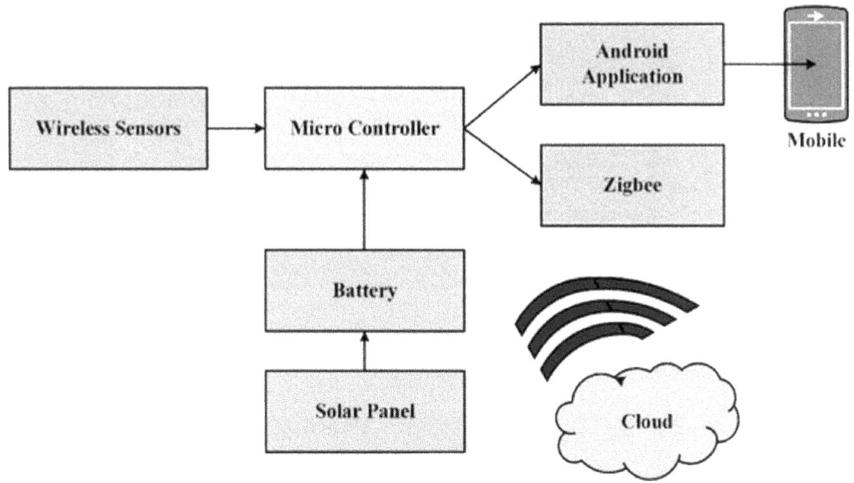

$$S_P \rightarrow P_S \rightarrow M_C \quad (3)$$

4. SUSTAINABLE COMPUTING BASED SIMULATION OF INTELLIGENT BORDER SURVEILLANCE USING MOBILE WIRELESS SENSOR NETWORKS

The efficient protection of the border wireless sensor network is used because sometimes troops cannot detect the intruder. Border protection is now become an essential concern all over the world due to the enhancement of terrorism. Even if the intruder can pass away from the troop, and the troop has no information about this, sensors can detect and inform the troop on the application about the intruder. For the sensor network detecting a target has become a critical application. The working of sensors needs to be more efficient; it depends on the arrangement of the sensors. We can achieve this arrangement before the deployment and distributing keys to sensor nodes. This model is efficient in terms of energy as a solar panel is also attached to the battery. We have used different sensors on the border, like a motion sensor, to detect the intruder. If an intruder is coming, our system can be inactive; otherwise, it can be in a passive state to save energy. This scenario is represented in Figure 7. In this diagram, sensors are deployed on the boundaries, transmitting the information to the base station. The base station then transfers the information to the cloud. In Figure 8, the border sensors share the information with other sensors that send the information to the base station. The working of this system is also explained in Eq 4.

Figure 7. Wireless sensors deployed on the borders

Figure 8. Wireless sensors sharing information

$$B_{or} = \begin{cases} if & I_n = 1 \quad S_e = 1 \\ else & \quad\quad\quad S_e = 0 \end{cases} \tag{4}$$

Insects are utilized for discovering pests around the boundary. In this case, the intruder has been discovered. Then detectors are accountable to some gateway node. The entry node admits the intrusion details are acquired. The entry node transmits a note onto the nearest boundary troop's cellular telephones, and the troop admits the intrusion details be acquired. Subsequently, troop arrives to grab the intruder if that is damaging to this nation. This action is demonstrated in Figure 9. The sensors have been sharing their information and moving it into the bottom channel. That yellowish lighting reveals that the detectors are still working conditions. The detectors, gateways, and boundary troops are connected using links, and sensors send data to the base station, as shown in Eq 5.

$$S_n = \left[\left(S_{mo} + I_n \left(S_{e,} D_e \right) \right) \rightarrow BS \right] \tag{5}$$

Figure 9. Sensors on the inactive border states

The energy consumption is in Joules of node 1, as shown in Figure 10, and Figure 11 shows the remaining energy of node one as a function of the time and battery consumed. When the node sends a message, it consumes 0.06 J. The sensors' energy consumption is due to sending and receiving data through sensors and their electric operations. The remaining energy decreases as a time function in sensors. In our Sustainable Computing based simulation, we have done a simulation for 3 seconds. Figures 6 and 7 show the energy consumed by sensors in 3 seconds.

Figure 10. Energy consumption of sensor 1 as a function of time

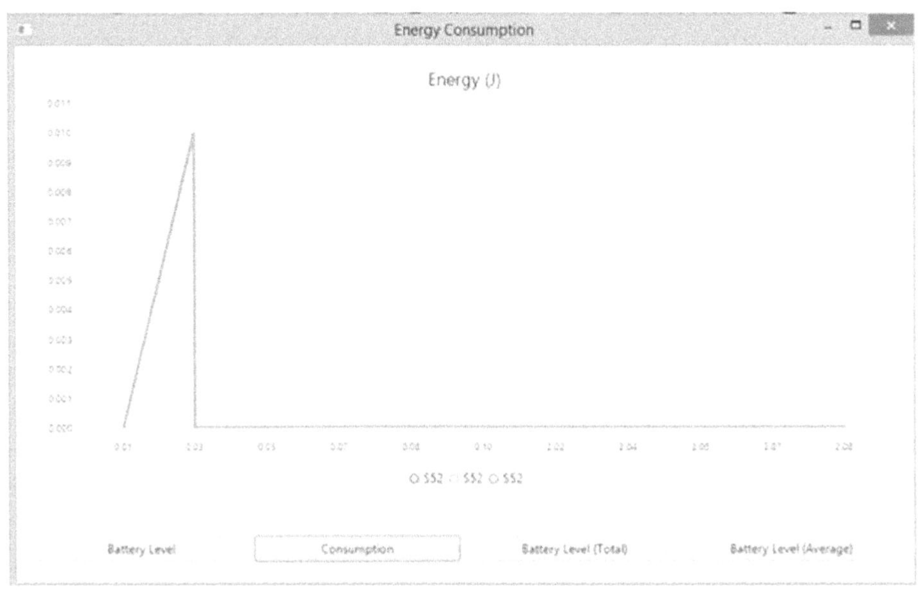

Figure 11. The remaining energy of sensor 1 as a function of time

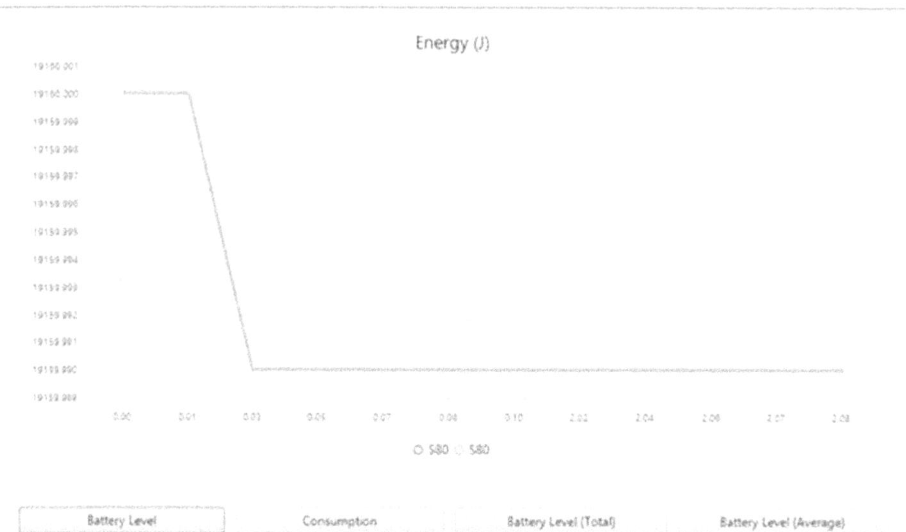

5. AUTHENTICATION PROTOCOL FOR THE SECURITY OF MOBILE APPLICATIONS

For better security of the application, we have proposed a security protocol. The security protocol is necessary because the soldier's mobile device can be stolen during the war. It can be going into the hands of the enemy in the situation when troops expire. In this condition, we have more sensitive information on the mobile, and we cannot afford to share this information with anyone. So, we have security on the application which is used on mobile devices. We have three major security factors. First is the login id, the second is a password, and the third security is fingerprint verification on the application. Each troop has a unique ID, and the soldier can set an authentication password on the application; also, troops have the fingerprint verification of the application. After processing these three steps, the soldier can enter the application.

This security protocol shows the two-way communication between the solider s and server si. The application's information is always stored on the cloud and the internet facility we have arranged on the battlefield with the Zigbee technology as we know the Zigbee Technology we have used for low range communication. So, we know that the battlefield area is more than the range of Zigbee technology. We have to deploy several Zigbee towers on the battlefield, and the communication between these towers is always shared. The mobile application should always connect with the internet to share communication between the soldiers. We can calculate the message period when hackers hack messages from one troop to another. If the message period is more than the casual period, we can identify that any cracker has altered the message. In this scenario, we have 2 phases of the protocol. The first is the registration protocol, and the second is the login and authentication phase.

Solider *si*	Server *s*

5.1 Registration Phase

Select $ID_{si,}$ PW_{si} and r_i Imprints F_{si}

Calculates $\overline{PW_{si}} = h_2\,(ID_{si}||PW_{si}||F_{si})$

$$\xrightarrow{\{PW_{si}, ID_{si}, r_i\}}$$

$A_{si} = h_2(ID_{si}||S_k)$

$B_{si} = A_{si} \oplus \overline{PW_{si}}$

$N_{si} = h_2\,(\overline{PW_{si}} \,||\, A_{si} \,||\, ID_{si})$

Generate r_1, $DID_{si} = S_{si}(ID_{si}\,||\,r_1) \oplus \overline{PW_{si}} \oplus r_i$

Store $\{B_{si}, DID_{si}, N_{si}\}$ in Cloud

$$\xleftarrow{Cloud\,\{C_{si}\}}$$

$g_{si} = F_{si} \oplus h_2\,(PW_{si}\,||\,ID_{si}\,||\,r_i)$

$E_{si} = r_i \oplus h_2\,(ID_{si}\,||\,PW_{si})$

Store g_{si} and E_{si} in C_{si}

Login and Authentication Protocol

$$Input\ ID_{si}, PW_{si}, F_{si}^{*}$$

$$F_{si} = g_{si} \oplus h_2 (ID_{si} \| PW_{si})$$

$$Verify\ d(F_{si}, F_{si}^{*}) \geq r$$

$$r_i = E_{si} \oplus h_2 (ID_{si} \| PW_{si})$$

$$\overline{PW_{si}} = h_2 (ID_{si} \| PW_{si} \| F_{si})$$

$$A_{si} = r_i \oplus \overline{PW_{si}}$$

$$N_{si}^{'} = h_2 (\overline{PW_{si}} \| A_{si} \| ID_{si})\ and$$

$$Check = N_{si}^{'} \stackrel{?}{=} N_{si}$$

$$BID_{si} = DID_{si} \oplus \overline{PW_{si}}$$

$$Generate\ b_i, Gsi = b_i \oplus h_2 (A_{si} \| ID_{si} \| t_1)$$

$$H_{si} = h_2(ID_{si} \| A_{si} \| b_i \| t_1)$$

$$\xrightarrow{\{BID_{si}, H_{si}, G_{si}, t_1\}}$$

Verify $(t_2 - t_1) < \Delta T$

$$(ID_{si} \| r_1) = D_{si}(BID_{si})$$

$$A_{si} = h_2(ID_{si} \| S_k)$$

$$b_i = G_{si} \oplus h_2(ID_{si} \| A_{si})$$

$$H'_{si} = h_2(ID_{si} \| A_{si} \| t_1 \| b_i)$$

$$Verify\ H'_{si} \stackrel{?}{=} H_{si}$$

Generate r_n

$$M_s = r_n \oplus h_2(ID_{si} \| A_{si})$$

$$PSD_{si} = E_{S_k}(ID_{si} \| r_n) \oplus BID_{si} \oplus b_i$$

$$H_s = h_2(A_{si} \| ID_{si} \| t_3)$$

$$\xleftarrow{\{M_S, H_s, t_3, PSD_{si}\}}$$

Verify $(t_4 - t_3) < \Delta T$

$$H'_s = h_2(A_{si} \| ID_{si} \| t_3)$$

$$Verify\ H'_s \stackrel{?}{=} H_s$$

$$DIS_{si} = DID_{si} \oplus PSD_{si} \oplus PSD_{si} \oplus b_i$$

$$\xleftrightarrow{S_k = h_2(A_{si} \| ID_{si} \| b_i)}$$

6. CASE STUDY OF GOOGLE PLAY STORE

Google play store has become the primary hub of applications, where thousands of developers upload thousands of applications daily. There is no check and balance to check the authenticity and duplicity of the application. There is not much information on the google play store's front end where any developer and user get any information. Even Google has no access to the application's source code. This application looks like a legitimate application that can harm users' integrity and cause users to lose trust in the google play store. Users should always download that application, which has a high rating and a maximum number of downloads.

This research work has scrapped thousands of applications with different categories from the Google play store. We have scrapped IoT, Network commutation, networking, and WSN with the free and paid applications, as shown in Figure 12. We merge these categories of applications separately and give them a class name of the WSN application. This paper has analyzed WSN applications based on rating attributes with a high rating value. The user should download those applications, and developers should develop these types of applications.

6.1 The Analysis of Free and Paid Applications

We have scarped thousands of free and paid applications of WSN applications. We have analyzed that 50% of free applications are developed and used by the users, and the same 50% equal ratio of paid applications developed and used by the users. This scenario is different from other scenarios; casually, the number of applications of paid applications is less than several free applications. We have analyzed what

Figure 12. Small sample screenshot of the WSN application

1	title	free	scoreText	score
2	Internet of Things (IOT)	TRUE	4.5	4.5
3	Internet of Things	TRUE	5	5
4	IoTool - Internet of Things (IoT) sensor platform	TRUE	4	4.034483
5	Android Things Toolkit	TRUE	4.5	4.529255
6	Internet of Things	TRUE	3.8	3.8
7	Learn Internet Of Things Full	TRUE	0	0
8	Data Communication and Computer Network (DCN)	TRUE	5	5
9	Data Communication and Computer Network	TRUE	4.7	4.736842
10	Learn Data Communication Computer Network Full	TRUE	5	5
11	Data Communications & Network	TRUE	4.5	4.515152
12	Data Communication And Network	TRUE	3.2	3.238095
13	Networking Basics	TRUE	4.2	4.164855
14	LINQQ-Business & Professional Networking Platformâ€¨	TRUE	4.4	4.42963
15	Shapr â€“ Meaningful Networking	TRUE	4	3.968192
16	Learn Networking Offline - Networking Tutorials	TRUE	5	5
17	Computer Networking	TRUE	4.4	4.382022
18	Networking Plus (Learn Computer Networking & CCNA)	TRUE	4.5	4.461538
19	Wireless Sensor Client	TRUE	3	3
20	iMonnit Mobile	TRUE	3.8	3.8
21	Sensor Node Free	TRUE	4	4
22	Sensor Networks Installer	TRUE	0	0

percentage of the free and paid application is the same in-WSN application after scraping. We have visualized this percentage in the shape of the Pie Chart, as shown in Figure 13.

6.2 Rating Trends of Free WSN-Related Applications

For a specific purpose, thousands of users download the software from the google play store. Such users have their background in connection with that program. Based on this experience, the user gives the application a ranking. Google Play Store sets the rating ratio between 0 and 5. A rating scale of 0 shows that this application is terrible, and a rating scale of 5 shows that this application is too good in terms of functionality. It provides a graph of how users scores on free WSN apps. It can envision that perhaps most people give free WSN apps 5 stars. Nonetheless, users do not think twice about giving 0 scores in the free WSN application because they are buying this application and are displeased by this, as displayed in Figure 14.

6.3 Rating Trends of Paid WSN Applications

It provides a graph of how users to rate apps for paying WSN apps. It can hope that most people offer paid WSN applications 4.5 stars. Nonetheless, as shown in Figure 15, users do not think twice about giving 0 scores in a paid WSN app since they purchase the app and are displeased by it.

7. CONCLUSION

The mobile WSN is the latest wireless technology for gathering information from a particular field of interest. Two of the essential service ranges are the software for

Figure 13. Percentage visualization of free and paid applications of WSN applications in the form of a pie chart

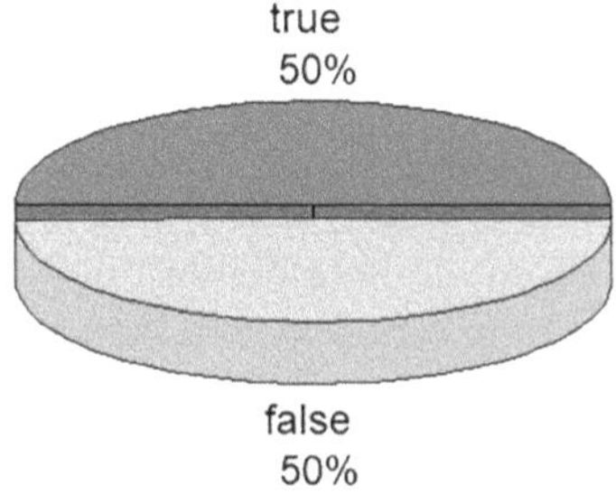

Figure 14. Rating trends of free WSN applications

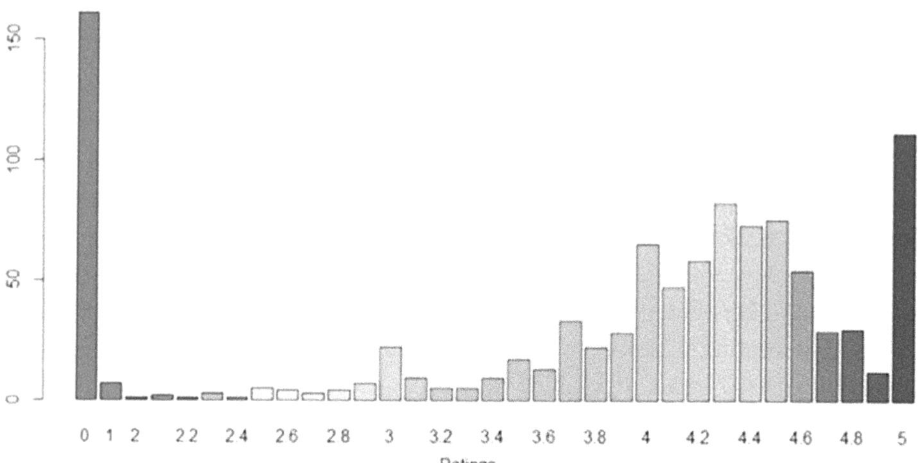

Figure 15. Rating trends of free WSN applications

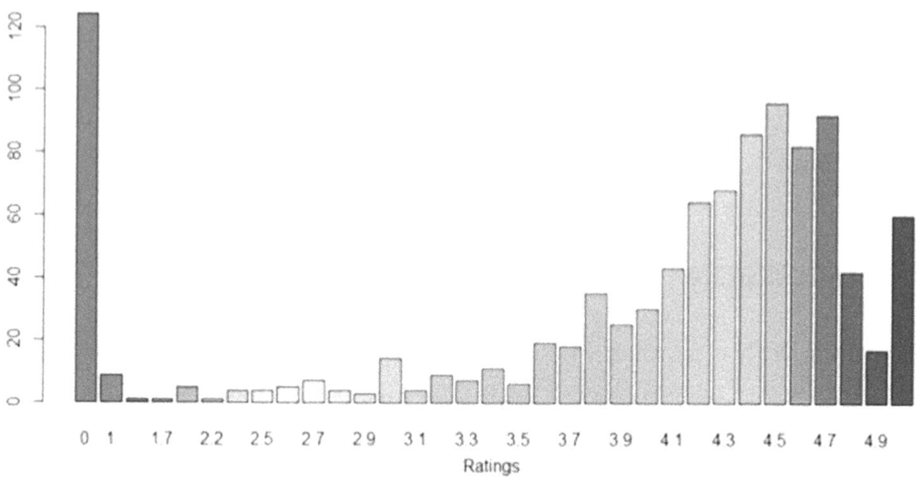

intrusion detection and border surveillance. The primary benefit of using mobile WSN applications is the temporal and high spatial data resolution resulting from deploying hundreds of low-cost sensor nodes along borders. The mobile WSN base border protection system is proposed for continuous monitoring in this work. The border troops, sensors, gateways, cloud, and android applications are assumed in this system. The intruder is caught, reported, and detected by this system. A border troop does not even detect it. After sending the information from the border, the sensor sends this information to the base station using the android application.

Using this application, the base station sends the data to the cloud and sends the message on the troop's mobile phone. The mobile WSN was developed for significant results because the solar panel is attached to the battery; this system has less battery consumption. We simulated border protection design using the mobile WSN technology on a CupCarbon simulator tool. We have analyzed that we can build an Android application for this critical mission where troops can be intimated about the intrusion and communicate with each other during the war. This application can guide the troop in the time of emergency on what the next step should be followed. We can check the status of different sensors deployed on the border with the help of the application. We have proposed a security protocol for the registration phase, login, and authentication protocol security. We have analyzed these applications based on the application's rating with Machine Learning techniques. This analyzed information helps the developers at the time of development of the application.

8. FUTURE WORK

We can deploy this proposed sachem in the real-time battlefield and check the proposed setup flaws in future work. We can change the Zigbee technology if we consider this not suitable for crucial situations. Also, we can change things according to the situation.

REFERENCES

Afzaal, H., & Zafar, N. A. (2017). *Modeling of IoT-based border protection system.* Paper presented at the Electrical Engineering and Computing Technologies (INTELLECT), 2017 First International Conference on Latest trends in.

Alippi, C., Anastasi, G., Di Francesco, M., & Roveri, M. (2009). Energy management in wireless sensor networks with energy-hungry sensors. *IEEE Instrumentation & Measurement Magazine*, *12*(2), 16–23. doi:10.1109/MIM.2009.4811133

Almurisi, N., & Tadisetty, S. (2022). Cloud-based virtualization environment for IoT-based WSN: Solutions, approaches and challenges. *Journal of Ambient Intelligence and Humanized Computing*, *13*(10), 1–23. doi:10.1007/s12652-021-03515-z PMID:35371335

Almusaylim, Z., & Jhanjhi, N. (2020). *Comprehensive review: Privacy protection of user in location-aware services of mobile cloud computing.* Academic Press.

Almusaylim, Z. A., Zaman, N., & Jung, L. T. (2018). *Proposing a data privacy aware protocol for roadside accident video reporting service using 5G in Vehicular Cloud Networks Environment.* Paper presented at the 2018 4th International Conference on Computer and Information Sciences (ICCOINS). 10.1109/ICCOINS.2018.8510588

Ambika, N. (2022). Enhancing Security in IoT Instruments Using Artificial Intelligence. In *IoT and Cloud Computing for Societal Good* (pp. 259–276). Springer. doi:10.1007/978-3-030-73885-3_16

Amutha, J., Nagar, J., & Sharma, S. (2020). A Distributed Border Surveillance (DBS) System for Rectangular and Circular Region of Interest with Wireless Sensor Networks in Shadowed Environments. *Wireless Personal Communications*, 1–21.

Bagnasco, S., Berzano, D., Guarise, A., Lusso, S., Masera, M., & Vallero, S. (2015). *Monitoring of IaaS and scientific applications on the Cloud using the Elasticsearch ecosystem.* Paper presented at the Journal of physics: Conference series. 10.1088/1742-6596/608/1/012016

Bhardwaj, K. K., Banyal, S., Sharma, D. K., & Al-Numay, W. (2022). Internet of things based smart city design using fog computing and fuzzy logic. *Sustainable Cities and Society*, *79*, 103712. doi:10.1016/j.scs.2022.103712

Boukerche, A., & Zhou, X. (2020). A Novel Hybrid MAC Protocol for Sustainable Delay-Tolerant Wireless Sensor Network. *IEEE Transactions on Sustainable Computing*, *5*(4), 455–467. doi:10.1109/TSUSC.2020.2973701

Bounceur, A., Clavier, L., Combeau, P., Marc, O., Vauzelle, R., Masserann, A., . . . Devendra, V. (2018). *Cupcarbon: A new platform for the design, simulation and 2d/3d visualization of radio propagation and interferences in iot networks.* Paper presented at the 2018 15th IEEE Annual Consumer Communications & Networking Conference (CCNC).

Crussell, J., Gibler, C., & Chen, H. (2012). *Attack of the clones: Detecting cloned applications on android markets.* Paper presented at the European Symposium on Research in Computer Security. 10.1007/978-3-642-33167-1_3

Deng, Q., Su, Y., Hu, S., Xiong, X., Juan, R., Zhang, Y., & Ma, H. (2018). *A Parallel Impedance Measurement System for Electrical Impedance Tomography System with Multi-Microcontroller-Unit Architecture.* Paper presented at the 2018 IEEE International Conference on Manipulation, Manufacturing and Measurement on the Nanoscale (3M-NANO). 10.1109/3M-NANO.2018.8552230

Eulaerts. (2022). Weak Signals in Border Management and Surveillance Technologies. Academic Press.

Humayun, M., Jhanjhi, N., Alruwaili, M., Amalathas, S. S., Balasubramanian, V., & Selvaraj, B. J. I. A. (2020). Privacy protection and energy optimization for 5G-aided industrial. *Internet of Things : Engineering Cyber Physical Human Systems*, *8*, 183665–183677.

Imran, L. B., Farhan, M., Latif, R. M. A., & Rafiq, A. (2018). Design of an IoT based warfare car robot using sensor network connectivity. *Proceedings of the 2nd International Conference on Future Networks and Distributed Systems*. 10.1145/3231053.3231121

Javaid, M., Haleem, A., Singh, R. P., & Suman, R. (2022). Enabling flexible manufacturing system (FMS) through the applications of industry 4.0 technologies. *Internet of Things and Cyber-Physical Systems*.

Khan, J. A., Qureshi, H. K., & Iqbal, A. (2015). Energy management in wireless sensor networks: A survey. *Computers & Electrical Engineering*, *41*, 159–176. doi:10.1016/j.compeleceng.2014.06.009

Khargharia, B., Hariri, S., Szidarovszky, F., Houri, M., El-Rewini, H., Khan, S. U., . . . Yousif, M. S. (2007). *Autonomic power & performance management for large-scale data centers.* Paper presented at the 2007 IEEE International Parallel and Distributed Processing Symposium. 10.1109/IPDPS.2007.370510

Koley, I., & Samanta, T. (2019). Mobile sink based data collection for energy efficient coordination in wireless sensor network using cooperative game model. *Telecommunication Systems*, *71*(3), 377–396. doi:10.1007/s11235-018-0507-4

Latif, R. M. A., Belhaouari, S. B., Saeed, S., Imran, L. B., Sadiq, M., & Farhan, M. (2020). *Integration of google play content and frost prediction using cnn: scalable iot framework for big data*. Academic Press.

Latif, R. M. A., Imran, L.-B., Farhan, M., Bah, M. J., Ali, G., & Abid, Y. A. (2019). *Real-time simulation of IoT based smart home live mirror using WSN.* Paper presented at the 2019 International Conference on Frontiers of Information Technology (FIT). 10.1109/FIT47737.2019.00019

Latif, R. M. A., Naeem, M. R., Rizwan, O., & Farhan, M. (2021). *A Smart Technique to Forecast Karachi Stock Market Share-Values using ARIMA Model.* Paper presented at the 2021 International Conference on Frontiers of Information Technology (FIT). 10.1109/FIT53504.2021.00065

Martín, C., Garrido, D., Llopis, L., Rubio, B., & Díaz, M. (2022). Facilitating the monitoring and management of structural health in civil infrastructures with an Edge/Fog/Cloud architecture. *Computer Standards & Interfaces*, *81*, 103600. doi:10.1016/j.csi.2021.103600

Muhammad, K., Lloret, J., & Baik, S. W. (2019). Intelligent and energy-efficient data prioritization in green smart cities: Current challenges and future directions. *IEEE Communications Magazine*, *57*(2), 60–65. doi:10.1109/MCOM.2018.1800371

Mukhtarov, F., Dieperink, C., & Driessen, P. (2018). The influence of information and communication technologies on public participation in urban water governance: A review of place-based research. *Environmental Science & Policy*, *89*, 430–438. doi:10.1016/j.envsci.2018.08.015

Papageorge, M. V., Freyman, B. J., Juskey, F. J., & Thome, J. R. (1995). *Integrated circuit package having a face-to-face IC chip arrangement*. Google Patents.

Patil, S. M., & Baig, M. M. (2018). *Survey on Creating ZigBee Chain Reaction using IoT*. Academic Press.

Ramzan, M., Awan, S. M., Aldabbas, H., Abid, A., Farhan, M., Khalid, S., & Latif, R. M. A. (2019). Internet of medical things for smart D3S to enable road safety. *International Journal of Distributed Sensor Networks*, *15*(8), 1550147719864883. doi:10.1177/1550147719864883

Rao, P. M., & Deebak, B. (2022). Security and privacy issues in smart cities/industries: Technologies, applications, and challenges. *Journal of Ambient Intelligence and Humanized Computing*, 1–37.

Rejeti, K., Murali, G., & Kumar, B. S. (2019). *An Accurate Methodology to Identify the Explosives Using Wireless Sensor Networks*. Paper presented at the International Conference on Sustainable Computing in Science, Technology and Management (SUSCOM), Amity University Rajasthan, Jaipur-India. 10.2139/ssrn.3362178

Ren, Q. (2018). Massive Collaborative Wireless Sensor Network Structure Based on Cloud Computing. *International Journal of Online and Biomedical Engineering*, *14*(11), 4–15. doi:10.3991/ijoe.v14i11.9499

Saleh, M., Jhanjhi, N., Abdullah, A., & Saher, R. (2022a). *IoTES (A Machine learning model) Design dependent encryption selection for IoT devices*. Paper presented at the 2022 24th International Conference on Advanced Communication Technology (ICACT).

Saleh, M., Jhanjhi, N., Abdullah, A., & Saher, R. (2022b). *Proposing encryption selection model for IoT devices based on IoT device design.* Paper presented at the 2022 24th International Conference on Advanced Communication Technology (ICACT). 10.23919/ICACT53585.2022.9728914

Sethi, P. (2020). Swarm Intelligence for Clustering in Wireless Sensor Networks. *Swarm Intelligence Optimization: Algorithms and Applications*, 263-273.

Shafiq, M., Ashraf, H., Ullah, A., Masud, M., Azeem, M., & Jhanjhi, N. (2021). *Robust cluster-based routing protocol for IoT-assisted smart devices in WSN.* Academic Press.

Shah, S. U. A., Manzoor, M. K., Latif, R. M. A., Farhan, M., & Ashiq, M. I. (2019). *A Novel Routing Protocol Based on Congruent Gravity Value for Underwater Wireless Sensor Networks.* Paper presented at the 2019 International Conference on Frontiers of Information Technology (FIT). 10.1109/FIT47737.2019.00018

Sharma, S., & Verma, V. K. (2022). An integrated exploration on internet of things and wireless sensor networks. *Wireless Personal Communications, 124*(3), 2735–2770. doi:10.1007/s11277-022-09487-3

Sheikh, H. F., & Ahmad, I. (2015). *An evolutionary technique for performance-energy-temperature optimized scheduling of parallel tasks on multi-core processors.* Academic Press.

Sheikh, H. F., Ahmad, I., Wang, Z., & Ranka, S. (2012). *An overview and classification of thermal-aware scheduling techniques for multi-core processing systems.* Academic Press.

Sheikh, H. F., Tan, H., Ahmad, I., & Ranka, S. (2012). *Energy-and performance-aware scheduling of tasks on parallel and distributed systems.* Academic Press.

Soto-Acosta, P., Del Giudice, M., & Scuotto, V. (2018). Emerging issues on business innovation ecosystems: The role of information and communication technologies (ICTs) for knowledge management (KM) and innovation within and among enterprises. *Baltic Journal of Management, 13*(3), 298–302. doi:10.1108/BJM-07-2018-398

Tripathi, B., Keil, S. J., Gulati, M., Cho, J. W., Machnicki, E. P., Herbeck, G. H., ... Dalal, A. (2019). *System on a chip with always-on processor which reconfigures SOC and supports memory-only communication mode.* Google Patents.

Ullah, A., Ishaq, N., Azeem, M., Ashraf, H., Jhanjhi, N., Humayun, M., ... Almusaylim, Z. (2021). *A survey on continuous object tracking and boundary detection schemes in IoT assisted wireless sensor networks.* Academic Press.

Ullo, S., Gallo, M., Palmieri, G., Amenta, P., Russo, M., Romano, G., . . . De Angelis, M. (2018). *Application of wireless sensor networks to environmental monitoring for sustainable mobility.* Paper presented at the 2018 IEEE International Conference on Environmental Engineering (EE). 10.1109/EE1.2018.8385263

Varshney, S., Kumar, C., Swaroop, A., Khanna, A., Gupta, D., Rodrigues, J. J., Pinheiro, P., & De Albuquerque, V. H. C. (2018). Energy efficient management of pipelines in buildings using linear wireless sensor networks. *Sensors (Basel)*, *18*(8), 2618. doi:10.3390/s18082618 PMID:30103372

Wu, Y., Wu, Y., Guerrero, J. M., & Vasquez, J. C. (2022). Decentralized transactive energy community in edge grid with positive buildings and interactive electric vehicles. *International Journal of Electrical Power & Energy Systems*, *135*, 107510. doi:10.1016/j.ijepes.2021.107510

Yang, W., Li, J., Zhang, Y., Li, Y., Shu, J., & Gu, D. (2014). APKLancet: tumor payload diagnosis and purification for android applications. *Proceedings of the 9th ACM symposium on Information, computer and communications security.* 10.1145/2590296.2590314

Zanella, A., Bui, N., Castellani, A., Vangelista, L., & Zorzi, M. (2014). *Internet of things for smart cities.* Academic Press.

Zhu, J. (2018). Methods and System for Providing Software Defined Microcontroller Unit (MCU). Google Patents.

Chapter 4
The Internet of Things (IoT) Is Revolutionizing Inventory Management

Imdad Ali Shah
School of Computing Science, Taylor's University, Malaysia

Areesha Sial
Mehran University of Engineering and Technology, Pakistan

Sarfraz Brohi
University of the West of England, UK

ABSTRACT

Every part of the supply chain has been affected by the rise of Industry 4.0 technologies. Many businesses have been trying out this modern technology to see if it can help them make more money. IoT devices make it simple for companies to keep track of an item's specific location, which helps inventory management (IM). The time it takes to find inventory is shortened as a result. The abundance of real-time data makes it possible to offer insightful information that supports strategic and tactical business decisions. Developing a supply chain into a fully integrated supply chain has several benefits. The differences between fourth-generation technology and earlier generations make it seem like traditional ways of restocking inventory don't adapt well enough to new technologies and can't handle IoT systems. Thanks to technological advancements, supply chains are undergoing rapid transformation.

1. INTRODUCTION

The application of AI to inventory management has emerged as one of the most widely used corporate strategies today. Computers and other devices, such as robots

DOI: 10.4018/979-8-3693-3816-2.ch004

controlled by computers, are essentially what artificial intelligence (AI) is all about. One of the most widely used technologies nowadays is AI. This machine performs jobs based on human experience and intelligence while processing vast volumes of data and identifying various data patterns. The management of inventory gives companies the ability to choose what products to order, when to order them, and in what numbers. The inventory is monitored from the time a product is purchased until it is sold. This technique identifies patterns and adjusts production accordingly to ensure that there is sufficient stock on hand to fulfil customer orders and that they are given timely warnings of any potential shortages (Stankovic, J. A, 2016, Mármol, F. G.,2016, Nespoli, P., 2017). The worldwide supply chain and every area of inventory management are being rapidly transformed by IoT. The Fourth Industrial Revolution is ushered in by the Internet of Things in a world where new technologies and ongoing innovation exist (Díaz-López, D., Dunhill J, 2020, Huertas Celdran A,2018, Fernandez Maim, 2019). Additionally, a McKinsey Global Institute estimate estimates that the IoT might contribute between $560 billion and $850 billion annually to logistics, supply chain management, and inventory management by 2025.

IoT will develop as soon as almost all technological goods on the market have internet access (Nguyen H, 2016, Cheng L, 2017, Cabaj K 2018. By 2020, there are predicted to be 26 billion linked devices worldwide, providing more communication than we had previously thought possible between the devices and their users (Xiao F, 2020, Luo P, 2020, Lee S, 2017). New technological innovations and inventions in the logistics and supply chain sector range from specialized integrations of tried-and-true methods (such as bitcoin AI platforms) to more sector-specific innovations. And it appears that technology is utterly transforming the logistics sector each year (Prabadevi, B., 2020, Lv, Z., 2020). We acknowledge that the term "Internet" is synonymous with revolution and the future, even though it may appear to be a regular part of our daily lives. And the truth is that since the Internet has become more accessible to everyone, our way of life has completely changed.

With the interconnectedness of all the assets in the supply chain, the Internet of Things provides "intelligent" to businesses and opens a world of opportunities. For example, it allows for real-time control of a product's path from when it leaves the warehouse to its destination. Utilizing the Internet of Things has advanced the sector's digitalization by enabling remote organisation, control, and automation of operations from any device with an internet connection, cutting costs and time so that human labour only contributes value (Tan, Y., Cheng, 2017, Li Y, Liu H, 2017, Anwar, 2018). In general, recruiting is finding and selecting the best candidates for a position so they can focus their efforts on realising their professional and organizational objectives. With the introduction of technologies like the internet of things (IoT), corporate analytics, and deep learning in the HR sector, Employers use them to improve their hiring practices and find the best candidates for open positions (Bannour, 2017). IoT is defined as cooperating between different systems and processes online with the primary goal of gathering data, analyzing it, and producing reports so quick decisions can be made, an overview of management and supply chain is in Figure 1.

Its origins may be traced back to the 1960s when the United States established a network strictly for military use. This was done so that, in the unlikely event of a foreign attack, military intelligence could be accessible from any location in the nation. Since then, a lot has changed. In the twenty-first century, all our devices are connected, and the internet has given us access to an almost limitless amount of knowledge that is always just a click away (Shah, I. A,2022, Shah, I. A., 2021, Shah, I. A., 2022, Chen-xu, N., 2015). Now that the glories of the internet are generally known to everybody, what do we mean when we refer to the Internet of Things? We shall attempt to summarise the meaning of the acronym IoT, even though its complexity matches our love of technology. IoT is a system that enables millions of objects to be connected via the internet and transport data over a specific network without any contact with humans. There is no shorter or simpler way to define it. Anyone who has already experienced the digital transformation wave quickly equates using the internet to create digital connections with commonplace items like a refrigerator. What about its application in the logistics sector (Wang, Y., 2016, Al-Najjar A, 2016). A prediction of a significant increase in the use of technology in this sector was all that the Internet of Things in the logistics business was about five years ago. This forecast has come true and gone above and beyond expectations. Along with artificial intelligence and big data, it is one of the first technical advancements that most allure business executives.

Figure 1. An overview of the management and supply chain
Chin (2018)

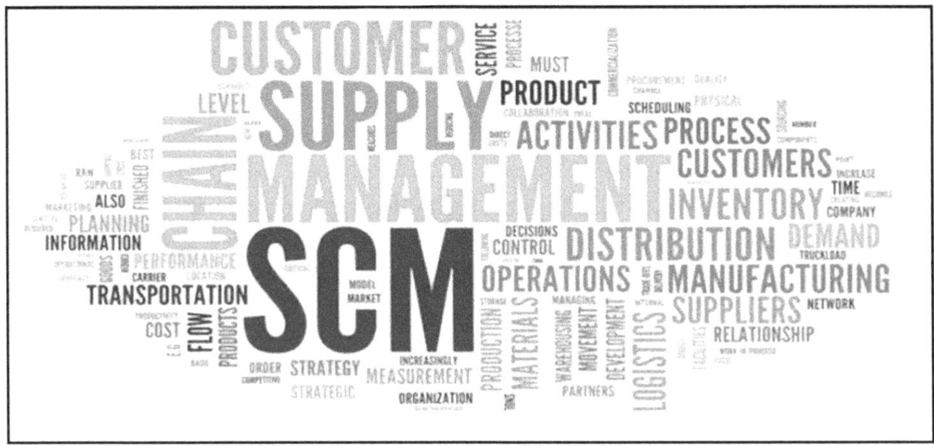

2. LITERATURE REVIEW

The organization is being helped by the organization's ability to adapt to the rapidly shifting business environment and support in auxiliary activities like hiring, performance management, training, etc., by the new technologies rising complexity. IoT focuses on enhancing the competitive edge in the recruitment field by analyzing the organization's unique job requirements and searching for suitable candidates through various online job portals and social media sites (Botelho, F., 2014, Ahmed El-Hassany, 2016, Suman Karki, 2018). Hiring managers have concentrated on finding a variety of profiles that will be suitable for the open positions in the organization and evaluating them by looking over their job profiles. The use of IoT technologies helps businesses rediscover talent by screening the talent pool that is currently available and looking for opportunities to cross-train the resources to use the capacity that is presently available, leverage the skills that are already present, and increase productivity. IoT is also concentrated on helping management manage inventory, which is crucial for a business to store the necessary items to support the manufacturing process and help the company manage costs effectively (Shah, I. A.,2022, Shah, I. A.,2022, Shah, I. A., 2022). The IoT, machine learning, and other sophisticated technologies are used by HR managers and logistics directors to plan, improve relationships with stakeholders, develop strategies, and effectively allocate resources. The IoT-powered technologies assist in preventing unconscious biases, assist in successfully screening candidates, and assist the organisation in improving sustainability and progress (Li, N., Jiang, 2017, Mace, J., 2018, Ouyang, J.,2014). Increased use of IoT has made it easier for businesses to connect, analyze, and evaluate data to make educated decisions. The cost of hiring has decreased thanks to the IoT's use in the hiring process. Since it is widely acknowledged that information about potential candidates is primarily mentioned in subjective elements, candidates frequently cite their skill set, job history, age, and other demographics allowing management to filter prospects swiftly.

These tools have greatly aided the organisation in tracking and evaluating the job profiles of candidates for open positions, which has allowed the recruiters to save time and money. The IoT makes it possible to engage candidates in real time, increase their awareness of the job description, and handle other particulars (Qian, Y., 2017, Liron Schiff, 2016). Chatbots allow for open communication between candidates and employers and assist in requesting the feedback and information needed from applicants. HR managers can make better decisions, forecast future organisational personnel needs, and select the best candidates by utilising the data analytics technologies that are now available. IoT supports hiring internal candidates by mapping internal candidates' skill sets, skill levels, competency bases, and other factors that may match the available positions (Wen, H., 2018, Timothy Zhu, 2017,

Pena, J. G, 2014). The IoT solutions also assist in obtaining employee data and comparing individuals to job criteria, improving their ability to choose the best candidate internally or externally. IoT benefits the organization and improves the recruiting market, increasing competition and lowering hiring costs for businesses (Muzafar, S., Hamid, B. 2020). IoT real-time data collection is a very recent technology. Early IoT adopters often set objectives to motivate activities with obvious revenue opportunities and competitive advantages.

Real-time warehousing has always been crucial but has never been more critical. The rise of online retailers is primarily to blame for this (Sharma, P. K.,2017, Steichen, M. 2017, Meng, Y.2012). Real-time stock visibility is made possible by the vast quantity of data that is currently accessible across IoT devices, mobile devices, and resellers. Companies can track product expiration dates thanks to connected IoT devices, dramatically reducing the risk of waste and product damage. IoT devices allow businesses to track the whereabouts of their products, which helps prevent product theft and loss. IoT tools are used in intelligent warehouse management to give warehouses, production facilities, and distribution centres real-time visibility. Using quality data from sensors and IoT systems strengthens current inventory management systems.

Managing an enterprise's materials used to manufacture items is known as inventory management. The component stock used as raw materials for manufacture is included in the inventory. It is a significant resource and is seen favorably by the company. Businesses spend money tracking, storing, and protecting their list (Ni, H., 2018, Chin, T.2018, Rahouti, M, 2021). Inventory mismanagement by a business can result in significant financial loss, which is frequently caused by either excess or surplus stock. Inventory management includes planning, managing, and optimising the amount of stock that must be purchased and the timing of that purchase. This ensures that neither too little nor too much stock is purchased, which could disrupt production or result in financial loss. Numerous studies have been done to increase the effectiveness of inventory management. They have significantly impacted business and inventory management, assisting organisations in running their operations more precisely and with less effort (Chin, T., 2018). For quick and precise retrieval, an inventory management system based on an intranet architecture was proposed.

Global businesses frequently have partners, operations, and entities across several countries and continents. It isn't easy to manage partners and businesses on a worldwide scale. Every inventory decision the company makes has the potential to generate significant financial gain or loss. Due to their international operations, their production, sales, and service centres frequently have multiple locations (Palvia, S., Aeron, 2018, Sharef, B. T., 2014, Correia, S. 2017). Much money may be saved by properly managing the inventory, which can then be put toward improving other parts of the business's operations. Customers may be satisfied because of a global inventory management system since the company may be able to deliver the goods within the anticipated time frame. A global inventory management system makes it easier to execute thorough multi-inventory searches and to have accurate information about all inventories that are currently in stock (He, Z, 2016, Kok, S. H.,2020). It illustrates an inventory management model used by multinational corporations. Suppliers, raw materials, work-in-progress, finished goods, and customers make up most of it. In the event of a worldwide firm, suppliers, production facilities, and customers would be spread out around the globe.

This is just a tiny example of the numerous ways the private sector is utilising IoT to increase effectiveness and efficiency while enabling new business models, IoT-driven inventory management in Figure 2.

Raw materials, most of the inventory, and finished commodities require storage space. It is directly influenced by the production volume that the company intends to carry out and client demand. Manufacturing hubs are frequently found in areas with convenient access to resources. These businesses efficiently use web applications and cloud-based tools to manage inventory (Kiran, S. R. A., 2021, Umrani, S., 2020, Abolhasan, M. 2015). The Industrial Internet of Things (IIoT), Industry 4.0, is the Internet of Things (IoT) applied to the manufacturing sector. The IIoT is the upcoming technology that will revolutionise businesses and manufacturing facilities with an emphasis on return on investment. IIoT involves connecting every machine in a business to a network and collecting data from the devices in the manufacturing process. Since every machine has many sensors, the data from those sensors may be transmitted in real-time to a cloud storage system across a communication network. The devices may be watched over and made to operate more effectively. The acquired

Figure 2. IoT-driven inventory management
Humayun (2020)

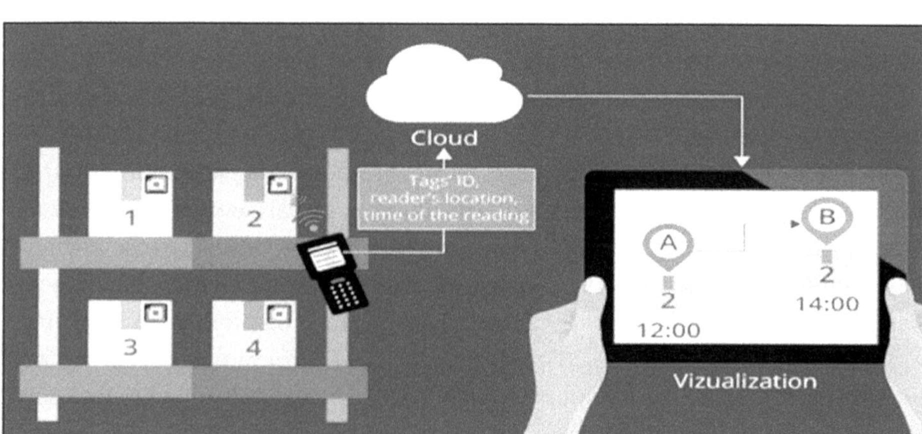

data can be utilised to analyze the corporate inventory management system and can be permanently kept in a cloud storage service (B. Dong et al, 2017, Huang, X., 2017, Mukherjee, B. K., 2020). The recorded data can extract useful information to help the enterprise's global inventory performance. The business can decrease losses and boost profits by identifying areas where inventory performance could be enhanced. IIoT increases the global enterprise's connection, efficiency, and scalability while saving money and time. Decision-makers can obtain highly accurate and reliable information from the collected data, which aids them in providing solutions to a company's challenging problems, such as how to enhance performance, cut costs, and safeguard the environment. The IoT is the most promising technology used in businesses due to its substantial benefits (Rahman, A., 2019, Islam, M. J., 2019). Several areas can be considered when integrating IoT into inventory management, including that returns and raw materials used to make the product are managed throughout the inventory management process. The ability to track and monitor perishable inventory in real-time during storage and transportation is essential for managing perishable inventory (Javaid, M., Ndiaye, M., 2020). By detecting an item's weight or height, RFID tags, barcodes, and sensors can automatically check inventory levels, prompting replenishment when supplies run low. More intelligent purchasing of raw materials and finished items may be made possible using analytics with backend database systems that give pricing and availability data. Industry analysts predict that IoT technology might help cut expenses associated with carrying inventories by up to 10%. Strategies for managing lists that are IoT-enabled help prevent delays brought on by out-of-stock components (Cheng, J., 2018, Shahid, H.,2021). International shipments can be tracked using IoT devices. Shipping companies use IoT devices to track the location and condition of containers, enabling clients to keep an eye on containers as they travel. Additionally, they can detect openings in containers and changes in temperature, pressure, and shocks that can harm delicate goods. This enhances shippers' and suppliers' accountability while enabling businesses to monitor their shipments and spot possible issues.

3. EVALUATION OF IoT IN INVENTORY MANAGEMENT

The Internet of Things (IoT) is here and poised to revolutionize many sectors, including inventory management. But before we can comprehend how IoT will affect inventory management and how we can optimise this. When the number of work-in-progress items is low, an IoT-based inventory management system gives producers accurate information about the flow of parts and resources by giving them up-to-date information about the state, location, and mobility of objects in stock (Kumar, M. S.,2020, Karakus, M., 2017). Establishing a digital infrastructure requires an Internet of Things inventory management system. It has a wide range of advantages. It improves the availability and readability of data. IoT in Inventory Management improvement supply chain in Figure 3.

The openness of things inventory management confers numerous benefits to a facility's operational effectiveness. More information is collected when more Internet of Things devices are used in a warehouse. This visibility gives them access to data about their operations that they would not have otherwise, which enables them to keep making improvements (Sahay, R., 2019, Jacquenet, C., 2016, Al Shuhaimi, F., 2016, Yassein, M. B., 2017). More than a billion different devices are connected to the Internet of Things, and each of these devices gathers information that could be useful to a facility. It could reveal the things that employees select most frequently throughout a particular season. The information can then be used by storage facilities to reorganise their inventory by combining items that are frequently chosen together to boost productivity.

3.1 Enhances Data Transparency and Visibility

The openness of IoT inventory management has numerous advantages for a facility's operating effectiveness. A warehouse will gather more data by employing more Internet of Things (IoT) sensors. They have access to operational data thanks to this visibility, which enables them to keep getting better (Chakraborty, 2021). More than 30 billion devices are part of the internet of things (IoT), each gathering data that a facility might find helpful.

Figure 3. The IoT in inventory management improvement supply chain
Humayun (2021)

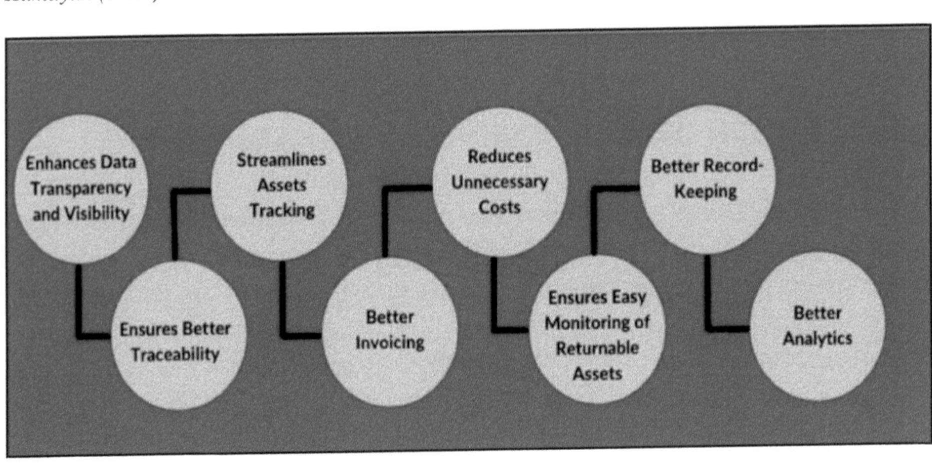

3.2 Ensures Better Traceability

With edge traceability throughout our supply chain, you can track your inventory from its point of origin to its destination. This makes it easier to meet customer needs. With the help of the Internet of Things' traceability features and blockchain, which creates a digital paper trail, you can track inventory from the factory to the customer (Shah, I. A., 2022, Holt, T. J., 2021). Accurate and real-time end-to-end details can help you optimise the procedures involved in inventory management, allowing you to make better use of your resources. We should keep track of and trace every item in your business's inventory to make it easier to see what you have, improve customer service, and lower the costs of keeping inventory.

3.3 Streamlines Assets Tracking

The previous asset monitoring systems, which consisted of tracking numbers and bar codes, are being phased out and replaced with IoT devices and sensors, which enable the tracking and management of commodities across the supply chain. Sensors connected to the Internet of Things can pinpoint the locations and times when shipments of packages have delays in transit. This paves the way for alternate routes and contingency planning, which speeds up the supply chain (Kamiya, S., 2021). These sensors allow businesses to track and record data about their items, including the times and temperatures at which they were stored, transported, and sold. With this information, IoT technology may assist businesses to enhance quality assurance, timely delivery, shipment, and forecasting. Monitor the movement of goods and property between companies. With the help of IoT asset tracking and blockchain-enabled solutions, you can create a digital trail of each step and safely record business transactions.

3.4 Better Invoicing

Cross-border transactions are common in global supply chains, but they can be cumbersome due to the number of participants, the amount of money being transferred, the different banking regulations in each country, and the sheer volume of paperwork involved. Considerable delays in payment may result from any inconsistencies, such as duplicate invoices. By using a distributed ledger that can't be changed, the Internet of Things and blockchain could speed up the movement of goods between marketplaces and make transactions safer, more efficient, and less expensive while protecting against fraud (Aliwa, E., 2021, Lim, M., Abdullah, A.2021). By adopting intelligent contracts powered by the blockchain, businesses can do away with the need to reconcile paperwork between numerous parties. These contracts can track the course of a shipment and, after delivery, fulfil the contract's payment obligations.

3.5 Reduces Unnecessary Costs

The team shouldn't need as much labour investment since they have access to many digital tools. The warehouse personnel can quickly track down and locate the products without searching the shelves.

3.6 Ensures Easy Monitoring of Returnable Assets

Using IoT for inventory management, anyone can follow recoverable transportation assets between locations and countries. Thanks to real-time asset tracking, businesses can quickly find and retrieve missing or stolen containers, even while they are in motion (ur Rehman, S., 2021). We can use technologies like predictions, data trills, fast notifications, and automated asset routing to speed up asset recovery and dispute settlement.

3.7 Better Record-Keeping

The customers get the appropriate products at the right time by improving inventory visibility. Keeping detailed records of your inventory lots can help you avoid unpleasant situations such as discovering an entire batch of finished goods.

3.8 Better Analytics

Businesses may employ advanced analytics to gain accurate insights into their operations thanks to the data produced by IoT technologies. Real-time performance monitoring and predictive analytics can work together. In addition to using methodologies, it also makes information accessible more quickly, significantly shortening supply-chain cycles.

4. IoT APPLICATIONS IN INVENTORY MANAGEMENT

Using the associated ID, IoT tracks the item's location, visualizes the results, and shows the updates instantly. Furthermore, it makes it possible for the warehouse management team to quickly check on the goods. The technology ensures efficiency while optimizing productivity. Figure 4 IoT applications in inventory management.

Figure 4. IoT applications in inventory management

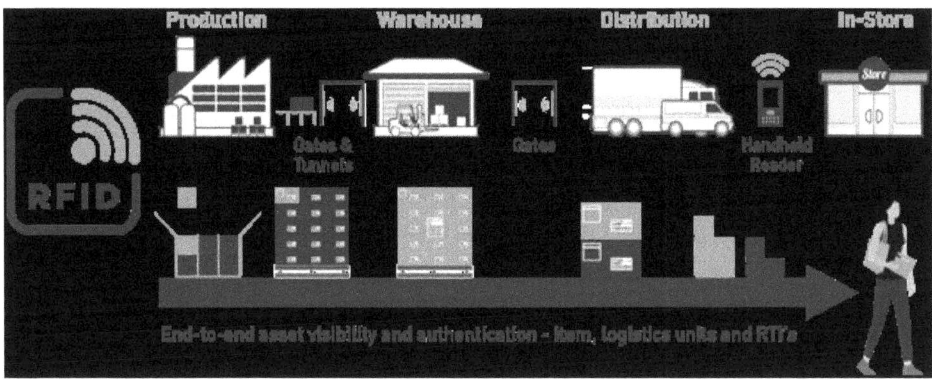

IoT apps provide real-time status updates on the inventory. This can help with emergency preparation and alternate plan-making since you can ascertain the precise location and cause of any transit delays. Courier services, e-commerce enterprises, and other vendors use the Internet of Things-powered live tracking and monitoring systems. IoT greatly minimizes wait times and communication lapses, which enhances customer support. Businesses are experimenting with micro-tracking technologies, which enable specific tracking of each courier item or product, to optimize their supply chain as 5G data transfer approaches. Micro-tracking in inventory management is made possible by cloud-based GPS and radio frequency identification, or RFID. These are cutting-edge 5G wireless data transfer technologies designed to capture data effectively and automatically. The warehouse management systems provide the most efficient use of resources to guarantee the facility's daily smooth and efficient operation. Many tasks, including managing human resources, transportation, tracking new and existing goods, and so forth, are included in a typical warehouse management process. Companies in various sectors are implementing performance-enhancing strategies by utilizing various IoT-enabled tools and applications to transform warehouses into intelligent spaces that incorporate robots, drones, and blockchain technology. IoT devices can gather and facilitate open communication between warehouse managers and logistics stakeholders, in addition to increasing supply chain efficiency.

5. OVERVIEW INVENTORY MANAGEMENT IN SUPPLY CHAIN

To maximise business value, it is essential to plan the supply chain in a way that minimises stock on hand. After this strategic task is complete, inventory control is crucial for managing any leftover inventories and ensuring the supply chain keeps up with the speed of international trade. The future of inventory management systems is being shaped by the speed with which robots and machine learning are being used in many other fields (Roopak, M., 2020, Srinivasan, K.,2021). Inventory managers have an overwhelming amount of data to sort through because data is collected at every stage of the global supply chain. Only if you can evaluate the data and apply it for inventory optimization does it have any value for supply chain management, and that is where AI comes in.

Despite these improvements in contemporary supply chain management, global supply networks nonetheless make inventory control more difficult. Considering this, effective inventory management is essential for supply chain planning (Shah, I. A., 2023, Khalil, M. I., 2021). Companies need to do a better job of highlighting the significance of the discipline, especially considering the logistical and financial difficulties encountered over the previous year.

The COVID-19 pandemic's irregular demand variations dispelled any qualms the globe had regarding the value of a responsive and adaptable supply chain. Today's supply chains must be quick and flexible to create benchmark inventory management capabilities where necessary. Careers in global supply chain management are more sought-after than ever. Professionals with advanced inventory management skills have fantastic job opportunities (Shah, I. A., 2023, Dimolianis, M., 2020). On the other hand, by maintaining a consistent inventory flow, effective inventory management can increase profitability, improve supply chain visibility, and improve operations. Currently, the gold standard for supply chain managers is inventory optimization.

6. DISCUSSION

IoT data provides the foundation for improving product quality and tracking and tracing capabilities. IoT technologies and the analytics that go with them are the foundations of world-class supply chains, inventory control, supplier integration, quality control of suppliers, and compliance upgrades.

An RFID tag broadcasts its identity to the tag reader through radio waves, allowing for data collection and automatic object identification. The tag has a microcircuit with a specific code and a data group and can be affixed to or inserted into a product. An antenna on the tag reader sends out radio waves, and the tag responds by sending the reader its data. In general, recruiting is finding and selecting the best candidates for a position so they can focus their efforts on realising their professional and organizational objectives. With the introduction of technologies like the internet of things (IoT), corporate analytics, and deep learning in the HR sector, Employers use them to improve their hiring practices and find the best candidates for open positions

(Glyptis, L., 2020, Lim, M.,2019). IoT is defined as cooperating between different systems and processes online with the primary goal of gathering data, analyzing it, and producing reports so quick decisions can be made.

These improvements are already in use in industry, where machines keep track of the pace and state of the assembly pieces and communicate this information to the following operators, along with precise directions on how and when to assemble the components via digital displays. RFID also helps anti-counterfeit strategies by enabling strong supply chain visibility and product verification through product traceability. RFID tags also become a product component as it moves down the supply chain to the point of sale. RFID technology needs specialized software dependent on service providers (Samsor, A. M., 2020, Shah, I. A., 2023, Jhanjhi, N. Z., Brohi,2019). This program manages the RFID reader, starts the scan to gather data from the tags, stores it on a local computer, or sends it to the cloud, RFID technology in the supply chain in Figure 5.

6.1 Chapter's Contribution and Discussion

In this chapter, we peer-review more than 100 research, survey, and review articles, including several book chapters on the evolution of IoT, in inventory management. Literature research reveals IoT opportunities in sustainable inventory management. A supply chain is beneficial. Given the contrast between the fourth generation and

Figure 5. RFID technology in the supply chain zetes

Getting Accurate Stock Details	You can't determine when to restock or which merchandise is doing well if you don't have proper stock information
Poor Processes	Operations might be slowed down and work can become error-prone if using outdated or manual techniques.
Changing Customer Demand	The tastes and wants of customers are always evolving. How will you be able to determine when and why their preferences change if your system is unable to observe trends
Using Warehouse Space Well	similar products are hard to find, staff members squander time. Getting inventory management right can help solve this problem
Trancing obsolete material	Almost all businesses experience this issue frequently. Not every product or material will be sold, and there will be a few materials that will become outmoded over time and be forgotten about by inventory managers.

previous technologies, typical inventory replenishment procedures cannot manage IoT systems. The use of IoT devices has made it simpler for companies to manage their inventory and reduce the time it takes to locate items. Real-time data provides valuable insights that support strategic and tactical decision-making, leading to more efficient and effective supply chain management. Furthermore, the integration of these technologies into the supply chain has several benefits, including better tracking, traceability, quality control, and compliance. By replacing outdated inventory management systems with IoT devices, businesses can improve overall efficiency and reduce waste. Another area where Industry 4.0 technologies have had a significant impact is warehousing. Warehouses have evolved from simply being storage facilities to essential business centers that enhance supply chain efficiency and speed. The use of automation and robotics in warehouses has streamlined processes and made it easier to manage inventory. Based on our chapter, we researched IoT opportunities in sustainable inventory management. It is challenging to obtain comprehensive knowledge of the authentic raw materials that have arrived, the availability of the proper materials, the monitoring of work in progress, and the timely shipping of the correct item to the right customer.

The application of AI to inventory management has emerged as one of the most widely used corporate strategies today. Computers and other devices, such as robots controlled by computers, are essentially what artificial intelligence (AI) is all about. One of the most widely used technologies nowadays is AI. This machine performs jobs based on human experience and intelligence while processing vast volumes of data and identifying various data patterns. The management of inventory gives companies the ability to choose what products to order, when to order them, and in what numbers. The inventory is monitored from the time a product is purchased until it is sold. IoT, is a vast network in which a vast number of physical objects with sensors and software are connected to the Internet and exchange information about their usage and operating environment. Through the network, the sensors continuously send data regarding the devices' operational status. IoT enables real-time data communication between devices without requiring human engagement.

IoT devices can help reduce errors and human labor while also speeding up processes and improving overall warehouse efficiency. IoT sensors are being installed in warehouses by businesses to monitor the movement and use of supplies and other assets. Businesses are also using sensors on shelves to provide inventory data in real time to their management system. By ensuring that inventory levels and equipment locations are properly identified and continuously monitored, IoT and smart warehouse management are helping to eliminate expensive and time-consuming errors. IoT is here and poised to revolutionize many sectors, including inventory management. But before we can comprehend how IoT will affect inventory management and how we can optimise this. When the number of work-in-progress items is low, an IoT-based inventory management system gives producers accurate information about the flow of parts and resources by giving them up-to-date information about the state, location, and mobility of objects in stock Kumar. Establishing a digital infrastructure requires an Internet of Things inventory management system. It has a wide range of advantages. It improves the availability and readability of data.

The openness of things inventory management confers numerous benefits to a facility's operational effectiveness. More information is collected when more Internet of Things devices are used in a warehouse. This visibility gives them access to data about their operations that they would not have otherwise, which enables them to keep making improvements. More than a billion different devices are connected to the Internet of Things, and each of these devices gathers information that could be useful to a facility. It could reveal the things that employees select most frequently throughout a particular season. IoT-based smart inventory management is the spark that ignites real-time visibility throughout production, distribution, and warehouse facilities, lowers inventory costs, and enhances predictive maintenance. Lower inventory carrying costs and fewer inventory management errors can be achieved by bolstering older inventory management systems with the high-quality and comprehensive data that IoT sensors and devices can deliver. Any company's system of record benefits from having IoT data linked into the ERP system, which guarantees the best data is always available for decision-making.

7. CONCLUSION

Industry 4.0 technologies have indeed had a significant impact on the supply chain, transforming the way businesses operate and making it easier to keep track of inventory and make data-driven decisions. The use of IoT devices has made it simpler for companies to manage their inventory and reduce the time it takes to locate items. Real-time data provides valuable insights that support strategic and tactical decision-making, leading to more efficient and effective supply chain management. Every part of the supply chain has been affected by the rise of Industry 4.0 technologies. Many businesses have been trying out this new technology to see if it can help them make more money. Developing a supply chain into a fully integrated supply chain has many benefits. The differences between fourth-generation technology and earlier generations make it seem like traditional ways of restocking inventory don't adapt well enough to new technologies and can't handle IoT systems. Thanks to technological advancements, supply chains are undergoing rapid transformation. The biggest problem with IM is when there is no requirement for information to make an informed choice. The use of devices of the IoT to replace outdated IM systems increases overall efficiency by enabling better tracking, traceability, quality control, and compliance.

8. FUTURE WORK

Over the past few years, warehouses have evolved into important business centres that boost supply chain efficiency and speed. The object of this chapter is to provide a review of applying IoT to inventory management by understanding the importance and role of inventory management in a supply chain. Our recommendations and solutions help new researchers and logistics companies get started. The researchers have needed to on IoT security issues in the context of Inventory Management.

REFERENCES

Abolhasan, M., Lipman, J., Ni, W., & Hagelstein, B. (2015). Software-defined wireless networking: Centralized, distributed, or hybrid? *IEEE Network*, *29*(4), 32–38. doi:10.1109/MNET.2015.7166188

Ahmed El-Hassany. (2016). SDNRacer: Concurrency Analysis for Software-defined Networks. In *37th ACM SIGPLAN Conference on Programming Language Design and Implementation (PLDI 16)*. ACM.

Al-Najjar, A., Layeghy, S., & Portmann, M. (2016). Pushing SDN to the end-host, network load balancing using OpenFlow. *Proc. PCCW'16*, 1–6. 10.1109/PERCOMW.2016.7457129

Al Shuhaimi, F., Jose, M., & Singh, A. V. (2016, September). Software defined network as solution to overcome security challenges in IoT. In *2016 5th International Conference on Reliability, Infocom Technologies and Optimization (Trends and Future Directions)(ICRITO)* (pp. 491-496). IEEE. 10.1109/ICRITO.2016.7785005

Aliwa, E., Rana, O., Perera, C., & Burnap, P. (2021). Cyberattacks and countermeasures for in-vehicle networks. *ACM Computing Surveys*, *54*(1), 1–37. doi:10.1145/3431233

Anwar, A., Cheng, Y., Huang, H., Han, J., Sim, H., Lee, D., . . . Butt, A. R. (2018, November). BESPOKV: Application tailored scale-out key-value stores. In SC18: International Conference for High Performance Computing, Networking, Storage and Analysis (pp. 14-29). IEEE.

Arief, A., Wahab, I. H. A., & Muhammad, M. (2021, May). Barriers and Challenges of e-Government Services: A Systematic Literature Review and Meta-Analyses. *IOP Conference Series. Materials Science and Engineering*, *1125*(1), 012027. doi:10.1088/1757-899X/1125/1/012027

Bannour, F., Souihi, S., & Mellouk, A. (2017). Distributed SDN control: Survey, taxonomy, and challenges. *IEEE Communications Surveys and Tutorials*, *20*(1), 333–354. doi:10.1109/COMST.2017.2782482

Botelho, F., Bessani, A., Ramos, F. M., & Ferreira, P. (2014, September). On the design of practical fault-tolerant SDN controllers. In *2014 third European workshop on software defined networks* (pp. 73-78). IEEE. 10.1109/EWSDN.2014.25

Cabaj, K., Gregorczyk, M., & Mazurczy, W. (2018). Softwaredefined networking-based crypto ransomware detection using http traffic characteristics. *Computers & Electrical Engineering*, *66*, 353–368. doi:10.1016/j.compeleceng.2017.10.012

Chakraborty, C., & Abougreen, A. N. (2021). Intelligent internet of things and advanced machine learning techniques for COVID-19. *EAI Endorsed Transactions on Pervasive Health and Technology*, *7*(26), e1.

Chen-xu, N., & Jie-sheng, W. (2015, July). Auto regressive moving average (ARMA) prediction method of bank cash flow time series. In *2015 34th Chinese Control Conference (CCC)* (pp. 4928-4933). IEEE.

Cheng, J., Chen, W., Tao, F., & Lin, C. L. (2018). Industrial IoT in 5G environment towards smart manufacturing. *Journal of Industrial Information Integration*, *10*, 10–19. doi:10.1016/j.jii.2018.04.001

Cheng, L., Li, Z., Zhang, Y., Zhang, Y., & Lee, I. (2017). Protecting interoperable clinical environment with authentication. *SIGBED Rev*, *14*(2), 34–43. doi:10.1145/3076125.3076129

Chin, T., Rahouti, M., & Xiong, K. (2018). Applying software-defined networking to minimize the end-to-end delay of network services. *Applied Computing Review*, *18*(1), 30–40. doi:10.1145/3212069.3212072

Chin, T., Xiong, K., & Rahouti, M. (2018). Kernel-Space Intrusion Detection Using Software-Defined Networking. *EAI Endorsed Transactions on Security and Safety*, *5*(15), e2.

Correia, S., Boukerche, A., & Meneguette, R. I. (2017). An architecture for hierarchical software-defined vehicular networks. *IEEE Communications Magazine*, *55*(7), 80–86. doi:10.1109/MCOM.2017.1601105 da Silva, L. E., & Coury, D. V. (2020). Network traffic prediction for detecting DDoS attacks in IEC 61850 communication networks. *Computers & Electrical Engineering*, *87*, 106793. doi:10.1016/j.compeleceng.2020.106793

Díaz-López, D., Dólera-Tormo, G., Gómez-Mármol, F., & Martínez-Pérez, G. (2016). Dynamic counter-measures for risk-based access control systems: An evolutive approach. *Future Generation Computer Systems*, *55*, 321–335. doi:10.1016/j.future.2014.10.012

Dimolianis, M., Pavlidis, A., & Maglaris, V. (2020, February). A multi-feature DDoS detection schema on P4 network hardware. In *2020 23rd Conference on Innovation in Clouds, Internet and Networks and Workshops (ICIN)* (pp. 1-6). IEEE. 10.1109/ICIN48450.2020.9059327

Dong, B. (2017). Software Defined Networking Based On-Demand Routing Protocol in Vehicle Ad-Hoc Networks. *ZTE Communications*, *15*(2), 11–18.

Dunhill, J. (2020). *Critical patient dies after cyber attack disables hospital computers*. https://www.iflscience.com/technology/critical-patient-dies-after-cyber-attack-disables-hospital-computers

Environment", *IEEE In 2018 4th International Conference on Computer and Information Sciences (ICCOINS)*, pp. 1-5, August 2018.

Glyptis, L., Christofi, M., Vrontis, D., Del Giudice, M., Dimitriou, S., & Michael, P. (2020). E-Government implementation challenges in small countries: The project manager's perspective. *Technological Forecasting and Social Change*, *152*, 119880. doi:10.1016/j.techfore.2019.119880

Hamid, B., Jhanjhi, N. Z., & Humayun, M. (2020). Digital Governance for Developing Countries Opportunities, Issues, and Challenges in Pakistan. In *Employing Recent Technologies for Improved Digital Governance* (pp. 36–58). IGI Global. doi:10.4018/978-1-7998-1851-9.ch003

He, Z., Zhang, D., Zhu, S., Cao, J., & Liu, X. (2016, September). Sdn enabled high performance multicast in vehicular networks. In *2016 IEEE 84th Vehicular Technology Conference (VTC-Fall)* (pp. 1-5). IEEE. 10.1109/VTCFall.2016.7881215

Holt, T. J., Stonhouse, M., Freilich, J., & Chermak, S. M. (2021). Examining ideologically motivated cyberattacks performed by far-left groups. *Terrorism and Political Violence*, *33*(3), 527–548. doi:10.1080/09546553.2018.1551213

Huang, X., Yu, R., Kang, J., He, Y., & Zhang, Y. (2017). Exploring mobile edge computing for 5G-enabled software defined vehicular networks. *IEEE Wireless Communications*, *24*(6), 55–63. doi:10.1109/MWC.2017.1600387

Huertas Celdran, A. (2018). Ice++: im-proving security, QoS, and high availability of medical cyber-physical systems through mobile edge computing. *IEEE 20th international conference one-health networking, applications and services (Healthcom),* 1–8.

Humayun, M., Hamid, B., Jhanjhi, N. Z., Suseendran, G., & Talib, M. N. (2021, August). 5G Network Security Issues, Challenges, Opportunities and Future Directions: A Survey. *Journal of Physics: Conference Series*, *1979*(1), 012037. doi:10.1088/1742-6596/1979/1/012037

Humayun, M., Jhanjhi, N. Z., Hamid, B., & Ahmed, G. (2020). Emerging smart logistics and transportation using IoT and blockchain. *IEEE Internet of Things Magazine*, *3*(2), 58–62. doi:10.1109/IOTM.0001.1900097

Islam, M. J., Mahin, M., Roy, S., Debnath, B. C., & Khatun, A. (2019, February). Distblacknet: A distributed secure black sdn-iot architecture with nfv implementation for smart cities. In *2019 International Conference on Electrical, Computer and Communication Engineering (ECCE)* (pp. 1-6). IEEE. 10.1109/ECACE.2019.8679167

Jacquenet, C., & Boucadair, M. (2016). A software-defined approach to IoT networking. *ZTE Communications*, *1*, 1–12.

Javaid, M., Haleem, A., Vaishya, R., Bahl, S., Suman, R., & Vaish, A. (2020). Industry 4.0 technologies and their applications in fighting COVID-19 pandemic. *Diabetes & Metabolic Syndrome*, *14*(4), 419–422. doi:10.1016/j.dsx.2020.04.032 PMID:32344370

Jhanjhi, N. Z., Brohi, S. N., & Malik, N. A. (2019, December). Proposing a rank and wormhole attack detection framework using machine learning. In *2019 13th International Conference on Mathematics, Actuarial Science, Computer Science and Statistics (MACS)* (pp. 1-9). IEEE.

Kamiya, S., Kang, J. K., Kim, J., Milidonis, A., & Stulz, R. M. (2021). Risk management, firm reputation, and the impact of successful cyberattacks on target firms. *Journal of Financial Economics*, *139*(3), 719–749. doi:10.1016/j.jfineco.2019.05.019

Karakus, M., & Durresi, A. (2017). A survey: Control plane scalability issues and approaches in software-defined networking (SDN). *Computer Networks*, *112*, 279–293. doi:10.1016/j.comnet.2016.11.017

Karki, S., Nguyen, B., & Zhang, X. (2018). QoS Support for Scientific Workflows Using Software-Defined Storage Resource Enclaves. In *2018 IEEE International Parallel and Distributed Processing Symposium (IPDPS 18)*. IEEE. 10.1109/IPDPS.2018.00020

Khalil, M. I., Jhanjhi, N. Z., Humayun, M., Sivanesan, S., Masud, M., & Hossain, M. S. (2021). Hybrid smart grid with sustainable energy efficient resources for smart cities. *Sustainable Energy Technologies and Assessments, 46*, 101211.

Kiran, S. R. A., Rajper, S., Shaikh, R. A., Shah, I. A., & Danwar, S. H. (2021). Categorization of CVE Based on Vulnerability Software By Using Machine Learning Techniques. *International Journal (Toronto, Ont.), 10*(3).

Kok, S. H., Azween, A., & Jhanjhi, N. Z. (2020). Evaluation metric for crypto-ransomware detection using machine learning. *Journal of Information Security and Applications*, *55*, 102646. doi:10.1016/j.jisa.2020.102646

Kumar, M. S., Raut, R. D., Narwane, V. S., & Narkhede, B. E. (2020). Applications of industry 4.0 to overcome the COVID-19 operational challenges. *Diabetes & Metabolic Syndrome*, *14*(5), 1283–1289. doi:10.1016/j.dsx.2020.07.010 PMID:32755822

Lee, S., Kim, J., Woo, S., Yoon, C., Scott-Hayward, S., Yegneswaran, V., Porras, P., & Shin, S. (2020). A comprehensive security assessment framework for software-defined networks. *Computers & Security*, *91*, 101720. doi:10.1016/j.cose.2020.101720

Li, N., Jiang, H., Feng, D., & Shi, Z. (2017). Customizable SLO and its near-precise enforcement for storage bandwidth. *ACM Transactions on Storage*, *13*(1), 1–25. doi:10.1145/2998454

Li, Y., Liu, H., & Yang, W. (2017). Predicting inter-data-center network traffic using elephant flow and sublink information. *IEEE Transactions on Network and Service Management*, *13*(4), 782–792.

Lim, M., Abdullah, A., & Jhanjhi, N. Z. (2021). Performance optimization of criminal network hidden link prediction model with deep reinforcement learning. *Journal of King Saud University. Computer and Information Sciences*, *33*(10), 1202–1210. doi:10.1016/j.jksuci.2019.07.010

Lim, M., Abdullah, A., Jhanjhi, N. Z., & Supramaniam, M. (2019). Hidden link prediction in criminal networks using the deep reinforcement learning technique. *Computers*, *8*(1), 8. doi:10.3390/computers8010008

Luo, Zou, Du, Jin, Liu, & Shen. (2020). Static detection of real-world buffer overflow induced by loop. *Computers & Security, 89*(101), 616.

Lv, Z., & Kumar, N. (2020). Software defined solutions for sensors in 6G/IoE. *Computer Communications*, *153*, 42–47. doi:10.1016/j.comcom.2020.01.060

Mace, J., Roelke, R., & Fonseca, R. (2018). Pivot tracing: Dynamic causal monitoring for distributed systems. *ACM Transactions on Computer Systems*, *35*(4), 1–28. doi:10.1145/3208104

Mármol, F. G., Pérez, M. G., & Pérez, G. M. (2016, July). I don't trust ICT: Research challenges in cyber security. In *IFIP International Conference on Trust Management* (pp. 129-136). Springer.

Meng, Y., & Li, W. (2012, December). Intelligent alarm filter using knowledge-based alert verification in network intrusion detection. In *International Symposium on Methodologies for Intelligent Systems* (pp. 115-124). Springer. 10.1007/978-3-642-34624-8_14

Mukherjee, B. K., Pappu, S. I., Islam, M. J., & Acharjee, U. K. (2020, February). An SDN based distributed IoT network with NFV implementation for smart cities. In *International Conference on Cyber Security and Computer Science* (pp. 539-552). Springer. 10.1007/978-3-030-52856-0_43

Muzafar, S., & Jhanjhi, N. Z. (2020). Success Stories of ICT Implementation in Saudi Arabia. In *Employing Recent Technologies for Improved Digital Governance* (pp. 151–163). IGI Global. doi:10.4018/978-1-7998-1851-9.ch008

Ndiaye, M., Oyewobi, S. S., Abu-Mahfouz, A. M., Hancke, G. P., Kurien, A. M., & Djouani, K. (2020). IoT in the wake of COVID-19: A survey on contributions, challenges and evolution. *IEEE Access : Practical Innovations, Open Solutions*, *8*, 186821–186839. doi:10.1109/ACCESS.2020.3030090 PMID:34786294

Nespoli, P., Papamartzivanos, D., Mármol, F. G., & Kambourakis, G. (2017). Optimal countermeasures selection against cyber attacks: A comprehensive survey on reaction frameworks. *IEEE Communications Surveys and Tutorials*, *20*(2), 1361–1396. doi:10.1109/COMST.2017.2781126

Nguyen, H., Acharya, B., Ivanov, R., Haeberlen, A., Phan, L. T. X., Sokolsky, O., Walker, J., Weimer, J., Hanson, W., & Lee, I. (2016) Cloud-based secure logger for medical devices. *Proceedings of the IEEE first international conference on connected health: applications, systems and engineering technologies (CHASE)*, 89–94. 10.1109/CHASE.2016.48

Ni, H., Rahouti, M., Chakrabortty, A., Xiong, K., & Xin, Y. (2018, August). A distributed cloud-based wide-area controller with sdn-enabled delay optimization. In 2018 IEEE Power & Energy Society General Meeting (PESGM) (pp. 1-5). IEEE. doi:10.1109/PESGM.2018.8586040

Ouyang, J., Lin, S., Jiang, S., Hou, Z., Wang, Y., & Wang, Y. (2014, February). SDF: Software-defined flash for web-scale internet storage systems. In *Proceedings of the 19th international conference on Architectural support for programming languages and operating systems* (pp. 471-484). 10.1145/2541940.2541959

Palvia, S., Aeron, P., Gupta, P., Mahapatra, D., Parida, R., Rosner, R., & Sindhi, S. (2018). *Online education: Worldwide status, challenges, trends, and implications*. Academic Press.

Pena, J. G. V., & Yu, W. E. (2014, April). Development of a distributed firewall using software defined networking technology. In *2014 4th IEEE International Conference on Information Science and Technology* (pp. 449-452). IEEE. 10.1109/ICIST.2014.6920514

Prabadevi, B., Jeyanthi, N., & Abraham, A. (2020). An analysis of security solutions for ARP poisoning attacks and its effects on medical computing. *International Journal of System Assurance Engineering and Management*, *11*(1), 1–14. doi:10.1007/s13198-019-00919-1

Qian, Y., Li, X., Ihara, S., Zeng, L., Kaiser, J., Süß, T., & Brinkmann, A. (2017, November). A configurable rule based classful token bucket filter network request scheduler for the lustre file system. In *Proceedings of the International Conference for High Performance Computing, Networking, Storage and Analysis* (pp. 1-12). 10.1145/3126908.3126932

Rahman, A., Islam, M. J., Sunny, F. A., & Nasir, M. K. (2019, December). DistBlockSDN: A distributed secure blockchain based SDN-IoT architecture with NFV implementation for smart cities. In *2019 2nd International Conference on Innovation in Engineering and Technology (ICIET)* (pp. 1-6). IEEE. 10.1109/ICIET48527.2019.9290627

Rahouti, M., Xiong, K., Ghani, N., & Shaikh, F. (2021). SYNGuard: Dynamic threshold-based SYN flood attack detection and mitigation in software-defined networks. *IET Networks*, *10*(2), 76–87. doi:10.1049/ntw2.12009

Roopak, M., Tian, G. Y., & Chambers, J. (2020, January). An intrusion detection system against ddos attacks in iot networks. In *2020 10th Annual Computing and Communication Workshop and Conference (CCWC)* (pp. 562-567). IEEE. 10.1109/CCWC47524.2020.9031206

Sahay, R., Meng, W., & Jensen, C. D. (2019). The application of Software Defined Networking on securing computer networks: A survey. *Journal of Network and Computer Applications*, *131*, 89–108. doi:10.1016/j.jnca.2019.01.019

Saleh, M., Jhanjhi, N. Z., Abdullah, A., & Saher, R. (2020). Design Challenges of Securing IoT Devices: A survey. *International Journal of Engineering Research & Technology (Ahmedabad)*, *13*(12), 5149–5165.

Samsor, A. M. (2020). *Challenges and Prospects of e-Government implementation in Afghanistan*. International Trade, Politics and Development.

Schiff, L., Schmid, S., & Kuznetsov, P. (2016). In-Band Synchronization for Distributed SDN Control Planes. *Computer Communication Review*, *46*(1), 37–43. doi:10.1145/2875951.2875957

Shah, I. A. (2022). Cybersecurity Issues and Challenges for E-Government During COVID-19: A Review. *Cybersecurity Measures for E-Government Frameworks*, 187-222.

Shah, I. A., Habeeb, R. A. A., Rajper, S., & Laraib, A. (2022). The Influence of Cybersecurity Attacks on E-Governance. In *Cybersecurity Measures for E-Government Frameworks* (pp. 77–95). IGI Global. doi:10.4018/978-1-7998-9624-1.ch005

Shah, I. A., Jhanjhi, N. Z., Amsaad, F., & Razaque, A. (2022). The Role of Cutting-Edge Technologies in Industry 4.0. In *Cyber Security Applications for Industry 4.0* (pp. 97–109). Chapman and Hall/CRC. doi:10.1201/9781003203087-4

Shah, I. A., Jhanjhi, N. Z., Humayun, M., & Ghosh, U. (2022). Health Care Digital Revolution During COVID-19. In *How COVID-19 is Accelerating the Digital Revolution* (pp. 17–30). Springer. doi:10.1007/978-3-030-98167-9_2

Shah, I. A., Jhanjhi, N. Z., & Laraib, A. (2023). Cybersecurity and Blockchain Usage in Contemporary Business. In *Handbook of Research on Cybersecurity Issues and Challenges for Business and FinTech Applications* (pp. 49–64). IGI Global.

Shah, I. A., & Rajper, S., & ZamanJhanjhi, N. (2021). Using ML and Data-Mining Techniques in Automatic Vulnerability Software Discovery. *International Journal (Toronto, Ont.)*, *10*(3).

Shah, I. A., Sial, Q., Jhanjhi, N. Z., & Gaur, L. (2023). Use Cases for Digital Twin. In Digital Twins and Healthcare: Trends, Techniques, and Challenges (pp. 102-118). IGI Global.

Shah, I. A., Sial, Q., Jhanjhi, N. Z., & Gaur, L. (2023). The Role of the IoT and Digital Twin in the Healthcare Digitalization Process: IoT and Digital Twin in the Healthcare Digitalization Process. In Digital Twins and Healthcare: Trends, Techniques, and Challenges (pp. 20-34). IGI Global.

Shah, I. A., Wassan, S., & Usmani, M. H. (2022). E-Government Security and Privacy Issues: Challenges and Preventive Approaches. In Cybersecurity Measures for E-Government Frameworks (pp. 61-76). IGI Global.

Shahid, H., Ashraf, H., Javed, H., Humayun, M., Jhanjhi, N. Z., & AlZain, M. A. (2021). Energy optimised security against wormhole attack in iot-based wireless sensor networks. *Computers, Materials & Continua*, *68*(2), 1967–1981. doi:10.32604/cmc.2021.015259

Sharef, B. T., Alsaqour, R. A., & Ismail, M. (2014). Vehicular communication ad hoc routing protocols: A survey. *Journal of Network and Computer Applications*, *40*, 363–396. doi:10.1016/j.jnca.2013.09.008

Sharma, P. K., Singh, S., Jeong, Y. S., & Park, J. H. (2017). Distblocknet: A distributed blockchains-based secure sdn architecture for iot networks. *IEEE Communications Magazine*, *55*(9), 78–85. doi:10.1109/MCOM.2017.1700041

Srinivasan, K., Garg, L., Datta, D., Alaboudi, A. A., Jhanjhi, N. Z., Agarwal, R., & Thomas, A. G. (2021). Performance comparison of deep cnn models for detecting driver's distraction. *CMC-Computers. Materials & Continua*, *68*(3), 4109–4124. doi:10.32604/cmc.2021.016736

Stankovic, J. A. (2016). Research directions for cyber-physical systems in wireless and mobile healthcare. *ACM Transactions on Cyber-Physical Systems*, *1*(1), 1–12. doi:10.1145/2899006

Steichen, M., Hommes, S., & State, R. (2017, September). ChainGuard—A firewall for blockchain applications using SDN with OpenFlow. In 2017 Principles, Systems and Applications of IP Telecommunications (IPTComm) (pp. 1-8). IEEE.

Tan, Y., Cheng, J., Zhu, H., Hu, Z., Li, B., & Liu, S. (2017, July). Real-time life prediction of equipment based on optimized ARMA model. In 2017 Prognostics and System Health Management Conference (PHM-Harbin) (pp. 1-6). IEEE. doi:10.1109/PHM.2017.8079318

Umrani, S., Rajper, S., Talpur, S. H., Shah, I. A., & Shujrah, A. (2020). Games based learning: A case of learning Physics using Angry Birds. *Indian Journal of Science and Technology*, *13*(36), 3778–3784. doi:10.17485/IJST/v13i36.853

ur Rehman, S., Khaliq, M., Imtiaz, S. I., Rasool, A., Shafiq, M., Javed, A. R., ... Bashir, A. K. (2021). DIDDOS: An approach for detection and identification of Distributed Denial of Service (DDoS) cyberattacks using Gated Recurrent Units (GRU). *Future Generation Computer Systems, 118*, 453-466.

Wang, Y., Jiang, D., Huo, L., & Zhao, Y. (2021). A new traffic prediction algorithm to software defined networking. *Mobile Networks and Applications*, *26*(2), 716–725. doi:10.1007/s11036-019-01423-3

Wen, H., Cao, Z., Zhang, Y., Cao, X., Fan, Z., Voigt, D., & Du, D. (2018, September). Joins: Meeting latency slo with integrated control for networked storage. In *2018 IEEE 26th International Symposium on Modeling, Analysis, and Simulation of Computer and Telecommunication Systems (MASCOTS)* (pp. 194-200). IEEE.

Xiao, F., Zhang, J., Huang, J., Gu, G., Wu, D., & Liu, P. (2020). *Unexpected data dependency creation and chaining: a new attack to sdn. 2020 IEEE Symposium on Security and Privacy.*

Yassein, M. B., Aljawarneh, S., Al-Rousan, M., Mardini, W., & Al-Rashdan, W. (2017, November). Combined software-defined network (SDN) and Internet of Things (IoT). In 2017 international conference on electrical and computing technologies and applications (ICECTA) (pp. 1-6). IEEE.

Zhu, T., Kozuch, M. A., & Harchol-Balter, M. 2017. WorkloadCompactor: Reducing Datacenter Cost While Providing Tail Latency SLO Guarantees. In *8th ACM Symposium on Cloud Computing (SoCC 17).* ACM. 10.1145/3127479.3132245

Chapter 5
Perspectives, Applications, Challenges, and Future Trends of IoT-Based Logistics

Kassim Kalinaki
https://orcid.org/0000-0001-8630-9110
Islamic University in Uganda, Uganda

Wasswa Shafik
https://orcid.org/0000-0002-9320-3186
Ndejje University, Uganda

Sarah Namuwaya
Public Procurement and Disposal of Public Assets, Uganda

Sumaya Namuwaya
Absa Bank Uganda Limited, Uganda

ABSTRACT

The emergence of the internet of things (IoT) has revolutionized many sectors of the economy, including logistics and supply chain management. By seamlessly integrating IoT into logistics operations, real-time tracking and monitoring of shipments becomes a reality, and optimizing routes and equipment performance becomes a breeze. Accordingly, supply chain operations have become streamlined like never before. This study delves into the various perspectives, applications, and challenges of deploying IoT in the logistics industry, offering a comprehensive overview for stakeholders, researchers, and students alike. With the potential for improved efficiency, effectiveness, and sustainability, the benefits of IoT in logistics are undeniable. The authors highlight future directions of this exciting field and learn how IoT shapes how we do business.

DOI: 10.4018/979-8-3693-3816-2.ch005

INTRODUCTION

Logistics refers to the orderly, efficient movement and storage of various goods and services, as well as any other associated information, from their place of origin to their site of utilization (Tran-Dang et al., 2022). This domain is progressively considered a core industry sector capable of boosting the economy's overall growth and playing an essential role in the efficient functioning of supply chains and global trade. Additionally, it is continuously becoming a vital factor for the success of many organizations in different sectors of the economy, including manufacturing, agriculture, and transportation, among others.

Getting goods and services to the right place at the right time and in a suitable condition to meet the needs of clients and businesses is the main objective of logistics (Alakaş & Eren, 2022). To realize that goal, various activities such as transportation, warehousing, distribution, information systems, and communication networks must be integrated efficiently and effectively. However, the complexity of supply chains and high labor costs have rendered the logistics industry a capital-intensive sector, negatively affecting the return on investments in the deployed logistics infrastructure (Song et al., 2021). Furthermore, the efficiency and effectiveness of local, regional, and global trade and supply chains are hampered, which minimizes the competitiveness of the firms and countries involved. Hence, there is a need for more ingenious methods to enhance the efficiency and effectiveness of logistical operations and minimize the costs involved.

The logistics sector has undergone tremendous transformation due to recent advancements in modern information and communication technologies (ICTs), which have made it possible to control the flow of goods, services, and information efficiently and effectively along the supply chain. ICT tools and systems are being deployed to plan and coordinate transportation routes, track and monitor the movement of goods, and manage inventory levels. Additionally, these technologies and tools make it easier for suppliers, manufacturers, distributors, retailers, warehouses, and customers to collaborate and communicate.(Lagorio et al., 2022).

Enabled by tremendous innovations in ICTs and key support techniques, including Big Data Analytics (BDA), IoT, and artificial intelligence (AI), smart logistics has added new dimensions that have optimized and transformed the traditional logistics industry (Ding et al., 2021). Smart logistics aims to enhance efficiency, minimize costs, and improve customer satisfaction using real-time data and automated decision-making. Additionally, smart logistics is supported by IoT technologies such as wireless sensor networks (WSN), radio frequency identification (RFID), and Global Positioning System (GPS), whose convergence allows for a seamless, ubiquitous, and pervasive communications network between them (Shee, 2023).

This interconnection enables smart logistics to attain end-to-end visibility and trackability, eventually enhancing the operational efficiency of logistics operations.

With IoT continuously becoming integrated into smart logistics, a massive amount of data from various heterogeneous devices is harvested. The complex relationships between several transactions inherent in the gathered data can be investigated using different mathematical and computational analysis techniques, such as big data analytics, to make well-informed decisions that enhance efficiency and effectiveness in the logistics industry (Song et al., 2021). For instance, using machine learning (ML) algorithms and historical data, smart logistics systems can predict demand for goods and services and optimize transportation routes and inventory levels accordingly (Chen et al., 2021). IoT integrated with logistics can revolutionize how goods and services are transported and delivered and create new business opportunities and efficiencies.

Contributions to the Chapter

Driven by the transformative potential of IoT in the logistics industry, this chapter delves into the following key contributions:

- An overview of logistics with IoT and its associated technologies, presenting a clear insight into the present state of the sector.
- Exploring the synergy of IoT and logistics operations, presenting perspectives from business, technology, and society.
- A detailed presentation of the different applications of IoT in logistics operations highlights the various ways IoT is being used to improve efficiency, effectiveness, and sustainability in logistics.
- Identification and discussion of the key challenges and obstacles that arise with integrating IoT into smart logistics operations.
- Finally, an exploration of future trends in the field of IoT in the logistics sector, providing insights into the exciting possibilities that lie ahead for this field.

Chapter Organization

Section 2 contains the different perspectives on integrating IoT in logistics. Section 3 provides the various applications of IoT in logistics operations. Section 4 showcases the real-world implementations of IoT in logistics and supply chains. The problems of integrating IoT in logistics operations are highlighted in Section 5. Future trends of IoT in logistics, along with the conclusion, are presented in sections 6 and 7, respectively.

BUSINESS, TECHNOLOGY, AND SOCIETAL PERSPECTIVES OF IoT IN LOGISTICS

There are several perspectives from which the integration of IoT into logistics operations can be viewed. This section discusses them, considering their importance in logistics operations and supply chain management.

Business Perspective

In today's fast-paced business landscape, staying ahead of the competition means embracing innovative technologies. IoT is one such technology that has the potential to revolutionize logistics operations, leading to significant improvements in efficiency and effectiveness. From deploying sensors and tracking devices to real-time monitoring of shipments, IoT in logistics is a game-changer, enabling businesses to optimize routes, improve equipment performance, and streamline supply chain operations (Tran-Dang et al., 2022). The deployment of IoT-enabled sensors and tracking devices enables real-time tracking and monitoring of shipments, allowing businesses to quickly respond to changes in demand, optimize routes, and reduce transit times. This leads to cost savings and improved customer satisfaction as goods are delivered faster and more efficiently (Lagorio et al., 2022).

In addition, IoT in logistics can significantly enhance the operational efficiency of supply chain operations in areas such as asset utilization, security, inventory control, fleet and traffic management, and safety. By gathering and analyzing real-time data from various devices and systems, businesses can make better-informed decisions, reduce costs, and improve the overall performance of their logistics operations (Öztuna, 2022). Through leveraging IoT technologies, companies can stay ahead of the competition and pave the way for a more sustainable future.

Technological Perspective

From a technological perspective, IoT involves the integration of sensors, connectivity, and software into physical devices and equipment, enabling them to communicate and exchange data pervasively. This requires a range of enabling technologies categorized into three categories: data acquisition, data connectivity, and data processing and storage. All these key technologies allow data collection, processing, and storage from many connected devices in logistical operations (Lagorio et al., 2022). Table 1 summarizes these categories and examples of deployed technologies in logistic processes.

Table 1. Summary of IoT-enabling technologies in logistics

Category	Technologies	References
Data acquisition	• Identification technologies include RFID, barcode, and near-field communication (NFC). • Tracking technologies include General Packet Radio Service (GPRS), GPS, BeiDou, Global Navigation Satellite System (GLONASS), Galileo, etc. • Sensing technologies include various humidity, vibration, temperature, and bio-sensor sensors.	(Ding et al., 2021; Kalinaki, Namuwaya, et al., 2023; Lagorio et al., 2022; Öztuna, 2022)
Connectivity	• Technologies For global coverage include 2G, 3G, 4G, 5G, and various satellites. • Technologies for long-range coverage include Sigfox, Low Power Wide Area (LPWA), Long Range (LoRa), Narrowband IoT (NB-IoT), etc. • Short-range technologies include ZigBee, Wireless Fidelity (WiFi), Bluetooth, etc.	
Data processing and storage	• Processing and analytics technologies include big data analytics, AI, ML, and other predictive algorithms. • Storage technologies include cloud computing and edge/fog computing.	

Societal Perspective

From a societal perspective, the integration of the IoT into logistics operations is a game-changer that can lead to improved sustainability of the industry and enhance safety for all stakeholders (Anusree & Balasubramanian, 2021; de Vass et al., 2020; Kaur et al., 2018; Nižetić et al., 2020). By enabling more efficient use of resources, such as fuel and transportation capacity, IoT in logistics plays a vital role in reducing the environmental impact of transportation and minimizing waste. Integrating the IoT into logistics operations is a transformative technology that offers a big chance to make the industry more efficient, effective, and sustainable, which is excellent for businesses, technology, and society.

APPLICATIONS OF IoT IN LOGISTICS AND SUPPLY CHAIN

IoT can bring tremendous benefits to the logistics industry. This section discusses the different ways in which IoT is transforming the logistics industry:

Real-Time Tracking of Assets

The integration of IoT technology permits the dynamic surveillance and tracing of consignments via the implementation of sensing devices and instruments that can be attached to shipments or placed in vehicles and other assets to track their location and status (Tan & Sidhu, 2022). This helps logistics companies optimize routes, reduce the risk of lost or damaged shipments, and improve efficiency. For instance, these sensors can collect data on the location through GPS technology to track shipments in real-time; temperature sensors can monitor the temperature of shipments to ensure that temperature-sensitive items are being transported and stored at the proper temperature; humidity sensors can monitor the humidity of shipments to ensure that humidity-sensitive items are being transported and stored at the appropriate humidity levels; vibration sensors can also be used to monitor the vibration of shipments to detect any damage or tampering during transport; and vision sensors can be used to capture the condition of the items being transported (Alsudani et al., 2023; Bhutta & Ahmad, 2021).

All the collected data from these sensors, along with other characteristics of the shipments being transported, is transmitted to a central server or cloud platform, which can then be accessed in real-time by logistics companies and their customers, enabling them to track the location and status of their shipments (Aljabhan, 2022). By collecting and transmitting this data in real-time, logistics companies can track the location and status of their shipments and act if any issues are detected. This helps enhance the efficiency and reliability of their operations and more significant shipments' visibility for clients.

Predictive Maintenance

This involves leveraging data and analytics to foretell the failure of assets or equipment, allowing the opportunity to plan maintenance proactively. In logistic operations, IoT sensors can monitor the performance of vehicles and other assets and alert maintenance teams when repairs or maintenance are needed (Gusmão Caiado et al., 2022). This can help prevent unexpected breakdowns and improve the overall reliability of logistics operations by providing real-time data on the performance of equipment and assets. For example, sensors can be placed on vehicles to monitor their performance, including tire pressure, fuel consumption, and engine temperature (Mohammad et al., 2021).

This data can be transmitted to a central server or cloud platform, where it can be analyzed to predict when maintenance or repairs will be needed. By using IoT to monitor the performance of equipment and assets in real time, logistics companies can proactively schedule maintenance and repairs rather than reacting to unexpected breakdowns. This helps to reduce downtime, improve the reliability of logistics operations, and ultimately save money by minimizing the cost of unforeseen repairs (Gusmão Caiado et al., 2022).

Improved Customer Service

IoT gives customers real-time tracking and status updates on their shipments so they can see how things are going and make better decisions. IoT improves customer care in the logistics industry through real-time tracking and updates to customers about the status of their shipments (de Vass et al., 2020; Hopkins & Hawking, 2018). This helps customers make better-informed decisions and improve their overall experience with the logistics company. For instance, if a customer is expecting a shipment and wants to know when it will be delivered, they can access real-time tracking information through an online portal or app provided by the logistics company (Alsudani et al., 2023).

This helps the customer plan their day and be prepared to receive the shipment when it arrives. Moreover, IoT can update customers on any shipment delays or issues. For example, if a shipment is delayed due to unforeseen circumstances, the customer can be notified in real time and provided with an updated delivery estimate (Nagarajan et al., 2022). This assists in reducing frustration and improves the overall customer experience. In a nutshell, by using IoT to provide real-time tracking and updates to customers, logistics companies can improve their customer care and build stronger customer relationships.

Inventory Management

IoT sensors can track inventory levels in warehouses and other storage facilities, enabling logistics companies to optimize their stock levels and reduce the risk of running out of stock (D. Kumar et al., 2022). IoT can help with inventory management in the logistics industry by providing real-time data on stock levels in warehouses and other storage facilities. This can help logistics companies optimize their stock levels and reduce the risk of running out of stock. For instance, IoT sensors can be placed on shelves or pallets to track the quantity of items in a warehouse (Mashayekhy et al., 2022). This data can be transmitted to a central server or cloud platform, where it can be analyzed to predict when stock is running low and needs replenishment. In addition, IoT can be used to track the movement of items within a warehouse, enabling logistics companies to optimize their storage layouts and ensure that things are being stored in the most efficient way possible. In summary, logistics companies can improve their efficiency and reduce the risk of running out of stock by using IoT to track inventory levels and optimize storage layouts. This leads to reduced costs and improved customer satisfaction.

Enhanced Safety

IoT devices can be used to monitor the safety of drivers and other employees, as well as the safety of shipments. Providing enhanced security in the logistics industry by monitoring the safety of drivers and other employees can help reduce the risk of accidents and improve overall safety in the sector (Tsang et al., 2022). For example, IoT sensors can be placed in vehicles to monitor the behavior of drivers, including things like speed, braking, and seatbelt usage (Khan et al., 2022). This data can be transmitted to a central server or cloud platform, where it can be analyzed to identify unsafe driving practices and provide feedback to drivers to help them improve their safety. In addition, IoT can be used to monitor the safety of shipments (Hoang et al., 2022). For example, sensors can be placed on shipments to monitor their temperature, humidity, and other factors to ensure they are transported and stored safely.

Supply Chain Visibility

IoT provides greater visibility into the supply chain, enabling logistics companies to identify bottlenecks and optimize their operations. IoT can provide greater visibility into the supply chain by collecting and transmitting data from various points in real time (Pundir et al., 2019). This data can include the location and status of shipments, the performance of equipment and assets, and the movement of goods within warehouses and other storage facilities. By collecting and analyzing this data, logistics companies can gain a more comprehensive view of their supply chain and identify bottlenecks or inefficiencies. This can help them optimize their operations and improve the overall efficiency of their supply chain. By providing more significant supply chain visibility to customers, logistics companies can build stronger relationships with their customers and improve their overall satisfaction. Customers can access real-time tracking and updates on the status of their shipments, enabling them to make better-informed decisions and plan their operations more effectively (Qader et al., 2022).

Using IoT to give logistics companies visibility into their supply chains can help them make their operations more efficient and transparent, saving them money and making their customers happier. The applications of IoT in logistics and supply chain management offer a myriad of advantages, including increased visibility, efficiency, safety, customer service, enhanced sustainability, and automation. As technology advances, the potential for further innovation and optimization in the logistics and supply chain industry remains vast, promising a future where IoT plays a central role in shaping a more connected, intelligent, and responsive global supply network.

REAL-WORLD CASES OF IoT iMPLEMENTATION IN LOGISTICS AND SUPPLY CHAIN

As depicted in the previous sections, the IoT has significantly transformed the logistics and supply chain industry by providing real-time data, enhancing visibility, and optimizing operational efficiency. This section highlights real-world cases that showcase the implementation of IoT in logistics and supply chains.

Maersk Line: Smart Containers (Asset Tracking and Condition Monitoring)

Maersk's implementation of IoT in their shipping containers demonstrates the value of real-time monitoring for perishable goods (Maersk, 2023; Pundir et al., 2019). The IoT sensors enable continuous tracking of containers' locations and conditions during transit. This technology ensures that temperature-sensitive items remain within the desired range, reducing the risk of spoilage. The data collected aids in optimizing shipping routes and conditions, ultimately improving the overall efficiency of Maersk's logistics operations.

Amazon Robotics: Warehouse Automation (Inventory Management and Order Fulfillment)

Amazon's use of IoT in warehouse automation showcases the impact of robotics and sensors on enhancing efficiency in inventory management and order fulfillment (Aldowah et al., 2020; Evans, 2023). Integrating IoT sensors and computer vision allows robots to navigate warehouses autonomously, locate products, and streamline order fulfillment. These speeds up the delivery process and minimizes inventory management errors, contributing to a more accurate and responsive supply chain.

DHL: IoT for End-to-End Supply Chain Visibility

DHL's implementation of IoT solutions emphasizes the importance of end-to-end visibility in supply chain operations (DHL, 2023; Shah et al., 2020). By incorporating sensors and tracking devices on shipments, DHL provides real-time information on the location and condition of goods. This visibility allows for better decision-making, minimizing delays, optimizing routes, and improving overall supply chain efficiency. DHL's approach showcases how IoT can be leveraged to enhance transparency across the entire logistics network.

Walmart - IoT in Cold Chain Management

Walmart's implementation of IoT in cold chain management underscores the critical role of real-time monitoring in ensuring the quality and safety of perishable goods (Radhakrishnan, 2021). By placing sensors in refrigerated trucks, Walmart can continuously monitor temperature conditions. Immediate alerts for temperature deviations allow for swift corrective actions, minimizing the risk of spoilage and maintaining the integrity of cold chain logistics. In this context, Walmart's use of IoT exemplifies how technology can address specific challenges in transporting temperature-sensitive products. These real-world examples highlight the diverse applications of IoT in logistics and supply chain management, showcasing how the technology is utilized to improve efficiency, reduce costs, and enhance overall visibility and control.

CHALLENGES OF IoT IN THE LOGISTICS OPERATIONS AND SUPPLY CHAIN

This section presents the IoT is challenges and hopes to face in terms of public development and more intelligent logistics. Even though IoT is everywhere, putting it in place leads to more technical, operational, economic, political, and social problems. In most cases, public information sharing is reported to involve security and privacy concerns. Because of this, showing these challenges helps researchers and business people find solutions to problems in the real world, as explained below.

Sustainable IoT Connection

Internet service disruptions appear to be one of the most significant obstacles to the correct operation of the IoT in managing supply chains and logistics (Hu et al., 2023). For instance, if an individual wants to make use of the most IoT opportunities that supply chain and logistics offer, one will need to set up a reliable network connection that is fast enough to let them gather and send data continuously, which may not be the case with the current internet attenuation (Mutie et al., 2023).

Employee Training

As the public becomes more autonomous online, it has not entirely accepted the technology, as seen in various sectors. For instance, even though IoT devices and software automate most of the supply chain's procedures, humans are still required to run those devices installed in cars, buildings, warehouses, and other places (Vidhate et al., 2022). To overcome this obstacle, the management of IoT service providers must offer the personnel proper training.

Security

Regarding implementing new ICTs in a company setting, data security is one of the most common causes of anxiety (Raza et al., 2023). When choosing a provider of supply chain IoT services, one is expected to consider and make sure that they pay special attention to finding any flaws in the way data is processed and stored and making certain that there are no leaks or threads from the outside (Alli et al., 2021).

Data Storage Concerns

The amount of data gathered by the sensors will increase in a manner that is proportional to the square root of the number of hours spent working. IoT has been used in the supply chain and logistics (Barut et al., 2022; Rahman et al., 2023), which has helped. Because of this, a significant amount of server capacity is needed to be able to store and process the information that has been received. In this case, businesses usually ask for supply chain management solutions using big data and the IoT.

Energy Consumption

IoT is made up of electronic devices that are made to work reliably for a long time. It is imperative in IoT systems used in industrial settings, where thousands of smaller IoT devices can be found (Fragapane et al., 2021; Vidhate et al., 2022). If the battery life of all IoT devices isn't very long, it can take a lot of time and money to keep a large-scale IoT system running. Because of this, it is essential to find ways to use less energy, and batteries last longer with limited energy usage during system communications.

Massive Volume of Information

Any IoT system will produce significant data, which must be moved, stored, and processed. Regarding the transfer and storage of millions or even terabytes of data, the usual methods used for these procedures are not particularly useful (Codinhoto et al., 2022; Madhavaram et al., 2022). IoT systems must use low-power, wide-area networking, NoSQL alternatives, and highly scalable cloud services to get around this problem.

Talent Shortage

Their study (Gupta & Quamara, 2020) found a severe lack of specialists who can build IoT systems, keep them running, and analyze the data IoT devices collect. This is because the education system can't keep up with new technological trends as they happen. Some are upgraded automatically, but some technical logistics require manual operation. This way, labor-intensive factors advance economic stress. Everything changes because of technology, including logistics. Connectivity and social media are raising customer expectations, which makes it more critical for a company's logistics to meet or exceed those expectations (Gomes et al., 2023). Logistics and how it is managed are changing due to technological advancements. For example, self-driving delivery vehicles, warehouse robots, and data insights that save time and money are all examples of how technology is changing logistics and how it is managed. Table 2 summarizes the difficulties encountered in IoT as applied to logistics operations and the related social, environmental, integration, and operational areas. In the next section, we'll discuss the technologies that will change supply and logistics as technology improves.

FUTURE IoT LOGISTICS AND SUPPLY CHAIN DIRECTIONS

With technological advancements, IoT in logistics and supply chains is expanding at both the industrial and consumer levels, with corporate benefits. Companies use it to collaborate across their partnerships. The supply chain has enthusiastically adopted it to manage and communicate essential product data during manufacture, warehousing, shipping, and delivery, regardless of how many organizations are involved. To standardize protocols among enterprises, a shared infrastructure is needed. As shown below, technology will significantly impact supply chains and logistics in the future.

3D Printing

Local and regional supply chains may shift or dissolve while using 3D printing since it reduces the need for long-distance shipping. Logistics operators may develop global 3D printing operations for on-demand orders in the growing aftermarket (Xiong et al., 2022). Local distribution centers' delay technology that raises customer expectations can optimize shipping operations creatively and profitably. In this age of technology, supply chain leaders who don't use new logistics technology will fall behind.

Table 2. Summary of the challenges of IoT in logistics operations and the related issues

Issue Category	Issue	Precise Description	References
Social Issues	Dynamic environments	Over time, users' actions, systems, and networks can change from intrusive to harmless.	(Hu et al., 2023)
	User acceptance and trust creation	IoT connects items under uncertain conditions. This makes trusting stakeholders difficult. IoT novices must trust it.	(K. D. Kumar et al., 2022)
	Government IOT legal frameworks	Problems could happen if IoT governance issues like accountability, transparency, and legitimacy are not addressed.	(Cahyono et al., 2023)
Environmental Issues	Disposal of wastes	IoT devices will increase e-waste using smart technologies like phones, computers, and accessories.	(Kadhim et al., 2023)
	Energy demands	Smart devices will rapidly consume more energy. Moreover, sustaining demand will be challenging with enhanced batteries and renewable sources, including solar and wind.	(Mugoni et al., 2023)
Integration Issues	Sharing Responsibilities	IoT-supported supply chains and personal health processes must make mistakes transparent.	(Kalinaki, Fahadi, et al., 2023; Z. Zhang et al., 2023)
	Innovative business models	Suppliers, manufacturers, and distributors should join the digital network and use the latest business standards.	(Al Rahamneh et al., 2023)
	The necessity for public standards	IoTs could be built using open-source software. Universal principles and procedures lag behind smart technologies.	(Z. Zhang et al., 2023)
	Finances	IoT-enabled supply chain cost pooling is complex. An IoT deployment's analytics or service may not justify the cost.	(Madhavaram et al., 2022)
	Interoperability and Scalability	IoT systems are very specialized and tailored, making supply chain scaling hard. Connecting devices and opening processes to promote interchange and reuse is complex.	(Barut et al., 2022)
Operational Issues	A lack of personal space	IoT difficulties go beyond data privacy and include customer voice recognition and vision.	(Fragapane et al., 2021)
	scarcity of security	Once the IoT is deployed, the security flaw seems minor.	(Hägele et al., 2023)
	Storage concerns	Smart gadgets generate more data, making it challenging to decide what to preserve and for how long. Energy demand will rise.	(Karmarkar, 2023)
	IoT lacks scenario planning and strategies.	Several organizations haven't set IoT goals and don't know how to use data sets to control the supply chain.	(Fragapane et al., 2021)
	Problems in Predicting Outcomes	IoT is a disruptive technology with unclear applications and uncertain effects.	(Calinescu et al., 2023)

Augmented Reality

Warehouse equipment can have barcode readers and other hands-free conveniences via heads-up visors or smart glasses. Augmented reality and cohesive management solutions increase efficiency. Due to the interconnectedness of the device, navigation, and assistance technologies make driving safer, product identification software verifies last-mile deliveries, and space optimization prompts optimized vehicle loading (Rejeb, Keogh, et al., 2021).

Big Data Analytics

Supply chains generate a constant stream of data that can be utilized to optimize the configuration of networks (Shafik et al., 2021). This data stream can aid in optimizing capacity utilization, predicting dangers, and suggesting new methods to generate revenue from supply chain components. Predictive insights enable organizations to make inventory adjustments in advance. This reduces the costs associated with warehousing and moves products closer to where they are needed.

Automation

Human-robot collaboration has recently become mainstream, with the dual goals of minimizing arduous physical labor and expanding staff numbers during labor shortages (D'Andrea, 2021). As the sophistication of future robots increases, picking, packaging, and sorting will become more prevalent, and humans or robots will make last-mile deliveries. An estimated 80% of the world's warehouses are still manually operated (Grosse & Glock, 2015). Robots armed with AI will load trailers onto automobiles most efficiently, eliminating the need for humans to do this physically tricky operation.

Self-Driving Vehicles

Reports indicate a staggering 53% of transportation costs go to the last mile of delivery (Barabas, 2023). As more than 40 companies test self-driving trucks and vans, they will likely change long-distance and last-mile deliveries in the coming years. Autonomous technology can help drivers with long, tiring trips by driving and guiding cars to some extent. Vehicles, forklifts, pallet stackers, and other machines used in warehouses and on-job sites can do some things independently (Engesser et al., 2023). The logistics industry will have to change its supply chain and data streams for auto parts to fit the new ways cars are made.

Digital Twins and Virtual Reality

To test, monitor, and manage machinery and processes, logistics companies increasingly simulate and digitally twin physical assets. MNM forecasts a $15.66 billion industry for digital twins by 2023 (Alsudani et al., 2023; Shafik & Kalinaki, 2023). Virtual reality creates immersive digital worlds for e-learning and safe training of hazardous processes. Digital visualization involves evaluating construction layouts and operational procedures, streamlining designs, and minimizing faults and costs. Virtual reality enables managers to test, operate, and maintain physical assets using IoT data.

Artificial Intelligence

The supply chain is pervasive, and therefore, organizations are now under pressure to adopt new technologies, such as AI, to remain competitive (Charles et al., 2023). This change generates a continuous flow of innovation, which promises increased supply chain performance. Today, performance might refer to enhanced connectivity, decision-making, the digital supply chain, big data analytics, and productivity. Some firms are resistant to new technologies since they are still operating comfortably.

Blockchain

The distribution industry could undergo a radical transformation by applying distributed ledger technology. Blockchains can eradicate paperwork from invoices, decrease waiting periods, stamp out fraudulent activity, and decrease supply chain costs by creating transparent and secure transactional links that simplify several layers of complexity (Kalinaki, Thilakarathne, et al., 2023). Blockchain technology must surmount the hurdles linked to its association with controversial cryptocurrencies and showcase its capacity to expand. In the future, the secure interconnection afforded by blockchain might considerably increase payment speeds and bring greater transparency to a sector whose bureaucratic complexities can be frustrating (Hasan & Salah, 2018; Li et al., 2022; Majeed et al., 2021; Rejeb, Rejeb, et al., 2021).

Cloud Logistics

Cloud-hosted analytics and procedures are the way of the future for logistics organizations, with half already using them and another fifth planning to do so. Cloud computing enables logistics firms to scale highly responsive on-demand and pay-per-use business models (Shafik et al., 2022; Y. Zhang et al., 2023). Despite data migration, security challenges, and significant data traffic, cloud logistics is increasingly tempting due to cost and time savings. As the public embraces technology and its related products and benefits in supply chain management, it improves planning, simplifies communication, and keeps track of and monitors activities (Xiaojun et al., 2023). An IoT platform can benefit small and large organizations with a defined goal. It is also vital to hire a quality design and development team. Digitally transitioning businesses must be adaptive to keep up with fast-evolving technology and business. A digital mindset and inventiveness are essential to achieving and surpassing business objectives.

CONCLUSION

IoT in the logistics industry is rapidly transforming how goods are tracked, transported, and delivered. The ability to monitor and track shipments in real-time, optimize routes and equipment performance, and streamline supply chain operations has opened new opportunities for businesses to improve efficiency, effectiveness, and sustainability. This chapter examines IoT's different perspectives, uses, and challenges in logistics. It also looks at the field's current state and where it's going in the future. From warehouse management to fleet tracking and predictive maintenance to last-mile delivery, the IoT is bringing about a paradigm shift in logistics operations. The ability to gather and analyze real-time data from various devices and systems allows for better decision-making, reduces costs, and improves customer satisfaction. Also, With the aid of IoT technologies such as RFID and GPS, real-time tracking and surveillance of consignments has become a reality. This lets logistics companies respond quickly to changes in demand, find the best routes, and cut down on transit times. Integrating IoT in logistics also presents opportunities to improve sustainability by reducing the environmental impact of transportation, minimizing waste, and optimizing the use of resources. It also enables the enhancement of security and compliance of logistics operations. However, implementing IoT in logistics operations is not without its challenges. Assuring the security and privacy of data, dealing with the sheer volume of data generated, and integrating new technologies with existing systems are just a few of the obstacles that must be overcome.

REFERENCES

Al Rahamneh, A. A., Alrawashdeh, S. T., Bawaneh, A. A., Alatyat, Z., Mohammad, A., Mohammad, A. A. S., & Al-Hawary, S. I. S. (2023). The effect of digital supply chain on lean manufacturing: A structural equation modelling approach. *Uncertain Supply Chain Management*, *11*(1), 391–402. doi:10.5267/j.uscm.2022.9.003

Alakaş, H. M., & Eren, T. (2022). *Integrated Systems and Utilization in Logistics*. doi:10.1007/978-981-16-5644-6_11

Aldowah, H., Rehman, S. U., Ghazal, S., Ivankova, G. V., Mochalina, E. P., & Goncharova, N. L. (2020). Internet of Things (IoT) in logistics. *IOP Conference Series. Materials Science and Engineering*, *940*(1), 012033. doi:10.1088/1757-899X/940/1/012033

Aljabhan, B. (2022). *A Comprehensive Analysis on the Adoption of IoT with Logistics and Supply Chain Management*. doi:10.1109/ICCSEA54677.2022.9936196

Alli, A. A., Kassim, K., Mutwalibi, N., Hamid, H., & Ibrahim, L. (2021). Secure Fog-Cloud of Things: Architectures, Opportunities and Challenges. In M. Ahmed & P. Haskell-Dowland (Eds.), *Secure Edge Computing* (1st ed., pp. 3–20). CRC Press. doi:10.1201/9781003028635-2

Alsudani, M. Q., Jaber, M. M., Ali, M. H., Abd, S. K., Alkhayyat, A., Kareem, Z. H., & Mohhan, A. R. (2023). Smart logistics with IoT-based enterprise management system using global manufacturing. *Journal of Combinatorial Optimization*, *45*(2), 1–31. doi:10.1007/s10878-022-00977-5

Anusree, P. S., & Balasubramanian, P. (2021). *IoT-Enabled Logistics for E-waste Management and Sustainability*. doi:10.1007/978-981-33-6691-6_9

Barabas, M. (2023). *Last Mile Delivery Costs: The Most Expensive Step in the Supply Chain*. Elite Extra. https://eliteextra.com/last-mile-delivery-costs-the-most-expensive-step-in-the-supply-chain/

Barut, A., Citil, M., Ahmed, Z., Sinha, A., & Abbas, S. (2022). How do economic and financial factors influence green logistics? A comparative analysis of E7 and G7 nations. *Environmental Science and Pollution Research International*, *30*(1), 1011–1022. doi:10.1007/s11356-022-22252-0 PMID:35908030

Bhutta, M. N. M., & Ahmad, M. (2021). Secure Identification, Traceability and Real-Time Tracking of Agricultural Food Supply during Transportation Using Internet of Things. *IEEE Access : Practical Innovations, Open Solutions*, *9*, 65660–65675. doi:10.1109/ACCESS.2021.3076373

Cahyono, Y., Purwoko, D., Koho, I. R., Setiani, A., Supendi, S., Setyoko, P. I., Sosiady, M., & Wijoyo, H. (2023). The role of supply chain management practices on competitive advantage and performance of halal agroindustry SMEs. *Uncertain Supply Chain Management*, *11*(1), 153–160. doi:10.5267/j.uscm.2022.10.012

Calinescu, T., Likhonosova, G., & Zelenko, O. (2023). Circular Economy: Ukraine's Reserves and the Consequences of the Global Recession. doi:10.1007/978-3-031-23463-7_16

Charles, V., Emrouznejad, A., & Gherman, T. (2023). A critical analysis of the integration of blockchain and artificial intelligence for supply chain. *Annals of Operations Research*, *327*(1), 7–47. doi:10.1007/s10479-023-05169-w PMID:36718465

Chen, Y.-T., Sun, E. W., Chang, M.-F., & Lin, Y.-B. (2021). Pragmatic real-time logistics management with traffic IoT infrastructure: Big data predictive analytics of freight travel time for Logistics 4.0. *International Journal of Production Economics*, *238*, 108157. doi:10.1016/j.ijpe.2021.108157

Codinhoto, R., Fialho, B. C., Pinti, L., & Fabricio, M. M. (2022). BIM and IoT for Facilities Management. In *Research Anthology on BIM and Digital Twins in Smart Cities* (pp. 407–429). IGI Global. doi:10.4018/978-1-6684-7548-5.ch019

D'Andrea, R. (2021). *Human–Robot Collaboration: The Future of Smart Warehousing*. doi:10.1007/978-3-030-61093-7_12

de Vass, T., Shee, H., & Miah, S. J. (2020). *Iot in supply chain management: a narrative on retail sector sustainability*. doi:10.1080/13675567.2020.1787970

DHL. (2023). *The value of IoT in supply chains*. DHL. https://www.dhl.com/global-en/delivered/digitalization/the-value-of-iot-in-supply-chains.html

Ding, Y., Jin, M., Li, S., & Feng, D. (2021). Smart logistics based on the internet of things technology: An overview. *International Journal of Logistics*, *24*(4), 323–345. doi:10.1080/13675567.2020.1757053

Engesser, V., Rombaut, E., Vanhaverbeke, L., & Lebeau, P. (2023). Autonomous Delivery Solutions for Last-Mile Logistics Operations: A Literature Review and Research Agenda. *Sustainability, 15*(3), 2774. doi:10.3390/su15032774

Evans, S. (2023). *Amazon Launches Heavy-Lifting Fulfillment Center Robot*. IoT World. https://www.iotworldtoday.com/robotics/amazon-launches-heavy-lifting-fulfillment-center-robot#close-modal

Fragapane, G., Hvolby, H. H., Sgarbossa, F., & Strandhagen, J. O. (2021). *Autonomous mobile robots in sterile instrument logistics: an evaluation of the material handling system for a strategic fit framework*. doi:10.1080/09537287.2021.1884914

Gomes, L. A. de V., de Faria, A. M., Braz, A. C., de Mello, A. M., Borini, F. M., & Ometto, A. R. (2023). Circular ecosystem management: Orchestrating ecosystem value proposition and configuration. *International Journal of Production Economics*, *256*, 108725. doi:10.1016/j.ijpe.2022.108725

Grosse, E. H., & Glock, C. H. (2015). The effect of worker learning on manual order picking processes. *International Journal of Production Economics*, *170*, 882–890. doi:10.1016/j.ijpe.2014.12.018

Gusmão Caiado, G., Luiz Goncalves Quelhas, O., Felipe Scavarda, L., Gayialis, S. P., Kechagias, E. P., Konstantakopoulos, G. D., & Papadopoulos, G. A. (2022). A Predictive Maintenance System for Reverse Supply Chain Operations. *Logistics*, *6*(1), 4. doi:10.3390/logistics6010004

Hägele, S., Grosse, E. H., & Ivanov, D. (2023). Supply chain resilience: A tertiary study. *International Journal of Integrated Supply Management*, *16*(1), 52. doi:10.1504/IJISM.2023.127660

Hasan, H. R., & Salah, K. (2018). Proof of Delivery of Digital Assets Using Blockchain and Smart Contracts. *IEEE Access : Practical Innovations, Open Solutions*, *6*, 65439–65448. doi:10.1109/ACCESS.2018.2876971

Hoang, M. T., Spandonidis, C., Sedikos, E., Giannopoulos, F., Petsa, A., Theodoropoulos, P., Chatzis, K., & Galiatsatos, N. (2022). A Novel Intelligent IoT System for Improving the Safety and Planning of Air Cargo Operations. *Signals*, *3*(1), 95–112. doi:10.3390/signals3010008

Hopkins, J., & Hawking, P. (2018). Big Data Analytics and IoT in logistics: A case study. *International Journal of Logistics Management*, *29*(2), 575–591. doi:10.1108/IJLM-05-2017-0109

Hu, H., Xu, J., Liu, M., & Lim, M. K. (2023). Vaccine supply chain management: An intelligent system utilizing blockchain, IoT and machine learning. *Journal of Business Research*, *156*, 113480. doi:10.1016/j.jbusres.2022.113480 PMID:36506475

Kadhim, J. Q., Aljazaery, I. A. (2023). *EBSCOhost | 161238003 | Enhancement of Online Education in Engineering College Based on Mobile Wireless Communication Networks and IOT*. International Journal of Emerging Technologies in Learning.

Kalinaki, K., Fahadi, M., Alli, A. A., Shafik, W., Yasin, M., & Mutwalibi, N. (2023). Artificial Intelligence of Internet of Medical Things (AIoMT) in Smart Cities: A Review of Cybersecurity for Smart Healthcare. In Handbook of Security and Privacy of AI-Enabled Healthcare Systems and Internet of Medical Things (pp. 271–292). CRC Press. https://doi.org/ doi:10.1201/9781003370321-11

Kalinaki, K., Namuwaya, S., Mwamini, A., & Namuwaya, S. (2023). Scaling Up Customer Support Using Artificial Intelligence and Machine Learning Techniques. In *Contemporary Approaches of Digital Marketing and the Role of Machine Intelligence* (pp. 23–45). IGI Global. doi:10.4018/978-1-6684-7735-9.ch002

Kalinaki, K., Thilakarathne, N. N., Mubarak, H. R., Malik, O. A., & Abdullatif, M. (2023). Cybersafe Capabilities and Utilities for Smart Cities. In *Cybersecurity for Smart Cities* (pp. 71–86). Springer., doi:10.1007/978-3-031-24946-4_6

Karmarkar, U. (2023). *Service industrialization*. Elgar Encyclopedia of Services. doi:10.4337/9781802202595.Service.Industrialization

Kaur, G., Tomar, P., & Singh, P. (2018). Design of Cloud-Based Green IoT Architecture for Smart Cities. *Studies in Big Data*, *30*, 315–333. doi:10.1007/978-3-319-60435-0_13

Khan, Y., Su'ud, M. B. M., Alam, M. M., Ahmad, S. F., Ahmad, A. Y. A. B., & Khan, N. (2022). Application of Internet of Things (IoT) in Sustainable Supply Chain Management. *Sustainability, 15*(1), 694. doi:10.3390/su15010694

Kumar, D., Kr Singh, R., Mishra, R., & Fosso Wamba, S. (2022). Applications of the internet of things for optimizing warehousing and logistics operations: A systematic literature review and future research directions. *Computers & Industrial Engineering*, *171*, 108455. doi:10.1016/j.cie.2022.108455

Kumar, K. D., Venkata Rathnam, T., Venkata Ramana, R., Sudhakara, M., & Poluru, R. K. (2022). Towards the Integration of Blockchain and IoT for Security Challenges in IoT. In *Research Anthology on Convergence of Blockchain, Internet of Things, and Security* (pp. 193–209). IGI Global. doi:10.4018/978-1-6684-7132-6.ch012

Lagorio, A., Zenezini, G., Mangano, G., & Pinto, R. (2022). A systematic literature review of innovative technologies adopted in logistics management. *International Journal of Logistics*, *25*(7), 1043–1066. doi:10.1080/13675567.2020.1850661

Li, D., Deng, L., Cai, Z., & Souri, A. (2022). Blockchain as a service models in the Internet of Things management: Systematic review. *Transactions on Emerging Telecommunications Technologies*, *33*(4), e4139. doi:10.1002/ett.4139

Madhavaram, S., Manis, K. T., Rashidi-Sabet, S., & Taylor, D. F. (2022). Capability bundling for effective supply chain management: An integrative framework and research agenda. *Journal of Business Logistics*. Advance online publication. doi:10.1111/jbl.12329

Maersk. (2023). *Remote Container Management*. Maersk. https://www.maersk.com/digital-solutions/captain-peter/services

Majeed, U., Khan, L. U., Yaqoob, I., Kazmi, S. M. A., Salah, K., & Hong, C. S. (2021). Blockchain for IoT-based smart cities: Recent advances, requirements, and future challenges. *Journal of Network and Computer Applications*, *181*, 103007. doi:10.1016/j.jnca.2021.103007

Mashayekhy, Y., Babaei, A., Yuan, X.-M., & Xue, A. (2022). Impact of Internet of Things (IoT) on Inventory Management: A Literature Survey. *Logistics*, *6*(2), 33. doi:10.3390/logistics6020033

Mohammad, S., Masuri, M. A. A., Salim, S., & Razak, M. R. A. (2021). Development of IoT Based Logistic Vehicle Maintenance System. *Proceeding - 2021 IEEE 17th International Colloquium on Signal Processing and Its Applications, CSPA 2021*, 127–132. 10.1109/CSPA52141.2021.9377290

Mugoni, E., Nyagadza, B., & Hove, P. K. (2023). Green reverse logistics technology impact on agricultural entrepreneurial marketing firms' operational efficiency and sustainable competitive advantage. *Sustainable Technology and Entrepreneurship*, *2*(2), 100034. doi:10.1016/j.stae.2022.100034

Mutie, M. D., Odock, S., & Litondo, K. (2023). Effect of green logistics practices on performance of logistics firms in Kenya. *DBA Africa Management Review*. http://erepository.uonbi.ac.ke/handle/11295/154439

Nagarajan, S. M., Deverajan, G. G., Chatterjee, P., Alnumay, W., & Muthukumaran, V. (2022). Integration of IoT based routing process for food supply chain management in sustainable smart cities. *Sustainable Cities and Society*, *76*, 103448. doi:10.1016/j.scs.2021.103448

Nižetić, S., Šolić, P., López-de-Ipiña González-de-Artaza, D., & Patrono, L. (2020). Internet of Things (IoT): Opportunities, issues and challenges towards a smart and sustainable future. *Journal of Cleaner Production*, *274*, 122877. doi:10.1016/j.jclepro.2020.122877 PMID:32834567

Öztuna, B. (2022). Logistics 4.0 and Technologic Applications. *Accounting, Finance, Sustainability, Governance and Fraud*, 9–27. doi:10.1007/978-981-16-5644-6_2

Pundir, A. K., Jagannath, J. D., & Ganapathy, L. (2019). Improving supply chain visibility using IoT-internet of things. *2019 IEEE 9th Annual Computing and Communication Workshop and Conference, CCWC 2019*, 156–162. 10.1109/CCWC.2019.8666480

Qader, G., Junaid, M., Abbas, Q., & Mubarik, M. S. (2022). Industry 4.0 enables supply chain resilience and supply chain performance. *Technological Forecasting and Social Change*, *185*, 122026. doi:10.1016/j.techfore.2022.122026

Radhakrishnan, S. (2021). *How Walmart Leverages IoT to Keep Your Ice Cream Frozen*. Walmart. https://corporate.walmart.com/news/2021/01/14/how-walmart-leverages-iot-to-keep-your-ice-cream-frozen

Rahman, A., Hasan, K., Kundu, D., Islam, M. J., Debnath, T., Band, S. S., & Kumar, N. (2023). On the ICN-IoT with federated learning integration of communication: Concepts, security-privacy issues, applications, and future perspectives. *Future Generation Computer Systems*, *138*, 61–88. doi:10.1016/j.future.2022.08.004

Raza, Z., Woxenius, J., Vural, C. A., & Lind, M. (2023). Digital transformation of maritime logistics: Exploring trends in the liner shipping segment. *Computers in Industry*, *145*, 103811. doi:10.1016/j.compind.2022.103811

Rejeb, A., Simske, J., Keogh, J. G., Rejeb, K., Simske, S. J., & Org, J. (2021). Blockchain technology in the smart city: a bibliometric review. *Quality & Quantity 2021 56:5*, *56*(5), 2875–2906. doi:10.1007/s11135-021-01251-2

Rejeb, A., Keogh, J. G., Leong, G. K., & Treiblmaier, H. (2021). Potentials and challenges of augmented reality smart glasses in logistics and supply chain management: A systematic literature review. *International Journal of Production Research*, *59*(12), 3747–3776. doi:10.1080/00207543.2021.1876942

Shafik, W., & Kalinaki, K. (2023). Smart City Ecosystem: An Exploration of Requirements, Architecture, Applications, Security, and Emerging Motivations. In Handbook of Research on Network-Enabled IoT Applications for Smart City Services (pp. 75–98). IGI Global. doi:10.4018/979-8-3693-0744-1.ch005

Shafik, W., Matinkhah, S. M., & Shokoor, F. (2022). Recommendation System Comparative Analysis: Internet of Things aided Networks. *EAI Endorsed Transactions on Internet of Things*, *8*(29), e5. doi:10.4108/eetiot.v8i29.1108

Shafik, W., Mojtaba Matinkhah, S., Shokoor, F., & Nur Sanda, M. (2021). Internet of Things-Based Energy Efficiency Optimization Model in Fog Smart Cities. *JOIV : International Journal on Informatics Visualization*, *5*(2), 105–112. doi:10.30630/joiv.5.2.373

Shah, S., Bolton, M., & Menon, S. (2020). A Study of Internet of Things (IoT) and its Impacts on Global Supply Chains. *Proceedings of International Conference on Computation, Automation and Knowledge Management, ICCAKM 2020*, 245–250. 10.1109/ICCAKM46823.2020.9051474

Shee, H. (2023). Internet of Things: Applications and Challenges for Supply Chain Management. The Palgrave Handbook of Supply Chain Management, 1–19. doi:10.1007/978-3-030-89822-9_78-1

Song, Y., Yu, F. R., Zhou, L., Yang, X., & He, Z. (2021). Applications of the Internet of Things (IoT) in Smart Logistics: A Comprehensive Survey. *IEEE Internet of Things Journal*, *8*(6), 4250–4274. doi:10.1109/JIOT.2020.3034385

Tan, W. C., & Sidhu, M. S. (2022). Review of RFID and IoT integration in supply chain management. *Operations Research Perspectives*, *9*, 100229. doi:10.1016/j.orp.2022.100229

Tran-Dang, H., Krommenacker, N., Charpentier, P., & Kim, D.-S. (2022). The Internet of Things for Logistics: Perspectives, Application Review, and Challenges. *IETE Technical Review*, *39*(1), 93–121. doi:10.1080/02564602.2020.1827308

Tsang, Y. P., Yang, T., Chen, Z. S., Wu, C. H., & Tan, K. H. (2022). How is extended reality bridging human and cyber-physical systems in the IoT-empowered logistics and supply chain management? *Internet of Things : Engineering Cyber Physical Human Systems*, *20*, 100623. doi:10.1016/j.iot.2022.100623

Vidhate, A. V., Saraf, C. R., Wani, M. A., Waghmare, S. S., & Edgar, T. (2022). Applying Blockchain Security for Agricultural Supply Chain Management. In *Research Anthology on Convergence of Blockchain, Internet of Things, and Security* (pp. 1229–1239). IGI Global. doi:10.4018/978-1-6684-7132-6.ch065

Xiaojun, L., Ming, S., & Yuzhuo, L. (2023). Research on logistics service recommendation model and application under mobile cloud environment. *Optik (Stuttgart)*, *273*, 170446. doi:10.1016/j.ijleo.2022.170446

Xiong, Y., Lu, H., Li, G. D., Xia, S. M., Wang, Z. X., & Xu, Y. F. (2022). Game changer or threat: The impact of 3D printing on the logistics supplier circular supply chain. *Industrial Marketing Management*, *106*, 461–475. doi:10.1016/j.indmarman.2022.03.002

Zhang, Y., Sóti, G., Hein, B., & Wurll, C. (2023). KI5GRob: Fusing Cloud Computing and AI for Scalable Robotic System in Production and Logistics. doi:10.1007/978-3-031-22216-0_47

Zhang, Z., Jin, J., Li, S., & Zhang, Y. (2023). Digital transformation of incumbent firms from the perspective of portfolios of innovation. *Technology in Society*, *72*, 102149. doi:10.1016/j.techsoc.2022.102149

Chapter 6
Logistics With the Internet of Things:
Challenges, Perspectives, and Applications

Imdad Ali Shah
School of Computing Science, Taylor's University, Malaysia

N. Z. Jhanjhi
https://orcid.org/0000-0001-8116-4733
School of Computing Science, Taylor's University, Malaysia

Humaira Ashraf
https://orcid.org/0000-0001-5067-3172
School of Computing Science, Taylor's University, Malaysia

ABSTRACT

The objective of logistics is to meet client demands in a timely and economical manner. The internet of things (IoT) vision allows numerous embedded, resource-constrained devices, things, and people to connect via the Internet protocol for constant data exchange. In this vision, logistics is a crucial player positioned to achieve complete visibility and transparency by utilizing pervasive interconnectivity to gather reliable and secure real-time data. It is essential for all retailers and logistics companies who want to preserve their leading positions to stay on top of logistical challenges and trends. A global supply chain disruption resulted from COVID-19's imbalance in the supply and demand for goods. 2020 saw a decrease in global productivity because of the pandemic and the lockdown. Due to this, the idea of digital transformation has gained traction during the past two years.

DOI: 10.4018/979-8-3693-3816-2.ch006

1. INTRODUCTION

We also discuss what IoT security is and why it matters. We also discuss how to secure networks, devices, and data in IoT environments. Development teams wish to ensure that their IoT projects are properly secured (J. Li, 2017, M. Liu, C. Qiu 2019). Read more about logistics challenges, IoT solutions, and IoT adoption outcomes. IoT adoption is high in industries with many assets, such as manufacturing, transportation, and utilities (L. Barreto, A. Trappey, S. Jeschke, 2017). Together with warehousing, these two industries were the front-runners in embedding connected systems even before the term "Internet of Things" was coined. These industries were thriving because of their (T. Qu, 2016, Y. Zhang, 2018) early adoption, which freed up other industrial segments to restructure their supply chain management. (T. Gregor, T. Gregor, Angelopoulos, 2017). The fact that IoT technology is complex and time-consuming contributes to the paucity of studies on the relationship between IoT and warehousing. Given that it forms the foundation for the strategy, how it will be implemented, and organisational traditions, this price must be far higher than the cost (Ramli, R. M., 2017, Meiyanti, R., Alguliyev, R., 2018). The value that a chain creates is necessary for every firm to exist. Understanding and meeting the value-based approach, or the demands of the customers, is at the heart of the company's strategy.

Customer attitudes have drastically changed from the last time as IoT utilisation has increased. Still, the topic hasn't been given a thorough investigation. The empirical studies from the papers chosen for this review discuss decision analysis. The deployment of IoT-related technology must be overseen by the logistics and warehousing sector. It is necessary to determine which technological systems are used the most frequently so their utility can be more thoroughly examined (Dhonju, G. R., Yang, L., Abebe, B. 2019). It's also critical to consider the implementation needs closely related to the ambition to seize fresh opportunities for expansion in logistics and industry. Some metrics that can be used for evaluation include stockout rate, orders despatched on time, shipment accuracy, and throughput. The majority of IoT technology studies also integrate data from several industries, leading to more conclusive findings that apply to a specific area (Alharmoodi, B. Y. R, Gouveia, L. B., 2020, Sharma, 2021). On the other hand, using data from multiple situations increases the possibility of confounding effects, which might result in incorrect results. Therefore, future studies utilising varied company data will be required to address this problem. They thus quickly recognised the advantages of new sensor types, communication technology, and service-oriented architecture. E-commerce has rapidly expanded in the global market in recent years, and logistics has had to contend with rising demand and a labour shortage and cheap wages. (Liu, D., Agbozo, E., Albrahim, R., 2018), Finding creative ways to optimize important processes to handle the problems ahead is currently the most pressing issue. Modern Internet-of-Things techniques will simplify and streamline the process, of physical connectivity through the Internet in Figure 1.

The Internet of Things is a network that enables anything to connect to the Internet to exchange data, facilitate communication, and enable intelligent searching, source identification, and location tracking. Service-oriented architecture and associated technologies are closely tied to the Internet of Things (Alqudah, M. A., 2021, Yang, R.,2020, Al-rawahna, A. S. M 2019). IoT technology standardization is crucial because it will promote better interoperability and lower entry barriers. (Suleimany, M., AlMendah, O. M, 2021), With the aid of proprietary technologies and inaccessible services, numerous manufacturers are developing vertical solutions. To transform this "Intranet of Things" into the more comprehensive "Internet of Things," standards must be developed.

This chapter is focused on the bellow points: -

- We discussed the IoT and logistics.
- We discussed logistics-related IoT Applications.
- Real-time location Tracking Mechanism
- We discussed security issues and challenges of the Internet of Things in logistics.
- We provided future work and recommendations.

Figure 1. IoT physical layers connectivity

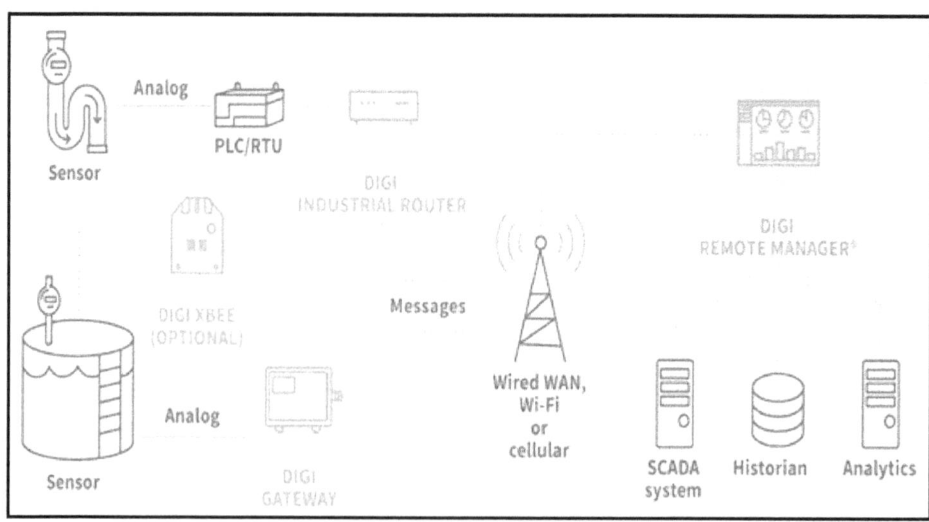

2. LITERATURE REVIEW

IoT has recently been used in intelligent logistics. Most primarily concentrate on IoT architecture and several IoT application elements in smart logistics. Only a tiny portion of these studies address issues with wireless communication technology, intelligent logistics development (Alguliyev, R., Joshi, P. R., 2018, Ari, A. A. A.,2020). The IoT revolution is just getting started, however. Less than 1% of all physical items that can be connected to the Internet have done so thus far. In terms of statistics, that means that, of the estimated 1.5 trillion objects on Earth, only about 15 billion are currently connected to the Internet. In a developed country, the typical customer is surrounded by dozens of connectable objects. These include home furnishings, apparel, wearable technology, cars, computers, consumer electronics, and communication gadgets. (Ferrag, M. A., 2020, Shah, I. A., 2022, Razuleu, L. A., 2018), We investigated the most important Internet of Things (IoT) technologies related to automated business process support in logistics. They introduced innovative products like WSN and RFID. Highlighted the latest requirements and potential for IoT-based cyber-physical logistics systems. Demonstrates the idea of CPLS, lists the fundamental technology layers, and uses a distribution center as an example of a real-world setting to illustrate the evolution of CPLS (Nzimakwe, T. I., Nautiyal, L., 2018, Pal SK, 2019). After analyzing the features of cloud computing and IoT, they provide solutions based on cloud computing and IoT to realise logistics information interchange and data sharing. Unfortunately, the authors only analyse and use a small portion of the IoT's core technologies, ignoring numerous others and their effects on smart logistics (AI). (Froehlich, 2020, Baharin, A. M.,2021, Ujjan, R. M. A.,2022). Logistics and transportation operations have long been fraught with dangers due to unpredictable weather, a high likelihood of fraud, and many assets to oversee. Logistics may now be regulated entirely with the help of the Internet of Things, eliminating any potential threats to the delivery process, or at least minimizing their effects. (Qi, R.,2017, Adjei-Bamfo, P., 2019, Qi, M.,2021) Businesses can use the Internet of Things to analyze routes, track the whereabouts of individual vehicles, and identify the most economical and environmentally friendly delivery strategies. A thorough understanding of the delivery process enables business owners to assess worker performance, reward best practices, respond quickly to issues that arise, and handle them skillfully to lower losses and risks. (Cheng, B.,2017, Gershon, D., AlEnezi, A., 2018), A significant advantage of IoT in logistics is increased public safety. Business managers can monitor their workforce's physical health and assess hazards using smart devices and wearables in logistics. Sensor-based apps can shield employers from hazardous materials, and drivers can be monitored to see whether they are following safety procedures. (Nagowah, S. D., Pradhan, P. 2018), Even technologies that track employees' routines and use the data to assess staff effectiveness exist. By using these insights, managers can better align operations, identify problems with time management or planning, and gain a better knowledge of employee efficiency. (Elezaj, O., Elezaj, O., Henriksen, H. Z 2018) Global logistics and transportation firms are embracing IoT and using big data and linked technologies to improve their operations' efficiency, sustainability, and effectiveness. the general architecture of logistics in Figure 2.

Here are a few noteworthy instances of IoT in logistics from top companies in the sector: DB Schenker, Nippon Express, DHL, and Maersk. (Chishiro, H., 2018, Chishiro, H, Máchová, R. 2017), thanks to the Internet of Things, logistics managers now have control and transparency over their operations that they could not have predicted. Technology can help streamline delivery and offer insights for better decision-making because of real-time data exchange and device-to-device connections.

As much data as possible can be gathered, analyzed, and reported on by the Internet of Things (IoT) devices. How about the previously mentioned predictive maintenance (Mahmood, Z., Le, N. T., 2016). The technicians may now plan downtime for when the equipment is already not in use, preventing delays in delivery times. Are you concerned that a storm may disrupt a shipment? The fleet can be automatically rerouted thanks to advanced analytics, keeping them safe and the load on schedule. An effective supply chain must deliver goods from the manufacturer to the final customer on time and by the requirements (Koo, E., Ma, L., Pathak, A., 2019). IoT has not been approached holistically, and the lack of cohesive concepts that unite IoT results in siloed systems that do not allow interoperability. This strategy is an expansion of the "IoT devices upload data only to a single application service provider"

Figure 2. The general architecture of logistics

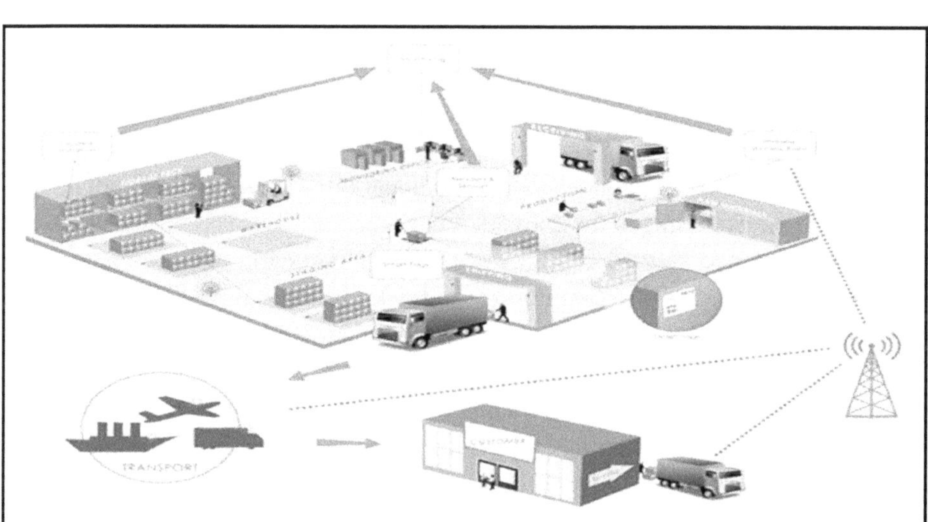

communication model for a single device to cloud communications. Businesses in the transportation and logistics sectors are far ahead of other industries and businesses in utilising the potential of data-driven technology (Maharaj, M. S,2019, Alguliyev, R., Distel, B., 2018). The logistics companies that convey goods have networks that are widely dispersed by nature, and they participate in the quick dissemination of information regarding the conditions of devices. IoT simply refers to networking physical items with sensors, software, and other technologies built in. Smart homes, smart cities, and other related developments are made possible by IoT technology. (Al-Nidawi, Sagarik, D., Alketbi, H., 2018). IoT helps to save time and energy and makes tasks appear simple and comfortable. It is used in every industry, including agriculture, healthcare, automobiles, and aerospace.

3. EVALUATION OF IoT AND LOGISTICS

IoT applications in the logistics sector go beyond just asset management and monitoring. However, detecting bottlenecks that can cause these assets to break down is its most practical application. Instead of relying on periodic inspection methods, the Internet of Things has enabled companies to adopt condition-based and predictive maintenance (Alexopoulos, 2019, Muzafar, S., 2022, Ujjan, R. M. A.,2022). These IoT prediction applications will assist businesses in spotting flaws before they have serious consequences. Companies in the logistics industry will be able to enhance their decision-making techniques and develop more efficient inspection and repair plans. Additionally, these proactive asset insights will assist businesses in lowering risks and downtime, leading to smooth process execution and on-time delivery operations. Managers of logistics oversee more than just the transportation of assets. They are also accountable for the cargo's security as well as the safety of the truck drivers. The buzz surrounding self-driving and autonomous cars are at an all-time high. Businesses will first introduce the idea of autonomous vehicles by utilising such IoT infrastructures in logistics (Muzafar, S, Hamid, B.,2020, Kumar, P.,2016). To create intelligent driving routes and directions, data about numerous cargo criteria will be evaluated and processed. As a result, logistics can save on operating expenses, cut down on traffic accidents, and guarantee timely freight delivery. Mobile phones are anticipated to have more mobile phones in 2020 than people on the planet, so mobile computing is likely to continue to develop. Sensor technology has advanced and become more accessible thanks to the consumerization of IT (Sharma, P., 2016, Shah, I. A.,2022, Humayun, M., 2020). Wireless communication will advance to a new degree of maturity with the transition to 5G, linking anything at any time. New data-based services will be made possible by big data and cloud technology.

- Along the supply chain.

Customers of businesses are requesting integrity control, particularly for sensitive commodities. Logistics organisations need transparency into the networks and assets being used to continuously improve efficiency and network utilization. Logistics solutions are required. (Alamri, M, Hamid, B., 2019, Hussain, S. J., 2021), Convergence of Logistics and Technology Trends IoT-enabled Capabilities15 IoT holds the possibility of significant benefits for logistics providers. (Shah, I. A., 2022), applications of IoT technology are expanding along with advances. The processes involved in managing inventories are a particular source of difficulty for each warehouse. To streamline inventory management, IoT and RFID technology predict future orders by monitoring factors like product durability, air humidity, temperature, and other factors that could lead to product damage. The IoT system's functionality and growth are based on RIFD technology (Shah, I. A., 2023, Ujjan, R. M. A., 2022). Autonomous systems must be customised for the storage environment to reduce the risk of collisions. By leaving a barrier in place, existing autonomous systems are frequently limited to moving across a limited number of previously established corridors. The creation of artificial intelligence that can make comparable decisions to those made by humans offers a potential remedy for these and other implementation-related issues. As storage capacity grows, there is a rising need for modern warehouse management technologies and the automation of warehouse operations. One of the issues that EU countries are dealing with is the decline in the number of workers available, increasing the possibility of warehouse technology development (Ujjan, Raja, 2020, Muzafar, S., 2022, Dawson, M., 2022, Gaur, L,2022). Adopting intelligent technologies that enhance storage procedures is frequently considered a reaction to such requirements. Glasses that alert a worker to an item to take are one example of technology. Using numerous sensors generates much information, which is then saved on the anticipated servers. The Big Data Concept is a new way of thinking for warehouse organisations and technologies that makes it possible to track and predict client requests, making stock management simpler. However, as a result, there are some difficulties and risks that must be adequately addressed in the installation of intelligent systems. Security is one of the fundamental issues with industry 4.0-based warehouses (Ujjan, R.M.A., 2022 Jhanjhi, N. Z, 2022). The current encryption techniques are no longer adequate to provide a high enough level of security. Additionally, there aren't enough software programs available to manage, examine, and print this much data. Customer service for logistics. They chose to use cloud computing technology, which stores data on servers that are frequently located in other countries due to its simplicity, convenience, speed, and ease of logistical organisation. (Ujjan, R. M. A., 2022) The security of such systems include restrictions on data available in addition to encryption protection.

However, the difficulties go beyond data protection and have the requirement to save operating expenses. Some of the warehouse and logistics activities will likely be outsourced and other businesses that do not focus on logistics will start to do so. In addition, augmented reality is a technology that has applications in warehouse systems. Real-time digital features can be added to reality using augmented reality, the general architecture of IoT in Figure 3.

4. REAL-TIME LOCATION TRACKING MECHANISM

It enables transportation firms to keep an eye on their cargo and trucks. You can monitor vehicle deliveries and enhance last-mile delivery with the route management solution. To improve supply chain management effectiveness, get tagged goods and vehicles' real-time locations displayed on the dashboard, applications IoT in the logistics in Figure 4.

5. SECURITY ISSUES AND CHALLENGES IN LOGISTICS AND IoT APPLICATIONS

A network of intelligent gadgets known as the "Internet of Things" connects and uses the internet to exchange data without human involvement. Smart technologies can

Figure 3. The general architecture of IoT

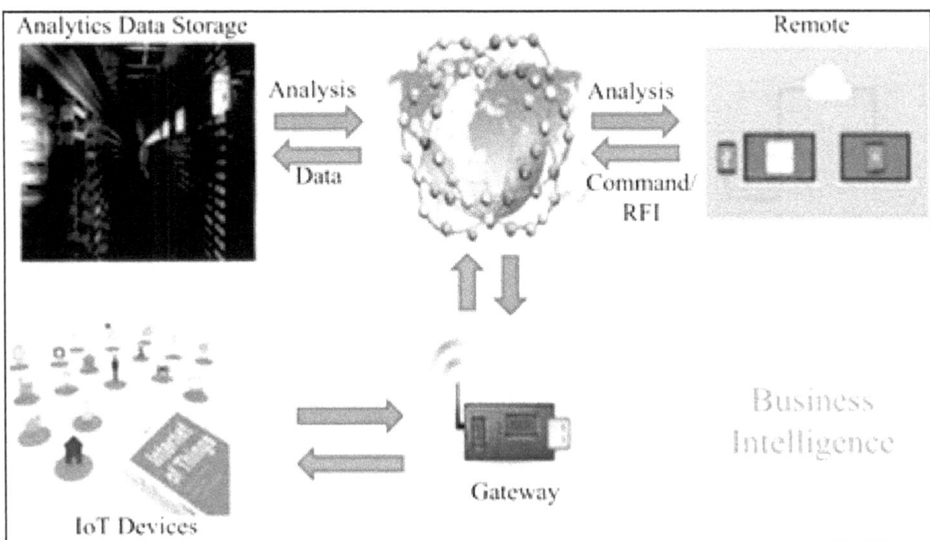

Figure 4. Overview of applications IoT in the logistics

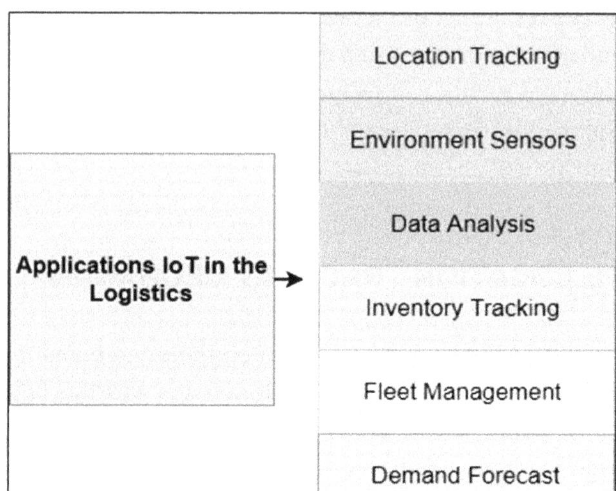

forecast demand IoT ecosystem's structured data also ensures transparency, which enables you to make timely decisions based on solid information. In conclusion, organized data is critical in streamlining the warehousing and shipping proc, and security IoT in the logistics in Figure 5.

Figure 5. Overview of security IoT in the logistics

Home automation	systems monitor and control home attributes like temperature, lighting, entertainment systems, appliances, and alarm systems
smart cities	Use data gathered by smart devices to improve infrastructure, public utilities, and services. Such devices can be connected sensors, lights, meters, waste bins, and air quality monitoring systems
Smart warehouses	use automated and interconnected technologies to help businesses increase productivity and efficiency. Common components of a smart warehouse include robots, drones, radio frequency identification (RFID) scanners, artificial intelligence-driven programs, and complex warehouse management software

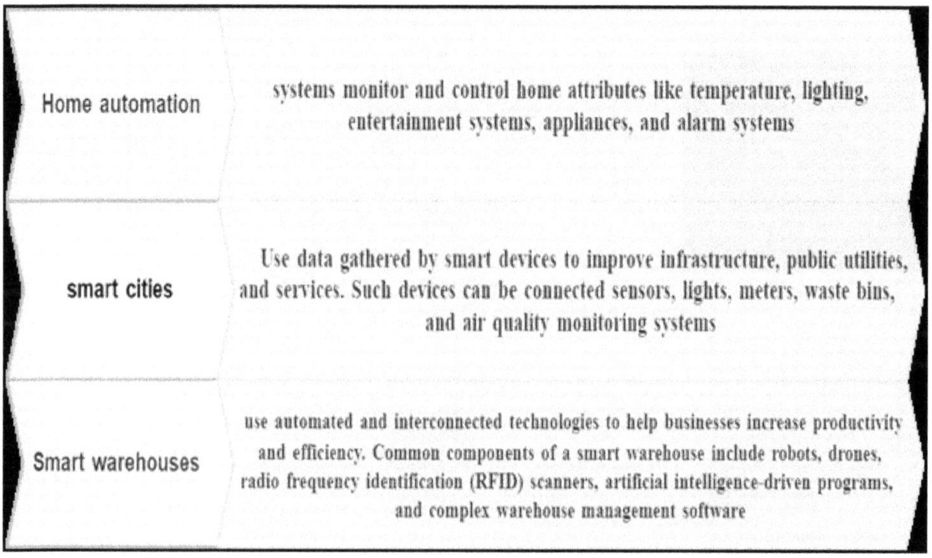

6. DISCUSSION

In a developed country, the typical customer is surrounded by dozens of connectable objects. These include home furnishings, apparel, wearable technology, cars, computers, consumer electronics, and communication gadgets. We investigated the most important Internet of Things (IoT) technologies related to automated business process support in logistics. They introduced innovative products like WSN and RFID. Highlighted the latest requirements and potential for IoT-based cyber-physical logistics systems. Demonstrates the idea of CPLS, lists the fundamental technology layers, and uses a distribution center as an example of a real-world setting to illustrate the evolution of CPLS. After analyzing the features of cloud computing and IoT, they provide solutions based on cloud computing and IoT to realise logistics information interchange and data sharing. Unfortunately, the authors only analyse and use a small portion of the IoT's core technologies, ignoring numerous others and their effects on smart logistics (AI). Logistics and transportation operations have long been fraught with dangers due to unpredictable weather, a high likelihood of fraud, and many assets to oversee. Logistics may now be regulated entirely with the help of the Internet of Things, eliminating any potential threats to the delivery process, or at least minimizing their effects. Businesses can use the Internet of Things to analyze routes, track the whereabouts of individual vehicles, and identify the most economical and environmentally friendly delivery strategies. A thorough understanding of the delivery process enables business owners to assess worker performance, reward best practices, respond quickly to issues that arise, and handle them skillfully to lower losses and risks. A significant advantage of IoT in logistics is increased public safety. Business managers can monitor their workforce's physical health and assess hazards using smart devices and wearables in logistics. Sensor-based apps can shield employers from hazardous materials, and drivers can be monitored to see whether they are following safety procedures.

For decades, it has been possible to track items using technology thanks to various information and communication technologies. Therefore, the logistics function can benefit from the advancements brought forth by the IoT. The right place aspect is guaranteed through location tracking. The correct quality is ensured by monitoring the product's condition. This data offers the required visibility for responding to unforeseen situations, taking appropriate action at the right moment, and streamlining the entire process. From a management standpoint, the food supply chain is complicated because it deals with perishable goods and has several participants throughout the chain. According to FAO estimates, 30–50% of the food produced in North America and Europe is wasted or lost, making up one-third of all food produced globally. Food supply networks are another essential component of every economy that cannot be offshored. Therefore, minimizing the formation of unnecessary food waste and ensuring food safety and efficiency along the entire food supply chain is a compelling potential of the application of IoT, which accounts for the increasing interest in this field.

Chapter's Contribution and Recommendations

Our contribution to this chapter is that production and logistics are evolving because of new digital and IoT technology. An expanding range of production and warehousing activities are being monitored, automated, and supported by such systems, whether learning more about these processes or regulating them more effectively. This technology is constantly evolving. Sensors are becoming more intelligent, adaptive, and energy efficient as they get smaller. They send data fed into increasingly complicated infrastructures to be analysed and analyzed-faster rates, monitoring the state of production gear even in adverse situations. A few IoT applications for logistics will quicken data-driven operations and follow current industry trends. Companies frequently lack the knowledge, assets, or employees necessary to evaluate the market for leading IoT technologies and determine what they can achieve regarding production and logistics. They are prevented from moving on with their digitalization programmes and prototype development for the same reasons. Help is available from the SCS Center for Applied Research. They are combining our expertise in software development, integration, and optimization with that of Fraunhofer IIS, our parent company, in the creation of sensors and other hardware. Since IT outsourcing is a significant economic trend in the age of digitization, academics have paid attention to the subject in the past ten years. A comparative empirical study of the logistics industries in Germany and Mexico is undertaken using a conceptual model as the foundation, and it is further strengthened by data obtained through in-depth interviews that shed light on the variables driving IT outsourcing in both countries. The logistics sector has adopted IoT to meet all these expectations and compete with other businesses. There was a time when there were too few employees, the markets were unstable, and the profit margins were skinny. This industry was severely hit. But everything changed gradually once IoT was adopted. For the Internet of Things (IoT) in the logistics sector, scalability is a major barrier that can be overcome in several ways. To manage the enormous amount of data produced by connected devices, a strong and dependable connectivity infrastructure is first and foremost necessary for large-scale IoT installations in logistics. This entails making certain that there is sufficient network bandwidth, minimal latency, and high availability to facilitate real-time logistics operation monitoring and control.

Logistics IoT scalability also requires resolving security and privacy issues. With an increase in connected devices comes an increase in the potential attack surface for malevolent actors. It is crucial to make sure that IoT devices, networks, and data are secure to avoid unwanted access, data breaches, and delays in logistics operations. IoT devices and data can be protected by putting robust encryption, authentication methods, and security protocols in place. The upkeep and administration of the physical infrastructure that supports IoT deployments are also part of the scalability challenge in IoT logistics. This covers the deployment and administration of supporting infrastructure, including gateways, servers, and cloud platforms, in addition to the installation, configuration, and continuing maintenance of IoT devices. For IoT logistics systems to be reliable and scalable, it becomes imperative to implement effective deployment and maintenance procedures together with strong device management systems.

7. CONCLUSION

logistics is a crucial player positioned to achieve complete visibility and transparency by utilizing pervasive interconnectivity to gather reliable and secure real-time data. It is essential for all retailers and logistics companies who want to preserve their leading positions to stay on top of logistical challenges and trends. A global supply chain disruption resulted from COVID-19's imbalance in the supply and demand for goods. 2020 saw a decrease in global productivity because of the pandemic and the lockdown. Due to this, the idea of digital transformation has gained traction during the past two years. For many years, manufacturers have been monitoring the industry 4.0 transformation. However, the concept is gaining traction as one survey revealed that more than half of all businesses intend to undergo a digital transformation following the epidemic. Despite the potential for enormous benefits, obstacles are still blocking the complete implementation of IoT in logistics. The logistics sector has adopted IoT to meet all these expectations and compete with other businesses. There was a time when there were too few employees, the markets were unstable, and the profit margins were skinny. This industry was severely hit. But everything changed gradually once IoT was adopted.

8. FUTURE WORK

For the IoT (IoT) in the logistics sector, scalability is a significant barrier that can be overcome in several ways. To manage the enormous amount of data produced by connected devices, a robust and dependable connectivity infrastructure is, first and foremost, necessary for large-scale IoT installations in logistics. This entails ensuring sufficient network bandwidth, minimal latency, and high availability to facilitate real-time logistics operation monitoring and control.

8.1 Scalability

The capacity to seamlessly integrate and manage a wide range of devices, sensors, and The capacity to seamlessly integrate and manage a wide range of devices, sensors, and platforms across many locations, suppliers, and stakeholders is essential to the scalability of IoT in logistics. This calls for creating frameworks, protocols, and interoperability standards that enable smooth data transfer and interoperability among diverse IoT systems and devices. The capacity to seamlessly integrate and manage a wide range of devices, sensors, and platforms across many locations, suppliers, and stakeholders is essential to the scalability of IoT in logistics. This calls for creating frameworks, protocols, and interoperability standards that enable smooth data transfer and interoperability among diverse IoT systems and devices. The scalability challenge in IoT logistics is the efficient administration and processing of IoT devices' enormous volume of data. Logistics operations have a large amount of data about inventories, shipping, tracking, and environmental factors. Implementing strong data management and analytics systems that can effectively process, store, and analyze this data to extract insightful information in real-time is essential to achieving scalability. Logistics IoT scalability also requires resolving security and privacy issues. With increased connected devices comes the potential attack surface for malevolent actors. It is crucial to ensure that IoT devices, networks, and data are secure to avoid unwanted access, data breaches, and delays in logistics operations. Implementing robust encryption, authentication methods, and security protocols can protect IoT devices and data. The upkeep and administration of the physical infrastructure that supports IoT deployments are also part of the scalability challenge in IoT logistics. This covers the deployment and administration of supporting infrastructure, including gateways, servers, and cloud platforms, and the installation, configuration, and continuing maintenance of IoT devices. For IoT logistics systems to be reliable and scalable, it becomes imperative to implement effective deployment and maintenance procedures together with robust device management systems.

8.2 Security

The security of IoT in logistics presents a variety of difficulties that should be carefully considered. It's among the most significant IoT supply chain challenges. First off, controlling and safeguarding the vast number of linked devices in the logistics ecosystem presents substantial difficulty. As more and more IoT devices connect to the cloud and one another, it is essential to make sure the data being transmitted is valid and intact. Since logistics operations sometimes entail the transportation of goods between various geographic sites, the physical security of IoT devices is a key concern. These gadgets are susceptible to loss, alteration, or illegal access, which could jeopardize the integrity of the logistics network. Large volumes of data are generated by IoT devices in logistics, and protecting this data at every stage of its lifespan is a significant concern. Every step of the process, from data collection and transfer to storage and analysis, needs to be properly secured to avoid unauthorized access or security lapses. Security measures have become more complex due to the variety of IoT devices used in logistics, which range from trackers and sensors to drones and autonomous cars. Constant upgrades and attention to detail are needed to ensure compatibility, standardization, and efficient security processes across many platforms and devices.

8.3 Integration

One of the biggest obstacles to IoT adoption in the logistics sector is integration. A variety of parties, each using a different set of systems and platforms, are involved in the logistics industry. These stakeholders include manufacturers, suppliers, distributors, retailers, and transportation providers. It is a difficult undertaking to integrate these various systems and devices to provide seamless data flow and interoperability.

8.4 Staff Skill

A significant obstacle confronting the logistics sector in the adoption of Internet of Things (IoT) technology is the requirement for proficient personnel capable of efficiently overseeing and managing IoT devices and systems. Professionals with a thorough understanding of network protocols, device connectivity, and data management are needed for IoT systems in logistics. Ensuring the smooth integration and interoperability of IoT devices throughout the logistics ecosystem might be challenging without this knowledge. To safeguard Internet of Things devices and networks from potential attacks and vulnerabilities, logistical staff members must be knowledgeable about cybersecurity principles and best practices. IoT devices are vulnerable to security breaches due to their interconnectedness, and logistics staff may find it difficult to protect sensitive data and stop unwanted access if they lack the necessary knowledge and training. Because IoT technologies are always evolving, logistics personnel must stay up-to-date on the newest developments and market trends. To effectively deploy and manage IoT solutions in the logistics industry, they must be knowledgeable about the latest IoT standards, protocols, and platforms. Technical difficulties with IoT devices need to be troubleshooted and resolved by qualified individuals who can identify issues, evaluate data, and put suitable fixes in place. This entails detecting problems with connectivity, identifying malfunctioning sensors or actuators, and fixing software or firmware bugs—all of which call for a high level of technical proficiency.

8.5 Data Quality

In the context of the Internet of Things, the logistics sector has several difficulties in guaranteeing data quality. First off, it can be debilitating to deal with the sheer amount and diversity of data produced by IoT devices. The logistics industry must deal with monitoring and integrating varied data streams from several sources because there are innumerable sensors, RFID tags, and other linked devices dispersed throughout the supply chain. Second, upholding data dependability and correctness is essential for efficient operations and sound decision-making. IoT devices could, however, experience problems with connectivity, power outages, or software bugs, which could result in inconsistent or inaccurate data. To address these problems and guarantee data integrity, strong data validation and verification processes are needed. Significant concerns exist regarding data security and privacy in the IoT-enabled logistics industry. The exchange of confidential data across networked devices increases the likelihood of cyberattacks, data breaches, and illegal access. Securing critical logistics data requires strong security measures like encryption, authentication mechanisms, and secure data transmission. One logistical difficulty is the compatibility of IoT devices and systems. As diverse devices and technologies are incorporated across the supply chain, it becomes increasingly difficult to guarantee smooth communication, data sharing, and interoperability. To facilitate seamless interoperability and optimize the potential advantages of IoT in logistics, standardization initiatives and the adoption of standardized protocols are crucial.

REFERENCES

Abebe, B. (2019). *E-government based land administration framework; trends, challenges and prospects* (Doctoral dissertation).

Adjei-Bamfo, P., Maloreh-Nyamekye, T., & Ahenkan, A. (2019). The role of e-government in sustainable public procurement in developing countries: A systematic literature review. *Resources, Conservation and Recycling*, *142*, 189–203. doi:10.1016/j.resconrec.2018.12.001

Agbozo, E., Alhassan, D., & Spassov, K. (2018, November). Personal data and privacy barriers to e-Government adoption, implementation and development in Sub-Saharan Africa. In *International Conference on Electronic Governance and Open Society: Challenges in Eurasia* (pp. 82–91). Springer. https://link.springer.com/chapter/10.1007/978-3-030-13283-5_7

Al-Nidawi, W. J. A., Al-Wassiti, S. K. J., Maan, M. A., & Othman, M. (2018). A review in E-government service quality measurement. *Indonesian Journal of Electrical Engineering and Computer Science*, *10*(3), 1257–1265. doi:10.11591/ijeecs.v10.i3.pp1257-1265

Al-rawahnaA. S. M.ChenS. C.HungC. W. (2019). The barriers of e-government success: An empirical study from Jordan. *Available at* SSRN 3498847. doi:10.2139/ssrn.3498847

Alamri, M., Jhanjhi, N. Z., & Humayun, M. (2019). Blockchain for Internet of Things (IoT) research issues challenges & future directions: A review. *Int. J. Comput. Sci. Netw. Secur*, *19*(1), 244–258.

Albrahim, R., Alsalamah, H., Alsalamah, S., & Aksoy, M. (2018). Access control model for modern virtual e-government services: Saudi Arabian case study. *International Journal of Advanced Computer Science and Applications*, *9*(8), 357–364. doi:10.14569/IJACSA.2018.090847

AlEnezi, A., AlMeraj, Z., & Manuel, P. (2018, April). Challenges of IoT based smart-government development. In *2018 21st Saudi Computer Society National Computer Conference (NCC)* (pp. 1-6). IEEE.

Alexopoulos, C., Lachana, Z., Androutsopoulou, A., Diamantopoulou, V., Charalabidis, Y., & Loutsaris, M. A. (2019, April). How machine learning is changing e-government. In *Proceedings of the 12th International Conference on Theory and Practice of Electronic Governance* (pp. 354-363). 10.1145/3326365.3326412

Alferidah, D. K., & Jhanjhi, N. Z. (2020). A review on security and privacy issues and challenges in internet of things. *International Journal of Computer Science and Network Security IJCSNS*, *20*(4), 263–286.

Alguliyev, R., Aliguliyev, R., & Yusifov, F. (2018). Role of Social Networks in E-government: Risks and Security Threats. *Online Journal of Communication and Media Technologies*, *8*(4), 363–376.

Alharmoodi, B. Y. R., & Lakulu, M. M. B. (2020). Transition from e-government to m-government: Challenges and opportunities-case study of UAE. *European Journal of Multidisciplinary Studies*, *5*(1), 61–67. doi:10.26417/453fgx96c

Alketbi, H. (2018). *An evaluation of e-government effectiveness in Dubai smart government departments* (Doctoral dissertation, Southampton Solent University). https://ssudl.solent.ac.uk/id/eprint/3809/

AlMendah, O. M. (2021). A Survey of Blockchain and E-governance applications: Security and Privacy issues. *Turkish Journal of Computer and Mathematics Education, 12*(10), 3117–3125.

Alqudah, M. A., & Muradkhanli, L. (2021). Artificial Intelligence in Electric Government; Ethical Challenges and Governance in Jordan. *Electronic Research Journal of Social Sciences and Humanities, 3*, 65–74.

Angelopoulos, K., Diamantopoulou, V., Mouratidis, H., Pavlidis, M., Salnitri, M., Giorgini, P., & Ruiz, J. F. (2017, August). A holistic approach for privacy protection in E-government. In *Proceedings of the 12th International Conference on Availability, Reliability and Security* (pp. 1-10). 10.1145/3098954.3098960

Ari, A. A. A., Ngangmo, O. K., Titouna, C., Thiare, O., Mohamadou, A., & Gueroui, A. M. (2020). *Enabling privacy and security in Cloud of Things: Architecture, applications, security & privacy challenges*. Applied Computing and Informatics.

Baharin, A. M., & Zolkipli, M. F. (2021). Review on Current Target of Mobile Attacks. *Borneo International Journal, 4*(2), 17-24.

Barreto, L., Amaral, A., & Pereira, T. (2017). Industry 4.0 implications in logistics: An overview. *Proc. Int. Conf. Manuf. Eng. Soc. (MESIC 2017),* 13, 1245–1252. 10.1016/j.promfg.2017.09.045

Cheng, B., Solmaz, G., Cirillo, F., Kovacs, E., Terasawa, K., & Kitazawa, A. (2017). FogFlow: Easy programming of IoT services over cloud and edges for smart cities. *IEEE Internet of Things Journal, 5*(2), 696–707. doi:10.1109/JIOT.2017.2747214

Chhajed, G. J., & Garg, B. R. (2022). Applying Decision Tree for Hiding Data in Binary Images for Secure and Secret Information Flow. In *Cybersecurity Measures for E-Government Frameworks* (pp. 175–186). IGI Global. doi:10.4018/978-1-7998-9624-1.ch011

Chishiro, H., Tsuchiya, Y., Chubachi, Y., Abu Bakar, M. S., & De Silva, L. C. (2017, June). Global PBL for environmental IoT. In *Proceedings of the 2017 International Conference on E-commerce, E-Business and E-Government* (pp. 65-71). 10.1145/3108421.3108437

Dawson, M., & Walker, D. (2022). Argument for Improved Security in Local Governments Within the Economic Community of West African States. *Cybersecurity Measures for E-Government Frameworks*, 96-106.

Dhonju, G. R., & Shakya, S. (2019). Analyzing Challenges for the Implementation of E-Government in Municipalities within Kathmandu Valley. *Journal of Science and Engineering*, *7*, 70–78. doi:10.3126/jsce.v7i0.26795

Distel, B. (2018). Bringing Light into the Shadows: A Qualitative Interview Study on Citizens' Non-Adoption of e-Government. *Electronic. Journal of E-Government*, *16*(2), 98–105.

Elezaj, O., Tole, D., & Baci, N. (2018). Big Data in e-Government Environments: Albania as a Case Study. *Academic Journal of Interdisciplinary Studies*, *7*(2), 117–124. doi:10.2478/ajis-2018-0052

Ferrag, M. A., Shu, L., Yang, X., Derhab, A., & Maglaras, L. (2020). Security and privacy for green IoT-based agriculture: Review, blockchain solutions, and challenges. *IEEE Access : Practical Innovations, Open Solutions*, *8*, 32031–32053. doi:10.1109/ACCESS.2020.2973178

Froehlich, A., Ringas, N., & Wilson, J. (2020). E-Governance in Africa and the World. In *Space Supporting Africa* (pp. 53–124). Springer. doi:10.1007/978-3-030-52260-5_2

Gaur, L., Ujjan, R. M. A., & Hussain, M. (2022). The Influence of Deep Learning in Detecting Cyber Attacks on E-Government Applications. In *Cybersecurity Measures for E-Government Frameworks* (pp. 107–122). IGI Global. doi:10.4018/978-1-7998-9624-1.ch007

Gershon, D., Prince, O., & Opoku, A. M. (2018). Promoting Inclusiveness and Participation in Governance: The Directions of Electronic Government in Ghana. *International Journal of Advanced Research*, *7*(3), 397–406. doi:10.21474/IJAR01/7931

Gouveia, L. B. (2020). e-Government and Smart Cities: Contexts and Challenges Taking from Digital Usage and Exploration. *UNU-EGOV| UM DSI PDSI talk.*

Gregor, T. (2017). Smart connected logistics. *Proc. Int. Sci. Conf. Sustain. Mod. Safe Transp. (TRANSCOM),* 192, 265–270.

Hamid, B., Jhanjhi, N. Z., & Humayun, M. (2020). Digital Governance for Developing Countries Opportunities, Issues, and Challenges in Pakistan. In *Employing Recent Technologies for Improved Digital Governance* (pp. 36–58). IGI Global. doi:10.4018/978-1-7998-1851-9.ch003

Hamid, B., Jhanjhi, N. Z., Humayun, M., Khan, A., & Alsayat, A. (2019, December). Cyber security issues and challenges for smart cities: A survey. In *2019 13th International Conference on Mathematics, Actuarial Science, Computer Science and Statistics (MACS)* (pp. 1-7). IEEE. 10.1109/MACS48846.2019.9024768

Henriksen, H. Z. (2018). One step forward and two steps back: e-Government policies in practice. In *Policy Analytics, Modelling, and Informatics* (pp. 79–97). Springer. doi:10.1007/978-3-319-61762-6_4

Humayun, M., Niazi, M., Jhanjhi, N. Z., Alshayeb, M., & Mahmood, S. (2020). Cyber security threats and vulnerabilities: A systematic mapping study. *Arabian Journal for Science and Engineering*, *45*(4), 3171–3189. doi:10.1007/s13369-019-04319-2

Hussain, M., Talpur, M. S. H., & Humayun, M. (2022). The Consequences of Integrity Attacks on E-Governance: Privacy and Security Violation. In *Cybersecurity Measures for E-Government Frameworks* (pp. 141–156). IGI Global. doi:10.4018/978-1-7998-9624-1.ch009

Hussain, S. J., Irfan, M., Jhanjhi, N. Z., Hussain, K., & Humayun, M. (2021). Performance enhancement in wireless body area networks with secure communication. *Wireless Personal Communications*, *116*(1), 1–22. doi:10.1007/s11277-020-07702-7 PMID:33558792

Jeschke, S., Brecher, C., Song, H., & Rawat, D. (2017). *Industrial Internet of Things: Cybermanufacturing Systems*. Springer. doi:10.1007/978-3-319-42559-7

Jhanjhi, N. Z., Ahmad, M., Khan, M. A., & Hussain, M. (2022). The impact of cyber attacks on e-governance during the covid-19 pandemic. In *Cybersecurity Measures for E-Government Frameworks* (pp. 123–140). IGI Global. doi:10.4018/978-1-7998-9624-1.ch008

Joshi, P. R., & Islam, S. (2018). E-government maturity model for sustainable e-government services from the perspective of developing countries. *Sustainability (Basel)*, *10*(6), 1882. doi:10.3390/su10061882

Koo, E. (2019). *Digital transformation of Government: from E-Government to intelligent E-Government* (Doctoral dissertation). Massachusetts Institute of Technology.

Kumar, P., Kunwar, R. S., & Sachan, A. (2016). A survey report on: Security & challenges in internet of things. In *Proc National Conference on ICT & IoT* (pp. 35-39). Academic Press.

Le, N. T., & Hoang, D. B. (2016, December). Can maturity models support cyber security? In *2016 IEEE 35th international performance computing and communications conference (IPCCC)* (pp. 1-7). 10.1109/PCCC.2016.7820663

Li, J., Yu, F. R., Deng, G., Luo, C., Ming, Z., & Yan, Q. (2017). Industrial Internet: A survey on the enabling technologies, applications, and challenges. IEEE Commun. Surveys Tuts., 19(3), 1504–1526.

Liu, D., & Carter, L. (2018, May). Impact of citizens' privacy concerns on e-government adoption. In *Proceedings of the 19th Annual International Conference on Digital Government Research: Governance in the Data Age* (pp. 1-6). 10.1145/3209281.3209340

Liu, M., Yu, F. R., Teng, Y., Leung, V. C. M., & Song, M. (2019, June). Performance optimization for blockchain-enabled industrial Internet of Things (IIoT) systems: A deep reinforcement learning approach. *IEEE Transactions on Industrial Informatics*, *15*(6), 3559–3570. doi:10.1109/TII.2019.2897805

Ma, L., & Zheng, Y. (2019). National e-government performance and citizen satisfaction: A multilevel analysis across European countries. *International Review of Administrative Sciences*, *85*(3), 506–526. doi:10.1177/0020852317703691

Máchová, R. (2017). Measuring the effects of open data on the level of corruption. In *Proceedings of the 21th International Conference Current Trends in Public Sector Research*. Masarykova univerzita.

Maharaj, M. S., & Munyoka, W. (2019). Privacy, security, trust, risk and optimism bias in e-government use: The case of two Southern African Development Community countries. *South African Journal of Information Management*, *21*(1), 1–9.

Mahmood, Z. (Ed.). (2016). *Connectivity frameworks for smart devices: the internet of things from a distributed computing perspective*. Springer. doi:10.1007/978-3-319-33124-9

Malhotra, H., Bhargava, R., & Dave, M. (2017, November). Challenges related to information security and its implications for evolving e-government structures: A comparative study between India and African countries. In *2017 International Conference on Inventive Computing and Informatics (ICICI)* (pp. 30-35). IEEE. 10.1109/ICICI.2017.8365370

Meiyanti, R., Utomo, B., Sensuse, D. I., & Wahyuni, R. (2018, August). E-government challenges in developing countries: a literature review. In *2018 6th International Conference on Cyber and IT Service Management (CITSM)* (pp. 1-6). IEEE. 10.1109/CITSM.2018.8674245

Muzafar, S., Humayun, M., & Hussain, S. J. (2022). Emerging Cybersecurity Threats in the Eye of E-Governance in the Current Era. In *Cybersecurity Measures for E-Government Frameworks* (pp. 43–60). IGI Global. doi:10.4018/978-1-7998-9624-1.ch003

Muzafar, S., & Jhanjhi, N. Z. (2020). Success Stories of ICT Implementation in Saudi Arabia. In *Employing Recent Technologies for Improved Digital Governance* (pp. 151–163). IGI Global. doi:10.4018/978-1-7998-1851-9.ch008

Nagowah, S. D., Sta, H. B., & Gobin-Rahimbux, B. A. (2018, October). An overview of semantic interoperability ontologies and frameworks for IoT. In *2018 Sixth International Conference on Enterprise Systems (ES)* (pp. 82-89). IEEE. 10.1109/ES.2018.00020

Nautiyal, L., Malik, P., & Agarwal, A. (2018). Cybersecurity system: an essential pillar of smart cities. In *Smart Cities* (pp. 25–50). Springer. doi:10.1007/978-3-319-76669-0_2

Nzimakwe, T. I. (2018). Government's Dynamic Approach to Addressing Challenges of Cybersecurity in South Africa. In Handbook of Research on Information and Cyber Security in the Fourth Industrial Revolution (pp. 364-381). IGI Global. doi:10.4018/978-1-5225-4763-1.ch013

Pal, S. K. (2019). Changing technological trends for E-governance. In *E-governance in India* (pp. 79-105). Palgrave Macmillan. https://link.springer.com/chapter/10.1007/978-981-13-8852-1_5

Pathak, A., AmazUddin, M., Abedin, M. J., Andersson, K., Mustafa, R., & Hossain, M. S. (2019). IoT based smart system to support agricultural parameters: A case study. *Procedia Computer Science*, *155*, 648–653. doi:10.1016/j.procs.2019.08.092

Pradhan, P., & Shakya, S. (2018). Big Data Challenges for e-Government Services in Nepal. *Journal of the Institute of Engineering*, *14*(1), 216–222. doi:10.3126/jie.v14i1.20087

Qi, M., & Wang, J. (2021). Using the Internet of Things e-government platform to optimize the administrative management mode. *Wireless Communications and Mobile Computing*, *2021*, 2021. doi:10.1155/2021/2224957

Qi, R., Feng, C., Liu, Z., & Mrad, N. (2017). Blockchain-powered internet of things, e-governance and e-democracy. In *E-Democracy for Smart Cities* (pp. 509–520). Springer. doi:10.1007/978-981-10-4035-1_17

Qiu, C., Yu, F. R., Yao, H., Jiang, C., Xu, F., & Zhao, C. (2019, June). Blockchain-based software-defined industrial Internet of Things: A dueling deep Q-learning approach. *IEEE Internet of Things Journal*, *6*(3), 4627–4639. doi:10.1109/JIOT.2018.2871394

Qu, T., Lei, S., Wang, Z., Nie, D., Chen, X., & Huang, G. (2016, April). IoT-based real-time production logistics synchronization system under smart cloud manufacturing. *International Journal of Advanced Manufacturing Technology*, *84*(1–4), 147–164. doi:10.1007/s00170-015-7220-1

Ramli, R. M. (2017). Challenges and issues in Malaysian e-government. *Electronic Government, an International Journal, 13*(3), 242-273.

Razuleu, L. A. (2018). *E-Governance and Its Associated Cybersecurity: The Challenges and Best Practices of Authentication and Authorization Among a Rapidly Growing E-government* (Doctoral dissertation). California State University, Northridge.

Sagarik, D., Chansukree, P., Cho, W., & Berman, E. (2018). E-government 4.0 in Thailand: The role of central agencies. *Information Polity*, *23*(3), 343–353. doi:10.3233/IP-180006

Shah, I. A. (2022). Cybersecurity Issues and Challenges for E-Government During COVID-19: A Review. *Cybersecurity Measures for E-Government Frameworks*, 187-222.

Shah, I. A., Habeeb, R. A. A., Rajper, S., & Laraib, A. (2022). The Influence of Cybersecurity Attacks on E-Governance. In *Cybersecurity Measures for E-Government Frameworks* (pp. 77–95). IGI Global. doi:10.4018/978-1-7998-9624-1.ch005

Shah, I. A., Jhanjhi, N. Z., Humayun, M., & Ghosh, U. (2022). Health Care Digital Revolution During COVID-19. In *How COVID-19 is Accelerating the Digital Revolution* (pp. 17–30). Springer. doi:10.1007/978-3-030-98167-9_2

Shah, I. A., Jhanjhi, N. Z., & Laraib, A. (2023). Cybersecurity and Blockchain Usage in Contemporary Business. In *Handbook of Research on Cybersecurity Issues and Challenges for Business and FinTech Applications* (pp. 49–64). IGI Global.

Sharma, P., Zawar, S., & Patil, S. B. (2016). Ransomware Analysis: Internet of Things (Iot) Security Issues, Challenges and Open Problems Inthe Context of Worldwide Scenario of Security of Systems and Malware Attacks. In *International conference on recent Innovation in Engineering and Management* (*Vol. 2*, No. 3, pp. 177-184). Academic Press.

Sharma, S. K., Metri, B., Dwivedi, Y. K., & Rana, N. P. (2021). Challenges common service centers (CSCs) face in delivering e-government services in rural India. *Government Information Quarterly*, *38*(2), 101573. doi:10.1016/j.giq.2021.101573

Suleimany, M. (2021, May). Smart Urban Management and IoT; Paradigm of E-Governance and Technologies in Developing Communities. In *2021 5th International Conference on Internet of Things and Applications (IoT)* (pp. 1-6). IEEE.

Trappey, A., Trappey, C., Fan, C., Hsu, A., Li, X., & Lee, I. (2017, September). IoT patent roadmap for smart logistic service providers in the context of industry 4.0. *Zhongguo Gongcheng Xuekan*, *40*(7), 593–602. doi:10.1080/02533839.2017.1362325

Ujjan, R. M. A., Hussain, K., & Brohi, S. N. (2022). The impact of Blockchain technology on advanced security measures for E-Government. In *Cybersecurity Measures for E-Government Frameworks* (pp. 157–174). IGI Global. doi:10.4018/978-1-7998-9624-1.ch010

Ujjan, R. M. A., Khan, N. A., & Gaur, L. (2022). E-Government Privacy and Security Challenges in the Context of Internet of Things. In *Cybersecurity Measures for E-Government Frameworks* (pp. 22–42). IGI Global. doi:10.4018/978-1-7998-9624-1.ch002

Ujjan, R. M. A., Pervez, Z., Dahal, K., Bashir, A. K., Mumtaz, R., & González, J. (2020). Towards sFlow and adaptive polling sampling for deep learning based DDoS detection in SDN. *Future Generation Computer Systems*, *111*, 763–779. doi:10.1016/j.future.2019.10.015

Ujjan, R. M. A., Taj, I., & Brohi, S. N. (2022). E-Government Cybersecurity Modeling in the Context of Software-Defined Networks. In *Cybersecurity Measures for E-Government Frameworks* (pp. 1–21). IGI Global. doi:10.4018/978-1-7998-9624-1.ch001

Ujjan, R. M. A., Taj, I., & Brohi, S. N. (2022). *E-Government Cybersecurity Modeling in the Context of Software-Defined Networks. In Cybersecurity Measures for E-Government Frameworks*. IGI Global.

Ujjan, R. M. A., Taj, I., & Brohi, S. N. (2022). E-Government Cybersecurity Modeling in the Context of Software-Defined Networks. In *Cybersecurity Measures for E-Government Frameworks* (pp. 1–21). IGI Global. doi:10.4018/978-1-7998-9624-1.ch001

Yang, L., Elisa, N., & Eliot, N. (2019). Privacy and security aspects of E-government in smart cities. In *Smart cities cybersecurity and privacy* (pp. 89–102). Elsevier. doi:10.1016/B978-0-12-815032-0.00007-X

Yang, R., & Wibowo, S. (2020). *Risks and Uncertainties in Citizens' Trust and Adoption of E-Government: A Proposed Framework*. Academic Press.

Zhang, Y., Guo, Z., Lv, J., & Liu, Y. (2018, September). A framework for smart production-logistics systems based on CPS and industrial IoT. *IEEE Transactions on Industrial Informatics*, *14*(9), 4019–4032. doi:10.1109/TII.2018.2845683

Chapter 7
Blockchain-Based Authentication for the Internet of Vehicles (BBA-IoV)

Rida Zehra
https://orcid.org/0009-0009-2468-3970
University of the West of England, UK

ABSTRACT

IoV has become an appealing application that can provide a wide range of mobile services for drivers. In order to mitigate traffic congestion and reduce the occurrence of accidents, vehicles can be provided with up-to-date information regarding the location, trajectory, speed, and other relevant details of adjacent vehicles. Such an open environment leaves a lot of room for malicious nodes to pass falsified and tampered information. Due to the potential relevance and sensitivity of the information, IoV must address the security and privacy concerns in the network. In this chapter, they propose an efficient IoV-based decentralised authentication mechanism based on the blockchain named BBA- IoV to ensure secure node communication. This method requires the exchange of keys to encrypt communication. From performance analysis, they show that this approach protects communication against several attacks such as Sybil, GPS spoofing, tampering, and fabrication attacks.

IoV is a transformation of Vehicular Ad Hoc Networks (VANETs) that can increase traffic efficiency. The evolution of sensing and communication technologies and their rapid usage in vehicular communication has made it possible for vehicles to connect with other road infrastructures to convey information in real time (Jiang et al., 2019). The growth of the Internet of Things (IoT) allows vehicles to be self-

DOI: 10.4018/979-8-3693-3816-2.ch007

sufficient and smarter and provides a platform to enable the IoV. According to (Li, 2012), the number of vehicles globally could rise to between two and five billion by 2050.

There are two main types of VANET communications, namely Vehicle-to-Vehicle (V2V) and Vehicle-to-Infrastructure(V2I) (Fangchun et al., 2014). Communication between vehicles in the IoV is possible, as well as with pedestrians, signs, and roadside units (Nakamoto, 2009). The communication can be related to route planning, road congestion, traffic issues, and emergency details that need to be secure; for example, the actual identity of a driver must not be disclosed.

In a rapidly evolving world where vehicles are becoming more interconnected, there are various security and privacy concerns that pose risks to the safety of drivers and passengers. These concerns include data manipulation, authenticity, and the potential disclosure of sensitive information. Thus, vehicles in the IoV are vulnerable to security threats by presenting false information that leads to serious risks; it is, therefore, necessary to fix these problems. In current studies such as (Aich et al., 2019; Leo et al., 2020; Qu et al., 2015), proposed methods are highly centralised, which means a single point of failure can damage the whole system -if the central authority is targeted data will be maliciously exploited -needs to be resolved. This issue is where the blockchain has been proposed and advocated as an adequate solution.

Blockchain is a decentralised ledger that employs a distributed data structure comprised of a sequential chain of blocks to store transaction information. The objective is to streamline peer-to-peer (P2P) transactions by eliminating the requirement for direct interactions between peers and any involvement from intermediaries. Several studies have explored the use of blockchain as a solution for vehicle authentication methods, such as (Al Ameen et al., 2012), whereby a blockchain-based authentication system seeks to solve centralised infrastructure, anonymity, and trust. They proposed a lightweight authentication system for automotive fog infrastructure. Similarly, an authentication system for vehicles using blockchain based on the services of fog was implemented in the paper (Sharma et al., 2018). The existing works mentioned above do not discuss integrating blockchain to provide authentication to both vehicle and service management. We present a novel architecture for the integration of blockchain into existing vehicular systems.

They, therefore, suggested an improved new approach to avoid the issue of authentication with blockchain technology. The use of blockchain technology has several benefits, including any vehicle can enter the block and can confirm that other vehicles are authentic without any third party. In the field of protection, safety, and performance, the integration of blockchain and IoT will potentially improve the current IoV network. The BBA-IoV method includes encryption techniques for generating and exchanging keys to ensure security. The RA is the transport authority under the BBA-IoV system that checks and issues the registration number for registered new vehicles. The RSU facilitates the vehicle's integration into the IoV network while concurrently delivering vehicle services. Interactions on the blockchain involve the external actors RA and RSU. Moreover, we used ECDH as a key protocol, while hybrid ECDH-AES is used for encryption and decryption. Firstly, the vehicle gets registered and then applies to access the network, for which validation and verification will be done by blockchain to ensure authenticity. Finally, we evaluate the performance of BBA-IoV by some experiments which clearly show that this approach can prevent different types of attacks such as Sybil attacks, GPS spoofing, tampering, fabrication, masquerading, and wormhole attacks. It has a low operation and storage cost as compared to some existing schemes (Xu et al., 2019), and it provides similar or better security than existing ones using less key size.

BACKGROUND

Preliminary Knowledge

Blockchain Technology

In 2008, Satoshi Nakamoto introduced two innovative ideas that had profound implications. Bitcoin is a decentralised digital cryptocurrency that operates without the need for a central network. The phrase "blockchain" is more prevalent than "cryptocurrency" (Nakamoto, 2009).

Blockchain refers to a distributed information structure that consists of a chain of blocks. It acts as a decentralised ledger, storing transaction logs. Blockchain involves conducting transactions over a peer-to-peer (P2P) network, where participants are not required to have knowledge of each other and there is no intermediary present. Blockchain is designed as a structured ledger, depicted in Figure 1, stored as a distributed database system, and connected to a preceding block. There are two essential parts of the block, the header and the transaction. It is divided into two main parts. The header of the previous block will include a real hash block and a link will be established between the two blocks. This is why a blockchain is named.

The transaction is the principal entity within the network of blockchains. A majority consensus system uses network nodes to validate each transaction before the blockchain is implemented. No data collected can be changed or removed, and it is possible to reinterpret the timeline of any transaction at any moment. A consensus must be achieved for verification and confirmation by individual miners, known as mining. Miners make mathematical consumer calculations and, in exchange,

Figure 1. The basic structure of the blockchain

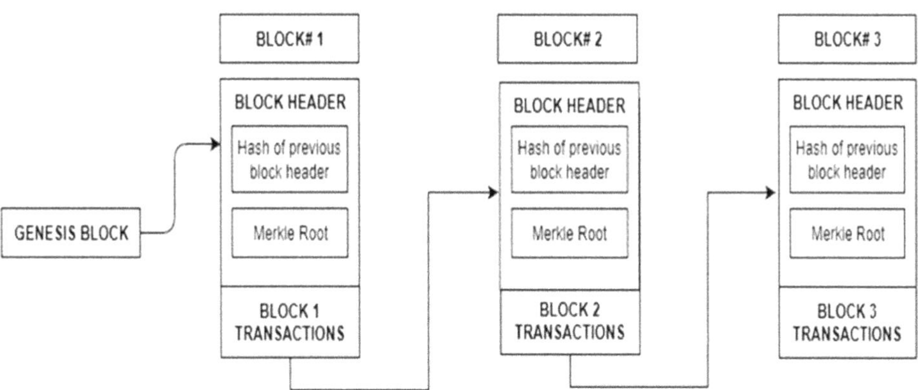

obtain rewards. This work can be hard to solve, but once it has been done, it can be easily checked.

Blockchain for IoV In the context of the IoV, blockchain refers to a decentralized and distributed ledger technology that securely records and verifies transactions related to connected vehicles and their associated data. The IoV involves the integration of communication technologies and smart devices in vehicles to enhance safety, efficiency, and overall transportation experience. Blockchain features for IoV serves several purposes as mentioned in in Table 1.

Related Work

This section focuses on studies pertaining to the mechanisms used for vehicle authentication. There are numerous research articles available in the literature. While the central server may be the bottleneck of the entire system, some of these do not use blockchain technology to guarantee the legitimacy of the vehicle on

Table 1. Features of the blockchain and its impact on IoV

Features	Impacts
Immutability	The transaction is duplicated on every node, ensuring fault tolerance.
Consensus	The decision-making process involves all participants.
Decentralised	IoV excludes third parties.
Security	To secure, utilise the cryptographic hash function.
Time Stamp	Sort the transactions in the correct order.
Non-repudiation	A sender cannot refuse a message.

the network. Until it fails, the server interrupts the entire system, such as (Priya & Karuppanan, 2011), which designs a stable and distributed architecture of the certification framework against fake certification. Furthermore, (Xu et al., 2019) provide a lightweight authentication scheme (LIAU), using a cryptographic key architecture and a hash function to create parameters for V2V authentication. Besides, the LIAU system has low coordination and time costs. Nevertheless, this method needs more capability to support a distributed architecture due to its centralised storage for record keeping. When an attack happens, the entire network is affected. Similar to (Xu et al., 2019), the authentication of vehicles is provided by reference (Tan et al., 2018), which specifies a certificate-free authentication and road message protocol called SCAR that needs no authentication certificates between vehicles or RSUs. RSUs are seen as a bridge between trustworthy and vehicular authorities. The data exchange between TA and RSU is carried out via a secure wired link, while contact with the V2V and the Vehicle-to-Road (V2R) is conducted via an open wireless channel. Nevertheless, it is dependent on a reliable intermediary to execute this protocol.

In contrast, Blockchain technology is an effective way to solve a decentralised approach to reliable interactions. Also, it discusses the possible authentication in IoV like (Lu et al., 2018) introduced an anonymous reputation system based on blockchain called BARS to build the confidentiality-proof confidence model for VANETs. Also, they found that the privacy of users is maintained throughout the authentication process. In order to do so, the vehicle must also alter confidentiality to avoid contact data from being connected in such a way that they often communicate with RSUs, which has a severe effect on the efficiency of VANETs. In comparison to (Lu et al., 2018), another (Lin et al., 2008) scheme called a blockchain-based ECPP was presented, with the PKI signature mechanism used to authenticate the vehicle's contact. The RSU uses a community ID approach to generate an anonymous short-term certificate in response to a request from the OBU. Despite the ECPP's conditional privacy feature, the OBU can still be linked because the affected RSUs keep using the same pseudonym for the entire OBU. It is also impossible to determine which compromised RSUs sent the message because the TA and the RSUs work together throughout the ECPP monitoring process.

Thus, our proposed method, BBA-IoV, is better related to the prevention of security attacks such as Sybil, GPS spoofing, masquerading, and Wormhole attacks, and has a better performance in terms of operation and communication cost, as discussed later in the chapter.

Attacks on Authentication in IoV

Let us now proceed to analyses several prevalent authentication attacks that target the IoV.

Sybil Attack

Multiple network identities are required to execute a sybil attack. A single node with several identities can exert simultaneous influence over the entire system in a wireless network, even though the network is controlled by multiple nodes. The dynamic nature of IoV necessitates that vehicles remain connected to the network and provides an opportunity for hackers to execute computer attacks (Daiyu et al., 2017). Such an attack can be known as one of the most serious IoV attacks. The main aim of this attack is to build networks according to its objectives. Attacker nodes (vehicles), for instance, have an attacker who may act by taking a route other than the desired route. Sybil attack are not just one of the most hazardous attack strategies, but they are also typically the most difficult to detect. The attacker means that the vehicle is in various locations by sending incorrect location data, which is increasingly dangerous for networks using regional routing (Samad et al., 2018).

GPS Spoofing Attack

GPS spoofing is a form of cyber-attack where the attacker generates false Global Positioning System (GPS) signals to deceive GPS receivers and provide inaccurate location information. This can have serious consequences, especially in systems and applications that rely on accurate GPS data, such as navigation systems, time synchronisation, and location-based services. GPS data plays a significant part in IoV applications, including navigation and payment applications (Mershad & Artail, 2013). Furthermore, a study of the false-position impact reveals that the total ratio of packet transmission can be decreased by almost 90% (Tim & Elmar, 2006).

Masquerading Attack

Masquerading refers to a security IoV attack that uses the same ID on many nodes, as the name implies. To get access to the unauthorised device, the intruder must first obtain a legitimate ID. This kind of assault is similar to Sybil, although it does not involve the use of many identities (Samad et al., 2018).

Wormhole Attack

In a wormhole attack, the intruder gains access to the network and then uses it to send and receive packets. Since data meant for one node ends up in other places, security is compromised. Wormholes render all IoV elements immune to their natural reaction (Ji et al., 2013).

METHOD

This section presents a method for blockchain-based authentication, enabling the vehicle to connect to the network as a legitimate entity. The registration process is also outlined within this section. Table 2 describes the notations used in this section.

Registration Phase

In this phase, prior to entering the vehicle network, the vehicle is required to undergo the initial registration process. The user follows specific registration steps to guarantee the successful registration of their vehicle. The registration steps are outlined as follows:

Step 1: Upon receiving the model number and license number from the service provider, the V_n forwards a registration request to the RA for the vehicle registration process. It is assumed that an authorised official verifies the

Table 2. Notations used

Notation	Description
R_p	denotes the public key of RA
R_s	denotes the private key of RA
V_p	denotes the public key of vehicle
V_s	denotes the private key of vehicle
V_r	vehicle registration number
V_n	specific vehicle
K_s	shared secret
E_k	encryption key
D_k	decryption key
L_i	driving license number
B_i	block number
M	model number

authenticity of the original information, with the details extending beyond the scope of this report.

Step 2: A request for the generation of keys, RA sends a key pair of R_p and V_p to calculate the K_s that are vital for the encryption and decryption of information discussed in this chapter later.

Step 3: RA sends V_r after the active key exchange on the vehicle that is encrypted with E_k and waits for the acceptance. In Equation 1, the V_r for the vehicle is computed.

Step 4: As in Figure 2, when an encrypted confirmation is obtained, RA will add a transaction to the blockchain. The registry transaction block comprises the transaction types V_r, D_k, and E_k. When a transaction is added to the database, RA can remove all the vehicles' records, including V_r, D_k, $E_{k,}$ *and* $K_{s,}$ from the registration temporary database.

Authentication Phase

Upon completion of registration, vehicles need only try to interact with the RSU to acquire the network and use the services they wish. To do this, the vehicle must

Figure 2. Shows the working of the registration process

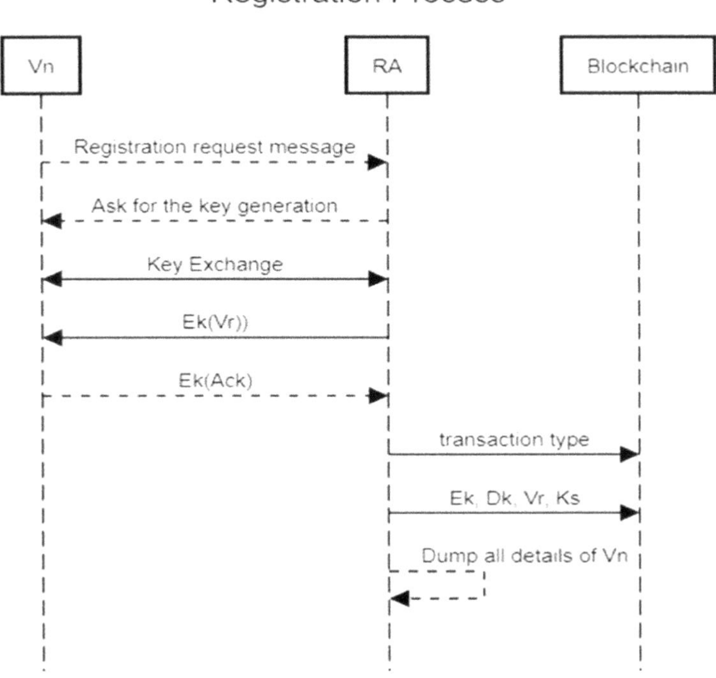

be authenticated by V_n. The authentication method has been split up into several steps, referred to in Figure 3.

Step 1: In addition to the request for the service connection, the V_r obtained by the method of registration is submitted to the RSU.

Step 2: Every RSU stores the request and waits for blockchain review in its local memory. RSU will check the Vr vehicle. When it matches existing information, RSU will mark the transaction legitimate, allow the network to access and issue a $B_{i,}$ and permit to access the network. If this is not the case, the RSU will mark it as an invalid transaction.

Equation 1 Calculate the vehicle registration number using the mode of driving license number and model number.

$$Vr = Li \Delta M$$

Step 3: RSU eliminates invalid local memory transactions, and if legitimate, RSU will use the blockchain as an authentication block.

Key Generation Algorithm

ECDH is a key protocol for a shared secret generation via a vulnerable medium. Every party has a public-private key pair elliptical. It is a Diffie-Hellman protocol elliptic cryptographic curve version. The ECDH secret key may be used explicitly for a key or a particular key, which then is encrypted through a symmetric key.

Encryption/Decryption Scheme

ECC does not explicitly provide a method of encryption such as RSA. In calculating a secret key for symmetric encryption and decryption, they have introduced a hybrid encryption framework using AES, meaning that both ECDH and AES are used.

EVALUATION AND RESULTS

This evaluation procedure takes place after the implementation step is completed, which includes security and performance analysis.

Figure 3. Depicts the authentication process

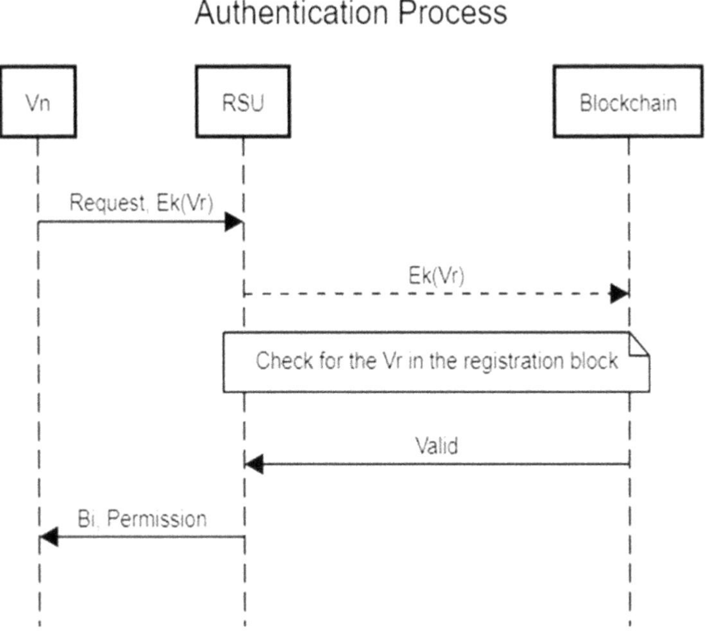

Attacks Analysis

An authentic user or vehicle transmitting data should be. The device must be able to differentiate between honest and dishonest vehicles. The Sybil attack enables the connection of numerous nodes to a network, posing a threat to the overall behavior of the network, as discussed in the above section. A wormhole attack is a type of security threat in wireless networks, particularly in ad hoc and sensor networks. In a wormhole attack, malicious nodes create a tunnel (or "wormhole") between two distant points in the network. GPS spoofing attacks highlight the need for robust security measures in systems that rely on accurate location data, especially in critical applications where the consequences of inaccurate information could be severe. The black-hole attack redirected every packet into the attacker and dropped a packet, which led to immediate vehicle decision-making and put human safety in danger. Replay attacks may subsequently reuse messages to deceive other network organisations. Fabrication attacks allow malicious nodes to send the entire network with false signals that lead to misinterpretation. Masquerading attacks enable the authorisation of an ID to enter illegally into the system. Many other threats, including message tampering and greyhole attacks, are also occurring.

All the methods mentioned earlier pose potential risks to authentication and should be mitigated. BBA-IoV plays a crucial role in helping devices thwart large-scale and harmful attacks, like the Sybil attack. This type of attack empowers a malicious node to generate counterfeit identities and introduce inaccurate information into the network. However, nodes (vehicles) can only have a few identities because the RA generates only one V_r against a single encrypted vehicle in BBA-IoV, as mentioned above. As a result, the possibility of fraudulent identities has been reduced. Therefore, the risk of false identities has been minimised.

In addition, the utilisation of timestamping is implemented to safeguard against wormhole and replay attacks in this procedure. A message-receiving node handles timestamp in the blockchain. If the difference between the real and the obtained timestamps exceeds the predetermined threshold, the message is disregarded or erased. Furthermore, as a safeguard against spoofing attacks, BBA-IoV requires that V_r be used only by an allowed entity; otherwise, it is labelled as invalid. The masking attack employs cryptographic encryption techniques that prevent the attacker from recognising an actual vehicle.

Moreover, all miners have reached a consensus on the transaction blocks recorded in the blockchain within the suggested mechanism. Blockchain hashing guarantees the sequencing and specifics of the blocks. Each block possesses its unique hashes. Manipulating the data in the block would modify the hash. If malicious nodes intend to modify the contents of the block or tamper with any element within it, they must alter the hash. Due to the interconnection of each block with the preceding block hash, calculating hashes becomes challenging, hence preventing the execution of a harmful action by an attacker.

Let us consider two scenarios in which the RSU or RA has been jeopardised. If the attackers breach the RSU, they cannot obtain the authentication ID of the vehicle because the authentic B_i is stored only in the blockchain. Second, even if RA is hacked, the original vehicle identifications and the actual owner of the vehicle are

Table 3. Comparison of security performance

Types of Attacks	Performance				
	PPAS	*LIAU*	*BARS*	*ECPP*	*BBA-IoV*
Sybil Attack	✓	✓	✓	✓	✓
Replay Attack	✓	✓	✓	✗	✓
GPS Spoofing	✓	✓	✗	✓	✓
Fabrication Attack	✓	✓	✓	✗	✓
Tampering Attack	✓	✓	✓	✗	✓
Masquerading Attack	✓	✓	✓	✓	✓

Note: ✓shows the methods that defense against the attacks,✗shows that do not.

still secure because RA dumps all original vehicle information. Thus, a malicious node cannot get a vehicle's identity.

Unlike traditional cloud computing, the BBA-IoV system does not use centralised storage. Blockchain keeps track of all transaction blocks that are exposed to all nodes on the network. If an attacker launches an attack, it must target any block containing the transaction.

This approach, in addition to authentication, provides other security functions. Confidentiality can be achieved, for example, because no one can access permitted information. The blockchain hash mechanism assures data integrity. Finally, they offer a non-repudiation guarantee, which is backed up by a specific vehicle registration number or block number provided by RA and RSU. Table 3 summarises the contribution of related methods to security attacks.

RESULT

This proposed framework allows for performance assessments based on the cryptographic algorithm used for public and private keys; AES is used to encrypt the message as the system key is symmetrical and is used to decrypt the message. ECDH is a one-way feature that makes calculations quick but makes it impossible to reverse the simulation results for the original values.

Security Analysis

The security aspect is evaluated in this section by employing specific parameters as detailed below:

i. ***Key Size:*** The key size is crucial to the cryptographic algorithm's security. The differences and similarities between RSA and ECDH are shown in Table 4. This algorithm is chosen based on a comparative analysis of other algorithms. The ECDH algorithm consumes lower power compared to other algorithms and provides the same level of security as RSA. The private keys are produced via a random process and consist of 64 hexadecimal digits. As a result of key compression, the public keys consist of 65 hexadecimal digits.

iii. ***Encryption with ECDH:*** The shared secret key, created by ECDH, can be utilised for symmetric encryption and decryption utilising asymmetric encryption algorithms like AES. The ECDH and AES hybrid method was implemented, as stated above. The brainpoolP256r1 curve has been utilised. In addition, both

Table 4. Security Comparison of two algorithms

Key Size(bits)	RSA key Size	ECDH Key Size
80	1024	160-223
112	2048	224-255
128	3072	256-383
192	7680	384-511
256	15360	512

the Vehicle Owner and RA parties desire to exchange information securely while preventing interception by a third-party man-in-the-middle (MIM). However, in order to decrypt it, they must first resolve the discrete logarithm problem.

Performance Analysis

This section provides an analysis of the storage cost, delay time, and communication cost associated with our proposed authentication scheme.

i. ***Delay Time:*** Initially, we examine the delay time of our suggested approach by employing ECDH. The primary advantage of utilising ECDH is the utilisation of larger key sizes, which offer more strength compared to the RSA algorithm. A regular ECDH key with a length of 256 bits possesses an RSA key with a length of 3072 bits, which is 10,000 times more potent than an RSA key with a length of 2048 bits. (Wayne-2014). In contrast, ECDH requires lower computational power and memory, leading to significantly faster speed and improved performance. The figure illustrates the time delay between RSA and ECDH with various key sizes configured.

ii. ***Communication and Storage Cost:*** The cost of communication and storage is another metric used to measure performance. All the parameter computation and exchange add up to a communication cost, which is proportional to the total amount of communication. During the communication phase of the BBA-IoV technique, a series of interactions were necessary among the RA, RSU, vehicle, and blockchain. The space required to store all the parameters on the blockchain is known as the storage cost. Whenever it allocates B_i to the vehicle, RSU has its local cache with low memory and erases it, as previously mentioned, whereas RA erases all the details. Three data structures make up

Figure 4. Shows the delay time comparison

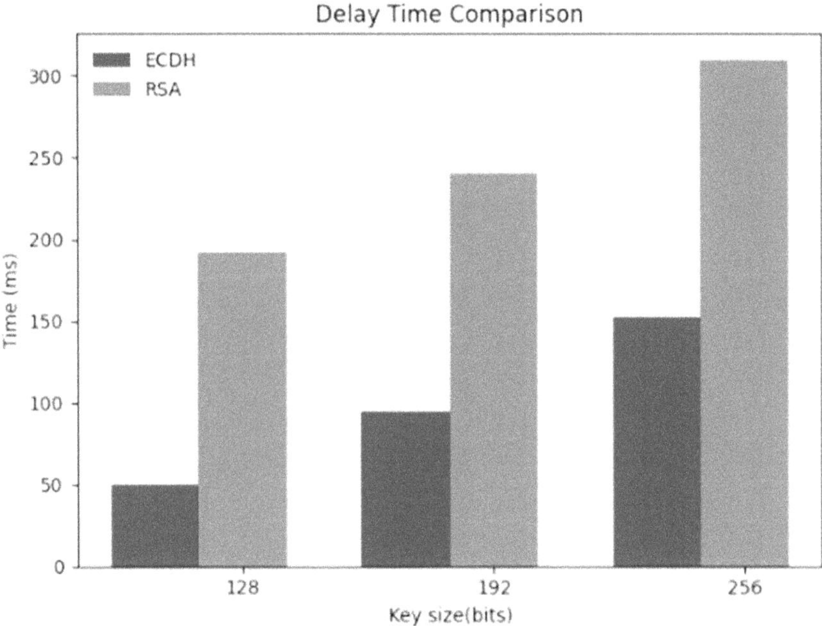

a blockchain: a 32-byte hash digest, a 4-byte timestamp, and an 8-byte nonce. In addition, there are two different block sizes available: 28 and 56. For each vehicle, two blocks are generated. Suppose they have *n* numbers of vehicles; storage overhead would be Equation 2:

Equation 2 calculates the storage cost.

$$StorageCost = \frac{n}{2}(32+4+8+28+56) = 64nbytes$$

In comparison to LIAU and SCAR, this method is therefore effective and has minimal storage and communication expenses, as stated in Figure 5.

iii. ***Operation Cost:*** The operation cost is the time it takes for the vehicle to register and validate itself. The longer it takes, the more complex the protocol becomes. Figure 6 depicts the operation time as compared with LIAU and ECCP. The storage and communication costs of LIAU are significant even though its operation time is marginally more than that of BBA-IOV.

Figure 5. Shows the cost comparison

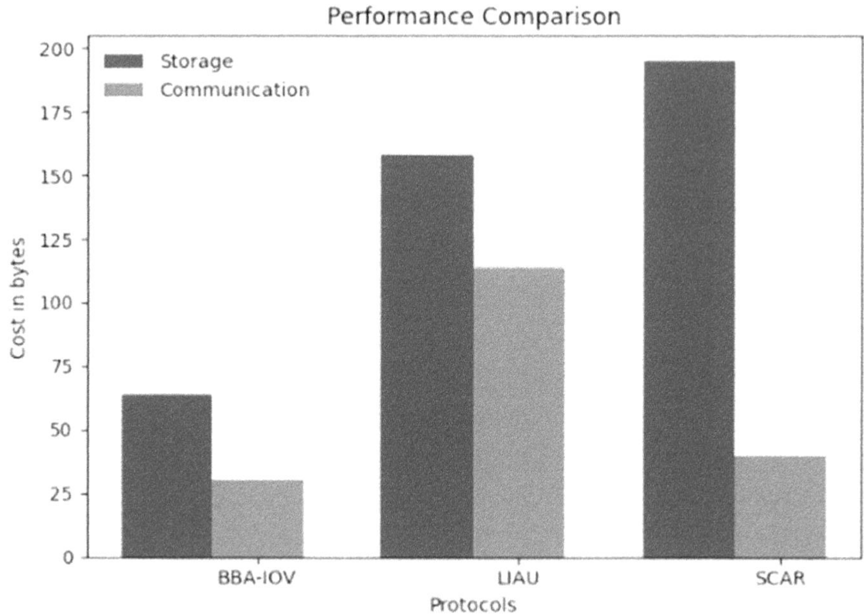

Figure 6. Shows the operation time comparison

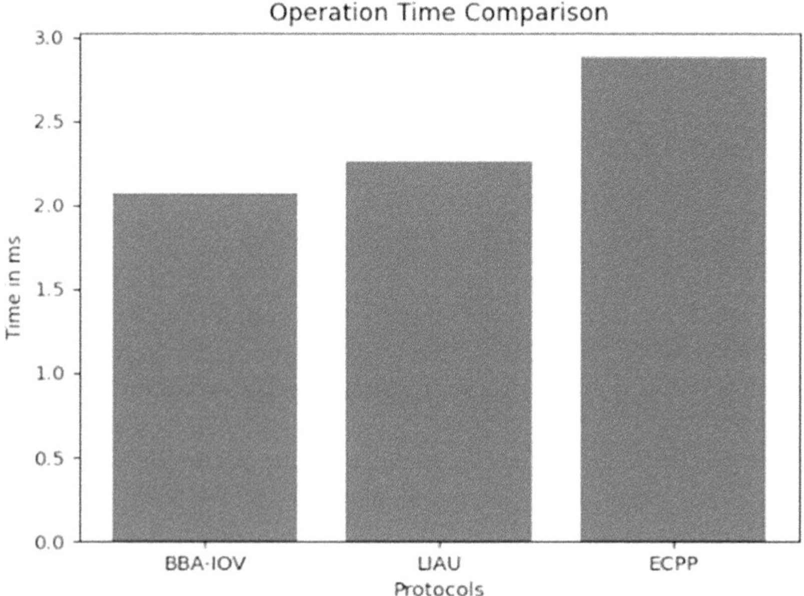

CONCLUSION

This article describes the implementation of an authentication scheme for vehicles using blockchain technology. The blockchain is briefly described, making it easily understandable. In addition, it highlighted the current issues of IoV and how they can be addressed using blockchain technology. It's important to note that blockchain is a cutting-edge technology that offers both anonymity and security without compromising the identity of the user. This proposed framework utilises a private blockchain, which enhances security by minimising the risk of authentication attacks. In addition, the authentication process for the vehicle is streamlined, enhancing the overall efficiency of the system. In addition, the hash functions within the blockchain ensure that the original data remains unaltered. Given the consensus feature of blockchain, transactions undergo verification prior to being added to the blockchain. The proposed mechanism delves into the exploration of incorporating additional features to enhance security services, including integrity, confidentiality, access control, and non-repudiation, in conjunction with authentication. Finally, this chapter thoroughly analyses the security of the proposed system and evaluates its performance.

REFERENCES

Aich, S., Chakraborty, S., Sain, M., Lee, H.-i., & Kim, H.-C. (2019). A Review on Benefits of IoT Integrated Blockchain based Supply Chain Management Implementations across Different Sectors with Case Study. *2019 21st International Conference on Advanced Communication Technology (ICACT),* 138-141. 10.23919/ICACT.2019.8701910

Al Ameen, M., Liu, J., & Kwak, K. (2012). Security and Privacy Issues in Wireless Sensor Networks for Healthcare Applications. *Journal of Medical Systems*, *36*(1), 93–101. doi:10.1007/s10916-010-9449-4 PMID:20703745

Ji, S., Chen, T., & Zhong, S. (2015, March 1). Wormhole Attack Detection Algorithms in Wireless Network Coding Systems. *IEEE Transactions on Mobile Computing*, *14*(3), 660–674. doi:10.1109/TMC.2014.2324572

Jiang, T., Fang, H., & Wang, H. (2019, June). Blockchain-Based Internet of Vehicles: Distributed Network Architecture and Performance Analysis. *IEEE Internet of Things Journal*, *6*(3), 4640–4649. doi:10.1109/JIOT.2018.2874398

Leinmüller, T., & Schoch, E. (2006). *Greedy Routing in Highway Scenarios: The Impact of Position Faking Nodes*. Academic Press.

Leo, M., Aymen, C., & Francine, K. (2020). Survey on blockchain-based applications in internet of vehicles. *Computers & Electrical Engineering*, *84*, 106646. Advance online publication. doi:10.1016/j.compeleceng.2020.106646

Li, Y. (2012). An overview of the DSRC/WAVE technology. Lecture Notes of the Institute for Computer Sciences. *Social-Informatics and Telecommunications Engineering, LNICST.*, *74*, 544–558. doi:10.1007/978-3-642-29222-4_38

Lu, R., Lin, X., Zhu, H., Ho, P.-H., & Shen, X. (2008). ECPP: Efficient Conditional Privacy Preservation Protocol for Secure Vehicular Communications. *IEEE INFOCOM 2008 - The 27th Conference on Computer Communications,* 1229-1237. 10.1109/INFOCOM.2008.179

Lu, Z., Liu, W., Wang, Q., Qu, G., & Liu, Z. (2018). A Privacy-Preserving Trust Model Based on Blockchain for VANETs. *IEEE Access : Practical Innovations, Open Solutions*, *6*, 45655–45664. doi:10.1109/ACCESS.2018.2864189

Mershad, K., & Artail, H. (2013, February). A Framework for Secure and Efficient Data Acquisition in Vehicular Ad Hoc Networks. *IEEE Transactions on Vehicular Technology*, *62*(2), 536–551. doi:10.1109/TVT.2012.2226613

Nakamoto, S. (2009). *Bitcoin: A peer-to-peer electronic cash system.* http://www.bitcoin.org/bitcoin.pdf

Priya, K., & Karuppanan, K. (2011). Secure privacy and distributed group authentication for VANET. *2011 International Conference on Recent Trends in Information Technology (ICRTIT),* 301-306. 10.1109/ICRTIT.2011.5972438

Qu, F., Wu, Z., Wang, F.-Y., & Cho, W. (2015, December). A Security and Privacy Review of VANETs. *IEEE Transactions on Intelligent Transportation Systems*, *16*(6), 2985–2996. doi:10.1109/TITS.2015.2439292

Samad, A., Alam, S., Shuaib, M., & Bokhari, M. (2018). *Internet of Vehicles (IoV).* Requirements, Attacks and Countermeasures.

Sharma, N., Chauhan, N., & Chand, N. (2018). Security challenges in Internet of Vehicles (IoV) environment. *2018 First International Conference on Secure Cyber Computing and Communication (ICSCCC),* 203-207. 10.1109/ICSCCC.2018.8703272

Tan, Choi, Kim, Pan, & Chung. (2018). Secure Certificateless Authentication and Road Message Dissemination Protocol in VANETs. Wireless Communications and Mobile Computing. doi:10.1155/2018/7978027

Wayne, T. (2014). *Benefits of Elliptic Curve Cryptography.* https://casecurity.org/2014/06/10/benefits-of-elliptic-curve-cryptography

Xu, D., Wu, Y., & Duan, Y. (2017). *Sybil Attack Detection Scheme Based on Data Flow Monitoring and RSSI ranging in WSN.* doi:10.25236/icmit.2017.19

Xu, H., Zeng, M., Hu, W., & Wang, J. (2019). Authentication-Based Vehicle-to-Vehicle Secure Communication for VANETs. Mobile Information Systems. doi:10.1155/2019/7016460

Yang, F., Wang, S., Li, J., Liu, Z., & Sun, Q. (2014, October). An overview of Internet of Vehicles. *China Communications*, *11*(10), 1–15. doi:10.1109/CC.2014.6969789

Chapter 8
Logistics Industry in the Context of the Blockchain Technology

Imdad Ali Shah
School of Computing Science, Taylor's University, Malaysia

Areeba Laraib
Mehran University of Engineering and Technology, Pakistan

Fida Hussain
Shaheed Benazir Bhutto Dewan University, Pakistan

ABSTRACT

Blockchain technology has garnered considerable interest from academics and businesses. One of the primary reasons to keep track of customer satisfaction and adoption is that customers don't use the product or service enough. Identifying the factors that influence the use and adoption of blockchain technologies will help solve the adoption problems effectively. Many significant firms, like Google, Amazon, and others, will embrace blockchain technology. It will indeed be found in the future and revolutionise logistics and transportation. Even though the advantages of blockchain technology have been well studied in the financial sector, using blockchain technology can help decrease significant logistical challenges such as border delays, product damage, errors, and multiple data entry.

INTRODUCTION

Logistics are becoming more complex as more parties participate directly or indirectly in supply chains. Communication and end-to-end visibility are getting more and more

DOI: 10.4018/979-8-3693-3816-2.ch008

challenging because of this complexity, leading to inefficient logistical processes. All parties in the supply chain have raised their standards for transparency, dependability, and customer service simultaneously. The blockchain is becoming more popular as a potential remedy for these problems. Although blockchain technology has a far more comprehensive range of uses, cryptocurrencies are where it is most employed and related. A distributed ledger (book) called blockchain has several applications. Contracts, cargo tracking, and financial transactions are only a few applications for it (AlShamsi, Yli-Huumo, J.,, 2017). A product may undergo more than 31 inspections by organisms while in transit; adding all of this up is very expensive. In addition, there has always been a tonne of paperwork to finish. The end-to-end transportation business is already inefficient, and the paperwork process worsens it (Berke, A, Moller, A.P., 2019). The absence of a single source of truth and a convoluted process fundamentally slows down the logistic process.

A decentralized organization must carry out all transactions, which also acts as a hub for process improvement and verification. Due to blockchain's digital nature, all documentation must be completed online, making the data accessible to everyone, anywhere (Mattila, J., Edvard Tijan et all., Yassine Issaoui, 2019). Making decisions with the aid of blockchain tracking can result in a more satisfying service for the customer. In this article, blockchain technology in logistics is highlighted, along with the future of blockchain technology and its uses. Overview of Blockchain Figure 1.

Blockchain helps with the tracing and verification of multi-step transactions that need to be able to be traced and verified. Blockchains reduce compliance expenses and quicken the processing of data transfers. The increased security consumers receive when conducting transactions is perhaps the most valuable benefit of utilizing blockchain technology. This function enhances trust between customers and business partners, safeguards personal information, and makes transaction tracing

Figure 1. Overview of blockchain

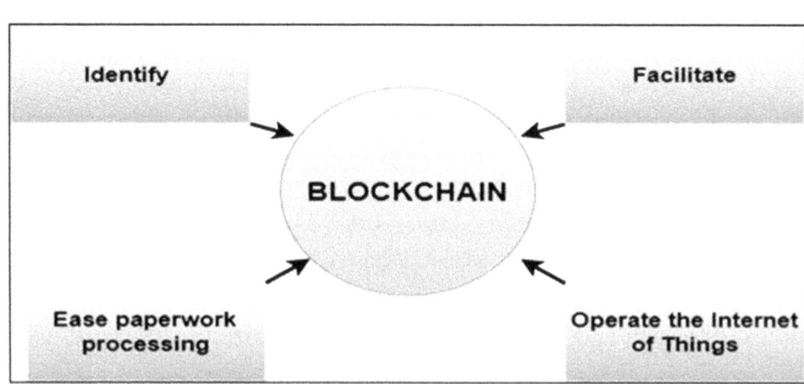

more transparent. Although blockchain technologies offer enormous potential, they are still not widely used across all industries.

(Alqahtani, M.,2020, Donalds, C.,2020, Harris, M. A.,2019). We must comprehend the theories and models from which these components are developed to get a comprehensive picture of the factors influencing the adoption of blockchain technology. To date, examining Blockchain technology assessments has revealed a lack of understanding of the key research techniques applied to Blockchain adoption and the main industries where Blockchain applications are deployed (Huang, K.,2021, Krishnaraju, V.2016, Galvez, J.F.,2018). Presented research on the knowledge and state of blockchain technology in supply chains and logistics. Their investigation found that integrating blockchain technology into logistical operations was very beneficial based on the data gathered throughout the testing.

Our chapter will focus on the following points: -

- We discussed the importance of blockchain technology in the logistics industry.
- We discussed the security issues and challenges of using blockchain technology in logistics.
- We have peer-reviewed on implementing blockchain technology in the logistics industry.
- We provided future work and recommendations.

LITERATURE REVIEW

The study made some insightful observations regarding the acceptance and usage of Blockchain technology in international logistics networks. There is hesitation regarding adopting blockchain because it is still a developing technology with limited standardization, which means there is no consensus on a standard paradigm. The lack of laws and usage guidelines breeds unrest among stakeholders (Alamri, M.,2019). Although blockchain technology simplifies transaction procedures, transaction times are nevertheless prolonged by slow transaction rates. It is not simple to adopt blockchain technology and integrate it into the current system; the process necessitates a management change, requiring staff to be addressed and instructed on its uses for benefits. Due to inputted data being immutable, blockchain technology protects the safety and integrity of transactions and documentation, reducing fraudulent operations. In logistics systems, a massive paper trail and physical paperwork are vulnerable to fraud, human error, and misplacement (Choi, B. G.,2017). AI may stage and store freight, and machine learning can optimize freight routes using the stored data. This example illustrates the vast opportunities and advantages the global logistics industry can gain from implementing Blockchain technology.

Furthermore, a blockchain-based digital government frequently improves accountability and confidence while streamlining operations, safeguarding data, and reducing misuse and fraud. Organisations, governments, and people share resources via an encrypted distributed ledger (Galvez, J.F.,2018, Liu, D.,2018). Governments and citizen data are protected by removing single points of failure. The preceding research reviews on blockchain technology are displayed in Table 1 below. Recently, this topic has drawn much interest and attention worldwide. We'll see that blockchain technology has been researched in various fields, including logistics, supply chain management, agriculture, healthcare, and the energy sector (Shah, I. A., 2022, Shah, I. A. Shah, I. A.,2022). The rules and laws controlling this technology were a topic of interest in other reviews. It can be shown that the previous assessments have forgotten to analyze the aspects affecting Blockchain acceptance. Little is known about the principal fields where blockchain applications are used and the primary research methodologies employed in their adoption (Shah, I. A.,2022, Ronchi, A. M.,2019, Simonova, A. 2020). Blockchain technology in logistics is examined along with the future of blockchain technology and its uses. This paper aims to study how blockchain technology may be implemented in logistics procedures, ascertain (Muller, S. R.,2020, Simonova, A.,2020) how it affects business transparency, and provide justifications for why blockchain technology should be applied across the supply chain. Blockchain uses in intelligent logistics are discussed in "Smart Logistics: Study of the Application of Blockchain Technology.

This was done by grouping the apps into four clusters information, transportation, financial, and management, and displaying the apps in each one. As discussed in "Blockchain provides many potential advantages for the logistics sector. Making sure that the origin and authenticity of products are known, proven, and shared enables organizations to increase efficiency, transparency, and traceability and make supply chains safer. On the other hand, businesses are waiting for a natural, game-changing solution to logistics issues. There is a lack of understanding and confidence regarding technology and its applications. Many company leaders are still unsure what blockchain is and how it is transforming the industry. Because blockchain is an underlying technology, and everything happens behind the scenes, it's difficult to explain how it may provide a new kind of infrastructure and a new means to digitize assets through tokens. The report states, " Businesses in the logistics sector are considering implementing it to obtain a competitive edge. It might be challenging to modify and adjust supply chains and logistics. Businesses generally (Twizeyimana, J. D.,2019, Yazdanmehr, A.,2020, Yoo, C. W.,2018) spend a lot of time and effort creating and perfecting their supply chains. Therefore, it is difficult to introduce new technology because of integration issues. The lack of experts with specific experience in (Shah, I. A.,2022, Shah, I. A.,2022, Shah, I. A.,2022) cryptocurrency and a thorough understanding of different types of crypto assets is another barrier to implementing blockchain in logistics. How the Blockchain would aid in lowering logistics costs and optimizing operations and research problems is discussed.

In today's corporate world, information about a company's transactions is frequently maintained discreetly, and there is often no master ledger of all activity. Contrarily, this data is commonly dispersed across internal departments and corporate divisions, making reconciling transactions a time-consuming and error-prone process (De Filippi, P.,2019, El Haddouti, S.,2019, Fan, K., 2018). A typical stock transaction, for instance, can be completed in a matter of microseconds. Still, the stock transfer may take much longer because the parties involved in the supply chain do not have access to each other's ledgers and cannot automatically confirm that the assets are owned and are, therefore transferable, blockchain and Logistics in Figure 2.

One of the most critical challenges to overcome in implementing blockchain in the supply chain is the need to include all the various parties. Additionally, the solution's implementation may be slowed by the information shared across the entire blockchain. Therefore, to properly deploy Blockchain technology in the supply chain, it is necessary first to analyse the requirements and goals of the many actors involved to create a business model that can demonstrate the solution's benefits (Agbo, C. C., 2019, Salam, S.,2021, Bao, J.2020). The blockchain is utilized in financial or cryptocurrency applications because it improves various applications' speed, security, usability, and confidentiality. Many businesses have created their research centres for the development of blockchain technology to investigate the

Figure 2. Blockchain and logistics

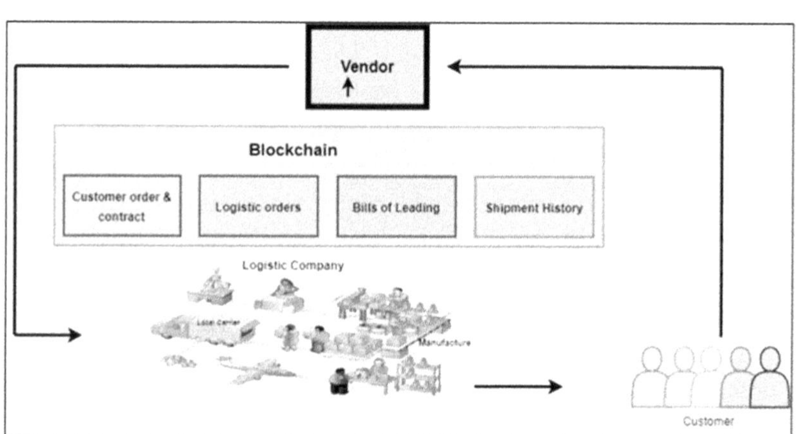

potential applications of this technology across numerous industries. A "widely distributed database that is completely capable of maintaining various (end-user) records of digital data or even events in such a way that it becomes almost impossible to tamper with or change the contents of those data packets in any way" is what is meant by the definition of blockchain. In other words, while adding data, accessing it, or even inspecting it is conceivable, changing or deleting the data itself is thought to be virtually impossible.

OVERVIEW OF BLOCKCHAIN TECHNOLOGY IN THE LOGISTICS INDUSTRY

One of the significant developments of 2021 has been blockchain technology. More and more businesses are participating in projects run by this online information system daily. There are many distinct purposes for which blockchain can be used. Various industries are working to create answers to their issues with it. The main concern in the logistics sector of the supply chain is how blockchain may enhance it. Blockchain technology can let businesses track their goods from the precise moment they are manufactured to the exact minute they are delivered. (Shah, I. A., 2021, Kiran, S. R. A., 2021, Umrani, S. 2020) it facilitates better information exchange between all parties participating in a process and even enables companies to automate payment procedures. The system operates in that each party receives a copy of the database or a portion of it. That party is then permitted to modify the database under conditions agreed upon by all parties (Kim, H. M.,2018, Han, M.,2018, Mengelkamp, E.,2018). Transporting raw materials or finished goods to clients is a logistical undertaking that involves several parties. To ensure the transactions are trustworthy, all logistics transactions are supported by various papers (Naik, N., 2020, Nawari, N. O.,2019, Su, Z.2018). In contrast to face-to-face transactions, where payment is made after the buyer has physically seen the product, global trade is conducted using routine trade paperwork. Additionally, unless you phone or email the other party, you cannot know what tasks or procedures they are working on in real-time. However, blockchain technology establishes a trusted ecosystem by ensuring that transaction data on blocks is impervious to fabrication or change (Shah, I. A.,2023, Shah, I. A.,2023, Low Xin Yuan 2023). The interface of the blockchain application with the physical world is one of its most crucial features, which necessitates using the right equipment and technology, like IoT. Due to blockchain technology's recent introduction, low acceptance, and complexity for many people and organizations, it is still not widely used in intelligent logistics. Logistics, technological advances, and the advent of the fourth industrial revolution helped create new problems (United Nations, 2018,

Zheng, Z.,2018, Singh, A. P.2020). These can hasten the technical integration of all logistics procedures. As a result, a brand-new idea known as "smart logistics" or "logistics 4.0" has emerged. In McFarlane's opinion, Intelligent logistics revolves around effective planning and management techniques. This is merely a primary classification of several recent initiatives, however. However, these applications impact various aspects of organisms, including their capacity for economic activity. Managers have complete visibility into the overall processes' operations status thanks to data collection and transmission in close to real-time, enabling them to make prompt decisions based on trustworthy information. (Kumar, M. S., 2021) examines the effect of the blockchain on several supply chain management goals using a case study methodology.

The study made some insightful observations regarding the acceptance and usage of Blockchain technology in international logistics networks. There is hesitation regarding adopting blockchain because it is still a developing technology with limited standardization, which means there is no consensus on a standard paradigm. The lack of laws and usage guidelines breeds unrest among stakeholders. Although blockchain technology simplifies transaction procedures, transaction times are nevertheless prolonged by slow transaction rates. It is not simple to adopt blockchain technology and integrate it into the current system; the process necessitates a management change, requiring staff to be addressed and instructed on its uses for benefits. Due to inputted data being immutable, blockchain technology protects the safety and integrity of transactions and documentation, reducing fraudulent operations. In logistics systems, a massive paper trail and physical paperwork are vulnerable to fraud, human error, and misplacement. AI may stage and store freight, and machine learning can optimize freight routes using the stored data. This example illustrates the vast opportunities and advantages the global logistics industry can gain from implementing Blockchain technology. and applications of blockchain clusters in logistics in Figure 3.

Figure 3. Applications of blockchain clusters in logistics

Information
Transport
Finance
Management

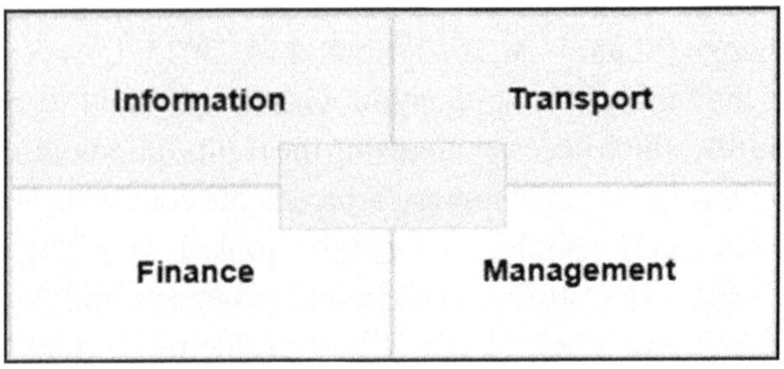

Information

The use of blockchain in information clusters entails recording orders, receipts, invoices, payments, and other official papers and registering each asset as it moves through supply chain nodes. Digital purchases are tracked simultaneously with physical ones.

Transport

Increased sustainability, decreased fraud, decreased administrative delays, decreased waste, and quicker problem identification are all benefits of integrating Blockchain into shipping Walmart, a large-format retailer, recently received a patent that will enable them to connect delivery drones to the Blockchain and enhance last-mile operations (Tosh, D. K., 2017). Blockchain technology might be crucial in minimizing these issues and enhancing logistics procedures. This innovation applies to all personnel, processes, and tools in the final supply chain segments.

Finance

Among other financial services, blockchain can be used for online payments and remittances. These services influence network-wide financial operations, product management, and supply chain processes. They will also facilitate the acquisition of goods and services by removing currency restrictions and transfer costs (Yang, T., 2017), enhancing corporate operations. Customer satisfaction and meeting their requirements will be prioritized.

Management

Smart logistics can be improved using Blockchain, which enhances management and makes supply networks more responsive. Additionally, near real-time data gathering and transmission give managers a comprehensive picture of the status of the entire process, enabling them to make quick decisions based on correct information. Even while blockchain has been utilized in international trade for some time, its importance has grown since the COVID-19 health crisis began, many advantages of blockchain in logistics technology. Figure 4 shows many advantages of blockchain in logistics technology.

The way we manage and keep data is being quickly transformed by blockchain technology. A blockchain is based on a network of data blocks secured and connected by encryption in place of a central database. Many industries, including cross-border trade logistics and global supply chains, benefit from the rise of blockchain.

Figure 4. Many advantages of blockchain in logistics technology

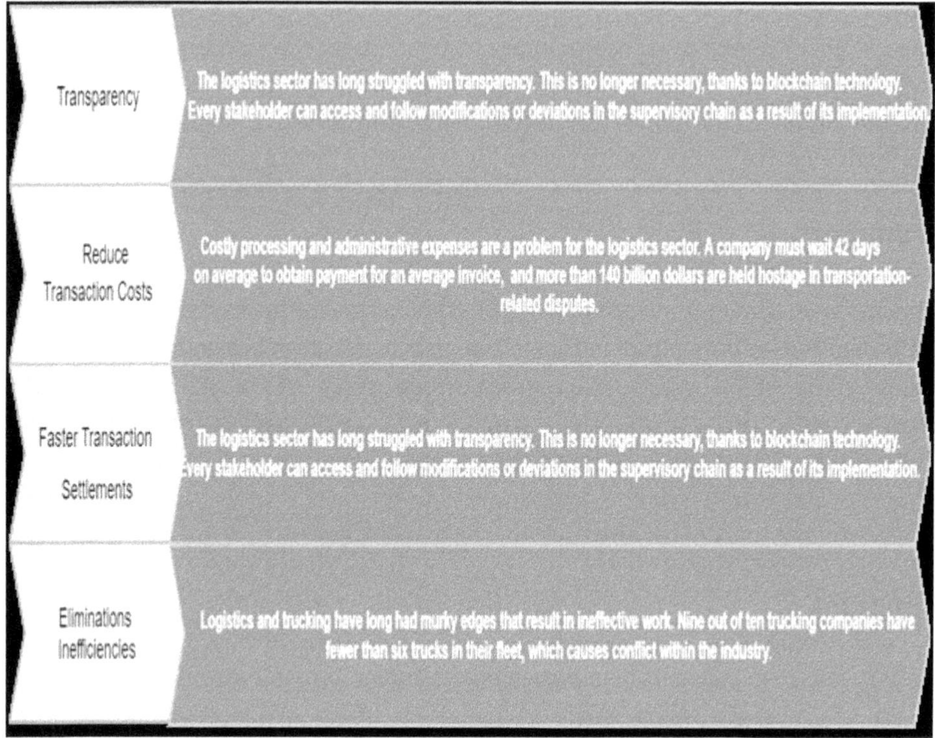

Blockchain can improve international shipment tracking, reduce administrative work by automating the documentation process, and secure transactions throughout the logistics chain (Shah, I. A., 2023, S Umrani, 2020). A recent conference on the use of blockchain in commerce and logistics was held in Singapore at the World Bank Hub for Infrastructure and Urban Development.

Frequently, end users cannot see where their things are or when they will come. The blockchain lessens the monopoly that some intermediaries currently have over important information. Any participant in the global supply chain has access to real-time data on the location of a shipment, the history of any documentation errors, and the identities of their partners (Cachin, C., 2017, McKinney, S. A., 2017). This might significantly increase the opportunities available to small and medium-sized businesses in the supply chain. The impact of blockchain on the financial markets is clear. It offers a mechanism to make safe, impenetrable logs of delicate activity, making it ideal for global financial transactions. By eliminating the intermediaries that existed in earlier decades, blockchain technology enables more affordable and effective methods of transferring and receiving money (Paintner, P., 2021). Despite the critical role that small and medium-sized enterprises play in the global economy, access to financing can be one of the significant problems these companies confront. For instance, small and medium-sized enterprises employ 50% of the world's workers and account for about 90% of all businesses. Giving those businesses a more straightforward way to accept payments, make payments, and increase income would only strengthen their position as global leaders. These businesses may fill financial shortages and respond to difficulties that may arise as they create or expand their businesses thanks to blockchain technology. Unfunded or underfunded projects sometimes face the danger of failing, yet decentralized financial arrangements give companies access to capital without using intermediaries (Ahmad, M. S., 2021). The supply chain is a complicated network, and even minor errors can have negative repercussions. Suppliers and transportation businesses can function more precisely and dependably by digitising and automating processes that were formerly paper-based. Additionally, blockchain-driven logistics could be game-changing for companies that depend on timely product delivery to clients, particularly at times when many supply lines are stymied.

DISCUSSION

Even if they anticipate several benefits in various logistics business areas, our study's findings show that most respondents and their firms are still wary about using blockchain. In general, queries about technology, in general, have gotten more positive feedback than inquiries about the state of technology now. This could mean that technology has advanced. Surprisingly, respondents who work for businesses with more excellent experience with blockchain tend to see more positive impact areas and fewer problems. One can anticipate that organizations with more excellent experience better understand the technology than their less experienced competitors. Interestingly, this may indicate a link between current Blockchain efforts and decisions made in the past to perform Blockchain projects (Millard, J., 2017, McKibbin, W.,2020). This could result in a division between businesses that continue to gain technology experience and those that stagnate at a low level of expertise. Most blockchain solutions are being created for the agriculture and food industries, as became evident throughout the review. The pharmaceutical and cross-sectoral sectors, however, are also important. Additionally, given that new frameworks were rarely suggested, academics appear to be content with developing solutions on top of Ethereum and Hyperledger Fabric (Lim, M.,2021). When use cases are considered, most solutions focus on the tracking and tracing of goods or fraud prevention. This is also evident in the obstacles raised since knowledge asymmetry, and unidentified provenance issues were commonly raised.

Internet of Things (IoT) devices have been frequently suggested as ways to solve the real-time openness of product information, and staff involvement is primarily relied upon. As seen by a sizable fraction of studies that do not discuss the usage or requirement of data integrity methods, the quality of data input into blockchain systems is not effectively addressed by current literature. Instead, research in academia has concentrated chiefly on the immutability and security of data after it is stored on the blockchain itself (Rodela, T. T., 2020). A potential bottleneck and avenue for dishonest individuals to introduce false data into the blockchain solution is the reliance on responsible third parties for data integrity assurance. Most recommended solutions have not yet been integrated with businesses and are now in the metrics testing phase. Lesser supply chain partners rarely discuss supported supply chain management methods (Ahmad, T.,2020, Lallie, H. S., 2021). This includes managing returns and consumer relationships, as well as developing and commercializing products. Despite being underutilized, the returns management process may be worth more investigation because of its function in locating chances for product improvement. Since blockchain technology is still in its early stages, many forces must join to overcome these constraints if it is to reach its full potential. Blockchain technology often reduces system failure risk significantly and addresses supply chain vulnerability issues (Samtani, S., 2020). Four categories and clusters of applications of blockchain technology can be made information, transportation, management, and finance. Regarding data, Blockchain's implementation enables safer monitoring, tracking, and validation of all data flows. By integrating blockchain technology into shipping, fraud, waste, and bureaucratic delays will be reduced, issues will be identified more quickly, and sustainability will be improved (Razaque, A., 2019). Blockchain can speed up company transactions by allowing parties buying goods and services to pay more and less, simplifying logistics transaction processes, and attracting more customers. Blockchain technology enhances management procedures by giving managers real time image of the entire logistics process in real-time and empowering them to make quick decisions based on information.

With its ability to guarantee traceability, security, and transparency, blockchain technology has the potential to solve issues with global supply chain management. "Being an emerging technology, the Blockchain seeks to store and transmit data in a secure, more open, and decentralized way," according to (Abubakar, A. M., 2019, Khan, N. A.,2019). Blockchain technology is used most frequently in peer-to-peer digital currencies like Bitcoin. A blockchain is essentially a distributed database, which means that all digital events that have taken place are recorded and shared among all users; once entered, the data cannot be changed. It kickstarts developing a self-sufficient, transparent, and scalable digital economy (Brohi, S. N., 2020). Blockchain technology, set in the twenty-first century, has significantly advanced logistics and supply chain management. A digital ledger of transactions that have been copied and propagated throughout all the nodes in the blockchain network is known as blockchain technology. Data and resource transfer between the point of origin and the point of consumption is known as global logistics. The development of Smart Logistics was facilitated by the fourth industrial revolution, which improved the technology's integration into all logistics procedures. Global logistics has benefited from the successful advancement of blockchain technology, which also makes decentralization and immutable data storage possible. Blockchain technology can reduce errors, product damage, order delays, and redundant data entry. (Pranggono, B., 2021, He, Y., 2021, Weil, T., 2020) respondents who work for businesses with more excellent experience with blockchain tend to see more positive impact areas and fewer problems. One can anticipate that organizations with more excellent experience better understand the technology than their less experienced competitors. Interestingly, this may indicate a link between current Blockchain efforts and decisions made in the past to perform Blockchain projects (which we use to gauge technical experience). This could result in a division between businesses that continue to gain technology experience and those that stagnate at a low level of expertise. Blockchain may have a good influence on their customers through cost savings. However, this impact area comes second because the technology is anticipated to benefit logistical service providers primarily. Communication with customers has the most significant impact. The fact that this effect area rates higher than the customer as a beneficiary shows that customer communication does help both the customer and the logistical service providers, challenging the Logistics Industry using blockchain technology in Figure 5.

Chapter Contribution and Discussion

This chapter contributes to one of the significant developments of 2021, which has been blockchain technology. More and more businesses are participating in projects run by this online information system daily. There are many distinct purposes for which blockchain can be used. Various industries are working to create answers to their issues with it. The main concern in the logistics sector of the supply chain is how blockchain may enhance it. Blockchain technology can let businesses track their goods from the precise moment they are manufactured to the exact minute they are delivered. Logistics are becoming more complex as more parties participate directly or indirectly in supply chains. Communication and end-to-end visibility are getting more and more challenging because of this complexity, leading to inefficient logistical processes. All parties in the supply chain have raised their standards for transparency, dependability, and customer service

Figure 5. The challenges logistics Industry using blockchain technology

Blockchain Adoption	Many influential people in the logistics sector are unaware of blockchain technology. Some people believe that fixing something that is not broken is useless.
Complex Industry	The term "logistics" refers to a wide range of distinct elements. The method is not straightforward to modify due to the complexity of deliveries and freight. Orders may need to transit through many jurisdictions depending on the logistics of each shipment, which exposes them to a lot of paperwork, delays, and human error.
Early Stages of Development	There aren't many engineers who are familiar with blockchain technology because of its infancy. This could make the implementation costly and difficult Since blockchain latency is not yet immediate, more work needs to be done on it. The blockchain might sustain serious harm, for instance. Organizations must come to a consensus to trust and deploy blockchain-based solutions in order to advance in this field and before the sector can completely accept the technology.
Data Concerns	Each transaction's data is stored by blockchain apps in a distributed ledger that is then used by all parties. In addition, there is still more information associated with the cryptographic algorithms. Finding a balance between simultaneously keeping data in their traditional databases and on the ledger eventually becomes challenging.

simultaneously. The blockchain is becoming more popular as a potential remedy for these problems. Although blockchain technology has a far more comprehensive range of uses, cryptocurrencies are where it is most employed and related. The logistic process is fundamentally slowed down by the absence of a single source of truth and a convoluted process. A decentralized organization must carry out all transactions, which also acts as a hub for process improvement and verification. Due to blockchain's digital nature, all documentation must be completed online, making the data accessible to everyone, anywhere.

Blockchain technology might be crucial in minimizing these issues and enhancing logistics procedures. This innovation applies to all personnel, processes, and tools in the final supply chain segments. Through cost savings, blockchain may have a good influence on their customers. However, this impact area comes second because the technology is anticipated to benefit logistical service providers primarily. Communication with customers has the most significant impact. The fact that this effect area rates higher than the customer as a beneficiary show that customer communication does help both the customer and the logistical service providers.

CONCLUSION

Blockchain technologies have drawn a lot of interest from both academia and business. One of the main reasons for conducting studies on customers' happiness and adoption is that their adoption rate is still low. Identifying the factors that influence the use and adoption of blockchain technologies will help solve the adoption problems effectively. Many significant firms, like Google, Amazon, and others, will embrace blockchain technology. It will indeed be found in the future and revolutionize logistics and transportation. Even though the advantages of blockchain technology have been well studied in the financial sector, using blockchain technology can help decrease significant logistical challenges such as border delays, product damage, errors, and multiple data entry. Logistics are becoming more complex as more parties participate directly or indirectly in supply chains. Communication and end-to-end visibility are getting more and more challenging because of this complexity, leading to inefficient logistical processes. All parties in the supply chain have raised their standards for transparency, dependability, and customer service simultaneously. Blockchain is becoming more popular as a potential remedy for these problems. The interaction of a blockchain application with the outside world is one of its most essential features, which calls for adopting appropriate tools and technologies like IoT. The potential of the blockchain is thrilling, but its execution may struggle to live up to its seamless, utopian pitch, much like self-driving vehicles and completely automated homes. The blockchain represents a significant advance in terms of technology, effectiveness, and transparency. However, just like humans, it may take a few generations for the new "genetics" to integrate into the existing systems fully. Blockchain is no exception to the rule that technical ages are remarkably short in search of fresh discoveries.

FUTURE WORK

Despite the innovative nature of the technology itself, its implementation in applications is beset with numerous limits and difficulties. Given the article's length, a brief but thorough treatment of the technical and non-technical obstacles to blockchain adoption in supply chains is provided. The retrieval and commit times of records in a blockchain are significantly slower than in a regular database. Additionally, it necessitates a significant increase in processing power, and the scalability of this power is a major worry. Furthermore, any systems dealing with the blockchain must be able to communicate with one another. The payment period must be brief and flexible to convert into any other currency, including FIAT money.

REFERENCES

Abubakar, A. M., Behravesh, E., Rezapouraghdam, H., & Yildiz, S. B. (2019). Applying artificial intelligence technique to predict knowledge hiding behavior. *International Journal of Information Management*, *49*, 45–57. doi:10.1016/j.ijinfomgt.2019.02.006

Agbo, C. C., Mahmoud, Q. H., & Eklund, J. M. (2019, June). Blockchain technology in healthcare: A systematic review. []. Multidisciplinary Digital Publishing Institute.]. *Health Care*, *7*(2), 56. PMID:30987333

Ahmad, M. S., & Shah, S. M. (2021). Moving Beyond the Crypto-Currency Success of Blockchain: A Systematic Survey. *Scalable Computing: Practice and Experience*, *22*(3), 321–346. doi:10.12694/scpe.v22i3.1853

AhmadT. (2020). Corona virus (covid-19) pandemic and work from home: Challenges of cybercrimes and cybersecurity. *Available at* SSRN 3568830. doi:10.2139/ssrn.3568830

Alamri, M., Jhanjhi, N. Z., & Humayun, M. (2019). Blockchain for Internet of Things (IoT) research issues challenges & future directions: A review. *Int. J. Comput. Sci. Netw. Secur*, *19*, 244–258.

AlShamsi, M., Al-Emran, M., & Shaalan, K. (2022). A Systematic Review on Blockchain Adoption. *Applied Sciences (Basel, Switzerland)*, *12*(9), 4245. doi:10.3390/app12094245

Bao, J., He, D., Luo, M., & Choo, K. K. R. (2020). A survey of blockchain applications in the energy sector. *IEEE Systems Journal*.

Brohi, S. N., Jhanjhi, N. Z., Brohi, N. N., & Brohi, M. N. (2020). Key Applications of State-of-the-Art technologies to mitigate and eliminate COVID-19. Berke, A. How Safe are Blockchains? *Harvard Business review*. https://hbr. org/2017/03/how-safe-are-blockchains-it-depends

Cachin, C., & Vukolić, M. (2017). Blockchain consensus protocols in the wild. *arXiv preprint arXiv:1707.01873*.

Choi, B. G., Jeong, E., & Kim, S. W. (2019). Multiple security certification system between blockchain based terminal and internet of things device: Implication for open innovation. *Journal of Open Innovation*, *5*(4), 87. doi:10.3390/joitmc5040087

De Filippi, P., Mannan, M., & Reijers, W. (2020). Blockchain as a confidence machine: The problem of trust & challenges of governance. Technology in Society, 62, Donalds, C., & Osei-Bryson, K. M. (2020). Cybersecurity compliance behavior: Exploring the influences of individual decision style and other antecedents. *International Journal of Information Management*, *51*, 102056.

Edvard, T. (2019). Blockchain Technology Implementation in Logistics. *Sustainability*.

El Haddouti, S., & El Kettani, M. D. E. C. (2019, April). Analysis of identity management systems using blockchain technology. In *2019 International Conference on Advanced Communication Technologies and Networking (CommNet)* (pp. 1-7). IEEE. 10.1109/COMMNET.2019.8742375

Fan, K., Wang, S., Ren, Y., Li, H., & Yang, Y. (2018). Medblock: Efficient and secure medical data sharing via blockchain. *Journal of Medical Systems*, *42*(8), 1–11. doi:10.1007/s10916-018-0993-7 PMID:29931655

Galvez, J. F., Mejuto, J., & Simal-Gandara, J. Future challenges on the use of blockchain for food traceability analysis. *TrAC Trends in Analytical Chemistry*. Science Direct. https://www.sciencedirect.com/science/article/abs/pii/S0268401219302877

Galvez, J. F., Mejuto, J., & Simal-Gandara, J. (2018). Future challenges on the use of blockchain for food traceability analysis. *Trends in Analytical Chemistry*, *107*, 222–232. doi:10.1016/j.trac.2018.08.011

Han, M., Li, Z., He, J., Wu, D., Xie, Y., & Baba, A. (2018, September). A novel blockchain-based education records verification solution. In *Proceedings of the 19th Annual SIG Conference on Information Technology Education* (pp. 178-183). IEEE. 10.1145/3241815.3241870

Harris, M. A., & Martin, R. (2019). Promoting cybersecurity compliance. In *Cybersecurity education for awareness and compliance* (pp. 54–71). IGI Global. https://www.igi-global.com/chapter/promoting-cybersecurity-compliance/225917 doi:10.4018/978-1-5225-7847-5.ch004

He, Y., Aliyu, A., Evans, M., & Luo, C. (2021). Health Care Cybersecurity Challenges and Solutions Under the Climate of COVID-19: Scoping Review. *Journal of Medical Internet Research*, *23*(4), e21747. https://www.jmir.org/2021/4/e21747/. doi:10.2196/21747 PMID:33764885

Hofbauer, D., Ivkic, I., & Tauber, M. (2019). *"On the Cost of Security Compliance in Information Systems." 10th International Multi-Conference on Complexity, Informatics and Cybernetics 2019*. IMCIC.

Huang, K., & Madnick, S. (2021, January). Does High Cybersecurity Capability Lead to Openness in Digital Trade? The Mediation Effect of E-Government Maturity. In *Proceedings of the 54th Hawaii International Conference on System Sciences* (p. 4352).

Issaoui, Y. (2019). *Smart Logistics: Study of The Application of Bolckchain Technology The 10th International Conference on Emerging Ubiquitous Systems and Pervasive Networks*. Springer. https://link.springer.com/article/10.1007/s12205-020-0188-x

Jabbar, S., Lloyd, H., Hammoudeh, M., Adebisi, B., & Raza, U. (2021). Blockchain-enabled supply chain: Analysis, challenges, and future directions. *Multimedia Systems*, *27*(4), 787–806. doi:10.1007/s00530-020-00687-0

Khan, N. A., Brohi, S. N., & Zaman, N. (2020). Ten deadly cyber security threats amid COVID-19 pandemic. *Tech*. https://www.techrxiv.org/articles/preprint/Ten_Deadly_Cyber_Security_Threats_Amid_COVID-19_Pandemic/12278792/1

Kim, C., & Kim, K. A. (2021). The institutional change from E-Government toward Smarter City; comparative analysis between royal borough of Greenwich, UK, and Seongdong-gu, South Korea. *Journal of Open Innovation*, *7*(1), 42. doi:10.3390/joitmc7010042

Kim, H. M., & Laskowski, M. (2018). Agriculture on the blockchain: Sustainable solutions for food, farmers, and financing. *Supply Chain Revolution, Barrow Books*.

Kiran, S. R. A., Rajper, S., Shaikh, R. A., Shah, I. A., & Danwar, S. H. (2021). Categorization of CVE Based on Vulnerability Software By Using Machine Learning Techniques. *International Journal (Toronto, Ont.)*, *10*(3).

Krishnaraju, V., Mathew, S. K., & Sugumaran, V. (2016). Web personalization for user acceptance of technology: An empirical investigation of E-government services. *Information Systems Frontiers*, *18*(3), 579–595. doi:10.1007/s10796-015-9550-9

Kumar, M. S., Vimal, S., Jhanjhi, N. Z., Dhanabalan, S. S., & Alhumyani, H. A. (2021). Blockchain based peer to peer communication in autonomous drone operation. *Energy Reports*.

Lallie, H. S., Shepherd, L. A., Nurse, J. R., Erola, A., Epiphaniou, G., Maple, C., & Bellekens, X. (2021). Cyber security in the age of covid-19: A timeline and analysis of cyber-crime and cyber-attacks during the pandemic. *Computers & Security*, *105*, 102248. https://www.sciencedirect.com/science/article/pii/S0167404821000729. doi:10.1016/j.cose.2021.102248 PMID:36540648

Li, L., He, W., Xu, L., Ash, I., Anwar, M., & Yuan, X. (2019). Investigating the impact of cybersecurity policy awareness on employees' cybersecurity behavior. *International Journal of Information Management*, *45*, 13–24. doi:10.1016/j.ijinfomgt.2018.10.017

Lim, M., Abdullah, A., & Jhanjhi, N. Z. (2021). Performance optimization of criminal network hidden link prediction model with deep reinforcement learning. *Journal of King Saud University. Computer and Information Sciences*, *33*(10), 1202–1210. doi:10.1016/j.jksuci.2019.07.010

Lindman, J., Tuunainen, V. K., & Rossi, M. (2017). Opportunities and risks of Blockchain Technologies–a research agenda.

Liu, C., Wang, N., & Liang, H. (2020). Motivating information security policy compliance: The critical role of supervisor-subordinate guanxi and organizational commitment. *International Journal of Information Management*, *54*, 102152. doi:10.1016/j.ijinfomgt.2020.102152

Liu, D., & Carter, L. (2018, May). Impact of citizens' privacy concerns on e-government adoption. In *Proceedings of the 19th Annual International Conference on Digital Government Research: Governance in the Data Age* (pp. 1-6). IEEE. 10.1145/3209281.3209340

Mattila, J., & Seppälä, T. (2017). Blockchains as a Path to a Network of Systems—An Emerging New Trend of the Digital Platforms in Industry and Society. Ideas. https://ideas.repec.org/p/rif/report/45.html

McKibbin, W., & Fernando, R. (2020). The economic impact of COVID-19. *Economics in the Time of COVID*, *19*, 45.

McKinney, S. A., Landy, R., & Wilka, R. (2017). Smart contracts, blockchain, and the next frontier of transactional law. *Wash. JL Tech. & Arts*, *13*, 313.

Mengelkamp, E., Gärttner, J., Rock, K., Kessler, S., Orsini, L., & Weinhardt, C. (2018). Designing microgrid energy markets: A case study: The Brooklyn Microgrid. *Applied Energy*, *210*, 870–880. https://dl.acm.org/doi/abs/10.1145/3241815.3241870. doi:10.1016/j.apenergy.2017.06.054

Millard, J. (2017). European Strategies for e-Governance to 2020 and Beyond. In *Government 3.0–Next Generation Government Technology Infrastructure and Services* (pp. 1–25). Springer. doi:10.1007/978-3-319-63743-3_1

Motahar, S. M., Mukhtar, M., Safie, N., Ma'arif, Y., & Mostafavi, S. (2018). Revisiting the Diversification on the Implementation of Open Source ERP Teaching Models. *Journal of Advanced Research in Dynamical and Control Systems,* (9), 2379- 2385 https://papers.ssrn.com/sol3/papers.cfm?abstract_id=3786555

Muller, S. R., & Lind, M. L. (2020). Factors in Information Assurance Professionals' Intentions to Adhere to Information Security Policies. [IJSSSP]. *International Journal of Systems and Software Security and Protection*, *11*(1), 17–32. doi:10.4018/IJSSSP.2020010102

Naik, N., & Jenkins, P. (2020, April). Self-Sovereign Identity Specifications: Govern your identity through your digital wallet using blockchain technology. In *2020 8th IEEE International Conference on Mobile Cloud Computing, Services, and Engineering (MobileCloud)* (pp. 90-95). IEEE.

Nawari, N. O., & Ravindran, S. (2019). Blockchain and the built environment: Potentials and limitations. *Journal of Building Engineering*, *25*, 100832. doi:10.1016/j.jobe.2019.100832

Paintner, P. (2021). *Blockchain technology in the area of e-Governance–Guidelines for implementation* [Doctoral dissertation, University NOVA].

Pranggono, B., & Arabo, A. (2021). COVID-19 pandemic cybersecurity issues. *Internet Technology Letters*, *4*(2), e247. doi:10.1002/itl2.247

Razaque, A., Amsaad, F., Khan, M. J., Hariri, S., Chen, S., Siting, C., & Ji, X. (2019). Survey: Cybersecurity vulnerabilities, attacks and solutions in the medical domain. *IEEE Access : Practical Innovations, Open Solutions*, *7*, 168774–168797. doi:10.1109/ACCESS.2019.2950849

RodelaT. T.TasnimS.MazumderH.FaizahF.SultanaA.HossainM. M. (2020). Economic Impacts of Coronavirus Disease (COVID-19) in Developing Countries. https://osf.io/preprints/socarxiv/wygpk/ doi:10.31235/osf.io/wygpk

Ronchi, A. M. (2019). e-Government: Background, Today's Implementation and Future Trends. In e-Democracy (pp. 93-196). Springer, Cham.

Salam, S., & Kumar, K. P. (2021). Survey on Applications of Blockchain in E-Governance. *REVISTA GEINTEC-GESTAO INOVACAO E TECNOLOGIAS, 11*(4), 3807-3822.

Samtani, S., Zhu, H., & Chen, H. (2020). Proactively Identifying Emerging Hacker Threats from the Dark Web: A Diachronic Graph Embedding Framework (D-GEF). [TOPS]. *ACM Transactions on Privacy and Security*, *23*(4), 1–33. doi:10.1145/3409289

Shah, I. A. (2022). Cybersecurity Issues and Challenges for E-Government During COVID-19: A Review. *Cybersecurity Measures for E-Government Frameworks*, 187-222.

Shah, I. A., Habeeb, R. A. A., Rajper, S., & Laraib, A. (2022). The Influence of Cybersecurity Attacks on E-Governance. In Cybersecurity Measures for E-Government doi:10.4018/978-1-7998-9624-1.ch005

Shah, I. A., Jhanjhi, N. Z., Humayun, M., & Ghosh, U. (2022). Health Care Digital Revolution During COVID-19. In *How COVID-19 is Accelerating the Digital Revolution* (pp. 17–30). Springer. doi:10.1007/978-3-030-98167-9_2

Shah, I. A., Jhanjhi, N. Z., Humayun, M., & Ghosh, U. (2022). Impact of COVID-19 on Higher and Post-secondary Education Systems. In *How COVID-19 is Accelerating the Digital Revolution* (pp. 71–83). Springer. doi:10.1007/978-3-030-98167-9_5

Shah, I. A., Jhanjhi, N. Z., & Laraib, A. (2023). Cybersecurity and Blockchain Usage in Contemporary Business. In *Handbook of Research on Cybersecurity Issues and Challenges for Business and FinTech Applications* (pp. 49–64). IGI Global.

Shah, I. A., & Rajper, S., & ZamanJhanjhi, N. (2021). Using ML and Data-Mining Techniques in Automatic Vulnerability Software Discovery. *International Journal (Toronto, Ont.)*, *10*(3).

Shah, I. A., Sial, Q., Jhanjhi, N. Z., & Gaur, L. (2023). Use Cases for Digital Twin. In Digital Twins and Healthcare: Trends, Techniques, and Challenges (pp. 102-118). IGI Global.

Shah, I. A., Sial, Q., Jhanjhi, N. Z., & Gaur, L. (2023). The Role of the IoT and Digital Twin in the Healthcare Digitalization Process: IoT and Digital Twin in the Healthcare Digitalization Process. In Digital Twins and Healthcare: Trends, Techniques, and Challenges (pp. 20-34). IGI Global.

Shah, I. A., Wassan, S., & Usmani, M. H. (2022). E-Government Security and Privacy Issues: Challenges and Preventive Approaches. In Cybersecurity Measures for E-Government Frameworks (pp. 61-76). IGI Global.

Simonova, A. (2020). *An Analysis of Factors Influencing National Institute of Standards and Technology Cybersecurity Framework Adoption in Financial Services: A Correlational Study* [Doctoral dissertation, Capella University].

Singh, A. P., Pradhan, N. R., Luhach, A. K., Agnihotri, S., Jhanjhi, N. Z., Verma, S., Kavita, Ghosh, U., & Roy, D. S. (2020). A novel patient-centric architectural framework for blockchain-enabled healthcare applications. *IEEE Transactions on Industrial Informatics, 17*(8), 5779–5789. doi:10.1109/TII.2020.3037889

Su, Z., Wang, Y., Xu, Q., Fei, M., Tian, Y. C., & Zhang, N. (2018). A secure charging scheme for electric vehicles with smart communities in energy blockchain. *IEEE Internet of Things Journal, 6*(3), 4601–4613. doi:10.1109/JIOT.2018.2869297

Tasca, P., & Tessone, C. J. (2017). Taxonomy of blockchain technologies. Principles of identification and classification. *arXiv preprint arXiv:1708.04872.*

Tosh, D. K., Shetty, S., Liang, X., Kamhoua, C., & Njilla, L. (2017, October). Consensus protocols for blockchain-based data provenance: Challenges and opportunities. In *2017 IEEE 8th Annual Ubiquitous Computing, Electronics and Mobile Communication Conference (UEMCON)* (pp. 469-474). IEEE.

Twizeyimana, J. D., & Andersson, A. (2019). The public value of E-Government–A literature review. *Government Information Quarterly, 36*(2), 167–178. doi:10.1016/j.giq.2019.01.001

Umrani, S., Rajper, S., Talpur, S. H., Shah, I. A., & Shujrah, A. (2020). -. *Indian Journal of Science and Technology.*

Weil, T., & Murugesan, S. (2020). IT Risk and Resilience-Cybersecurity Response to COVID-19. *IT Professional, 22*(3), 4–10. https://store.computer.org/csdl/magazine/it/2020/03/09098180/1k2pKv7b7zO. doi:10.1109/MITP.2020.2988330

Xia, Q., Sifah, E. B., Smahi, A., Amofa, S., & Zhang, X. (2017). BBDS: Blockchain-based data sharing for electronic medical records in cloud environments. *Information (Basel), 8*(2), 44. doi:10.3390/info8020044

Yang, T., Guo, Q., Tai, X., Sun, H., Zhang, B., Zhao, W., & Lin, C. (2017, November). Applying blockchain technology to decentralized operation in future energy internet. In *2017 IEEE Conference on Energy Internet and Energy System Integration (EI2)* (pp. 1-5). IEEE. 10.1109/EI2.2017.8244418

Yazdanmehr, A., Wang, J., & Yang, Z. (2020). Peers matter: The moderating role of social influence on information security policy compliance. *Information Systems Journal, 30*(5), 791–844. doi:10.1111/isj.12271

Yli-Huumo, J., Ko, D., Choi, S., Park, S., & Smolander, K. (2016). Where is current research on blockchain technology?—A systematic review. *PLoS One*, *11*(10), e0163477. doi:10.1371/journal.pone.0163477 PMID:27695049

Yoo, C. W., Sanders, G. L., & Cerveny, R. P. (2018). Exploring the influence of flow and psychological ownership on security education, training and awareness effectiveness and security compliance. *Decision Support Systems*, *108*, 107–118. doi:10.1016/j.dss.2018.02.009

Zheng, Z., Xie, S., Dai, H. N., Chen, X., & Wang, H. (2018). Blockchain challenges and opportunities: A survey. *International Journal of Web and Grid Services, 14*(4), 352-375. https://www.inderscienceonline.com/doi/abs/10.1504/IJWGS.2018.095647

Chapter 9
A Comprehensive Exploration of DDoS Attacks and Cybersecurity Imperatives in the Digital Age

Humaira Ashraf
https://orcid.org/0000-0001-5067-3172
Taylor's University, Malaysia

Noor Zaman Jhanjhi
https://orcid.org/0000-0001-8116-4733
Taylor's University, Malaysia

Sarfraz Brohi
University of the West of England, UK

Saira Muzafar
King Faisal University, Saudi Arabia

ABSTRACT

This study emphasizes the critical role of cybersecurity in safeguarding digital infrastructure, ensuring passenger safety, and maintaining operational integrity. By highlighting the multifaceted challenges of DDoS attacks, the document advocates for a comprehensive and forward-thinking approach. The imperative need for robust security measures, a cybersecurity-aware culture, and continuous vigilance against emerging threats is underscored. This proactive stance is vital for fortifying the transportation sector against the evolving landscape of digital threats, ensuring uninterrupted and secure operations.

DOI: 10.4018/979-8-3693-3816-2.ch009

INTRODUCTION: AN OVERVIEW

On a cheerful Christmas morning in 2014, as people around the world unwrapped their gift-wrapped presents, a sinister event unfolded in the digital realm. Gamers excitedly powered up their new game consoles and eagerly awaited online gaming experiences, only to be met with a frustrating "Service Unavailable" message. Soon, news of a Distributed Denial of Service (DDoS) attack targeting gaming sites spread, and users expressed their anger on the companies' social media platforms. Lizard Squad, a group of malicious actors, was later identified as the culprits behind this disruptive attack. This incident resulted in significant financial losses and severely tarnished the affected companies' reputations, taking years to recover (Aamir et al., 2013).

Importance of Cybersecurity in the Digital Age

The significance of cybersecurity in the digital era is immense, considering the widespread influence of technology in our personal, professional, and societal domains (Ping et al., 2023). Following are the primary factors that emphasize the importance of cybersecurity:

1. Protection of Confidential and Sensitive Information

In the current age of extensive digital storage of personal and sensitive data, ensuring cybersecurity is of utmost importance to protect information such as financial records, healthcare data, and personally identifiable information (PII), can identify a person when used by itself or in conjunction with other pertinent data (Hamilton et al., 2023).

2. Data breach prevention:

Implementing robust cybersecurity protocols is crucial in order to thwart illegal entry and safeguard against data breaches. A breach can result in significant consequences, such as monetary deficits, harm to one's standing, and legal sanctions (Muzafar & Jhanjhi, 2020).

3. Protecting Intellectual Property:

Businesses depend on online platforms to host and exchange intellectual property, trade secrets, and private information. Cybersecurity safeguards these assets, hence maintaining the competitiveness and innovation of enterprises.

4. Ensuring Smooth & Secure Business Continuity:

The growing reliance of organizations on digital infrastructure and cybersecurity precautions are essential for maintaining ongoing operations. Implementing measures to safeguard against cyber threats is crucial for ensuring uninterrupted business operations and mitigating potential financial damages(Xuan et al., 2023).

5. Mitigating Reputational Damage:

A cybersecurity breach has the potential to damage the reputation of individuals, corporations, and institutions. Safeguarding against cyber-attacks is crucial for preserving confidence and credibility among stakeholders, customers, and the public.

6. Threats to National Security:

The interconnectivity of digital networks presents significant national security vulnerabilities. The importance of cybersecurity lies in safeguarding crucial infrastructure, government networks, and defense systems against potentially devastating cyber-attacks (Muzafar et al., 2022).

7. Preserving Personal Identity and Privacy:

People commonly disclose a plethora of personal information on the internet. Implementing cybersecurity measures is crucial in order to safeguard persons against identity theft, financial fraud, and several other cybercrimes.

8. Implications for the Global Economy:

Cybersecurity breaches can have a widespread impact on the global economy. Assaults on financial institutions, supply lines, and multinational firms have the potential to cause economic turmoil and interrupt worldwide commerce.

The digital environment keeps evolving, with cyber threats emerging persistently. Hence, cybersecurity is a continuous activity that necessitates adjusting to emerging threats, weaknesses, and technologies, rather than being a one-time undertaking. Cybersecurity plays a crucial role in upholding the reliability, secrecy, and accessibility of digital systems. With the increasing dependence on technology, there is a greater need to establish strong cybersecurity measures in order to safeguard individuals, organizations, and society as a whole in the digital era.

Understanding DDoS Attacks

To understand DDoS attacks, let's break down the term into its two components: "Distributed" and "Denial of Service." At its core, a Denial-of-Service attack seeks to render a service unavailable, thereby denying access to legitimate users. This is often achieved by overwhelming the resources required to provide the service (Muzafar et al., 2022). One highly effective method involves generating a multitude of phony requests from various, "distributed" sources, drowning out genuine requests.

To illustrate, consider owning a corner bakery. To complete a transaction, several elements are needed, including customers knowing how to find your store, reaching your store, and paying for their purchases. The attackers can disrupt these elements:

1. **Address Lookup**: Attackers may disrupt the process by overwhelming address lookup services or directory assistance with fake queries.
2. **Access**: They can physically block access to your store, preventing customers from entering.
3. **Payment Processing**: Attackers may flood your payment processing service with a high volume of low-value transactions, causing delays.

DDoS attacks usually involve a large volume of partially legitimate actions, making it challenging to distinguish attackers from legitimate users (Aamir et al., 2013).

The Effectiveness of DDoS Attacks

DDoS attacks are highly effective due to their simplicity and the extensive digital landscape we inhabit. The goal of these assaults is to flood a target's network with so much traffic that genuine users are unable to access it. DDoS assaults' success can vary based on a number of factors, including the magnitude and complexity of the assault, the network of the target architecture, and the efficiency of its mitigation techniques. Unlike software vulnerabilities that require in-depth understanding, DDoS attacks can be executed without deep technical knowledge (Chun et al., 2023). The proliferation of connected devices, including smartphones and Internet-of-Things (IoT) devices, provides attackers with ample sources.

In our highly connected world, anyone can rent a botnet and launch DDoS attacks with relative ease, increasing the chances of a successful attack. Defenders, on the other hand, must protect against numerous attacks, while attackers only need one successful attempt to achieve their goals.

DDoS assaults can be initiated in a variety of methods, but the basic sequence is as follows:

1. The attacker chooses a target. This might be a website, an online service, or any other resource accessible via a network.
2. The attacker establishes a botnet. This is often accomplished by infecting computers with malware that grants the attacker access to the devices.
3. The attacker instructs the botnet to overwhelm the victim with traffic. This may be accomplished in a number of methods, including sending SYN floods, UDP floods, or HTTP floods.
4. The influx of traffic overwhelms the target's resources, rendering them inaccessible to genuine users.

Perpetrators and Motivations Behind DDoS Attacks

DDoS attackers come from various backgrounds and motivations can be driven by diverse intentions, and offenders may possess distinct objectives while initiating such attacks. One group includes criminals seeking financial gain. They offer DDoS-for-hire services, often disguised as stress testing . Payment is typically made in untraceable currencies like Bitcoin, and some even offer refunds if the attack doesn't succeed. Criminals might also demand ransoms from targets, threatening larger DDoS attacks if their demands are not met.

While some DDoS attacks are financially motivated, others may be ideologically driven, seeking to make a political or social statement by disrupting services. Hacktivist groups, for example, may use DDoS attacks to express their grievances or protest certain actions.

In essence, the motives behind DDoS attacks are varied, ranging from financial gain to political activism, and they continue to pose significant challenges in the digital landscape (Aamir et al., 2013).

DDoS attacks. Common motivations for DDoS attacks include:

1. Hacktivism

Hacktivists employ Distributed Denial of Service (DDoS) attacks as a means of achieving their social or political objectives. They might focus on targeting companies, countries, or individuals that they view as opponents, utilizing DDoS as a method of expressing protest or activism.

2. Competitive Advantage

To secure a competitive advantage, business rivals may employ DDoS attacks. Engaging in the deliberate interference of a competitor's internet-based services can result in monetary setbacks, harm to one's standing, and potentially attract clients to the party that launched the attack.

3. Extortion

Certain offenders initiate Distributed Denial of Service (DDoS) assaults to coerce monetary payment from the target. They issue a threatening ultimatum to either prolong or intensify the attack unless a sum of money is handed over. The technique described is commonly referred to as a ransom-driven Distributed Denial of Service (DDoS) attack.

4. Cyber Warfare

Nation-states or groups sponsored by states may employ Distributed Denial of Service (DDoS) assaults as a component of more extensive cyber warfare operations. These assaults may target competitor nations, essential infrastructure, or government organizations with the intention of disrupting their operations.

5. **Disruption for Ideological Reasons:**

Certain attackers may be driven by ideological motives, aiming to undermine the digital presence of entities that contradict their beliefs or principles. This motivation can be attributed to divergences in religious, cultural, or ideological beliefs.

6. **Criminal Intent**

Cybercriminals may initiate Distributed Denial of Service (DDoS) attacks to obtain financial benefits. Through the disruption of internet services, criminals can cause diversions, so facilitating the execution of additional harmful actions such as data stealing, deception, or network penetration.

7. Evaluating Security Measures:

DDoS assaults are occasionally employed to assess an organization's cybersecurity safeguards. Attackers may initiate a Distributed Denial of Service (DDoS) assault to assess the efficacy of countermeasures, pinpoint weaknesses, and ready themselves for more sophisticated cyber offensives.

8. **Vandalism and Mischief:**

Certain individuals may initiate DDoS attacks purely for the pleasure of creating disruption and turmoil. The underlying drive behind this motivation is mostly focused on inflicting harm or demonstrating one's technical expertise, rather than being driven by strategic considerations.

UNDERSTANDING DDoS ATTACKS

A Distributed Denial of Service (DDoS) assault is an intentional and malicious effort to disrupt the regular operation of a specific server, service, or network by inundating it with an excessive amount of internet traffic. A DDoS attack, in contrast to a standard DoS attack, is executed by several sources that are typically spread across different areas. The objective of a Distributed Denial of Service (DDoS) assault is to render a website, online service, or network resource inaccessible to its intended users.

DDoS Attack Types and Characteristics

A comprehensive understanding of DDoS attack types and characteristics is crucial.

1: Fundamental Categories of DDoS Attacks

DDoS attacks fall into three primary categories based on the protocols and mechanisms targeted:

1. **Protocol-Based Attacks:** These attacks focus on major network protocols like UDP, TCP, and others, including ICMP, GRE, IPIP, ESP, AH, SCTP, OSPF, SWIPE, TLSP, Compaq_PEE, and more. Examples include IP Null Attacks, SYN Floods, UDP Floods, and Ping of Death.
2. **OSI Model-Based Attacks:** These attacks align with the OSI model's seven layers, affecting the physical, data link, network, and transport layers. Examples include MAC flooding, ICMP floods, and SYN/ACK floods.
3. **Mechanism-Based Attacks:** These attacks employ diverse mechanisms like flood attacks, vulnerability exploitation in the network protocol stack, and application layer (L7) DDoS attacks, such as HTTP floods (Afek et al., 2016, Nayak, R.P et al., 2021).

2: The Anatomy of DDoS Attacks

Understanding the mechanics involved in DDoS attacks, from initiation to impact:

- **Attack Initiation:** Involves botnet formation, recruitment, compromise, command and control, and synchronization.
- **Attack Phases:** Includes flooding the network, resource exhaustion, and application layer attacks.
- **Attack Scale:** Discusses magnitude and duration, highlighting the varying scale of DDoS attacks.

Example: The 2016 Dyn DDoS Attack

The 2016 Dyn DDoS attack serves as an illustrative example, showcasing the global ramifications of DDoS attacks and their complexity.

3: Motivations and Attackers

Understanding the motivations that drive DDoS attacks, which range from financial gain and hacktivism to personal vendettas and competitive rivalry.

Case Study: The 2016 Dyn DDoS Attack

This case study illustrates how the Mirai botnet was harnessed for profit-driven disruption, highlighting the potential for financial gain and hacktivist-driven attacks.

4: Understanding DDoS Attack Patterns

Classifying DDoS attacks into various patterns, including volume-based attacks, protocol-based attacks, and application layer attacks.

Example: The 2018 GitHub DDoS Attack

The 2018 GitHub DDoS attack, with a staggering 1.35 terabits per second (Tbps) of traffic, emphasizes the significance of understanding volume-based attack patterns.

DoS Attacks in IoT

Let's explore DoS attacks in more detail and their implications in the context of the Internet of Things (IoT):

1. Types of DoS Attacks:
    - **Volume-Based Attacks:** These involve overwhelming the target with a massive volume of traffic. This can be accomplished using techniques like flooding the target with a high number of requests.

  - **Protocol-Based Attacks:** Attackers exploit vulnerabilities in network protocols to disrupt the target. For example, the attacker might use a flood of half-open connections, which consumes server resources.
  - **Application Layer Attacks:** These attacks focus on exploiting vulnerabilities in the application layer of a network protocol stack, like HTTP or HTTPS. Commonly, this involves sending a high number of legitimate looking but malicious requests.

2. IoT Implications:

DoS attacks, and especially DDoS attacks, have significant implications for the IoT:

- **Botnet Attacks:** IoT devices are often susceptible to compromise because they may have weak security or default credentials. As a result, they can be easily enlisted into botnets for use in DDoS attacks. The sheer number of IoT devices increases the scale and impact of these attacks.(Al-Fuqaha et al., 2015).
- **IoT Device Overload:** Overloading IoT devices with traffic or requests can cause them to become unresponsive, affecting their intended functions. This can be a serious problem, especially in scenarios where IoT devices control critical infrastructure, like smart cities or industrial processes (Alrawais et al., 2017).
- **Data Loss and Privacy:** IoT devices often collect and transmit sensitive data. A DoS attack on an IoT device can result in data loss and privacy breaches, which can have legal and regulatory consequences (Al-Fuqaha et al., 2015).
- **Service Disruption:** In scenarios where IoT is used for services like remote healthcare monitoring or smart home automation, a DoS attack can disrupt these services, potentially endangering lives or causing significant inconvenience.

CYBERSECURITY IN TRANSPORTATION INDUSTRY

The transportation sector, a linchpin of modern society, has greatly enhanced operational efficiency and passenger experiences through advanced technologies. However, this digital transformation has exposed it to multifaceted cyber threats that jeopardize passenger safety, data integrity, and critical services (Mecheva & Kakanakov, 2020).

Major Cybersecurity Threats to the Transportation Industry

1. **Distributed Denial of Service (DDoS) Attacks:** DDoS attacks can disrupt transportation systems by overwhelming networks and infrastructure, rendering critical systems inoperative. This can result in flight delays, traffic congestion, or other transportation disruptions.
2. **Ransomware:** Transportation organizations, including airports, ports, and logistics companies, are attractive targets for ransomware attacks. These attacks can encrypt essential systems and data, demanding a ransom for decryption keys. If successful, they can lead to significant downtime and financial losses. Attacks using ransomware have nearly increased, from 13% in 2021 to 25% in 2022, making them the most significant threat facing the industry. They are quickly followed by risks relating to data (breach, leak), as hackers target customer, employee, and intellectual property information in addition to credentials in order to make money. Since there are no known groups that target the transportation sector specifically, the attacks are thought to be of an opportunistic character.
3. **Data Breaches:** Personal data, payment information, and sensitive operational data are often stored within transportation systems. Data breaches can compromise this information, leading to privacy violations, financial loss, and legal consequences.
4. **IoT Vulnerabilities:** The Internet of Things (IoT) is widely used in transportation, but IoT devices can be exploited to gain unauthorized access to systems or disrupt operations. Insecure IoT devices can create significant security vulnerabilities.
5. **Phishing and Social Engineering:** Employees in the transportation industry may be targeted with phishing attacks or social engineering tactics. Successful attacks can lead to unauthorized access to systems or the theft of sensitive information.
6. **Malware and Viruses:** Malicious software can infect transportation systems, causing data corruption, system disruptions, and unauthorized access. Malware can spread through email attachments, infected software, or compromised websites.
7. **Insider Threats:** Disgruntled employees, contractors, or vendors can pose a significant risk. Insider threats may intentionally sabotage systems or steal sensitive data.
8. **Supply Chain Attacks:** Transportation organizations rely on a complex network of suppliers and partners. A breach in the supply chain can introduce vulnerabilities into the transportation infrastructure.
9. **Critical Infrastructure Attacks:** Attacks on critical transportation infrastructure, such as power grids, communication networks, and air traffic control systems, can result in widespread disruptions and potential safety risks.

Historical Context of Cybersecurity Threats in the Transportation Industry

Understanding the historical context of cybersecurity threats in transportation is vital for recognizing patterns, vulnerabilities, and the evolving nature of these threats. This chapter delves into historical incidents involving various cyber threats and their impact on the industry's security landscape.

1: Distributed Denial of Service (DDoS) Attacks

- **South Korean Airlines (2011):** A DDoS attack disrupted booking systems, leading to flight delays and passenger inconvenience (Pandita, Kumar, & Pandita, 2019)
- **British Airways (2015):** A DDoS attack affected British Airways' website and mobile app, causing operational disruptions and passenger check-in difficulties.
- **San Francisco Municipal Transportation Agency (2016):** A ransomware attack, coupled with a DDoS attack, disrupted San Francisco's public transit system (Muni), resulting in operational issues and free rides for passengers (Pandita, Kumar, & Pandita, 2019)
- **Singapore Airlines (2019):** A series of DDoS attacks targeted Singapore Airlines, impacting its website and mobile app, thus affecting customer services. (Pandita, Kumar, & Pandita, 2019)

2: Ransomware Attacks

- **WannaCry (2017):** The global WannaCry ransomware attack targeted various transportation companies, causing IT system failures and operational delays (Pandita, Kumar, & Pandita, 2019).

3: Insider Threats

- **Disgruntled Employee (2018):** An incident in 2018 saw a disgruntled employee sabotage a transportation company's computer system, leading to service disruptions. (Pandita, Kumar, & Pandita, 2019).

4: IoT Vulnerabilities

- **Connected Car Vulnerabilities (2019):** Vulnerabilities in connected car systems were discovered in 2019, highlighting the potential for remote exploitation.

5: Phishing Attacks

- **Multiple Incidents:** Various transportation companies have fallen victim to phishing attacks targeting employees and passengers, resulting in data breaches and operational disruptions. (Pandita, Kumar, & Pandita, 2019).

6: Supply Chain Attacks

- **Software Vendor Attack (2020):** In 2020, a supply chain attack on a software vendor exposed transportation companies to data breaches and operational disruptions. (Pandita, Kumar, & Pandita, 2019).

7: Weak Authentication

- **Multiple Incidents:** Several transportation companies have experienced security breaches due to weak authentication practices, leading to unauthorized access and data breaches.

8: Software Vulnerabilities

- **Data Breaches and Disruptions:** Vulnerabilities in software have led to data breaches and operational disruptions for transportation companies.

Understanding the diverse historical incidents in the transportation industry provides a contextual backdrop to the evolving landscape of cyber threats and the need for robust cybersecurity measures. It illuminates the importance of preparing for and responding to such challenges effectively.

Understanding DDoS Attacks and Their Impact on the Transportation Industry

DDoS attacks, which originated 27 years ago, have evolved into prolonged, sophisticated threats capable of causing extended disruptions. The transport sector is a prominent target for these assaults because of its reliance on linked systems and crucial role in the global economy. These attacks have become more frequent in recent years. DDoS assaults have the potential to significantly affect the transportation sector, leading to extensive disruptions and financial losses. Distributed Denial of Service (DDoS) attacks can have a significant impact on transportation systems that rely on Internet of Things (IoT) devices. Here's how DDoS attacks can affect IoT in transportation (Alrawais et al., 2017, Gopi, Net al., 2021):

1. **Flight and train delays and cancellations:** Denial-of-service (DDoS) attacks have the potential to interfere with online reservation platforms and systems, causing delays in passenger boarding and check-in. Trains and aircraft may be completely cancelled in extreme circumstances.
2. **Compromised safety systems:** To regulate air traffic, track conditions, and operate traffic lights, transportation systems rely on complex computer networks. DDoS assaults have the ability to compromise these systems, which might result in mishaps and safety risks.
3. **Supply chain disruptions:** The transportation sector is essential to the flow of commodities and goods. Supply chains can be disrupted by DDoS

assaults on ports and logistics firms, which might result in shortages and price rises.

4. **Financial losses:** Because DDoS assaults can cause delay, lost income, and the expenses of resolving the attack, transportation businesses may suffer large financial losses (Afek et al., 2016)
5. **Disruption of Traffic Management Systems:** DDoS attacks targeting traffic management systems can disrupt the real-time traffic data collection, communication between traffic lights and sensors, and the ability to adjust signal timings. This can lead to traffic congestion, accidents, and inefficient transportation systems.
6. **Impaired Fleet Management**: DDoS attacks on IoT devices used for fleet management can disrupt real-time vehicle tracking, communication between vehicles and central systems, and the ability to optimize routes. This can lead to delays, fuel inefficiency, and potential safety issues.
7. **Public Transportation Delays**: DDoS attacks against IoT systems used in public transportation can lead to inaccurate scheduling, delays in service updates, and payment processing disruptions, inconveniencing passengers and affecting public transportation reliability.
8. **Parking Problems**: DDoS attacks targeting IoT parking systems can make it impossible for drivers to access real-time information about available parking spaces, pay for parking, or locate their vehicles. This can lead to increased traffic congestion and user frustration.
9. **Traffic Safety Risks**: DDoS attacks on IoT systems used for connected vehicles can disrupt communication between vehicles and infrastructure, potentially leading to accidents, especially in situations where real-time data is critical for safety, such as at intersections.
10. **Supply Chain Disruptions**: Transportation is worldwide, which means that intricate supply chains are involved. All aspects of the transportation ecosystem are susceptible to disruption from cyberattacks on manufacturers, suppliers, or logistical partners. DDoS attacks on IoT devices in logistics and supply chain management can lead to disruptions in the transportation of goods, causing delays, loss of perishable goods, and disruptions in the supply chain (Agrawal & Tapaswi, 2019).
11. **Environmental Impact**: DDoS attacks can disrupt IoT systems monitoring environmental data and air quality, potentially impacting the ability to make real-time adjustments for environmental sustainability in transportation.
12. **Navigation Apps**: DDoS attacks on navigation and mobility apps can disrupt the ability of users to receive real-time traffic updates, route planning, and other transportation information, which can result in navigation difficulties and inefficiencies. (Agrawal & Tapaswi, 2019).

13. **Autonomous Vehicles**: DDoS attacks on IoT systems in autonomous vehicles can be especially dangerous. These attacks can disrupt communication between autonomous vehicles and infrastructure, making it impossible for vehicles to navigate safely or make critical decisions. There's a big attack surface due to the growing dependence on connected and autonomous cars. Unauthorized access, tampering with navigation systems, and even remote control are just a few of the cybersecurity risks that can seriously jeopardize the safety of autonomous vehicles that are connected.
14. Integration of 5G Networks with IoT:

While the adoption of 5G networks and a plethora of IoT devices improves connectivity, they also present new security risks. More network-connected devices equate to more possible points of entry for cybercriminals. To guard against known vulnerabilities, make sure that all IoT devices have end-to-end encryption, put in place stringent access controls, and update and patch them often (Akram Abdul-Ghani et al., 2018).

In essence, DDoS attacks on IoT in transportation can lead to a breakdown of communication and data exchange between devices, vehicles, and infrastructure, potentially causing accidents, delays, inefficiencies, and safety risks. The reliance on real-time data and communication in modern transportation systems makes them vulnerable to DDoS attacks, and organizations must invest in robust security measures and contingency plans to mitigate the impact of such attacks (Akram Abdul-Ghani et al., 2018).

SECURING TRANSPORTATION SYSTEMS

The transportation industry is at a pivotal juncture where it must proactively address the escalating cybersecurity threats that have the potential to disrupt critical services. As we navigate the evolving landscape of threats and vulnerabilities, it's essential to explore the future challenges that lie ahead and the innovative solutions that promise to enhance transportation security (Akram Abdul-Ghani et al., 2018).

Future Challenges in Transportation Cybersecurity

1. **Emerging Technologies and IoT Expansion**: With the rapid proliferation of Internet of Things (IoT) devices in the transportation sector, new attack vectors emerge. IoT devices often have limited security measures, making them susceptible to compromise. The exponential growth in connected vehicles,

smart infrastructure, and real-time data collection introduces new challenges in securing these devices against DDoS attacks.

2. **SDN Based Vulnerabilities:** Software-Defined Networking (SDN) offers notable benefits in improving the efficacy and adaptability of transportation systems. However, it also brings up fresh hurdles in the realm of cybersecurity. Software-Defined Networking (SDN) implements a centralized controller that effectively oversees and governs the entire network. This centered architecture results in a singular vulnerability and a larger potential for attacks. Cyber attackers may focus their attacks on the SDN controller in order to infiltrate and compromise the entire transportation network (Muzafar & Jhanjhi, 2022). With the ongoing evolution and use of SDN technologies in the transportation industry, there may be various future challenges due to increased attack surface.
3. **Artificial Intelligence and Machine Learning-Powered Attacks**: As attackers become more sophisticated, they leverage AI and machine learning to develop evasive tactics. These technologies enable adaptive attacks that can dynamically change their behavior to avoid detection. AI-driven DDoS attacks can be challenging to identify and mitigate in real time.
4. **Insider Threats and Human Error**: Disgruntled employees, vendors, or contractors continue to pose a significant threat to transportation cybersecurity. As organizations grow more complex, managing insider threats and human error becomes increasingly challenging. Preventing unintentional data breaches and sabotage remains a critical challenge.
5. **Zero-Day Vulnerabilities and Advanced Persistent Threats (APTs)**: Cybercriminals are constantly searching for zero-day vulnerabilities – unknown flaws in software or hardware. When exploited, these vulnerabilities can lead to devastating DDoS attacks. Coupled with APTs that infiltrate systems for long-term espionage, zero-day vulnerabilities become a potent threat (Al-Duwairi et al., 2020).

Innovations in Transportation Cybersecurity

Due to technical advancements following are the innovations for secure transportation systems.

1. **Machine Learning and AI Defense Systems**: In response to AI-powered attacks, the transportation industry is leveraging machine learning and AI for defense. AI-driven security systems can analyze network traffic patterns, detect anomalies, and adapt in real time to counteract evolving threats. These systems can identify and mitigate DDoS attacks more effectively (Alrawais et al., 2017).

2. **Blockchain for Secure Data Sharing**: Blockchain technology is gaining prominence in securing data sharing within transportation ecosystems. Blockchain ensures data integrity, privacy, and secure transactions. By using decentralized and tamper-resistant ledgers, transportation organizations can securely share critical information and maintain transparency (Julie et al., n.d.).
3. **Cybersecurity Information Sharing and Collaboration**: The transportation industry is fostering increased collaboration among organizations to share threat intelligence and best practices. Public and private entities are working together to establish robust defense mechanisms and improve overall security.
4. **Zero-Day Detection and Patch Management**: To counter the threat of zero-day vulnerabilities, transportation organizations are investing in advanced intrusion detection systems that can identify suspicious activity indicating a zero-day exploit. Rapid patch management and mitigation strategies are being developed to respond to these threats as soon as they are detected.
5. **Biometric Authentication and Multifactor Authentication (MFA)**: Enhancing access control and identity management is crucial. Biometric authentication methods, such as fingerprint or facial recognition, are being integrated into transportation systems. Additionally, multifactor authentication (MFA) adds an extra layer of security by requiring users to provide multiple forms of identification.
6. **Quantum-Safe Cryptography**: As quantum computing advances, it poses a threat to existing cryptographic systems. Quantum-safe or post-quantum cryptography is emerging to safeguard data against quantum attacks. The transportation sector is exploring quantum-resistant encryption methods to protect sensitive information.
7. **Threat Hunting and Red Teaming**: Transportation organizations are taking a proactive stance by conducting threat hunting and red teaming exercises. These activities simulate potential cyberattacks, helping organizations identify weaknesses and enhance their incident response capabilities.

The Future of Transportation Cybersecurity

The future of transportation cybersecurity is undoubtedly a dynamic landscape. As cyber threats continue to evolve and diversify, the transportation industry must adapt to secure critical systems. Collaboration between the public and private sectors, alongside innovative technologies, will play a pivotal role in ensuring the security, reliability, and efficiency of transportation services (Anand et al., 2020).

The challenges and innovations outlined here represent a snapshot of the ongoing efforts to safeguard the transportation industry. By staying at the forefront of cybersecurity developments and adopting cutting-edge technologies, the transportation sector can navigate the road ahead with resilience and confidence, even in the face of evolving DDoS attacks and emerging threats.

1. Safety of Networked Automobiles

New cybersecurity threats are brought about by the proliferation of linked infrastructure and driverless cars. To guarantee passenger safety and uphold confidence, it is crucial to safeguard linked automobiles. To prevent cyber-attacks, for instance, it's essential to employ techniques like intrusion detection system implementation, communication channel security, and software and firmware protection for cars.

2. Security of Supply Chains in the Digital Age

Supply chain security has grown in importance as supply chain and logistics procedures change. Additionally, critical tactics like vendor risk management, secure data exchange, blockchain technology for traceability, and ongoing supply chain network monitoring are essential for boosting security and fending off disruptive cyberattacks. By utilizing blockchain technology, organizations may create supply chain traceability that is accountable and transparent. Additionally, strong vendor risk management and safe data-sharing procedures aid in the reduction of vulnerabilities. Continuous monitoring also guarantees the early detection of possible dangers.

3. Intrusions into Intelligent Transportation Systems (ITS) through Cyberspace

Transportation operations are made more efficient by Intelligent Transportation Systems (ITS), which utilize cutting edge technologies. Still, they are vulnerable to cyberattacks that might tamper with signals, interfere with traffic, and jeopardize data security. The protection of critical infrastructure and the maintenance of the integrity and dependability of ITS so depend on the implementation of strong cybersecurity measures such network segmentation, encryption, and anomaly detection systems.

4. Defending Important Infrastructure

While vital to transportation, critical infrastructure—such as ports, airports, and railroads—is also susceptible to cybersecurity threats. For this reason, putting into practice sensible tactics like access restrictions, video monitoring, physical security measures, and intrusion detection systems is essential to reducing risks and guarding against future disruptions.

5. Security of IoT in Intelligent Logistics

By utilizing sensors, RFID tags, and GPS tracking devices, the Internet of Things (IoT) has revolutionized logistical operations. But it's imperative that the cybersecurity issues around IoT devices in logistics are addressed. Vulnerability management, secure firmware updates, data encryption, and device authentication are important components. Furthermore, to safeguard data integrity, stop illegal access, and keep intelligent logistics systems running smoothly, strong IoT security measures are necessary.

6. Smart Warehouse Cybersecurity

Cyber-attacks target warehouses more frequently as they adopt automation and digitization. To guarantee the safety of intelligent warehouses, cybersecurity protocols are necessary. The implementation of access restrictions for robots and automation systems, the security of warehouse management systems, and thorough cybersecurity training for staff members are a few examples.

7. Transportation Data Privacy

In the transportation sector, data privacy has become a crucial issue. Transportation firms need to give data privacy a priority in order to maintain regulatory compliance, win over stakeholders and customers, and grow their trust in the face of massive data generation. This covers things like how crucial it is to abide by laws like the General Data Protection Regulation (GDPR), how to use data anonymization strategies, and how to safeguard sensitive data using encryption.

8. Business Continuity Planning and Incident Response

For enterprises to reduce the effect of cyber catastrophes, strong business continuity policies and efficient incident response procedures are essential. Early discovery, containment, and recovery are the main elements of incident response planning. To properly handle new threats, it's also critical to update reaction strategies and conduct testing on a regular basis. (Anand et al., 2020)

9. Recognize the vital services and assets you possess:

Determine the services that you have made available to the public internet as well as their weaknesses. Assign resources a priority according to their availability and importance to the mission. Adopt measures (such as server hardening and patching) to reduce the likelihood of an attack. Check if the web application firewall (WAF) is set up in a Deny state and protects your important assets (Anirudh et al., 2017).

10. Recognize the methods via which users join your network:

Determine the many ways your user base, whether onsite or virtually through virtual private networks (VPNs), connects to your organization's network. Determine probable chokepoints in the network and any countermeasures that could reduce the amount of time that important staff are interrupted.

11. Become a member of a DDoS defense service:

While DDoS protection is offered by many internet service providers (ISPs), specialist DDoS protection services may offer stronger defenses against more sophisticated or extensive DDoS attacks. By signing up for a DDoS protection service, you can safeguard systems and services from attacks by having it monitor network traffic, verify the existence of an assault, locate the attack's origin, and redirect hostile traffic off your network. Once a key asset and service review is finished, organizations should sign up for a DDoS protection service.

12. Recognize your defenses against specialized edge networks:

For information on certain managed services that protect against DDoS assaults, get in touch with a managed service provider (MSP). Customizing edge defenses can be facilitated by MSPs that offer various technologies on the "edge." The downtime brought on by DDoS attacks can be minimized with edge defense services. While legitimate people are much more likely to visit your websites and web apps, edge defense, detection, and mitigation services lower the likelihood that malicious traffic will reach its destination.

13. Create and assess designs for colocation, load balancing, and high availability:

Examine the architecture of the systems and networks to remove any potential single points of failure, such as single-node hosting of high-value assets (HVAs). Make that HVAs can load-balance (LB) over several nodes and/or provide high availability (HA). One useful tactic for maintaining company continuity is the colocation of HVAC services. But the greatest defense against DDoS is to thwart the attack with DdoS defenses in your local datacenter or upstream service provider defenses.

14. Create a plan for your organization's DDoS reaction:

Your firm should follow the response strategy as it identifies, mitigates, and quickly recovers from DDoS attacks. Throughout a DDoS attack, all internal stakeholders—including network defenders and leaders inside your organization—as well as service providers should be aware of their respective roles and obligations. The plan should, at the very least, involve identifying and validating DDoS attacks, deploying mitigations, monitoring, and recovery. Al-Duwairi et al., 2020).

CONCLUSION

A denial-of-service (DDoS) attack aims to interfere with the target's regular operations, rendering it unavailable to its intended users for a set period of time or permanently. DDoS assaults can affect websites, network infrastructure, and a range of online services. Modern transportation sector's reliance on digital technologies, networking, and automation makes cybersecurity crucial. Securing transportation systems is indispensable for ensuring passenger safety, preserving operational integrity, and securing sensitive data. Cybersecurity, specifically DDoS assaults in the transportation industry is a complex and diverse problem that necessitates a thorough and forward-thinking strategy. To strengthen the resilience and safety of its digital infrastructure, proactive cybersecurity measures and a strong response strategy are essential to protect against the disruptive impacts of DDoS assaults in the transportation industry. The transportation industry can achieve this by installing strong security measures, promoting a culture of cybersecurity awareness, and maintaining updates on emerging threats.

REFERENCES

Aamir, M., Zaidi, M. A., Zulfikar, S., & Bhutto, A. (2013). A Survey on DDoS Attack and Defense Strategies: From Traditional Schemes to Current Techniques. *Interdisciplinary Information Sciences*, *19*(2), 173–200. doi:10.4036/iis.2013.173

Afek, Y., Bremler-Barr, A., Cohen, E., Feibish, S. L., & Shagam, M. (2016). *Efficient Distinct Heavy Hitters for DNS DDoS Attack Detection*. Research Gate. https://doi.org/ doi:10.1145/1235

Agrawal, N., & Tapaswi, S. (2019). Defense Mechanisms against DDoS Attacks in a Cloud Computing Environment: State-of-the-Art and Research Challenges. *IEEE Communications Surveys and Tutorials, 21*(4), 3769–3795. doi:10.1109/COMST.2019.2934468

Akram Abdul-Ghani, H., Konstantas, D., & Mahyoub, M. (2018). A Comprehensive IoT Attacks Survey based on a Building-blocked Reference Model. *IJACSA). International Journal of Advanced Computer Science and Applications, 9*(3). www.ijacsa.thesai.org

Al-Duwairi, B., Al-Kahla, W., AlRefai, M. A., Abdelqader, Y., Rawash, A., & Fahmawi, R. (2020). SIEM-based detection and mitigation of IoT-botnet DDoS attacks. [IJECE]. *Iranian Journal of Electrical and Computer Engineering, 10*(2), 2182–2191. doi:10.11591/ijece.v10i2.pp2182-2191

Al-Fuqaha, A., Guizani, M., Mohammadi, M., Aledhari, M., & Ayyash, M. (2015). Internet of Things: A Survey on Enabling Technologies, Protocols, and Applications. *IEEE Communications Surveys and Tutorials, 17*(4), 2347–2376. doi:10.1109/COMST.2015.2444095

Alrawais, A., Alhothaily, A., Hu, C., & Cheng, X. (2017). Fog Computing for the Internet of Things: Security and Privacy Issues. *IEEE Internet Computing, 21*(2), 34–42. doi:10.1109/MIC.2017.37

Anand, P., Singh, Y., Selwal, A., Singh, P. K., Felseghi, R. A., & Raboaca, M. S. (2020). IoVT: Internet of Vulnerable Things? Threat Architecture, Attack Surfaces, and Vulnerabilities in Internet of Things and Its Applications towards Smart Grids. *Energies, 13*(18), 4813. doi:10.3390/en13184813

Anirudh, M., Arul Thileeban, S., & Nallathambi, D. J. (2017). Use of honeypots for mitigating DoS attacks targeted on IoT networks. *International Conference on Computer, Communication, and Signal Processing: Special Focus on IoT, ICCCSP 2017*. IEEE. 10.1109/ICCCSP.2017.7944057

ChunT. J.EnL. J.XuenM. T. Y.XuanY. M.MuzafarS. (2023). Secured Software Development and Importance of Secure Software Development Life Cycle. Authorea Preprints. doi:10.36227/techrxiv.24548416.v1

Gopi, R., Sathiyamoorthi, V., Selvakumar, S., Manikandan, R., Chatterjee, P., Jhanjhi, N. Z., & Luhach, A. K. (2021). Enhanced method of ANN based model for detection of DDoS attacks on multimedia internet of things. *Multimedia Tools and Applications*, 1–19.

Hamilton, G., Williams, M., & Khan, T. M. (2023). Securing Personally Identifiable Information (PII) in Personal Financial Statements. *Lecture Notes in Networks and Systems, 652 LNNS*, 709–728. https://doi.org/ doi:10.1007/978-3-031-28073-3_48/ FIGURES/4

Julie, G., Nayahi, J. J. V., & Zaman, N. (n.d.). *Blockchain technology : fundamentals, applications, and case studies*. Routledge. https://www.routledge.com/Blockchain-Technology-Fundamentals-Applications-and-Case-Studies/Julie-Nayahi-Jhanjhi/p/book/9780367431372

Mecheva, T., & Kakanakov, N. (2020). Cybersecurity in Intelligent Transportation Systems. *Computers, 9*(4), 83. doi:10.3390/computers9040083

Muzafar, S., & Jhanjhi, N. (2022). DDoS Attacks on Software Defined Network: Challenges and Issues. *2022 International Conference on Business Analytics for Technology and Security, ICBATS 2022, 2022-Janua*. IEEE. 10.1109/ICBATS54253.2022.9780662

Muzafar, S., & Jhanjhi, N. Z. (2020). *Success Stories of ICT Implementation in Saudi Arabia*. IGI Global. *Https://Services.Igi-Global.Com/Resolvedoi/Resolve.Aspx?Doi=10.4018/978-1-7998-1851-9.Ch008*, 151–163. doi:10.4018/978-1-7998-1851-9.ch008

Nayak, R. P., Sethi, S., Bhoi, S. K., Sahoo, K. S., Tabbakh, T. A., & Almusaylim, Z. A. (2021). TBDDoSA-MD: Trust-Based DDoS Misbehave Detection Approach in Software-defined Vehicular Network (SDVN). *Computers, Materials & Continua, 69*(3).

PingS. W.WahJ. C. J.JieL. W.HanJ. B. Y.MuzafarS. (2023). *Secure Software Development: Issues and Challenges*. https://arxiv.org/abs/2311.11021v1

Siddiqui, F. J., Ashraf, H., & Ullah, A. (2020). Dual server based security system for multimedia Services in Next Generation Networks. *Multimedia Tools and Applications, 79*(11-12), 7299–7318. doi:10.1007/s11042-019-08406-2

XuanY. M.XuenM. T. Y.MuzafarS. (2023). *Cloud Computing Migration: A Thoughtful Decision*. doi:10.20944/preprints202311.0850.v1

Chapter 10
Digital Safeguards:
Navigating Cyber Threats in the Logistics Industry Framework

Muhammad Tayyab
Taylor's University, Malaysia

Khizar Hameed
https://orcid.org/0000-0003-1203-2010
University of Tasmania, Australia

Noor Zaman Jhanjhi
https://orcid.org/0000-0001-8116-4733
Taylor's University, Malaysia

Amer Zaheer
Shifa Tameer-e-Millat University, Islamabad, Pakistan

Faizan Qamar
Universiti Kebangsaan Malaysia, Malaysia

ABSTRACT

The rapid integration of internet and technological advancements over the past two decades has reshaped the global landscape, leading to transformative changes in various sectors.The emergence of Industry 4.0, conceptualized in 2011, has particularly revolutionized manufacturing and logistics by advocating for systematic digitalization technology integration to enhance efficiency and reduce costs. However, this technological evolution, while fostering efficiency and process optimization, also introduces vulnerabilities to cyber threats. The logistics sector, heavily reliant on interconnected systems like internet of things, faces potential risks from cyberattacks that target sensitive data across the interconnected supply chain. This chapter aims to address the intricate relationship between digitalization and the logistics sector, emphasizing the crucial role of digital safeguards in navigating cyber dangers. Furthermore, the chapter delves into the significance of visibility in supply-chain operations and explores technologies and practices for enhancing supply-chain visibility.

DOI: 10.4018/979-8-3693-3816-2.ch010

1. INTRODUCTION

Internet and technological advancements have been widely adopted for the past two decades, and the world has been redefined as a result of technological advancements, which have allowed for the expansion of teleconferencing, telemedicine, and telemarketing, as well as altered the nature of human interactions. An idea for the increasing digitization of industrial processes called "Industry 4.0" emerged in 2011 from a German technological innovation initiative (Kagermann, 2014). Industry 4.0, the fourth industrial revolution, posits that businesses in the manufacturing and logistics sectors can achieve better efficiency and reduced costs by systematically integrating digitalization technology into their operations. Ultimately, this integration will help the business develop and maintain its competitive edge in the long run. Numerous enabling technologies associated with Industry 4.0 have also played a role in the dramatic shift in the corporate environment (Mubarak & Petraite, 2020). A significant technology in this context is the Internet of Things (IoT), which describes networks of networked, uniquely identifying devices that may communicate with each other dynamically and intelligently (Atzori et al., 2017). It is a network design that includes hardware components, software applications, and platforms that intelligently connect and share data amongst themselves; the term "Industrial Internet of Things" (IIoT) describes its common use in industrial settings like production and supply chains (Barreto et al., 2017). It is anticipated that by the year 2027, the global expenditure on the digital transformation of the logistics industry will amount to approximately $95 billion (Wolak et al., 2019). According to the digital industries barometer, the logistics and transport sector is positioned fifth globally out of eleven industries, with a digital transformation adoption score of 6.61 (Du et al., 2023).

Increased efficiency and process optimization are hallmarks of modern logistics, which depend highly on digital technologies and communication infrastructure (Lu et al., 2003). With the help of these innovations, online retailers can keep tabs on shipments, communicate with clients and business associates, and easily collect vital sales data (Cheung & Michael, 2021). On the other hand, growing dependence on technology makes systems more vulnerable to cyberattacks, which can negatively affect businesses and the services they provide to their customers. Cyberattacks can target sensitive data in several locations due to the interconnected nature of the logistics business (Alshurideh et al., 2023). The more connections there are in a supply chain, the more susceptible it is to attacks. Integrating systems allows for the exchange of information, and supply chains are a vital part of this complex global network. For example, fraudsters can break into a company's network, steal sensitive information, and then demand payment to decrypt the data by using information about inventory, delivery and arrival timings, and locations (Zhang et al., 2023).

The importance of authoring this book chapter is to highlight the role of digitalisation in the logistics sector, followed by a discussion of the landscape of digital safeguards and how to navigate cyber dangers in the logistics industry. To that end, we established the following goals, which resulted in the following essential noteworthy contributions. It begins with an in-depth examination of the current cybersecurity scenario in the logistics sector. Furthermore, it offers a thorough understanding of the logistics business structure, as well as the ramifications of rising connection and technology use. Furthermore, it includes a thorough overview of digital safeguards for cybersecurity in logistics, as well as risk assessment, tactics, and communication patterns in logistics. Aside from that, this chapter discusses the importance of visibility in supply-chain operations, as well as the technology and methods for improving supply-chain visibility. This chapter also includes a full examination of incident response and recovery in logistics. Finally, toward the end, various open challenges and potential opportunities in the logistics sector are discussed.

The specific contributions of the chapter are as follows.

- An in-depth discussion on the current cyber threat landscape in the logistic sector.
- A detailed understanding of the logistics industry framework along with the implications of increased connectivity and technology adoption.
- A comprehensive discussion on the digital safeguards for cybersecurity in logistics, along with the risk assessment and strategies and communication patterns in logistics.
- A detailed discussion on the significance of visibility in supply-chain operations, along with the technologies and practices for enhancing supply-chain visibility.
- A comprehensive discussion on incident response and recovery in logistics.
- An array of open challenges and future opportunities in the logistic sector.

The chapter is structured as follows: Section 2 addresses the cyber threat picture in the logistics business, including potential cyber-attacks and recent incidents. Section 3 provides a comprehensive overview and explanation of the logistics sector framework. Section 4 explains the digital precautions for logistics cybersecurity. Section 5 discusses the concept of supply-chain visibility and security in logistics. The section 6 presents an overview of incident response and recovery in logistics. Section 7 focuses on the numerous modern technologies for digital protections in logistics businesses. The section 8 describes regulatory compliance and standards in the logistics industry. Section 9 covered future trends and considerations. Section 10 concludes the book chapter.

2. CYBER THREAT LANDSCAPE IN LOGISTICS

Logistics, like any other sector that uses different ICT technologies such as IoT, Fog computing, cloud computing, and so on, are vulnerable to cyber assaults. This is especially true during the COVID-19 pandemic when the industry is experiencing a boom (Remko, 2020).

2.1. Current Cyber Threats

2.1.1. Exploration of Prevalent Cyber Threats Targeting the Logistics Sector

In tandem with logistics industry advancements, there has been a corresponding growth in the number of internal and external users and applications able to access acquisition data. Many cybercriminals have set their sights on the logistics industry because of its vital role in the world economy. Supply chain service detours, monetary losses, and the possible exploitation of highly confidential data are some serious outcomes that can result from cybersecurity issues in the logistics business. Assessing a supply chain attack's potential threats and consequences is essential for ensuring safety and resilience in an increasingly dependent society on worldwide, linked digital supply chains (Taeihagh & Hazel, 2019).

This section examines the potential cyber risks that commonly target the internal and external logistics and supply chain operations. The logistics industry is frequently subjected to cyber threats, as depicted in Figure 1. Below are several potential cyber threats that can impact logistics (Colicchia et al., 2019; Syed & Syed, 2022):

- **Denial of Services (DoS):** For many reasons, cybercriminals have recently focused their attention on the transportation and logistics industry, a particularly vulnerable sector of the economy. A denial-of-service (DoS) attack can have far-reaching implications since the attackers take over the targeted organization or systems and interrupt the logistics workflow for thousands of other organizations. On top of that, as of late, attackers have been using ransomware attacks in conjunction with denial-of-service attacks, which have the potential to greatly impact the operational logistics supply chain across all transportation modalities.
- **Data Breaches and Insider Threats:** Logistics organizations are vulnerable to insider threats and data breaches, which can take the form of current or former employees, third-party contractors, or even customers. These individuals can compromise systems inadvertently or maliciously, accessing sensitive information like financial records and employee files. Damage to

Figure 1. Prevalent cyber threats targeting the logistics sector

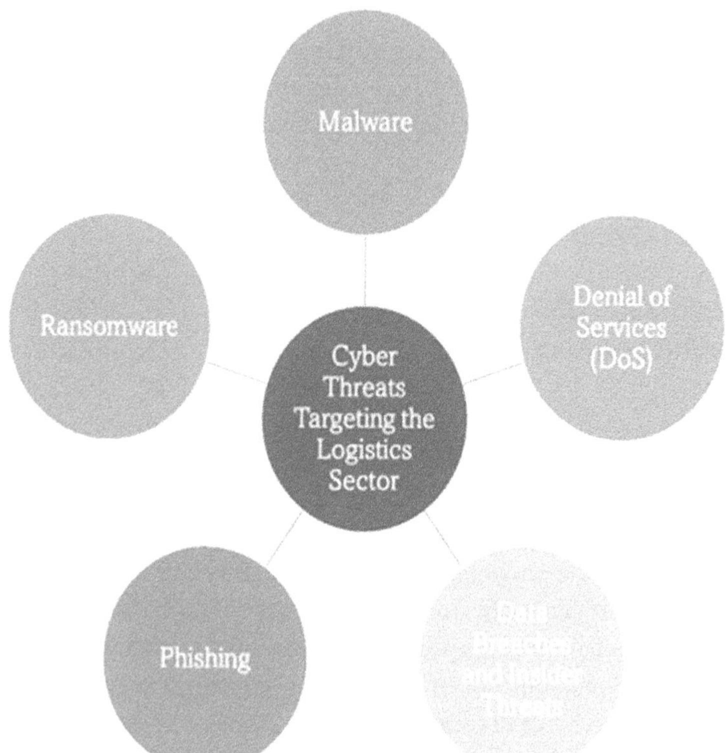

reputation, financial losses, and legal ramifications can result from insider threats and data breaches caused by malware attacks in the logistics sector. Victims of identity theft and those who trade on the dark web may potentially profit from stolen information.

- **Phishing:** The shipping and logistics industry is a common target of phishing schemes, in which perpetrators assume the identities of reputable companies such as DHL, Swiss Post, FedEx, Australia Post, and the United States Postal Service. In phishing, a malicious actor poses as a trustworthy entity in an effort to trick victims into divulging important information. Phishing schemes often target logistics organizations because of their constant interaction with customers, particularly due to the widespread use of electronic delivery status updates.
- **Ransomware:** The logistics industry is seeing a rise in the complexity of ransomware attacks, with bad actors increasingly aiming their attacks against supply chains to cripple an organization's ecosystem as a whole rather than merely a single company. Ransomware has the potential to incapacitate

businesses and service companies, causing significant delays in meeting their responsibilities to you while they endeavor to reinstate their services. Because of this, many things have gone wrong, including ships or trucks becoming stranded at stations and ports, empty supermarket shelves, and medicine being out of stock.

- **Malware:** In malware attacks, the perpetrators install malicious software on a targeted system with the intention of gaining unauthorized access and maybe stealing sensitive data. Malware attacks on logistics and transportation networks can impede shipments or compromise traffic control systems, posing serious safety risks.

2.1.2 Examples of Recent Cyber Incidents Affecting Supply Chain Operations

The sophistication and frequency of cyber attacks targeting supply chains are rising significantly. In recent years, businesses and their subcontractors, retailers, and third-party vendors of services have been vulnerable to cyberattacks because of the dependency on ICT technologies and complex interaction methods. This way, malicious actors can access the targeted organizations by jeopardizing a completely trusted portion or some part of a program or process inside the supply chain. Furthermore, attackers can actively catch their victims off guard by doing this, as they can easily bypass commonly used security measures. This section investigates recent cyber attack incidents that have significantly impacted supply chain operations by analyzing the methods of cyber attacks employed against various organizations and applications (Gihon, n.d.).

The JetBrains TeamCity CI/CD tool became known to have a critical-rated vulnerability in September 2023, exploited by hackers from SolarWinds. In the event exploited, this vulnerability could grant attackers full administrative authority over the server's configuration and allow them to execute remote code execution. An important authentication bypass vulnerability was the focus of this cyber attack because of the damage it could do and the fact that attackers with access to HTTP(s) could use it to run remote code and take over the affected servers' administrative functions. Consequently, this attack could open the door to supply chain attacks.

In October 2023, Okta, a company that offers services for managing identities and authentication, said that hackers had gained access to sensitive client information by stealing login credentials for its consumer support management platform. In recent support situations, the threat actor may access data posted by some Okta customers. Furthermore, cybercriminals frequently target Okta because of major corporations like Microsoft's widespread usage of their software. Consequently, if attackers manage to breach their systems, they might launch software supply chain attacks, gaining access to the networks of their clients.

The MOVEit, a widely used application in the United States for securely transferring classified files, was compromised in June 2023 by a supply chain attack that specifically targeted individuals of the MOVEit Transfer utility, which is owned by Progress Software, an American company. Several organizations whose supply chains utilize the MOVEit application have experienced a data intrusion due to this attack; as a consequence, the information of their customers and/or employees has been compromised.

Mandiant Consulting responded in March 2023 to a supply chain compromise that impacted the 3CX Desktop App software, which facilitates user voice, video, and chat communications. As part of this attack, the hackers could access the victim's system, execute malicious code, and then compromise the programs by including a malicious library file in the bundle, which fetched an encrypted file with command and control information.

Applied Materials, a semiconductor firm, was the victim of a supply chain cyber attack in February 2023 that interrupted shipments and was estimated to cost $250 million. Although the firm has not confirmed it, rumors have circulated that industrial equipment provider MKS Instruments was the target of the hack since the business declared a ransomware assault on February 3 and postponed its fourth-quarter results call as a result.

On 3 February 2022, 22 flights were delayed by up to 20 minutes at Zurich Airport (ZRH) due to a ransomware attack that affected Swissport, an example of a cyberattack at airport ground services and air cargo operator (i.e., logistics industry). The organisation asserts that the BlackCat ransomware gang was responsible for the attack on their IT systems. While the majority of key systems and applications were unharmed, a few systems had to be temporarily shut down because of the impact on various servers.

A supply chain attack in December 2022 infected nightly versions of the free and open-source machine learning toolkit PyTorch with malware. Torchtriton is a dependency of PyTorch, and the attack was made feasible by compromising its Python Package Index (PyPI) source repository. After downloading the Triton package, the malicious software was programmed to run and upload confidential data from the victim's PC. The Linux nightly releases of PyTorch were the only ones affected by the vulnerability; users of the stable package were unaffected.

2.2 Vulnerabilities in the Logistics Framework

2.2.1 Identification of Key Vulnerabilities Within the Logistics Industry Framework

The operations and profitability of logistics and supply networks are susceptible to a wide range of risks and vulnerabilities (Supply Chain Vulnerability, n.d.). Figure 2 shows the possible vulnerabilities in the logistics framework.

- **Natural Disasters:** Earthquakes, storms, and floods are examples of natural disasters that can potentially cause severe disruptions, which can result in delayed shipments and damaged commodities.
- **Unexpected Delays in Transportation:** numerous factors can cause disruptions in the transportation of commodities, including power limits,

Figure 2. Vulnerabilities in the logistics framework

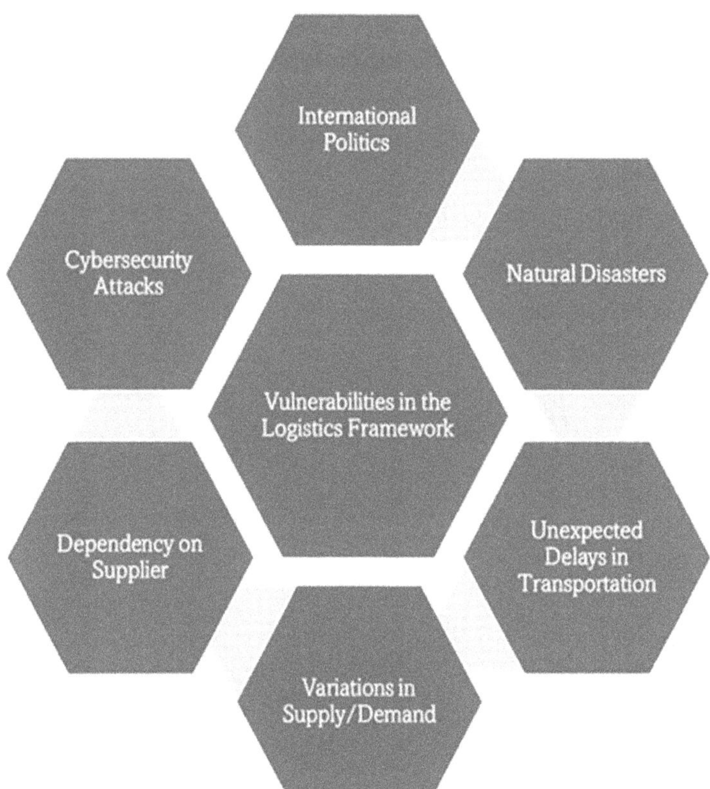

accidents, strikes, and congestion at terminals; these can all lead to increased costs and delays.

- **Variations in Supply/Demand:** Inventory management challenges and supply-demand imbalances may emerge due to the swift consumer demand fluctuations, market dynamics, and economic circumstances.
- **Dependency on Supplier:** Disruptions to the supply chain may result from elements such as reliance on a solitary source, supplier insolvency, quality concerns, or delivery setbacks.
- **Cybersecurity Attacks:** An increase in the peril of cyberattacks on logistical systems and data intrusions has resulted from the expanding prevalence of digitalization, which has increased the likelihood of disruptions and the loss of sensitive information.
- **International Politics:** There are a number of factors that can generate uncertainty and have an impact on international trade, including instability in politics, disagreements over trade, penalties, and policy changes.

2.2.2 Discussion on Potential Points of Entry for Cyber Threats

The most advanced criminals of today have a methodical strategy to find their next victim. The content of this piece breaks out the typical hacking process and identifies the most common avenues of entry that bad actors use to launch attacks (The most common entry points for a cyber attack, n.d.). Figure 3 showing the common entry points of entry for cyber threats.

Figure 3. Potential points of entry for cyber threats

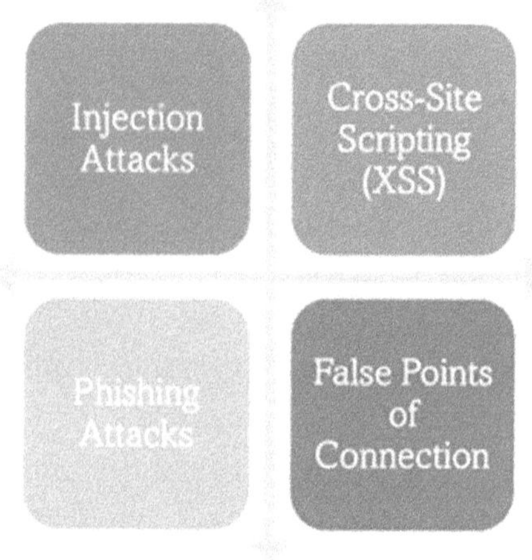

- **Injection Attacks:** When input is not properly validated, illicit programs or commands might be executed, leading to injection attacks. An intruder may be able to access private information or even take over the system if this happens. Various injection attacks, including injection of SQL, cross-site scripting, etc., are possible.
- **Cross-Site Scripting (XSS):** An attacker can exploit a security hole known as cross-site scripting (XSS) to inject harmful code into a website, which unsuspecting users can execute. Among the code's malevolent functions is the ability to steal user data and run instructions on the user's PC. Sending a maliciously constructed payload to a logged-in user on a susceptible website is one way to abuse XSS. Any of these methods—email, URL, or attachment—can convey the payload. When consumers visit third-party websites that contain XSS vulnerabilities, attackers can inject spyware into such sites.
- **Phishing Attacks:** Phishing is a form of social engineering utilized by malicious actors to coerce the target user into divulging confidential data or personally identifiable information (PII). These malicious actors might, for instance, send fraudulent emails purporting to originate from a reputable organization or individual with the intention of obtaining sensitive data such as credit card or password information. There is a likelihood that the emails may encompass attachments or hyperlinks to perilous websites, which may instruct the recipient to install malware onto their device.
- **False Points of Connection:** Exploiting aberrant access points is one of the most prevalent strategies cyber adversaries employ to enter businesses illicitly. Fraudsters have swiftly established unauthorized wireless access points to gain rapid access to networks. Detecting or identifying them may prove challenging due to their apparent legitimacy as access points.

3. UNDERSTANDING THE LOGISTICS INDUSTRY FRAMEWORK

3.1 Components of the Logistics Framework

Logistics management is essential for firms to effectively manage their supply chain, despite its complexity. Logistics operations and activities inside the supply chain are defined by the logistics framework. One must first comprehend the essential elements that can establish and maintain uniformity in the transfer of products from producer to retailer or end user in order to comprehend the logistical framework and the operations that comprise it .

3.1.1 Breakdown of the Key Components of the Logistics Industry Framework

As the industry evolves and demands more efficient logistics to deliver products to distributors and consumers, it is essential to possess a thorough understanding of the key components of logistics management. For effective management of supply chain operations, the logistics framework consists of the following six main parts (Axestrack, n.d.; Key Elements of Logistics Management, n.d.), as showing in the Figure 4:

- **Storage, Warehousing and Materials Handling:** The modern world necessitates proper storage and preservation of commodities and materials due to the unpredictable nature of market supply and demand, making a surplus of items necessary to meet customers' unexpected demands. Warehouse management systems (WMS) play a crucial role in this implementation by making sure goods are facile to store, move, and transport, optimize storage capacities and equipment, and reduce distribution and transportation costs. This helps supply chain operations run smoothly.
- **Inventory:** Inventory management plays a crucial role in logistical systems by establishing the optimal storage location and determining when and how much stock should be ordered to meet customer demands. So, to make things easier and simpler, digital inventory control and administration regulates supply-side activities; with good inventory management, businesses may avoid having excess or shortage of products/items. It goes so far as to forecast customer demand, which allows for more organized and effective order planning.
- **Packaging and Unitizations:** Logistics management, which emphasizes the correct handling and storage of items, relies heavily on packaging and unitization in terms of the essentiality of goods and their condition in the supply chain. Unitization can be defined as the process of grouping or bundling cargo, enclosing it in packaging, and loading it onto or within a larger unit. Additionally, unitization streamlines the process of storing and transporting goods and commodities.
- **Transport:** Transport is also regarded as the most essential element of a framework for logistics management, as it coordinates and facilitates the delivery of goods to their ultimate destination via various means (freight trains, automobiles, maritime shipping, etc.). Consequently, it attains a multitude of advantages, including decreased expenses, diminished environmental impacts, prompt deliveries, and an emphasis on transportation optimization

to guarantee the timely arrival of products or items at the doorstep of the consumer.

- **Information and Control:** The integration of cutting-edge technologies, encompassing sophisticated hardware, software, and processes, can furnish organizations with data-driven decisions that enhance supply chain management efficiency. This paradigm represents the prospective development in the logistics sector. Organizations are increasingly adopting cutting-edge technologies such as Blockchain, Artificial Intelligence, the Internet of Things, and Big Data to attain complete supply chain transparency. Nonetheless, ensuring the uninterrupted flow of information and exercising authority over data control are critical and formidable elements of the logistic framework. These components underscore the significance of obtaining valuable insights and effectively managing demand.
- **Fleet Management:** Companies nowadays pour a lot of money into fleet management, purchasing new cars to add to the current fleet and investing in software, hardware, and cloud-based services to make customer delivery services, drivers, and fleets more efficient. Consequently, logistics would be

incomplete without commercial vehicle management and monitoring, including tasks like optimizing asset use, enhancing fleet maintenance planning, and controlling expenses.

3.1.2 Overview of the Interconnected Nature of Logistics Operations

Logistics framework refers to the comprehensive interconnected network of processes, individuals, assets, and undertakings entailed in producing, distributing, and shipping products and services to final consumers. The components comprising the logistic framework are those involved in production and distribution. These processes—purchasing, operations, and logistics—are designed to facilitate the manufacturing and distribution of products and services on behalf of businesses. It encompasses diverse procedures, including the acquisition of raw materials, the manufacturing process, the storage and transportation of products, and the final retail sale. In the

Figure 4. Breakdown of the key components of the logistics industry framework

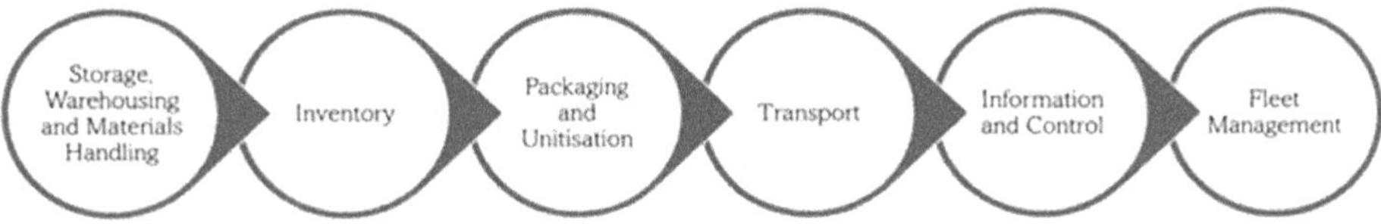

contemporary era, characterized by widespread interconnectivity and globalization, supply chain management is critical in determining businesses' success across diverse industries (Al-Banna et al., 2023).

In logistics operations, Information/data also played an important role that has the potential to transformed into the primary asset required for effective supply chain management. From various sources, including logistics operation monitoring, production process monitoring, inventory level tracking, and consumer behavior analysis, the supply chain generates enormous amounts of data. This information is vital for facilitating informed decision-making throughout the entire supply chain (Ali et al., 2023).

However, in recent times, supply chain management has been significantly impacted. by modifications made when there was a substantial shift in both the supply and demand of goods and services, as has been the case during the coronavirus (COVID-19) epidemic. There has been minimal damage to either the productive capacity or the underlying mechanisms of the markets. The markets maintain their traditional operational patterns. Nonetheless, the disruptions caused by the coronavirus may result in substantial modifications to the organizational structures and types of supply networks.

3.2 Digital Transformation in Logistics

This section examines the dynamic domain of logistics' digital transformation, investigates the state-of-the-art technologies that propel this revolution, and reveals the emergent trends reconfiguring the sector. By acquiring an all-encompassing comprehension of these technologies and trends, one can discern their tremendous influence on the logistics domain, thereby bestowing an advantage on organizations that adopt them.

3.2.1 Examination of the Ongoing Digital Transformation in Logistics

Digital transformation describes the shift toward more digital logistics methods to better serve companies and their customers by making logistics systems more efficient, effective, and responsive. The logistics domain is experiencing an unprecedented revolution propelled by digital transformation. Amidst the swift pace of technological progress, the logistics sector adopts cutting-edge technologies to optimize processes, increase effectiveness, and satisfy continuously expanding customer demands. Many logistics organizations are only beginning to understand the effects of digital transformation on their internal operations, in addition to the increasing demand to digitize their supply chain management systems. For example, numerous technologies, including statistical analysis and real-time monitoring, are transforming the transportation, warehousing, and delivery of goods (Gregory, 1998).

Although the logistics industry greatly benefits from digital technology, many problems persist, and many people in the field are still unhappy. On the other hand, there are a lot of unforeseen advantages that organizations may reap from digital technology, which are enhancing supply chain capabilities and day-today personnel management systems. In light of this, why is adopting digital technologies in the logistics industry so critical? The significance of this change in perspective is examined in the following points via a succession of crucial indicators (Cichosz et al., 2020):

- **Supply Chain Enhancement:** By utilizing AI-powered algorithms and sophisticated analytics, supply chain operations are enhanced through the ability to forecast demand, optimize supplies, and allocate resources strategically.
- **Maximized Productivity:** The utilization of digital technology has the potential to optimize operations and maximized productivity, thereby enhancing overall efficiency across the supply chain and mitigating errors related to human labor.
- **Monitoring in Real-Time:** By leveraging intelligent technologies such as RFID, sensors, and internet of things-based network devices, organizations can gain instantaneous visibility into their shipments. This capability enhances their capacity to trace and monitor shipments in the event of supply chain disruptions or losses.
- **Risk Mitigation:** By leveraging real-time data and analytics, organizational leaders can preemptively identify and mitigate potential risks, thereby safeguarding the sustainability and robustness of their companies.
- **Operational Flexibility and Reactivity:** The ability to rapidly respond to shifting client needs and adapt to ever-changing market conditions is made possible for organizations through the process of digital transformation in order to enhance the operational flexibility and reactivity

3.2.2 Implications of Increased Connectivity and Technology Adoption

The implications of greater connectivity and the use of numerous critical technologies are altering the logistics industry and driving digital transformation in logistics. An essential step towards transforming logistics companies' operations, enhancing productivity, streamlining processes, and improving client relations is the rising trend of merging/combining diverse organizations and subsequently integrating different ICT systems. Even though numerous digital technologies are causing a revolution in the logistics sector, the following are some of the most important digital technologies (illustrating in Figure 5) driving this digital transformation that the industry has come to accept (Digital, n.d.).

- **Internet of Things (IoT):** The Internet of Things (IoT) is a system of networked computing devices, sensors, and networks that may gather and share data to allow the monitoring and tracking of goods, automobiles, and stocks in real time. In addition, it helps with supply chain accessibility, strategic selection, and logistics operation effectiveness by revealing the whereabouts, circumstances, and current state of assets.
- **Cloud Computing:** The cloud computing paradigm provides Internet-accessible, scalable, flexible, efficient, and on-demand computing resources automatically configured and priced on a pay-as-you-go basis. Cloud-based integrated solutions facilitate secure and instantaneous communication, exchange of information, and integration among various systems and stakeholders for logistic organizations operating in the supply chain and logistics industry. In addition, cloud-based technologies offer a centralized repository for collecting, processing, and evaluating data, enabling the smooth flow of information and supporting flexible and versatile logistics operations.
- **Artificial Intelligence (AI):** Artificial intelligence (AI) revolutionizes logistics by automating operations, processing enormous quantities of data, and facilitating intelligent decision-making, which allows for better demand pattern prediction, route optimization, forecast accuracy, and inventory management. On the other hand, ML algorithms can learn from data to incrementally enhance operational efficiency, which in turn decreases costs and increases client retention.
- **Analytics with Big Data:** A logistics network built on the IoT can collect and process the massive amounts of data produced by logistics operations, allowing businesses to get valuable insights through analytics and boost their efficiency. For instance, logistics companies can leverage big data analytics to extract actionable insights from massive datasets; this allows for better demand planning, improvement of routes, mitigation of risks, and analysis of customer behavior; ultimately, it leads to data-driven choices, boosts performance, and improves satisfaction among consumers.
- **Robotics and Automation:** The implementation of robotics and automation technologies are transforming the logistics sector by enabling stack inspection, administration, and order fulfillment. Integrating diverse autonomous systems—including robotic limbs, automated piloted vehicles, and self-sufficient mobile robots—capable of performing repetitive tasks with greater precision and efficacy facilitates this process. By implementing

these technologies, warehouse layouts may be optimized, human error may be mitigated, and operational productivity may be enhanced.

- **Blockchain Technology:** Logistics companies can use blockchain technology's decentralized, distributed, secure, and transparent transactions through immutable ledgers. This technology can improve supply chain visibility, traceability, and trust between companies and customers. It can also streamline processes across supply chain stakeholders, reduce fraudulent activity, improve regulatory compliance, and expedite the management of agreements, documentation, and transactions.

4. DIGITAL SAFEGUARDS FOR CYBERSECURITY IN LOGISTICS

4.1 Risk Assessment and Mitigation

Managing risks effectively is of the utmost importance in the ever-changing logistics industry, where many variables converge to enable the transportation of products. Many obstacles plague the logistics sector, such as interruptions in the supply chain, risks to data security, difficulties in meeting regulatory requirements, and even natural catastrophes. In the absence of proper risk mitigation strategies being

Figure 5. Digital technologies in logistics

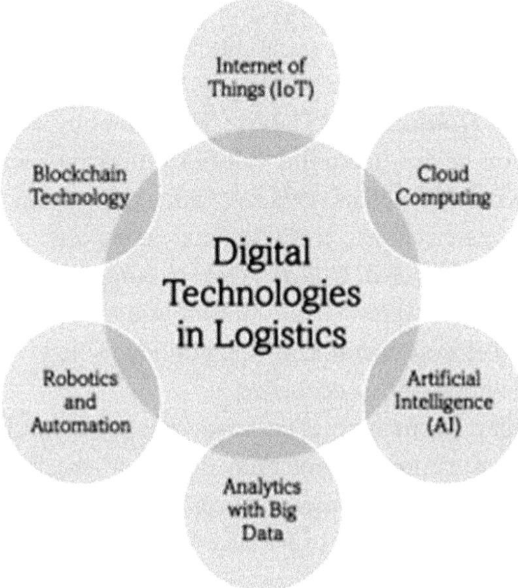

implemented, these challenges may lead to significant project setbacks, escalated costs, and reputational harm for the company in question.

4.1.1 Strategies for Conducting Comprehensive Risk Assessments in Logistics

A multitude of natural disasters can manifest, including but not limited to digital assaults, supply chain disruptions, inventory stock-outs, typhoons, and floods; man-made crises include but are not limited to catastrophes such as cyberattacks and floods. Profound setbacks to operations related to logistics and a multitude of adverse consequences may ensue as a consequence of these catastrophes. The most important steps in performing thorough logistics risk assessments are as follows (Panjehfouladgaran et al., 2020):

- **Natural Disasters:** Unpredictable occurrences in the logistics industry, such as natural disasters (e.g., wildfires, hurricanes, earthquakes, or floods), can disrupt the supply chain and cause significant harm to logistics operations. In addition to material costs and property damage, these events can increase expenses. Understanding the logistic risks associated with these catastrophes is an essential component of the suitable risk assessment methodology.
- **Establishing Trust with Vendors:** Problems with long-term vendor reliability, whether owing to financial instability or production issues, can cause supply chain disruptions, and when a critical supplier fails to deliver the necessary parts or goods, it can harm the entire logistics network. Prolonged interruptions can damage a company's brand and diminish customer trust, thus it's vital to check supplier reliability and have backup plans/items ready, as the part of risk assessment.
- **Transportation Holdups and Delays:** There are numerous potential causes of transportation delays, including but not limited to excessive traffic, road closures, and vehicle mechanical issues. Such delays may have financial and non-financial repercussions on the logistics company and its clients in the form of delayed shipments. Consequently, a comprehensive risk assessment is necessary, which is required to implement a detailed alternative plan for the journey, and closely monitoring the individuals involved can significantly reduce the likelihood of this occurring.
- **Product Quality Assurance:** The term "quality control assurance" refers to the process of evaluating potential threats to the integrity of goods in transit. In sectors where customer safety and product quality are of the utmost importance, the consequences of product damage or loss during shipment can

be devastating. Therefore, to limit this risk, it is vital to apply strict quality control techniques and ensure secure packing.

- **Adherence to Regulations:** Logistics operations must always be mindful of regulatory compliance to avoid monetary sanctions, legal proceedings, and damage to the company's reputation. Therefore, it is critical to be informed about the constantly changing legislation and to develop and implement effective compliance methods to lessen the impact of this risk.

4.1.2 Mitigation Measures to Address Identified Risks and Vulnerabilities

This section explains the mitigation measures to address identified risks and vulnerabilities (Menoni et al., 2012).

- **Emergency Preparedness:** Logistics organizations should create thorough and alternate disaster preparedness plans that detail specific actions to follow in the event of a variety of unanticipated crisis scenarios; this is what emergency preparedness is all about. A logistical organization's preparations should address at least the following: safeguarding inventory, guaranteeing personnel safety, and assuring uninterrupted operations. This will help decrease risk in the event of any situation and minimize expenditures and delays.
- **Diversifying the Supply Chain Process:** Suppose a logistical organization relies on a single supplier or route. In that case, it is more likely to be vulnerable to interruptions caused by incidents like catastrophic weather, strikes by employees, or sudden alterations to regulations. To diversify the supply chain, one must expand their network of distribution channels and suppliers. Adopting this mitigation method allows for seamless adaptability to unexpected problems and redundancy of products and procedures.
- **Protection Against Financial Losses Through Insurance:** Logistics companies ought to consider insurance options that are customized to their particular requirements, as sufficient protection can serve as a means of survival during challenging circumstances. Although insurance cannot prevent the occurrence of catastrophes, it can certainly mitigate their devastation. In addition, these plans may provide reimbursement for expenses related to business disruption, inventory loss and replacement, and restorations to damaged assets.
- **Legal Readiness and Compliance with Regulations:** It is crucial to adhere to all relevant safety laws and regulations. To circumvent penalties and legal complications, it is imperative to stay abreast of the always evolving

regulations and ensure that your logistics activities are in compliance with them. To ensure the protection of your interests in the event of disruptions, it is advisable to be lawfully prepared. This entails establishing contractual agreements that clearly delineate your obligations and potential legal obligations with vendors and business partners.

- **Strategic Alliances:** Strategic alliances with the use of collaborative and communications skills during times of crisis are critical elements in the field of logistics, as is the capacity to establish enduring partnerships with shipping companies, suppliers, and other relevant parties. Additionally, when individuals can communicate and provide mutual support, they are more adept at responding to disruptions in a coordinated fashion, thereby ensuring that all parties remain aligned.
- **Use of Modern ICT Tools and Continuous Monitoring:** Risk management in logistics is reliant heavily on contemporary information and communication technologies (ICT). As an illustration, ICT solutions, such as cloud services, databases, RFID sensors, and others, can assist logistics companies in enhancing their tracking and monitoring activities. Reduce the severity of potential catastrophes if your organization can respond rapidly to changes and disruptions. By enabling you to monitor shipments, reserve inventory levels, and demand fluctuations, these technologies can provide you with critical information regarding your supply chain.
- **Employee Education and Training:** Initiating training and education programs is an essential next step for logistic firms after utilizing and depolying current ICT systems. These programs should be a part of the organization's risk management plan and employee welcome packages. When disaster strikes, your employees are the first line of defense for your firm. To ensure they can handle the situation effectively, it is important to train your staff on emergency response processes and practice disaster scenarios on a regular basis.
- **Ongoing Evaluation and Enhancement:** Lastly, logistic organizations consider risk management as an ongoing activity that necessitates reviewing the internal and external processes of the supply chain on a regular basis and updating risk management plans to account for new or changing hazards. Organizations can use ICT techniques like machine learning approaches to strengthen their resilience in the face of future disruptions by conducting post-disaster evaluations and learning from the lessons learned. Utilizing predictive modeling and statistical analysis, organizations can enhance their readiness for and management of risks. Businesses have the ability to avert potential catastrophes by analyzing historical data and current market trends in order to identify such issues.

4.2 Endpoint Security

To get access to systems, cyber attackers frequently aim for endpoints. To get around this, there is a cybersecurity solution called endpoint security that prevents cyberthreats and unwanted activities from endpoints. This section discusses the necessity of endpoint security in the supply chain and how sectors can protect themselves by establishing contingency plans to address cybersecurity risks.

4.2.1 Importance of Securing Endpoints in Logistics Operations

Supply chain efficiency was of the utmost importance during the height of the COVID-19 epidemic to meet the critical needs of hospitals, stores, and other essential organizations. However, COVID-19 has changed the focus for sectors targeting cybersecurity as an impending threat to business following a challenging year for most supply chains.

Since COVID-19, the world has gained a better understanding of the magnitude of the threats, and endpoint security can offer significant protection for devices connected to a Logistics network. End device management and maintenance becomes more challenging and perilous when information technology staff are overwhelmed or unorganized supply-chain processes introduce security holes.

In light of the complexity of the processes/devices involved in supply chain management, businesses need device management systems that cover all aspects of the risk supply chain, including manufacturing, transportation, activities, and servicing. Organizations can improve the end device security posture from beginning to end across their infrastructure by utilizing endpoint security services (Closs & McGarrell, 2004).

4.2.2 Best Practices for Endpoint Protection and Monitoring

Advanced endpoint security solutions go beyond simple antivirus software to thwart various threats, including newly discovered and old malware, file-less attacks, vulnerabilities, and post-intrusion approaches. Endpoint security solutions may frequently isolate infected endpoints, stopping attacks from propagating to other endpoints. This is useful since threat actors may utilize endpoints as a backdoor into a company's network.

Consider these potential best practices for endpoint monitoring and protection when you evaluate an endpoint security solution (Kadrich, 2007).

- **A Solitary Lightweight Protocol/Agent:** Smaller businesses should use a single agent or lightweight protocols for endpoint threat prevention, detection, and response instead of deploying cumbersome agents that constantly monitor your endpoints for attack signatures.

- **Robust Endpoint Security Measures:** The most effective endpoint security solutions can block malware at every stage of an attack, from discovery and penetration to installation and behavior, by combining numerous security databases, such as incursions and signature engines.
- **Cloud-based Solutions:** When it comes to end-point security, a cloud-based solution is ideal for remote workers since it not only simplifies operations and gets rid of cumbersome on-premises servers, but it can also scale up fast to handle additional users and data.
- **A Robust Pre-built Detecting System:** To identify covert cyber threats, it is ideal to have a strong pre-built detection system that incorporates a wide range of machine learning and analytics methodologies. On the other hand, there is a wide range of capabilities and usability among these solutions in the public eye.
- **Visibility for Faster Inquiry and Reaction:** In order to decrease response times, organizations should select security solutions that offer a comprehensive view of incidents together with detailed investigative information, rather than those that are compartmentalized and produce infinite warnings without any useful context.

4.3 Secure Communication Protocols/Technologies

Logistics and supply chain management include the procedures, personnel, and technologies employed to acquire resources and components, manufacture finished goods, and transport them to consumers. The efficient execution of day-to-day activities depends on logistics and supply chain management communication systems/protocols. The management of logistics and supply chains is not an exception to the rule that communication connections are necessary for any company involved in transporting goods from one location to another. But they take on an even greater significance when unexpected disasters and crisis situations strike.

4.3.1 Exploration of Secure Communication Protocols for Data Exchange

Communication is key if you're involved in a logistical operation involving transporting items. Supply chain communications rely on established protocols and technologies to constantly contact important field players in various places and monitor all shipments' statuses in real-time.

A wide variety of protocols, methods, and requirements for communication are involved in logistics management.

- **Email:** The use of email facilitates communication and information sharing between assignment managers and logistics operations.
- **Voice Communication:** Through various mobile services and cellphones, logistical operations and clients can communicate in real-time via voice communication protocol.
- **Text Messages:** Logistics operators, assignment managers, and clients often use text messaging as a communication mechanism to promptly communicate and update each other about any scenario.
- **Radio Frequency Identification (RFID) Tags:** Shipped goods can have their unique identifiers communicated with the use of tiny devices called radio frequency identification (RFID) tags.
- **IoT-based Smart Devices:** Smart devices connected to the Internet of Things (IoT) transfer data from the warehouse to a main computer system, where it may be stored and used to make quick decisions based on intelligence.
- **Online Messaging Platforms:** By utilizing these protocols, logistics operations and transportation managers are able to store and manage data as well as communicate with one another.

4.3.2 Implementation of Encryption and Secure Channels

Logistics companies face a substantial threat from supply chain vulnerabilities. It is of the utmost importance to guarantee the security and confidentiality of supply chain activities in a globally integrated market. This section delves into the ways in which these vulnerabilities can be mitigated and the supply chain protected through the use of secure channels and encryption.

One effective method to reduce supply chain risks is to implement secure file transfer protocols. Businesses may protect their sensitive data and make sure it stays discreet, intact, and available by using secure communication techniques, authentication, and encryption. The use of secure communication channels, such as those employed by secure file transfer solutions, is critical in achieving data integrity and confidentiality, two of the most important aspects of data security. The data is protected from illegal access by using sophisticated encryption methods in these secure communication channels. Companies may be sure that no one other than authorized personnel can read and decode their data by encrypting it both while it's in motion and when it's stored. As a result, businesses can rest easy knowing their data is secure against intrusion and manipulation.

5. SUPPLY CHAIN VISIBILITY AND SECURITY

The term "supply chain visibility" describes a company's ability to observe and comprehend all the steps and components that make up its supply chain. A transparent supply chain allows for easy monitoring of inventory levels, shipments, and the efficiency of all parties involved in real-time. Effective supply chain visibility Within the supply chain allows access to the most recent information regarding the status of commodities and their location across the supply chain.

5.1 Importance of Visibility

Supply chain visibility is critical for enhancing operational effectiveness, mitigating risks, and delivering value to clients and the organization. It is an indispensable element within the framework of modern supply chain management.

5.1.1 Discussion on the Significance of Visibility in Supply Chain Operations

Amidst the dynamic nature of the contemporary business environment, the significance of supply chain visibility is underscored by the subsequent advan-tages that augment said visibility. This increases a business's ability to make more informed decisions and maintain a competitive advantage in the marketplace (Kalaiarasan et al., 2023).

- **Satisfy Customer Demands:** In order to accommodate shifting consumer demands, supply channels must possess the capacity for transforming. You can ascertain the necessary measures to realign your supply chain with consumer preferences with a supply chain advisor who possesses extensive knowledge of such transformations and offers comprehensive insight into supply chain operations.
- **Reducing Downtime:** By proactively identifying potential locations of disruptions, logistic organizations can decrease the likelihood that such disruptions will result in complications. Furthermore, outcomes are exceedingly satisfactory, and issues are significantly reduced when a supply chain is managed with robust data analysis and communication.
- **Results Influenced by Analytical Data:** The analytical data gathered from various logistics operations resources, along with the insights of a seasoned consultant, empowers shippers to make better decisions. With this data, shippers can see their supply chain and access a wealth of information (Tayyab & Marjani, 2021a).

- **Maximized Efficiency:** The utilization of data to inform supply chain decisions obviates the necessity of passively awaiting guidance on the subsequent course of action to maximize the efficiency of logistic operations. Being cognizant of impending events enables one to accelerate progress, directly impacting supply chain visibility. Furthermore, this is intricately linked to the process of increasing agility to facilitate the monitoring of inventory, the evaluation of supplier efficacy, and tracing product flow for businesses.
- **Maintaining Compliance and Fostering Sustainability:** The supply chain's environmental impact can be better understood with the help of visibility, which in turn helps with compliance with standards and regulations. This is especially important in industries where supply chain integrity and traceability are paramount, such as healthcare, aerospace, and pharmaceuticals (Tayyab & Marjani, 2021b).

5.1.2 Technologies and Practices for Enhancing Supply Chain Visibility

In order to improve and enhance supply chain visibility, there are numerous methods available; however, the most appropriate method will be determined by the company and the products, as well as the technologies and practices that they choose to implement.

Potential technologies and practices that organizations can implement to improve the visibility of their supply chains are outlined here (Cheng et al., 2023).

- **Streamlining Supply-chain Processes:** In the streamlining process of the supply chain, simplifying the supply chain is possible due to the methodical enhancements implemented in its operations. To accomplish this objective by reducing expenses, boosting overall output, and eradicating inefficiencies, a comprehensive examination and restructuring of the procurement, production, transportation, and delivery procedures may be undertaken. Improving the efficiency of the supply chain is a key component of modern company strategies since it helps companies stay competitive and resilient in dynamic marketplaces.
- **Real-time Interaction With Suppliers:** The creation of open lines of communication and technical interfaces with vendors and business associates allows for the smooth flow of information while also guaranteeing that everyone is using the same set of records.
- **Interactive Logistics Connection:** The logistics connections practices delineate the methodology through which various components of a supply

chain are strategically harmonized and synchronized to enhance information flow, cooperation, and communication. Furthermore, it encompasses integrating data, systems, and processes throughout the complete supply chain, commencing with acquiring basic materials and concluding with the shipment of completed products to customers.

- **Visualizing the Supply Chain in One Frame:** A strategic tool for better understanding the interdependent web of businesses and individuals engaged in the creation and delivery of a product or service, supply chain mapping entails creating a graphical representation of this network. By incorporating this procedure into your logistical framework, you can better understand your supply chain ecosystem as a whole, from the movement of materials and information to the flow of funds. You can also better identify important players, evaluate their interdependencies, and find areas of inefficiency or risk.
- **Supply Chain Software / Technologies:** By employing supply chain monitoring software and solutions, monitoring the precise trajectory that goods traverse from their initial location to their ultimate endpoint becomes feasible. Supply chain transparency software can furnish users with transparent and unambiguous information about every phase of the supply chain. You will be capable of thoroughly comprehending the activities that transpire within the supply network by employing its assistance. To achieve this, an extensive array of data sources and technologies are integrated to facilitate real-time tracking and evaluation of products, inventory, and logistics-related activities (Suja, 2022).

By employing state-of-the-art technologies like the IoT, RFID, and Global Positioning System (GPS) tracking, one can obtain real-time access to current information concerning the whereabouts and state of commodities. Furthermore, a deeper comprehension of supply chain trends, potential risks, and opportunities for enhancement can be achieved by employing data analytics and artificial intelligence, which can offer substantial insights. Ultimately, this procedure guarantees that all participants within the supply chain employ compatible data formats and systems, thereby reducing errors and facilitating information sharing. Additionally, the implementation of these technologies aids in the safeguarding of confidential supply chain data against cyber threats and unauthorized entry. This practice aids in preserving the confidentiality and integrity of the data.

5.2 Data Integrity Measures

A straightforward explanation of the importance of data integrity measures is that it is a critical enabler of decision-making and estimation, particularly when disruption is at its peak. Having high data integrity measures to achieve data confidentiality and integrity implies that you have correct, accurate, and unmodifiable data (Hameed et al., 2017).

5.2.1 Ensuring Data Integrity Throughout the Supply Chain

It is critical to assess the integrity of your logistics systems in order to obtain accurate data that can be utilized to enhance your operations, processes, and overall performance. In order to ensure data integrity, the system is required to monitor and record various metrics, including the total number of errors encountered, the time required to retrieve data, and the presence of missing information, such as customs clearance documents. Ensuring the preservation of data integrity is crucial for accessing reliable, authentic, and precise information. Consequently, one can monitor progress, enhance communication with personnel and external vendors, and make decisions grounded in dependable information. Here are a few scenarios where having accurate data can be beneficial. For example, ensuring data integrity is crucial for monitoring supplier performance, as it helps identify issues, develop solutions, amend contracts, and foster relationships with suppliers. In addition, data integrity in supply-chain agility is achieved by highlighting different spots in the event of a disruption, allowing for the determination of which shipments will be impacted and the effective and efficient transition from maritime transport to air freight, among other changes. Likewise, it is imperative to identify any deficiencies in information and furnish the requisite documentation when engaging with external collaborators to minimize communication setbacks. Last but certainly not least, in addition to the external vendors, the integrity of the data is also beneficial in the logistic organization from the point of view of informing the internal team members. This is done to ensure that the teams are aware of any delays, the reasons for the delays, and any new delivery dates. This allows the teams to prepare and plan for any inevitable changes.

5.2.2 Safeguards Against Data Tampering and Manipulation

A system that identifies eliminates, and corrects low-quality data is critical in logistics because it can provide real-time data, alert you when data is incorrect, and enable you to connect with vendors when something is missing; these functions can enhance confidence. Furthermore, logistical organizations require a dependable method for making prompt and intelligent decisions based on current information in case of an error.

The following are potential safeguards against data manipulation and tampering (Duggineni, 2023):

- **Come Up With Cyber Security Steps:** By integrating these cybersecurity standards into contractual agreements and enabling the monitoring of data flows, organizations can enhance their confidence in the secure transmission of data to other entities along their supply chain. One can effectively mitigate numerous future issues pertaining to data security concerns by incorporating explicit language concerning cybersecurity requirements into sourcing contracts. In addition, the contractual specifications and standard should be specified in the agreement so that suppliers and partners are required to implement a minimum level of precautions to ensure the security of their software and hardware.
- **Determine Safe Ways to Communicate Data Transfer:** Data supply chains involve the movement of data rather than the physical components often associated with supply chains. The constant movement of data occurs when it is either exported to other programs or sent to third parties so that they can provide services. In addition, encrypting data in transit and implementing a system to track and trace the current and potential data flows throughout your data supply chain are both essential components of safe data transfer procedures.
- **Implement Rule Management for Handling Emergencies:** Implementing an automated rules management system for handling emergencies significantly simplifies identifying and promptly correcting data quality errors, thereby averting further expenses or delays. The ability to detect discrepancies in data instantaneously enables one to address issues without delay; delay and increased costs can result from missing or incomplete information. Furthermore, these management systems can verify the precise time and date of shipping departures, update pre-established collection dates, and incorporate essential clearance documents, including product codes and packaging lists.
- **Build Flexible Systems Seamlessly Adapt to New Circumstances:** The current data-driven operations, data supply chains, and agile infrastructures all face the same problem of complying with ever-evolving privacy standards, which are imposed on a global scale. Businesses must carefully evaluate the storage and sharing of data, as well as who has access to it, in order to avoid financial, legal, and reputational consequences that can result from violating privacy requirements.

- **Staff Education and Development:** To lessen the impact of potential threats on the data supply chain, fostering a cyber-aware corporate culture is important. The importance of company data, its various cyber threats, and the telltale signals of typical online attacks (such as shady email messages and inconsistent system setups) can be addressed through well-designed cyber education and awareness programs.
- **Implement and Deploy Effective intrusion detection Systems:** While it's true that no security measure can completely thwart cybercriminals, there are a number of ways to keep them out of your IT infrastructure. Behavioral analysis, specialized intrusion detection systems, and network-level scanning applications can help identify those who have managed to get past your perimeter defenses and are now trying to steal sensitive information.

6. INCIDENT RESPONSE AND RECOVERY IN LOGISTICS

Incident and response in logistic is considered as a comprehensive exploration that can handle the cybersecurity incidents and ensured to recover the business continuity within the specific system. It is also challenges to address the security challenges and requirements to the logistic sector. Following are the key parameters that are considered as efficient incident and recovery elements in logistic sector.

- **Understanding Incident Response:** The logistic industry now a days driven by the digital transformation and interconnected systems, which has faced an evolving landscape of cybersecurity challenges. The incident response can be elaborated on the process of detecting, analyzing, and mitigating the security challenges, needs. It also emphasizes the need for a swift and a proper organized response to the system which can then be further analyzed by the experts to fix.
- **Identification of Logistics-specific Threats:** The process of identification of cybersecurity threats in logistics systems where the experts tried their efforts to finding out all the vulnerabilities so that the logistics environments can be work smoothly. Furthermore, it also deals with the various cybersecurity threat resembles in the logistics domain like attacks in supply chain, or disruption in supply chain, data breaches, attacks in inventory management systems, potential vulnerabilities in logistics, insider threats, and ransomware attacks within the smart devices used in logistics operations.
- **Incident Response Framework:** Framework for incident response can be composed of response teams that initiate the initial response to any threats in the logistic environment. As the logistics industry has been become a

increasingly dependent on digital technologies, need for the robust and efficient response framework to secure against the paramount cybersecurity threats. A resilient incident response framework may involves guidelines for establishing the secure environment, protocols, and procedures starting from lower end until the top management system. This also include the composition of an response team, having defined roles and responsibilities, communication mechanism or protocols that ensures the proper coordinated reply against any cybersecurity attack.

- **Risk Assessment and Preparedness:** As the logistics industry is the backbone of the economy of a country because of its interconnected of complex network. With the passage of time, the industry is continuously evolving with numbers of new technological features. Such involvements may open numerous gateways for vulnerabilities. The process of making the logistics industry aware of all kind of security threats that may occur at any stage is the risk assessment. This can also be defined as the proactively identification of vulnerabilities in the logistic systems. Most important risk assessments includes security audits, penetration testing, regular testing for operational tools that enables the logistic industry to prepare against the potential attacks.
- **Recovery and Continuity Measures:** For every systems that continuously improving with the passage of time with number of new features, the recovery after any cybersecurity attacks is considered as the pivotal element for the system. In logistics sector, the systems not only consider the mechanism to escalate from the cybersecurity threats but also provide a proper solution that develop a robust recovery and continuity strategies. Furthermore, it discusses the process of system restoration, data recovery, and prioritizing critical logistics operations to minimize downtime.

In addition to all of above methods to overcome the cyber threats for logistics companies, incident response and recovery also provides a robust framework and effective practices that efficiently provides response to the cyber threats, cyber secruity attacks. This also provide the comprehensive approach that can mitigate the potential damages, ensures the resiliency and continuity of logistical operational activities even facing cyberattacks.

6.1 Developing Incident Response Plans

This section of book chapter discusses about the guidelines for the development of robust incident response plan that tailored to the logistics industry. Recognizing the uniqueness and challenging nature of incident response mechanism, the guidelines encompass a step by step approach to develop a robust and effective incident response strategic system. The key elements that includes the identification of critical assets, effective responsibilities, and development of effective and efficient communication protocol.

Guidelines for Robust Plans

In the logistics sector, creating a detailed incident response plan involves specific guidelines. This includes defining a structured plan tailored to the logistics industry's unique challenges and vulnerabilities. It encompasses identifying potential threats, assessing their potential impact, and outlining steps for detection, response, and recovery.

Swift Response Strategies

The logistics industry requires prompt and effective response strategies to cyber incidents. This involves establishing a tiered response system that outlines roles, responsibilities, and communication channels during an incident. Swift response strategies would detail containment procedures, system isolation, preservation of evidence, and notification protocols.

6.2 Recovery Measures

Post-Incident Recovery Procedures: After an incident, the logistics industry needs well-defined recovery procedures. This includes a step-by-step recovery plan that focuses on restoring affected systems and services. This phase involves system restoration, data recovery, and ensuring business continuity.

Learning from Successful Recovery: Learning from successful recovery efforts is crucial. This involves analyzing the recovery process after each incident. It's essential to identify what worked well, what could be improved, and how these lessons can be incorporated into future recovery strategies. Documenting these lessons learned is critical for continuous improvement.

In essence, effective incident response plans and recovery measures in the logistics industry involve proactive planning, swift response strategies, structured recovery procedures, and a continuous learning process. This ensures the industry is equipped to face cyber incidents and can rapidly recover while fortifying its defenses against future threats.

7. ADVANCED TECHNOLOGIES FOR DIGITAL SAFEGUARDS

The logistic industry, is now working and moving towards digital transformation, that is increasingly reliant on the advanced technologies to its fortify its digital safeguards in the modern era. Going in detail into this section of the study, enhancing cybersecurity measures within the logistic sector have been explored.

7.1 Blockchain for Immutable Transaction Security

One of the most secure and latest security features that have been used worldwide in different areas to secure the systems against cybersecurity threats. It has been explored as a revolutionary tools for ensuring security in the financial sector of logistics sector while performing different online transactions (Tayyab et al., n.d.). The distributed nature of blockchain ensures the transparent and secure lodgers that not only reduces the risk of fraudulent but also provide security to all activities within the supply chain of logistic industry. Moreover, in logistic industry, blockchain and its applications is providing the security to the transactional data, verifying the authenticity of goods, and maintained the trustworthy level in the logistic ecosystem which increase the trust level of customers.

7.2 Artificial Intelligence (AI) for Predictive Cyber Threat Analysis

AI is considered as the most active and most reliable tools that can provide a critical predictive components for cyber threats analysis for logistic operations. This study also discovers how the powerful AL algorithms can able to analyse and identify different patters, potential cyber threats, predict potential vulnerabilities within the logistic network using vast and real-time dataset. Using empowered AI and ML algorithms, logistics industry can proactively address the challenging cybersecurity attacks before they escalate (Rangaraju, 2023).

7.3 Internet of Things (IoT) for Enhanced Visibility and Security

Logistics industry has enhances the visibility and security in logistics operations by the integration of IoTs devices (Kaur et al., 2023). Powerful IoT enabled sensors and devices have not only provided the real-time monitoring of cargo, shipments, warehouses conditions, transportation fleets but also provided the off-side security. Such integration of IoTs with logistics industry has provided the real-time security by enabling rapid response to the incident or anomalies and potential breaches.

7.4 Cyber-Physical Systems (CPS) for Integrated Security Measures

Cyber-physical systems (CPS) has been considered as a holistic approach that can integrate security measures in logistic sector. In normal circumstances, CPS combines with complex computational components with processes to enable the most powerful, secure, and interconnected logistics environment (Wang et al., n.d.). Moreover, the use of CPS ensures the automating of security protocols and providing the confidentiality of data and creating most secure and resilient logistic infrastructure.

7.5 Autonomous Systems and Robotics for Secure Operations

As the logistic sector is improving with the passage of time, new innovative technologies have been provided evolutionary measures, the logistic industry have developed with new features. One of the features is the development of autonomous systems and robotics have contributed the logistics to secure the logistic operations (Ding et al., 2023). Moreover, the development of unmanned vehicles, drones and robotics systems is mitigating the security risks by reducing the human interaction in the critical systems. Using autonomous robotics, the human error can be reduced and the efficiency have been increased significantly.

7.6 Cloud-Based Security Solutions for Scalable Protection

More interestingly, beside the autonomous and robotics features have been integrated with logistic industry, the usage of cloud based systems have become indispensable because of data and services. Cloud based systems have become more reliable, efficient, scalable, and adaptive tools for logistics industry (Suman et al., 2023). There have different platforms which provide secure storage, real-time vulnerabilities assessment, flexible cybersecurity measures, and provide confidentiality to the logistic systems. Cloud platforms delve into the advantages of leveraging cloud solutions to safeguard logistics data, facilitate secure collaborations, and ensure seamless scalability.

7.7 Biometric Authentication for Access Control

Security can also be enhanced by the integration of biometric features like fingerprints or face scanner for logistic industry. To access the critical section of logistic industry, such security measures plays a pivotal role. These features not only boost the confidence level of logistics man power but also improves the logistic infrastructure

(Huang, 2023). Biometric security provides the identity verification and prevents unauthorized access to the system. The integration of these technologies promises not only enhanced security measures but also a resilient foundation for the future of cybersecurity in the logistics industry.

8. REGULATORY COMPLIANCE AND STANDARDS

Due to the increase number of cyber security attacks in logistic industry, there are many features that have been developed to overcome the loss created by cyber security attacks. Following are the few key factors that play a pivotal role in defense against such cyber security attacks in logistic industry. Moreover, this section explores the significance of regulatory frameworks and standards in strengthen the cybersecurity posture of logistics operations (Abhay, 2023).

8.1 Regulatory Frameworks Shaping Logistics Cybersecurity

Exploring the complex features of cybersecurity regulations in the logistic sector is very crucial. Such regulatory frameworks may includes the General Data Protection Regulation (GDPR), the Health Insurance Portability and Accountability Act (HIPAA), and regional data protection laws (Sharma et al., 2023). These cybersecurity features highlights the impact of rules and regulations on logistics sector that emphasizes the urge for compliance's to secure the sensitive informations (Darmayanti & Dwipayana, 2023).

8.2 International Standards for Cybersecurity Resilience

Logistic sector legally operates in a globally interconnected environment, necessitating adherence to international cybersecurity standards like ISO/IEC 270001 or ISO standards. Such standards bound or outlines best practices for information security management in logistic sector (Grima et al., 2023). International standards defines how the cybersecurity reisliences with logistics sector by securing the information and provide confidentiality to the systems and man power.

8.3 Industry-Specific Compliance Requirements

In the logistics sector, there are different section which may have unique compliance requirements. Such unique requirements make the logistic sector most important to secure from cyber crimes. Industry-specific compliance requirements specify different rules, regulations and standards that are unique challenges and characteristics of the logistic industry which need to address (Progoulakis et al., 2023). These compliances are design to provide the safety, security, and efficiency of logistics operations along with the legal and operational obligations.

8.4 Emerging Regulatory Trends in Logistics Cybersecurity

Emerging trends in logistic industry have made the future of logistics cybersecurity most important in all areas. The algorithms which are used to provide data privacy, cross border data flows and regulations are the key parameters of the regulatory trends in logistics (Poyhonen et al., 2023). Furthermore, how logistics companies can anticipate, mitigate, and adapt to such trends that can proactively addresses the cybersecurity challenges in the logistic industry.

8.5 Legal Implications of Non-Compliance

Due to larger numbers of innovative features in the logistics industry which opens many loopholes for attackers. Such loopholes which are not compliance with cybersecurity regulations can then leads to severe legal consequences for the system (Martto et al., 2023). As logistic industry operates throughout the countries with different law of the lands however, the operational laws are same up to larger interest. If the features that is against the regulations of cybersecurity can face several consequences. It underscores the importance of proactive compliance measures to mitigate legal risks and maintain the trust of customers and stakeholders (Alqahtani et al., 2023). By exploring the intersection of regulatory compliance and cybersecurity in the logistics industry, this chapter equips logistics professionals with a comprehensive understanding of the regulatory landscape. Adhering to established frameworks and standards not only enhances cybersecurity resilience but also contributes to the overall integrity and trustworthiness of logistics operations.

9. FUTURE TRENDS AND CONSIDERATIONS IN LOGISTICS CYBERSECURITY

Logistic industry is keep on growing and propels into the future with numbers of new innovative features based on AI and ML empowered algorithms, while fostering continuous improvements in digital safeguards become paramount (Jaiswal et al., 2023). There have been reported many cyber threats and attacks in logistic industry which have or have been effecting the industry financially and economically (Kalkha et al., 2023). This section, few of the future trends and considerations have been explored in logistic industry while keeping the scenario of cybersecurity attacks.

Following are the few areas that can be the future trends for logistic sector to be explored.

9.1 Emerging Cyber Threats

This study has explored the emerging cyber threats that have been poised to challenge the logistics cybersecurity. Maintly, it evaluate the numbers of evolving attacks like AI-driven attacks, ransomware attacks, or vulnerabilites in supply chain management. Logistic professional by taking care comprehensively through all these attacks, can then proactively strategies defense mechanisms to protect and safeguard the critical operations.

- **AI-Driven Threats:** The numner of threats evaluation in logistics have increased with the integration AI driven attacks (Shrivastava, 2023). These kinds of attacks need to be care while developing a mechanisms for logistics industry based on AI and new features.
- **Ransomware Variants Targeting Logistics Infrastructure:** This is the kind of attack which encrypt all kind of data present in the administration system and user cannot able to even access that data which is the property of administration (Meers et al., 2023). As the logistic industry is growing with number new and amazaing AI features, this kind of attacks have been reported continuously.

To overcome such attacks, there is need of online storage or backup of existing data on daily or timely basis, so that if it happens with the system, there should be way to overcome such thing and safe the dataset (Afenyo & Livingstone, 2023).

- **Supply Chain Vulnerabilities:** Supply chain is the backbone of any logistic sector because, if the supply chain got some problems either tangible or non tangible, then the whole logistic environment will suffer financially as well as other losses. A Growing Concern As logistics relies heavily on interconnected supply chains, vulnerabilities in the supply chain become attractive targets for cyber adversaries (Shrivastava, 2023). This section discusses potential threats to the supply chain, ranging from third-party breaches to compromised IoT devices. It highlights the need for comprehensive risk assessments and collaborative approaches to fortify the entire logistics ecosystem (Iqbal, 2023).

9.2 Continuous Improvement Strategies

There should a mechanism in which the logistic sector improves and update with the secure passage so that during that even, no one can access the system internally or externally. Cybersecurity attacks are able to get access the system and can demage the data or update into the logistic environment. Following are the two methods that can be used for continuous improvement strategies in the logistics sector (Liu et al., 2023).

- **Dynamic Training Programs:** While improving the system it is difficult to identify the human error or human involvement because in the logistic sector there can be numbers of user and employees who are using the system to maintain the supply chain and other operational duties (Malagon-Su´arez & Orjuela-Castro, 2023). In this method, a dynamic approach is used to improve the system so that the system may not suffer during the up-gradation process.
- **Adaptive Technologies:** The landscape of cybersecurity technologies is in perpetual motion. This section discusses the importance of adopting adaptive technologies that can evolve to counter emerging threats (Junejo et al., 2023). It explores the role of machine learning, threat intelligence platforms, and automated response systems in creating a dynamic defense architecture (Kalkha et al., 2023).

The merger between regulatory compliance and continuous improvement has been discussed by adhering to evolving the cybersecurity regulations and different components. These regulations can serve as a catalyst for ongoing improvement and then can be the part of the system maintenance. Similarly, by integrating the digital safeguard with the logistic sector, regulatory framework for different logistics sector can ensure compliance with the advancing the improvement with cybersecurity resilience.

10. CONCLUSION

Logistic sector has been evolved with the number of AI based features that improved with technological advancements over the past two decades and reshaped the global landscape and leading towards the transformative changes among various sector of the industry. The rapidly evolution landscape of the industry 4.0, driven by innovative technological advancements like IoTs, and Industrial Internet of things (IIoTs), has dramatically advanced the logistic sector. In this study, numbers of technological evolutions, process optimization, threat detection using AI based tools and mitigating the cyber security threats in the logistic sector have been discussed. Furthermore, This chapter aims to address the intricate relationship between digitalization and the logistics sector, emphasizing the crucial role of digital safeguards in navigating cyber dangers or threats. However, the flip side of this digital revolution is the escalating vulnerability to cyberattacks, a consequence of increased interconnectivity and reliance on technology. This study also provided some future research areas for further improvement by the logistic sector. Furthermore, this study has illuminated both the challenges and opportunities within the contemporary logistics sector concerning digitalization and cybersecurity dynamics. By addressing open challenges and recognizing potential future opportunities, this study provides a holistic overview of the evolving landscape where digitalization and cybersecurity intersect in the logistics domain. As the logistics industry continues to navigate this dynamic terrain, a proactive approach to digital safeguards and cybersecurity will be pivotal for ensuring sustained growth, security, and efficiency.

REFERENCES

Abhay, K. (2023). Grover. Out of the frying pan and into the fire? uncovering the impact of fsma's sanitary food transportation rule on the food logistics industry. *Business Horizons*, *66*(2), 203–214. doi:10.1016/j.bushor.2022.06.003

Afenyo, M., & Livingstone, D. (2023). Caesar. Maritime cybersecurity threats: Gaps and directions for future research. *Ocean and Coastal Management*, *236*, 106493. doi:10.1016/j.ocecoaman.2023.106493

Al-Banna, A., Rana, Z. A., Yaqot, M., & Menezes, B. (2023). Interconnectedness between supply chain resilience, industry 4.0, and investment. *Logistics*, *7*(3), 50. doi:10.3390/logistics7030050

Ali, S. M., Ashraf, M. A., Hasin, M. M. T., & Ahmed, S. (2023). Drivers for internet of things (iot) adoption in supply chains: Implications for sustainability in the post-pandemic era. *Computers & Industrial Engineering*, *183*, 109515. doi:10.1016/j.cie.2023.109515

Alqahtani, F., Selviaridis, K., & Stevenson, M. (2023). The effectiveness of performance-based contracting in the defence sector: A systematic literature review. *Journal of Purchasing and Supply Management*, *29*(5), 100877. doi:10.1016/j.pursup.2023.100877

Alshurideh, M., Alquqa, E., Alzoubi, H., Kurdi, B., & Hamadneh, S. (2023). The effect of information security on e-supply chain in the uae logistics and distribution industry. *Uncertain Supply Chain Management*, *11*(1), 145–152. doi:10.5267/j.uscm.2022.11.001

Atzori, L., Iera, A., & Morabito, G. (2017). Understanding the internet of things: Definition, potentials, and societal role of a fast evolving paradigm. *Ad Hoc Networks*, *56*, 122–140. doi:10.1016/j.adhoc.2016.12.004

Axestrack. (n.d.). The 6 Major Components of Logistics Management. Axestrack.

Barreto, L., Amaral, A., & Pereira, T. (2017). Industry 4.0 implications in logistics: An overview. *Procedia Manufacturing*, *13*, 1245–1252. doi:10.1016/j.promfg.2017.09.045

Cheng, L. T., Tei, Z., Yeo, S. F., Lai, K.-H., Kumar, A., & Chung, L. (2023). Nexus among blockchain visibility, supply chain integration and supply chain performance in the digital transformation era. *Industrial Management & Data Systems*, *123*(1), 229–252. doi:10.1108/IMDS-12-2021-0784

Cheung, K.-F., & Michael, G. H. (2021). Bell, and Jyotirmoyee Bhattacharjya. Cybersecurity in logistics and supply chain management: An overview and future research directions. *Transportation Research Part E, Logistics and Transportation Review*, *146*, 102217. doi:10.1016/j.tre.2020.102217

Cichosz, M., Wallenburg, C. M., & Michael Knemeyer, A. (2020). Digital transformation at logistics service providers: Barriers, success factors and leading practices. *International Journal of Logistics Management*, *31*(2), 209–238. doi:10.1108/IJLM-08-2019-0229

Closs & McGarrell. (2004). *Enhancing security throughout the supply chain*. IBM Center for the Business of Government.

Colicchia, C., Creazza, A., & David, A. (2019). Managing cyber and information risks in supply chains: Insights from an exploratory analysis. *Supply Chain Management*, *24*(2), 215–240. doi:10.1108/SCM-09-2017-0289

Darmayanti, N. L., & Dwipayana, A. D. (2023). Logistics industry readinessinapplication policy over dimension overloading (odol). *ASTONJADRO*, *12*(2), 454–460.

Digital, C. (n.d.). *The Digital Transformation of Logistics: An Overview of Technologies and Trends*. copperdigital.medium.com

Ding, S., Lu, S., Xu, Y., Korkali, M., & Cao, Y. (2023). Review of cybersecurity for integrated energy systems with integration of cyber-physical systems. *Energy Conversion and Economics*, *4*(5), 334–345. doi:10.1049/enc2.12097

Du, S., Zhang, H., & Kong, Y. (2023). Sustainability implications of the arctic shipping route for shanghai port logistics in the post-pandemic era. *Sustainability (Basel)*, *15*(22), 16017. doi:10.3390/su152216017

Duggineni, S. (2023). Data integrity and risk. *Open Journal of Optimization*, *12*(2), 25–33. doi:10.4236/ojop.2023.122003

Gihon. (n.d.). *The Weak Link: Recent Supply Chain Attacks Examined*. cy-berint.com

Gregory, N. (1998). Logistics, strategy and structure: A conceptual framework. *International Journal of Operations & Production Management*, *18*(1), 37–52. doi:10.1108/01443579810192772

Grima, Thalassinos, Cristea, Kadlubek, Maditinos, & Peiseniece. (2023). *Digital transformation, strategic resilience, cyber security and risk management*. Academic Press.

Hameed, K., Haseeb, J., Tayyab, M., & Junaid, M. (2017). Secure provenance in wireless sensor networks-a survey of provenance schemes. In 2017 International Conference on Communication, Computing and Digital Systems (C-CODE) (pp. 11–16). IEEE.

Huang, Q. (2023). Enhancing university logistics management through iot technology in the context of bioinformatics engineering. *Journal of Commercial Biotechnology*, *28*(3).

Iqbal, H. (2023). Machine learning for intelligent data analysis and automation in cybersecurity: Current and future prospects. *Annals of Data Science*, *10*(6), 1473–1498. doi:10.1007/s40745-022-00444-2

Jaiswal, N., Misra, A., Khang, A., & Misra, P. K. (2023). The role of internet of things technologies in business and production. In *AI-Aided IoT Technologies and Applications for Smart Business and Production* (pp. 1–13). CRC Press. doi:10.1201/9781003392224-1

Junejo, A. K., Breza, M., & Julie, A. (2023). McCann. Threat modeling for communication security of iot-enabled digital logistics. *Sensors (Basel)*, *23*(23), 9500. doi:10.3390/s23239500 PMID:38067872

Kadrich, M. (2007). *Endpoint security*. Addison-Wesley Professional.

Kagermann, H. (2014). Change through digitization—value creation in the age of industry 4.0. In *Management of permanent change* (pp. 23–45). Springer.

Kalaiarasan, R., Agrawal, T. K., Olhager, J., Wiktorsson, M., & Hauge, J. B. (2023). Supply chain visibility for improving inbound logistics: A design science approach. *International Journal of Production Research*, *61*(15), 5228–5243. doi:10.1080/00207543.2022.2099321

Kalkha, H., Khiat, A., Bahnasse, A., & Ouajji, H. (2023). The rising trends of smart e-commerce logistics. *IEEE Access : Practical Innovations, Open Solutions*, *11*, 33839–33857. doi:10.1109/ACCESS.2023.3252566

Kaur, R., Gabrijelčič, D., & Klobučar, T. (2023). Artificial intelligence for cybersecurity: Literature review and future research directions. *Information Fusion*, *97*, 101804. doi:10.1016/j.inffus.2023.101804

Key Elements of Logistics Management. (n.d.) https://www.mojro.com/resource-key-elements-of-logistics-management

Liu, Y., Tao, X., Li, X., Colombo, A., & Hu, S. (2023). *Artificial intelligence in smart logistics cyber-physical systems: State-of-the-arts and potential applications*. IEEE Transactions on Industrial Cyber-Physical Systems.

Lu, J., Yu, C.-S., Liu, C., & James, E. (2003). Technology acceptance model for wireless internet. *Internet Research*, *13*(3), 206–222. doi:10.1108/10662240310478222

Malagon-Su´arez & Orjuela-Castro. (2023). Challenges and trends in logistics 4.0. *Ingenier´ıa*, 28.

Martto, J., Diaz, S., Hassan, B., Mannan, S., Singh, P., Villasuso, F., & Baobaid, O. (2023). Esg strategies in the oil and gas industry from the maritime & logistics perspectiveopportunities & risks. In Abu Dhabi International Petroleum Exhibition and Conference. SPE.

Meers, J., Halliday, S., & Tomlinson, J. (2023). "Creative non-compliance": Complying with the "spirit of the law" not the "letter of the law" under the covid-19 lockdown restrictions. *Deviant Behavior*, *44*(1), 93–111. doi:10.1080/01639625.2021.2014286

Menoni, S., Molinari, D., Parker, D., Ballio, F., & Tapsell, S. (2012). Assessing multifaceted vulnerability and resilience in order to design riskmitigation strategies. *Natural Hazards*, *64*(3), 2057–2082. doi:10.1007/s11069-012-0134-4

Mubarak, M. F., & Petraite, M. (2020). Industry 4.0 technologies, digital trust and technological orientation: What matters in open innovation? *Technological Forecasting and Social Change*, *161*, 120332. doi:10.1016/j.techfore.2020.120332

Panjehfouladgaran, Frederick, & Lim. (2020). Reverse logistics risk management: identification, clustering and risk mitigation strategies. *Management Decision*, *58*(7):1449–1474.

Poyhonen, J., Simola, J., & Lehto, M. (2023). Basic elements of cyber security for a smart terminal process. In *The Proceedings of the... International Conference on Cyber Warfare and Security*. Academic Conferences International Ltd.

Progoulakis, I., Nikitakos, N., Dalaklis, D., Christodoulou, A., Dalaklis, A., & Yaacob, R. (2023). Digitalization and cyber physical security aspects in maritime transportation and port infrastructure. In Smart Ports and Robotic Systems: Navigating the Waves of Techno-Regulation and Governance (pp. 227–248). Springer. doi:10.1007/978-3-031-25296-9_12

Rangaraju, S. (2023). Ai sentry: Reinventing cybersecurity through intelligent threat detection. *EPH-International Journal of Science And Engineering*, *9*(3), 30–35. doi:10.53555/ephijse.v9i3.211

Remko, V. H. (2020). Research opportunities for a more resilient post-covid-19 supply chain–closing the gap between research findings and industry practice. *International Journal of Operations & Production Management*, *40*(4), 341–355. doi:10.1108/IJOPM-03-2020-0165

Sharma, M., Luthra, S., Joshi, S., Kumar, A., & Jain, A. (2023). Green logistics driven circular practices adoption in industry 4.0 era: A moderating effect of institution pressure and supply chain flexibility. *Journal of Cleaner Production*, *383*, 135284. doi:10.1016/j.jclepro.2022.135284

Shrivastava, S. (2023). Recent trends in supply chain management of business-tobusiness firms: A review and future research directions. *Journal of Business and Industrial Marketing*, *38*(12), 2673–2693. doi:10.1108/JBIM-02-2023-0122

Suja, A. (2022). Machine learning-based wearable devices for smart healthcare application with risk factor monitoring. In *Empowering Sustainable Industrial 4.0 Systems With Machine Intelligence* (pp. 174–185). IGI Global.

Suman, O. P., Saini, L. K., & Kumar, S. (2023). Cloud-based data protection and secure backup solutions: A comprehensive review of ensuring business continuity. In *2023 Third International Conference on Secure Cyber Computing and Communication (ICSCCC)* (pp. 821–826). IEEE. 10.1109/ICSCCC58608.2023.10176503

Supply Chain Vulnerability: Identifying and Mitigating Risks. (n.d.). magaya.com

Syed, N. F., & Syed, W. (2022). Traceability in supply chains: A cyber security analysis. *Computers & Security*, *112*, 102536. doi:10.1016/j.cose.2021.102536

Taeihagh, A., & Hazel, S. M. L. (2019). Governing autonomous vehicles: Emerging responses for safety, liability, privacy, cybersecurity, and industry risks. *Transport Reviews*, *39*(1), 103–128. doi:10.1080/01441647.2018.1494640

Tayyab, Marjani, Jhanjhi, Abaker, Hashem, & Usmani. (n.d.). *A watermark-based secure model for data security against security attacks for machine learning algorithms*. Academic Press.

Tayyab, M., & Marjani, M. (2021a). A light-weight watermarking-based framework on dataset using deep learning algorithms. In *2021 National Computing Colleges Conference (NCCC)* (pp. 1–6). IEEE.

Tayyab, M., & Marjani, M. (2021b). Cryptographic based secure model on dataset for deep learning algorithms. *CMC Comput. Mater. Contin*, *69*, 1183–1200.

The most common entry points for a cyber attack. (n.d.). guptadeepak.com

Wang, Li, Liu, & Zhang. (n.d.). Real-time cyber-physical security solution leveraging an integrated learning-based approach: An integrated learningbased cyber-physical security solution. *ACM Transactions on Sensor Networks*.

Wolak, Lysionok, Kosturek, Wi´sniewski, Wawryszuk, Kawa, Davidson, Ma´ckowiak, Starzyk, & Kulikowska-Wielgus. (2019). *Technological revolution. Directions in the development of the transport-forwarding-logistics (tfl) sector.* Academic Press.

Zhang, Q., Shi, L., & Sun, S. (2023). Optimization of intelligent logistics system based on big data collection techniques. In *The International Conference on Cyber Security Intelligence and Analytics* (pp. 378–387). Springer. 10.1007/978-3-031-31860-3_40

Chapter 11
Securing the Supply Chain:
Cybersecurity Strategies for Logistics Resilience

Siva Raja Sindiramutty
Taylor's University, Malaysia

Chong Eng Tan
https://orcid.org/0000-0002-3990-3501
Universiti Malaysia Sarawak, Malaysia

Wei Wei Goh
Taylor's University, Malaysia

Sumathi Balakrishnan
Taylor's University, Malaysia

Norhidayah Hamzah
https://orcid.org/0009-0002-2715-001X
Taylor's University, Malaysia

Rehan Akbar
https://orcid.org/0000-0002-3703-5974
Florida International University, USA

ABSTRACT

The exponential growth of digital connectivity in the logistics landscape has heightened the significance of cybersecurity. This chapter delves into the intricate fabric of securing supply chains against evolving cyber threats, aiming to equip logistics professionals with actionable strategies for resilience. Beginning with analysing the prevailing cyber threat landscape, it illuminates common vulnerabilities and highlights recent impactful attacks targeting supply chains. Understanding the nexus between cybersecurity and logistics resilience becomes pivotal, emphasizing the need for continuous operations amidst adversities. To fortify this resilience, the chapter meticulously navigates through risk assessment methodologies, mitigation strategies, and the imperative role of supply chain visibility. It elaborates on vendor and partner management protocols, advocating for stringent cybersecurity considerations within contractual agreements. Moreover, it outlines robust incident response plans and recovery strategies essential for mitigating cyber incidents' ramifications.

DOI: 10.4018/979-8-3693-3816-2.ch011

INTRODUCTION

Background

Overview of the Growing Importance of Cybersecurity in the Logistics Industry

Cybersecurity has become a crucial concern in the logistics industry due to the increasing reliance on digital systems and technologies for managing supply chains and operations (Singh et al., 2023; Adeyemo et al., 2019). The logistics sector extensively utilizes interconnected networks, cloud-based platforms, and IoT (Internet of Things) devices, exposing it to various cyber threats (Singh et al., 2023). With the rise in cyberattacks targeting logistics, such as ransomware attacks on shipping companies and data breaches in inventory management systems, the need for robust cybersecurity measures has become more evident. The evolution of logistics towards digitalization and automation, including the integration of AI-driven solutions and autonomous vehicles, has further heightened cybersecurity concerns (Abed & Anupam, 2022; Alferidah & Jhanjhi, 2020). These advancements offer efficiency and optimization but also widen the attack surface for cyber adversaries, necessitating proactive security strategies. Additionally, the globalization of supply chains and the interconnected nature of logistics networks across international borders increase the complexity of security challenges (Manners-Bell, 2020). Regulatory bodies and industry standards have responded by emphasizing cybersecurity frameworks tailored for the logistics sector. Compliance with regulations such as GDPR and ISO 27001 has become imperative for logistics companies to safeguard sensitive customer information and maintain data integrity (Rebe, 2023). Moreover, partnerships between logistics firms and cybersecurity providers have emerged to develop specialized solutions addressing industry-specific vulnerabilities (Zawaideh et al., 2023). Investments in cybersecurity awareness and training programs have also gained traction within logistics organizations (Almoaigel & Abuabid, 2023; Alkinani et al., 2021). Educating employees about potential threats like phishing attacks and social engineering has become essential in fortifying the human element of cybersecurity. Furthermore, the integration of encryption protocols and authentication mechanisms within logistics software and systems has been crucial in preventing unauthorized access and data breaches (Mostafa et al., 2023; Almusaylim et al., 2018).

In conclusion, the growing importance of cybersecurity in the logistics industry stems from the industry's digital transformation, increased cyber threats, and the complexity of interconnected networks. As logistics continue to evolve with technological advancements, concerted efforts towards robust cybersecurity measures, regulatory compliance, industry collaboration, and employee education remain imperative to mitigate risks and ensure the secure functioning of supply chain operations. Figure 1 shows the significance of cybersecurity within the manufacturing sector.

Introduction to the Complexities and Vulnerabilities of the Supply Chain in the Digital Era.

The evolution of the digital era has brought about significant advancements and complexities in supply chain management, revolutionizing how businesses operate globally. In this era, the supply chain is no longer confined to physical entities but encompasses a network of interconnected systems, technologies, and processes. The integration of digital technologies, such as the Internet of Things (IoT), blockchain, artificial intelligence, and big data analytics, has led to increased efficiency and connectivity across the supply chain (Li et al., 2023; Brohi et al., 2020). However, with these advancements come vulnerabilities and challenges that pose substantial risks to supply chain operations. One of the critical complexities lies in the increased

Figure 1. The significance of cybersecurity within the manufacturing sector
(Wipro, n.d.)

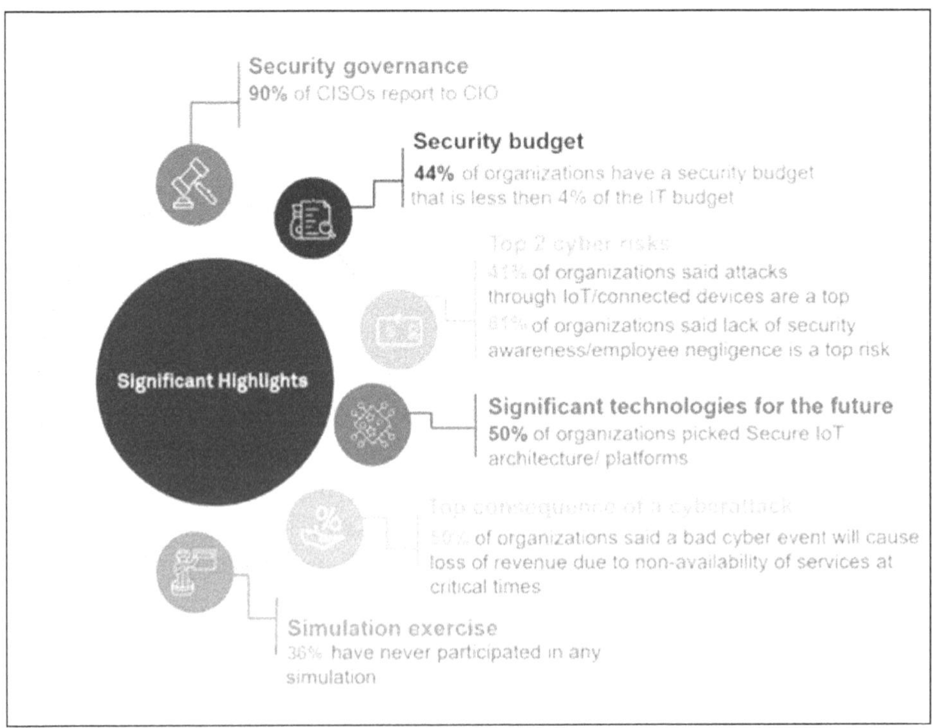

interdependence among supply chain entities. A disruption or failure in one part of the chain can swiftly propagate across interconnected nodes, leading to significant disruptions and financial losses (Gao et al., 2023; Chesti et al., 2020). Moreover, the reliance on digital infrastructure exposes supply chains to cybersecurity threats and data breaches. Another complexity arises from the globalization of supply chains, where companies source materials, components, and products from diverse geographical locations. Political instability, trade conflicts, and natural disasters in one region can severely impact the entire supply chain, highlighting the need for robust risk management strategies (Manners-Bell, 2020b). Additionally, the rapid pace of technological advancements introduces challenges related to the management of obsolete technologies and the adaptation of new ones. Furthermore, the sheer volume of data generated within digital supply chains presents challenges regarding data governance, privacy, and ethical considerations (Wylde et al., 2023; Diwaker et al., 2019). Ensuring data security and compliance with regulations such as the General Data Protection Regulation (GDPR) is crucial to maintaining trust and mitigating risks associated with data misuse (Evans et al., 2022). While the digital era has revolutionized supply chain management, it has also introduced intricate complexities and vulnerabilities. Addressing these challenges requires a holistic approach that involves adopting resilient strategies, enhancing cybersecurity measures, fostering collaboration among supply chain partners, and continuously adapting to technological innovations while prioritizing ethical considerations and regulatory compliance.

Objectives

Clear Articulation of the Chapter's Objectives

The primary objective of this chapter is to illuminate the critical intersection between cybersecurity and the logistics industry, emphasizing the imperative need for robust strategies to safeguard the intricate supply chain networks. We aim to provide a comprehensive overview of the evolving cyber threat landscape, delineating the various threats that pose substantial risks to logistics operations. Through real-world examples and case studies, we intend to illustrate the tangible impact of cyber incidents on supply chains, highlighting the urgency for proactive cybersecurity measures. Moreover, this chapter seeks to elucidate the concept of logistics resilience within the realm of cybersecurity, elucidating its significance in maintaining continuous and secure operations amidst cyber threats. We aim to delve into existing resilience frameworks applicable to logistics, conducting a comparative analysis to discern their efficacy in fortifying supply chain resilience. Furthermore, a pivotal objective is the provision of actionable strategies. This includes a detailed exploration of risk assessment methodologies and mitigation strategies specific to logistics, emphasizing supply chain visibility, effective vendor and partner management, and robust incident response and recovery plans. Additionally, we aim to discuss the integration of cutting-edge technologies and best practices for enhanced cybersecurity while addressing regulatory compliance and industry standards governing logistics cybersecurity. Ultimately, this chapter endeavours to equip readers with a comprehensive understanding of cybersecurity's pivotal role in fortifying logistics resilience. It aims to empower industry practitioners, decision-makers, and stakeholders with tangible strategies, insights from successful implementations, and a forward-thinking outlook on emerging trends, enabling them to proactively safeguard supply chains against evolving cyber threats.

Emphasis on Providing Actionable Strategies for Enhancing Cybersecurity and Resilience in Logistics Operations.

This chapter places a distinct emphasis on offering actionable strategies tailored to bolster cybersecurity and resilience within the logistics sector. Recognizing the escalating cyber threats facing supply chains, our focus lies in equipping logistics professionals with practical, implementable approaches to fortify their defences and ensure operational continuity. Central to our objectives is the provision of comprehensive risk assessment methodologies specifically designed for logistics operations. We aim to delineate a detailed process for identifying vulnerabilities and threats within supply chains, accompanied by pragmatic strategies for mitigating these risks effectively. Furthermore, the chapter delves into the pivotal role of supply chain visibility, advocating for technologies and practices that enhance traceability, transparency, and control, thereby strengthening cybersecurity measures.

Additionally, we prioritize the elucidation of vendor and partner management best practices, elucidating methods to assess and enhance the cybersecurity posture of external stakeholders. This includes insightful discussions on contractual considerations for embedding robust cybersecurity protocols within vendor agreements. Moreover, our chapter navigates the terrain of incident response and recovery planning, elucidating the development of agile and resilient strategies to swiftly counter cyber incidents, minimize disruptions, and facilitate rapid recovery. By presenting a blend of innovative technologies, industry standards, and successful case studies, we aim to empower logistics professionals with a holistic toolkit of actionable strategies. These insights are tailored to not only navigate the current threat landscape but also to proactively address future challenges, ensuring that logistics operations are fortified against evolving cyber threats while maintaining resilience and continuity.

Chapter Contributions

Strategic Insights: This chapter provides strategic insights into the critical nexus between cybersecurity and the logistics industry. It offers a comprehensive understanding of the evolving cyber threat landscape and its specific implications for supply chain operations.

Actionable Frameworks: Emphasizing practicality, the chapter offers actionable frameworks and methodologies tailored for logistics operations. These frameworks encompass risk assessment, supply chain visibility enhancement, vendor management protocols, and incident response planning.

Real-world Relevance: By integrating case studies and examples, this chapter highlights the tangible impact of cyber incidents on logistics. It showcases successful implementations, lessons learned, and innovative solutions adopted in the face of cybersecurity challenges.

Technological Integration: It explores the integration of cutting-edge technologies, such as blockchain and AI, elucidating their role in fortifying cybersecurity within logistics. Case studies illustrate successful technological implementations relevant to the industry.

Compliance Guidance: The chapter provides a succinct overview of relevant regulations and industry standards governing logistics cybersecurity. It offers practical recommendations for aligning with these standards and exceeding compliance requirements.

Future-oriented Outlook: Lastly, this chapter presents a forward-thinking perspective by anticipating future trends and challenges in cybersecurity for logistics. It encourages ongoing vigilance, adaptation, and innovation to stay ahead of the evolving threat landscape.

Chapter Organization

Introduction: The chapter commences with an Introduction segment that outlines the growing significance of cybersecurity in logistics operations. It elucidates the complexities and vulnerabilities prevalent in the supply chain amidst the digital era, culminating in a clear articulation of the chapter's objectives.

Cyber Threat Landscape in Logistics: This section provides an in-depth analysis of the prevailing cyber threats facing the logistics sector. It explores various cyber-attack examples targeting supply chain vulnerabilities, accompanied by a discussion on the potential impacts of these threats on logistics operations, supported by relevant case studies.

Understanding Logistics Resilience: Focusing on resilience within the context of cybersecurity, this segment defines and emphasizes the importance of logistics resilience. It explores existing resilience frameworks applicable to logistics, conducting a comparative analysis to assess their effectiveness in maintaining continuous operations.

Cybersecurity Strategies for Logistics Resilience: This substantial section delineates actionable strategies for enhancing cybersecurity within logistics operations. It covers areas such as risk assessment, supply chain visibility, vendor and partner management, incident response, and recovery planning.

Technology Integration and Best Practices: Addressing technological facets, this part delves into advanced authentication, encryption, data protection practices, and the exploration of emerging technologies like blockchain and AI pertinent to logistics cybersecurity.

Regulatory Compliance and Standards: Providing guidance, this section highlights relevant cybersecurity regulations impacting the logistics industry, alongside insights into industry-specific standards. It offers recommendations for compliance and surpassing industry benchmarks.

Case Studies and Practical Applications: Here, the chapter examines successful implementations and real-world applications, drawing lessons, best practices, challenges faced, and innovative solutions adopted within logistics cybersecurity.

Future Trends and Considerations: The final section anticipates future trends in the evolving threat landscape, discusses upcoming technological advancements and emphasizes the importance of ongoing vigilance and adaptation in logistics cybersecurity.

Figure 2. Landscape of cybersecurity

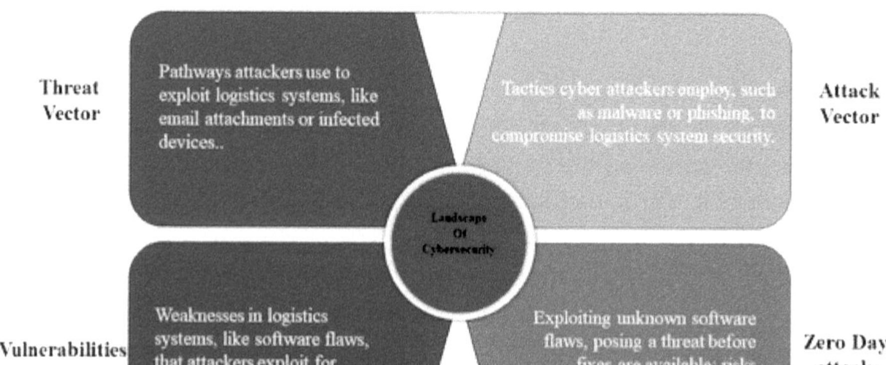

CYBER THREAT LANDSCAPE IN LOGISTICS

Overview of Cyber Threats

Examination of Common Cyber Threats Facing the Logistics Sector

The logistics sector faces numerous cyber threats that endanger the security and integrity of its operations. Cyber threats in this industry have evolved, becoming more sophisticated and impactful, posing significant challenges to organizations. One prevalent threat is phishing attacks, where malicious actors deceive employees through deceptive emails or messages to gain unauthorized access to sensitive information (Hummer & Byrne, 2023). Another concerning threat is ransomware, a type of malware that encrypts critical data, disrupting logistics operations until a ransom is paid. Furthermore, supply chain attacks have emerged as a grave concern, where attackers compromise one part of the supply chain to infiltrate the entire network, potentially causing widespread disruptions (Çınar, 2023; Fatima-Tuz-Zahra et al., 2020). Figure 2 shows the landscape of cybersecurity threats.

Additionally, the logistics sector faces risks from insider threats, wherein employees or former employees misuse their access privileges to steal or leak sensitive information (Sun et al., 2023). Moreover, the Internet of Things (IoT) devices used extensively in logistics present vulnerabilities that can be exploited by cyber attackers to gain unauthorized access to networks. The reliance on outdated or unpatched software and systems also poses a significant risk, as these systems may have known vulnerabilities that hackers can exploit (Altulaihan et al., 2023). The logistics industry's increasing reliance on cloud computing services exposes it to potential security breaches if not properly secured (Akbar et al., 2023). Social engineering attacks, such as pretexting and baiting, manipulate individuals into divulging sensitive information, making them a persistent threat to logistics companies (Ribeiro et al., 2023). Additionally, distributed denial-of-service (DDoS) attacks are a concern, overwhelming logistics networks with traffic, and disrupting services.

In conclusion, the logistics sector confronts multifaceted cyber threats that jeopardize its operations, data security, and customer trust. The landscape of cyber threats continues to evolve, demanding a proactive approach to implementing robust cybersecurity measures to safeguard against these diverse risks. Organizations must invest in employee training, regularly update their systems, adopt encryption technologies, and establish incident response plans to mitigate the impact of cyber threats on the logistics industry.

Examples of Recent Cyber-Attacks Targeting Supply Chain Vulnerabilities

In recent years, cyber-attacks targeting supply chains have become increasingly prevalent, posing significant threats to organizations worldwide. Numerous high-profile incidents underscore the vulnerability of supply chains to malicious activities. For instance, the SolarWinds supply chain attack in 2020 compromised software updates, affecting approximately 18,000 customers, including government agencies and major corporations (Clinton, 2023; Gaur et al., 2021). Similarly, the Kaseya ransomware attack in 2021 exploited vulnerabilities in the company's software management system, impacting hundreds of businesses through compromised IT service providers (Jacob, 2023). Moreover, the Colonial Pipeline ransomware attack in 2021 disrupted fuel supplies across the East Coast of the United States, highlighting the severe consequences of targeting critical infrastructure within supply chains (Madhira et al., 2023; Gaur, Singh, et al., 2021). Similarly, the JBS cyber-attack, also in 2021, affected the global meat supply chain, emphasizing the broad-reaching impact cyber-attacks can have on essential industries (Jackson, 2023). Furthermore, the Microsoft Exchange Server breach in early 2021 revealed vulnerabilities in email systems, enabling unauthorized access to sensitive information in various organizations (Deborah et al., 2023). Another noteworthy incident includes the Accellion File Transfer Appliance (FTA) cyber-attacks in 2021, where threat actors exploited vulnerabilities in the FTA software to access data from multiple organizations, affecting numerous sectors (*Cyber Threats and Engagements in 2022*, n.d.). Additionally, the ASUS supply chain attack in 2019 involved compromised software updates, leading to the distribution of malware to numerous ASUS computers (Andreoli et al., 2023). Furthermore, the Log4j vulnerability discovered in late 2021 posed a significant threat to various systems and supply chains globally due to its widespread use in software applications (Siavvas et al., 2023; Ghosh et al., 2020). This vulnerability allowed threat actors to execute arbitrary code, potentially compromising sensitive information and impacting supply chain operations across industries.

In conclusion, recent cyber-attacks targeting supply chains have exhibited the grave repercussions of exploiting vulnerabilities within interconnected systems. These incidents emphasize the critical need for enhanced cybersecurity measures, supply chain resilience, and collaborative efforts among organizations and governments to mitigate and prevent future attacks on supply chains.

Impact on the Supply Chain

Discussion on the Potential Consequences of Cyber Threats on Logistics Operations

Cyber threats pose significant risks to the smooth functioning of logistics operations, potentially leading to severe consequences for businesses and global supply chains. Instances such as the NotPetya ransomware attack in 2017 disrupted the operations of Maersk, a major shipping company, causing substantial financial losses and logistical chaos (Möller, 2023). These threats can impede various facets of logistics, including transportation, inventory management, and communication systems, leading to delays, financial losses, and compromised data integrity (Mızrak, 2023; Gopi et al., 2021). The potential consequences of cyber threats on logistics operations include operational disruptions. For instance, ransomware attacks like WannaCry have targeted transportation systems, halted operations and caused delays in cargo movement (Al-Hawawreh et al., 2024; Hussain et al., 2019). Furthermore, compromised communication channels due to cyber-attacks can hinder coordination between different elements of the supply chain, impacting delivery schedules and inventory management (Green, 2023; Humayun et al., 2022).

Moreover, cyber incidents can lead to financial losses and increased operating costs. The cost of recovery and system restoration following an attack, coupled with potential revenue losses due to disrupted operations, can significantly impact the financial health of logistics companies. Additionally, reputational damage resulting from cyber-attacks can erode customer trust and confidence in logistics providers, potentially leading to the loss of business relationships (Chatterjee et al., 2023; Jhanjhi et al., 2021). Cyber threats also jeopardize the security and integrity of sensitive data within logistics systems. Breaches in data security can expose confidential information, such as customer details or shipment schedules, leading to potential data manipulation or theft (Al-Zubaidie & Shyaa, 2023). Such compromises in data integrity can result in incorrect inventory management, causing further disruptions across the supply chain.

In conclusion, cyber threats pose multifaceted risks to logistics operations, encompassing operational disruptions, financial losses, compromised data integrity, and reputational damage. Logistics companies must invest in robust cybersecurity measures and contingency plans to mitigate these risks and ensure the resilience and reliability of global supply chains.

Case Studies Illustrate the Real-World Impact of Cyber Incidents on The Supply Chain

Cyber incidents have increasingly disrupted supply chains, leading to significant real-world impacts on businesses globally. Several case studies highlight the severity and diverse consequences of these incidents, demonstrating the vulnerabilities within supply chain networks. The SolarWinds breach of 2020 exemplifies the far-reaching effects of cyber incidents on supply chains. This sophisticated attack affected numerous organizations, including government agencies and corporations, showcasing the potential for supply chain disruptions caused by third-party breaches (Shinde, 2021; Kumar et al., 2015). Another pivotal case study is the NotPetya malware attack in 2017. This ransomware targeted various companies, paralyzing operations within their supply chains. Maersk, a global shipping company, reported losses of over $300 million due to this cyber incident, highlighting the financial ramifications of supply chain disruptions (Manners-Bell, 2020c; Lim et al., 2020). Moreover, the 2018 cyber-attack on British Airways' supply chain systems resulted in compromised customer data, affecting nearly 500,000 customers. This breach underscored the importance of cybersecurity measures across all segments of the supply chain to safeguard sensitive information (Yeboah-Ofori & Opoku-Boateng, 2023). The JBS cyber-attack in 2021, impacting one of the world's largest meat suppliers, led to production halts across multiple facilities. This event emphasized the vulnerability of critical infrastructure within supply chains and highlighted the need for robust cybersecurity protocols (Husain et al., 2023; Muzammal et al., 2020).

Additionally, the Colonial Pipeline ransomware attack in 2021 disrupted fuel distribution across the eastern United States, causing shortages and price spikes. This incident shed light on the cascading effects of cyber disruptions on essential services and the economy (Gao et al., 2023b; Sankar et al., 2020; Sindiramutty et al., 2024). These case studies underscore the pervasive impact of cyber incidents on supply chains, including financial losses, operational disruptions, compromised data, and public trust erosion. They emphasize the necessity for comprehensive cybersecurity strategies, collaboration among supply chain partners, and proactive measures to mitigate potential threats and strengthen resilience (Mızrak, 2023a; Sindiramutty et al., 2024a). In conclusion, the outlined case studies elucidate the tangible and detrimental effects of cyber incidents on supply chains. Implementing robust cybersecurity measures and fostering a culture of vigilance across the entire supply chain network is imperative to mitigate risks and ensure continuity in today's digitally interconnected business landscape.

Figure 3. Resilience of the logistics industry in terms of cybersecurity
(Boyes, 2015)

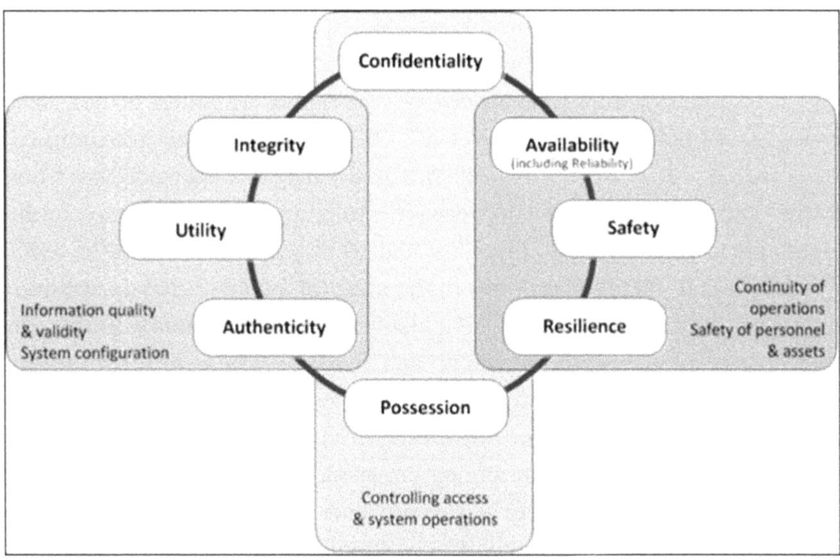

UNDERSTANDING LOGISTICS RESILIENCE

Definition and Importance

Defining Logistics Resilience in the Context of Cybersecurity

Logistics resilience in the context of cybersecurity refers to the capacity of a logistics system to withstand and recover from cyber threats while ensuring the continuous flow of goods and services. It involves the integration of security measures within logistical operations to mitigate risks posed by cyberattacks, ensuring the reliability and stability of supply chains. Cyber threats, ranging from malware attacks to data breaches, can disrupt logistical networks, impacting transportation, inventory management, and overall operations (Hammad et al., 2023; Singhal et al., 2020). The resilience of logistics in cybersecurity encompasses various elements. Firstly, it involves proactive measures to identify vulnerabilities within the supply chain and logistics infrastructure (Rivera et al., 2023). Conducting risk assessments and implementing robust cybersecurity protocols, including encryption techniques and firewalls, helps fortify systems against potential cyber threats (Khalil, 2023). Additionally, establishing redundancies and backup systems within logistical networks can minimize disruptions caused by cyber incidents. Figure 3 shows the Resilience of the logistics industry in terms of cybersecurity.

Moreover, collaboration and coordination among stakeholders play a pivotal role in enhancing logistics resilience against cyber threats. Close collaboration between government agencies, private enterprises, and cybersecurity experts is essential to share threat intelligence and best practices (Ainslie et al., 2023). Training and awareness programs for employees are crucial in reinforcing a culture of cybersecurity within logistics operations (Álvarez et al., 2023). Furthermore, adaptability and flexibility are integral aspects of logistics resilience in cybersecurity. Constant monitoring and updating of security measures to align with evolving cyber threats are imperative (Safitra et al., 2023). This adaptability also extends to the ability to swiftly recover and restore operations in the event of a cyber incident, minimizing the impact on the supply chain. In conclusion, logistics resilience in the context of cybersecurity is a multifaceted approach that integrates proactive measures, collaboration, adaptability, and recovery strategies within logistics operations to mitigate the risks posed by cyber threats. By implementing robust cybersecurity protocols, fostering collaboration among stakeholders, and ensuring adaptability, logistical systems can effectively withstand and recover from cyber incidents, maintaining the continuity and reliability of supply chains.

Explanation of Why Resilience is Crucial for Maintaining Continuous Operations

Resilience stands as a critical factor in ensuring the seamless continuation of operations in various domains. It encompasses the ability to adapt, recover, and maintain functionality amidst adversity (Steen et al., 2023). In today's dynamic and unpredictable world, resilience serves as a cornerstone for organizational, societal, and individual sustainability. The importance of resilience is underscored by its multifaceted impact on different aspects of operations. Resilience acts as a shield against disruptions, safeguarding operations from potential threats such as natural disasters, cyber-attacks, and economic downturns (Saeed et al., 2023). Organizations equipped with resilient systems and processes display greater capacity to absorb shocks and swiftly return to normal functioning. This ability to bounce back is crucial in maintaining continuous operations during unforeseen circumstances. Moreover, resilience fosters innovation and growth within organizations (Suhandiah et al., 2023). By promoting a culture of adaptability and learning from setbacks, resilient entities leverage challenges as opportunities for improvement and advancement (Ismail et al., 2023). This resilience-driven mindset encourages the exploration of new avenues and enhances organizational agility in a rapidly changing environment. Resilience also plays a pivotal role in ensuring the mental and emotional well-being of individuals within an operational setting (O'Donnell et al., 2022). Studies indicate that resilient individuals demonstrate better stress management and coping mechanisms, resulting in improved performance and sustained productivity, even under pressure. Furthermore, a resilient operational framework contributes to building trust and credibility among stakeholders (Chowdhury et al., 2022). Consistent delivery and reliability, despite challenges, strengthen relationships with clients, partners, and communities, fostering long-term sustainability and growth (Ceynowa et al., 2023).

In conclusion, resilience stands as an indispensable component for maintaining continuous operations across various sectors. Its ability to shield against disruptions, foster innovation, support mental well-being, and bolster stakeholder trust emphasizes its paramount importance in the fabric of operational sustainability.

Resilience Frameworks

Overview of Existing Resilience Frameworks Applicable to the Logistics Industry

The logistics industry faces multifaceted challenges due to its complex network, operational intricacies, and external uncertainties (Jussila et al., 2016). To address these challenges, various resilience frameworks have been developed to enhance the industry's adaptability and responsiveness to disruptions (Apasrawirote & Yawised, 2023). One prominent framework is the Supply Chain Resilience Assessment Framework (SCRAF), which emphasizes the evaluation of vulnerabilities and capabilities across the supply chain (C. Li, 2024). SCRAF enables logistics entities to identify weak links and implement strategies to mitigate risks and build resilience. The Resilience Engineering Framework (REF) focuses on system design and the integration of adaptive capacities within logistics operations (Yodo & Wang, 2016). REF highlights the need for flexibility, redundancy, and diversity to enhance resilience (Sharifi, 2023). The Dynamic Resilience Framework (DRF) emphasizes continuous adaptation and learning within logistics systems. DRF underscores the importance of real-time monitoring, quick decision-making, and agile responses to disruptions (Shishodia et al., 2021). Additionally, the Risk-Opportunity-Resilience (ROR) framework integrates risk management with resilience strategies, acknowledging that disruptions can also present opportunities for innovation and growth (Hause & Kihlström, 2022b). These frameworks collectively contribute to enhancing the resilience of the logistics industry by providing structured methodologies to assess vulnerabilities, mitigate risks, and foster adaptive capacities. However, their implementation requires tailored approaches considering the specific context and dynamics of each logistics operation.

Figure 4. Cybersecurity and operational resilience
(Machin, 2022)

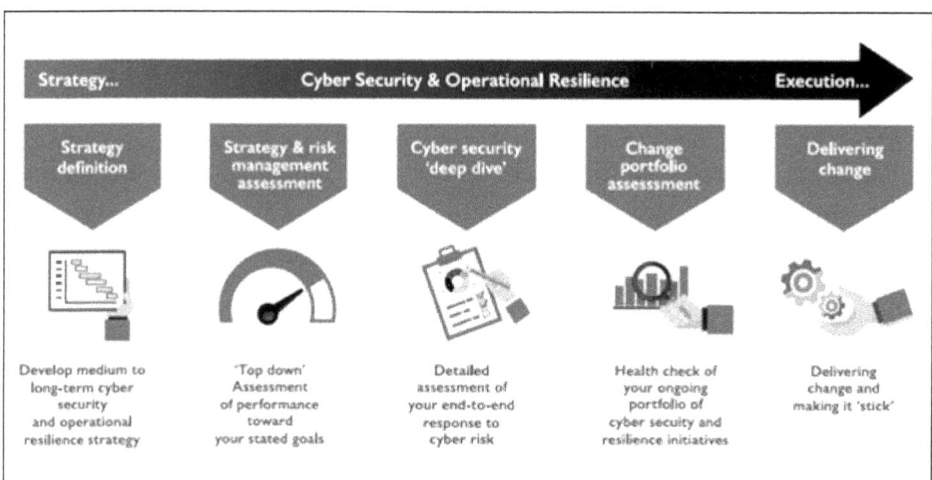

CYBERSECURITY STRATEGIES FOR LOGISTICS RESILIENCE

Risk Assessment and Mitigation

Detailed Process for Conducting Risk Assessments in Logistics

Risk assessments in logistics involve a systematic evaluation of potential hazards and vulnerabilities within the supply chain to mitigate possible disruptions and losses. The process comprises several key steps to ensure comprehensive identification and management of risks. The first step involves defining the scope and objectives of the assessment, which helps in setting clear parameters for the evaluation. Subsequently, gathering relevant data from various sources, such as historical records, industry reports, and expert opinions, aids in understanding the existing risks in logistics (Pattnaik & Shah, 2023). The identification of potential risks follows, where different types of risks, including natural disasters, supplier failures, or transportation issues, are recognized and categorized based on their impact and probability (Liu et al., 2024). Utilizing techniques like SWOT analysis or risk matrices assists in prioritizing these risks. The next step involves assessing the severity and likelihood of occurrence of identified risks, which allows for the quantification of risks in the logistics process (Barongo et al., 2023). Figure 4 shows cybercesurity and operational resilience.

After evaluating the risks, developing risk mitigation strategies becomes crucial. This stage involves brainstorming and selecting appropriate risk response measures, such as risk avoidance, transfer, reduction, or acceptance (Windapo & Chiswanda,

2023). Implementing these strategies necessitates collaboration among stakeholders and allocation of resources (Hegab et al., 2023). Simultaneously, continuous monitoring and periodic reassessment are vital to adapt to dynamic environments and emerging risks (Da Silva et al., 2023). Communication plays a pivotal role throughout the risk assessment process. Effective communication among stakeholders ensures a shared understanding of risks and strategies, facilitating swift responses to potential disruptions (Al-Wathinani et al., 2023). Moreover, documentation of the entire risk assessment process is essential for future reference and analysis. In conclusion, the process of conducting risk assessments in logistics involves several interlinked steps, starting from defining the scope to continuous monitoring and documentation. It's a dynamic process requiring collaborative efforts, data-driven decisions, and constant adaptation to ensure the resilience of the supply chain against potential threats and vulnerabilities.

Strategies for Mitigating Identified Risks and Vulnerabilities

Identifying and addressing risks and vulnerabilities is crucial in ensuring the safety and stability of any system or organization. Several strategies have been proposed to mitigate these challenges. One fundamental approach involves conducting regular risk assessments to pinpoint potential threats (Peng et al., 2023). Once identified, a proactive response is essential, involving the implementation of robust security measures (Kilag, 2023). Education and training play a pivotal role in mitigating risks, as highlighted by Posamentier et al. (2022). Providing employees with adequate knowledge about potential threats and cybersecurity best practices significantly reduces the likelihood of vulnerabilities being exploited (Bandari, 2023). Moreover, instilling a culture of security consciousness within an organization enhances vigilance against potential risks (Azzani et al., 2024). Employing encryption techniques is another critical strategy for safeguarding sensitive data. Encryption adds an extra layer of security, making it difficult for unauthorized individuals to access confidential information (Nikose & Srinivas, 2023). Regularly updating software and systems is equally important as outdated systems are more susceptible to exploitation (Kioskli et al., 2023). Implementing a robust incident response plan is imperative. Having a clear protocol in place enables swift and effective action in the event of a security breach. Additionally, fostering collaboration and information sharing among different departments and stakeholders bolsters the overall security posture of an organization (Ramadhianto et al., 2023). Regular audits and assessments, both internal and external, are vital for evaluating the effectiveness of implemented security measures (Rizvi et al., 2023). These evaluations help in identifying any gaps or weaknesses that require immediate attention and rectification. Employing a multifaceted approach that encompasses proactive risk assessment, employee education, technological safeguards, incident response planning, and continuous evaluations is essential for mitigating identified risks and vulnerabilities.

Supply Chain Visibility

Importance of Visibility in the Supply Chain for Cybersecurity

In today's interconnected business landscape, maintaining robust cybersecurity measures within the supply chain is crucial for safeguarding sensitive information and maintaining operational integrity. Visibility, referring to the ability to monitor and comprehend activities across the supply chain, emerges as a cornerstone for enhancing cybersecurity resilience (Chindrus & Caruntu, 2023). A lack of visibility within the supply chain can exacerbate vulnerabilities, leaving businesses susceptible to cyber threats (Zhang et al., 2021). Thus, establishing comprehensive visibility mechanisms is imperative to proactively identify and mitigate potential cyber risks.

Visibility plays a pivotal role in understanding the flow of information and assets within the supply chain ecosystem. It allows stakeholders to gain real-time insights into activities, detect anomalies, and promptly respond to security breaches (Davies et al., 2022). Improved visibility aids in identifying weak links and potential entry points for cyber-attacks, enabling the implementation of targeted security measures (Pour et al., 2023). Moreover, enhanced visibility fosters transparency and accountability among supply chain partners, facilitating collaboration in addressing cybersecurity concerns. With the rise of interconnected systems and the integration of technologies like IoT and cloud computing, visibility becomes increasingly complex but simultaneously critical (Krupitzer & Stein, 2023). Lack of visibility across multiple layers of the supply chain can create blind spots, hindering the ability to assess and respond effectively to cyber threats (Rahman et al., 2023). However, with robust visibility measures, businesses can proactively monitor the entire supply chain network, enabling timely threat detection and incident response (Aljohani, 2023).

In conclusion, visibility within the supply chain is fundamental for bolstering cybersecurity defences and mitigating potential risks. By leveraging visibility tools and technologies, businesses can attain a comprehensive understanding of their supply chain operations, enabling them to fortify security measures, enhance collaboration, and mitigate vulnerabilities effectively. Embracing robust visibility strategies is pivotal in safeguarding against evolving cyber threats and ensuring the resilience of the supply chain ecosystem.

Technologies and Practices for Enhancing Visibility and Traceability

In the current business landscape, enhancing visibility and traceability is crucial across various industries. Technologies and practices play a pivotal role in achieving this objective by providing insights, transparency, and accountability throughout the supply chain. Visibility and traceability enable businesses to track products, monitor processes, and maintain quality standards, fostering customer trust and satisfaction (Sharma et al., 2023). RFID (Radio Frequency Identification) technology is widely used for enhancing visibility in supply chains (Reyes, 2023). It enables real-time tracking of assets and inventory, facilitating accurate monitoring of product movements. IoT (Internet of Things) devices also contribute significantly by collecting and transmitting data across interconnected systems. These devices facilitate monitoring, analytics, and decision-making in logistics and production processes.

Blockchain technology ensures traceability and transparency by creating an immutable record of transactions (Saranya & Maheswari, 2023). Its decentralized nature enhances data security and authenticity, providing a trustworthy system for recording supply chain activities (S. Li et al., 2023). Furthermore, advanced analytics and AI-driven solutions interpret vast amounts of data, offering actionable insights (Zaripova et al., 2023). These technologies empower businesses to optimize operations and respond promptly to changes or disruptions. Implementing standardized practices such as GS1 standards ensures uniformity in data exchange and product identification. This promotes interoperability among different stakeholders, enhancing visibility across the supply chain (Razak et al., 2021). Additionally, adopting lean and Six Sigma methodologies aids in streamlining processes, reducing errors, and enhancing traceability. In conclusion, technologies like RFID, IoT, and blockchain, coupled with standardized practices and methodologies, significantly enhance visibility and traceability within supply chains. These innovations not only improve operational efficiency but also contribute to building trust and meeting the increasing demands of consumers and regulatory bodies in today's dynamic business environment.

Vendor and Partner Management

Best Practices for Assessing and Ensuring the Cybersecurity Posture of Vendors and Partners

In today's interconnected digital landscape, safeguarding sensitive data and systems against cyber threats extends beyond a company's internal defences. Collaborating with vendors and partners necessitates ensuring a robust cybersecurity posture throughout the supply chain. Employing best practices in assessing and securing these external entities is crucial to mitigate potential risks. Initiating a comprehensive risk assessment process is fundamental. This involves evaluating vendors' security protocols, data handling procedures, and compliance with industry standards (Wallis & Dorey, 2023). Establishing clear cybersecurity requirements within contracts and agreements is pivotal. These clauses should outline specific security measures and expectations, emphasizing the importance of adherence to established protocols (Wu et al., 2022b). Regular audits and assessments serve as proactive measures to ensure continuous compliance and adherence to cybersecurity standards. Utilizing standardized assessment frameworks such as the NIST Cybersecurity Framework or ISO 27001 aids in benchmarking security practices (Alshar'e, 2023). Moreover, implementing third-party security certifications can validate a vendor's commitment to cybersecurity.

Fostering a culture of collaboration and communication between the company and its vendors is imperative (Hotha, 2023). Conducting cybersecurity training and workshops for vendors ensures awareness of evolving threats and best practices. Additionally, establishing incident response protocols in collaboration with vendors helps in the prompt and efficient mitigation of potential breaches (Auzina et al., 2023). Utilizing technological solutions such as encryption, multi-factor authentication, and intrusion detection systems fortifies data protection. They are employing continuous monitoring tools to aid in real-time threat detection and response. Regularly updating and patching systems and software mitigates vulnerabilities. Lastly, maintaining a dynamic and adaptive approach is essential. Continuous evaluation and improvement of vendor cybersecurity practices align with the ever-evolving threat landscape (Thomas & Sule, 2022).

In conclusion, safeguarding a company's cybersecurity extends to assessing and ensuring the robustness of vendor and partner practices. Employing comprehensive risk assessments, contractual obligations, standardized frameworks, collaborative efforts, technological solutions, and a dynamic approach is pivotal in mitigating risks and fortifying the overall cybersecurity posture within a supply chain.

Contractual Considerations for Cybersecurity in Vendor Agreements

In contemporary business landscapes, where digital interconnectedness prevails, contractual considerations play a pivotal role in ensuring robust cybersecurity measures. Vendors, serving as third-party entities, often handle sensitive information, necessitating stringent clauses to protect data integrity and confidentiality (Kumbhare et al., 2023). In crafting vendor agreements, several key considerations are imperative to fortify cybersecurity frameworks. Defining clear cybersecurity obligations is paramount. Specific delineation of security protocols, compliance standards, and data protection measures within the contract is essential to establish accountability and expectations (Oladoyinbo et al., 2023). Clauses specifying encryption protocols and incident response procedures in case of a breach are fundamental safeguards. Conducting thorough risk assessments and audits becomes pivotal. Implementing periodic evaluations of vendor systems and security controls aids in identifying vulnerabilities and enforcing necessary upgrades (Chauhan & Shiaeles, 2023). Including clauses mandating regular security assessments and audits within the agreement promotes a proactive approach to cybersecurity. Figure 5 shows the enterprise's general security strategy

Moreover, liability allocation is a critical aspect. Clearly defining responsibilities and liabilities in the event of a breach or data compromise is crucial for mitigating financial and legal repercussions (Puspita & Boydston, 2023). Including indemnification clauses outlining the consequences and responsibilities in case of security incidents is imperative. Additionally, the inclusion of termination and exit strategies holds significance. Incorporating provisions for contract termination in the case of repeated security violations or failure to comply with cybersecurity standards safeguards the contracting party from prolonged exposure to potential risks (Parker, 2023). Similarly, specifying data ownership and return or destruction protocols post-contract termination ensures the protection of proprietary information (Goldby & Okonjo, 2023). In conclusion, crafting comprehensive vendor agreements with robust cybersecurity clauses is imperative to safeguard sensitive data and mitigate risks associated with third-party engagements. Clear delineation of obligations, regular assessments, defined liability, and termination strategies form the foundation of secure vendor agreements, facilitating a proactive approach to cybersecurity management.

Figure 5. Enterprise general security strategy
(Di Nardo, 2022)

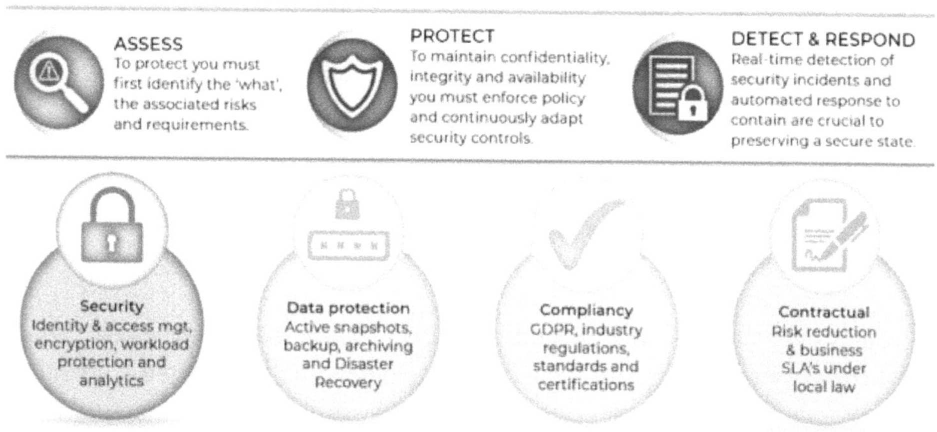

Incident Response and Recovery

Development of Robust Incident Response Plans for Logistics Operations

Incident response planning is critical in safeguarding logistics operations against disruptions and ensuring the continuity of supply chains. Robust incident response plans (IRPs) are essential to mitigate risks and manage unforeseen events effectively. This section outlines key considerations and strategies to develop effective IRPs tailored to logistics operations. Understanding the diverse nature of incidents in logistics is crucial (Sarkar et al., 2022). IRPs should encompass a wide range of potential disruptions, including natural disasters, cyber-attacks, infrastructure failures, and human errors (Magableh & Mistarihi, 2023). Conducting risk assessments aids in identifying vulnerabilities and evaluating potential impacts, forming the foundation of an effective IRP (Maghsoudi et al., 2023). Collaboration and communication among stakeholders are pivotal. Establishing clear lines of communication internally and externally with suppliers, partners, and relevant authorities facilitates swift response and coordination during crises. Regular drills and simulations enhance preparedness and validate the efficacy of the IRP.

Additionally, leveraging technology and data-driven approaches enhances incident response capabilities. Implementing real-time monitoring systems and utilizing predictive analytics enable early detection of potential threats, allowing proactive measures to be taken to minimize disruptions (Cornwell et al., 2023). Furthermore, flexibility and adaptability are integral to IRPs. Plans should be dynamic, allowing for adjustments based on the evolving nature of threats and changing operational environments (Poudel et al., 2023). Regular reviews and updates ensure the relevance and effectiveness of the IRP over time.

In conclusion, developing robust IRPs for logistics operations requires a comprehensive approach that considers various threats, emphasizes collaboration, integrates technology and allows for adaptability. By implementing these strategies, organizations can enhance their resilience and mitigate the impact of incidents on their supply chains.

Strategies for Swift Recovery and Minimizing the Impact of Cyber Incidents

In today's interconnected digital landscape, the logistics industry faces escalating threats from cyber incidents that can disrupt operations and compromise sensitive data. Adopting proactive measures is crucial to swiftly recover and mitigate the impact of such incidents in logistics operations. This report delineates strategies essential for bolstering cybersecurity in logistics.

Fostering a culture of cybersecurity awareness among employees is fundamental (Alotaibi et al., 2023). Regular training sessions should be conducted to educate staff on identifying and responding to potential cyber threats promptly (Shukur et al., 2023). Implementing robust access controls and authentication mechanisms ensures restricted entry to sensitive logistical data, minimizing vulnerabilities. Maintaining up-to-date software and systems is paramount (Shukur et al., 2023). Regular patches and updates should be applied to safeguard against known vulnerabilities. Employing intrusion detection and prevention systems (IDPS) aids in real-time monitoring and immediate response to suspicious activities (Ntizikira et al., 2024). Establishing resilient backup and recovery protocols is crucial. Regularly backing up critical logistical data in secure off-site locations shields against data loss in case of a cyber incident (Dhandabani & Tyagi, 2023). Having a well-defined incident response plan (IRP) enables swift action, reducing downtime and potential damage caused by cyber breaches.

Collaborating with cybersecurity experts and fostering partnerships within the industry (Ayala et al., 2023) enhances knowledge sharing and enables access to the latest threat intelligence. They are engaging in continuous risk assessments and audits to aid in identifying potential vulnerabilities and fortifying cybersecurity measures in logistics operations. In conclusion, the evolving nature of cyber threats necessitates a multifaceted approach to fortify cybersecurity in logistics operations. By prioritizing employee training, system updates, robust backup protocols, industry collaborations, and regular risk assessments, logistics companies can mitigate the impact of cyber incidents and facilitate a swift recovery, ensuring the integrity and efficiency of their operations.

TECHNOLOGY INTEGRATION AND BEST PRACTICES

Advanced Authentication and Access Controls

Exploration of Advanced Authentication Methods for Securing Access

Traditional username-password authentication methods are susceptible to various security threats, prompting the exploration and development of advanced authentication techniques. This report investigates the efficacy of several advanced authentication methods in enhancing access security. Biometric authentication

Figure 6. Advanced authentication software and framework
(Cyberres, 2023)

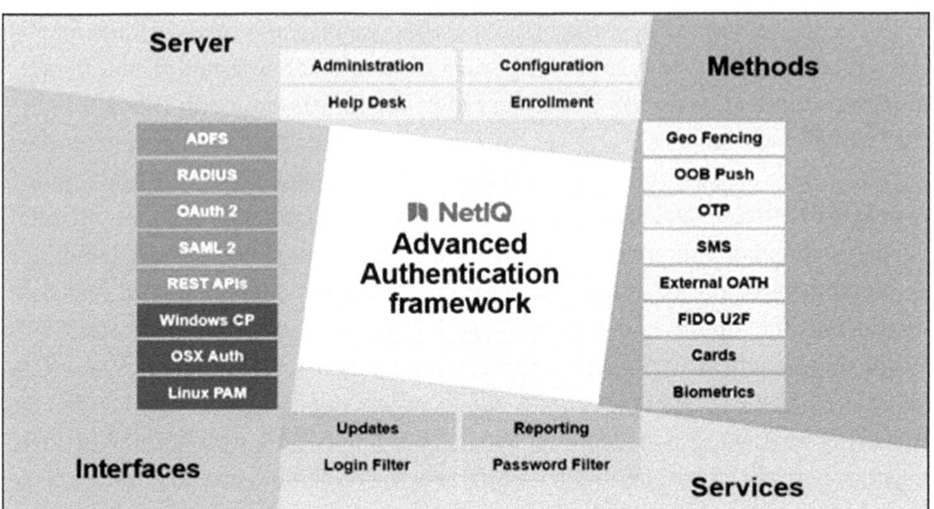

stands as a prominent advanced method, utilizing unique physical or behavioural traits for identity verification (Das et al., 2023). Biometrics such as fingerprint, iris, and facial recognition offer enhanced security by being inherently unique to individuals (Strauß, 2023). Multi-factor authentication (MFA) combines two or more authentication factors, typically something a user knows, has, or is. MFA significantly fortifies security by requiring multiple proofs of identity before granting access. Hardware-based authentication tokens provide an added layer of security by generating one-time passwords or cryptographic keys (Teffandi et al., 2023). These tokens reduce the risk of unauthorized access, particularly in remote environments. Context-aware authentication systems analyze various contextual factors like device location, time, and user behaviour to assess the legitimacy of access attempts (More & Sakhare, 2023). Contextual information strengthens security by recognizing anomalies and potentially fraudulent access. Figure 6 shows advanced authentication software and framework.

Blockchain-based authentication mechanisms offer decentralized and tamper-resistant identity verification (Diro et al., 2024). By leveraging blockchain's immutability, authentication records become highly secure and transparent. Risk-based authentication dynamically adjusts security measures based on risk levels associated with access attempts. This method minimizes disruptions for regular users while tightening security in high-risk scenarios. Adaptive authentication systems continuously monitor and adapt security protocols based on evolving threats and user behaviour (Safitra et al., 2023b). These systems employ machine learning algorithms to detect patterns and anomalies, thus strengthening security measures proactively. In conclusion, the exploration of advanced authentication methods has provided a diverse array of tools to bolster access security. Biometrics, MFA, hardware tokens, contextual analysis, blockchain, risk-based, and adaptive authentication represent pivotal advancements in thwarting unauthorized access attempts. Employing a combination of these methods tailored to specific security needs is essential in fortifying access control and protecting sensitive information.

Implementation of Access Controls to Safeguard Critical Systems and Data

Access controls play a crucial role in safeguarding critical systems and data within organizations, ensuring that only authorized individuals have appropriate access rights. Effective implementation of access controls is imperative to prevent unauthorized access, data breaches, and potential cyber threats (Omotunde & Ahmed, 2023). This involves the use of various strategies and technologies, such as authentication methods, authorization protocols, and encryption techniques (Q. Lin et al., 2024). Authentication mechanisms, including passwords, biometrics, and multi-factor authentication, are fundamental in verifying users' identities before granting access (Carrillo-Torres et al., 2023). Moreover, authorization protocols define what resources or data a user can access based on their authenticated identity and assigned privileges (Sutradhar et al., 2024). Role-based access control (RBAC) and attribute-based access control (ABAC) are widely used authorization models that manage user permissions efficiently. Encryption technologies, such as data encryption at rest and in transit, are essential in protecting sensitive information from unauthorized viewing or modification (Abiodun et al., 2023). Additionally, implementing least privilege principles limits user access to only the resources necessary for their tasks, reducing the attack surface and minimizing potential security risks. Regular monitoring and auditing of access controls are vital to identify anomalies, detect potential security breaches, and ensure compliance with security policies and regulations (Apeh et al., 2023). Continuous assessments and updates of access control systems are necessary to adapt to evolving security threats and technological advancements. Figure 7 shows examples of 5 best authentication methods.

In conclusion, the implementation of access controls is a critical component of cybersecurity strategies. Organizations must deploy a comprehensive approach encompassing authentication, authorization, encryption, the principle of least privilege, and continuous monitoring to safeguard critical systems and sensitive data from unauthorized access and potential security threats.

Figure 7. Five best types of authentication method

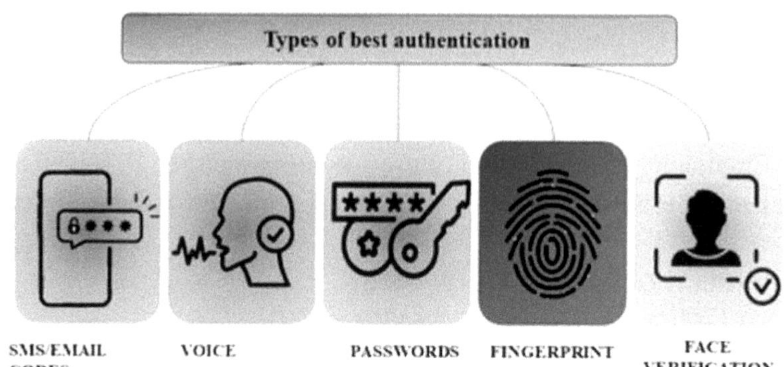

Encryption and Data Protection

Importance of Encryption in Protecting Sensitive Data

Encryption plays a pivotal role in safeguarding sensitive information across digital platforms and is considered a cornerstone in ensuring data security (Weippl & Schrittwieser, 2023). It involves the process of converting plaintext data into a coded format, making it indecipherable without the corresponding decryption key. This transformation aids in preventing unauthorized access and potential data breaches, thereby upholding confidentiality (Weippl & Schrittwieser, 2023). Encryption is crucial in protecting sensitive data because it shields personal information, such as financial details, healthcare records, and private communications, from being intercepted or accessed by cybercriminals.

One of the key reasons encryptions hold paramount importance in data protection is its role in securing data during transmission. When data is transmitted over networks or the internet, encryption ensures that even if intercepted, the data remains incomprehensible to unauthorized individuals (Madavarapu et al., 2023). Moreover, encryption assists in complying with regulatory requirements such as the General Data Protection Regulation (GDPR) by providing a method to secure personal data and prevent unauthorized access. This compliance is crucial for organizations dealing with customer information, enhancing trust and credibility. Additionally, encryption helps maintain the integrity of data by safeguarding it from tampering or unauthorized modifications (Duggineni, 2023). It ensures that data remains unaltered during storage or transmission, thus preserving its accuracy and reliability (T et al., 2023). Moreover, encryption mitigates the risks associated with data theft and cyberattacks, thereby reducing potential financial losses and reputational damage to individuals and organizations. In conclusion, encryption serves as a crucial safeguard in protecting sensitive data by preventing unauthorized access, securing data during transmission, ensuring regulatory compliance, preserving data integrity, and mitigating cybersecurity risks. Its implementation is fundamental in today's digital landscape to ensure the confidentiality, integrity, and security of sensitive information.

Best Practices for Data Protection Throughout the Logistics Process

Data protection is paramount in the logistics industry to safeguard sensitive information and maintain the integrity of operations. Implementing best practices ensures the secure handling, storage, and transmission of data throughout the logistics process. Encryption stands as a fundamental measure in securing data. By encrypting sensitive information during storage and transit, logistics companies can prevent unauthorized access and mitigate the risk of data breaches. Moreover, regular encryption key updates enhance security measures and thwart potential threats (Farah et al., 2023; Azam, Dulloo, Majeed, Wan, Xin, & Sindiramutty, 2023). Access control mechanisms play a pivotal role in data protection. Implementing role-based access (RBAC) ensures that only authorized personnel can access specific information, reducing the likelihood of internal data breaches (Saxena & Alam, 2023). Additionally, multi-factor authentication (MFA) adds an extra layer of security, requiring multiple forms of verification before granting access. Regular data backups are crucial to mitigate the impact of data loss due to system failures or cyberattacks (Rajkumar et al., 2023). Scheduled backups stored in secure off-site locations ensure data recoverability and business continuity in the event of an unforeseen incident. Training and educating employees about data security protocols and best practices are vital. Employees should understand the significance of safeguarding sensitive information, recognize potential threats, and adhere to established security protocols (Olaniyi et al., 2023; Azam et al., 2023). Vendor risk management is essential, requiring logistics companies to evaluate and monitor the security practices of third-party service providers (Valashiya & Luke, 2022). A comprehensive assessment ensures that vendors comply with data protection standards, minimizing potential vulnerabilities in the logistics chain.

Implementing robust firewalls and intrusion detection systems (IDS) fortifies network security. Firewalls act as barriers against unauthorized access, while IDS monitor network traffic for suspicious activities, enabling timely detection and response to potential threats. Regular security audits and assessments help identify vulnerabilities and assess compliance with data protection regulations (Fadhil et al., 2023). Addressing identified gaps promptly strengthens overall security posture. Lastly, maintaining compliance with relevant data protection regulations such as

GDPR, HIPAA, or CCPA is imperative (Lyons & Fitzgerald, 2023). Adhering to legal requirements ensures that data handling practices align with industry standards and protect against legal repercussions. In conclusion, safeguarding data throughout the logistics process demands a multi-faceted approach. Encryption, access control, backups, employee training, vendor management, network security measures, regular assessments, and compliance with regulations collectively form the foundation for robust data protection in logistics operations.

Emerging Technologies

Examination of Emerging Technologies, Such as Blockchain and AI, for Enhancing Cybersecurity

Cybersecurity remains a critical concern in today's digital landscape due to the constant evolution of cyber threats. As organizations grapple with the complexities of safeguarding sensitive data and systems, emerging technologies like Blockchain and Artificial Intelligence (AI) offer promising avenues to enhance cybersecurity measures. These innovative solutions address various vulnerabilities in traditional security approaches.

Blockchain technology, recognized for its decentralized and immutable nature, plays a pivotal role in fortifying cybersecurity. Its foundation lies in creating a secure and transparent ledger system resistant to tampering and unauthorized access (Batool, 2023; Sindiramutty, 2023). Through cryptographic techniques and distributed consensus mechanisms, Blockchain ensures data integrity and reduces the risk of data manipulation or unauthorized alterations (Juma et al., 2023; Ananna et al., 2023). Its decentralized structure mitigates single points of failure, strengthening resilience against cyber-attacks (Dai, 2023; Azam, Dulloo, et al., 2023). Simultaneously, AI-driven solutions present a formidable defence against sophisticated cyber threats. AI algorithms, particularly machine learning models, enable real-time threat detection by analyzing vast datasets to identify anomalous patterns and behaviours (Iqbal, 2023). These systems continually adapt and learn from new threats, enhancing predictive capabilities and empowering proactive cybersecurity measures.

Furthermore, the amalgamation of Blockchain and AI amplifies cybersecurity capabilities synergistically. Integrating Blockchain's tamper-proof ledger with AI's predictive analysis fortifies data protection and confidentiality (Rane et al., 2023; Azam, Tajwar, et al., 2023). AI algorithms leveraging Blockchain's secure environment bolster authentication processes, ensuring the integrity of identities and access controls. Despite their potential, these technologies also present challenges. Blockchain encounters scalability issues and regulatory concerns, while AI grapples with ethical considerations and adversarial attacks. Additionally, the rapid evolution of cyber threats demands continual advancements in these technologies to stay ahead of malicious actors (D & Tyagi, 2023; Azam et al., 2023). In conclusion, Blockchain and AI offer innovative pathways to fortify cybersecurity measures, providing robust defences against evolving threats. However, acknowledging their potential, addressing inherent challenges, and ensuring responsible deployment remain imperative in leveraging these technologies effectively.

Case Studies Illustrating Successful Implementations of These Technologies in Logistics

Blockchain technology and artificial intelligence (AI) have emerged as transformative tools for enhancing cybersecurity within the logistics industry. By leveraging decentralized ledgers and advanced algorithms, these innovations offer secure, transparent, and efficient solutions. Several case studies highlight the successful integration of blockchain and AI in fortifying cybersecurity within logistics operations.

Case Study 1: Maersk's Implementation of Blockchain

Maersk, a global shipping giant, implemented blockchain to enhance supply chain security and efficiency. By partnering with IBM, Maersk developed a blockchain-based platform named TradeLens, enabling secure data sharing among multiple stakeholders. The system's transparency and immutability significantly reduced paperwork, minimized errors, and heightened security against cyber threats (Lorenz-Meyer & Santos, 2023).

Case Study 2: IBM's Watson AI in Logistics Security

IBM Watson, an AI-powered system, has been instrumental in bolstering cybersecurity in logistics. Its cognitive computing capabilities analyze vast amounts of data to detect anomalies and potential security breaches in real time. Watson's machine learning algorithms continuously learn from patterns, improving threat detection and response mechanisms (Kumari & Muthulakshmi, 2023).

Case Study 3: FedEx's Blockchain Adoption

FedEx deployed blockchain to enhance shipment tracking and security. By implementing a blockchain-based platform, FedEx ensured end-to-end visibility of parcels, reducing instances of tampering and enhancing cybersecurity (Bodemer, 2023). The immutable nature of blockchain records provided a secure audit trail, mitigating risks associated with data manipulation.

Case Study 4: DHL's AI-Powered Cybersecurity Measures

DHL integrated AI-driven cybersecurity measures to safeguard logistics operations. Using predictive analytics and AI algorithms, DHL preemptively identifies potential threats and vulnerabilities across its supply chain network (Soumpenioti & Panagopoulos, 2023). This proactive approach significantly reduces the likelihood of cyber-attacks and data breaches.

The successful integration of blockchain and AI in logistics has revolutionized cybersecurity practices. Through case studies like Maersk's TradeLens, IBM's Watson, FedEx's blockchain adoption, and DHL's AI-driven security measures, the industry has witnessed enhanced data security, transparency, and operational efficiency. These implementations serve as pivotal examples of how blockchain and AI technologies fortify cybersecurity within logistics, ensuring secure and resilient supply chain operations.

REGULATORY COMPLIANCE AND STANDARDS

Overview of Relevant Regulations

Summary of Cybersecurity Regulations Impacting the Logistics Industry

Cybersecurity regulations are crucial for safeguarding sensitive data and operations within the logistics industry. These regulations encompass various aspects that aim to mitigate cyber threats and ensure the security of logistics operations and data. Several key regulations significantly impact this sector, aiming to enhance resilience against cyber threats and protect critical infrastructure. The International Maritime Organization's (IMO) guidelines on maritime cybersecurity set out measures to enhance the resilience of the global shipping industry against cyber risks, emphasizing the importance of risk management and incorporating cybersecurity into safety management systems (Afenyo & Caesar, 2023).

The Cybersecurity Maturity Model Certification (CMMC) is particularly influential in the logistics industry (Bruce, 2023). This framework by the Department

Figure 8. Cybersecurity enterprise policies

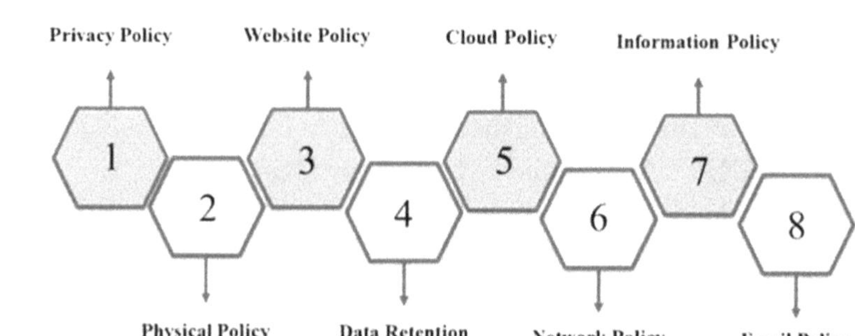

of Defense outlines cybersecurity standards necessary for contractors working with the U.S. government, ensuring the protection of Controlled Unclassified Information (CUI). Moreover, the European Union's General Data Protection Regulation (GDPR) imposes stringent rules on data protection, impacting logistics operations handling personal data (Blind et al., 2023). It mandates companies to adopt robust cybersecurity measures to protect personal information and defines severe penalties for non-compliance. The Cybersecurity Framework by the National Institute of Standards and Technology (NIST) provides guidelines applicable across industries, aiding logistics companies in assessing and improving their cybersecurity posture by emphasizing risk-based approaches and continuous improvement (Qureshi et al., 2023).

In addition, the Security and Exchange Commission's (SEC) guidance on cybersecurity disclosures requires publicly traded companies, including those in logistics, to disclose cybersecurity risks and incidents to investors and customers (Jiang, 2024). The International Air Transport Association (IATA) also emphasizes cybersecurity through its guidelines for air cargo supply chain security, aiming to secure air cargo processes against cyber threats, ensuring safe and efficient operations. The Transported Asset Protection Association's (TAPA) standards (Wensveen, 2023), focus on supply chain security and include cybersecurity measures to prevent cargo theft and enhance overall supply chain resilience. The United States Transportation Security Administration (TSA) provides cybersecurity guidelines and recommendations for enhancing the security of transportation systems, impacting logistics operations within the country (Marassi & Marrone, 2023). Furthermore, the Federal Motor Carrier Safety Administration (FMCSA) highlights the importance of cybersecurity in the transportation sector, ensuring the protection of critical infrastructure and sensitive information (Chirayath, 2023). In conclusion, adherence to cybersecurity regulations is pivotal for the logistics industry's security and resilience (Khan et al., 2023). Compliance with these regulations is essential to protect sensitive data, maintain operational continuity, and uphold trust in the global supply chain network.

Industry Standards

Examination Of Cybersecurity Standards Specific to Logistics

Frameworks and Standards

Logistics cybersecurity adheres to various frameworks and standards. The International Organization for Standardization (ISO) sets benchmarks, such as ISO 27001, focusing on information security management systems. Additionally, the National Institute of Standards and Technology (NIST) provides guidelines, especially NIST SP 800-53, offering security controls for federal information systems and organizations (Khan et al., 2023).

Transportation and Supply Chain Security

The transportation sector is governed by specific cybersecurity standards. For instance, the Transportation Security Administration (TSA) in the United States has implemented the Transportation Systems Sector Cybersecurity Framework Implementation Guide to safeguard critical infrastructure (Dorn, 2023). Moreover, supply chain security standards like the Cybersecurity Maturity Model Certification (CMMC) are vital for defence contractors to ensure cybersecurity practices throughout the supply chain.

Risk Management and Compliance

Logistics cybersecurity heavily focuses on risk management and compliance measures. The European Union Agency for Cybersecurity (ENISA) offers guidelines for enhancing the resilience of cybersecurity capabilities, emphasizing risk assessment and management (Jacobs, 2023). Furthermore, compliance with regulations like the General Data Protection Regulation (GDPR) is imperative to protect personal data within logistics operations (Miadzvetskaya, 2023).

Collaborative Initiatives

Collaboration among stakeholders is crucial in fortifying logistics cybersecurity. Organizations like the Cybersecurity and Infrastructure Security Agency (CISA) promote information sharing and collaborative efforts to combat cyber threats in the logistics sector (Özkan & Tüysüzoğlu, 2023). Additionally, the World Economic Forum (WEF) facilitates discussions and initiatives to address cybersecurity challenges in global supply chains (WEF, 2021).

CASE STUDIES AND PRACTICAL APPLICATIONS

Successful Implementations

In-Depth Analysis of Successful Cybersecurity Implementations in Logistics

Cybersecurity plays a pivotal role in safeguarding the integrity, confidentiality, and availability of information systems within the logistics sector. An in-depth analysis of successful cybersecurity implementations in logistics reveals key strategies and practices utilized to mitigate evolving cyber threats. According to Alqudhaibi et al. (2023), a proactive approach to cybersecurity involves continuous risk assessment, emphasizing the identification of vulnerabilities across networks, devices, and software. Successful implementations often integrate robust encryption mechanisms multi-factor authentication and intrusion detection systems to fortify defenses against unauthorized access and data breaches.

Collaboration and partnerships, as highlighted by Panyushkina (2023) emerge as critical components in addressing cybersecurity challenges within the logistics ecosystem. Effective collaborations between industry stakeholders, government entities, and cybersecurity experts foster information sharing and collective efforts to combat emerging threats. Furthermore, adherence to industry standards and compliance frameworks, such as ISO 27001 ensures a structured approach to managing information security risks, enhancing the resilience of logistics operations (Al-Dosari & Fetais, 2023). Continuous employee training and awareness campaigns are imperative in fostering a culture of cybersecurity vigilance. Employees, often considered the weakest link, need to be equipped with knowledge about phishing attempts, social engineering tactics, and best practices in handling sensitive data (Strand, 2023). Additionally, the implementation of robust incident response plans enables swift and effective responses to cyber incidents, minimizing their impact on logistics operations.

Integration of advanced technologies like Artificial Intelligence (AI) and Machine Learning (ML) bolsters cybersecurity capabilities within logistics (Nguyen et al., 2022). AI-driven anomaly detection and predictive analytics enhance threat detection and enable proactive measures against potential breaches (Ajala, 2024). Moreover, the adoption of blockchain technology ensures data integrity and transparency across the supply chain, reducing the risk of tampering or unauthorized access to critical information. In conclusion, successful cybersecurity implementations in logistics demand a multi-faceted approach encompassing technological advancements, collaboration, employee training, and regulatory compliance. By adopting these strategies, logistics entities can fortify their defences, effectively mitigating cyber threats and ensuring the secure and uninterrupted flow of goods and information.

Challenges and Solutions

Exploration of Challenges Faced During Cybersecurity Implementations

Cybersecurity implementation encounters multifaceted challenges in today's digital landscape, hindering the effective safeguarding of systems and data. As highlighted by Ghasemshirazi et al. (2023), one of the foremost challenges involves the ever-evolving nature of cyber threats. Malicious actors continuously adapt and diversify their tactics, rendering traditional defence mechanisms less effective (Rehman et al., 2024). A critical issue identified by Brown (2018) involves the shortage of skilled cybersecurity professionals, creating a workforce gap that impairs organizations' abilities to address threats effectively (Adetoye & Fong, 2023). This gap is compounded by the rapid advancement of technology, requiring continuous training and skill updates. Additionally, compliance with diverse regulations and standards poses a significant challenge. Organizations often struggle to align their cybersecurity measures with multiple regulatory frameworks, leading to confusion and potential compliance gaps (Rawindaran et al., 2023).

Interconnected systems and the proliferation of Internet of Things (IoT) devices introduce new vulnerabilities (John et al., 2023). Securing these diverse endpoints becomes increasingly challenging due to their varied nature and potential entry points for cyber threats. Moreover, the expanding attack surface, including cloud-based services, amplifies the difficulty of protecting sensitive information (Sheik et al., 2023). The lack of standardized security protocols across different cloud platforms further complicates this issue. Financial constraints present a formidable challenge in implementing robust cybersecurity measures. Allocating adequate resources for comprehensive security infrastructure often clashes with budgetary limitations, leaving organizations exposed to potential risks (Kumar, 2024). Furthermore, the constant tension between security and user experience hampers effective implementation. Striking a balance between stringent security protocols and user-friendly interfaces remains a persistent challenge.

In conclusion, the landscape of cybersecurity implementation faces a myriad of challenges ranging from the adaptive nature of threats to the scarcity of skilled professionals, compliance complexities, IoT vulnerabilities, cloud security concerns, financial limitations, and the balancing act between security and usability. Addressing these challenges demands a concerted effort from stakeholders, including organizations, policymakers, and cybersecurity professionals, to develop adaptive strategies and collaborative approaches to mitigate risks effectively.

Innovative Solutions and Adaptations to Overcome Challenges

Addressing the multifaceted challenges within cybersecurity implementation demands innovative solutions and adaptive strategies in the face of evolving threats. One promising avenue involves leveraging advancements in artificial intelligence (AI) and machine learning (ML) technologies (Rane et al., 2023b). AI-powered systems can analyze vast amounts of data to detect anomalies and potential threats, aiding in proactive threat mitigation (Telo, 2017). Similarly, blockchain technology offers decentralized and tamper-resistant data storage, enhancing security and transparency (Musa et al., 2023). Embracing these emerging technologies could fortify defences against evolving threats. Furthermore, collaboration and information sharing among industry peers and governmental bodies play a pivotal role (Susha et al., 2023). Initiatives such as Information Sharing and Analysis Centers (ISACs) facilitate the exchange of threat intelligence and best practices, fostering a collective defence approach. Similarly, public-private partnerships can bridge the cybersecurity skills gap by facilitating knowledge transfer and training initiatives. Such collaborations enhance the collective resilience of the cybersecurity ecosystem. Another adaptive approach involves a shift towards a risk-based cybersecurity framework (Melaku, 2023). Prioritizing critical assets and vulnerabilities enables organizations to allocate resources effectively. Additionally, automation and orchestration tools streamline security operations, enabling rapid response and reducing human error. Implementing these frameworks and tools helps organizations adapt to the dynamic threat landscape.

Education and awareness initiatives are crucial in building a cyber-resilient culture. Training programs not only empower employees with cybersecurity knowledge but also cultivate a proactive security mindset (Tolossa, 2023). Additionally, gamification of cybersecurity training enhances engagement and retention of security best practices among staff. A well-informed and vigilant workforce becomes a formidable line of defence against cyber threats. Moreover, the integration of security-by-design principles in the product development lifecycle (PDL) emphasizes embedding security measures from the outset (Casola et al., 2024). Incorporating robust security protocols in IoT devices and cloud services reduces vulnerabilities at the source. Standardization efforts across various platforms and industries further bolster security measures and interoperability.

FUTURE TRENDS AND CONSIDERATIONS

Evolving Threat Landscape

Discussion on the Evolving Nature of Cyber Threats and Their Implications for Logistics

Cyber threats have become increasingly sophisticated and diverse, posing significant challenges to the logistics industry. The nature of these threats is continuously evolving, presenting new risks and implications for logistics operations worldwide (Pandey et al., 2020). The reliance on digital technologies and interconnected systems within the logistics sector has amplified vulnerabilities, making it a prime target for cyber-attacks (Soderi et al., 2023). As logistics heavily depends on data management and automation any breach in cybersecurity can disrupt supply chains, leading to substantial financial losses and reputational damage. One of the critical implications of cyber threats on logistics is the potential disruption of supply chains

(Kendzierskyj et al., 2023). Attackers target supply chain networks to infiltrate and manipulate sensitive data, causing delays in delivery schedules and compromising the integrity of goods. Furthermore, the increased integration of Internet of Things (IoT) devices in logistics introduces new entry points for cyber threats (R. Sharma & Arya, 2022). These interconnected devices, if compromised, can disrupt operations and compromise the safety and security of goods in transit.

Moreover, the evolving nature of cyber threats requires continuous adaptation and investment in cybersecurity measures Companies need to implement robust security protocols, conduct regular risk assessments, and provide employee training to mitigate these risks (Melaku, 2023b). Additionally, collaboration and information sharing among stakeholders within the logistics ecosystem are crucial to combat cyber threats effectively. The implications of cyber threats on logistics extend beyond financial losses; they can impact customer trust and confidence (Tiwari et al., 2023). Customers expect secure and timely delivery of goods, and any disruptions due to cyber-attacks can lead to dissatisfaction and potential loss of clientele. Hence, investing in cybersecurity not only protects the logistics infrastructure but also maintains customer loyalty and satisfaction (Williams et al., 2022). In conclusion, the evolving nature of cyber threats poses significant challenges to the logistics industry, necessitating proactive measures to safeguard against potential disruptions. With the increasing reliance on digital technologies and interconnected systems, securing the logistics infrastructure is paramount to maintaining operational efficiency, protecting sensitive data, and ensuring the smooth flow of goods across supply chains (Aithal, 2023). Figure 9 shows the essential eight cybersecurity maturity model.

Anticipation of Future Challenges and Trends

As the landscape of technology continues to evolve rapidly, the realm of cybersecurity within the logistics sector faces several anticipated challenges and upcoming trends. One of the foremost concerns is the rise of AI-powered cyber-attacks. Artificial intelligence and machine learning, while beneficial for logistics operations, can also be exploited by cybercriminals to launch more sophisticated and adaptive attacks, necessitating advanced defence mechanisms (Schmitt, 2023). Additionally, the proliferation of 5G technology introduces both opportunities and risks for logistics security. While 5G enables faster and more reliable communication, its widespread adoption expands the attack surface, potentially leading to more significant vulnerabilities in the logistics network infrastructure (Salahdine et al., 2023). Securing the diverse endpoints and data transmitted through 5G networks will become imperative to prevent potential breaches.

The Internet of Things (IoT) will continue to play a pivotal role in logistics, but its rapid expansion also amplifies security concerns. The increasing number

Figure 9. The essential eight cybersecurity maturity model
(FocusNet, 2023)

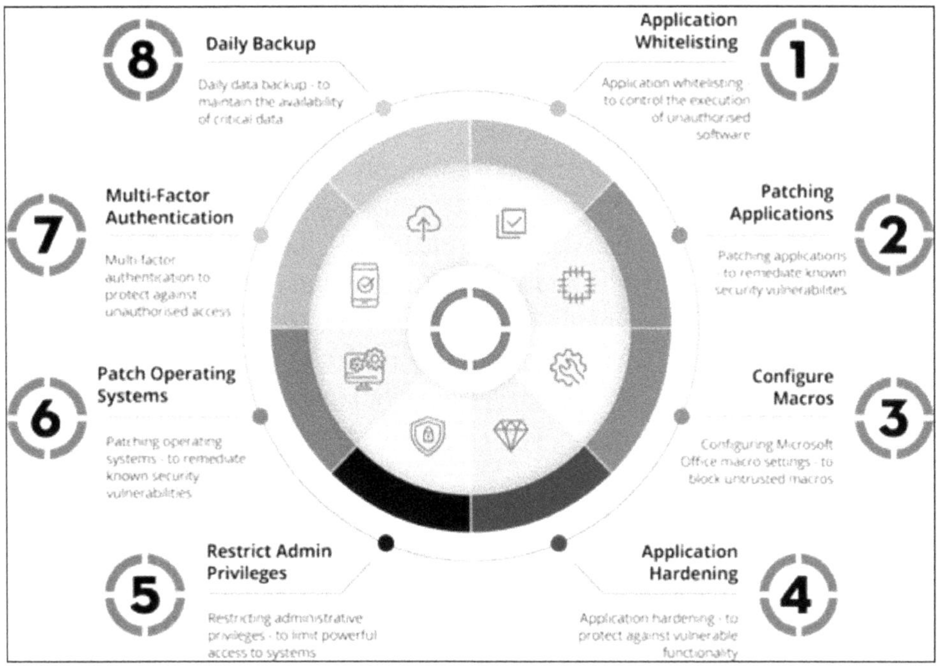

of interconnected devices in logistics operations presents challenges in ensuring their security and protecting against IoT-based cyber-attacks. Strengthening IoT device security protocols and implementing robust encryption measures will be critical to mitigate these risks (N. K. Pandey et al., 2023). Moreover, the growing complexity of supply chain networks, including the incorporation of blockchain technology for enhanced transparency and traceability, poses both opportunities and challenges for cybersecurity (A. Singh et al., 2022). While blockchain can improve data integrity and trust in supply chains, its implementation requires careful consideration of security measures to prevent potential vulnerabilities and cyber threats. Furthermore, the emergence of quantum computing introduces a paradigm shift in cybersecurity (Rasool et al., 2023). While quantum computing holds the promise of solving complex problems more efficiently, it also poses a threat to traditional encryption methods. Thus, the logistics industry must anticipate the need for quantum-resistant encryption to safeguard sensitive data from future quantum-enabled cyber threats. In conclusion, the anticipation of future challenges and trends in cybersecurity for logistics necessitates a proactive approach. As technologies continue to advance, logistics companies must invest in innovative cybersecurity solutions, collaborate with experts, and continually adapt their strategies to mitigate potential risks and ensure the resilience of their operations in the face of evolving cyber threats.

Technological Advancements

Exploration of Upcoming Technologies and Their Potential Impact on Logistics Cybersecurity

Cybersecurity in logistics faces evolving challenges due to rapid technological advancements. Emerging technologies like the Internet of Things (IoT), blockchain, and Artificial Intelligence (AI) offer promising opportunities yet pose significant security concerns (Bothra et al., 2023). The integration of IoT devices into logistics networks enhances operational efficiency but expands the attack surface, increasing vulnerabilities. Blockchain's decentralized ledger system secures data integrity and transparency, yet its adoption in logistics requires addressing scalability and interoperability issues to prevent cyber threats (Ugochukwu et al., 2023). Artificial Intelligence (AI) and Machine Learning (ML) algorithms optimize logistics processes but also present cybersecurity risks (Goel et al., 2022). AI-powered predictive analytics improve decision-making but are susceptible to adversarial attacks, demanding robust defences. Quantum computing's potential threatens conventional encryption methods, urging the development of quantum-resistant security measures in logistics (Kop et al., 2023). Additionally, the adoption of 5G technology enhances connectivity in logistics, yet its vulnerabilities to network breaches necessitate heightened cybersecurity protocols (Jahankhani et al., 2023). The convergence of these technologies amplifies cybersecurity concerns in logistics. Supply chain digitization and the reliance on interconnected systems heighten the risk of cyber threats, including data breaches and ransomware attacks. Ensuring end-to-end encryption, implementing robust authentication protocols, and deploying intrusion detection systems become imperative (Wagner et al., 2023). Collaborative efforts among stakeholders, including logistics companies, technology providers, and regulatory bodies, are crucial in establishing standardized security protocols and frameworks. Continuous investment in research and development is pivotal to innovative adaptive cybersecurity measures. Proactive threat intelligence gathering and analysis are essential for preemptive defence against evolving cyber threats (Dehghantanha et al., 2018). Furthermore, fostering cybersecurity awareness and training among logistics personnel is vital to fortify the human element, often the weakest link in security. Figure 10 shows the benefits of future technology blockchain in the logistics industry.

Figure 10. Benefits of blockchain in the logistics industry
(Burak & Burak, 2024)

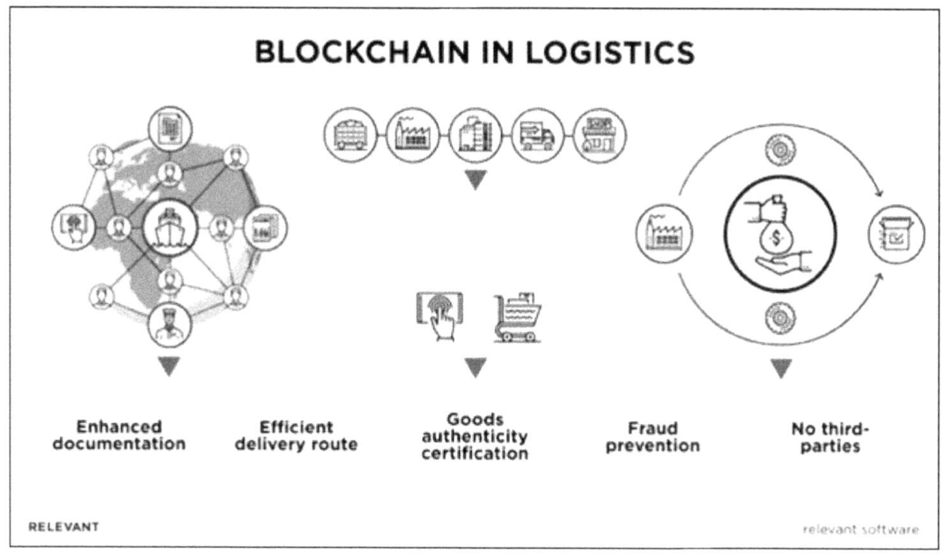

Considerations for Staying Ahead of the Cybersecurity Curve

In the fast-evolving landscape of cybersecurity, staying ahead of potential threats demands proactive measures and constant vigilance. Understanding the dynamics of emerging technologies and their associated risks is fundamental. Regular assessments of vulnerabilities, system weaknesses, and potential entry points for cyber threats are critical. Emphasizing a robust cybersecurity posture involves a multi-layered defence strategy, including encryption, firewalls, and intrusion detection systems (Amro et al., 2023).

Continuous monitoring and real-time threat intelligence gathering are paramount in identifying and responding to evolving cyber threats. Leveraging AI and Machine Learning for anomaly detection and predictive analysis enhances the capability to foresee and prevent potential breaches. Moreover, fostering a culture of cybersecurity awareness and training among employees is indispensable, as human error remains a prevalent factor in security breaches (Jeffrey et al., 2023). Ensuring compliance with evolving regulatory frameworks and industry standards is crucial to mitigate risks. Collaborative partnerships with cybersecurity experts, sharing best practices, and conducting regular audits and simulations of cyber-attack scenarios are effective measures (SL et al., 2023). Establishing incident response plans and conducting drills to test the efficiency of these protocols is essential for a timely and effective response to cyber incidents.

Furthermore, the integration of innovative technologies such as blockchain for secure data transactions and decentralized storage enhances resilience against cyber threats. Quantum-safe encryption methods and post-quantum cryptography are emerging areas that warrant exploration to counter future threats posed by quantum computing (Wynn & Jones, 2023). Maintaining a proactive stance against cyber threats involves constant adaptation and evolution. It requires a holistic approach encompassing technological advancements, robust protocols, employee education, compliance adherence, and industry collaboration. By embracing these considerations and integrating them into cybersecurity strategies, organizations can better position themselves to stay ahead of the cybersecurity curve.

CONCLUSION

Summary of Key Findings

Recapitulation of Key Strategies and Considerations for Securing the Supply Chain in Logistics

Securing the supply chain in logistics demands a multifaceted approach that integrates robust cybersecurity strategies and proactive measures. Key considerations to fortify the supply chain against evolving cyber threats include:

Comprehensive Risk Assessment and Mitigation: Initiating a thorough risk assessment process within logistics operations is crucial. Identifying vulnerabilities and potential threats enables the development of targeted mitigation strategies. Implementing a proactive approach to address risks significantly enhances resilience.

Enhanced Supply Chain Visibility: Heightened visibility across the supply chain is pivotal for cybersecurity. Leveraging advanced technologies and practices for improved traceability ensures early threat detection and prompt response, mitigating potential disruptions.

Rigorous Vendor and Partner Management: Strengthening cybersecurity extends beyond internal measures. Effective assessment and continuous monitoring of vendor cybersecurity posture are essential. Formulating clear contractual agreements that prioritize cybersecurity compliance is fundamental to securing partnerships.

Efficient Incident Response and Recovery Plans: Establishing robust incident response plans is imperative. These plans must encompass swift action protocols to contain threats, minimize downtime, and restore operations efficiently. Timely recovery procedures mitigate the fallout from cyber incidents.

Integration of Advanced Technologies: Embracing advanced authentication methods, stringent access controls, encryption, and emerging technologies like blockchain and AI fortify cybersecurity defences. Implementing these technologies augments data protection and reduces vulnerabilities.

By aligning with regulatory compliance, adhering to industry standards, and learning from successful case studies, logistics entities can fortify their cybersecurity posture. Anticipating future trends, staying abreast of technological advancements, and fostering a culture of vigilance and innovation will be pivotal in sustaining resilient supply chains amidst evolving cyber threats. This comprehensive approach ensures a robust defence mechanism, safeguarding logistics operations against potential cyber adversaries and ensuring continuous, secure, and efficient supply chain management.

Reinforcement of the Importance of Cybersecurity in Maintaining Resilience

Cybersecurity stands as the linchpin in preserving the resilience of logistics operations within the intricate supply chain ecosystem. Its significance cannot be overstated, as it serves as the primary safeguard against multifaceted threats that could jeopardize the continuity and reliability of logistics services. Maintaining resilience in logistics necessitates a robust cybersecurity framework that anticipates, detects, mitigates, and recovers from potential cyber threats. Cybersecurity acts as the bulwark shielding critical infrastructure, sensitive data, and operational functionalities from malicious intrusions, ensuring uninterrupted operations. The interconnected nature of modern logistics amplifies the importance of cybersecurity. As logistics operations increasingly rely on digital platforms, IoT devices, and cloud-based systems, the vulnerability surface expands, making it imperative to fortify defences against evolving cyber threats. Without adequate cybersecurity measures in place, logistics systems become susceptible to disruptions, leading to cascading consequences that permeate the entire supply chain. Moreover, cybersecurity catalyzes building trust among stakeholders. Customers, partners, and suppliers place immense trust in logistics providers to secure their data and uphold the integrity of the supply chain. Maintaining robust cybersecurity not only safeguards sensitive information but also fosters trust and credibility, bolstering relationships and enhancing the reputation of logistics entities in the industry. In conclusion, cybersecurity remains the cornerstone of resilience in logistics. It is not merely a reactive measure but a proactive strategy that underpins the entire operational continuity. By prioritizing cybersecurity, logistics entities fortify their defences, preserve operational resilience, and reinforce trust, thereby ensuring the sustained functionality and reliability of the supply chain in an ever-evolving digital landscape.

Future Outlook

Reflection on the Future Landscape of Cybersecurity in Logistics

The future landscape of cybersecurity in logistics holds both unprecedented challenges and remarkable opportunities, propelled by rapid technological advancements and evolving threat vectors. As logistics operations increasingly integrate digital solutions and emerging technologies, the cybersecurity landscape is set to witness profound transformations. One of the defining facets of the future cybersecurity landscape in logistics is the continuous evolution of cyber threats. The proliferation of interconnected devices, IoT (Internet of Things) sensors, AI-driven systems, and cloud-based platforms will expand the attack surface, offering adversaries new entry points. As a result, logistics entities will confront more sophisticated and targeted cyber threats that demand adaptive, preemptive defence mechanisms. The integration of cutting-edge technologies like blockchain, AI, and machine learning holds promise for fortifying cybersecurity within logistics. Blockchain's immutable and decentralized ledger system can enhance data integrity, supply chain transparency, and secure transactions. AI and machine learning applications are poised to revolutionize threat detection, predictive analytics, and automated response mechanisms, empowering logistics operations with proactive defence capabilities.

However, these technological advancements will also present challenges, particularly concerning the skill gap in cybersecurity expertise and the need for continual adaptation. Logistics organizations will face the critical task of recruiting and nurturing cybersecurity talent capable of navigating the intricacies of emerging technologies and evolving cyber threats. Moreover, regulatory frameworks and compliance standards will undergo refinement to address the dynamic nature of cybersecurity risks within logistics. Stricter regulations and industry standards will compel logistics entities to reassess their cybersecurity strategies, ensuring alignment and adherence to evolving compliance requirements. The future landscape of cybersecurity in logistics demands a proactive and holistic approach. It necessitates investments in innovative technologies, continual education and training, collaboration among industry stakeholders, and a heightened focus on resilience-building measures. In essence, the future of cybersecurity in logistics heralds a paradigm shift toward proactive defence strategies leveraging emerging technologies. Adapting to these changes will be paramount, empowering logistics entities to navigate the evolving threat landscape, fortify cyber defences, and ensure the resilience and security of the global supply chain in the digital era.

Encouragement for Ongoing Vigilance, Adaptation, and Innovation in the Face of Evolving Cyber Threats

In the ever-evolving landscape of cybersecurity, the imperative for ongoing vigilance, adaptation, and innovation cannot be overstated. The dynamic nature of cyber threats demands a steadfast commitment to proactive measures, continuous evolution, and a culture of innovation within logistics operations. Vigilance stands as the first line of defence against the myriad of cyber threats targeting the logistics industry. It necessitates a constant state of awareness, proactive monitoring, and threat intelligence gathering. Remaining vigilant involves staying abreast of emerging threat vectors, understanding evolving attack methodologies, and swiftly adapting to emerging risks. Moreover, adaptation lies at the core of resilience. As cyber threats continue to evolve in sophistication and diversity, the ability to adapt existing cybersecurity strategies and technologies becomes paramount. Logistics entities must remain agile, ready to recalibrate their defence mechanisms and adopt innovative solutions to counter emerging threats effectively.

Furthermore, fostering a culture of innovation is pivotal. Embracing novel technologies, exploring cutting-edge cybersecurity solutions, and investing in research and development initiatives are key elements in staying ahead of cyber adversaries. Innovation breeds resilience, empowering logistics operations to proactively anticipate threats and proactively mitigate risks. Encouraging interdisciplinary collaboration and knowledge sharing is also essential. Engaging diverse expertise, sharing best practices, and participating in collaborative forums enable the collective intelligence needed to combat evolving cyber threats effectively. By fostering a collaborative environment, the industry can strengthen its defences against multifaceted cyber adversaries. In conclusion, the journey toward cybersecurity resilience in logistics hinges upon ongoing vigilance, adaptation, and relentless innovation. Embracing these principles equips logistics entities with the agility and resilience required to navigate the ever-changing threat landscape. By fostering a culture that values vigilance, encourages adaptive strategies, and promotes innovation, the logistics industry can fortify its defences and maintain a robust cybersecurity posture, ensuring the continued security and integrity of global supply chains.

REFERENCES

Abed, A. K., & Anupam, A. (2022). Review of security issues in Internet of Things and artificial intelligence-driven solutions. *Security and Privacy*, *6*(3), e285. doi:10.1002/spy2.285

Abiodun, M. K., Adeniyi, A. E., Victor, A. O., Awotunde, J. B., Atanda, O. G., & Adeniyi, J. K. (2023). Detection and Prevention of Data Leakage in Transit Using LSTM Recurrent Neural Network with Encryption Algorithm. *2023 International Conference on Science, Engineering and Business for Sustainable Development Goals (SEB-SDG)*. IEEE. 10.1109/SEB-SDG57117.2023.10124503

Adetoye, B., & Fong, R. C. (2023). Building a resilient cybersecurity workforce: a multidisciplinary solution to the problem of high turnover of cybersecurity analysts. In Advanced sciences and technologies for security applications (pp. 61–87). Springer. doi:10.1007/978-3-031-20160-8_5

Adeyemo, V. E., Abdullah, A., Jhanjhi, N. Z., Supramaniam, M., & Balogun, A. O. (2019). Ensemble and Deep-Learning Methods for Two-Class and Multi-Attack Anomaly Intrusion Detection: An Empirical study. *International Journal of Advanced Computer Science and Applications*, *10*(9). doi:10.14569/IJACSA.2019.0100969

Afenyo, M., & Caesar, L. D. (2023). Maritime cybersecurity threats: Gaps and directions for future research. *Ocean and Coastal Management*, *236*, 106493. doi:10.1016/j.ocecoaman.2023.106493

Ainslie, S., Thompson, D. G., Maynard, S. B., & Ahmad, A. (2023). Cyber-threat intelligence for security decision-making: A review and research agenda for practice. *Computers & Security*, *132*, 103352. doi:10.1016/j.cose.2023.103352

Aithal, P. S. (2023, June 30). *How to create business value through technological innovations using ICCT Underlying Technologies*. SSRN. https://papers.ssrn.com/sol3/papers.cfm?abstract_id=4541179

AjalaO. A. (2024). Leveraging AI/ML for anomaly detection, threat prediction, and automated response. *Pre Print*. doi:10.20944/preprints202401.0159.v1

Akbar, H. S., Zubair, M., & Malik, M. S. (2023). The Security Issues and challenges in Cloud Computing. *International Journal for Electronic Crime Investigation*, *7*(1), 13–32. doi:10.54692/ijeci.2023.0701125

Al-Dosari, K., & Fetais, N. (2023). Risk-Management Framework and Information-Security Systems for Small and Medium Enterprises (SMEs): A Meta-Analysis Approach. *Electronics (Basel)*, *12*(17), 3629. doi:10.3390/electronics12173629

Al-Hawawreh, M., Alazab, M., Ferrag, M. A., & Hossain, M. S. (2024). Securing the Industrial Internet of Things against ransomware attacks: A comprehensive analysis of the emerging threat landscape and detection mechanisms. *Journal of Network and Computer Applications*, *223*, 103809. doi:10.1016/j.jnca.2023.103809

Al-Wathinani, A. M., Barten, D. G., Borowska-Stefańska, M., Gołda, P., AlDulijan, N. A., Alhallaf, M. A., Samarkandi, L. O., Almuhaidly, A. S., Goniewicz, M., Samarkandi, W. O., & Goniewicz, K. (2023). Driving Sustainable disaster Risk reduction: A rapid review of the policies and strategies in Saudi Arabia. *Sustainability (Basel)*, *15*(14), 10976. doi:10.3390/su151410976

Al-Zubaidie, M., & Shyaa, G. S. (2023). Applying detection leakage on hybrid cryptography to secure transaction information in E-Commerce apps. *Future Internet*, *15*(8), 262. doi:10.3390/fi15080262

Alferidah, D. K., & Jhanjhi, N. Z. (2020). Cybersecurity Impact over Bigdata and IoT Growth. *2020 International Conference on Computational Intelligence (ICCI)*. IEEE. 10.1109/ICCI51257.2020.9247722

Aljohani, A. (2023). Predictive analytics and machine learning for Real-Time supply chain risk mitigation and agility. *Sustainability (Basel)*, *15*(20), 15088. doi:10.3390/su152015088

Alkinani, M. H., Almazroi, A. A., Jhanjhi, N. Z., & Khan, N. A. (2021). 5G and IoT Based Reporting and Accident Detection (RAD) System to Deliver First Aid Box Using Unmanned Aerial Vehicle. *Sensors (Basel)*, *21*(20), 6905. doi:10.3390/s21206905 PMID:34696118

Almoaigel, M. F., & Abuabid, A. (2023). Implementation of Cybersecurity Situation Awareness Model in Saudi SMES. *International Journal of Advanced Computer Science and Applications*, *14*(11). Advance online publication. doi:10.14569/IJACSA.2023.01411110

Almusaylim, Z. A., Jhanjhi, N. Z., & Jung, L. T. (2018). Proposing A Data Privacy Aware Protocol for Roadside Accident Video Reporting Service Using 5G In Vehicular Cloud Networks Environment. *2018 4th International Conference on Computer and Information Sciences (ICCOINS)*. IEEE. 10.1109/ICCOINS.2018.8510588

Alotaibi, S. S., Furnell, S., & He, Y. (2023). Towards a framework for the personalization of cybersecurity awareness. In IFIP advances in information and communication technology (pp. 143–153). Springer. doi:10.1007/978-3-031-38530-8_12

Alqudhaibi, A., Albarrak, M., Aloseel, A., Jagtap, S., & Salonitis, K. (2023). Predicting cybersecurity threats in critical Infrastructure for Industry 4.0: A proactive approach based on attacker motivations. *Sensors (Basel)*, *23*(9), 4539. doi:10.3390/s23094539 PMID:37177743

Alshar'e, M. (2023). Cyber Security Framework Selection: Comparision OF NIST and ISO27001. *Applied Computing Journal*, 245–255. doi:10.52098/acj.202364

Altulaihan, E., Alismail, A., & Frikha, M. (2023). A survey on web application penetration testing. *Electronics (Basel)*, *12*(5), 1229. doi:10.3390/electronics12051229

Álvarez, C., Hinojosa, C., González, S. A., & Rojas, L. (2023). Towards cybersecure maritime supply chains in Latin America and the Caribbean. In Lecture notes in logistics (pp. 425–450). Springer. doi:10.1007/978-3-031-32032-3_19

Amro, A., Gkioulos, V., & Katsikas, S. K. (2023). Assessing Cyber Risk in Cyber-Physical Systems Using the ATT&CK Framework. *ACM Transactions on Privacy and Security*, *26*(2), 1–33. doi:10.1145/3571733

Ananna, F. F., Nowreen, R., Jahwari, S. S. R. A., Costa, E., Angeline, L., & Sindiramutty, S. R. (2023). Analysing Influential factors in student academic achievement: Prediction modelling and insight. *International Journal of Emerging Multidisciplinaries Computer Science & Artificial Intelligence*, *2*(1). doi:10.54938/ijemdcsai.2023.02.1.254

Ananna, F. F., Nowreen, R., Jahwari, S. S. R. A., Costa, E., Angeline, L., & Sindiramutty, S. R. (2023). Analysing Influential factors in student academic achievement: Prediction modelling and insight. *International Journal of Emerging Multidisciplinaries Computer.*

Andreoli, A., Lounis, A., Debbabi, M., & Hanna, A. (2023). On the prevalence of software supply chain attacks: Empirical study and investigative framework. *Forensic Science International Digital Investigation*, *44*, 301508. doi:10.1016/j.fsidi.2023.301508

Apasrawirote, D., & Yawised, K. (2023). The emerging of business resilience plans (BRPs) in dealing with business turbulence. *Management Research Review*, *47*(1), 141–161. doi:10.1108/MRR-04-2022-0273

Apeh, A. J., Hassan, A. O., Oyewole, O. O., Fakeyede, O. G., Okeleke, P. A., & Adaramodu, O. R. (2023). GRC STRATEGIES IN MODERN CLOUD INFRASTRUCTURES: A REVIEW OF COMPLIANCE CHALLENGES. *Computer Science & IT Research Journal*, *4*(2), 111–125. doi:10.51594/csitrj.v4i2.609

Auzina, I., Volkova, T., Noreña-Chavez, D., Kadłubek, M., & Thalassinos, E. (2023). Cyber Incident Response Managerial Approaches for enhancing Small–Medium-Size enterprise's cyber maturity. In Contemporary studies in economic and financial analysis (pp. 175–190). doi:10.1108/S1569-37592023000111A012

Ayala, A. D., Endicott-Popovsky, B., & Hinrichs, R. J. (2023). CyberAlumni a cybersecurity collaboratory. *Journal of the Colloquium for Information Systems Security Education*, *10*(1), 5. doi:10.53735/cisse.v10i1.160

Azam, H., Dulloo, M. I., Majeed, M. H., Wan, J. P. H., Xin, L. T., & Sindiramutty, S. R. (2023). Cybercrime Unmasked: Investigating cases and digital evidence. *International Journal of Emerging Multidisciplinaries Computer Science & Artificial Intelligence*, *2*(1). doi:10.54938/ijemdcsai.2023.02.1.255

Azam, H., Dulloo, M. I., Majeed, M. H., Wan, J. P. H., Xin, L. T., & Sindiramutty, S. R. (2023). Cybercrime Unmasked: Investigating cases and digital evidence. *International Journal of Emerging Multidisciplinaries Computer Science & Artificial Intelligence*, *2*(1). doi:10.54938/ijemdcsai.2023.02.1.255

Azam, H., Dulloo, M. I., Majeed, M. H., Wan, J. P. H., Xin, L. T., Tajwar, M. A., & Sindiramutty, S. R. (2023). Defending the digital Frontier: IDPS and the battle against Cyber threat. *International Journal of Emerging Multidisciplinaries Computer Science & Artificial Intelligence*, *2*(1). doi:10.54938/ijemdcsai.2023.02.1.253

Azam, H., Dulloo, M. I., Majeed, M. H., Wan, J. P. H., Xin, L. T., Tajwar, M. A., & Sindiramutty, S. R. (2023). Defending the digital Frontier: IDPS and the battle against Cyber threat. *International Journal of Emerging Multidisciplinaries Computer Science & Artificial Intelligence*, *2*(1). doi:10.54938/ijemdcsai.2023.02.1.253

Azam, H., Tajwar, M. A., Mayhialagan, S., Davis, A. J., Yik, C. J., Ali, D., & Sindiramutty, S. R. (2023). Innovations in Security: A study of cloud Computing and IoT. *International Journal of Emerging Multidisciplinaries Computer Science & Artificial Intelligence*, *2*(1). doi:10.54938/ijemdcsai.2023.02.1.252

Azam, H., Tajwar, M. A., Mayhialagan, S., Davis, A. J., Yik, C. J., Ali, D., & Sindiramutty, S. R. (2023). Innovations in Security: A study of cloud Computing and IoT. *International Journal of Emerging Multidisciplinaries Computer Science & Artificial Intelligence*, *2*(1). doi:10.54938/ijemdcsai.2023.02.1.252

AzamH.TanM.PinL. T.SyahmiM. A.QianA. L. W.JingyanH.UddinH.SindiramuttyS. R. (2023). Wireless Technology Security and Privacy: A Comprehensive Study. Preprints. doi:10.20944/preprints202311.0664.v1

Azam, H., Tan, M., Pin, L. T., Syahmi, M. A., Qian, A. L. W., Jingyan, H., Uddin, H., & Sindiramutty, S. R. (2023). *Wireless Technology Security and Privacy: A Comprehensive.*

Azzani, I. K., Purwantoro, S. A., & Almubarok, H. Z. (2024). Enhancing awareness of cyber crime: A crucial element in confronting the challenges of hybrid warfare In Indonesia. *Defense and Security Studies*, *5*, 1–9. doi:10.37868/dss.v5.id255

Bandari, V. (2023, January 20). *Enterprise Data Security Measures: A comparative review of effectiveness and risks across different industries and organization types*. TenorsGate. https://research.tensorgate.org/index.php/IJBIBDA/article/view/3

Barongo, O. G., Numfor, S. A., & Kosacka-Olejnik, M. (2023). Modeling a reverse logistics supply Chain for End-of-Life Vehicle Recycling Risk Management: A Fuzzy Risk Analysis approach. *Sustainability (Basel)*, *15*(3), 2142. doi:10.3390/su15032142

Batool, F. (2023, December 31). *Blockchain Empowered Network Security: A Critical analysis of detection Approaches and Innovations*. IJASC. https://ijasc.com/index.php/ijasc/article/view/43

Blind, K., Niebel, C., & Rammer, C. (2023). The impact of the EU General data protection regulation on product innovation. *Industry and Innovation*, 1–41. doi:10.1080/13662716.2023.2271858

BodemerO. (2023). Revolutionizing Worldwide Operations through Blockchain: A Marxian Perspective. *TechRhiv*. doi:10.36227/techrxiv.24006402.v1

Bothra, P., Karmakar, R., Bhattacharya, S., & De, S. (2023). How can applications of blockchain and artificial intelligence improve performance of Internet of Things? – A survey. *Computer Networks*, *224*, 109634. doi:10.1016/j.comnet.2023.109634

Boyes, H. (2015). Cybersecurity and Cyber-Resilient supply chains. *TIM Review*. https://timreview.ca/article/888

BrohiS. N.JhanjhiN. Z.BrohiN. N.BrohiM. N. (2020). Key Applications of State-of-the-Art Technologies to Mitigate and Eliminate COVID-19. TechRxiv. doi:10.36227/techrxiv.12115596.v2

Bruce, G. (2023). Cybersecurity compliance requirements for USA Department of Defense Contractors - Dragons at the gate. In Lecture Notes in Computer Science (pp. 290–308). Springer. doi:10.1007/978-3-031-35822-7_20

Burak, A., & Burak, A. (2024, January 15). *New technology in logistics trends to keep an eye on in 2024*. Relevant Software. https://relevant.software/blog/new-technology-in-logistics-trends/

Carrillo-Torres, D., Díaz, J. P., Cantoral-Ceballos, J. A., & Vargas-Rosales, C. (2023). A novel Multi-Factor authentication algorithm based on image recognition and user established relations. *Applied Sciences (Basel, Switzerland)*, *13*(3), 1374. doi:10.3390/app13031374

Casola, V., De Benedictis, A., Mazzocca, C., & Orbinato, V. (2024). Secure Software Development and Testing: A Model-based Methodology. *Computers & Security*, *137*, 103639. doi:10.1016/j.cose.2023.103639

Ceynowa, W., Przybyłowski, A., Wojtasik, P., & Ciskowski, Ł. (2023). ICT adoption for sustainable logistics development in the HoReCa and wholesale sectors. *Sustainability (Basel)*, *15*(4), 3746. doi:10.3390/su15043746

Chatterjee, P., Das, D., & Rawat, D. B. (2023). Use of Federated Learning and Blockchain towards Securing Financial Services. *arXiv (Cornell University)*. https://doi.org//arxiv.2303.12944 doi:10.48550

Chauhan, M., & Shiaeles, S. (2023). An analysis of cloud security frameworks, problems and proposed solutions. *Network (Bristol, England)*, *3*(3), 422–450. doi:10.3390/network3030018

Chesti, I. A., Humayun, M., Sama, N. U., & Jhanjhi, N. Z. (2020). Evolution, Mitigation, and Prevention of Ransomware. *2020 2nd International Conference on Computer and Information Sciences (ICCIS)*. IEEE. 10.1109/ICCIS49240.2020.9257708

Chindrus, C., & Caruntu, C. F. (2023). Securing the Network: A Red and Blue Cybersecurity Competition case study. *Information (Basel)*, *14*(11), 587. doi:10.3390/info14110587

Chirayath, S. S. (2023). Insider Threats and Strategies to Manage Insider Risk. In SpringerLink. doi:10.1007/978-981-99-5005-8_7

Chowdhury, S., Rodríguez-Espíndola, O., Dey, P. K., & Budhwar, P. (2022). Blockchain technology adoption for managing risks in operations and supply chain management: Evidence from the UK. *Annals of Operations Research*, *327*(1), 539–574. doi:10.1007/s10479-021-04487-1 PMID:35095153

Çınar, B. (2023). Supply chain cybersecurity: Risks, challenges, and strategies for a globalized world. *Journal of Engineering Research and Reports*, *25*(9), 196–210. doi:10.9734/jerr/2023/v25i9993

Clinton, L. (2023). *Fixing American Cybersecurity: Creating a Strategic Public-Private Partnership*. Georgetown University Press.

Cornwell, N., Bilson, C., Gepp, A., Stern, S., & Vanstone, B. J. (2023). Modernising operational risk management in financial institutions via data-driven causal factors analysis: A pre-registered report. *Pacific-Basin Finance Journal*, *77*, 101906. doi:10.1016/j.pacfin.2022.101906

Cyber Threats and Engagements in 2022. (n.d.). DTIC. https://apps.dtic.mil/sti/citations/trecms/AD1208002

Cyberres. (2023). *Advanced Authentication Software & Authentication Framework*. CyberRES. https://www.microfocus.com/en-us/cyberres/identity-access-management/advanced-authentication

D, L., & Tyagi, A. K. (2023). *Privacy preservation and secured data storage in cloud computing*. IGI Global.

Da Silva, R. F., De Andrade Melani, A. H., De Carvalho Michalski, M. Â., & De Souza, G. F. M. (2023). Reliability and risk centered maintenance: A novel method for supporting maintenance management. *Applied Sciences (Basel, Switzerland)*, *13*(19), 10605. doi:10.3390/app131910605

Dai, J. (2023). *Cyber resilience enhancement for microgrid digitalization*. doi:10.32657/10356/171843

Das, T., Harshey, A., Mishra, V., & Srivastava, A. (2023). An Introduction to Biometric Authentication Systems. Springer. doi:10.1007/978-981-99-1377-0_26

Davies, P., Liu, Y., Cooper, M., & Xing, Y. (2022). Supply chains and ecosystems for servitization: A systematic review and future research agenda. *International Marketing Review*, *40*(4), 667–692. doi:10.1108/IMR-10-2021-0318

Deborah, L. J., Vijayakumar, P., Gupta, B. B., & Pelusi, D. (2023). *Secure data management for online learning applications*. CRC Press. doi:10.1201/9781003264538

Dehghantanha, A., Conti, M., & Dargahi, T. (2018). *Cyber Threat intelligence*. Springer. doi:10.1007/978-3-319-73951-9

Dhandabani, L. D., & Tyagi, A. K. (2023). *Privacy preservation and secured data storage in cloud computing*. Engineering Science Reference.

Di Nardo, C. (2022, September 16). *Cybersecurity strategy: what are the key aspects to consider?* DeltalogiX. https://deltalogix.blog/en/2022/09/14/cybersecurity-strategy-what-are-the-key-aspects-to-consider/

Diro, A., Zhang, L., Saini, A., Kaisar, S., & Hiep, P. C. (2024). Leveraging zero knowledge proofs for blockchain-based identity sharing: A survey of advancements, challenges and opportunities. *Journal of Information Security and Applications*, *80*, 103678. doi:10.1016/j.jisa.2023.103678

Diwaker, C., Tomar, P., Solanki, A., Nayyar, A., Jhanjhi, N. Z., Abdullah, A., & Supramaniam, M. (2019). A new model for predicting Component-Based software reliability using soft computing. *IEEE Access : Practical Innovations, Open Solutions*, *7*, 147191–147203. doi:10.1109/ACCESS.2019.2946862

Dorn, T. M. (2023). *U.S. critical infrastructure: Its Importance and Vulnerabilities to Cyber and Unmanned Systems*. Page Publishing Inc.

Duggineni, S. (2023). Data integrity and risk. *Open Journal of Optimization*, *12*(02), 25–33. doi:10.4236/ojop.2023.122003

Evans, R., Hajli, N., & Nisar, T. M. (2022). Privacy-Enhancing factors and Consumer concerns: The moderating effects of the General Data Protection Regulation. *British Journal of Management*, *34*(4), 2075–2092. doi:10.1111/1467-8551.12685

FadhilI. S. M.NizarN.RostamR. J. (2023). Security and Privacy Issues in Cloud Computing. *TEchRIv*. doi:10.36227/techrxiv.23506905.v1

Farah, M. B., Al-Kadri, M. O., Ahmed, Y., Abouzariba, R., & Bellekens, X. (2023). Cyber Incident Scenarios in the Maritime Industry: Risk Assessment and Mitigation Strategies. *2023 IEEE International Conference on Cyber Security and Resilience (CSR)*. IEEE. 10.1109/CSR57506.2023.10224972

Fatima-Tuz-Zahra. Jhanjhi, N. Z., Brohi, S. N., Malik, N. A., & Humayun, M. (2020). Proposing a Hybrid RPL Protocol for Rank and Wormhole Attack Mitigation using Machine Learning. *2020 2nd International Conference on Computer and Information Sciences*. IEEE.

FocusNet. (2023, September 20). *Cyber Security Services*. FocusNet Technology. https://www.focusnet.com.au/cyber-security/

Gao, X., Ye, Y., Gong, S., Chen, L., & Wang, T. (2023a). Empirical patterns of interdependencies among critical infrastructures in cascading disasters: Evidence from a comprehensive multi-case analysis. *International Journal of Disaster Risk Reduction*, *95*, 103862. doi:10.1016/j.ijdrr.2023.103862

Gao, X., Ye, Y., Gong, S., Chen, L., & Wang, T. (2023b). Empirical patterns of interdependencies among critical infrastructures in cascading disasters: Evidence from a comprehensive multi-case analysis. *International Journal of Disaster Risk Reduction*, *95*, 103862. doi:10.1016/j.ijdrr.2023.103862

Gaur, L., Afaq, A., Solanki, A., Singh, G., Sharma, S., Jhanjhi, N. Z., My, H. T., & Le, D. (2021). Capitalizing on big data and revolutionary 5G technology: Extracting and visualizing ratings and reviews of global chain hotels. *Computers & Electrical Engineering*, *95*, 107374. doi:10.1016/j.compeleceng.2021.107374

Gaur, L., Singh, G., Solanki, A., Jhanjhi, N. Z., Bhatia, U., Sharma, S., & Verma, S. Kavita, Petrović, N., Muhammad, F. I., & Kim, W. (2021). Disposition of youth in predicting sustainable development goals using the Neuro - fuzzy and random forest algorithms. *Human-Centric Computing and Information Sciences*. https://repository.usp.ac.fj/12807/

Ghasemshirazi, S., Shirvani, G., & Alipour, M. A. (2023). Zero Trust: applications, challenges, and opportunities. *arXiv (Cornell University)*. https://doi.org//arxiv.2309.03582 doi:10.48550

Ghosh, G., Kavita, Verma, S., Jhanjhi, N. Z., & Talib, M. N. (2020). Secure surveillance system using chaotic image encryption technique. *IOP Conference Series. Materials Science and Engineering*, *993*(1), 012062. doi:10.1088/1757-899X/993/1/012062

Goel, A., Goel, A., & Kumar, A. (2022). The role of artificial neural network and machine learning in utilizing spatial information. *Spatial Information Research*, *31*(3), 275–285. doi:10.1007/s41324-022-00494-x

Goldby, M., & Okonjo, J. (2023). Smart contracts: balancing innovation and consumer protection in insurance law and regulation. Edward Elgar Publishing eBooks. doi:10.4337/9781802205893.00035

Gopi, R., Sathiyamoorthi, V., Selvakumar, S., Ramesh, M., Chatterjee, P., Jhanjhi, N. Z., & Luhach, A. K. (2021). Enhanced method of ANN based model for detection of DDoS attacks on multimedia internet of things. *Multimedia Tools and Applications*, *81*(19), 26739–26757. doi:10.1007/s11042-021-10640-6

Green, C. (2023). Best practices in supplier relationship management and response when supply is disrupted by cyber attack : An incident response framework. *PubMed*, *17*(1), 6–15. https://pubmed.ncbi.nlm.nih.gov/37537763

Hammad, M., Jillani, R., Ullah, S., Namoun, A., Tufail, A., Kim, K., & Shah, H. (2023). Security Framework for Network-Based Manufacturing Systems with Personalized Customization: An Industry 4.0 Approach. *Sensors (Basel)*, *23*(17), 7555. doi:10.3390/s23177555 PMID:37688011

Hause, M., & Kihlström, L. (2022a). Tilting at Windmills: Drivers, risk, opportunity, resilience and the 2021 Texas electricity grid failure. *INCOSE International Symposium*, *32*(1), 545–564. doi:10.1002/iis2.12948

Hause, M., & Kihlström, L. (2022b). Tilting at Windmills: Drivers, risk, opportunity, resilience and the 2021 Texas electricity grid failure. *INCOSE International Symposium*, *32*(1), 545–564. doi:10.1002/iis2.12948

Hegab, H., Shaban, I. S., Jamil, M., & Khanna, N. (2023). Toward sustainable future: Strategies, indicators, and challenges for implementing sustainable production systems. *Sustainable Materials and Technologies*, *36*, e00617. doi:10.1016/j.susmat.2023.e00617

Hotha, K. K. (2023). Unleashing the Power of Innovation in CDMOs through Customer-Centricity and Culture of Service. *American Journal of Industrial and Business Management*, *13*(04), 234–246. doi:10.4236/ajibm.2023.134016

Humayun, M., Alsaqer, M., & Jhanjhi, N. Z. (2022). Energy optimization for smart cities using IoT. *Applied Artificial Intelligence*, *36*(1), 2037255. doi:10.1080/08839514.2022.2037255

Hummer, D., & Byrne, J. M. (2023). *Handbook on crime and technology*. Edward Elgar Publishing. doi:10.4337/9781800886643

Husain, M. S., Faisal, M., Sadia, H., Ahmad, T., & Shukla, S. (2023). *Advances in cyberology and the advent of the Next-Gen information revolution*. IGI Global. doi:10.4018/978-1-6684-8133-2

Hussain, S. J., Ahmed, U., Liaquat, H., Mir, S., Jhanjhi, N. Z., & Humayun, M. (2019). IMIAD: Intelligent Malware Identification for Android Platform. *2019 International Conference on Computer and Information Sciences (ICCIS)*. IEEE. 10.1109/ICCISci.2019.8716471

Iqbal, S. Z. (2023, December 31). *Role of Artificial Intelligence in Enhancing Network Security: A comprehensive analysis*. IJASC. https://ijasc.com/index.php/ijasc/article/view/46

Ismail, A., Hidajat, P. T., Dora, Y. M., Prasatia, F. E., & Pranadani, A. (2023). *Leading the digital transformation: Evidence from Indonesia*. Asadel Publisher.

Jackson, E. (2023). New risks to the missing middle of global meat supply chains. In SAGE Business Cases Originals eBooks. doi:10.4135/9781071920510

Jacob, S. (2023). *The Rapid Increase of Ransomware Attacks Over the 21st Century and Mitigation Strategies to Prevent Them from Arising*.

Jacobs, B. (2023). A comparative study of EU and US regulatory approaches to cybersecurity in space. *Air and Space Law*, *48*(4 /5), 477–492. doi:10.54648/AILA2023052

Jahankhani, H., Kendzierskyj, S., & Hussien, O. (2023). Approaches and methods for regulation of security risks in 5G and 6G. In Advanced sciences and technologies for security applications (pp. 43–70). doi:10.1007/978-3-031-33631-7_2

Jeffrey, N., Tan, Q., & Flecha, J. R. V. (2023). A review of Anomaly detection Strategies to detect Threats to Cyber-Physical Systems. *Electronics (Basel)*, *12*(15), 3283. doi:10.3390/electronics12153283

Jhanjhi, N. Z., Humayun, M., & Almuayqil, S. N. (2021). Cyber security and privacy issues in industrial internet of things. *Computer Systems Science and Engineering*, *37*(3), 361–380. doi:10.32604/csse.2021.015206

Jiang, W. (2024). Cybersecurity Risk and Audit Pricing—A Machine Learning-Based analysis. *Journal of Information Systems*, 1–27. doi:10.2308/ISYS-2023-019

John, F. L., Lakshmi, D., & Kuncharam, M. (2023). *Introduction to the Internet of Things*. Wiley. doi:10.1002/9781119812524.ch1

Juma, M., AlAttar, F., & Touqan, B. (2023). Securing big data integrity for industrial IoT in smart manufacturing based on the Trusted Consortium Blockchain (TCB). *Iot*, *4*(1), 27–55. doi:10.3390/iot4010002

Jussila, A., Mainela, T., & Nätti, S. (2016). Formation of strategic networks under high uncertainty of a megaproject. *Journal of Business and Industrial Marketing*, *31*(5), 575–586. doi:10.1108/JBIM-03-2014-0055

Kamil, Y., Lund, S., & Islam, M. S. (2023). Information security objectives and the output legitimacy of ISO/IEC 27001: Stakeholders' perspective on expectations in private organizations in Sweden. *Information Systems and e-Business Management*, *21*(3), 699–722. doi:10.1007/s10257-023-00646-y

Kendzierskyj, S., Jahankhani, H., Jamal, A., Hussien, O., & Yang, L. (2023). The Role of Blockchain with a Cybersecurity Maturity Model in the Governance of Higher Education Supply Chains. In Advanced sciences and technologies for security applications (pp. 1–35). Springer. doi:10.1007/978-3-031-33627-0_1

Khalil, M. I. (2023, July 15). *Advanced cybersecurity measures in IT service operations and their crucial role in safeguarding enterprise data in a connected world*. Eigen Pub. https://studies.eigenpub.com/index.php/erst/article/view/14

Khan, S. K., Shiwakoti, N., Stasinopoulos, P., & Warren, M. (2023). Cybersecurity regulatory challenges for connected and automated vehicles – State-of-the-art and future directions. *Transport Policy*, *143*, 58–71. doi:10.1016/j.tranpol.2023.09.001

Kilag, O. K. T. (2023, July 13). *Managing cybersecurity Risks in educational technology Environments: Strategies and best practices*. GRN Journal. http://grnjournal.us/index.php/STEM/article/view/357

Kioskli, K., Fotis, T., Nifakos, S., & Mouratidis, H. (2023). The importance of conceptualising the Human-Centric approach in maintaining and promoting Cybersecurity-Hygiene in healthcare 4.0. *Applied Sciences (Basel, Switzerland)*, *13*(6), 3410. doi:10.3390/app13063410

KopM.AboyM.De JongE.GasserU.MinssenT.CohenI. G.BrongersmaM. L.QuintelT. FloridiL.LaflammeR. (2023). Towards responsible quantum technology. *Social Science Research Network*. doi:10.2139/ssrn.4393248

Krishnan, S., Thangaveloo, R., Rahman, S. B. A., & Sindiramutty, S. R. (2021). Smart Ambulance Traffic Control system. *Trends in Undergraduate Research*, *4*(1), c28–c34. doi:10.33736/tur.2831.2021

Krishnan, S., Thangaveloo, R., Rahman, S. B. A., & Sindiramutty, S. R. (2021). Smart Ambulance Traffic Control system. *Trends in Undergraduate Research*, *4*(1), c28–c34. doi:10.33736/tur.2831.2021

Krupitzer, C., & Stein, A. (2023). Unleashing the potential of digitalization in the Agri-Food Chain for integrated food systems. *Annual Review of Food Science and Technology*, *15*(1), annurev-food-012422-024649. doi:10.1146/annurev-food-012422-024649 PMID:37931153

Kumar, B. S. B. (2024). *A comprehensive analysis of key factors causing various kinds of cyber-attacks in higher educational institute's*. https://journalra.org/index.php/jra/article/view/1115

Kumar, T., Pandey, B., Mussavi, S. H., & Jhanjhi, N. Z. (2015). CTHS based energy efficient Thermal Aware Image ALU design on FPGA. *Wireless Personal Communications*, *85*(3), 671–696. doi:10.1007/s11277-015-2801-8

Kumari, S., & Muthulakshmi, P. (2023). *Artificial Intelligence—Blockchain Enabled Technology for Internet of Things*. Wiley. doi:10.1002/9781394213726.ch18

Kumbhare, A., Thakur, P., Patnaik, B. R. K., & Midiyam, K. (2023). Blockchain's data integrity and reliability. In Advances in business information systems and analytics book series (pp. 231–250). Springer. doi:10.4018/978-1-6684-7808-0.ch013

Li, C. (2024, January 4). *Graph Neural Networks for Tabular Data Learning: A Survey with Taxonomy and Directions*. arXiv.org. https://arxiv.org/abs/2401.02143

Li, J. H., Herdem, M. S., Nathwani, J., & Wen, J. Z. (2023). Methods and applications for Artificial Intelligence, Big Data, Internet of Things, and Blockchain in smart energy management. *Energy and AI*, *11*, 100208. doi:10.1016/j.egyai.2022.100208

Li, S., Zhou, T., Yang, H., & Wang, P. (2023). Blockchain-Based Secure Storage and Access Control Scheme for Supply Chain Ecological Business Data: A Case study of the Automotive industry. *Sensors (Basel)*, *23*(16), 7036. doi:10.3390/s23167036 PMID:37631574

Lim, M., Abdullah, A., Jhanjhi, N. Z., & Khan, M. K. (2020). Situation-Aware Deep Reinforcement Learning link Prediction model for evolving criminal networks. *IEEE Access : Practical Innovations, Open Solutions*, *8*, 16550–16559. doi:10.1109/ACCESS.2019.2961805

Lin, B., & Lin, B. (2023). Constructing an adaptability evaluation framework for community-based disaster management using an earthquake event. *International Journal of Disaster Risk Reduction*, *93*, 103774. doi:10.1016/j.ijdrr.2023.103774

Lin, Q., Li, X., Cai, K., Mohan, P., & Paulraj, D. (2024). Secure Internet of Medical Things (IoMT) based on ECMQV-MAC Authentication Protocol and EKMC-SCP Blockchain Networking. *Information Sciences*, *654*, 119783. doi:10.1016/j.ins.2023.119783

Liu, Y., Ma, X., Qiao, W., Ma, L., & Han, B. (2024). A novel methodology to model disruption propagation for resilient maritime transportation systems–a case study of the Arctic maritime transportation system. *Reliability Engineering & System Safety*, *241*, 109620. doi:10.1016/j.ress.2023.109620

Lorenz-Meyer, F., & Santos, V. (2023). Blockchain in the shipping industry: A proposal for the use of blockchain for SMEs in the maritime industry. *Procedia Computer Science*, *219*, 807–814. doi:10.1016/j.procs.2023.01.354

Lyons, V., & Fitzgerald, T. (2023). *The privacy leader Compass: A Comprehensive Business-Oriented Roadmap for Building and Leading Practical Privacy Programs*. CRC Press. doi:10.1201/9781003383017

Machin, D. (2022, April 16). *Cyber security and operational resilience*. Berkeley Partnership. https://www.berkeleypartnership.com/news-and-insights/insights/cyber-security-and-operational-resilience

Madavarapu, J. B., Yalamanchili, R. K., & Mandhala, V. N. (2023). *An Ensemble Data Security on Cloud Healthcare Systems*. IEEE. doi:10.1109/ICOSEC58147.2023.10276231

Madhira, N., Pelletier, J. M., Johnson, D., & Mishra, S. (2023). Code red: A nuclear nightmare-navigating ransomware response at an Eastern European power plant. *Journal of Information Technology Teaching Cases, 204388692311559*. doi:10.1177/20438869231155934

Magableh, G. M., & Mistarihi, M. Z. (2023). Global Supply Chain Nervousness (GSCN). *Sustainability (Basel), 15*(16), 12115. doi:10.3390/su151612115

Maghsoudi, A., Harpring, R., Piotrowicz, W., & Kedziora, D. (2023). Digital technologies for cash and voucher assistance in disasters: A cross-case analysis of benefits and risks. *International Journal of Disaster Risk Reduction, 96*, 103827. doi:10.1016/j.ijdrr.2023.103827

Manners-Bell, J. (2020a). *Supply chain Risk management: How to Design and Manage Resilient Supply Chains*. Kogan Page Publishers.

Manners-Bell, J. (2020b). *Supply chain Risk management: How to Design and Manage Resilient Supply Chains*. Kogan Page Publishers.

Manners-Bell, J. (2020c). *Supply chain Risk management: How to Design and Manage Resilient Supply Chains*. Kogan Page Publishers.

Marassi, L., & Marrone, S. (2023). What would happen if hackers attacked the railways? Consideration of the need for ethical codes in the railway transport systems. In Smart innovation, systems and technologies (pp. 289–296). Springer. doi:10.1007/978-981-99-3592-5_27

Melaku, H. M. (2023a). Context-Based and Adaptive Cybersecurity Risk Management Framework. *Risks, 11*(6), 101. doi:10.3390/risks11060101

Melaku, H. M. (2023b). A dynamic and adaptive cybersecurity governance framework. *Journal of Cybersecurity and Privacy, 3*(3), 327–350. doi:10.3390/jcp3030017

Miadzvetskaya, Y. (2023, May 10). *Data Governance Act: on International Transfers of Non-Personal Data and GDPR Mimesis*. SSRN. https://papers.ssrn.com/sol3/papers.cfm?abstract_id=4444051

Mızrak, F. (2023a). Integrating cybersecurity risk management into strategic management: a comprehensive literature review. *Journal of Business, Economics and Finance*. doi:10.17261/Pressacademia.2023.1807

Mızrak, F. (2023b). Managing Risks And Crises In The Logistics Sector: A Comprehensive Analysis Of Strategies And Prioritization Using Ahp Method. *Meriç Uluslararası Sosyal Ve Stratejik Araştırmalar Dergisi, 7*(Özel Sayı), 114–148. doi:10.54707/meric.1335033

Möller, D. P. F. (2023). Ransomware Attacks and Scenarios: Cost Factors and Loss of Reputation. Springer. doi:10.1007/978-3-031-26845-8_6

More, P., & Sakhare, S. (2023). Context-Aware device classification and clustering for smarter and secure connectivity in internet of things. *EAI Endorsed Transactions on Industrial Networks and Intelligent Systems*, *10*(3), e5. doi:10.4108/eetinis.v10i3.3874

Mostafa, A. M., Ezz, M., Elbashir, M. K., Alruily, M., Hamouda, E., Alsarhani, M., & Said, W. (2023). Strengthening cloud security: An innovative Multi-Factor Multi-Layer authentication framework for cloud user authentication. *Applied Sciences (Basel, Switzerland)*, *13*(19), 10871. doi:10.3390/app131910871

Musa, H., Krichen, M., Altun, A. A., & Ammi, M. (2023). Survey on Blockchain-Based Data Storage Security for Android Mobile Applications. *Sensors (Basel)*, *23*(21), 8749. doi:10.3390/s23218749 PMID:37960449

Muzammal, S. M., Murugesan, R. K., Jhanjhi, N. Z., & Jung, L. T. (2020). SMTrust: Proposing Trust-Based Secure Routing Protocol for RPL Attacks for IoT Applications. *2020 International Conference on Computational Intelligence (ICCI)*. Springer. 10.1109/ICCI51257.2020.9247818

Nguyen, D. K., Sermpinis, G., & Stasinakis, C. (2022). Big data, artificial intelligence and machine learning: A transformative symbiosis in favour of financial technology. *European Financial Management*, *29*(2), 517–548. doi:10.1111/eufm.12365

Nikose, A., & Srinivas, K. (2023). TRO-CP-ABE: A secure and flexible layer with traceability and easy revocation in ciphertext-policy attribute-based encryption. *International Journal of Internet Technology and Secured Transactions*, *13*(2), 196. doi:10.1504/IJITST.2023.129585

Ntizikira, E., Wang, L., Alblehai, F., Saleem, K., & Lodhi, M. A. (2023). Secure and Privacy-Preserving intrusion detection and prevention in the internet of unmanned aerial vehicles. *Sensors (Basel)*, *23*(19), 8077. doi:10.3390/s23198077 PMID:37836907

Ntizikira, E., Wang, L., Chen, J., & Saleem, K. (2024). Honey-block: Edge assisted ensemble learning model for intrusion detection and prevention using defense mechanism in IoT. *Computer Communications*, *214*, 1–17. doi:10.1016/j.comcom.2023.11.023

O'Donnell, S., Quigley, E., Hayden, J., Adamis, D., Gavin, B., & McNicholas, F. (2022). Psychological distress among healthcare workers post COVID-19 pandemic: From the resilience of individuals to healthcare systems. *Irish Journal of Psychological Medicine*, *40*(3), 508–512. doi:10.1017/ipm.2022.35 PMID:35938227

OladoyinboT. O.AdebiyiO. O.UgonniaJ. C.OlaniyiO. A.OkunleyeO. J. (2023). Evaluating and establishing baseline security requirements in cloud computing: an enterprise Risk Management approach. *Social Science Research Network*. doi:10.2139/ssrn.4612909

Olaniyi, O. O., Asonze, C. U., Ajayi, S. S., Olabanji, S., & Adigwe, C. S. (2023). A Regressional Study on the Impact of Organizational Security Culture and Transformational Leadership on Social Engineering Awareness among Bank Employees: The Interplay of Security Education and Behavioral Change. *Asian Journal of Economics. Business and Accounting*, *23*(23), 128–143. doi:10.9734/ajeba/2023/v23i231176

Omotunde, H., & Ahmed, M. (2023). A Comprehensive Review of Security Measures in Database Systems: Assessing Authentication, Access Control, and Beyond. *Mesopotamian*, 115–133. doi:10.58496/MJCSC/2023/016

Özkan, A., & Tüysüzoğlu, G. (2023). *Security studies: Classic to Post-Modern Approaches*. Rowman & Littlefield.

Pandey, N. K., Kumar, K., Saini, G., & Mishra, A. K. (2023). Security issues and challenges in cloud of things-based applications for industrial automation. *Annals of Operations Research*. doi:10.1007/s10479-023-05285-7 PMID:37361100

Pandey, S., Singh, R. K., Gunasekaran, A., & Kaushik, A. (2020). Cyber security risks in globalized supply chains: Conceptual framework. *Journal of Global Operations and Strategic Sourcing*, *13*(1), 103–128. doi:10.1108/JGOSS-05-2019-0042

Panyushkina, E. (2023). Modern challenges of the digital ecosystem of transport and logistics. *E3S Web of Conferences, 383*, 03008. doi:10.1051/e3sconf/202338303008

Parker, M. I. (2023). Managing threats to health data and information: toward security. Elsevier. doi:10.1016/B978-0-323-90802-3.00016-2

Pattnaik, M., & Shah, T. (2023). Role of Big Data to Boost Corporate Decision Making. *2023 2nd International Conference on Edge Computing and Applications (ICECAA)*. Springer. 10.1109/ICECAA58104.2023.10212179

Peng, Y., Welden, N., & Renaud, F. G. (2023). A framework for integrating ecosystem services indicators into vulnerability and risk assessments of deltaic social-ecological systems. *Journal of Environmental Management*, *326*, 116682. doi:10.1016/j.jenvman.2022.116682 PMID:36375428

Posamentier, J., Seibel, K., & DyTang, N. (2022). Preventing Youth Suicide: A Review of School-Based Practices and How Social–Emotional Learning Fits into Comprehensive efforts. *Trauma, Violence & Abuse*, *24*(2), 746–759. doi:10.1177/15248380211039475 PMID:35139714

Poudel, S., Arafat, M. Y., & Moh, S. (2023). Bio-Inspired Optimization-Based Path Planning Algorithms in Unmanned Aerial Vehicles: A survey. *Sensors (Basel)*, *23*(6), 3051. doi:10.3390/s23063051 PMID:36991762

Pour, M. S., Nader, C., Friday, K., & Bou-Harb, E. (2023). A comprehensive survey of recent internet measurement techniques for cyber security. *Computers & Security*, *128*, 103123. doi:10.1016/j.cose.2023.103123

Puspita, N. Y., & Boydston, N. G. W. P. (2023). Framing the responsibility of Public-Private Partnerships (PPPs) on space technology in international law. *Padjadjaran Journal of International Law*, *7*(2), 172–192. doi:10.23920/pjil.v7i2.1352

Qureshi, K. N., O'Keeffe, G., O'Farrell, S., & Costelloe, G. (2023). Cybersecurity Standards and Policies for CPS in IOE. In Internet of things (pp. 177–192). doi:10.1007/978-3-031-45162-1_11

Rahman, M. A., Wuest, T., & Shafae, M. (2023). Manufacturing cybersecurity threat attributes and countermeasures: Review, meta-taxonomy, and use cases of cyberattack taxonomies. *Journal of Manufacturing Systems*, *68*, 196–208. doi:10.1016/j.jmsy.2023.03.009

Rajkumar, V. S., Ştefanov, A., Presekal, A., Pálenský, P., & Rueda, J. L. (2023). Cyber Attacks on power grids: Causes and propagation of cascading failures. *IEEE Access : Practical Innovations, Open Solutions*, *11*, 103154–103176. doi:10.1109/ACCESS.2023.3317695

Ramadhianto, R., Toruan, T. S. L., Kertopati, S. N. H., & Almubaroq, H. Z. (2023). Analysis of presidential regulations concerning cyber security to bolster defense policy management. *Defense and Security Studies*, *4*, 84–93. doi:10.37868/dss.v4.id244

RaneN.ChoudharyS.RaneJ. (2023a). Blockchain and Artificial Intelligence (AI) integration for revolutionizing security and transparency in finance. *Social Science Research Network*. doi:10.2139/ssrn.4644253

Rane, N., Choudhary, S., & Rane, J. (2023b). *Leading-edge Artificial Intelligence (AI), Machine Learning (ML), Blockchain, and Internet of Things (IoT) technologies for enhanced wastewater treatment systems*. Social Science Research Network. doi:10.2139/ssrn.4641557

RasoolR. U.AhmadH. F.RafiqueW.QayyumA.QadirJ.AnwarZ. (2023). Quantum Computing for Healthcare: A Review. TechRxiv. doi:10.36227/techrxiv.17198702.v4

Rawindaran, N., Nawaf, L., Alarifi, S., Alghazzawi, D., Carroll, F., Katib, I., & Hewage, C. (2023). Enhancing Cyber Security Governance and Policy for SMEs in Industry 5.0: A Comparative Study between Saudi Arabia and the United Kingdom. *Digital*, *3*(3), 200–231. doi:10.3390/digital3030014

Razak, G. M., Hendry, L., & Stevenson, M. (2021). Supply chain traceability: A review of the benefits and its relationship with supply chain resilience. *Production Planning and Control*, *34*(11), 1114–1134. doi:10.1080/09537287.2021.1983661

Rebe, N. (2023). *Regulating Cyber Technologies: Privacy vs security*. World Scientific. doi:10.1142/q0379

Rehman, Z., Gondal, I., Ge, M., Dong, H., Gregory, M. A., & Tari, Z. (2024). Proactive Defense Mechanism: Enhancing IoT Security through Diversity-based Moving Target Defense and Cyber Deception. *Computers & Security*, *103685*, 103685. doi:10.1016/j.cose.2023.103685

Reyes, P. (2023). Radio Frequency identification (RFID) and supply chain management. Springer. doi:10.1007/978-3-030-89822-9_109-1

Ribeiro, R., Mateus-Coelho, N., & Mamede, H. S. (2023). Improving social engineering resilience in enterprises. *ARIS2 - Advanced Research on Information Systems Security, 3*(1), 34–65. doi:10.56394/aris2.v3i1.30

Rivera, A. D. T., Mendoza-Becerril, M. A., & Pereira, V. A. (2023). The Resilience of the Renewable Energy Electromobility Supply Chain: Review and Trends. *Sustainability (Basel)*, *15*(14), 10838. doi:10.3390/su151410838

Rizvi, S. S., Zwerling, T., Thompson, B., Faiola, S., Campbell, S., Fisanick, S., & Hutnick, C. (2023). A modular framework for auditing IoT devices and networks. *Computers & Security*, *132*, 103327. doi:10.1016/j.cose.2023.103327

Saah, A. E. N., Yee, J., & Choi, J. M. (2023). Securing Construction Workers' Data Security and Privacy with Blockchain Technology. *Applied Sciences (Basel, Switzerland)*, *13*(24), 13339. doi:10.3390/app132413339

Saeed, S., Altamimi, S. A., Alkayyal, N. A., Alshehri, E., & Alabbad, D. A. (2023). Digital Transformation and Cybersecurity Challenges for businesses Resilience: Issues and recommendations. *Sensors (Basel)*, *23*(15), 6666. doi:10.3390/s23156666 PMID:37571451

Safitra, M. F., Lubis, M., & Fakhrurroja, H. (2023a). Counterattacking Cyber Threats: A framework for the Future of Cybersecurity. *Sustainability (Basel)*, *15*(18), 13369. doi:10.3390/su151813369

Safitra, M. F., Lubis, M., & Fakhrurroja, H. (2023b). Counterattacking Cyber Threats: A framework for the Future of Cybersecurity. *Sustainability (Basel)*, *15*(18), 13369. doi:10.3390/su151813369

Salahdine, F., Han, T., & Zhang, N. (2023). 5G, 6G, and Beyond: Recent advances and future challenges. *Annales des Télécommunications*, *78*(9–10), 525–549. doi:10.1007/s12243-022-00938-3

Sankar, S., Ramasubbareddy, S., Luhach, A. K., Deverajan, G. G., Alnumay, W. S., Jhanjhi, N. Z., Ghosh, U., & Sharma, P. K. (2020). Energy efficient optimal parent selection based routing protocol for Internet of Things using firefly optimization algorithm. *Transactions on Emerging Telecommunications Technologies*, *32*(8), e4171. doi:10.1002/ett.4171

Saranya, P., & Maheswari, R. (2023). Proof of Transaction (POTX) based traceability system for an agriculture supply chain. *IEEE Access : Practical Innovations, Open Solutions*, *11*, 10623–10638. doi:10.1109/ACCESS.2023.3240772

Sarkar, B. D., Shankar, R., & Kar, A. K. (2022). Port logistic issues and challenges in the Industry 4.0 era for emerging economies: An India perspective. *Benchmarking*, *30*(1), 50–74. doi:10.1108/BIJ-08-2021-0499

Saxena, U. R., & Alam, T. (2023). Provisioning trust-oriented role-based access control for maintaining data integrity in cloud. *International Journal of Systems Assurance Engineering and Management*, *14*(6), 2559–2578. doi:10.1007/s13198-023-02112-x

Schmitt, M. (2023). Securing the digital world: Protecting smart infrastructures and digital industries with artificial intelligence (AI)-enabled malware and intrusion detection. *Journal of Industrial Information Integration*, *36*, 100520. doi:10.1016/j.jii.2023.100520

Sharifi, A. (2023). Resilience of urban social-ecological-technological systems (SETS): A review. *Sustainable Cities and Society*, *99*, 104910. doi:10.1016/j.scs.2023.104910

Sharma, A., Bhatia, T., Singh, R., & Sharma, A. (2023). Developing the framework of blockchain-enabled agri-food supply chain. *Business Process Management Journal*. doi:10.1108/BPMJ-01-2023-0035

Sharma, R., & Arya, R. (2022). Security threats and measures in the Internet of Things for smart city infrastructure: A state of art. *Transactions on Emerging Telecommunications Technologies*, *34*(11), e4571. doi:10.1002/ett.4571

Sheik, A. T., Maple, C., Epiphaniou, G., & Dianati, M. (2023). Securing Cloud-Assisted connected and Autonomous Vehicles: An In-Depth threat Analysis and risk assessment. *Sensors (Basel)*, *24*(1), 241. doi:10.3390/s24010241 PMID:38203103

Shinde, A. (2021). *Introduction to cyber security: Guide to the World of Cyber Security*. Notion Press.

Shirsat, A., Muthukaruppan, V., Hu, R., Paduani, V., Xu, B., Song, L., Li, Y., Liu, N., Baran, M., Lubkeman, D., & Tang, W. (2023). A secure and adaptive hierarchical Multi-Timescale framework for resilient load restoration using a community microgrid. *IEEE Transactions on Sustainable Energy*, *14*(2), 1057–1075. doi:10.1109/TSTE.2023.3251099

Shishodia, A., Sharma, R., Rajesh, R., & Munim, Z. H. (2021). Supply chain resilience: A review, conceptual framework and future research. *International Journal of Logistics Management*, *34*(4), 879–908. doi:10.1108/IJLM-03-2021-0169

Shukur, B. S., Aljanabi, M., & Ali, A. H. (2023). ChatGPT: Exploring the Role of Cybersecurity in the Protection of Medical Information. *Journals. Mesopotamian. Press*, 18–21. doi:10.58496/MJCS/2023/004

Siavvas, M., Tsoukalas, D., Kalouptsoglou, I., Manganopoulou, E., Manolis, G. D., Kehagias, D., & Tzovaras, D. (2023). Security Monitoring during Software Development: An Industrial Case Study. *Applied Sciences (Basel, Switzerland)*, *13*(12), 6872. doi:10.3390/app13126872

Sindiramutty, S. R. (2023). Autonomous Threat Hunting: a future paradigm for AI-Driven Threat intelligence. *arXiv (Cornell University)*. https://doi.org//arxiv.2401.00286 doi:10.48550

Sindiramutty, S. R. (2023). Autonomous Threat Hunting: a future paradigm for AI-Driven Threat intelligence. *arXiv (Cornell University)*. https://doi.org//arxiv.2401.00286 doi:10.48550

Sindiramutty, S. R., Jhanjhi, N. Z., Ray, S. K., Jazri, H., Khan, N. A., & Gaur, L. (2024). Metaverse: Virtual Meditation. In Metaverse Applications for Intelligent Healthcare (pp. 93–158). IGI Global. doi:10.4018/978-1-6684-9823-1.ch003

Sindiramutty, S. R., Jhanjhi, N. Z., Ray, S. K., Jazri, H., Khan, N. A., Gaur, L., Gharib, A., & Manchuri, A. R. (2024a). Metaverse: Virtual Gyms and Sports. In Metaverse Applications for Intelligent Healthcare (pp. 24–92). IGI Global. doi:10.4018/978-1-6684-9823-1.ch003

Singh, A., Gutub, A., Nayyar, A., & Khan, M. K. (2022). Redefining food safety traceability system through blockchain: Findings, challenges and open issues. *Multimedia Tools and Applications*, *82*(14), 21243–21277. doi:10.1007/s11042-022-14006-4 PMID:36276604

Singh, R. K., Mishra, R., Gupta, S., & Mukherjee, A. A. (2023). Blockchain applications for secured and resilient supply chains: A systematic literature review and future research agenda. *Computers & Industrial Engineering*, *175*, 108854. doi:10.1016/j.cie.2022.108854

Singhal, V., Jain, S. P., Anand, D., Singh, A., Verma, S., Kavita, Rodrigues, J. J. P. C., Jhanjhi, N. Z., Ghosh, U., Jo, O., & Iwendi, C. (2020). Artificial Intelligence Enabled Road Vehicle-Train Collision Risk Assessment Framework for Unmanned railway level crossings. *IEEE Access : Practical Innovations, Open Solutions*, *8*, 113790–113806. doi:10.1109/ACCESS.2020.3002416

SL. S. D., MV, M. K., Prashanth, B., & Y, V. S. M. (2023). Malware analysis and intrusion detection in Cyber-Physical systems. IGI Global.

Soderi, S., Masti, D., & Lun, Y. Z. (2023). Railway Cyber-Security in the Era of Interconnected Systems: A survey. *IEEE Transactions on Intelligent Transportation Systems*, *24*(7), 6764–6779. doi:10.1109/TITS.2023.3254442

Soumpenioti, V., & Panagopoulos, A. (2023). AI Technology in the Field of Logistics. *2023 18th International Workshop on Semantic and Social Media Adaptation & Personalization*. IEEE. 10.1109/SMAP59435.2023.10255203

Steen, R., Haug, O. J., & Patriarca, R. (2023). Business continuity and resilience management: A conceptual framework. *Journal of Contingencies and Crisis Management*. doi:10.1111/1468-5973.12501

Strand, S. S. (2023). *An investigation into cyber security risk mitigation and the human factor in developing a cyber security culture - A comparative analysis of two maritime companies in Norway*. Open Archive. https://openarchive.usn.no/usn-xmlui/handle/11250/3076275

StraußS. (2023). The body as permanent digital identity? Societal and ethical implications of biometrics as mainstream technology. tecnoscienza.unibo.it. doi:10.6092/issn.2038-3460/17611

Suhandiah, S., Suhariadi, F., Yulianti, P., & Abbas, A. (2023). Autonomy and feedback on innovative work behavior: The role of resilience as a mediating factor in Indonesian Islamic banks. *Cogent Business & Management*, *10*(1), 2178364. doi:10.1080/23311975.2023.2178364

Sun, N., Zhu, C., Zhang, Y., & Liu, Y. (2023). An Identity Privacy-Preserving Scheme against Insider Logistics Data Leakage Based on One-Time-Use Accounts. *Future Internet*, *15*(11), 361. doi:10.3390/fi15110361

Susha, I., Rukanova, B., Zuiderwijk, A., Gil-García, J. R., & Gascó-Hernández, M. (2023). Achieving voluntary data sharing in cross sector partnerships: Three partnership models. *Information and Organization*, *33*(1), 100448. doi:10.1016/j.infoandorg.2023.100448

Sutradhar, S., Karforma, S., Bose, R., Roy, S., Djebali, S., & Bhattacharyya, D. (2024). Enhancing identity and access management using Hyperledger Fabric and OAuth 2.0: A block-chain-based approach for security and scalability for healthcare industry. *Internet of Things and Cyber-Physical Systems*, *4*, 49–67. doi:10.1016/j.iotcps.2023.07.004

T, V. K., Rajasekaran, P., Jeevika, L., Lavan, S., & Tharshan, R. (2023). Data Preservation in Chatbot with Cloud Deployment. *2023 7th International Conference on Trends in Electronics and Informatics (ICOEI)*. IEEE. doi:10.1109/ICOEI56765.2023.10125731

Talluri, S., Kull, T., Yíldíz, H., & Yoon, J. (2013). Assessing the efficiency of risk mitigation strategies in supply chains. *Journal of Business Logistics*, *34*(4), 253–269. doi:10.1111/jbl.12025

Teffandi, N., Feryputri, N. A., Hasanuddin, M. O., Syafalni, I., & Sutisna, N. (2023). GRAIN Algorithm Implementation for Lightweight Hardware-Based OTP Authentication. *2023 International Conference on Electrical Engineering and Informatics (ICEEI)*. IEEE. 10.1109/ICEEI59426.2023.10346638

Telo, J. (2017, January 17). *AI for Enhanced Healthcare Security: An Investigation of Anomaly Detection, Predictive Analytics, Access Control, Threat Intelligence, and Incident Response*. https://research.tensorgate.org/index.php/JAAHM/article/view/16

Thomas, G., & Sule, M. (2022). A service lens on cybersecurity continuity and management for organizations' subsistence and growth. *Organizational Cybersecurity Journal*, *3*(1), 18–40. doi:10.1108/OCJ-09-2021-0025

Tiwari, S., Sharma, P., Choi, T., & Lim, A. (2023). Blockchain and third-party logistics for global supply chain operations: Stakeholders' perspectives and decision roadmap. *Transportation Research Part E, Logistics and Transportation Review, 170*, 103012. doi:10.1016/j.tre.2022.103012

Tolossa, D. (2023). Importance of cybersecurity awareness training for employees in business. *VIDYA - a JOURNAL OF GUJARAT UNIVERSITY, 2*(2), 104–107. doi:10.47413/vidya.v2i2.206

Ugochukwu, N. A., Goyal, S. B., Rajawat, A. S., Verma, C., & Illés, Z. (2023). Enhancing Logistics with The Internet of Things: A Secured and Efficient Distribution and Storage Model Utilizing Blockchain Innovations and Interplanetary File System. *IEEE Access : Practical Innovations, Open Solutions, 1*. doi:10.1109/ACCESS.2023.3339754

Valashiya, M. C., & Luke, R. (2022). Enhancing supply chain information sharing with third party logistics service providers. *International Journal of Logistics Management, 34*(6), 1523–1542. doi:10.1108/IJLM-11-2021-0522

Wagner, E., Heye, D., Serror, M., Kunze, I., Wehrle, K., & Henze, M. (2023). *MADTLS: Fine-grained middlebox-aware end-to-end security for industrial communication. arXiv*. Cornell University., doi:10.1145/3634737.3637640

Wallis, T., & Dorey, P. (2023). Implementing partnerships in energy supply chain cybersecurity resilience. *Energies, 16*(4), 1868. doi:10.3390/en16041868

Weippl, E., & Schrittwieser, S. (2023). Introduction to Security and Privacy. In SpringerLink (pp. 397–414). doi:10.1007/978-3-031-45304-5_26

WensveenJ. G. (2023). *Air transportation*. doi:10.4324/9780429346156

Windapo, A., & Chiswanda, F. (2023). Perspectives of severity in the choice of risk management techniques. *E3S Web of Conferences, 409*, 03016. doi:10.1051/e3sconf/202340903016

Wipro. (n.d.). *Importance of cybersecurity in the manufacturing industry*. WiPro. https://www.wipro.com/cybersecurity/cybersecurity-in-the-manufacturing-industry/

Wu, X., Du, Y., Fan, T., Guo, J., Ren, J., Wu, R., & Zheng, T. (2022a). Threat analysis for space information network based on network security attributes: A review. *Complex & Intelligent Systems, 9*(3), 3429–3468. doi:10.1007/s40747-022-00899-z

Wu, X., Du, Y., Fan, T., Guo, J., Ren, J., Wu, R., & Zheng, T. (2022b). Threat analysis for space information network based on network security attributes: A review. *Complex & Intelligent Systems, 9*(3), 3429–3468. doi:10.1007/s40747-022-00899-z

Wylde, V., Prakash, E., Hewage, C., & Platts, J. (2023). Ethical challenges in the use of digital technologies: AI and big data. In Advanced sciences and technologies for security applications (pp. 33–58). Springer. doi:10.1007/978-3-031-09691-4_3

Wynn, M. G., & Jones, P. (2023). Corporate digital responsibility and the business implications of quantum computing. *Advances in Environmental and Engineering Research*, *04*(04), 1–15. doi:10.21926/aeer.2304053

Yeboah-Ofori, A., & Opoku-Boateng, F. A. (2023). Mitigating cybercrimes in an evolving organizational landscape. *Continuity & Resilience Review*, *5*(1), 53–78. doi:10.1108/CRR-09-2022-0017

Yodo, N., & Wang, P. (2016). Engineering Resilience Quantification and System Design Implications: A Literature Survey. *Journal of Mechanical Design*, *138*(11), 111408. doi:10.1115/1.4034223

Zaripova, R., Kosulin, V., Shkinderov, M., & Rakhmatullin, I. (2023). Unlocking the potential of artificial intelligence for big data analytics. *E3S Web of Conferences*, *460*, 04011. doi:10.1051/e3sconf/202346004011

Zawaideh, F., Abu-Ulbeh, W., Majdalawi, Y. I., Zakaria, M. D., Jusoh, J. A., & Das, S. (2023). E-Commerce Supply Chains with Considerations of Cyber-Security. *2023 International Conference on Computer Science and Emerging Technologies (CSET)*. IEEE. 10.1109/CSET58993.2023.10346738

Zhang, H., Jia, F., & You, J. (2021). Striking a balance between supply chain resilience and supply chain vulnerability in the cross-border e-commerce supply chain. *International Journal of Logistics*, *26*(3), 320–344. doi:10.1080/13675567.2021.1948978

Compilation of References

Aamir, M., Zaidi, M. A., Zulfikar, S., & Bhutto, A. (2013). A Survey on DDoS Attack and Defense Strategies: From Traditional Schemes to Current Techniques. *Interdisciplinary Information Sciences*, *19*(2), 173–200. doi:10.4036/iis.2013.173

Abdul-Hussein, M. (2023). *Review: Network Intrusion Detection Systems for Attack Detection and Prevention.* iasj.net. https://www.iasj.net/iasj/download/c6544ecec16b3966

Abebe, B. (2019). *E-government based land administration framework; trends, challenges and prospects* (Doctoral dissertation).

Abebe, B. (2019). *E-government based land administration framework; trends, challenges and prospects* (Doctoral dissertation). https://ir.bdu.edu.et/handle/123456789/10878

Abed, A. K., & Anupam, A. (2022). Review of security issues in Internet of Things and artificial intelligence-driven solutions. *Security and Privacy*, *6*(3), e285. doi:10.1002/spy2.285

Abhay, K. (2023). Grover. Out of the frying pan and into the fire? uncovering the impact of fsma's sanitary food transportation rule on the food logistics industry. *Business Horizons*, *66*(2), 203–214. doi:10.1016/j.bushor.2022.06.003

Abiodun, M. K., Adeniyi, A. E., Victor, A. O., Awotunde, J. B., Atanda, O. G., & Adeniyi, J. K. (2023). Detection and Prevention of Data Leakage in Transit Using LSTM Recurrent Neural Network with Encryption Algorithm. *2023 International Conference on Science, Engineering and Business for Sustainable Development Goals (SEB-SDG).* IEEE. 10.1109/SEB-SDG57117.2023.10124503

Abolhasan, M., Lipman, J., Ni, W., & Hagelstein, B. (2015). Software-defined wireless networking: Centralized, distributed, or hybrid? *IEEE Network*, *29*(4), 32–38. doi:10.1109/MNET.2015.7166188

Abubakar, A. M., Behravesh, E., Rezapouraghdam, H., & Yildiz, S. B. (2019). Applying artificial intelligence technique to predict knowledge hiding behavior. *International Journal of Information Management*, *49*, 45–57. doi:10.1016/j.ijinfomgt.2019.02.006

Accenture. (2020a). *CYBER THREATSCAPE REPORT 2020 - Accenture Security*. Retrieved May 12, 2023, from https://www.readkong.com/page/cyber-threatscape-report-2020-accenture-security-6648512

Accenture. (2020b). *The Cost of Cybercrime: Annual Study by Accenture*. Retrieved May 12, 2023, from https://iapp.org/resources/article/the-cost-of-cybercrime-annual-study-by-accenture/

Adetoye, B., & Fong, R. C. (2023). Building a resilient cybersecurity workforce: a multidisciplinary solution to the problem of high turnover of cybersecurity analysts. In Advanced sciences and technologies for security applications (pp. 61–87). Springer. doi:10.1007/978-3-031-20160-8_5

Adjei-Bamfo, P., Maloreh-Nyamekye, T., & Ahenkan, A. (2019). The role of e-government in sustainable public procurement in developing countries: A systematic literature review. *Resources, Conservation and Recycling*, *142*, 189–203. doi:10.1016/j.resconrec.2018.12.001

Admin. (2022a, January 20). *The impact of e-commerce on the logistics industry*. Globalia Blog. https://www.globalialogisticsnetwork.com/blog/2021/10/07/e-commerce-and-logistics-how-the-logistics-industry-is-changing-due-to-the-rise-of-e-commerce/

Admin. (2022b). Cybersecurity for Small Business: Overview, Importance, Challenges and Tips. *Stealthlabs*. https://www.stealthlabs.com/blog/cybersecurity-for-small-business-overview-importance-challenges-and-tips/

Afek, Y., Bremler-Barr, A., Cohen, E., Feibish, S. L., & Shagam, M. (2016). *Efficient Distinct Heavy Hitters for DNS DDoS Attack Detection*. Research Gate. https://doi.org/ doi:10.1145/1235

Afenyo, M., & Livingstone, D. (2023). Caesar. Maritime cybersecurity threats: Gaps and directions for future research. *Ocean and Coastal Management*, *236*, 106493. doi:10.1016/j.ocecoaman.2023.106493

Afzaal, H., & Zafar, N. A. (2017). *Modeling of IoT-based border protection system*. Paper presented at the Electrical Engineering and Computing Technologies (INTELLECT), 2017 First International Conference on Latest trends in.

Agbo, C. C., Mahmoud, Q. H., & Eklund, J. M. (2019, June). Blockchain technology in healthcare: A systematic review. []. Multidisciplinary Digital Publishing Institute.]. *Health Care*, *7*(2), 56. PMID:30987333

Agbozo, E., Alhassan, D., & Spassov, K. (2018, November). Personal data and privacy barriers to e-Government adoption, implementation and development in Sub-Saharan Africa. In *International Conference on Electronic Governance and Open Society: Challenges in Eurasia* (pp. 82–91). Springer. https://link.springer.com/chapter/10.1007/978-3-030-13283-5_7

Agrawal, N., & Tapaswi, S. (2019). Defense Mechanisms against DDoS Attacks in a Cloud Computing Environment: State-of-the-Art and Research Challenges. *IEEE Communications Surveys and Tutorials*, *21*(4), 3769–3795. doi:10.1109/COMST.2019.2934468

Ahmad, T. (2019). Technology Convergence and Cybersecurity: A Critical Analysis of Cybercrime Trends in India. *27th Convergence India Pragati Maidan*, 29-31. https://papers.ssrn.com/sol3/papers.cfm?abstract_id=3326232

Ahmad, M. S., & Shah, S. M. (2021). Moving Beyond the Crypto-Currency Success of Blockchain: A Systematic Survey. *Scalable Computing: Practice and Experience*, *22*(3), 321–346. doi:10.12694/scpe.v22i3.1853

Ahmad, T. (2020). Corona virus (covid-19) pandemic and work from home: Challenges of cybercrimes and cybersecurity. *SSRN*, *3568830.* doi:10.2139/ssrn.3568830

Ahmed El-Hassany. (2016). SDNRacer: Concurrency Analysis for Software-defined Networks. In *37th ACM SIGPLAN Conference on Programming Language Design and Implementation (PLDI 16).* ACM.

Aich, S., Chakraborty, S., Sain, M., Lee, H.-i., & Kim, H.-C. (2019). A Review on Benefits of IoT Integrated Blockchain based Supply Chain Management Implementations across Different Sectors with Case Study. *2019 21st International Conference on Advanced Communication Technology (ICACT),* 138-141. 10.23919/ICACT.2019.8701910

Ainslie, S., Thompson, D. G., Maynard, S. B., & Ahmad, A. (2023). Cyber-threat intelligence for security decision-making: A review and research agenda for practice. *Computers & Security*, *132*, 103352. doi:10.1016/j.cose.2023.103352

Aithal, P. S. (2023, June 30). *How to create business value through technological innovations using ICCT Underlying Technologies*. SSRN. https://papers.ssrn.com/sol3/papers.cfm?abstract_id=4541179

Ajaikumar, B. K., Varsha, R., & Dey, P. (2021). OVID-19, cytokines, inflammation, and spices: How are they related? *Life Sciences*, *284*, 119–201. doi:10.1016/j.lfs.2021.119201

AjalaO. A. (2024). Leveraging AI/ML for anomaly detection, threat prediction, and automated response. *Pre Print.* doi:10.20944/preprints202401.0159.v1

Akbar, H. S., Zubair, M., & Malik, M. S. (2023). The Security Issues and challenges in Cloud Computing. *International Journal for Electronic Crime Investigation*, *7*(1), 13–32. doi:10.54692/ijeci.2023.0701125

Akram Abdul-Ghani, H., Konstantas, D., & Mahyoub, M. (2018). A Comprehensive IoT Attacks Survey based on a Building-blocked Reference Model. *IJACSA). International Journal of Advanced Computer Science and Applications*, *9*(3). www.ijacsa.thesai.org

Al Ameen, M., Liu, J., & Kwak, K. (2012). Security and Privacy Issues in Wireless Sensor Networks for Healthcare Applications. *Journal of Medical Systems*, *36*(1), 93–101. doi:10.1007/s10916-010-9449-4 PMID:20703745

Al Rahamneh, A. A., Alrawashdeh, S. T., Bawaneh, A. A., Alatyat, Z., Mohammad, A., Mohammad, A. A. S., & Al-Hawary, S. I. S. (2023). The effect of digital supply chain on lean manufacturing: A structural equation modelling approach. *Uncertain Supply Chain Management*, *11*(1), 391–402. doi:10.5267/j.uscm.2022.9.003

Al Shuhaimi, F., Jose, M., & Singh, A. V. (2016, September). Software defined network as solution to overcome security challenges in IoT. In *2016 5th International Conference on Reliability, Infocom Technologies and Optimization (Trends and Future Directions)(ICRITO)* (pp. 491-496). IEEE. 10.1109/ICRITO.2016.7785005

Alaba, F. A., Kocak, A., & Kantarcioglu, M. (2019). Cloud Security for Logistics Cybersecurity: Issues, Challenges and Countermeasures. *IEEE Access : Practical Innovations, Open Solutions*, *7*, 93092–93107. doi:10.1109/ACCESS.2019.2922457

Alakaş, H. M., & Eren, T. (2022). *Integrated Systems and Utilization in Logistics*. doi:10.1007/978-981-16-5644-6_11

Alamri, M., Jhanjhi, N. Z., & Humayun, M. (2019). Blockchain for Internet of Things (IoT) research issues challenges & future directions: A review. *Int. J. Comput. Sci. Netw. Secur*, *19*, 244–258. https://seap.taylors.edu.my/file/rems/publication/109566_6018_1.pdf

Al-Banna, A., Rana, Z. A., Yaqot, M., & Menezes, B. (2023). Interconnectedness between supply chain resilience, industry 4.0, and investment. *Logistics*, *7*(3), 50. doi:10.3390/logistics7030050

Albrahim, R., Alsalamah, H., Alsalamah, S., & Aksoy, M. (2018). Access control model for modern virtual e-government services: Saudi Arabian case study. *International Journal of Advanced Computer Science and Applications*, *9*(8), 357–364. doi:10.14569/IJACSA.2018.090847

Al-Dosari, K., & Fetais, N. (2023). Risk-Management Framework and Information-Security Systems for Small and Medium Enterprises (SMEs): A Meta-Analysis Approach. *Electronics (Basel)*, *12*(17), 3629. doi:10.3390/electronics12173629

Aldowah, H., Rehman, S. U., Ghazal, S., Ivankova, G. V., Mochalina, E. P., & Goncharova, N. L. (2020). Internet of Things (IoT) in logistics. *IOP Conference Series. Materials Science and Engineering*, *940*(1), 012033. doi:10.1088/1757-899X/940/1/012033

Al-Duwairi, B., Al-Kahla, W., AlRefai, M. A., Abdelqader, Y., Rawash, A., & Fahmawi, R. (2020). SIEM-based detection and mitigation of IoT-botnet DDoS attacks. [IJECE]. *Iranian Journal of Electrical and Computer Engineering*, *10*(2), 2182–2191. doi:10.11591/ijece.v10i2.pp2182-2191

AlEnezi, A., AlMeraj, Z., & Manuel, P. (2018, April). Challenges of IoT based smart-government development. In *2018 21st Saudi Computer Society National Computer Conference (NCC)* (pp. 1-6). IEEE.

Alexandre, D., & Dmitry, I. (2021). Ripple Effect and Supply Chain Disruption Management: New Trends and Research Directions. *International Journal of Production Research*, *59*(1), 102–109. doi:10.1080/00207543.2021.1840148

Alexopoulos, C., Lachana, Z., Androutsopoulou, A., Diamantopoulou, V., Charalabidis, Y., & Loutsaris, M. A. (2019, April). How machine learning is changing e-government. In *Proceedings of the 12th International Conference on Theory and Practice of Electronic Governance* (pp. 354-363). 10.1145/3326365.3326412

Alferidah, D. K., & Zaman, N. (2020). *Cybersecurity Impact over Bigdata and IoT Growth.* doi:10.1109/ICCI51257.2020.9247722

Alferidah, D. K., & Jhanjhi, N. Z. (2020). A review on security and privacy issues and challenges in internet of things. *International Journal of Computer Science and Network Security IJCSNS, 20*(4), 263–286.

Al-Fuqaha, A., Guizani, M., Mohammadi, M., Aledhari, M., & Ayyash, M. (2015). Internet of Things: A Survey on Enabling Technologies, Protocols, and Applications. *IEEE Communications Surveys and Tutorials, 17*(4), 2347–2376. doi:10.1109/COMST.2015.2444095

Alguliyev, R., Aliguliyev, R., & Yusifov, F. (2018). Role of Social Networks in E-government: Risks and Security Threats. *Online Journal of Communication and Media Technologies, 8*(4), 363–376. https://www.ojcmt.net/article/role-of-social-networks-in-e-government-risks-and-security-threats-3957

Alharmoodi, B. Y. R., & Lakulu, M. M. B. (2020). Transition from e-government to m-government: Challenges and opportunities-case study of UAE. *European Journal of Multidisciplinary Studies, 5*(1), 61–67. doi:10.26417/453fgx96c

Al-Hawawreh, M., Alazab, M., Ferrag, M. A., & Hossain, M. S. (2024). Securing the Industrial Internet of Things against ransomware attacks: A comprehensive analysis of the emerging threat landscape and detection mechanisms. *Journal of Network and Computer Applications, 223*, 103809. doi:10.1016/j.jnca.2023.103809

Alhawawsha, M., & Panchenko, T. (2020, January). Open Data Platform Architecture and Its Advantages for an Open E-Government. In *International Conference on Computer Science, Engineering and Education Applications* (pp. 631–639). Springer. https://link.springer.com/chapter/10.1007/978-3-030-55506-1_56

Ali, R. M., Jaafar, H. S., & Mohamad, S. (2008). *Logistics and Supply Chain in Malaysia: Issues and Challenges.* Research Gate. https://www.researchgate.net/profile/Harlina_Jaafar2/publication/228710182_Logistics_and_Supply_Chain_in_Malaysia_Issues_and_Challenges/links/02bfe51090cfde3894000000.pdf

Alippi, C., Anastasi, G., Di Francesco, M., & Roveri, M. (2009). Energy management in wireless sensor networks with energy-hungry sensors. *IEEE Instrumentation & Measurement Magazine, 12*(2), 16–23. doi:10.1109/MIM.2009.4811133

Ali, S. M., Ashraf, M. A., Hasin, M. M. T., & Ahmed, S. (2023). Drivers for internet of things (iot) adoption in supply chains: Implications for sustainability in the post-pandemic era. *Computers & Industrial Engineering, 183*, 109515. doi:10.1016/j.cie.2023.109515

Aliwa, E., Rana, O., Perera, C., & Burnap, P. (2021). Cyberattacks and countermeasures for in-vehicle networks. *ACM Computing Surveys, 54*(1), 1–37. doi:10.1145/3431233

Aljabhan, B. (2022). *A Comprehensive Analysis on the Adoption of IoT with Logistics and Supply Chain Management.* doi:10.1109/ICCSEA54677.2022.9936196

Aljohani, A. (2023). Predictive analytics and machine learning for Real-Time supply chain risk mitigation and agility. *Sustainability (Basel), 15*(20), 15088. doi:10.3390/su152015088

Alketbi, H. (2018). *An evaluation of e-government effectiveness in Dubai smart government departments* (Doctoral dissertation, Southampton Solent University). https://ssudl.solent.ac.uk/id/eprint/3809/

Alkinani, M. H., Almazroi, A. A., Jhanjhi, N. Z., & Khan, N. A. (2021). 5G and IoT Based Reporting and Accident Detection (RAD) System to Deliver First Aid Box Using Unmanned Aerial Vehicle. *Sensors (Basel), 21*(20), 6905. doi:10.3390/s21206905 PMID:34696118

Alli, A. A., Kassim, K., Mutwalibi, N., Hamid, H., & Ibrahim, L. (2021). Secure Fog-Cloud of Things: Architectures, Opportunities and Challenges. In M. Ahmed & P. Haskell-Dowland (Eds.), *Secure Edge Computing* (1st ed., pp. 3–20). CRC Press. doi:10.1201/9781003028635-2

AlMendah, O. M. (2021). A Survey of Blockchain and E-governance applications: Security and Privacy issues. *Turkish Journal of Computer and Mathematics Education, 12*(10), 3117–3125. https://turcomat.org/index.php/turkbilmat/article/view/4964

Al-Mhiqani, M. N., Ahmad, R., Abidin, Z. Z., Yassin, W., Hassan, A., Abdulkareem, K. H., Ali, N. S., & Yunos, Z. (2020). A Review of Insider Threat Detection: Classification, Machine Learning Techniques, Datasets, Open Challenges, and Recommendations. *Applied Sciences (Basel, Switzerland), 10*(15), 5208. doi:10.3390/app10155208

Almoaigel, M. F., & Abuabid, A. (2023). Implementation of Cybersecurity Situation Awareness Model in Saudi SMES. *International Journal of Advanced Computer Science and Applications, 14*(11). Advance online publication. doi:10.14569/IJACSA.2023.01411110

Almurisi, N., & Tadisetty, S. (2022). Cloud-based virtualization environment for IoT-based WSN: Solutions, approaches and challenges. *Journal of Ambient Intelligence and Humanized Computing, 13*(10), 1–23. doi:10.1007/s12652-021-03515-z PMID:35371335

Almusaylim, Z. A., Zaman, N., & Jung, L. T. (2018). *Proposing a data privacy aware protocol for roadside accident video reporting service using 5G in Vehicular Cloud Networks Environment.* Paper presented at the 2018 4th International Conference on Computer and Information Sciences (ICCOINS). 10.1109/ICCOINS.2018.8510588

Almusaylim, Z., & Jhanjhi, N. (2020). *Comprehensive review: Privacy protection of user in location-aware services of mobile cloud computing.* Academic Press.

Almusaylim, Z. A., & Jhanjhi, N. Z. (2020). Comprehensive review: Privacy protection of user in location-aware services of mobile cloud computing. *Wireless Personal Communications, 111*(1), 541–564. doi:10.1007/s11277-019-06872-3

Al-Mushayt, O. S. (2019). Automating E-government services with artificial intelligence. *IEEE Access : Practical Innovations, Open Solutions, 7*, 146821–146829. doi:10.1109/ACCESS.2019.2946204

Al-Najjar, A., Layeghy, S., & Portmann, M. (2016). Pushing SDN to the end-host, network load balancing using OpenFlow. *Proc. PCCW'16*, 1–6. 10.1109/PERCOMW.2016.7457129

Al-Nidawi, W. J. A., Al-Wassiti, S. K. J., Maan, M. A., & Othman, M. (2018). A review in E-government service quality measurement. *Indonesian Journal of Electrical Engineering and Computer Science*, *10*(3), 1257–1265. doi:10.11591/ijeecs.v10.i3.pp1257-1265

Alotaibi, S. S., Furnell, S., & He, Y. (2023). Towards a framework for the personalization of cybersecurity awareness. In IFIP advances in information and communication technology (pp. 143–153). Springer. doi:10.1007/978-3-031-38530-8_12

Alqahtani, F., Selviaridis, K., & Stevenson, M. (2023). The effectiveness of performance-based contracting in the defence sector: A systematic literature review. *Journal of Purchasing and Supply Management*, *29*(5), 100877. doi:10.1016/j.pursup.2023.100877

Alqudah, M. A., & Muradkhanli, L. (2021). Artificial Intelligence in Electric Government; Ethical Challenges and Governance in Jordan. *Electronic Research Journal of Social Sciences and Humanities, 3*, 65-74. https://papers.ssrn.com/sol3/papers.cfm?abstract_id=3806600

Alqudah, M. A., & Muradkhanli, L. (2021). Artificial Intelligence in Electric Government; Ethical Challenges and Governance in Jordan. *Electronic Research Journal of Social Sciences and Humanities*, *3*, 65–74.

Alqudhaibi, A. (2023). *Predicting Cybersecurity Threats in Critical Infrastructure for Industry 4.0: A Proactive Approach Based on Attacker Motivations*. MDPI. doi:10.3390/s23094539

Al-rawahna, A. S. M., Chen, S. C., & Hung, C. W. (2019). The barriers of e-government success: An empirical study from Jordan. *SSRN*, *3498847*. doi:10.2139/ssrn.3498847

Alrawais, A., Alhothaily, A., Hu, C., & Cheng, X. (2017). Fog Computing for the Internet of Things: Security and Privacy Issues. *IEEE Internet Computing*, *21*(2), 34–42. doi:10.1109/MIC.2017.37

AlShamsi, M., Al-Emran, M., & Shaalan, K. (2022). A Systematic Review on Blockchain Adoption. *Applied Sciences (Basel, Switzerland)*, *12*(9), 4245. doi:10.3390/app12094245

Alshar'e, M. (2023). Cyber Security Framework Selection: Comparision OF NIST and ISO27001. *Applied Computing Journal*, 245–255. doi:10.52098/acj.202364

Al-Shboul, M., Rababah, O., Ghnemat, R., & Al-Saqqa, S. (2014). Challenges and factors affecting the implementation of e-government in Jordan. *Journal of Software Engineering and Applications*, *7*(13), 1111–1127. doi:10.4236/jsea.2014.713098

Alshurideh, M., Alquqa, E., Alzoubi, H., Kurdi, B., & Hamadneh, S. (2023). The effect of information security on e-supply chain in the uae logistics and distribution industry. *Uncertain Supply Chain Management*, *11*(1), 145–152. doi:10.5267/j.uscm.2022.11.001

Al-Soud, A. R., Al-Yaseen, H., & Al-Jaghoub, S. H. (2014). Jordan's e-Government at the crossroads. *Transforming Government: People, Process and Policy*. https://www.emerald.com/insight/content/doi/10.1108/TG-10-2013-0043/full/html

Alsudani, M. Q., Jaber, M. M., Ali, M. H., Abd, S. K., Alkhayyat, A., Kareem, Z. H., & Mohhan, A. R. (2023). Smart logistics with IoT-based enterprise management system using global manufacturing. *Journal of Combinatorial Optimization*, *45*(2), 1–31. doi:10.1007/s10878-022-00977-5

Altulaihan, E., Alismail, A., & Frikha, M. (2023). A survey on web application penetration testing. *Electronics (Basel)*, *12*(5), 1229. doi:10.3390/electronics12051229

Álvarez, C., Hinojosa, C., González, S. A., & Rojas, L. (2023). Towards cybersecure maritime supply chains in Latin America and the Caribbean. In Lecture notes in logistics (pp. 425–450). Springer. doi:10.1007/978-3-031-32032-3_19

Al-Wathinani, A. M., Barten, D. G., Borowska-Stefańska, M., Gołda, P., AlDulijan, N. A., Alhallaf, M. A., Samarkandi, L. O., Almuhaidly, A. S., Goniewicz, M., Samarkandi, W. O., & Goniewicz, K. (2023). Driving Sustainable disaster Risk reduction: A rapid review of the policies and strategies in Saudi Arabia. *Sustainability (Basel)*, *15*(14), 10976. doi:10.3390/su151410976

Al-Zubaidie, M., & Shyaa, G. S. (2023). Applying detection leakage on hybrid cryptography to secure transaction information in E-Commerce apps. *Future Internet*, *15*(8), 262. doi:10.3390/fi15080262

Amah, U., Mart, J., & Oyetoro, A. (2023). *Cloud Security Governance Guidelines*. doi:10.14293/PR2199.000062.v1

Ambika, N. (2022). Enhancing Security in IoT Instruments Using Artificial Intelligence. In *IoT and Cloud Computing for Societal Good* (pp. 259–276). Springer. doi:10.1007/978-3-030-73885-3_16

Amin, M. A., Rahman, A., & Shahriar, A. (2020). *Application of Theory of Constraints in Supply Chain Management*. ResearchGate. https://www.researchgate.net/publication/348050072_Application_of_Theory_of_Constraints_in_Supply_Chain_Management

Amir Latif, R. M., Hussain, K., Jhanjhi, N. Z., Nayyar, A., & Rizwan, O. (2020). A remix IDE: Smart contract-based framework for the healthcare sector by using Blockchain technology. *Multimedia Tools and Applications*, 1–24. https://link.springer.com/article/10.1007/s11042-020-10087-1

Amro, A., Gkioulos, V., & Katsikas, S. K. (2023). Assessing Cyber Risk in Cyber-Physical Systems Using the ATT&CK Framework. *ACM Transactions on Privacy and Security*, *26*(2), 1–33. doi:10.1145/3571733

Amutha, J., Nagar, J., & Sharma, S. (2020). A Distributed Border Surveillance (DBS) System for Rectangular and Circular Region of Interest with Wireless Sensor Networks in Shadowed Environments. *Wireless Personal Communications*, 1–21.

Anand, P., Singh, Y., Selwal, A., Singh, P. K., Felseghi, R. A., & Raboaca, M. S. (2020). IoVT: Internet of Vulnerable Things? Threat Architecture, Attack Surfaces, and Vulnerabilities in Internet of Things and Its Applications towards Smart Grids. *Energies*, *13*(18), 4813. doi:10.3390/en13184813

Ananna, F. F., Nowreen, R., Jahwari, S. S. R. A., Costa, E., Angeline, L., & Sindiramutty, S. R. (2023). Analysing Influential factors in student academic achievement: Prediction modelling and insight. *International Journal of Emerging Multidisciplinaries Computer.*

Ananna, F. F., Nowreen, R., Jahwari, S. S. R. A., Costa, E., Angeline, L., & Sindiramutty, S. R. (2023). Analysing Influential factors in student academic achievement: Prediction modelling and insight. *International Journal of Emerging Multidisciplinaries Computer Science & Artificial Intelligence, 2*(1). doi:10.54938/ijemdcsai.2023.02.1.254

Andrejić, M. (2019). Research in logistics service quality: A systematic literature review. *Transport, 35*(2), 224–235. doi:10.3846/transport.2019.11388

Andreoli, A., Lounis, A., Debbabi, M., & Hanna, A. (2023). On the prevalence of software supply chain attacks: Empirical study and investigative framework. *Forensic Science International Digital Investigation, 44*, 301508. doi:10.1016/j.fsidi.2023.301508

Angadi, A. A., Varol, C., & Shashidhar, N. (2023). Penetration Testing: Smart Home IoT Devices. In Lecture Notes in Computer Science (pp. 33–46). Springer Science+Business Media. doi:10.1007/978-3-031-23582-5_3

Angelopoulos, K., Diamantopoulou, V., Mouratidis, H., Pavlidis, M., Salnitri, M., Giorgini, P., & Ruiz, J. F. (2017, August). A holistic approach for privacy protection in E-government. In *Proceedings of the 12th International Conference on Availability* (pp. 1–10). Reliability and Security. doi:10.1145/3098954.3098960

Anirudh, M., Arul Thileeban, S., & Nallathambi, D. J. (2017). Use of honeypots for mitigating DoS attacks targeted on IoT networks. *International Conference on Computer, Communication, and Signal Processing: Special Focus on IoT, ICCCSP 2017*. IEEE. 10.1109/ICCCSP.2017.7944057

Annadurai, C., Nelson, I., Devi, K., Manikandan, R., Zaman, N., Masud, M., & Sheikh, A. (2022). Biometric Authentication-Based Intrusion Detection Using Artificial Intelligence Internet of Things in Smart City. *Energies, 15*(19), 7430. doi:10.3390/en15197430

Anusree, P. S., & Balasubramanian, P. (2021). *IoT-Enabled Logistics for E-waste Management and Sustainability*. doi:10.1007/978-981-33-6691-6_9

Anwar, A., Cheng, Y., Huang, H., Han, J., Sim, H., Lee, D., . . . Butt, A. R. (2018, November). BESPOKV: Application tailored scale-out key-value stores. In SC18: International Conference for High Performance Computing, Networking, Storage and Analysis (pp. 14-29). IEEE.

Apasrawirote, D., & Yawised, K. (2023). The emerging of business resilience plans (BRPs) in dealing with business turbulence. *Management Research Review, 47*(1), 141–161. doi:10.1108/MRR-04-2022-0273

Apeh, A. J., Hassan, A. O., Oyewole, O. O., Fakeyede, O. G., Okeleke, P. A., & Adaramodu, O. R. (2023). GRC STRATEGIES IN MODERN CLOUD INFRASTRUCTURES: A REVIEW OF COMPLIANCE CHALLENGES. *Computer Science & IT Research Journal, 4*(2), 111–125. doi:10.51594/csitrj.v4i2.609

Arabadzhyiev, D., Popovych, Y., Lytvynchuk, I., Bakbergen, K., & Kyrychenko, Y. (2021). Digital Society: Regulatory and Institutional Support of Electronic Governance in Modern Realities. In *SHS Web of Conferences* (Vol. 100, p. 03008). EDP Sciences. https://www.shsconferences.org/articles/shsconf/abs/2021/11/shsconf_iscsai2021_03008/shsconf_iscsai2021_03008.html

Ari, A. A. A., Ngangmo, O. K., Titouna, C., Thiare, O., Mohamadou, A., & Gueroui, A. M. (2020). *Enabling privacy and security in Cloud of Things: Architecture, applications, security & privacy challenges*. Applied Computing and Informatics.

Arief, A., Wahab, I. H. A., & Muhammad, M. (2021, May). Barriers and Challenges of e-Government Services: A Systematic Literature Review and Meta-Analyses. *IOP Conference Series. Materials Science and Engineering*, *1125*(1), 012027. doi:10.1088/1757-899X/1125/1/012027

Atzori, L., Iera, A., & Morabito, G. (2017). Understanding the internet of things: Definition, potentials, and societal role of a fast evolving paradigm. *Ad Hoc Networks*, *56*, 122–140. doi:10.1016/j.adhoc.2016.12.004

Auzina, I., Volkova, T., Noreña-Chavez, D., Kadłubek, M., & Thalassinos, E. (2023). Cyber Incident Response Managerial Approaches for enhancing Small–Medium-Size enterprise's cyber maturity. In Contemporary studies in economic and financial analysis (pp. 175–190). doi:10.1108/S1569-37592023000111A012

AV-TEST. (2021). *Malware Statistics & Trends Report | AV-TEST*. Retrieved May 12, 2023, from https://www.av-test.org/en/statistics/malware/

Axestrack. (n.d.). The 6 Major Components of Logistics Management. Axestrack.

Ayala, A. D., Endicott-Popovsky, B., & Hinrichs, R. J. (2023). CyberAlumni a cybersecurity collaboratory. *Journal of the Colloquium for Information Systems Security Education*, *10*(1), 5. doi:10.53735/cisse.v10i1.160

Azam, H., Tan, M., Pin, L. T., Syahmi, M. A., Qian, A. L. W., Jingyan, H., Uddin, H., & Sindiramutty, S. R. (2023). *Wireless Technology Security and Privacy: A Comprehensive*.

Azam, H., Dulloo, M. I., Majeed, M. H., Wan, J. P. H., Xin, L. T., & Sindiramutty, S. R. (2023). Cybercrime Unmasked: Investigating cases and digital evidence. *International Journal of Emerging Multidisciplinaries Computer Science & Artificial Intelligence*, *2*(1). doi:10.54938/ijemdcsai.2023.02.1.255

Azam, H., Dulloo, M. I., Majeed, M. H., Wan, J. P. H., Xin, L. T., Tajwar, M. A., & Sindiramutty, S. R. (2023). Defending the digital Frontier: IDPS and the battle against Cyber threat. *International Journal of Emerging Multidisciplinaries Computer Science & Artificial Intelligence*, *2*(1). doi:10.54938/ijemdcsai.2023.02.1.253

Azam, H., Tajwar, M. A., Mayhialagan, S., Davis, A. J., Yik, C. J., Ali, D., & Sindiramutty, S. R. (2023). Innovations in Security: A study of cloud Computing and IoT. *International Journal of Emerging Multidisciplinaries Computer Science & Artificial Intelligence*, *2*(1). doi:10.54938/ijemdcsai.2023.02.1.252

AzamH.TanM.PinL. T.SyahmiM. A.QianA. L. W.JingyanH.UddinH.SindiramuttyS. R. (2023). Wireless Technology Security and Privacy: A Comprehensive Study. Preprints. doi:10.20944/preprints202311.0664.v1

Azzani, I. K., Purwantoro, S. A., & Almubarok, H. Z. (2024). Enhancing awareness of cyber crime: A crucial element in confronting the challenges of hybrid warfare In Indonesia. *Defense and Security Studies*, *5*, 1–9. doi:10.37868/dss.v5.id255

Bagheri, M. S., Hamid, A. B. A., Soltanic, I., Mardani, A., & Soltan, E. K. H. (2013). The Role of Supply Chain Antecedents on Supply Chain Agility in SMEs: The Conceptual Framework. *Jurnal Teknologi*, *66*(1). Advance online publication. doi:10.11113/jt.v66.1826

Bagnasco, S., Berzano, D., Guarise, A., Lusso, S., Masera, M., & Vallero, S. (2015). *Monitoring of IaaS and scientific applications on the Cloud using the Elasticsearch ecosystem.* Paper presented at the Journal of physics: Conference series. 10.1088/1742-6596/608/1/012016

Baharin, A. M., & Zolkipli, M. F. (2021). Review on Current Target of Mobile Attacks. *Borneo International Journal, 4*(2), 17-24.

Bandari, V. (2023, January 20). *Enterprise Data Security Measures: A comparative review of effectiveness and risks across different industries and organization types.* TenorsGate. https://research.tensorgate.org/index.php/IJBIBDA/article/view/3

Bannour, F., Souihi, S., & Mellouk, A. (2017). Distributed SDN control: Survey, taxonomy, and challenges. *IEEE Communications Surveys and Tutorials*, *20*(1), 333–354. doi:10.1109/COMST.2017.2782482

Bao, J., He, D., Luo, M., & Choo, K. K. R. (2020). A survey of blockchain applications in the energy sector. *IEEE Systems Journal.*

Barabas, M. (2023). *Last Mile Delivery Costs: The Most Expensive Step in the Supply Chain.* Elite Extra. https://eliteextra.com/last-mile-delivery-costs-the-most-expensive-step-in-the-supply-chain/

Barongo, O. G., Numfor, S. A., & Kosacka-Olejnik, M. (2023). Modeling a reverse logistics supply Chain for End-of-Life Vehicle Recycling Risk Management: A Fuzzy Risk Analysis approach. *Sustainability (Basel)*, *15*(3), 2142. doi:10.3390/su15032142

Barreto, L., Amaral, A., & Pereira, T. (2017). Industry 4.0 implications in logistics: An overview. *Proc. Int. Conf. Manuf. Eng. Soc. (MESIC 2017),* 13, 1245–1252. 10.1016/j.promfg.2017.09.045

Barut, A., Citil, M., Ahmed, Z., Sinha, A., & Abbas, S. (2022). How do economic and financial factors influence green logistics? A comparative analysis of E7 and G7 nations. *Environmental Science and Pollution Research International*, *30*(1), 1011–1022. doi:10.1007/s11356-022-22252-0 PMID:35908030

Batool, F. (2023, December 31). *Blockchain Empowered Network Security: A Critical analysis of detection Approaches and Innovations.* IJASC. https://ijasc.com/index.php/ijasc/article/view/43

Beck, K., Beedle, M., Van Bennekum, A., Cockburn, A., Cunningham, W., Fowler, M., . . . Thomas, D. (2001). *Manifesto for agile software development*. Agile Alliance. https://agilemanifesto.org/

Bhagat, C., Sharma, B., & Kumar Mishra, A. (2021). *Assessment of E Governance for National Development–A Case Study of Province 1 Nepal*. https://papers.ssrn.com/sol3/papers.cfm?abstract_id=3857194

Bhardwaj, K. K., Banyal, S., Sharma, D. K., & Al-Numay, W. (2022). Internet of things based smart city design using fog computing and fuzzy logic. *Sustainable Cities and Society*, *79*, 103712. doi:10.1016/j.scs.2022.103712

Bhutta, M. N. M., & Ahmad, M. (2021). Secure Identification, Traceability and Real-Time Tracking of Agricultural Food Supply during Transportation Using Internet of Things. *IEEE Access : Practical Innovations, Open Solutions*, *9*, 65660–65675. doi:10.1109/ACCESS.2021.3076373

Bhuvana, M., & Vasantha, S. (2021). The Impact of COVID-19 on Rural Citizens for Accessing E-Governance Services: A Conceptual Model Using the Dimensions of Trust and Technology Acceptance Model. *Recent Advances in Technology Acceptance Models and Theories, 335*, 471. https://www.ncbi.nlm.nih.gov/pmc/articles/PMC7979245/

Blind, K., Niebel, C., & Rammer, C. (2023). The impact of the EU General data protection regulation on product innovation. *Industry and Innovation*, 1–41. doi:10.1080/13662716.2023.2271858

BodemerO. (2023). Revolutionizing Worldwide Operations through Blockchain: A Marxian Perspective. *TechRhiv*. doi:10.36227/techrxiv.24006402.v1

Botelho, F., Bessani, A., Ramos, F. M., & Ferreira, P. (2014, September). On the design of practical fault-tolerant SDN controllers. In *2014 third European workshop on software defined networks* (pp. 73-78). IEEE. 10.1109/EWSDN.2014.25

Bothra, P., Karmakar, R., Bhattacharya, S., & De, S. (2023). How can applications of blockchain and artificial intelligence improve performance of Internet of Things? – A survey. *Computer Networks*, *224*, 109634. doi:10.1016/j.comnet.2023.109634

Boukerche, A., & Zhou, X. (2020). A Novel Hybrid MAC Protocol for Sustainable Delay-Tolerant Wireless Sensor Network. *IEEE Transactions on Sustainable Computing*, *5*(4), 455–467. doi:10.1109/TSUSC.2020.2973701

Bounceur, A., Clavier, L., Combeau, P., Marc, O., Vauzelle, R., Masserann, A., . . . Devendra, V. (2018). *Cupcarbon: A new platform for the design, simulation and 2d/3d visualization of radio propagation and interferences in iot networks*. Paper presented at the 2018 15th IEEE Annual Consumer Communications & Networking Conference (CCNC).

Bowersox, D. J., Closs, D. J., & Cooper, M. E. (2002). *Supply Chain Logistics Management*. http://ci.nii.ac.jp/ncid/BB09911482

Bowersox, D., Closs, D., & Cooper, M. (2019). *Supply chain logistics management*. McGraw-Hill Education.

Boyes, H. (2015). Cybersecurity and Cyber-Resilient supply chains. *TIM Review*. https://timreview.ca/article/888

Bozhilov, N. (2023, March 10). *Case Study: How Logistics Benefits from a Managed Cyber Security Approach – The Logistics Point*. http://www.thelogisticspoint.com/2023/03/10/case-study-how-logistics-benefits-from-a-managed-cyber-security-approach/

Bradley, C., & Barrera, D. (2023). Towards Characterizing IoT Software Update Practices. In Lecture Notes in Computer Science (pp. 406–422). Springer Science+Business Media. doi:10.1007/978-3-031-30122-3_25

Brohi, S. N., Jhanjhi, N. Z., Brohi, N. N., & Brohi, M. N. (2020). Key Applications of State-of-the-Art technologies to mitigate and eliminate COVID-19. Berke, A. How Safe are Blockchains? *Harvard Business review*. https://hbr. org/2017/03/how-safe-are-blockchains-it-depends

Brohi, S. N., Jhanjhi, N. Z., Brohi, N. N., & Brohi, M. N. (2020). *Key Applications of State-of-the-Art technologies to mitigate and eliminate COVID-19*. file:///C:/Users/imdad/Downloads/Key%20Applications%20of%20State-of-the-Art%20Technologies%20to%20Mitigate%20and%20Eliminate%20COVID-19%20(1).pdf

BrohiS. N.JhanjhiN. Z.BrohiN. N.BrohiM. N. (2020). Key Applications of State-of-the-Art Technologies to Mitigate and Eliminate COVID-19. TechRxiv. doi:10.36227/techrxiv.12115596.v2

Bruce, G. (2023). Cybersecurity compliance requirements for USA Department of Defense Contractors - Dragons at the gate. In Lecture Notes in Computer Science (pp. 290–308). Springer. doi:10.1007/978-3-031-35822-7_20

Burak, A., & Burak, A. (2024, January 15). *New technology in logistics trends to keep an eye on in 2024*. Relevant Software. https://relevant.software/blog/new-technology-in-logistics-trends/

Burrell, D. N. (2020). Understanding the talent management intricacies of remote cybersecurity teams in covid-19 induced telework organizational ecosystems. *Land Forces Academy Review*, *25*(3), 232-244. https://www.armyacademy.ro/reviste/rev3_2020/Burrell.pdf

Burrell, D. N., Bhargava, N., Bradley-Swanson, O. T., Harmon, M. W., Wright, J., Springs, D., & Dawson, M. (2020). Supply Chain and Logistics Management and an Open Door Policy Concerning Cyber Security Introduction. *International Journal of Management and Sustainability*, *9*(1), 1–10. doi:10.18488/journal.11.2020.91.1.10

Cabaj, K., Gregorczyk, M., & Mazurczy, W. (2018). Softwaredefined networking-based crypto ransomware detection using http traffic characteristics. *Computers & Electrical Engineering*, *66*, 353–368. doi:10.1016/j.compeleceng.2017.10.012

Cachin, C., & Vukolić, M. (2017). Blockchain consensus protocols in the wild. *arXiv preprint arXiv:1707.01873*.

Cahyono, Y., Purwoko, D., Koho, I. R., Setiani, A., Supendi, S., Setyoko, P. I., Sosiady, M., & Wijoyo, H. (2023). The role of supply chain management practices on competitive advantage and performance of halal agroindustry SMEs. *Uncertain Supply Chain Management*, *11*(1), 153–160. doi:10.5267/j.uscm.2022.10.012

Calinescu, T., Likhonosova, G., & Zelenko, O. (2023). Circular Economy: Ukraine's Reserves and the Consequences of the Global Recession. doi:10.1007/978-3-031-23463-7_16

Carrapico, H., & Farrand, B. (2020). Discursive continuity and change in the time of Covid-19: The case of EU cybersecurity policy. *Journal of European Integration*, *42*(8), 1111–1126. doi: 10.1080/07036337.2020.1853122

Carrillo-Torres, D., Díaz, J. P., Cantoral-Ceballos, J. A., & Vargas-Rosales, C. (2023). A novel Multi-Factor authentication algorithm based on image recognition and user established relations. *Applied Sciences (Basel, Switzerland)*, *13*(3), 1374. doi:10.3390/app13031374

Cartwright, A., & Cartwright, E. (2023). The economics of ransomware attacks on integrated supply chain networks. *Digital Threats : Research and Practice*, *4*(4), 1–14. Advance online publication. doi:10.1145/3579647

Casola, V., De Benedictis, A., Mazzocca, C., & Orbinato, V. (2024). Secure Software Development and Testing: A Model-based Methodology. *Computers & Security*, *137*, 103639. doi:10.1016/j.cose.2023.103639

CBS News. (2017, July 1). *NotPetya ransomware attack cost FedEx $300M*. CBS News. https://www.cbsnews.com/news/notpetya-ransomware-attack-cost-fedex-300m/

Ceynowa, W., Przybyłowski, A., Wojtasik, P., & Ciskowski, Ł. (2023). ICT adoption for sustainable logistics development in the HoReCa and wholesale sectors. *Sustainability (Basel)*, *15*(4), 3746. doi:10.3390/su15043746

Chakraborty, C., & Abougreen, A. N. (2021). Intelligent internet of things and advanced machine learning techniques for COVID-19. *EAI Endorsed Transactions on Pervasive Health and Technology*, *7*(26), e1.

Chandra, N. A., Ramli, K., Ratna, A. P., & Gunawan, T. S. (2022). Information Security Risk Assessment Using Situational Awareness Frameworks and Application Tools. *Risks*, *10*(8), 165. doi:10.3390/risks10080165

Charles, V., Emrouznejad, A., & Gherman, T. (2023). A critical analysis of the integration of blockchain and artificial intelligence for supply chain. *Annals of Operations Research*, *327*(1), 7–47. doi:10.1007/s10479-023-05169-w PMID:36718465

Chatterjee, P., Das, D., & Rawat, D. B. (2023). Use of Federated Learning and Blockchain towards Securing Financial Services. *arXiv (Cornell University)*. https://doi.org//arxiv.2303.12944 doi:10.48550

Chauhan, M., & Shiaeles, S. (2023). An analysis of cloud security frameworks, problems and proposed solutions. *Network (Bristol, England)*, *3*(3), 422–450. doi:10.3390/network3030018

Chaurasiya, S. K., Biswas, A., Nayyar, A., Jhanjhi, N. Z., & Banerjee, R. (2023). DEICA: A differential evolution-based improved clustering algorithm for IoT-based heterogeneous wireless sensor networks. *International Journal of Communication Systems*, *36*(5), e5420. Advance online publication. doi:10.1002/dac.5420

Cheng, B., Solmaz, G., Cirillo, F., Kovacs, E., Terasawa, K., & Kitazawa, A. (2017). FogFlow: Easy programming of IoT services over cloud and edges for smart cities. *IEEE Internet of Things Journal*, *5*(2), 696–707. doi:10.1109/JIOT.2017.2747214

Cheng, J., Chen, W., Tao, F., & Lin, C. L. (2018). Industrial IoT in 5G environment towards smart manufacturing. *Journal of Industrial Information Integration*, *10*, 10–19. doi:10.1016/j.jii.2018.04.001

Cheng, L. T., Tei, Z., Yeo, S. F., Lai, K.-H., Kumar, A., & Chung, L. (2023). Nexus among blockchain visibility, supply chain integration and supply chain performance in the digital transformation era. *Industrial Management & Data Systems*, *123*(1), 229–252. doi:10.1108/IMDS-12-2021-0784

Cheng, L., Li, Z., Zhang, Y., Zhang, Y., & Lee, I. (2017). Protecting interoperable clinical environment with authentication. *SIGBED Rev*, *14*(2), 34–43. doi:10.1145/3076125.3076129

Chen-xu, N., & Jie-sheng, W. (2015, July). Auto regressive moving average (ARMA) prediction method of bank cash flow time series. In *2015 34th Chinese Control Conference (CCC)* (pp. 4928-4933). IEEE.

Chen, Y.-T., Sun, E. W., Chang, M.-F., & Lin, Y.-B. (2021). Pragmatic real-time logistics management with traffic IoT infrastructure: Big data predictive analytics of freight travel time for Logistics 4.0. *International Journal of Production Economics*, *238*, 108157. doi:10.1016/j.ijpe.2021.108157

Chesti, I. A., Humayun, M., Sama, N. U., & Jhanjhi, N. Z. (2020). Evolution, Mitigation, and Prevention of Ransomware. *2020 2nd International Conference on Computer and Information Sciences (ICCIS)*. IEEE. 10.1109/ICCIS49240.2020.9257708

Cheung, K., Bell, M. G., & Bhattacharjya, J. (2021). Cybersecurity in logistics and supply chain management: An overview and future research directions. *Transportation Research Part E, Logistics and Transportation Review*, *146*, 102217. doi:10.1016/j.tre.2020.102217

Chhajed, G. J., & Garg, B. R. (2022). Applying Decision Tree for Hiding Data in Binary Images for Secure and Secret Information Flow. In *Cybersecurity Measures for E-Government Frameworks* (pp. 175–186). IGI Global. doi:10.4018/978-1-7998-9624-1.ch011

Chindrus, C., & Caruntu, C. F. (2023). Securing the Network: A Red and Blue Cybersecurity Competition case study. *Information (Basel)*, *14*(11), 587. doi:10.3390/info14110587

Chin, T., Rahouti, M., & Xiong, K. (2018). Applying software-defined networking to minimize the end-to-end delay of network services. *Applied Computing Review*, *18*(1), 30–40. doi:10.1145/3212069.3212072

Chin, T., Xiong, K., & Rahouti, M. (2018). Kernel-Space Intrusion Detection Using Software-Defined Networking. *EAI Endorsed Transactions on Security and Safety*, *5*(15), e2.

Chirayath, S. S. (2023). Insider Threats and Strategies to Manage Insider Risk. In SpringerLink. doi:10.1007/978-981-99-5005-8_7

Chishiro, H., Tsuchiya, Y., Chubachi, Y., Abu Bakar, M. S., & De Silva, L. C. (2017, June). Global PBL for environmental IoT. In *Proceedings of the 2017 International Conference on E-commerce, E-Business and E-Government* (pp. 65-71). 10.1145/3108421.3108437

Choi, B. G., Jeong, E., & Kim, S. W. (2019). Multiple security certification system between blockchain based terminal and internet of things device: Implication for open innovation. *Journal of Open Innovation*, *5*(4), 87. doi:10.3390/joitmc5040087

Choudhury, R. (2020). *Logistics Market - Global Industry Analysis, Size, Share, Growth, Trends, and Forecast, 2020-2027*. Transparency Market Research.

Chowdhury, S., Rodríguez-Espíndola, O., Dey, P. K., & Budhwar, P. (2022). Blockchain technology adoption for managing risks in operations and supply chain management: Evidence from the UK. *Annals of Operations Research*, *327*(1), 539–574. doi:10.1007/s10479-021-04487-1 PMID:35095153

Chow, G., Heaver, T. D., & Henriksson, L. (1994). Logistics Performance. *International Journal of Physical Distribution & Logistics Management*, *24*(1), 17–28. doi:10.1108/09600039410055981

Christopher, M. (2016). *Logistics & supply chain management*. Pearson Education Limited.

Christopher, M. (2021). Logistics and Supply Chain Management. In Communications in computer and information science. Springer Science+Business Media. doi:10.1007/978-3-030-89743-7

Chung, S., & Lee, J. (2021). Secure Data Transmission Using an Advanced Encryption Algorithm in IoT-Based Logistics Applications. *Electronics (Basel)*, *10*(4), 388.

ChunT. J.EnL. J.XuenM. T. Y.XuanY. M.MuzafarS. (2023). Secured Software Development and Importance of Secure Software Development Life Cycle. Authorea Preprints. doi:10.36227/techrxiv.24548416.v1

Cichosz, M., Wallenburg, C. M., & Michael Knemeyer, A. (2020). Digital transformation at logistics service providers: Barriers, success factors and leading practices. *International Journal of Logistics Management*, *31*(2), 209–238. doi:10.1108/IJLM-08-2019-0229

Çınar, B. (2023). Supply chain cybersecurity: Risks, challenges, and strategies for a globalized world. *Journal of Engineering Research and Reports*, *25*(9), 196–210. doi:10.9734/jerr/2023/v25i9993

CIS. (2021). *CIS Controls*. Retrieved May 12, 2023, from https://www.cisecurity.org/controls

CISA. (2021, May 10). *Home Page | CISA*. Retrieved May 11, 2023, from https://www.cisa.gov/ncas/current-activity/2021/01/14/artificial-intelligence-ai-cybersecurity

Clinton, L. (2023). *Fixing American Cybersecurity: Creating a Strategic Public-Private Partnership*. Georgetown University Press.

Closs & McGarrell. (2004). *Enhancing security throughout the supply chain.* IBM Center for the Business of Government.

Cloud Security Alliance. (2019). *Top Threats to Cloud Computing, Version 4*. https://downloads.cloudsecurityalliance.org/assets/research/top-threats/tc_v4.pdf

Cloud Security Alliance. (2020). *Cloud Controls Matrix*. Retrieved May 12, 2023, from https://cloudsecurityalliance.org/artifacts/cloud-controls-matrix-v3-0-1/

Codinhoto, R., Fialho, B. C., Pinti, L., & Fabricio, M. M. (2022). BIM and IoT for Facilities Management. In *Research Anthology on BIM and Digital Twins in Smart Cities* (pp. 407–429). IGI Global. doi:10.4018/978-1-6684-7548-5.ch019

Colicchia, C., Creazza, A., & David, A. (2019). Managing cyber and information risks in supply chains: Insights from an exploratory analysis. *Supply Chain Management*, *24*(2), 215–240. doi:10.1108/SCM-09-2017-0289

Collidu. (2022, December 7). *Cybersecurity Awareness*. https://www.collidu.com/presentation-cybersecurity-awareness

Committee on National Security Systems. (2016). *CNSS Instruction No. 1253: Security Categorization and Control Selection for National Security Systems. Committee on National Security Systems.* Retrieved May 11, 2023, from https://www.dcsa.mil/portals/91/documents/ctp/nao/CNSSI_No1253.pdf

Cornwell, N., Bilson, C., Gepp, A., Stern, S., & Vanstone, B. J. (2023). Modernising operational risk management in financial institutions via data-driven causal factors analysis: A pre-registered report. *Pacific-Basin Finance Journal*, *77*, 101906. doi:10.1016/j.pacfin.2022.101906

Correia, S., Boukerche, A., & Meneguette, R. I. (2017). An architecture for hierarchical software-defined vehicular networks. *IEEE Communications Magazine*, *55*(7), 80–86. doi:10.1109/MCOM.2017.1601105

Cosco. (2018, July 25). *COSCO Shipping Lines Falls Victim to Cyber Attack.* Offshore Energy. Retrieved May 12, 2023, from https://www.offshore-energy.biz/cosco-shipping-lines-falls-victim-to-cyber-attack/

Coveware. (2023, April 28). *Ransomware Quarterly Reports. Coveware: Ransomware Recovery First Responders.* Retrieved May 12, 2023, from https://www.coveware.com/ransomware-quarterly-reports

Cowgill, B., & Stevenson, M. T. (2020, May). Algorithmic social engineering. In *AEA Papers and Proceedings* (Vol. 110, pp. 96-100). https://www.aeaweb.org/articles?id=10.1257/pandp.20201037

Cradduck, L. (2019). E-conveyancing: a consideration of its risks and rewards. *Property Management*. https://www.emerald.com/insight/content/doi/10.1108/PM-04-2019-0021/full/html

CrowdStrike. (2022, February 15). *2021 Global Threat Report*. crowdstrike.com. Retrieved May 12, 2023, from https://www.crowdstrike.com/global-threat-report-2021/

Crussell, J., Gibler, C., & Chen, H. (2012). *Attack of the clones: Detecting cloned applications on android markets*. Paper presented at the European Symposium on Research in Computer Security. 10.1007/978-3-642-33167-1_3

Cyber Threats and Engagements in 2022. (n.d.). DTIC. https://apps.dtic.mil/sti/citations/trecms/AD1208002

Cyberres. (2023). *Advanced Authentication Software & Authentication Framework*. CyberRES. https://www.microfocus.com/en-us/cyberres/identity-access-management/advanced-authentication

Cybersecurity 2.0. (2021). Retrieved May 13, 2023, from https://www.dhl.com/global-en/home/insights-and-innovation/thought-leadership/trend-reports/cybersecurity-supply-chain.html

Cybersecurity Responsibility. (n.d.). https://www.sketchbubble.com/en/presentation-cybersecurity-responsibility.html

Cyberstar. (2021, August 30). *The Maritime Industry is Rethinking Cyber Security resilience. We're Here to Help*. https://www.zkcyberstar.com/2021/08/30/the-maritime-industry-is-rethinking-cyber-security-were-here-to-help/

D, L., & Tyagi, A. K. (2023). *Privacy preservation and secured data storage in cloud computing*. IGI Global.

D'Andrea, R. (2021). *Human–Robot Collaboration: The Future of Smart Warehousing*. doi:10.1007/978-3-030-61093-7_12

da Silva, L. E., & Coury, D. V. (2020). Network traffic prediction for detecting DDoS attacks in IEC 61850 communication networks. *Computers & Electrical Engineering*, *87*, 106793. doi:10.1016/j.compeleceng.2020.106793

Da Silva, R. F., De Andrade Melani, A. H., De Carvalho Michalski, M. Â., & De Souza, G. F. M. (2023). Reliability and risk centered maintenance: A novel method for supporting maintenance management. *Applied Sciences (Basel, Switzerland)*, *13*(19), 10605. doi:10.3390/app131910605

Dahwan, A. A., & Raju, V. (2021). The Infleuence of Online Services and Telecommunication Infrastructure on the Implementation of E-government in Military Institutions in Yemen. *Annals of the Romanian Society for Cell Biology*, 1698–1710. https://www.annalsofrscb.ro/index.php/journal/article/view/2689

Dai, J. (2023). *Cyber resilience enhancement for microgrid digitalization*. doi:10.32657/10356/171843

Darmayanti, N. L., & Dwipayana, A. D. (2023). Logistics industry readinessinapplication policy over dimension overloading (odol). *ASTONJADRO*, *12*(2), 454–460.

Das, T., Harshey, A., Mishra, V., & Srivastava, A. (2023). An Introduction to Biometric Authentication Systems. Springer. doi:10.1007/978-981-99-1377-0_26

Davies, P., Liu, Y., Cooper, M., & Xing, Y. (2022). Supply chains and ecosystems for servitization: A systematic review and future research agenda. *International Marketing Review*, *40*(4), 667–692. doi:10.1108/IMR-10-2021-0318

Dawson, M., & Walker, D. (2022). Argument for Improved Security in Local Governments Within the Economic Community of West African States. *Cybersecurity Measures for E-Government Frameworks*, 96-106.

De Filippi, P., Mannan, M., & Reijers, W. (2020). Blockchain as a confidence machine: The problem of trust & challenges of governance. Technology in Society, 62, Donalds, C., & Osei-Bryson, K. M. (2020). Cybersecurity compliance behavior: Exploring the influences of individual decision style and other antecedents. *International Journal of Information Management*, *51*, 102056.

de Vass, T., Shee, H., & Miah, S. J. (2020). *Iot in supply chain management: a narrative on retail sector sustainability*. doi:10.1080/13675567.2020.1787970

Deborah, L. J., Vijayakumar, P., Gupta, B. B., & Pelusi, D. (2023). *Secure data management for online learning applications*. CRC Press. doi:10.1201/9781003264538

Dehghantanha, A., Conti, M., & Dargahi, T. (2018). *Cyber Threat intelligence*. Springer. doi:10.1007/978-3-319-73951-9

Deloitte. (2021). *Global supply chain disruption and future strategies survey*. Retrieved from https://www2.deloitte.com/content/dam/Deloitte/us/Documents/strategy/global-supply-chain-disruption-and-future-strategies-survey.pdf

Deng, Q., Su, Y., Hu, S., Xiong, X., Juan, R., Zhang, Y., & Ma, H. (2018). *A Parallel Impedance Measurement System for Electrical Impedance Tomography System with Multi-Microcontroller-Unit Architecture*. Paper presented at the 2018 IEEE International Conference on Manipulation, Manufacturing and Measurement on the Nanoscale (3M-NANO). 10.1109/3M-NANO.2018.8552230

Department of Defense. (2020). *Cybersecurity Maturity Model Certification*. Chief Information Officer. Retrieved May 10, 2023, from https://dodcio.defense.gov/CMMC/About/

Dhandabani, L. D., & Tyagi, A. K. (2023). *Privacy preservation and secured data storage in cloud computing*. Engineering Science Reference.

DHL. (2023). *The value of IoT in supply chains*. DHL. https://www.dhl.com/global-en/delivered/digitalization/the-value-of-iot-in-supply-chains.html

Dhonju, G. R., & Shakya, S. (2019). Analyzing Challenges for the Implementation of E-Government in Municipalities within Kathmandu Valley. *Journal of Science and Engineering*, *7*, 70–78. doi:10.3126/jsce.v7i0.26795

Di Nardo, C. (2022, September 16). *Cybersecurity strategy: what are the key aspects to consider?* DeltalogiX. https://deltalogix.blog/en/2022/09/14/cybersecurity-strategy-what-are-the-key-aspects-to-consider/

Díaz-López, D., Dólera-Tormo, G., Gómez-Mármol, F., & Martínez-Pérez, G. (2016). Dynamic counter-measures for risk-based access control systems: An evolutive approach. *Future Generation Computer Systems*, *55*, 321–335. doi:10.1016/j.future.2014.10.012

Digital, C. (n.d.). *The Digital Transformation of Logistics: An Overview of Technologies and Trends*. copperdigital.medium.com

Dimolianis, M., Pavlidis, A., & Maglaris, V. (2020, February). A multi-feature DDoS detection schema on P4 network hardware. In *2020 23rd Conference on Innovation in Clouds, Internet and Networks and Workshops (ICIN)* (pp. 1-6). IEEE. 10.1109/ICIN48450.2020.9059327

Ding, D., Han, Q.-L., Xiang, Y., Ge, X., & Zhang, X.-M. (2018). A survey on security control and attack detection for industrial cyber-physical systems. *Neurocomputing*, *275*, 1674–1683. doi:10.1016/j.neucom.2017.10.009

Ding, S., Lu, S., Xu, Y., Korkali, M., & Cao, Y. (2023). Review of cybersecurity for integrated energy systems with integration of cyber-physical systems. *Energy Conversion and Economics*, *4*(5), 334–345. doi:10.1049/enc2.12097

Ding, Y., Jin, M., Li, S., & Feng, D. (2021). Smart logistics based on the internet of things technology: An overview. *International Journal of Logistics*, *24*(4), 323–345. doi:10.1080/13675567.2020.1757053

Diro, A., Zhang, L., Saini, A., Kaisar, S., & Hiep, P. C. (2024). Leveraging zero knowledge proofs for blockchain-based identity sharing: A survey of advancements, challenges and opportunities. *Journal of Information Security and Applications*, *80*, 103678. doi:10.1016/j.jisa.2023.103678

Distel, B. (2018). Bringing Light into the Shadows: A Qualitative Interview Study on Citizens' Non-Adoption of e-Government. *Electronic. Journal of E-Government*, *16*(2), 98–105.

Diwaker, C., Tomar, P., Solanki, A., Nayyar, A., Jhanjhi, N. Z., Abdullah, A., & Supramaniam, M. (2019). A new model for predicting Component-Based software reliability using soft computing. *IEEE Access : Practical Innovations, Open Solutions*, *7*, 147191–147203. doi:10.1109/ACCESS.2019.2946862

Dmitry, I., & Alexandre, D. (2021). A digital supply chain twin for managing the disruption risks and resilience in the era of Industry 4.0. *Production Planning and Control*, *32*(9), 775–788. doi:10.1080/09537287.2020.1768450

Dong, B. (2017). Software Defined Networking Based On-Demand Routing Protocol in Vehicle Ad-Hoc Networks. *ZTE Communications*, *15*(2), 11–18.

Dorn, T. M. (2023). *U.S. critical infrastructure: Its Importance and Vulnerabilities to Cyber and Unmanned Systems*. Page Publishing Inc.

Dorr, B., Bhatia, A., Dalton, A., Mather, B., Hebenstreit, B., Santhanam, S., . . . Strzalkowski, T. (2020, April). Detecting asks in social engineering attacks: Impact of linguistic and structural knowledge. In *Proceedings of the AAAI Conference on Artificial Intelligence* (Vol. 34, No. 5, pp. 7675-7682). https://ojs.aaai.org/index.php/AAAI/article/view/6269

Dubey, A., Saquib, Z., & Dwivedi, S. (2015). *Electronic authentication for e-Government services-a survey*. https://digital-library.theiet.org/content/conferences/10.1049/cp.2015.0299

Duggineni, S. (2023). Data integrity and risk. *Open Journal of Optimization*, *12*(2), 25–33. doi:10.4236/ojop.2023.122003

Dunhill, J. (2020). *Critical patient dies after cyber attack disables hospital computers*. https://www.iflscience.com/technology/critical-patient-dies-after-cyber-attack-disables-hospital-computers

Du, S., Zhang, H., & Kong, Y. (2023). Sustainability implications of the arctic shipping route for shanghai port logistics in the post-pandemic era. *Sustainability (Basel)*, *15*(22), 16017. doi:10.3390/su152216017

Edge, C., & Trouton, R. (2023). MDM Internals. In Apress eBooks (pp. 207–279). doi:10.1007/978-1-4842-9156-6_4

Edvard, T. (2019). Blockchain Technology Implementation in Logistics. *Sustainability*.

El Haddouti, S., & El Kettani, M. D. E. C. (2019, April). Analysis of identity management systems using blockchain technology. In *2019 International Conference on Advanced Communication Technologies and Networking (CommNet)* (pp. 1-7). IEEE. 10.1109/COMMNET.2019.8742375

Elezaj, O., Tole, D., & Baci, N. (2018). Big Data in e-Government Environments: Albania as a Case Study. *Academic Journal of Interdisciplinary Studies*, *7*(2), 117–124. doi:10.2478/ajis-2018-0052

Elijah, A. V., Abdullah, A., Zaman, N., Supramaniam, M., & Abdullateef, B. N. (2019). Ensemble and Deep-Learning Methods for Two-Class and Multi-Attack Anomaly Intrusion Detection: An Empirical Study. *International Journal of Advanced Computer Science and Applications*, *10*(9). Advance online publication. doi:10.14569/IJACSA.2019.0100969

Engesser, V., Rombaut, E., Vanhaverbeke, L., & Lebeau, P. (2023). Autonomous Delivery Solutions for Last-Mile Logistics Operations: A Literature Review and Research Agenda. *Sustainability*, *15*(3), 2774. doi:10.3390/su15032774

Enginerasoft. (2023, March 24). *Why is it important to back up data in logistics?* Enginerasoft. Enginerasoft. https://enginerasoft.com/why-is-it-important-to-back-up-data-in-logistics/

ENISA. (2021). *Post-Quantum Cryptography: Anticipating Threats and Preparing the Future*. Retrieved May 10, 2023, from https://www.enisa.europa.eu/news/enisa-news/post-quantum-cryptography-anticipating-threats-and-preparing-the-future

ENISA. (n.d.). *Understanding the increase in Supply Chain Security Attacks*. https://www.enisa.europa.eu/news/enisa-news/understanding-the-increase-in-supply-chain-security-attacks

Entrepreneurship and management. (2021). http://economicresearch.pl/Books/index.php/eep/catalog/view/85/87/122-1

Environment", *IEEE In 2018 4th International Conference on Computer and Information Sciences (lCCOINS)*, pp. 1-5, August 2018.

Erdogan, G., Halvorsrud, R., Boletsis, C., Tverdal, S., & Pickering, J. (2023). *Cybersecurity Awareness and Capacities of SMEs*. doi:10.5220/0011609600003405

Eulaerts. (2022). Weak Signals in Border Management and Surveillance Technologies. Academic Press.

European Union. (2016). *General Data Protection Regulation (GDPR)*. https://eur-lex.europa.eu/legal-content/EN/TXT/?uri=CELEX:32016R0679

Evans, S. (2023). *Amazon Launches Heavy-Lifting Fulfillment Center Robot*. IoT World. https://www.iotworldtoday.com/robotics/amazon-launches-heavy-lifting-fulfillment-center-robot#close-modal

Evans, R., Hajli, N., & Nisar, T. M. (2022). Privacy-Enhancing factors and Consumer concerns: The moderating effects of the General Data Protection Regulation. *British Journal of Management*, *34*(4), 2075–2092. doi:10.1111/1467-8551.12685

F5 Lab. (2012). *Application protection reprt*. F5 Lab. Retrieved May 12, 2023, from https://www.f5.com/content/dam/f5-labs-v2/article/pdfs/F5-Labs-2021-Application-Protection-Report-24AUG21.pdf

Factor Analysis of Information Risk. (2021). *What is the FAIR Institute?* FAIR Institute. Retrieved May 11, 2023, from https://www.fairinstitute.org/

FadhilI. S. M.NizarN.RostamR. J. (2023). Security and Privacy Issues in Cloud Computing. *TEchRIv*. doi:10.36227/techrxiv.23506905.v1

Fan, K., Wang, S., Ren, Y., Li, H., & Yang, Y. (2018). Medblock: Efficient and secure medical data sharing via blockchain. *Journal of Medical Systems*, *42*(8), 1–11. doi:10.1007/s10916-018-0993-7 PMID:29931655

Farah, M. B., Al-Kadri, M. O., Ahmed, Y., Abouzariba, R., & Bellekens, X. (2023). Cyber Incident Scenarios in the Maritime Industry: Risk Assessment and Mitigation Strategies. *2023 IEEE International Conference on Cyber Security and Resilience (CSR)*. IEEE. 10.1109/CSR57506.2023.10224972

Fatima-Tuz-Zahra. Jhanjhi, N. Z., Brohi, S. N., Malik, N. A., & Humayun, M. (2020). Proposing a Hybrid RPL Protocol for Rank and Wormhole Attack Mitigation using Machine Learning. *2020 2nd International Conference on Computer and Information Sciences*. IEEE.

Fedele, A., & Roner, C. (2021). Dangerous games: A literature review on cybersecurity investments. *Journal of Economic Surveys*, *36*(1), 157–187. doi:10.1111/joes.12456

FedRAMP. (2020). *FedRAMP*. Retrieved May 11, 2023, from https://www.gsa.gov/technology/government-it-initiatives/fedramp

Fernando, Y., Tseng, M., Wahyuni-Td, I. S., De Sousa Jabbour, A. B. L., Jabbour, C. J. C., & Foropon, C. (2022). Cyber supply chain risk management and performance in industry 4.0 era: Information system security practices in Malaysia. *Journal of Industrial and Production Engineering*, *40*(2), 102–116. doi:10.1080/21681015.2022.2116495

Ferrag, M. A., Shu, L., Yang, X., Derhab, A., & Maglaras, L. (2020). Security and privacy for green IoT-based agriculture: Review, blockchain solutions, and challenges. *IEEE Access : Practical Innovations, Open Solutions*, *8*, 32031–32053. doi:10.1109/ACCESS.2020.2973178

Ferreira, A., & Cruz-Correia, R. (2021). COVID-19 and cybersecurity: Finally, an opportunity to disrupt? *JMIRx Med*, *2*(2), e21069. doi:10.2196/21069 PMID:34032816

FocusNet. (2023, September 20). *Cyber Security Services.* FocusNet Technology. https://www.focusnet.com.au/cyber-security/

Fosso, J., Wamba, S., Roubaud, D., & Foropon, C. (2021). Empirical investigation of data analytics capability and organizational flexibility as complements to supply chain resilience. *International Journal of Production Research*, *59*(1), 110–128. doi:10.1080/00207543.2019.1582820

Foster, I., Larson, J. D., Masich, M., Snoeren, A. C., Savage, S., & Levchenko, K. (2015). *Security by Any Other Name.* doi:10.1145/2810103.2813607

Fragapane, G., Hvolby, H. H., Sgarbossa, F., & Strandhagen, J. O. (2021). *Autonomous mobile robots in sterile instrument logistics: an evaluation of the material handling system for a strategic fit framework.* doi:10.1080/09537287.2021.1884914

Froehlich, A., Ringas, N., & Wilson, J. (2020). E-Governance in Africa and the World. In *Space Supporting Africa* (pp. 53–124). Springer. doi:10.1007/978-3-030-52260-5_2

Galvez, J. F., Mejuto, J., & Simal-Gandara, J. Future challenges on the use of blockchain for food traceability analysis. *TrAC Trends in Analytical Chemistry.* Science Direct. https://www.sciencedirect.com/science/article/abs/pii/S0268401219302877

Galvez, J. F., Mejuto, J., & Simal-Gandara, J. (2018). Future challenges on the use of blockchain for food traceability analysis. *Trends in Analytical Chemistry*, *107*, 222–232. doi:10.1016/j.trac.2018.08.011

Gao, X., Ye, Y., Gong, S., Chen, L., & Wang, T. (2023a). Empirical patterns of interdependencies among critical infrastructures in cascading disasters: Evidence from a comprehensive multi-case analysis. *International Journal of Disaster Risk Reduction*, *95*, 103862. doi:10.1016/j.ijdrr.2023.103862

Gartner. (2021). Gartner Top Security Projects for 2020-2021. Gartner. Retrieved May 12, 2023, from https://www.gartner.com/smarterwithgartner/gartner-top-security-projects-for-2020-2021

Gaur, L., Singh, G., Solanki, A., Jhanjhi, N. Z., Bhatia, U., Sharma, S., & Verma, S. Kavita, Petrović, N., Muhammad, F. I., & Kim, W. (2021). Disposition of youth in predicting sustainable development goals using the Neuro - fuzzy and random forest algorithms. *Human-Centric Computing and Information Sciences*. https://repository.usp.ac.fj/12807/

Gaur, L., Zaman, N., Bakshi, S., & Gupta, P. (2022). Analyzing Consequences of Artificial Intelligence on Jobs using Topic Modeling and Keyword Extraction. In *2022 2nd International Conference on Innovative Practices in Technology and Management (ICIPTM)*. 10.1109/ICIPTM54933.2022.9754064

Gaur, L., Afaq, A., Solanki, A., Singh, G., Sharma, S., Jhanjhi, N. Z., My, H. T., & Le, D. (2021). Capitalizing on big data and revolutionary 5G technology: Extracting and visualizing ratings and reviews of global chain hotels. *Computers & Electrical Engineering*, *95*, 107374. doi:10.1016/j.compeleceng.2021.107374

Gaur, L., Bhatia, U., Jhanjhi, N. Z., Muhammad, G., & Masud, M. (2021). Medical image-based detection of COVID-19 using Deep Convolution Neural Networks. *Multimedia Systems*, 1–10. https://link.springer.com/article/10.1007/s00530-021-00794-6 PMID:33935377

Gaur, L., Ujjan, R. M. A., & Hussain, M. (2022). The Influence of Deep Learning in Detecting Cyber Attacks on E-Government Applications. In *Cybersecurity Measures for E-Government Frameworks* (pp. 107–122). IGI Global. doi:10.4018/978-1-7998-9624-1.ch007

Gershon, D., Prince, O., & Opoku, A. M. (2018). Promoting Inclusiveness and Participation in Governance: The Directions of Electronic Government in Ghana. *International Journal of Advanced Research*, *7*(3), 397–406. doi:10.21474/IJAR01/7931

Ghosh, G., Kavita, Verma, S., Jhanjhi, N. Z., & Talib, M. N. (2020). Secure surveillance system using chaotic image encryption technique. *IOP Conference Series. Materials Science and Engineering*, *993*(1), 012062. doi:10.1088/1757-899X/993/1/012062

Gihon. (n.d.). *The Weak Link: Recent Supply Chain Attacks Examined*. cy-berint.com

Global, I. (2020, September 30). A Guide to the NIST Cybersecurity Framework. *Dark Reading*. https://www.darkreading.com/physical-security/a-guide-to-the-nist-cybersecurity-framework

Glyptis, L., Christofi, M., Vrontis, D., Del Giudice, M., Dimitriou, S., & Michael, P. (2020). E-Government implementation challenges in small countries: The project manager's perspective. *Technological Forecasting and Social Change*, *152*, 119880. doi:10.1016/j.techfore.2019.119880

Gnusarev, V. (2019). Logistics in global supply chains. Advances in Economics. *Business and Management Research*, *88*, 177–181. doi:10.2991/978-94-6239-284-6_27

Goel, A., Goel, A., & Kumar, A. (2022). The role of artificial neural network and machine learning in utilizing spatial information. *Spatial Information Research*, *31*(3), 275–285. doi:10.1007/s41324-022-00494-x

Goldby, M., & Okonjo, J. (2023). Smart contracts: balancing innovation and consumer protection in insurance law and regulation. Edward Elgar Publishing eBooks. doi:10.4337/9781802205893.00035

Gomes, L. A. de V., de Faria, A. M., Braz, A. C., de Mello, A. M., Borini, F. M., & Ometto, A. R. (2023). Circular ecosystem management: Orchestrating ecosystem value proposition and configuration. *International Journal of Production Economics*, *256*, 108725. doi:10.1016/j.ijpe.2022.108725

Gonzalez-Granadillo, G., Gonzalez-Zarzosa, S., & Diaz, R. (2021). Security Information and Event Management (SIEM): Analysis, Trends, and Usage in Critical Infrastructures. *Sensors (Basel)*, *21*(14), 4759. doi:10.3390/s21144759 PMID:34300500

Gopi, R., Sathiyamoorthi, V., Selvakumar, S., Manikandan, R., Chatterjee, P., Jhanjhi, N. Z., & Luhach, A. K. (2021). Enhanced method of ANN based model for detection of DDoS attacks on multimedia internet of things. *Multimedia Tools and Applications*, 1–19.

Gorla, N., & Somers, T. M. (2014). The impact of IT outsourcing on information systems success. *Information & Management*, *51*(3), 320–335. doi:10.1016/j.im.2013.12.002

Gouveia, L. B. (2020). e-Government and Smart Cities: Contexts and Challenges Taking from Digital Usage and Exploration. *UNU-EGOV| UM DSI PDSI talk.*

Gouveia, L. B. (2020). e-Government and Smart Cities: Contexts and Challenges Taking from Digital Usage and Exploration. *UNU-EGOV| UM DSI PDSI talk.* https://bdigital.ufp.pt/handle/10284/8554

Green, C. (2023). Best practices in supplier relationship management and response when supply is disrupted by cyber attack : An incident response framework. *PubMed, 17*(1), 6–15. https://pubmed.ncbi.nlm.nih.gov/37537763

Gregor, T. (2017). Smart connected logistics. *Proc. Int. Sci. Conf. Sustain. Mod. Safe Transp. (TRANSCOM),* 192, 265–270.

Gregory, N. (1998). Logistics, strategy and structure: A conceptual framework. *International Journal of Operations & Production Management*, *18*(1), 37–52. doi:10.1108/01443579810192772

Grima, Thalassinos, Cristea, Kadlubek, Maditinos, & Peiseniece. (2023). *Digital transformation, strategic resilience, cyber security and risk management.* Academic Press.

Grosse, E. H., & Glock, C. H. (2015). The effect of worker learning on manual order picking processes. *International Journal of Production Economics*, *170*, 882–890. doi:10.1016/j.ijpe.2014.12.018

Gupta, R., & Agarwal, S. P. (2017). A Comparative Study of Cyber Threats in Emerging Economies. *Globus: An International Journal of Management & IT, 8*(2), 24-28. https://globusjournal.com/wp-content/uploads/2018/07/826Ruchika.pdf

Gusmão Caiado, G., Luiz Goncalves Quelhas, O., Felipe Scavarda, L., Gayialis, S. P., Kechagias, E. P., Konstantakopoulos, G. D., & Papadopoulos, G. A. (2022). A Predictive Maintenance System for Reverse Supply Chain Operations. *Logistics, 6*(1), 4. doi:10.3390/logistics6010004

Hägele, S., Grosse, E. H., & Ivanov, D. (2023). Supply chain resilience: A tertiary study. *International Journal of Integrated Supply Management, 16*(1), 52. doi:10.1504/IJISM.2023.127660

Hall, R. C., Hoppa, M. A., & Hu, Y. (2023). An Empirical Study of Password Policy Compliance. *Journal of the Colloquium for Information Systems Security Education, 10*(1), 8. doi:10.53735/cisse.v10i1.156

Hameed, K., Haseeb, J., Tayyab, M., & Junaid, M. (2017). Secure provenance in wireless sensor networks-a survey of provenance schemes. In 2017 International Conference on Communication, Computing and Digital Systems (C-CODE) (pp. 11–16). IEEE.

Hamid, B., Jhanjhi, N. Z., Humayun, M., Khan, A., & Alsayat, A. (2019, December). Cyber security issues and challenges for smart cities: A survey. In *2019 13th International Conference on Mathematics, Actuarial Science, Computer Science and Statistics (MACS)* (pp. 1-7). IEEE. 10.1109/MACS48846.2019.9024768

Hamid, B., Jhanjhi, N. Z., & Humayun, M. (2020). Digital Governance for Developing Countries Opportunities, Issues, and Challenges in Pakistan. In *Employing Recent Technologies for Improved Digital Governance* (pp. 36–58). IGI Global. doi:10.4018/978-1-7998-1851-9.ch003

Hamilton, G., Williams, M., & Khan, T. M. (2023). Securing Personally Identifiable Information (PII) in Personal Financial Statements. *Lecture Notes in Networks and Systems, 652 LNNS*, 709–728. https://doi.org/ doi:10.1007/978-3-031-28073-3_48/FIGURES/4

Hammad, M., Jillani, R., Ullah, S., Namoun, A., Tufail, A., Kim, K., & Shah, H. (2023). Security Framework for Network-Based Manufacturing Systems with Personalized Customization: An Industry 4.0 Approach. *Sensors (Basel), 23*(17), 7555. doi:10.3390/s23177555 PMID:37688011

Hammi, B., Zeadally, S., & Nebhen, J. (2023). Security threats, countermeasures, and challenges of digital supply chains. *ACM Computing Surveys, 55*(14s), 1–40. Advance online publication. doi:10.1145/3588999

Han, M., Li, Z., He, J., Wu, D., Xie, Y., & Baba, A. (2018, September). A novel blockchain-based education records verification solution. In *Proceedings of the 19th Annual SIG Conference on Information Technology Education* (pp. 178-183). IEEE. 10.1145/3241815.3241870

Haran, M. H. (2016). Framework Based Approach for the Mitigation of Insider Threats in E-governance IT Infrastructure. *International Journal of Scientific Research, 3*(4), 5–10. https://citeseerx.ist.psu.edu/viewdoc/download?doi=10.1.1.566.4423&rep=rep1&type=pdf

Harris, M. A., & Martin, R. (2019). Promoting cybersecurity compliance. In *Cybersecurity education for awareness and compliance* (pp. 54–71). IGI Global. https://www.igi-global.com/chapter/promoting-cybersecurity-compliance/225917 doi:10.4018/978-1-5225-7847-5.ch004

Hasan, H. R., & Salah, K. (2018). Proof of Delivery of Digital Assets Using Blockchain and Smart Contracts. *IEEE Access : Practical Innovations, Open Solutions*, *6*, 65439–65448. doi:10.1109/ACCESS.2018.2876971

Hause, M., & Kihlström, L. (2022a). Tilting at Windmills: Drivers, risk, opportunity, resilience and the 2021 Texas electricity grid failure. *INCOSE International Symposium*, *32*(1), 545–564. doi:10.1002/iis2.12948

He, Z., Zhang, D., Zhu, S., Cao, J., & Liu, X. (2016, September). Sdn enabled high performance multicast in vehicular networks. In *2016 IEEE 84th Vehicular Technology Conference (VTC-Fall)* (pp. 1-5). IEEE. 10.1109/VTCFall.2016.7881215

Health Information Trust Alliance. (2021). *HITRUST CSF*. https://hitrustalliance.net/hitrust-csf/

Hegab, H., Shaban, I. S., Jamil, M., & Khanna, N. (2023). Toward sustainable future: Strategies, indicators, and challenges for implementing sustainable production systems. *Sustainable Materials and Technologies*, *36*, e00617. doi:10.1016/j.susmat.2023.e00617

Henriksen, H. Z. (2018). One step forward and two steps back: e-Government policies in practice. In *Policy Analytics, Modelling, and Informatics* (pp. 79–97). Springer. doi:10.1007/978-3-319-61762-6_4

Herawati, A. R., Warsono, H., Afrizal, T., & Saputra, J. (2021). *The Challenges of Industrial Revolution 4.0: An Evidence from Public Administration Ecology in Indonesia*. http://www.ieomsociety.org/singapore2021/papers/846.pdf

He, Y., Aliyu, A., Evans, M., & Luo, C. (2021). Health Care Cybersecurity Challenges and Solutions Under the Climate of COVID-19: Scoping Review. *Journal of Medical Internet Research*, *23*(4), e21747. doi:10.2196/21747 PMID:33764885

Hiscox. (2019). *The hiscox cyber readiness report 2019*. https://www.sciencedirect.com/science/article/pii/S0167404821000729

Hitachi, Ltd. (2020). *JP1 Intelligent Governance : Hitachi ICT Solutions*. Retrieved May 13, 2023, from https://www.hitachi.asia/ict-solutions/solutions/sms/jp1-it-compliance/?gclid=CjwKCAjwx_eiBhBGEiwA15gLN3IaGHvkl2SSzzorz10SRCZvdlRraeyTFofPf69bsZEO4fB7pgjQshoC7hwQAvD_BwE#assetmgmt

Hoang, M. T., Spandonidis, C., Sedikos, E., Giannopoulos, F., Petsa, A., Theodoropoulos, P., Chatzis, K., & Galiatsatos, N. (2022). A Novel Intelligent IoT System for Improving the Safety and Planning of Air Cargo Operations. *Signals, 3*(1), 95–112. doi:10.3390/signals3010008

Hoerl, R., & Snee, R. D. (2012). *Statistical Thinking: Improving Business Performance*. http://ci.nii.ac.jp/ncid/BA55971443

Hofbauer, D., Ivkic, I., & Tauber, M. (2019). *"On the Cost of Security Compliance in Information Systems." 10th International Multi-Conference on Complexity, Informatics and Cybernetics 2019*. IMCIC.

Holt, T. J., Stonhouse, M., Freilich, J., & Chermak, S. M. (2021). Examining ideologically motivated cyberattacks performed by far-left groups. *Terrorism and Political Violence*, *33*(3), 527–548. doi:10.1080/09546553.2018.1551213

Hong, B., Shao, B., Guo, J., Fu, J., Li, C., & Zhu, B. (2023). Dynamic Bayesian network risk probability evolution for third-party damage of natural gas pipelines. *Applied Energy*, *333*, 120620. doi:10.1016/j.apenergy.2022.120620

Hopkins, J., & Hawking, P. (2018). Big Data Analytics and IoT in logistics: A case study. *International Journal of Logistics Management*, *29*(2), 575–591. doi:10.1108/IJLM-05-2017-0109

Hotha, K. K. (2023). Unleashing the Power of Innovation in CDMOs through Customer-Centricity and Culture of Service. *American Journal of Industrial and Business Management*, *13*(04), 234–246. doi:10.4236/ajibm.2023.134016

Huang, K., & Madnick, S. (2021, January). Does High Cybersecurity Capability Lead to Openness in Digital Trade? The Mediation Effect of E-Government Maturity. In *Proceedings of the 54th Hawaii International Conference on System Sciences* (p. 4352).

Huang, K., Siegel, M., & Madnick, S. (2018). Systematically understanding the cyber attack business: A survey. *ACM Computing Surveys*, *51*(4), 1–36. doi:10.1145/3199674

Huang, Q. (2023). Enhancing university logistics management through iot technology in the context of bioinformatics engineering. *Journal of Commercial Biotechnology*, *28*(3).

Huang, X., Yu, R., Kang, J., He, Y., & Zhang, Y. (2017). Exploring mobile edge computing for 5G-enabled software defined vehicular networks. *IEEE Wireless Communications*, *24*(6), 55–63. doi:10.1109/MWC.2017.1600387

Huertas Celdran, A. (2018). Ice++: im-proving security, QoS, and high availability of medical cyber-physical systems through mobile edge computing. *IEEE 20th international conference one-health networking, applications and services (Healthcom),* 1–8.

Hu, H., Xu, J., Liu, M., & Lim, M. K. (2023). Vaccine supply chain management: An intelligent system utilizing blockchain, IoT and machine learning. *Journal of Business Research*, *156*, 113480. doi:10.1016/j.jbusres.2022.113480 PMID:36506475

Humayun, M., Jhanjhi, N. Z., Hamid, B., & Ahmed, G. (2020). Emerging smart logistics and transportation using IoT and blockchain. *IEEE Internet of Things Magazine, 3*(2), 58-62. https://ieeexplore.ieee.org/abstract/document/9125435

Humayun, M., Zaman, N., Talib, M. N., Shah, M. H., & Suseendran, G. (2021b). Cybersecurity for Data Science: Issues, Opportunities, and Challenges. In Lecture notes in networks and systems (pp. 435–444). Springer International Publishing. doi:10.1007/978-981-16-3153-5_46

Humayun, M., Alsaqer, M., & Jhanjhi, N. Z. (2022). Energy optimization for smart cities using IoT. *Applied Artificial Intelligence*, *36*(1), 2037255. doi:10.1080/08839514.2022.2037255

Humayun, M., Hamid, B., Jhanjhi, N. Z., Suseendran, G., & Talib, M. N. (2021, August). 5G Network Security Issues, Challenges, Opportunities and Future Directions: A Survey. *Journal of Physics: Conference Series*, *1979*(1), 012037. doi:10.1088/1742-6596/1979/1/012037

Humayun, M., Jhanjhi, N., Alruwaili, M., Amalathas, S. S., Balasubramanian, V., & Selvaraj, B. J. I. A. (2020). Privacy protection and energy optimization for 5G-aided industrial. *Internet of Things : Engineering Cyber Physical Human Systems*, *8*, 183665–183677.

Humayun, M., Niazi, M., Zaman, N., Alshayeb, M., & Mahmood, S. (2020). Cyber Security Threats and Vulnerabilities: A Systematic Mapping Study. *Arabian Journal for Science and Engineering*, *45*(4), 3171–3189. doi:10.1007/s13369-019-04319-2

Humayun, M., Zaman, N., Hamid, B., & Ahmed, G. (2020). Emerging Smart Logistics and Transportation Using IoT and Blockchain. *IEEE Internet of Things Magazine*, *3*(2), 58–62. doi:10.1109/IOTM.0001.1900097

Hummer, D., & Byrne, J. M. (2023). *Handbook on crime and technology*. Edward Elgar Publishing. doi:10.4337/9781800886643

Husain, M. S., Faisal, M., Sadia, H., Ahmad, T., & Shukla, S. (2023). *Advances in cyberology and the advent of the Next-Gen information revolution*. IGI Global. doi:10.4018/978-1-6684-8133-2

Hussain, M., Talpur, M. S. H., & Humayun, M. (2022). The Consequences of Integrity Attacks on E-Governance: Privacy and Security Violation. In *Cybersecurity Measures for E-Government Frameworks* (pp. 141–156). IGI Global. doi:10.4018/978-1-7998-9624-1.ch009

Hussain, S. J., Ahmed, U., Liaquat, H., Mir, S., Jhanjhi, N. Z., & Humayun, M. (2019). IMIAD: Intelligent Malware Identification for Android Platform. *2019 International Conference on Computer and Information Sciences (ICCIS)*. IEEE. 10.1109/ICCISci.2019.8716471

Hussain, S. J., Irfan, M., Jhanjhi, N. Z., Hussain, K., & Humayun, M. (2021). Performance enhancement in wireless body area networks with secure communication. *Wireless Personal Communications*, *116*(1), 1–22. doi:10.1007/s11277-020-07702-7 PMID:33558792

IBM. (2020). *Cost of a data breach 2022*. IBM. Retrieved May 12, 2023, from https://www.ibm.com/reports/data-breach

IBM. (2023). *X-Force Threat Intelligence Index*. IBM Security. Retrieved May 12, 2023, from https://www.cert.hu/sites/default/files/xforce_threat_intelligence_index_2021_90037390usen.pdf

Ilves, T. H. (2016). The consequences of cyber attacks. *Journal of International Affairs*, *70*(1), 175–181.

Imran, L. B., Farhan, M., Latif, R. M. A., & Rafiq, A. (2018). Design of an IoT based warfare car robot using sensor network connectivity. *Proceedings of the 2nd International Conference on Future Networks and Distributed Systems*. 10.1145/3231053.3231121

International Electrotechnical Commission. (2018). *An Overview of ISA/IEC 62443 Standards Security of Industrial Automation and Control Systems.* ISA. Retrieved May 10, 2023, from https://gca.isa.org/hubfs/ISAGCA%20Quick%20Start%20Guide%20FINAL.pdf

International Organization for Standardization. (2022, November 29). *ISO/IEC 15408-1:2022 Information security, cybersecurity and privacy protection — Evaluation criteria for IT security — Part 1: Introduction and general model.* ISO. Retrieved May 10, 2023, from https://www.iso.org/standard/72891.html

International Organization for Standardization. (2022a). *ISO/IEC 27001 Information security management systems.* ISO. Retrieved May 10, 2023, from https://www.iso.org/standard/27001

Iqbal, S. Z. (2023, December 31). *Role of Artificial Intelligence in Enhancing Network Security: A comprehensive analysis.* IJASC. https://ijasc.com/index.php/ijasc/article/view/46

Iqbal, H. (2023). Machine learning for intelligent data analysis and automation in cybersecurity: Current and future prospects. *Annals of Data Science*, *10*(6), 1473–1498. doi:10.1007/s40745-022-00444-2

ISACA. (2020). https://www.studocu.com/row/document/islamic-university-of-madinah/system-integration/cobit-2019-framework-introduction-and-methodology-1/24868396

ISACA. (2021). *How Effective Is Your Cybersecurity Audit?* Retrieved May 13, 2023, from https://www.isaca.org/resources/isaca-journal/issues/2022/volume-3/how-effective-is-your-cybersecurity-audit

Islam, M. J., Mahin, M., Roy, S., Debnath, B. C., & Khatun, A. (2019, February). Distblacknet: A distributed secure black sdn-iot architecture with nfv implementation for smart cities. In *2019 International Conference on Electrical, Computer and Communication Engineering (ECCE)* (pp. 1-6). IEEE. 10.1109/ECACE.2019.8679167

Ismail, A., Hidajat, P. T., Dora, Y. M., Prasatia, F. E., & Pranadani, A. (2023). *Leading the digital transformation: Evidence from Indonesia.* Asadel Publisher.

ISO. (2019). *ISO/IEC 27001:2013 Information technology -- Security techniques -- Information security management systems -- Requirements.* https://www.iso.org/obp/ui/#iso:std:iso-iec:27001:ed-2:v1:en

Issaoui, Y. (2019). *Smart Logistics: Study of The Application of Bolckchain Technology The 10th International Conference on Emerging Ubiquitous Systems and Pervasive Networks.* Springer. https://link.springer.com/article/10.1007/s12205-020-0188-x

ITRC. (2022, January 21). *Identity Theft Resource Center's 2021 Annual Data Breach Report Sets New Record for Number of Compromises - ITRC.* Retrieved May 13, 2023, from https://www.idtheftcenter.org/post/identity-theft-resource-center-2021-annual-data-breach-report-sets-new-record-for-number-of-compromises/

Jabbar, S., Lloyd, H., Hammoudeh, M., Adebisi, B., & Raza, U. (2021). Blockchain-enabled supply chain: Analysis, challenges, and future directions. *Multimedia Systems*, *27*(4), 787–806. doi:10.1007/s00530-020-00687-0

Jackson, E. (2023). New risks to the missing middle of global meat supply chains. In SAGE Business Cases Originals eBooks. doi:10.4135/9781071920510

Jacob, S. (2023). *The Rapid Increase of Ransomware Attacks Over the 21st Century and Mitigation Strategies to Prevent Them from Arising*.

Jacobs, B. (2023). A comparative study of EU and US regulatory approaches to cybersecurity in space. *Air and Space Law*, *48*(4 /5), 477–492. doi:10.54648/AILA2023052

Jacquenet, C., & Boucadair, M. (2016). A software-defined approach to IoT networking. *ZTE Communications*, *1*, 1–12.

Jahankhani, H., Kendzierskyj, S., & Hussien, O. (2023). Approaches and methods for regulation of security risks in 5G and 6G. In Advanced sciences and technologies for security applications (pp. 43–70). doi:10.1007/978-3-031-33631-7_2

Jaiswal, N., Misra, A., Khang, A., & Misra, P. K. (2023). The role of internet of things technologies in business and production. In *AI-Aided IoT Technologies and Applications for Smart Business and Production* (pp. 1–13). CRC Press. doi:10.1201/9781003392224-1

Javaid, M., Haleem, A., Singh, R. P., & Suman, R. (2022). Enabling flexible manufacturing system (FMS) through the applications of industry 4.0 technologies. *Internet of Things and Cyber-Physical Systems*.

Javaid, M., Haleem, A., Singh, R. P., & Suman, R. (2023). Towards insighting Cybersecurity for Healthcare domains: A comprehensive review of recent practices and trends. *Chinese Root Global Impact*, *1*, 100016. doi:10.1016/j.csa.2023.100016

Javaid, M., Haleem, A., Vaishya, R., Bahl, S., Suman, R., & Vaish, A. (2020). Industry 4.0 technologies and their applications in fighting COVID-19 pandemic. *Diabetes & Metabolic Syndrome*, *14*(4), 419–422. doi:10.1016/j.dsx.2020.04.032 PMID:32344370

Javelin. (2021). *2021 Identity Fraud Study: Shifting Angles*. Javelin. Retrieved May 12, 2023, from https://javelinstrategy.com/content/2021-identity-fraud-report-shifting-angles-identity-fraud

JayakumarP.BrohiS. N.ZamanN. (2021). Artificial Intelligence and Military Applications: Innovations, Cybersecurity Challenges & Open Research Areas. *Preprint.org*. doi:10.20944/preprints202108.0047.v1

Jazri, H., & Jat, D. S. (2016, November). A quick cybersecurity wellness evaluation framework for critical organizations. In *2016 International Conference on ICT in Business Industry & Government (ICTBIG)* (pp. 1-5). IEEE. https://ieeexplore.ieee.org/abstract/document/7892725

Jeffrey, N., Tan, Q., & Flecha, J. R. V. (2023). A review of Anomaly detection Strategies to detect Threats to Cyber-Physical Systems. *Electronics (Basel)*, *12*(15), 3283. doi:10.3390/electronics12153283

Jeschke, S., Brecher, C., Song, H., & Rawat, D. (2017). *Industrial Internet of Things: Cybermanufacturing Systems*. Springer. doi:10.1007/978-3-319-42559-7

Jhanjhi, N. Z., Brohi, S. N., & Malik, N. A. (2019, December). Proposing a rank and wormhole attack detection framework using machine learning. In *2019 13th International Conference on Mathematics, Actuarial Science, Computer Science and Statistics (MACS)* (pp. 1-9). IEEE.

Jhanjhi, N. Z., Ahmad, M., Khan, M. A., & Hussain, M. (2022). The impact of cyber attacks on e-governance during the covid-19 pandemic. In *Cybersecurity Measures for E-Government Frameworks* (pp. 123–140). IGI Global. doi:10.4018/978-1-7998-9624-1.ch008

Jhanjhi, N. Z., Humayun, M., & Almuayqil, S. N. (2021). Cyber security and privacy issues in industrial internet of things. *Computer Systems Science and Engineering*, *37*(3), 361–380. doi:10.32604/csse.2021.015206

Jiang, T., Fang, H., & Wang, H. (2019, June). Blockchain-Based Internet of Vehicles: Distributed Network Architecture and Performance Analysis. *IEEE Internet of Things Journal*, *6*(3), 4640–4649. doi:10.1109/JIOT.2018.2874398

Jiang, W. (2024). Cybersecurity Risk and Audit Pricing—A Machine Learning-Based analysis. *Journal of Information Systems*, 1–27. doi:10.2308/ISYS-2023-019

Ji, S., Chen, T., & Zhong, S. (2015, March 1). Wormhole Attack Detection Algorithms in Wireless Network Coding Systems. *IEEE Transactions on Mobile Computing*, *14*(3), 660–674. doi:10.1109/TMC.2014.2324572

John, F. L., Lakshmi, D., & Kuncharam, M. (2023). *Introduction to the Internet of Things*. Wiley. doi:10.1002/9781119812524.ch1

Joshi, P. R., & Islam, S. (2018). E-government maturity model for sustainable e-government services from the perspective of developing countries. *Sustainability (Basel)*, *10*(6), 1882. doi:10.3390/su10061882

Joshi, S. (2015). E-Governance in Uttar Pradesh: Challenges and Prospects. *The Indian Journal of Public Administration*, *61*(2), 229–240. doi:10.1177/0019556120150203

Julie, G., Nayahi, J. J. V., & Zaman, N. (n.d.). *Blockchain technology : fundamentals, applications, and case studies*. Routledge. https://www.routledge.com/Blockchain-Technology-Fundamentals-Applications-and-Case-Studies/Julie-Nayahi-Jhanjhi/p/book/9780367431372

Juma, M., AlAttar, F., & Touqan, B. (2023). Securing big data integrity for industrial IoT in smart manufacturing based on the Trusted Consortium Blockchain (TCB). *Iot*, *4*(1), 27–55. doi:10.3390/iot4010002

Junejo, A. K., Breza, M., & Julie, A. (2023). McCann. Threat modeling for communication security of iot-enabled digital logistics. *Sensors (Basel), 23*(23), 9500. doi:10.3390/s23239500 PMID:38067872

Jussila, A., Mainela, T., & Nätti, S. (2016). Formation of strategic networks under high uncertainty of a megaproject. *Journal of Business and Industrial Marketing, 31*(5), 575–586. doi:10.1108/JBIM-03-2014-0055

Kadhim, J. Q., Aljazaery, I. A. (2023). *EBSCOhost | 161238003 | Enhancement of Online Education in Engineering College Based on Mobile Wireless Communication Networks and IOT.* International Journal of Emerging Technologies in Learning.

Kadrich, M. (2007). *Endpoint security.* Addison-Wesley Professional.

Kagermann, H. (2014). Change through digitization—value creation in the age of industry 4.0. In *Management of permanent change* (pp. 23–45). Springer.

Kalaiarasan, R., Agrawal, T. K., Olhager, J., Wiktorsson, M., & Hauge, J. B. (2023). Supply chain visibility for improving inbound logistics: A design science approach. *International Journal of Production Research, 61*(15), 5228–5243. doi:10.1080/00207543.2022.2099321

Kalinaki, K., Fahadi, M., Alli, A. A., Shafik, W., Yasin, M., & Mutwalibi, N. (2023). Artificial Intelligence of Internet of Medical Things (AIoMT) in Smart Cities: A Review of Cybersecurity for Smart Healthcare. In Handbook of Security and Privacy of AI-Enabled Healthcare Systems and Internet of Medical Things (pp. 271–292). CRC Press. https://doi.org/ doi:10.1201/9781003370321-11

Kalinaki, K., Namuwaya, S., Mwamini, A., & Namuwaya, S. (2023). Scaling Up Customer Support Using Artificial Intelligence and Machine Learning Techniques. In *Contemporary Approaches of Digital Marketing and the Role of Machine Intelligence* (pp. 23–45). IGI Global. doi:10.4018/978-1-6684-7735-9.ch002

Kalinaki, K., Thilakarathne, N. N., Mubarak, H. R., Malik, O. A., & Abdullatif, M. (2023). Cybersafe Capabilities and Utilities for Smart Cities. In *Cybersecurity for Smart Cities* (pp. 71–86). Springer., doi:10.1007/978-3-031-24946-4_6

Kalinin, M. O., Krundyshev, V., & Zegzhda, P. D. (2021). Cybersecurity Risk Assessment in Smart City Infrastructures. *Machines, 9*(4), 78. doi:10.3390/machines9040078

Kalkha, H., Khiat, A., Bahnasse, A., & Ouajji, H. (2023). The rising trends of smart e-commerce logistics. *IEEE Access : Practical Innovations, Open Solutions, 11*, 33839–33857. doi:10.1109/ACCESS.2023.3252566

Kamil, Y., Lund, S., & Islam, M. S. (2023). Information security objectives and the output legitimacy of ISO/IEC 27001: Stakeholders' perspective on expectations in private organizations in Sweden. *Information Systems and e-Business Management, 21*(3), 699–722. doi:10.1007/s10257-023-00646-y

Kamiya, S., Kang, J. K., Kim, J., Milidonis, A., & Stulz, R. M. (2021). Risk management, firm reputation, and the impact of successful cyberattacks on target firms. *Journal of Financial Economics*, *139*(3), 719–749. doi:10.1016/j.jfineco.2019.05.019

Karakus, M., & Durresi, A. (2017). A survey: Control plane scalability issues and approaches in software-defined networking (SDN). *Computer Networks*, *112*, 279–293. doi:10.1016/j.comnet.2016.11.017

Karki, S., Nguyen, B., & Zhang, X. (2018). QoS Support for Scientific Workflows Using Software-Defined Storage Resource Enclaves. In *2018 IEEE International Parallel and Distributed Processing Symposium (IPDPS 18)*. IEEE. 10.1109/IPDPS.2018.00020

Karmarkar, U. (2023). *Service industrialization*. Elgar Encyclopedia of Services. doi:10.4337/9781802202595.Service.Industrialization

Karpenko, O., Kuczabski, A., & Havryliak, V. (2021). Mechanisms for providing cybersecurity during the COVID-19 pandemic: Perspectives for Ukraine. *Security and Defence Quarterly*. http://yadda.icm.edu.pl/yadda/element/bwmeta1.element.doi-10_35467_sdq_133158

Kaspersky. (2019, May 26). *Brand Reputation Costs $200,000 to Repair*. Retrieved May 12, 2023, from https://www.kaspersky.com/about/press-releases/2015_brand-reputation-costs--200000-to-repair

Kaur, G., Tomar, P., & Singh, P. (2018). Design of Cloud-Based Green IoT Architecture for Smart Cities. *Studies in Big Data*, *30*, 315–333. doi:10.1007/978-3-319-60435-0_13

Kaur, K., Garg, S., Aujla, G. S., Kumar, N., Rodrigues, J. J., & Guizani, M. (2018). Edge computing in the industrial internet of things environment: Software-defined-networks-based edge-cloud interplay. *IEEE Communications Magazine*, *56*(2), 44–51. doi:10.1109/MCOM.2018.1700622

Kaur, R., Gabrijelčič, D., & Klobučar, T. (2023). Artificial intelligence for cybersecurity: Literature review and future research directions. *Information Fusion*, *97*, 101804. doi:10.1016/j.inffus.2023.101804

Kayapinar, Ö., & Lorcu, F. (2020). The Role of Technology Level and Logistics Performance on the Relationship Between Logistics Service Quality and Firm Performance. In *Advances in logistics, operations, and management science book series* (pp. 107–135). Routledge. doi:10.4018/978-1-7998-4601-7.ch006

Kendzierskyj, S., Jahankhani, H., Jamal, A., Hussien, O., & Yang, L. (2023). The Role of Blockchain with a Cybersecurity Maturity Model in the Governance of Higher Education Supply Chains. In Advanced sciences and technologies for security applications (pp. 1–35). Springer. doi:10.1007/978-3-031-33627-0_1

Key Elements of Logistics Management. (n.d.) https://www.mojro.com/resource-key-elements-of-logistics-management

Khalil, M. I. (2023, July 15). *Advanced cybersecurity measures in IT service operations and their crucial role in safeguarding enterprise data in a connected world.* Eigen Pub. https://studies.eigenpub.com/index.php/erst/article/view/14

Khalil, M. I., Jhanjhi, N. Z., Humayun, M., Sivanesan, S., Masud, M., & Hossain, M. S. (2021). Hybrid smart grid with sustainable energy efficient resources for smart cities. *Sustainable Energy Technologies and Assessments, 46*, 101211.

Khan, A., Jhanjhi, N. Z., & Sujatha, R. (2022b). Emerging Industry Revolution IR 4.0 Issues and Challenges. In Cyber Security Applications for Industry 4.0 (pp. 151-169). Chapman and Hall/CRC.

Khan, N. A., Brohi, S. N., & Zaman, N. (2020). Ten deadly cyber security threats amid COVID-19 pandemic. *Tech.* https://www.techrxiv.org/articles/preprint/Ten_Deadly_Cyber_Security_Threats_Amid_COVID-19_Pandemic/12278792/1

Khan, N. A., Brohi, S. N., & Zaman, N. (2020). *Ten deadly cyber security threats16amid COVID-19 pandemic.* https://www.techrxiv.org/articles/preprint/Ten_Deadly_Cyber_Security_Threats_Amid_COVID-19_Pandemic/12278792/1

Khan, Y., Su'ud, M. B. M., Alam, M. M., Ahmad, S. F., Ahmad, A. Y. A. B., & Khan, N. (2022). Application of Internet of Things (IoT) in Sustainable Supply Chain Management. *Sustainability, 15*(1), 694. doi:10.3390/su15010694

Khan, A., Jhanjhi, N. Z., & Humayun, M. (2022). The Role of Cybersecurity in Smart Cities. In *Cyber Security Applications for Industry 4.0* (pp. 195–208). Chapman and Hall/CRC. doi:10.1201/9781003203087-9

Khan, A., Jhanjhi, N. Z., Humayun, M., & Ahmad, M. (2020). The Role of IoT in Digital Governance. In *Employing Recent Technologies for Improved Digital Governance* (pp. 128–150). IGI Global. doi:10.4018/978-1-7998-1851-9.ch007

Khandpur, R. P., Ji, T., Jan, S., Wang, G., Lu, C. T., & Ramakrishnan, N. (2017, November). Crowdsourcing cybersecurity: Cyber attack detection using social media. In *Proceedings of the 2017 ACM on Conference on Information and Knowledge Management* (pp. 1049-1057). https://dl.acm.org/doi/abs/10.1145/3132847.3132866

Khan, J. A., Qureshi, H. K., & Iqbal, A. (2015). Energy management in wireless sensor networks: A survey. *Computers & Electrical Engineering, 41*, 159–176. doi:10.1016/j.compeleceng.2014.06.009

Khan, S. K., Shiwakoti, N., Stasinopoulos, P., & Warren, M. (2023). Cybersecurity regulatory challenges for connected and automated vehicles – State-of-the-art and future directions. *Transport Policy, 143*, 58–71. doi:10.1016/j.tranpol.2023.09.001

Khargharia, B., Hariri, S., Szidarovszky, F., Houri, M., El-Rewini, H., Khan, S. U., . . . Yousif, M. S. (2007). *Autonomic power & performance management for large-scale data centers.* Paper presented at the 2007 IEEE International Parallel and Distributed Processing Symposium. 10.1109/IPDPS.2007.370510

Khatoun, R., & Zeadally, S. (2017). Cybersecurity and privacy solutions in smart cities. *IEEE Communications Magazine*, *55*(3), 51–59. doi:10.1109/MCOM.2017.1600297CM

Kilag, O. K. T. (2023, July 13). *Managing cybersecurity Risks in educational technology Environments: Strategies and best practices.* GRN Journal. http://grnjournal.us/index.php/STEM/article/view/357

Kim, A. (2023, March 30). *20 Critical Security Controls | SANS Institute*. https://www.sans.org/webcasts/20-critical-security-controls-96685/

Kim, H. M., & Laskowski, M. (2018). Agriculture on the blockchain: Sustainable solutions for food, farmers, and financing. *Supply Chain Revolution, Barrow Books.*

Kim, C., & Kim, K. A. (2021). The institutional change from E-Government toward Smarter City; comparative analysis between royal borough of Greenwich, UK, and Seongdong-gu, South Korea. *Journal of Open Innovation*, *7*(1), 42. doi:10.3390/joitmc7010042

Kim, J. H., Seo, B., Choi, K., & Sung, S. (2023). Ballistic Penetration Test and Simulation of Metallic Aircraft Wing Fuel Tank. *International Journal of Aeronautical and Space Sciences*, *24*(1), 303–314. doi:10.1007/s42405-022-00565-1

Kioskli, K., Fotis, T., Nifakos, S., & Mouratidis, H. (2023). The importance of conceptualising the Human-Centric approach in maintaining and promoting Cybersecurity-Hygiene in healthcare 4.0. *Applied Sciences (Basel, Switzerland)*, *13*(6), 3410. doi:10.3390/app13063410

Kiran, S. R. A., Rajper, S., Shaikh, R. A., Shah, I. A., & Danwar, S. H. (2021). Categorization of CVE Based on Vulnerability Software By Using Machine Learning Techniques. *International Journal (Toronto, Ont.)*, *10*(3).

Kirkwood, S. (2022). *Cybersecurity in Logistics: How to Protect Your Supply Chain from Cyberattacks.* Evans Distribution Systems. https://www.evansdist.com/cybersecurity-in-logistics/

Kok, S. H., Azween, A., & Jhanjhi, N. Z. (2020). Evaluation metric for crypto-ransomware detection using machine learning. *Journal of Information Security and Applications*, *55*, 102646. doi:10.1016/j.jisa.2020.102646

Koley, I., & Samanta, T. (2019). Mobile sink based data collection for energy efficient coordination in wireless sensor network using cooperative game model. *Telecommunication Systems*, *71*(3), 377–396. doi:10.1007/s11235-018-0507-4

Koo, E. (2019). *Digital transformation of Government: from E-Government to intelligent E-Government* (Doctoral dissertation). Massachusetts Institute of Technology.

KopM.AboyM.De JongE.GasserU.MinssenT.CohenI. G.BrongersmaM. L.QuintelT.FloridiL. LaflammeR. (2023). Towards responsible quantum technology. *Social Science Research Network*. doi:10.2139/ssrn.4393248

Korir, G., Thiga, M., & Rono, L. (2019). *Implementing the Tool for Assessing Organisation Information Security Preparedness in E-Governance Implementation*. https://www.easpublisher.com/media/features_articles/EASJECS_210_284-299.pdf

Kozma, D., Varga, P., & Hegedűs, C. (2019). *Supply Chain Management and Logistics 4.0 - A Study on Arrowhead Framework Integration*. doi:10.1109/ICITM.2019.8710670

Krehel, O. (2021, August 31). *LIFARS Cybersecurity Firm provides Incident Response, Digtial Forensics, Ransomware Solutions*. LIFARS, a SecurityScorecard Company. Retrieved May 13, 2023, from https://www.lifars.com/about/

Krishnan, S., Thangaveloo, R., Rahman, S. B. A., & Sindiramutty, S. R. (2021). Smart Ambulance Traffic Control system. *Trends in Undergraduate Research*, *4*(1), c28–c34. doi:10.33736/tur.2831.2021

Krishnaraju, V., Mathew, S. K., & Sugumaran, V. (2016). Web personalization for user acceptance of technology: An empirical investigation of E-government services. *Information Systems Frontiers*, *18*(3), 579–595. doi:10.1007/s10796-015-9550-9

Kron. (2022). *Cybersecurity in the Logistics Industry*. Kron. Retrieved May 11, 2023, from https://krontech.com/cybersecurity-in-the-logistics-industry

Krupitzer, C., & Stein, A. (2023). Unleashing the potential of digitalization in the Agri-Food Chain for integrated food systems. *Annual Review of Food Science and Technology*, *15*(1), annurev-food-012422-024649. doi:10.1146/annurev-food-012422-024649 PMID:37931153

Krykavskyi, Ye., Pokhylchenko, O., Fertsch M. (2019). *Lohistyka ta upravlinnia lantsiuhamy postavok* [Logistics and Supply Chain Management]. 848s.

Krykavskyy, Ye., Pokhylchenko, O., & Hayvanovych, N. (2019) Digitalization of Supply Chains: New Paradigm. *Contemporary Issues in Economy*, 103-112. http://economicresearch.pl/Books/index.php/eep/catalog/view/55/57/86-2

Krykavskyy, Y., Hayvanovych, N., Pokhylchenko, O., Leonova, S., Dovhun, O., & Chornopyska, N. (2021). *Competence determinants of logistics landscape*. Contemporary Issues in Economy.

Kshetri, N. (2018). 1 Blockchain's roles in meeting key supply chain management objectives. *International Journal of Information Management*, *39*, 80–89. doi:10.1016/j.ijinfomgt.2017.12.005

Kumar, B. S. B. (2024). *A comprehensive analysis of key factors causing various kinds of cyber-attacks in higher educational institute's*. https://journalra.org/index.php/jra/article/view/1115

Kumar, P., Kunwar, R. S., & Sachan, A. (2016). A survey report on: Security & challenges in internet of things. In *Proc National Conference on ICT & IoT* (pp. 35-39). Academic Press.

Kumar, D., Kr Singh, R., Mishra, R., & Fosso Wamba, S. (2022). Applications of the internet of things for optimizing warehousing and logistics operations: A systematic literature review and future research directions. *Computers & Industrial Engineering*, *171*, 108455. doi:10.1016/j.cie.2022.108455

Kumari, S., & Muthulakshmi, P. (2023). *Artificial Intelligence—Blockchain Enabled Technology for Internet of Things*. Wiley. doi:10.1002/9781394213726.ch18

Kumar, K. D., Venkata Rathnam, T., Venkata Ramana, R., Sudhakara, M., & Poluru, R. K. (2022). Towards the Integration of Blockchain and IoT for Security Challenges in IoT. In *Research Anthology on Convergence of Blockchain, Internet of Things, and Security* (pp. 193–209). IGI Global. doi:10.4018/978-1-6684-7132-6.ch012

Kumar, M. S., Raut, R. D., Narwane, V. S., & Narkhede, B. E. (2020). Applications of industry 4.0 to overcome the COVID-19 operational challenges. *Diabetes & Metabolic Syndrome*, *14*(5), 1283–1289. doi:10.1016/j.dsx.2020.07.010 PMID:32755822

Kumar, M. S., Vimal, S., Jhanjhi, N. Z., Dhanabalan, S. S., & Alhumyani, H. A. (2021). Blockchain based peer to peer communication in autonomous drone operation. *Energy Reports*, *7*, 7925–7939. doi:10.1016/j.egyr.2021.08.073

Kumar, T., Pandey, B., Mussavi, S. H., & Jhanjhi, N. Z. (2015). CTHS based energy efficient Thermal Aware Image ALU design on FPGA. *Wireless Personal Communications*, *85*(3), 671–696. doi:10.1007/s11277-015-2801-8

Kumar, V., Malik, N., Singla, J., Zaman, N., Amsaad, F., & Razaque, A. (2022). Light Weight Authentication Scheme for Smart Home IoT Devices. *Cryptography*, *6*(3), 37. doi:10.3390/cryptography6030037

Kumbhare, A., Thakur, P., Patnaik, B. R. K., & Midiyam, K. (2023). Blockchain's data integrity and reliability. In Advances in business information systems and analytics book series (pp. 231–250). Springer. doi:10.4018/978-1-6684-7808-0.ch013

Kuypers, M., Heon, G., Martin, P., & Paté-Cornell, M. L. (2014). *Cyber security: The risk of supply chain vulnerabilities in an enterprise firewall*. ResearchGate. https://www.researchgate.net/publication/288365610_Cyber_security_The_risk_of_supply_chain_vulnerabilities_in_an_enterprise_firewall

Lagorio, A., Zenezini, G., Mangano, G., & Pinto, R. (2022). A systematic literature review of innovative technologies adopted in logistics management. *International Journal of Logistics*, *25*(7), 1043–1066. doi:10.1080/13675567.2020.1850661

Lallie, H. S., Shepherd, L. A., Nurse, J. R., Erola, A., Epiphaniou, G., Maple, C., & Bellekens, X. (2021). Cyber security in the age of covid-19: A timeline and analysis of cyber-crime and cyber-attacks during the pandemic. *Computers & Security*, *105*, 102248. doi:10.1016/j.cose.2021.102248 PMID:36540648

Latif, R. M. A., Belhaouari, S. B., Saeed, S., Imran, L. B., Sadiq, M., & Farhan, M. (2020). *Integration of google play content and frost prediction using cnn: scalable iot framework for big data*. Academic Press.

Latif, R. M. A., Imran, L.-B., Farhan, M., Bah, M. J., Ali, G., & Abid, Y. A. (2019). *Real-time simulation of IoT based smart home live mirror using WSN.* Paper presented at the 2019 International Conference on Frontiers of Information Technology (FIT). 10.1109/FIT47737.2019.00019

Latif, R. M. A., Naeem, M. R., Rizwan, O., & Farhan, M. (2021). *A Smart Technique to Forecast Karachi Stock Market Share-Values using ARIMA Model.* Paper presented at the 2021 International Conference on Frontiers of Information Technology (FIT). 10.1109/FIT53504.2021.00065

Lau, L. (2018, February 23). *Cybercrime "pandemic" may have cost the world $600 billion last year.* CNBC. https://www.cnbc.com/2018/02/22/cybercrime-pandemic-may-have-cost-the-world-600-billion-last-year.html

Le Blond, S., Gilbert, C., Upadhyay, U., Gomez-Rodriguez, M., & Choffnes, D. R. (2017). A Broad View of the Ecosystem of Socially Engineered Exploit Documents. *NDSS*. https://www.ndss-symposium.org/wp-content/uploads/2017/09/ndss2017_03B-4_LeBlond_paper.pdf

Le, N. T., & Hoang, D. B. (2016, December). Can maturity models support cyber security? In *2016 IEEE 35th international performance computing and communications conference (IPCCC)* (pp. 1-7). 10.1109/PCCC.2016.7820663

Lee, S., Abdullah, A., Jhanjhi, N., & Kok, S. (2021). Classification of botnet attacks in IoT smart factory using honeypot combined with machine learning. *PeerJ. Computer Science*, *7*, e350. doi:10.7717/peerj-cs.350 PMID:33817000

Lee, S., Kim, J., Woo, S., Yoon, C., Scott-Hayward, S., Yegneswaran, V., Porras, P., & Shin, S. (2020). A comprehensive security assessment framework for software-defined networks. *Computers & Security*, *91*, 101720. doi:10.1016/j.cose.2020.101720

Leinmüller, T., & Schoch, E. (2006). *Greedy Routing in Highway Scenarios: The Impact of Position Faking Nodes*. Academic Press.

Lenko, F. (2021). Specifics of RFID Based Access Control Systems Used in Logistics Centers. *Transportation Research Procedia*, *55*, 1613–1619. doi:10.1016/j.trpro.2021.07.151

Leo, M., Aymen, C., & Francine, K. (2020). Survey on blockchain-based applications in internet of vehicles. *Computers & Electrical Engineering*, *84*, 106646. Advance online publication. doi:10.1016/j.compeleceng.2020.106646

Li, C. (2024, January 4). *Graph Neural Networks for Tabular Data Learning: A Survey with Taxonomy and Directions*. arXiv.org. https://arxiv.org/abs/2401.02143

Li, J., Yu, F. R., Deng, G., Luo, C., Ming, Z., & Yan, Q. (2017). Industrial Internet: A survey on the enabling technologies, applications, and challenges. IEEE Commun. Surveys Tuts., 19(3), 1504–1526.

Liang, Y., Qi, G., Wei, K., & Chen, J. (2017). Exploring the determinant and influence mechanism of e-Government cloud adoption in government agencies in China. *Government Information Quarterly*, *34*(3), 481–495. doi:10.1016/j.giq.2017.06.002

Li, D., Deng, L., Cai, Z., & Souri, A. (2022). Blockchain as a service models in the Internet of Things management: Systematic review. *Transactions on Emerging Telecommunications Technologies*, *33*(4), e4139. doi:10.1002/ett.4139

Li, J. H., Herdem, M. S., Nathwani, J., & Wen, J. Z. (2023). Methods and applications for Artificial Intelligence, Big Data, Internet of Things, and Blockchain in smart energy management. *Energy and AI*, *11*, 100208. doi:10.1016/j.egyai.2022.100208

Li, L., He, W., Xu, L., Ash, I., Anwar, M., & Yuan, X. (2019). Investigating the impact of cybersecurity policy awareness on employees' cybersecurity behavior. *International Journal of Information Management*, *45*, 13–24. doi:10.1016/j.ijinfomgt.2018.10.017

Lim, M., Abdullah, A., & Jhanjhi, N. Z. (2019). Performance optimization of criminal network hidden link prediction model with deep reinforcement learning. *Journal of King Saud University-Computer and Information Sciences*. https://onlinelibrary.wiley.com/doi/abs/10.1002/ett.4171

Lim, M., Abdullah, A., Jhanjhi, N. Z., & Supramaniam, M. (2019). Hidden link prediction in criminal networks using the deep reinforcement learning technique. *Computers, 8*(1), 8. https://www.mdpi.com/2073-431X/8/1/8

Lim, M., Abdullah, A., & Jhanjhi, N. Z. (2021). Performance optimization of criminal network hidden link prediction model with deep reinforcement learning. *Journal of King Saud University. Computer and Information Sciences*, *33*(10), 1202–1210. doi:10.1016/j.jksuci.2019.07.010

Lim, M., Abdullah, A., Jhanjhi, N. Z., & Khan, M. K. (2020). Situation-Aware Deep Reinforcement Learning link Prediction model for evolving criminal networks. *IEEE Access : Practical Innovations, Open Solutions*, *8*, 16550–16559. doi:10.1109/ACCESS.2019.2961805

Lim, M., Abdullah, A., Jhanjhi, N. Z., & Supramaniam, M. (2019). Hidden link prediction in criminal networks using the deep reinforcement learning technique. *Computers*, *8*(1), 8. doi:10.3390/computers8010008

Li, N., Jiang, H., Feng, D., & Shi, Z. (2017). Customizable SLO and its near-precise enforcement for storage bandwidth. *ACM Transactions on Storage*, *13*(1), 1–25. doi:10.1145/2998454

Lin, B., & Lin, B. (2023). Constructing an adaptability evaluation framework for community-based disaster management using an earthquake event. *International Journal of Disaster Risk Reduction*, *93*, 103774. doi:10.1016/j.ijdrr.2023.103774

Lindman, J., Tuunainen, V. K., & Rossi, M. (2017). Opportunities and risks of Blockchain Technologies–a research agenda.

Linkov, I., Trump, B. D., Poinsatte-Jones, K., & Florin, M. V. (2018). Governance strategies for a sustainable digital world. *Sustainability (Basel)*, *10*(2), 440. doi:10.3390/su10020440

Lin, Q., Li, X., Cai, K., Mohan, P., & Paulraj, D. (2024). Secure Internet of Medical Things (IoMT) based on ECMQV-MAC Authentication Protocol and EKMC-SCP Blockchain Networking. *Information Sciences*, *654*, 119783. doi:10.1016/j.ins.2023.119783

Lin, X. (2022). Network Security Technology of Supply Chain Management Based on Internet of Things and Big Data. *Computational Intelligence and Neuroscience*, *2022*, 1–12. doi:10.1155/2022/7753086 PMID:35774432

Li, S., Zhou, T., Yang, H., & Wang, P. (2023). Blockchain-Based Secure Storage and Access Control Scheme for Supply Chain Ecological Business Data: A Case study of the Automotive industry. *Sensors (Basel)*, *23*(16), 7036. doi:10.3390/s23167036 PMID:37631574

Liu, Z., Wei, W., Wang, L., Ten, C. W., & Rho, Y. (2020). An Actuarial Framework for Power System Reliability Considering Cybersecurity Threats. *IEEE Transactions on Power Systems*. https://dl.acm.org/doi/abs/10.1145/3386723.3387847

Liu, C., Wang, N., & Liang, H. (2020). Motivating information security policy compliance: The critical role of supervisor-subordinate guanxi and organizational commitment. *International Journal of Information Management*, *54*, 102152. doi:10.1016/j.ijinfomgt.2020.102152

Liu, D., & Carter, L. (2018, May). Impact of citizens' privacy concerns on e-government adoption. In *Proceedings of the 19th Annual International Conference on Digital Government Research: Governance in the Data Age* (pp. 1-6). 10.1145/3209281.3209340

Liu, J., Wang, C., Li, C., Li, N., Deng, J., & Pan, J. Z. (2021). DTN: Deep triple network for topic specific fake news detection. *Journal of Web Semantics*, *100646*, 100646. doi:10.1016/j.websem.2021.100646

Liu, M., Yu, F. R., Teng, Y., Leung, V. C. M., & Song, M. (2019, June). Performance optimization for blockchain-enabled industrial Internet of Things (IIoT) systems: A deep reinforcement learning approach. *IEEE Transactions on Industrial Informatics*, *15*(6), 3559–3570. doi:10.1109/TII.2019.2897805

Liu, Y., Ma, X., Qiao, W., Ma, L., & Han, B. (2024). A novel methodology to model disruption propagation for resilient maritime transportation systems–a case study of the Arctic maritime transportation system. *Reliability Engineering & System Safety*, *241*, 109620. doi:10.1016/j.ress.2023.109620

Liu, Y., Tao, X., Li, X., Colombo, A., & Hu, S. (2023). *Artificial intelligence in smart logistics cyber-physical systems: State-of-the-arts and potential applications*. IEEE Transactions on Industrial Cyber-Physical Systems.

Li, Y. (2012). An overview of the DSRC/WAVE technology. Lecture Notes of the Institute for Computer Sciences. *Social-Informatics and Telecommunications Engineering, LNICST.*, *74*, 544–558. doi:10.1007/978-3-642-29222-4_38

Li, Y., Liu, H., & Yang, W. (2017). Predicting inter-data-center network traffic using elephant flow and sublink information. *IEEE Transactions on Network and Service Management*, *13*(4), 782–792.

Lorenz-Meyer, F., & Santos, V. (2023). Blockchain in the shipping industry: A proposal for the use of blockchain for SMEs in the maritime industry. *Procedia Computer Science*, *219*, 807–814. doi:10.1016/j.procs.2023.01.354

Lu, R., Lin, X., Zhu, H., Ho, P.-H., & Shen, X. (2008). ECPP: Efficient Conditional Privacy Preservation Protocol for Secure Vehicular Communications. *IEEE INFOCOM 2008 - The 27th Conference on Computer Communications,* 1229-1237. 10.1109/INFOCOM.2008.179

Luh, R., Marschalek, S., Kaiser, M., Janicke, H., & Schrittwieser, S. (2017). Semantics-aware detection of targeted attacks: A survey. *Journal of Computer Virology and Hacking Techniques*, *13*(1), 47–85. doi:10.1007/s11416-016-0273-3

Lu, J., Yu, C.-S., Liu, C., & James, E. (2003). Technology acceptance model for wireless internet. *Internet Research*, *13*(3), 206–222. doi:10.1108/10662240310478222

Luo, Y., & Zhang, H. (2019). Global logistics management and sustainable economic development. In S. O. Idowu, W. Leal Filho, & S. M. Mifsud (Eds.), Handbook of Research on Global Business Opportunities (pp. 228-240). IGI Global. doi:10.4018/978-1-5225-7180-3.ch011

Luo, Zou, Du, Jin, Liu, & Shen. (2020). Static detection of real-world buffer overflow induced by loop. *Computers & Security, 89*(101), 616.

Lu, Z., Liu, W., Wang, Q., Qu, G., & Liu, Z. (2018). A Privacy-Preserving Trust Model Based on Blockchain for VANETs. *IEEE Access : Practical Innovations, Open Solutions*, *6*, 45655–45664. doi:10.1109/ACCESS.2018.2864189

Lv, Z., & Kumar, N. (2020). Software defined solutions for sensors in 6G/IoE. *Computer Communications*, *153*, 42–47. doi:10.1016/j.comcom.2020.01.060

Lv, Z., Li, X., Wang, W., Zhang, B., Hu, J., & Feng, S. (2018). Government affairs service platform for smart city. *Future Generation Computer Systems*, *81*, 443–451. doi:10.1016/j.future.2017.08.047

Lyons, V., & Fitzgerald, T. (2023). *The privacy leader Compass: A Comprehensive Business-Oriented Roadmap for Building and Leading Practical Privacy Programs*. CRC Press. doi:10.1201/9781003383017

M, S. S., D, H., & Vallem, R. R. (2023). Cyber Security System Based on Machine Learning Using Logistic Decision Support Vector. *Mesopotamian Journal of Cybersecurity,* 64–72. doi:10.58496/MJCS/2023/011

Mace, J., Roelke, R., & Fonseca, R. (2018). Pivot tracing: Dynamic causal monitoring for distributed systems. *ACM Transactions on Computer Systems*, *35*(4), 1–28. doi:10.1145/3208104

Machin, D. (2022, April 16). *Cyber security and operational resilience.* Berkeley Partnership. https://www.berkeleypartnership.com/news-and-insights/insights/cyber-security-and-operational-resilience

Máchová, R. (2017). Measuring the effects of open data on the level of corruption. In *Proceedings of the 21th International Conference Current Trends in Public Sector Research*. Masarykova univerzita.

Madavarapu, J. B., Yalamanchili, R. K., & Mandhala, V. N. (2023). *An Ensemble Data Security on Cloud Healthcare Systems*. IEEE. doi:10.1109/ICOSEC58147.2023.10276231

Madhavaram, S., Manis, K. T., Rashidi-Sabet, S., & Taylor, D. F. (2022). Capability bundling for effective supply chain management: An integrative framework and research agenda. *Journal of Business Logistics*. Advance online publication. doi:10.1111/jbl.12329

Madhira, N., Pelletier, J. M., Johnson, D., & Mishra, S. (2023). Code red: A nuclear nightmare-navigating ransomware response at an Eastern European power plant. *Journal of Information Technology Teaching Cases, 204388692311559*. doi:10.1177/20438869231155934

Maersk. (2017). *Cyber attack update - A.P. Møller - Mærsk A/S. A.P. Møller - Mærsk a/S.* Retrieved May 12, 2023, from https://investor.maersk.com/news-releases/news-release-details/cyber-attack-update

Maersk. (2023). *Remote Container Management*. Maersk. https://www.maersk.com/digital-solutions/captain-peter/services

Magableh, G. M., & Mistarihi, M. Z. (2023). Global Supply Chain Nervousness (GSCN). *Sustainability (Basel)*, *15*(16), 12115. doi:10.3390/su151612115

Maghsoudi, A., Harpring, R., Piotrowicz, W., & Kedziora, D. (2023). Digital technologies for cash and voucher assistance in disasters: A cross-case analysis of benefits and risks. *International Journal of Disaster Risk Reduction*, *96*, 103827. doi:10.1016/j.ijdrr.2023.103827

Maharaj, M. S., & Munyoka, W. (2019). Privacy, security, trust, risk and optimism bias in e-government use: The case of two Southern African Development Community countries. *South African Journal of Information Management*, *21*(1), 1–9.

Mahmood, T., & Afzal, U. (2013*). Security Analytics: Big Data Analytics for cybersecurity: A review of trends, techniques and tools*. doi:10.1109/NCIA.2013.6725337

Mahmood, Z. (Ed.). (2016). *Connectivity frameworks for smart devices: the internet of things from a distributed computing perspective*. Springer. doi:10.1007/978-3-319-33124-9

Majeed, U., Khan, L. U., Yaqoob, I., Kazmi, S. M. A., Salah, K., & Hong, C. S. (2021). Blockchain for IoT-based smart cities: Recent advances, requirements, and future challenges. *Journal of Network and Computer Applications*, *181*, 103007. doi:10.1016/j.jnca.2021.103007

Ma, L., & Zheng, Y. (2019). National e-government performance and citizen satisfaction: A multilevel analysis across European countries. *International Review of Administrative Sciences*, *85*(3), 506–526. doi:10.1177/0020852317703691

Malagon-Su´arez & Orjuela-Castro. (2023). Challenges and trends in logistics 4.0. *Ingenier´ıa*, 28.

Malhotra, H., Bhargava, R., & Dave, M. (2017). Implementation of E-Governance projects: Development, Threats & Targets. *JIMS8I-International Journal of Information Communication and Computing Technology, 5*(2), 292-298. https://www.indianjournals.com/ijor.aspx?target=ijor:jims8i&volume=5&issue=2&article=001

Malhotra, H., Bhargava, R., & Dave, M. (2017, November). Challenges related to information security and its implications for evolving e-government structures: A comparative study between India and African countries. In *2017 International Conference on Inventive Computing and Informatics (ICICI)* (pp. 30-35). IEEE. 10.1109/ICICI.2017.8365370

Mallick, P., Salling, K. B., Pigosso, D. C. A., & McAloone, T. C. (2023). Closing the loop: Establishing reverse logistics for a circular economy, a systematic review. *Journal of Environmental Management, 328*, 117017. doi:10.1016/j.jenvman.2022.117017 PMID:36521223

Managers, S. (2022, February 24). *Role Of Technology In Logistics And Supply Chain Management*. https://genxfreight.co.uk/role-of-information-technology-in-logistics-and-supply-chain-management/

Mandiant. (2021). *M-trends 2021: Insights into Today's Top Cyber Trends and Attacks*. Mandiant. https://www.mandiant.com/resources/reports/m-trends-2021

Mangan, J., Lalwani, C., & Butcher, T. (2008). *Global Logistics and Supply Chain Management*. http://ci.nii.ac.jp/ncid/BA88939934

Manners-Bell, J. (2020a). *Supply chain Risk management: How to Design and Manage Resilient Supply Chains*. Kogan Page Publishers.

Manners-Bell, J. (2020b). *Supply chain Risk management: How to Design and Manage Resilient Supply Chains*. Kogan Page Publishers.

Manners-Bell, J. (2020c). *Supply chain Risk management: How to Design and Manage Resilient Supply Chains*. Kogan Page Publishers.

Marassi, L., & Marrone, S. (2023). What would happen if hackers attacked the railways? Consideration of the need for ethical codes in the railway transport systems. In Smart innovation, systems and technologies (pp. 289–296). Springer. doi:10.1007/978-981-99-3592-5_27

Mármol, F. G., Pérez, M. G., & Pérez, G. M. (2016, July). I don't trust ICT: Research challenges in cyber security. In *IFIP International Conference on Trust Management* (pp. 129-136). Springer.

Martín, C., Garrido, D., Llopis, L., Rubio, B., & Díaz, M. (2022). Facilitating the monitoring and management of structural health in civil infrastructures with an Edge/Fog/Cloud architecture. *Computer Standards & Interfaces, 81*, 103600. doi:10.1016/j.csi.2021.103600

Martto, J., Diaz, S., Hassan, B., Mannan, S., Singh, P., Villasuso, F., & Baobaid, O. (2023). Esg strategies in the oil and gas industry from the maritime & logistics perspectiveopportunities & risks. In Abu Dhabi International Petroleum Exhibition and Conference. SPE.

Mashayekhy, Y., Babaei, A., Yuan, X.-M., & Xue, A. (2022). Impact of Internet of Things (IoT) on Inventory Management: A Literature Survey. *Logistics, 6*(2), 33. doi:10.3390/logistics6020033

Mattila, J., & Seppälä, T. (2017). Blockchains as a Path to a Network of Systems—An Emerging New Trend of the Digital Platforms in Industry and Society. Ideas. https://ideas.repec.org/p/rif/report/45.html

McAfee. (2020). *Cloud Adoption and Risk Report.* McAfee. Retrieved May 12, 2023, from https://mscdss.ds.unipi.gr/wp-content/uploads/2018/10/Cloud-Adoption-Risk-Report-2019.pdf

McKevitt, J. (2017, June 29). *Maersk, FedEx cases show how cyberattacks can roil global logistics*. Supply Chain Dive. https://www.supplychaindive.com/news/FedEx-TNT-Express-cybersecurity-attack-ransomware/446078/

McKibbin, W., & Fernando, R. (2020). The economic impact of COVID-19. *Economics in the Time of COVID-19, 45*. https://www.incae.edu/sites/default/files/covid-19.pdf#page=52

McKibbin, W., & Fernando, R. (2020). The economic impact of COVID-19. *Economics in the Time of COVID*, *19*, 45.

McKinney, S. A., Landy, R., & Wilka, R. (2017). Smart contracts, blockchain, and the next frontier of transactional law. *Wash. JL Tech. & Arts*, *13*, 313.

Mecheva, T., & Kakanakov, N. (2020). Cybersecurity in Intelligent Transportation Systems. *Computers, 9*(4), 83. doi:10.3390/computers9040083

Meers, J., Halliday, S., & Tomlinson, J. (2023). "Creative non-compliance": Complying with the "spirit of the law" not the "letter of the law" under the covid-19 lockdown restrictions. *Deviant Behavior*, *44*(1), 93–111. doi:10.1080/01639625.2021.2014286

Mehrotra, K. (2021). Data Privacy & Protection. *SSRN*, *3858581*. https://papers.ssrn.com/sol3/papers.cfm?abstract_id=3858581

Meiyanti, R., Utomo, B., Sensuse, D. I., & Wahyuni, R. (2018, August). E-government challenges in developing countries: a literature review. In *2018 6th International Conference on Cyber and IT Service Management (CITSM)* (pp. 1-6). IEEE. 10.1109/CITSM.2018.8674245

Melaku, H. M. (2023a). Context-Based and Adaptive Cybersecurity Risk Management Framework. *Risks*, *11*(6), 101. doi:10.3390/risks11060101

Melaku, H. M. (2023b). A dynamic and adaptive cybersecurity governance framework. *Journal of Cybersecurity and Privacy*, *3*(3), 327–350. doi:10.3390/jcp3030017

Mengelkamp, E., Gärttner, J., Rock, K., Kessler, S., Orsini, L., & Weinhardt, C. (2018). Designing microgrid energy markets: A case study: The Brooklyn Microgrid. *Applied Energy*, *210*, 870–880. https://dl.acm.org/doi/abs/10.1145/3241815.3241870. doi:10.1016/j.apenergy.2017.06.054

Meng, Y., & Li, W. (2012, December). Intelligent alarm filter using knowledge-based alert verification in network intrusion detection. In *International Symposium on Methodologies for Intelligent Systems* (pp. 115-124). Springer. 10.1007/978-3-642-34624-8_14

Menoni, S., Molinari, D., Parker, D., Ballio, F., & Tapsell, S. (2012). Assessing multifaceted vulnerability and resilience in order to design riskmitigation strategies. *Natural Hazards*, *64*(3), 2057–2082. doi:10.1007/s11069-012-0134-4

Mensah, I. K. (2019). Impact of government capacity and E-government performance on the adoption of E-Government services. *International Journal of Public Administration*. https://www.tandfonline.com/doi/10.1080/01900692.2019.1628059

Mershad, K., & Artail, H. (2013, February). A Framework for Secure and Efficient Data Acquisition in Vehicular Ad Hoc Networks. *IEEE Transactions on Vehicular Technology*, *62*(2), 536–551. doi:10.1109/TVT.2012.2226613

Miadzvetskaya, Y. (2023, May 10). *Data Governance Act: on International Transfers of Non-Personal Data and GDPR Mimesis*. SSRN. https://papers.ssrn.com/sol3/papers.cfm?abstract_id=4444051

Millard, J. (2017). European Strategies for e-Governance to 2020 and Beyond. In *Government 3.0–Next Generation Government Technology Infrastructure and Services* (pp. 1–25). Springer. doi:10.1007/978-3-319-63743-3_1

Mızrak, F. (2023a). Integrating cybersecurity risk management into strategic management: a comprehensive literature review. *Journal of Business, Economics and Finance*. doi:10.17261/Pressacademia.2023.1807

Mızrak, F. (2023b). Managing Risks And Crises In The Logistics Sector: A Comprehensive Analysis Of Strategies And Prioritization Using Ahp Method. *Meriç Uluslararası Sosyal Ve Stratejik Araştırmalar Dergisi, 7*(Özel Sayı), 114–148. doi:10.54707/meric.1335033

Mohammad, S., Masuri, M. A. A., Salim, S., & Razak, M. R. A. (2021). Development of IoT Based Logistic Vehicle Maintenance System. *Proceeding - 2021 IEEE 17th International Colloquium on Signal Processing and Its Applications, CSPA 2021*, 127–132. 10.1109/CSPA52141.2021.9377290

Möller, D. P. F. (2023). Ransomware Attacks and Scenarios: Cost Factors and Loss of Reputation. Springer. doi:10.1007/978-3-031-26845-8_6

More, P., & Sakhare, S. (2023). Context-Aware device classification and clustering for smarter and secure connectivity in internet of things. *EAI Endorsed Transactions on Industrial Networks and Intelligent Systems*, *10*(3), e5. doi:10.4108/eetinis.v10i3.3874

Mostafa, A. M., Ezz, M., Elbashir, M. K., Alruily, M., Hamouda, E., Alsarhani, M., & Said, W. (2023). Strengthening cloud security: An innovative Multi-Factor Multi-Layer authentication framework for cloud user authentication. *Applied Sciences (Basel, Switzerland)*, *13*(19), 10871. doi:10.3390/app131910871

Motahar, S. M., Mukhtar, M., Safie, N., Ma'arif, Y., & Mostafavi, S. (2018). Revisiting the Diversification on the Implementation of Open Source ERP Teaching Models. *Journal of Advanced Research in Dynamical and Control Systems,* (9), 2379- 2385 https://papers.ssrn.com/sol3/papers.cfm?abstract_id=3786555

Mubarak, M. F., & Petraite, M. (2020). Industry 4.0 technologies, digital trust and technological orientation: What matters in open innovation? *Technological Forecasting and Social Change, 161*, 120332. doi:10.1016/j.techfore.2020.120332

Muda, J., Tumsa, S., Tuni, A., & Sharma, D. P. (2020). Cloud-Enabled E-Governance Framework for Citizen Centric Services. *Journal of Computer and Communications, 8*(7), 63–78. doi:10.4236/jcc.2020.87006

Mugoni, E., Nyagadza, B., & Hove, P. K. (2023). Green reverse logistics technology impact on agricultural entrepreneurial marketing firms' operational efficiency and sustainable competitive advantage. *Sustainable Technology and Entrepreneurship, 2*(2), 100034. doi:10.1016/j.stae.2022.100034

Muhammad, K., Lloret, J., & Baik, S. W. (2019). Intelligent and energy-efficient data prioritization in green smart cities: Current challenges and future directions. *IEEE Communications Magazine, 57*(2), 60–65. doi:10.1109/MCOM.2018.1800371

Mukherjee, D. (2023). *Network Segmentation: Enables enhance security and control access of critical assets.* CXOToday.com. https://www.cxotoday.com/cxo-bytes/network-segmentation-enables-enhance-security-and-control-access-of-critical-assets/

Mukherjee, B. K., Pappu, S. I., Islam, M. J., & Acharjee, U. K. (2020, February). An SDN based distributed IoT network with NFV implementation for smart cities. In *International Conference on Cyber Security and Computer Science* (pp. 539-552). Springer. 10.1007/978-3-030-52856-0_43

Mukhtarov, F., Dieperink, C., & Driessen, P. (2018). The influence of information and communication technologies on public participation in urban water governance: A review of place-based research. *Environmental Science & Policy, 89*, 430–438. doi:10.1016/j.envsci.2018.08.015

Muller, S. R., & Lind, M. L. (2020). Factors in Information Assurance Professionals' Intentions to Adhere to Information Security Policies. [IJSSSP]. *International Journal of Systems and Software Security and Protection, 11*(1), 17–32. doi:10.4018/IJSSSP.2020010102

Musa, H., Krichen, M., Altun, A. A., & Ammi, M. (2023). Survey on Blockchain-Based Data Storage Security for Android Mobile Applications. *Sensors (Basel), 23*(21), 8749. doi:10.3390/s23218749 PMID:37960449

Mutie, M. D., Odock, S., & Litondo, K. (2023). Effect of green logistics practices on performance of logistics firms in Kenya. *DBA Africa Management Review.* http://erepository.uonbi.ac.ke/handle/11295/154439

Muzafar, S., & Jhanjhi, N. (2022). DDoS Attacks on Software Defined Network: Challenges and Issues. *2022 International Conference on Business Analytics for Technology and Security, ICBATS 2022, 2022-Janua*. IEEE. 10.1109/ICBATS54253.2022.9780662

Muzafar, S., Humayun, M., & Hussain, S. J. (2022). Emerging Cybersecurity Threats in the Eye of E-Governance in the Current Era. In *Cybersecurity Measures for E-Government Frameworks* (pp. 43–60). IGI Global. doi:10.4018/978-1-7998-9624-1.ch003

Muzafar, S., & Jhanjhi, N. Z. (2020). Success Stories of ICT Implementation in Saudi Arabia. In *Employing Recent Technologies for Improved Digital Governance* (pp. 151–163). IGI Global. doi:10.4018/978-1-7998-1851-9.ch008

Muzaki, R., Briliyant, O. C., Hasditama, M. A., & Ritchi, H. (2020). *Improving Security of Web-Based Application Using ModSecurity and Reverse Proxy in Web Application Firewall.* doi:10.1109/IWBIS50925.2020.9255601

Muzammal, S. M., Murugesan, R. K., Jhanjhi, N. Z., & Jung, L. T. (2020). SMTrust: Proposing Trust-Based Secure Routing Protocol for RPL Attacks for IoT Applications. *2020 International Conference on Computational Intelligence (ICCI)*. Springer. 10.1109/ICCI51257.2020.9247818

Mwangi, N. M. (2015). *E-government adoption by Kenya ministries* (Doctoral dissertation, University of Nairobi). http://erepository.uonbi.ac.ke/handle/11295/94091

Naeem, M., Shahbaz, M., & Shafiq, M. (2020). Cyber Security Risks and Challenges in Logistics Industry: Incident Response Planning. *International Journal of Advanced Computer Science and Applications*, *11*(11), 40–47.

Nagarajan, S. M., Deverajan, G. G., Chatterjee, P., Alnumay, W., & Muthukumaran, V. (2022). Integration of IoT based routing process for food supply chain management in sustainable smart cities. *Sustainable Cities and Society*, *76*, 103448. doi:10.1016/j.scs.2021.103448

Nagowah, S. D., Sta, H. B., & Gobin-Rahimbux, B. A. (2018, October). An overview of semantic interoperability ontologies and frameworks for IoT. In *2018 Sixth International Conference on Enterprise Systems (ES)* (pp. 82-89). IEEE. 10.1109/ES.2018.00020

Nagy, G., Illés, B., & Bányai, Á. (2018). Impact of Industry 4.0 on production logistics. *IOP Conference Series*, *448*, 012013. 10.1088/1757-899X/448/1/012013

Naik, N., & Jenkins, P. (2020, April). Self-Sovereign Identity Specifications: Govern your identity through your digital wallet using blockchain technology. In *2020 8th IEEE International Conference on Mobile Cloud Computing, Services, and Engineering (MobileCloud)* (pp. 90-95). IEEE.

Najmi, K. Y., AlZain, M. A., Masud, M., Jhanjhi, N. Z., Al-Amri, J., & Baz, M. (2021). A survey on security threats and countermeasures in IoT to achieve users confidentiality and reliability. *Materials Today: Proceedings*. https://www.sciencedirect.com/science/article/pii/S221478532102469X

Nakamoto, S. (2009). *Bitcoin: A peer-to-peer electronic cash system*. http://www.bitcoin.org/bitcoin.pdf

Narasimhan, K. (2005). The Goal: A Process of Ongoing Improvement. *Measuring Business Excellence*, *9*(1), 76. Advance online publication. doi:10.1108/13683040510588882

National Institute of Standards and Technology. (2018). *Framework for Improving Critical Infrastructure Cybersecurity, Version 1.1*. doi:10.6028/NIST.CSWP.04162018

National Institute of Standards and Technology. (2021). *NIST Special Publication 800-53: Security and Privacy Controls for Information Systems and Organizations*. https://csrc.nist.gov/publications/detail/sp/800-53/rev-5/final

National Institute of Standards and Technology. (2023, April 17). *Small Business Cybersecurity Corner | NIST*. NIST. Retrieved May 12, 2023, from https://www.nist.gov/itl/smallbusinesscyber

Nautiyal, L., Malik, P., & Agarwal, A. (2018). Cybersecurity system: an essential pillar of smart cities. In *Smart Cities* (pp. 25–50). Springer. doi:10.1007/978-3-319-76669-0_2

Nawari, N. O., & Ravindran, S. (2019). Blockchain and the built environment: Potentials and limitations. *Journal of Building Engineering*, *25*, 100832. doi:10.1016/j.jobe.2019.100832

Nayak, R. P., Sethi, S., Bhoi, S. K., Sahoo, K. S., Tabbakh, T. A., & Almusaylim, Z. A. (2021). TBDDoSA-MD: Trust-Based DDoS Misbehave Detection Approach in Software-defined Vehicular Network (SDVN). *Computers, Materials & Continua*, *69*(3).

Nayyar, A., Jain, R., Mahapatra, B., & Singh, A. P. (2019). Cyber Security Challenges for Smart Cities. In *Practice, progress, and proficiency in sustainability* (pp. 27–54). IGI Global. doi:10.4018/978-1-5225-8085-0.ch002

NCCoE. (2021, October 21). *National Cybersecurity Center of Excellence (NCCoE) Zero Trust Cybersecurity: Implementing a Zero Trust Architecture*. Federal Register. Retrieved May 10, 2023, from https://www.federalregister.gov/documents/2020/10/21/2020-23292/national-cybersecurity-center-of-excellence-nccoe-zero-trust-cybersecurity-implementing-a-zero-trust

NCES. (2020). *Chapter 5-Protecting Your System: Physical Security, from Safeguarding Your Technology*. NCES Publication 98-297 (National Center for Education Statistics). Retrieved May 13, 2023, from https://nces.ed.gov/pubs98/safetech/chapter5.asp

Ndiaye, M., Oyewobi, S. S., Abu-Mahfouz, A. M., Hancke, G. P., Kurien, A. M., & Djouani, K. (2020). IoT in the wake of COVID-19: A survey on contributions, challenges and evolution. *IEEE Access : Practical Innovations, Open Solutions*, *8*, 186821–186839. doi:10.1109/ACCESS.2020.3030090 PMID:34786294

Nespoli, P., Papamartzivanos, D., Mármol, F. G., & Kambourakis, G. (2017). Optimal countermeasures selection against cyber attacks: A comprehensive survey on reaction frameworks. *IEEE Communications Surveys and Tutorials*, *20*(2), 1361–1396. doi:10.1109/COMST.2017.2781126

Neustar. (2020). *Cyber threats and trends: Q1 2020 report*. https://www.home.neustar/resources/research-reports/cyber-threats-and-trends-q1-2020-report

Ng, C. (2018). *The future of logistics: Five technologies that will self-orchestrate the supply chain.* PwC.

Nguyen, H., Acharya, B., Ivanov, R., Haeberlen, A., Phan, L. T. X., Sokolsky, O., Walker, J., Weimer, J., Hanson, W., & Lee, I. (2016) Cloud-based secure logger for medical devices. *Proceedings of the IEEE first international conference on connected health: applications, systems and engineering technologies (CHASE),* 89–94. 10.1109/CHASE.2016.48

Nguyen, D. K., Sermpinis, G., & Stasinakis, C. (2022). Big data, artificial intelligence and machine learning: A transformative symbiosis in favour of financial technology. *European Financial Management, 29*(2), 517–548. doi:10.1111/eufm.12365

Ni, H., Rahouti, M., Chakrabortty, A., Xiong, K., & Xin, Y. (2018, August). A distributed cloud-based wide-area controller with sdn-enabled delay optimization. In 2018 IEEE Power & Energy Society General Meeting (PESGM) (pp. 1-5). IEEE. doi:10.1109/PESGM.2018.8586040

Nikose, A., & Srinivas, K. (2023). TRO-CP-ABE: A secure and flexible layer with traceability and easy revocation in ciphertext-policy attribute-based encryption. *International Journal of Internet Technology and Secured Transactions, 13*(2), 196. doi:10.1504/IJITST.2023.129585

NIST. (2020). *Cybersecurity Framework.* https://www.nist.gov/cyberframework

Nižetić, S., Šolić, P., López-de-Ipiña González-de-Artaza, D., & Patrono, L. (2020). Internet of Things (IoT): Opportunities, issues and challenges towards a smart and sustainable future. *Journal of Cleaner Production, 274,* 122877. doi:10.1016/j.jclepro.2020.122877 PMID:32834567

Norris, D., Joshi, A., & Finin, T. (2015, June). *Cybersecurity challenges to American state and local governments. In 15th European Conference on eGovernment.* Academic Conferences and Publishing Int. Ltd. https://ebiquity.umbc.edu/paper/abstract/id/774/Cybersecurity-Challenges-to-American-State-and-Local-Governments

Nosiri, U. D., & Ndoh, J. A. (2018). E-Governance. *South East Journal of Political Science, 4*(1). https://journals.aphriapub.com/index.php/SEJPS/article/view/833

Novet, J. (2017, August 16). *Shipping company Maersk says June cyberattack could cost it up to $300 million.* CNBC. Retrieved May 12, 2023, from https://www.cnbc.com/2017/08/16/maersk-says-notpetya-cyberattack-could-cost-300-million.html

Nozari, H., & Edalatpanah, S. A. (2023). Smart Systems Risk Management in IoT-Based Supply Chain. In *Industrial and applied mathematics* (pp. 251–268). Springer Nature. doi:10.1007/978-981-19-9909-3_11

NSKT Global. (2021). https://nsktglobal.com/what-are-the-biggest-cybersecurity-threats-in-2021-

Ntizikira, E., Wang, L., Alblehai, F., Saleem, K., & Lodhi, M. A. (2023). Secure and Privacy-Preserving intrusion detection and prevention in the internet of unmanned aerial vehicles. *Sensors (Basel), 23*(19), 8077. doi:10.3390/s23198077 PMID:37836907

Ntizikira, E., Wang, L., Chen, J., & Saleem, K. (2024). Honey-block: Edge assisted ensemble learning model for intrusion detection and prevention using defense mechanism in IoT. *Computer Communications*, *214*, 1–17. doi:10.1016/j.comcom.2023.11.023

Nzimakwe, T. I. (2018). Government's Dynamic Approach to Addressing Challenges of Cybersecurity in South Africa. In Handbook of Research on Information and Cyber Security in the Fourth Industrial Revolution (pp. 364-381). IGI Global. doi:10.4018/978-1-5225-4763-1.ch013

O'Donnell, S., Quigley, E., Hayden, J., Adamis, D., Gavin, B., & McNicholas, F. (2022). Psychological distress among healthcare workers post COVID-19 pandemic: From the resilience of individuals to healthcare systems. *Irish Journal of Psychological Medicine*, *40*(3), 508–512. doi:10.1017/ipm.2022.35 PMID:35938227

Okereafor, K., & Adebola, O. (2020). Tackling the cybersecurity impacts of the coronavirus outbreak as a challenge to internet safety. *Int J IT Eng*, *8*(2). https://papers.ssrn.com/sol3/papers.cfm?abstract_id=3568830

OladoyinboT. O.AdebiyiO. O.UgonniaJ. C.OlaniyiO. A.OkunleyeO. J. (2023). Evaluating and establishing baseline security requirements in cloud computing: an enterprise Risk Management approach. *Social Science Research Network*. doi:10.2139/ssrn.4612909

Olaniyi, O. O., Asonze, C. U., Ajayi, S. S., Olabanji, S., & Adigwe, C. S. (2023). A Regressional Study on the Impact of Organizational Security Culture and Transformational Leadership on Social Engineering Awareness among Bank Employees: The Interplay of Security Education and Behavioral Change. *Asian Journal of Economics. Business and Accounting*, *23*(23), 128–143. doi:10.9734/ajeba/2023/v23i231176

Omotunde, H., & Ahmed, M. (2023). A Comprehensive Review of Security Measures in Database Systems: Assessing Authentication, Access Control, and Beyond. *Mesopotamian*, 115–133. doi:10.58496/MJCSC/2023/016

Ouyang, J., Lin, S., Jiang, S., Hou, Z., Wang, Y., & Wang, Y. (2014, February). SDF: Software-defined flash for web-scale internet storage systems. In *Proceedings of the 19th international conference on Architectural support for programming languages and operating systems* (pp. 471-484). 10.1145/2541940.2541959

Oxford Analytica. (2016). Estonia's e-governance model may be unique. *Emerald Expert Briefings*. https://www.emerald.com/insight/content/doi/10.1108/OXAN-DB214505/full/html

Özkan, A., & Tüysüzoğlu, G. (2023). *Security studies: Classic to Post-Modern Approaches*. Rowman & Littlefield.

Öztuna, B. (2022). Logistics 4.0 and Technologic Applications. *Accounting, Finance, Sustainability, Governance and Fraud*, 9–27. doi:10.1007/978-981-16-5644-6_2

Paintner, P. (2021). *Blockchain technology in the area of e-Governance–Guidelines for implementation* [Doctoral dissertation, University NOVA].

Pal, S. K. (2019). Changing technological trends for E-governance. In *E-governance in India* (pp. 79-105). Palgrave Macmillan. https://link.springer.com/chapter/10.1007/978-981-13-8852-1_5

Palvia, S., Aeron, P., Gupta, P., Mahapatra, D., Parida, R., Rosner, R., & Sindhi, S. (2018). *Online education: Worldwide status, challenges, trends, and implications*. Academic Press.

Pandey, N. K., Kumar, K., Saini, G., & Mishra, A. K. (2023). Security issues and challenges in cloud of things-based applications for industrial automation. *Annals of Operations Research*. doi:10.1007/s10479-023-05285-7 PMID:37361100

Pandey, S., Singh, R. K., Gunasekaran, A., & Kaushik, A. (2020). Cyber security risks in globalized supply chains: Conceptual framework. *Journal of Global Operations and Strategic Sourcing*, *13*(1), 103–128. doi:10.1108/JGOSS-05-2019-0042

Panjehfouladgaran, Frederick, & Lim. (2020). Reverse logistics risk management: identification, clustering and risk mitigation strategies. *Management Decision*, *58*(7):1449–1474.

Panyushkina, E. (2023). Modern challenges of the digital ecosystem of transport and logistics. *E3S Web of Conferences, 383*, 03008. doi:10.1051/e3sconf/202338303008

Papageorge, M. V., Freyman, B. J., Juskey, F. J., & Thome, J. R. (1995). *Integrated circuit package having a face-to-face IC chip arrangement*. Google Patents.

Parker, M. I. (2023). Managing threats to health data and information: toward security. Elsevier. doi:10.1016/B978-0-323-90802-3.00016-2

Pathak, A., AmazUddin, M., Abedin, M. J., Andersson, K., Mustafa, R., & Hossain, M. S. (2019). IoT based smart system to support agricultural parameters: A case study. *Procedia Computer Science*, *155*, 648–653. doi:10.1016/j.procs.2019.08.092

Patil, S. M., & Baig, M. M. (2018). *Survey on Creating ZigBee Chain Reaction using IoT*. Academic Press.

Pattnaik, M., & Shah, T. (2023). Role of Big Data to Boost Corporate Decision Making. *2023 2nd International Conference on Edge Computing and Applications (ICECAA)*. Springer. 10.1109/ICECAA58104.2023.10212179

Payment Card Industry Security Standards Council. (2019). *Payment Card Industry Data Security Standard (PCI DSS) version 3.2.1*. Retrieved from https://www.pcisecuritystandards.org/documents/PCI_DSS_v3-2-1.pdf

PCI Security Standards Council. (2021). *Payment Card Industry (PCI) Data Security Standard (DSS)*. https://www.pcisecuritystandards.org/pci-security-standards/pci-dss

Pena, J. G. V., & Yu, W. E. (2014, April). Development of a distributed firewall using software defined networking technology. In *2014 4th IEEE International Conference on Information Science and Technology* (pp. 449-452). IEEE. 10.1109/ICIST.2014.6920514

Peng, C., Xu, M., Xu, S., & Hu, T. (2017). Modeling and predicting extreme cyber attack rates via marked point processes. *Journal of Applied Statistics*, *44*(14), 2534–2563. doi:10.1080/02664763.2016.1257590

Peng, Y., Welden, N., & Renaud, F. G. (2023). A framework for integrating ecosystem services indicators into vulnerability and risk assessments of deltaic social-ecological systems. *Journal of Environmental Management*, *326*, 116682. doi:10.1016/j.jenvman.2022.116682 PMID:36375428

Pertiwi, D. A., Yusuf, M., & Efrilianda, D. A. (2022). Operational Supply Chain Risk Management on Apparel Industry Based on Supply Chain Operation Reference (SCOR). *Journal of Information System Exploration and Research*, *1*(1), 17–24. doi:10.52465/joiser.v1i1.103

PingS. W.WahJ. C. J.JieL. W.HanJ. B. Y.MuzafarS. (2023). *Secure Software Development: Issues and Challenges*. https://arxiv.org/abs/2311.11021v1

Ponemon Institute. (2020). *Cost of Insider Threats: Global Report 2020*. IBM. Retrieved May 12, 2023, from https://www.ibm.com/downloads/cas/LQZ4RONE

Ponemon Institute. (2020b). *The 2020 state of cybersecurity in small and medium-sized businesses*. Retrieved May 13, 2023, from https://www.ponemon.org/research/ponemon-library/security/security.html

Ponnusamy, V., Zaman, N., & Humayun, M. (2020). Fostering Public-Private Partnership. In *Advances in electronic government, digital divide, and regional development book series* (pp. 237–255). IGI Global. doi:10.4018/978-1-7998-1851-9.ch012

Posamentier, J., Seibel, K., & DyTang, N. (2022). Preventing Youth Suicide: A Review of School-Based Practices and How Social–Emotional Learning Fits into Comprehensive efforts. *Trauma, Violence & Abuse*, *24*(2), 746–759. doi:10.1177/15248380211039475 PMID:35139714

Poudel, S., Arafat, M. Y., & Moh, S. (2023). Bio-Inspired Optimization-Based Path Planning Algorithms in Unmanned Aerial Vehicles: A survey. *Sensors (Basel)*, *23*(6), 3051. doi:10.3390/s23063051 PMID:36991762

Pour, M. S., Nader, C., Friday, K., & Bou-Harb, E. (2023). A comprehensive survey of recent internet measurement techniques for cyber security. *Computers & Security*, *128*, 103123. doi:10.1016/j.cose.2023.103123

Poyhonen, J., Simola, J., & Lehto, M. (2023). Basic elements of cyber security for a smart terminal process. In *The Proceedings of the... International Conference on Cyber Warfare and Security*. Academic Conferences International Ltd.

Prabadevi, B., Jeyanthi, N., & Abraham, A. (2020). An analysis of security solutions for ARP poisoning attacks and its effects on medical computing. *International Journal of System Assurance Engineering and Management*, *11*(1), 1–14. doi:10.1007/s13198-019-00919-1

Prabakar, D., Sundarrajan, M., Manikandan, R., Zaman, N., Masud, M., & Alqhatani, A. (2023). Energy Analysis-Based Cyber Attack Detection by IoT with Artificial Intelligence in a Sustainable Smart City. *Sustainability (Basel)*, *15*(7), 6031. doi:10.3390/su15076031

Pradhan, P., & Shakya, S. (2018). Big Data Challenges for e-Government Services in Nepal. *Journal of the Institute of Engineering*, *14*(1), 216–222. doi:10.3126/jie.v14i1.20087

Pranggono, B., & Arabo, A. (2021). COVID-19 pandemic cybersecurity issues. *Internet Technology Letters*, *4*(2), e247. doi:10.1002/itl2.247

Priyadarshini, I., Chatterjee, J. M., Sujatha, R., Zaman, N., Karime, A., & Masud, M. (2021). Exploring Internet Meme Activity during COVID-19 Lockdown Using Artificial Intelligence Techniques. *Applied Artificial Intelligence*, *36*(1), 2014218. Advance online publication. doi:10.1080/08839514.2021.2014218

Priya, K., & Karuppanan, K. (2011). Secure privacy and distributed group authentication for VANET. *2011 International Conference on Recent Trends in Information Technology (ICRTIT)*, 301-306. 10.1109/ICRTIT.2011.5972438

Progoulakis, I., Nikitakos, N., Dalaklis, D., Christodoulou, A., Dalaklis, A., & Yaacob, R. (2023). Digitalization and cyber physical security aspects in maritime transportation and port infrastructure. In Smart Ports and Robotic Systems: Navigating the Waves of Techno-Regulation and Governance (pp. 227–248). Springer. doi:10.1007/978-3-031-25296-9_12

Pundir, A. K., Jagannath, J. D., & Ganapathy, L. (2019). Improving supply chain visibility using IoT-internet of things. *2019 IEEE 9th Annual Computing and Communication Workshop and Conference, CCWC 2019*, 156–162. 10.1109/CCWC.2019.8666480

Puspita, N. Y., & Boydston, N. G. W. P. (2023). Framing the responsibility of Public-Private Partnerships (PPPs) on space technology in international law. *Padjadjaran Journal of International Law*, *7*(2), 172–192. doi:10.23920/pjil.v7i2.1352

Qader, G., Junaid, M., Abbas, Q., & Mubarik, M. S. (2022). Industry 4.0 enables supply chain resilience and supply chain performance. *Technological Forecasting and Social Change*, *185*, 122026. doi:10.1016/j.techfore.2022.122026

Qian, Y., Li, X., Ihara, S., Zeng, L., Kaiser, J., Süß, T., & Brinkmann, A. (2017, November). A configurable rule based classful token bucket filter network request scheduler for the lustre file system. In *Proceedings of the International Conference for High Performance Computing, Networking, Storage and Analysis* (pp. 1-12). 10.1145/3126908.3126932

Qi, M., & Wang, J. (2021). Using the Internet of Things e-government platform to optimize the administrative management mode. *Wireless Communications and Mobile Computing*, *2021*, 1–11. doi:10.1155/2021/2224957

Qi, R., Feng, C., Liu, Z., & Mrad, N. (2017). Blockchain-powered internet of things, e-governance and e-democracy. In *E-Democracy for Smart Cities* (pp. 509–520). Springer. doi:10.1007/978-981-10-4035-1_17

Qiu, C., Yu, F. R., Yao, H., Jiang, C., Xu, F., & Zhao, C. (2019, June). Blockchain-based software-defined industrial Internet of Things: A dueling deep Q-learning approach. *IEEE Internet of Things Journal*, *6*(3), 4627–4639. doi:10.1109/JIOT.2018.2871394

Qu, F., Wu, Z., Wang, F.-Y., & Cho, W. (2015, December). A Security and Privacy Review of VANETs. *IEEE Transactions on Intelligent Transportation Systems*, *16*(6), 2985–2996. doi:10.1109/TITS.2015.2439292

Qureshi, K. N., O'Keeffe, G., O'Farrell, S., & Costelloe, G. (2023). Cybersecurity Standards and Policies for CPS in IOE. In Internet of things (pp. 177–192). doi:10.1007/978-3-031-45162-1_11

Qu, T., Lei, S., Wang, Z., Nie, D., Chen, X., & Huang, G. (2016, April). IoT-based real-time production logistics synchronization system under smart cloud manufacturing. *International Journal of Advanced Manufacturing Technology*, *84*(1–4), 147–164. doi:10.1007/s00170-015-7220-1

Radhakrishnan, S. (2021). *How Walmart Leverages IoT to Keep Your Ice Cream Frozen*. Walmart. https://corporate.walmart.com/news/2021/01/14/how-walmart-leverages-iot-to-keep-your-ice-cream-frozen

Rahman, A., Islam, M. J., Sunny, F. A., & Nasir, M. K. (2019, December). DistBlockSDN: A distributed secure blockchain based SDN-IoT architecture with NFV implementation for smart cities. In *2019 2nd International Conference on Innovation in Engineering and Technology (ICIET)* (pp. 1-6). IEEE. 10.1109/ICIET48527.2019.9290627

Rahman, A., Hasan, K., Kundu, D., Islam, M. J., Debnath, T., Band, S. S., & Kumar, N. (2023). On the ICN-IoT with federated learning integration of communication: Concepts, security-privacy issues, applications, and future perspectives. *Future Generation Computer Systems*, *138*, 61–88. doi:10.1016/j.future.2022.08.004

Rahman, M. A., Wuest, T., & Shafae, M. (2023). Manufacturing cybersecurity threat attributes and countermeasures: Review, meta-taxonomy, and use cases of cyberattack taxonomies. *Journal of Manufacturing Systems*, *68*, 196–208. doi:10.1016/j.jmsy.2023.03.009

Rahouti, M., Xiong, K., Ghani, N., & Shaikh, F. (2021). SYNGuard: Dynamic threshold-based SYN flood attack detection and mitigation in software-defined networks. *IET Networks*, *10*(2), 76–87. doi:10.1049/ntw2.12009

Rajkumar, V. S., Ştefanov, A., Presekal, A., Pálenský, P., & Rueda, J. L. (2023). Cyber Attacks on power grids: Causes and propagation of cascading failures. *IEEE Access : Practical Innovations, Open Solutions*, *11*, 103154–103176. doi:10.1109/ACCESS.2023.3317695

Rajmohan, R., Kumar, T. A., Pavithra, M., Sandhya, S. G., Julie, E. G., Nayahi, J. J. V., & Jhanjhi, N. Z. (2020). Blockchain: Next-generation technology for industry 4.0. *Blockchain Technology*, 177-198. https://www.taylorfrancis.com/chapters/edit/10.1201/9781003004998-11/blockchain-rajmohan-ananth-kumar-pavithra-sandhya

Ramadan, R. A., Aboshosha, B. W., Alshudukhi, J. S., Alzahrani, A. J., El-Sayed, A., & Dessouky, M. M. (2021). Cybersecurity and Countermeasures at the Time of Pandemic. *Journal of Advanced Transportation*, *2021*, 1–19. doi:10.1155/2021/6627264

Ramadhianto, R., Toruan, T. S. L., Kertopati, S. N. H., & Almubaroq, H. Z. (2023). Analysis of presidential regulations concerning cyber security to bolster defense policy management. *Defense and Security Studies*, *4*, 84–93. doi:10.37868/dss.v4.id244

Ramli, R. M. (2017). Challenges and issues in Malaysian e-government. *Electronic Government, an International Journal, 13*(3), 242-273.

Ramli, R. M. (2017). Challenges and issues in Malaysian e-government. *Electronic Government, an International Journal, 13*(3), 242-273. https://www.inderscienceonline.com/doi/abs/10.1504/EG.2017.086685

Ramzan, M., Awan, S. M., Aldabbas, H., Abid, A., Farhan, M., Khalid, S., & Latif, R. M. A. (2019). Internet of medical things for smart D3S to enable road safety. *International Journal of Distributed Sensor Networks*, *15*(8), 1550147719864883. doi:10.1177/1550147719864883

Ramzi, E. H., & Weerakkody, V. (2010). *E-Government implementation Challenges: A Case study*. https://aisel.aisnet.org/cgi/viewcontent.cgi?article=1318&context=amcis2010

Rana, N. P., Dwivedi, Y. K., & Williams, M. D. (2013). Analysing challenges, barriers and CSF of egov adoption. *Transforming Government: People, Process and Policy*. https://www.emerald.com/insight/content/doi/10.1108/17506161311325350/full/html

RaneN.ChoudharyS.RaneJ. (2023a). Blockchain and Artificial Intelligence (AI) integration for revolutionizing security and transparency in finance. *Social Science Research Network*. doi:10.2139/ssrn.4644253

Rane, N., Choudhary, S., & Rane, J. (2023b). *Leading-edge Artificial Intelligence (AI), Machine Learning (ML), Blockchain, and Internet of Things (IoT) technologies for enhanced wastewater treatment systems*. Social Science Research Network. doi:10.2139/ssrn.4641557

Rangaraju, S. (2023). Ai sentry: Reinventing cybersecurity through intelligent threat detection. *EPH-International Journal of Science And Engineering*, *9*(3), 30–35. doi:10.53555/ephijse.v9i3.211

Rao, P. M., & Deebak, B. (2022). Security and privacy issues in smart cities/industries: Technologies, applications, and challenges. *Journal of Ambient Intelligence and Humanized Computing*, 1–37.

RasoolR. U.AhmadH. F.RafiqueW.QayyumA.QadirJ.AnwarZ. (2023). Quantum Computing for Healthcare: A Review. TechRxiv. doi:10.36227/techrxiv.17198702.v4

Ravi, N., Verma, S., Jhanjhi, N. Z., & Talib, M. N. (2021, August). Securing VANET Using Blockchain Technology. In *Journal of Physics: Conference Series* (Vol. 1979, No. 1, p. 012035). IOP Publishing. https://iopscience.iop.org/article/10.1088/1742-6596/1979/1/012035/meta

Rawindaran, N., Nawaf, L., Alarifi, S., Alghazzawi, D., Carroll, F., Katib, I., & Hewage, C. (2023). Enhancing Cyber Security Governance and Policy for SMEs in Industry 5.0: A Comparative Study between Saudi Arabia and the United Kingdom. *Digital*, *3*(3), 200–231. doi:10.3390/digital3030014

Razak, G. M., Hendry, L., & Stevenson, M. (2021). Supply chain traceability: A review of the benefits and its relationship with supply chain resilience. *Production Planning and Control, 34*(11), 1114–1134. doi:10.1080/09537287.2021.1983661

Razaque, A., Amsaad, F., Khan, M. J., Hariri, S., Chen, S., Siting, C., & Ji, X. (2019). Survey: Cybersecurity vulnerabilities, attacks and solutions in the medical domain. *IEEE Access : Practical Innovations, Open Solutions, 7*, 168774–168797. doi:10.1109/ACCESS.2019.2950849

Raza, Z., Woxenius, J., Vural, C. A., & Lind, M. (2023). Digital transformation of maritime logistics: Exploring trends in the liner shipping segment. *Computers in Industry, 145*, 103811. doi:10.1016/j.compind.2022.103811

Razuleu, L. (2018). *E-Governance and its associated cybersecurity: The challenges and best practices of authentication and authorization among a rapidly growing e-government.* https://scholarworks.calstate.edu/concern/theses/qj72pb20t

Razuleu, L. A. (2018). *E-Governance and Its Associated Cybersecurity: The Challenges and Best Practices of Authentication and Authorization Among a Rapidly Growing E-government* (Doctoral dissertation). California State University, Northridge.

Rebe, N. (2023). *Regulating Cyber Technologies: Privacy vs security.* World Scientific. doi:10.1142/q0379

RedGoat. (2023, April 18). *Maersk incident response.* Red Goat. https://red-goat.com/why-you-should-test-your-incident-response-a-review-of-the-maersk-incident/

Rehman, Z., Gondal, I., Ge, M., Dong, H., Gregory, M. A., & Tari, Z. (2024). Proactive Defense Mechanism: Enhancing IoT Security through Diversity-based Moving Target Defense and Cyber Deception. *Computers & Security, 103685*, 103685. doi:10.1016/j.cose.2023.103685

Rejeb, A., Simske, J., Keogh, J. G., Rejeb, K., Simske, S. J., & Org, J. (2021). Blockchain technology in the smart city: a bibliometric review. *Quality & Quantity 2021 56:5, 56*(5), 2875–2906. doi:10.1007/s11135-021-01251-2

Rejeb, A., Keogh, J. G., Leong, G. K., & Treiblmaier, H. (2021). Potentials and challenges of augmented reality smart glasses in logistics and supply chain management: A systematic literature review. *International Journal of Production Research, 59*(12), 3747–3776. doi:10.1080/00207543.2021.1876942

Rejeb, A., Rejeb, K., Simske, S. J., & Treiblmaier, H. (2021). Blockchain Technologies in Logistics and Supply Chain Management: A Bibliometric Review. *Logistics, 5*(4), 72. doi:10.3390/logistics5040072

Rejeti, K., Murali, G., & Kumar, B. S. (2019). *An Accurate Methodology to Identify the Explosives Using Wireless Sensor Networks.* Paper presented at the International Conference on Sustainable Computing in Science, Technology and Management (SUSCOM), Amity University Rajasthan, Jaipur-India. 10.2139/ssrn.3362178

Remko, V. H. (2020). Research opportunities for a more resilient post-covid-19 supply chain–closing the gap between research findings and industry practice. *International Journal of Operations & Production Management*, *40*(4), 341–355. doi:10.1108/IJOPM-03-2020-0165

Ren, Q. (2018). Massive Collaborative Wireless Sensor Network Structure Based on Cloud Computing. *International Journal of Online and Biomedical Engineering*, *14*(11), 4–15. doi:10.3991/ijoe.v14i11.9499

Reyes, P. (2023). Radio Frequency identification (RFID) and supply chain management. Springer. doi:10.1007/978-3-030-89822-9_109-1

Ribeiro, R., Mateus-Coelho, N., & Mamede, H. S. (2023). Improving social engineering resilience in enterprises. *ARIS2 - Advanced Research on Information Systems Security, 3*(1), 34–65. doi:10.56394/aris2.v3i1.30

Rivera, A. D. T., Mendoza-Becerril, M. A., & Pereira, V. A. (2023). The Resilience of the Renewable Energy Electromobility Supply Chain: Review and Trends. *Sustainability (Basel)*, *15*(14), 10838. doi:10.3390/su151410838

Rizvi, S. S., Zwerling, T., Thompson, B., Faiola, S., Campbell, S., Fisanick, S., & Hutnick, C. (2023). A modular framework for auditing IoT devices and networks. *Computers & Security*, *132*, 103327. doi:10.1016/j.cose.2023.103327

Robinson. (2021). *4 Ways to Prepare Your Global Supply Chain for Cyber-Threats*. C.H. Robinson. Retrieved May 13, 2023, from https://www.chrobinson.com/en-us/resources/blog/4-ways-prepare-global-supply-chain-cyber-threats/

RodelaT. T.TasnimS.MazumderH.FaizahF.SultanaA.HossainM. M. (2020). Economic Impacts of Coronavirus Disease (COVID-19) in Developing Countries. doi:10.31235/osf.io/wygpk

Rohan, R., Pal, D., Hautamäki, J., Funilkul, S., Chutimaskul, W., & Thapliyal, H. (2023). A systematic literature review of cybersecurity scales assessing information security awareness. *Heliyon*, *9*(3), e14234. doi:10.1016/j.heliyon.2023.e14234 PMID:36938452

Ronchi, A. M. (2019). e-Government: Background, Today's Implementation and Future Trends. In e-Democracy (pp. 93-196). Springer, Cham.

Roopak, M., Tian, G. Y., & Chambers, J. (2020, January). An intrusion detection system against ddos attacks in iot networks. In *2020 10th Annual Computing and Communication Workshop and Conference (CCWC)* (pp. 562-567). IEEE. 10.1109/CCWC47524.2020.9031206

Rowe, A. (2023). 12 Cyber Security Measures That Every Small Business Must Take. *Tech.co.* https://tech.co/vpn/cyber-security-measures

Saah, A. E. N., Yee, J., & Choi, J. M. (2023). Securing Construction Workers' Data Security and Privacy with Blockchain Technology. *Applied Sciences (Basel, Switzerland)*, *13*(24), 13339. doi:10.3390/app132413339

Sadiq, A. A. I., Haning, M. T., Nara, N., & Rusdi, M. (2021). Learning Organization on the Implementation of E-Government in the City of Makassar. *Journal Dimensie Management and Public Sector*, *2*(3), 12–21. doi:10.48173/jdmps.v2i3.111

Saeed, S., Almuhaideb, A. M., Kumar, N., Zaman, N., & Zikria, Y. B. (Eds.). (2023). *Handbook of Research on Cybersecurity Issues and Challenges for Business and FinTech Applications*. IGI Global. doi:10.4018/978-1-6684-5284-4

Saeed, S., Altamimi, S. A., Alkayyal, N. A., Alshehri, E., & Alabbad, D. A. (2023). Digital Transformation and Cybersecurity Challenges for businesses Resilience: Issues and recommendations. *Sensors (Basel)*, *23*(15), 6666. doi:10.3390/s23156666 PMID:37571451

Safitra, M. F., Lubis, M., & Fakhrurroja, H. (2023a). Counterattacking Cyber Threats: A framework for the Future of Cybersecurity. *Sustainability (Basel)*, *15*(18), 13369. doi:10.3390/su151813369

Sagarik, D., Chansukree, P., Cho, W., & Berman, E. (2018). E-government 4.0 in Thailand: The role of central agencies. *Information Polity*, *23*(3), 343–353. doi:10.3233/IP-180006

Sahay, R., Meng, W., & Jensen, C. D. (2019). The application of Software Defined Networking on securing computer networks: A survey. *Journal of Network and Computer Applications*, *131*, 89–108. doi:10.1016/j.jnca.2019.01.019

Salahdine, F., Han, T., & Zhang, N. (2023). 5G, 6G, and Beyond: Recent advances and future challenges. *Annales des Télécommunications*, *78*(9–10), 525–549. doi:10.1007/s12243-022-00938-3

Salam, S., & Kumar, K. P. (2021). Survey on Applications of Blockchain in E-Governance. *REVISTA GEINTEC-GESTAO INOVACAO E TECNOLOGIAS, 11*(4), 3807-3822.

Saleem, J., Adebisi, B., Ande, R., & Hammoudeh, M. (2017, July). A state of the art survey-Impact of cyber attacks on SME's. In *Proceedings of the International Conference on Future Networks and Distributed Systems*. https://dl.acm.org/doi/abs/10.1145/3102304.3109812

Saleh, M., Jhanjhi, N., Abdullah, A., & Saher, R. (2022a). *IoTES (A Machine learning model) Design dependent encryption selection for IoT devices.* Paper presented at the 2022 24th International Conference on Advanced Communication Technology (ICACT).

Saleh, M., Jhanjhi, N., Abdullah, A., & Saher, R. (2022b). *Proposing encryption selection model for IoT devices based on IoT device design.* Paper presented at the 2022 24th International Conference on Advanced Communication Technology (ICACT). 10.23919/ICACT53585.2022.9728914

Saleh, M., Jhanjhi, N. Z., Abdullah, A., & Saher, R. (2020). Design Challenges of Securing IoT Devices: A survey. *International Journal of Engineering Research & Technology (Ahmedabad)*, *13*(12), 5149–5165.

Samad, A., Alam, S., Shuaib, M., & Bokhari, M. (2018). *Internet of Vehicles (IoV)*. Requirements, Attacks and Countermeasures.

Samsor, A. M. (2020). *Challenges and Prospects of e-Government implementation in Afghanistan*. International Trade, Politics and Development.

Samtani, S., Zhu, H., & Chen, H. (2020). Proactively Identifying Emerging Hacker Threats from the Dark Web: A Diachronic Graph Embedding Framework (D-GEF). *ACM Transactions on Privacy and Security (TOPS), 23*(4), 1-33. https://dl.acm.org/doi/abs/10.1145/3409289

Samtani, S., Zhu, H., & Chen, H. (2020). Proactively Identifying Emerging Hacker Threats from the Dark Web: A Diachronic Graph Embedding Framework (D-GEF). [TOPS]. *ACM Transactions on Privacy and Security*, *23*(4), 1–33. doi:10.1145/3409289

Samuel, K. E., Goury, M., Gunasekaran, A., & Spalanzani, A. (2011). Knowledge management in supply chain: An empirical study from France. *The Journal of Strategic Information Systems*, *20*(3), 283–306. doi:10.1016/j.jsis.2010.11.001

Sangki, J. (2018). Vision of future e-government via new e-government maturity model: Based on Korea's e-government practices. *Telecommunications Policy*, *42*(10), 860–871. doi:10.1016/j.telpol.2017.12.002

Sankar, S., Ramasubbareddy, S., Luhach, A. K., Deverajan, G. G., Alnumay, W. S., Jhanjhi, N. Z., Ghosh, U., & Sharma, P. K. (2020). Energy efficient optimal parent selection based routing protocol for Internet of Things using firefly optimization algorithm. *Transactions on Emerging Telecommunications Technologies*, *32*(8), e4171. doi:10.1002/ett.4171

Saranya, P., & Maheswari, R. (2023). Proof of Transaction (POTX) based traceability system for an agriculture supply chain. *IEEE Access : Practical Innovations, Open Solutions*, *11*, 10623–10638. doi:10.1109/ACCESS.2023.3240772

Sari, R. T. K., & Hindarto, D. (2023). Implementation of Cyber-Security Enterprise Architecture Food Industry in Society 5.0 Era. *Sinkron : Jurnal Dan Penelitian Teknik Informatika*, *8*(2), 1074–1084. doi:10.33395/sinkron.v8i2.12377

Sarkar, B. D., Shankar, R., & Kar, A. K. (2022). Port logistic issues and challenges in the Industry 4.0 era for emerging economies: An India perspective. *Benchmarking*, *30*(1), 50–74. doi:10.1108/BIJ-08-2021-0499

Saxena, U. R., & Alam, T. (2023). Provisioning trust-oriented role-based access control for maintaining data integrity in cloud. *International Journal of Systems Assurance Engineering and Management*, *14*(6), 2559–2578. doi:10.1007/s13198-023-02112-x

Scarfone, K., Hoffman, P., & Souppaya, M. (2009). Guide to enterprise telework and remote access security. *NIST Special Publication, 800*, 46. https://csrc.nist.rip/library/alt-SP800-46r1.pdf

Şcheau, M. C., Achim, M. V., Găbudeanu, L., Vaidean, V. L., Vilcea, A., & Apetri, L. (2023). Proposals of Processes and Organizational Preventive Measures against Malfunctioning of Drones and User Negligence. *Drones (Basel)*, *7*(1), 64. doi:10.3390/drones7010064

Schiff, L., Schmid, S., & Kuznetsov, P. (2016). In-Band Synchronization for Distributed SDN Control Planes. *Computer Communication Review*, *46*(1), 37–43. doi:10.1145/2875951.2875957

Schinas, O., & Metzger, D. (2023). Cyber-seaworthiness: A critical review of the literature. *Marine Policy*, *151*, 105592. doi:10.1016/j.marpol.2023.105592

Schmitt, M. (2023). Securing the digital world: Protecting smart infrastructures and digital industries with artificial intelligence (AI)-enabled malware and intrusion detection. *Journal of Industrial Information Integration*, *36*, 100520. doi:10.1016/j.jii.2023.100520

Security, H. N. (2021, June 28). *What are the most common cybersecurity challenges SMEs face today? Help Net Security*. Help Net Security. https://www.helpnetsecurity.com/2021/07/07/smes-cybersecurity-challenges/

Sethi, P. (2020). Swarm Intelligence for Clustering in Wireless Sensor Networks. *Swarm Intelligence Optimization: Algorithms and Applications*, 263-273.

Shafik, W., & Kalinaki, K. (2023). Smart City Ecosystem: An Exploration of Requirements, Architecture, Applications, Security, and Emerging Motivations. In Handbook of Research on Network-Enabled IoT Applications for Smart City Services (pp. 75–98). IGI Global. doi:10.4018/979-8-3693-0744-1.ch005

Shafik, W., Matinkhah, S. M., & Shokoor, F. (2022). Recommendation System Comparative Analysis: Internet of Things aided Networks. *EAI Endorsed Transactions on Internet of Things*, *8*(29), e5. doi:10.4108/eetiot.v8i29.1108

Shafik, W., Mojtaba Matinkhah, S., Shokoor, F., & Nur Sanda, M. (2021). Internet of Things-Based Energy Efficiency Optimization Model in Fog Smart Cities. *JOIV : International Journal on Informatics Visualization*, *5*(2), 105–112. doi:10.30630/joiv.5.2.373

Shafiq, M., Ashraf, H., Ullah, A., Masud, M., Azeem, M., & Jhanjhi, N. (2021). *Robust cluster-based routing protocol for IoT-assisted smart devices in WSN*. Academic Press.

Shah, I. A. (2022). Cybersecurity Issues and Challenges for E-Government During COVID-19: A Review. *Cybersecurity Measures for E-Government Frameworks*, 187-222.

Shah, I. A., Sial, Q., Jhanjhi, N. Z., & Gaur, L. (2023). The Role of the IoT and Digital Twin in the Healthcare Digitalization Process: IoT and Digital Twin in the Healthcare Digitalization Process. In Digital Twins and Healthcare: Trends, Techniques, and Challenges (pp. 20-34). IGI Global.

Shah, I. A., Sial, Q., Jhanjhi, N. Z., & Gaur, L. (2023). Use Cases for Digital Twin. In Digital Twins and Healthcare: Trends, Techniques, and Challenges (pp. 102-118). IGI Global.

Shah, I. A., Wassan, S., & Usmani, M. H. (2022). E-Government Security and Privacy Issues: Challenges and Preventive Approaches. In Cybersecurity Measures for E-Government Frameworks (pp. 61-76). IGI Global.

Shah, S. U. A., Manzoor, M. K., Latif, R. M. A., Farhan, M., & Ashiq, M. I. (2019). *A Novel Routing Protocol Based on Congruent Gravity Value for Underwater Wireless Sensor Networks.* Paper presented at the 2019 International Conference on Frontiers of Information Technology (FIT). 10.1109/FIT47737.2019.00018

Shah, I. A., Habeeb, R. A. A., Rajper, S., & Laraib, A. (2022). The Influence of Cybersecurity Attacks on E-Governance. In *Cybersecurity Measures for E-Government Frameworks* (pp. 77–95). IGI Global. doi:10.4018/978-1-7998-9624-1.ch005

Shah, I. A., Jhanjhi, N. Z., Amsaad, F., & Razaque, A. (2022). The Role of Cutting-Edge Technologies in Industry 4.0. In *Cyber Security Applications for Industry 4.0* (pp. 97–109). Chapman and Hall/CRC. doi:10.1201/9781003203087-4

Shah, I. A., Jhanjhi, N. Z., Humayun, M., & Ghosh, U. (2022). Health Care Digital Revolution During COVID-19. In *How COVID-19 is Accelerating the Digital Revolution* (pp. 17–30). Springer. doi:10.1007/978-3-030-98167-9_2

Shah, I. A., Jhanjhi, N. Z., Humayun, M., & Ghosh, U. (2022). Impact of COVID-19 on Higher and Post-secondary Education Systems. In *How COVID-19 is Accelerating the Digital Revolution* (pp. 71–83). Springer. doi:10.1007/978-3-030-98167-9_5

Shah, I. A., Jhanjhi, N. Z., & Laraib, A. (2023). Cybersecurity and Blockchain Usage in Contemporary Business. In *Handbook of Research on Cybersecurity Issues and Challenges for Business and FinTech Applications* (pp. 49–64). IGI Global.

Shah, I. A., Rajper, S., & ZamanJhanjhi, N. (2021). Using ML and Data-Mining Techniques in Automatic Vulnerability Software Discovery. *International Journal (Toronto, Ont.)*, *10*(3).

Shah, I. A., Zaman, N., & Laraib, A. (2022). Cybersecurity and Blockchain Usage in Contemporary Business. In *Advances in information security, privacy, and ethics book series* (pp. 49–64). IGI Global., doi:10.4018/978-1-6684-5284-4.ch003

Shahid, H., Ashraf, H., Javed, H., Humayun, M., Jhanjhi, N. Z., & AlZain, M. A. (2021). Energy optimised security against wormhole attack in iot-based wireless sensor networks. *Computers, Materials & Continua*, *68*(2), 1967–1981. doi:10.32604/cmc.2021.015259

Shah, S., Bolton, M., & Menon, S. (2020). A Study of Internet of Things (IoT) and its Impacts on Global Supply Chains. *Proceedings of International Conference on Computation, Automation and Knowledge Management, ICCAKM 2020*, 245–250. 10.1109/ICCAKM46823.2020.9051474

Sharef, B. T., Alsaqour, R. A., & Ismail, M. (2014). Vehicular communication ad hoc routing protocols: A survey. *Journal of Network and Computer Applications*, *40*, 363–396. doi:10.1016/j.jnca.2013.09.008

Sharifi, A. (2023). Resilience of urban social-ecological-technological systems (SETS): A review. *Sustainable Cities and Society*, *99*, 104910. doi:10.1016/j.scs.2023.104910

Sharma, P., Zawar, S., & Patil, S. B. (2016). Ransomware Analysis: Internet of Things (Iot) Security Issues, Challenges and Open Problems Inthe Context of Worldwide Scenario of Security of Systems and Malware Attacks. In *International conference on recent Innovation in Engineering and Management* (*Vol. 2*, No. 3, pp. 177-184). Academic Press.

Sharma, T. (2021). *Evolving Phishing Email Prevention Techniques: A Survey to Pin Down Effective Phishing Study Design Concepts*. https://www.ideals.illinois.edu/handle/2142/109179

Sharma, A., Bhatia, T., Singh, R., & Sharma, A. (2023). Developing the framework of blockchain-enabled agri-food supply chain. *Business Process Management Journal*. doi:10.1108/BPMJ-01-2023-0035

Sharma, M., Luthra, S., Joshi, S., Kumar, A., & Jain, A. (2023). Green logistics driven circular practices adoption in industry 4.0 era: A moderating effect of institution pressure and supply chain flexibility. *Journal of Cleaner Production*, *383*, 135284. doi:10.1016/j.jclepro.2022.135284

Sharma, N., Chauhan, N., & Chand, N. (2018). Security challenges in Internet of Vehicles (IoV) environment. *2018 First International Conference on Secure Cyber Computing and Communication (ICSCCC),* 203-207. 10.1109/ICSCCC.2018.8703272

Sharma, P. K., Singh, S., Jeong, Y. S., & Park, J. H. (2017). Distblocknet: A distributed blockchains-based secure sdn architecture for iot networks. *IEEE Communications Magazine*, *55*(9), 78–85. doi:10.1109/MCOM.2017.1700041

Sharma, R., & Arya, R. (2022). Security threats and measures in the Internet of Things for smart city infrastructure: A state of art. *Transactions on Emerging Telecommunications Technologies*, *34*(11), e4571. doi:10.1002/ett.4571

Sharma, S. K., Metri, B., Dwivedi, Y. K., & Rana, N. P. (2021). Challenges common service centers (CSCs) face in delivering e-government services in rural India. *Government Information Quarterly*, *38*(2), 101573. doi:10.1016/j.giq.2021.101573

Sharma, S., & Verma, V. K. (2022). An integrated exploration on internet of things and wireless sensor networks. *Wireless Personal Communications*, *124*(3), 2735–2770. doi:10.1007/s11277-022-09487-3

Shee, H. (2023). Internet of Things: Applications and Challenges for Supply Chain Management. The Palgrave Handbook of Supply Chain Management, 1–19. doi:10.1007/978-3-030-89822-9_78-1

Sheik, A. T., Maple, C., Epiphaniou, G., & Dianati, M. (2023). Securing Cloud-Assisted connected and Autonomous Vehicles: An In-Depth threat Analysis and risk assessment. *Sensors (Basel)*, *24*(1), 241. doi:10.3390/s24010241 PMID:38203103

Sheikh, H. F., & Ahmad, I. (2015). *An evolutionary technique for performance-energy-temperature optimized scheduling of parallel tasks on multi-core processors*. Academic Press.

Sheikh, H. F., Ahmad, I., Wang, Z., & Ranka, S. (2012). *An overview and classification of thermal-aware scheduling techniques for multi-core processing systems*. Academic Press.

Sheikh, H. F., Tan, H., Ahmad, I., & Ranka, S. (2012). *Energy-and performance-aware scheduling of tasks on parallel and distributed systems*. Academic Press.

Shinde, A. (2021). *Introduction to cyber security: Guide to the World of Cyber Security*. Notion Press.

Shirsat, A., Muthukaruppan, V., Hu, R., Paduani, V., Xu, B., Song, L., Li, Y., Liu, N., Baran, M., Lubkeman, D., & Tang, W. (2023). A secure and adaptive hierarchical Multi-Timescale framework for resilient load restoration using a community microgrid. *IEEE Transactions on Sustainable Energy*, *14*(2), 1057–1075. doi:10.1109/TSTE.2023.3251099

Shishodia, A., Sharma, R., Rajesh, R., & Munim, Z. H. (2021). Supply chain resilience: A review, conceptual framework and future research. *International Journal of Logistics Management*, *34*(4), 879–908. doi:10.1108/IJLM-03-2021-0169

Shrivastava, S. (2023). Recent trends in supply chain management of business-tobusiness firms: A review and future research directions. *Journal of Business and Industrial Marketing*, *38*(12), 2673–2693. doi:10.1108/JBIM-02-2023-0122

Shukur, B. S., Aljanabi, M., & Ali, A. H. (2023). ChatGPT: Exploring the Role of Cybersecurity in the Protection of Medical Information. *Journals. Mesopotamian. Press*, 18–21. doi:10.58496/MJCS/2023/004

Siavvas, M., Tsoukalas, D., Kalouptsoglou, I., Manganopoulou, E., Manolis, G. D., Kehagias, D., & Tzovaras, D. (2023). Security Monitoring during Software Development: An Industrial Case Study. *Applied Sciences (Basel, Switzerland)*, *13*(12), 6872. doi:10.3390/app13126872

Siddiqui, F. J., Ashraf, H., & Ullah, A. (2020). Dual server based security system for multimedia Services in Next Generation Networks. *Multimedia Tools and Applications*, *79*(11-12), 7299–7318. doi:10.1007/s11042-019-08406-2

Simatupang, T. M., Wright, A. F., & Sridharan, R. (2004). Applying the theory of constraints to supply chain collaboration. *Supply Chain Management*, *9*(1), 57–70. doi:10.1108/13598540410517584

Simonova, A. (2020). *An Analysis of Factors Influencing National Institute of Standards and Technology Cybersecurity Framework Adoption in Financial Services: A Correlational Study* [Doctoral dissertation, Capella University].

Şimşit, Z. T., Günay, N. S., & Vayvay, O. (2014). Theory of Constraints: A Literature Review. *Procedia: Social and Behavioral Sciences*, *150*, 930–936. doi:10.1016/j.sbspro.2014.09.104

Sindiramutty, S. R., Jhanjhi, N. Z., Ray, S. K., Jazri, H., Khan, N. A., & Gaur, L. (2024). Metaverse: Virtual Meditation. In Metaverse Applications for Intelligent Healthcare (pp. 93–158). IGI Global. doi:10.4018/978-1-6684-9823-1.ch003

Singh, S. (2016, September 22). Future Of Logistics: Five Technologies That Will Self-Orchestrate The Supply Chain. *Forbes*. https://www.forbes.com/sites/sarwantsingh/2016/09/22/future-of-logistics-5-technologies-that-will-self-orchestrate-the-supply-chain/?sh=5202b1155a63

Singh, A. P., Pradhan, N. R., Luhach, A. K., Agnihotri, S., Jhanjhi, N. Z., Verma, S., Kavita, Ghosh, U., & Roy, D. S. (2020). A novel patient-centric architectural framework for blockchain-enabled healthcare applications. *IEEE Transactions on Industrial Informatics*, *17*(8), 5779–5789. doi:10.1109/TII.2020.3037889

Singh, A., Gutub, A., Nayyar, A., & Khan, M. K. (2022). Redefining food safety traceability system through blockchain: Findings, challenges and open issues. *Multimedia Tools and Applications*, *82*(14), 21243–21277. doi:10.1007/s11042-022-14006-4 PMID:36276604

Singhal, V., Jain, S. P., Anand, D., Singh, A., Verma, S., Kavita, Rodrigues, J. J. P. C., Jhanjhi, N. Z., Ghosh, U., Jo, O., & Iwendi, C. (2020). Artificial Intelligence Enabled Road Vehicle-Train Collision Risk Assessment Framework for Unmanned railway level crossings. *IEEE Access : Practical Innovations, Open Solutions*, *8*, 113790–113806. doi:10.1109/ACCESS.2020.3002416

Singh, R. K., Mishra, R., Gupta, S., & Mukherjee, A. A. (2023). Blockchain applications for secured and resilient supply chains: A systematic literature review and future research agenda. *Computers & Industrial Engineering*, *175*, 108854. doi:10.1016/j.cie.2022.108854

Sithole, V. E. (2015). *An e-governance training model for public managers: The case of selected Free State Provincial departments* (Doctoral dissertation). https://repository.nwu.ac.za/handle/10394/16320

SL. S. D., MV, M. K., Prashanth, B., & Y, V. S. M. (2023). Malware analysis and intrusion detection in Cyber-Physical systems. IGI Global.

Sobb, T. M., Turnbull, B., & Moustafa, N. (2020). Supply Chain 4.0: A Survey of Cyber Security Challenges, Solutions and Future Directions. *Electronics (Basel)*, *9*(11), 1864. doi:10.3390/electronics9111864

Soderi, S., Masti, D., & Lun, Y. Z. (2023). Railway Cyber-Security in the Era of Interconnected Systems: A survey. *IEEE Transactions on Intelligent Transportation Systems*, *24*(7), 6764–6779. doi:10.1109/TITS.2023.3254442

Song, Y., Yu, F. R., Zhou, L., Yang, X., & He, Z. (2021). Applications of the Internet of Things (IoT) in Smart Logistics: A Comprehensive Survey. *IEEE Internet of Things Journal*, *8*(6), 4250–4274. doi:10.1109/JIOT.2020.3034385

Soni, V., Anand, R., Dey, P. K., Dash, A. P., & Banwet, D. K. (2017). Quantifying e-governance efficacy towards Indian–EU strategic dialogue. *Transforming Government: People, Process and Policy*. https://www.emerald.com/insight/content/doi/10.1108/TG-06-2017-0031/full/html

Soni, V., Dey, P. K., Anand, R., Malhotra, C., & Banwet, D. K. (2017). Digitizing grey portions of e-governance. *Transforming Government: People, Process and Policy*. https://www.emerald.com/insight/content/doi/10.1108/TG-11-2016-0076/full/html

Sony, A. L. (2015). Solving e-Governance Challenges in India through the Incremental Adoption to Cloud Service. *Law: J. Higher Sch. Econ.*, 169. https://heinonline.org/HOL/LandingPage?handle=hein.journals/pravo2015&div=15&id=&page=

Soto-Acosta, P., Del Giudice, M., & Scuotto, V. (2018). Emerging issues on business innovation ecosystems: The role of information and communication technologies (ICTs) for knowledge management (KM) and innovation within and among enterprises. *Baltic Journal of Management*, *13*(3), 298–302. doi:10.1108/BJM-07-2018-398

Soumpenioti, V., & Panagopoulos, A. (2023). AI Technology in the Field of Logistics. *2023 18th International Workshop on Semantic and Social Media Adaptation & Personalization*. IEEE. 10.1109/SMAP59435.2023.10255203

Srinivasan, K., Garg, L., Datta, D., Alaboudi, A. A., Jhanjhi, N. Z., Agarwal, R., & Thomas, A. G. (2021). Performance comparison of deep cnn models for detecting driver's distraction. *CMC-Computers. Materials & Continua*, *68*(3), 4109–4124. doi:10.32604/cmc.2021.016736

Srinivasan, M. (2016). The role of logistics in e-commerce. *International Journal of Management and Social Sciences Research*, *5*(4), 52–56.

Stankovic, J. A. (2016). Research directions for cyber-physical systems in wireless and mobile healthcare. *ACM Transactions on Cyber-Physical Systems*, *1*(1), 1–12. doi:10.1145/2899006

Stark, J. (2017). Productivity improvements in transport logistics. Journal of Supply Chain Management. *Logistics and Procurement*, *1*(2), 111–119. doi:10.1108/JSCLP-08-2017-0024

Steen, R., Haug, O. J., & Patriarca, R. (2023). Business continuity and resilience management: A conceptual framework. *Journal of Contingencies and Crisis Management*. doi:10.1111/1468-5973.12501

Steichen, M., Hommes, S., & State, R. (2017, September). ChainGuard—A firewall for blockchain applications using SDN with OpenFlow. In 2017 Principles, Systems and Applications of IP Telecommunications (IPTComm) (pp. 1-8). IEEE.

Stellios, I., Kotzanikolaou, P., Psarakis, M., Alcaraz, C., & Lopez, J. (2018). A survey of iot-enabled cyberattacks: Assessing attack paths to critical infrastructures and services. *IEEE Communications Surveys and Tutorials*, *20*(4), 3453–3495. doi:10.1109/COMST.2018.2855563

Strand, S. S. (2023). *An investigation into cyber security risk mitigation and the human factor in developing a cyber security culture - A comparative analysis of two maritime companies in Norway*. Open Archive. https://openarchive.usn.no/usn-xmlui/handle/11250/3076275

StraußS. (2023). The body as permanent digital identity? Societal and ethical implications of biometrics as mainstream technology. tecnoscienza.unibo.it. doi:10.6092/issn.2038-3460/17611

Suhandiah, S., Suhariadi, F., Yulianti, P., & Abbas, A. (2023). Autonomy and feedback on innovative work behavior: The role of resilience as a mediating factor in Indonesian Islamic banks. *Cogent Business & Management*, *10*(1), 2178364. doi:10.1080/23311975.2023.2178364

Suja, A. (2022). Machine learning-based wearable devices for smart healthcare application with risk factor monitoring. In *Empowering Sustainable Industrial 4.0 Systems With Machine Intelligence* (pp. 174–185). IGI Global.

Sujatha, R., & Prakash, G. (2022). *Cyber Security Applications for Industry 4.0, Chapman and Hall/CRC Cyber-Physical Systems Series*. CRC Press.

Suki, N. M., Sharif, A., & Afshan, S. (2021). The role of logistics performance for sustainable development in top Asian countries: Evidence from advance panel estimations. *Sustainable Development (Bradford)*, *29*(4), 595–606. doi:10.1002/sd.2160

Suleimany, M. (2021, May). Smart Urban Management and IoT; Paradigm of E-Governance and Technologies in Developing Communities. In *2021 5th International Conference on Internet of Things and Applications (IoT)* (pp. 1-6). IEEE.

Suleimany, M. (2021, May). Smart Urban Management and IoT; Paradigm of E-Governance and Technologies in Developing Communities. In *2021 5th International Conference on Internet of Things and Applications (IoT)* (pp. 1-6). IEEE. https://ieeexplore.ieee.org/abstract/document/9469713

Suman, O. P., Saini, L. K., & Kumar, S. (2023). Cloud-based data protection and secure backup solutions: A comprehensive review of ensuring business continuity. In *2023 Third International Conference on Secure Cyber Computing and Communication (ICSCCC)* (pp. 821–826). IEEE. 10.1109/ICSCCC58608.2023.10176503

Sun, N., Zhu, C., Zhang, Y., & Liu, Y. (2023). An Identity Privacy-Preserving Scheme against Insider Logistics Data Leakage Based on One-Time-Use Accounts. *Future Internet*, *15*(11), 361. doi:10.3390/fi15110361

Supply Chain Vulnerability: Identifying and Mitigating Risks. (n.d.). magaya.com

Susha, I., Rukanova, B., Zuiderwijk, A., Gil-García, J. R., & Gascó-Hernández, M. (2023). Achieving voluntary data sharing in cross sector partnerships: Three partnership models. *Information and Organization*, *33*(1), 100448. doi:10.1016/j.infoandorg.2023.100448

Sutradhar, S., Karforma, S., Bose, R., Roy, S., Djebali, S., & Bhattacharyya, D. (2024). Enhancing identity and access management using Hyperledger Fabric and OAuth 2.0: A block-chain-based approach for security and scalability for healthcare industry. *Internet of Things and Cyber-Physical Systems*, *4*, 49–67. doi:10.1016/j.iotcps.2023.07.004

Su, Z., Wang, Y., Xu, Q., Fei, M., Tian, Y. C., & Zhang, N. (2018). A secure charging scheme for electric vehicles with smart communities in energy blockchain. *IEEE Internet of Things Journal*, *6*(3), 4601–4613. doi:10.1109/JIOT.2018.2869297

Syed, N. F., & Syed, W. (2022). Traceability in supply chains: A cyber security analysis. *Computers & Security*, *112*, 102536. doi:10.1016/j.cose.2021.102536

Symantec. (2021). *Symantec Internet Security Threat Report*. Bradcom. Retrieved May 12, 2023, from https://docs.broadcom.com/doc/istr-03-jan-en

T, V. K., Rajasekaran, P., Jeevika, L., Lavan, S., & Tharshan, R. (2023). Data Preservation in Chatbot with Cloud Deployment. *2023 7th International Conference on Trends in Electronics and Informatics (ICOEI)*. IEEE. doi:10.1109/ICOEI56765.2023.10125731

Taeihagh, A., & Hazel, S. M. L. (2019). Governing autonomous vehicles: Emerging responses for safety, liability, privacy, cybersecurity, and industry risks. *Transport Reviews*, *39*(1), 103–128. doi:10.1080/01441647.2018.1494640

Taj, I., & Zaman, N. (2022). Towards Industrial Revolution 5.0 and Explainable Artificial Intelligence: Challenges and Opportunities. *International Journal of Computing and Digital Systems*, *12*(1), 285–310. doi:10.12785/ijcds/120124

Talluri, S., Kull, T., Yíldíz, H., & Yoon, J. (2013). Assessing the efficiency of risk mitigation strategies in supply chains. *Journal of Business Logistics*, *34*(4), 253–269. doi:10.1111/jbl.12025

Tampubolon, S., & Purba, H. H. (2021). Lean six sigma implementation, a systematic literature review. *International Journal of Production Management and Engineering*, *9*(2), 125. doi:10.4995/ijpme.2021.14561

Tan, Choi, Kim, Pan, & Chung. (2018). Secure Certificateless Authentication and Road Message Dissemination Protocol in VANETs. Wireless Communications and Mobile Computing. doi:10.1155/2018/7978027

Tan, Y., Cheng, J., Zhu, H., Hu, Z., Li, B., & Liu, S. (2017, July). Real-time life prediction of equipment based on optimized ARMA model. In 2017 Prognostics and System Health Management Conference (PHM-Harbin) (pp. 1-6). IEEE. doi:10.1109/PHM.2017.8079318

Tan, W. C., & Sidhu, M. S. (2022). Review of RFID and IoT integration in supply chain management. *Operations Research Perspectives*, *9*, 100229. doi:10.1016/j.orp.2022.100229

Tasca, P., & Tessone, C. J. (2017). Taxonomy of blockchain technologies. Principles of identification and classification. *arXiv preprint arXiv:1708.04872.*

Tayyab, Marjani, Jhanjhi, Abaker, Hashem, & Usmani. (n.d.). *A watermark-based secure model for data security against security attacks for machine learning algorithms*. Academic Press.

Tayyab, M., & Marjani, M. (2021a). A light-weight watermarking-based framework on dataset using deep learning algorithms. In *2021 National Computing Colleges Conference (NCCC)* (pp. 1–6). IEEE.

Tayyab, M., & Marjani, M. (2021b). Cryptographic based secure model on dataset for deep learning algorithms. *CMC Comput. Mater. Contin*, *69*, 1183–1200.

Teffandi, N., Feryputri, N. A., Hasanuddin, M. O., Syafalni, I., & Sutisna, N. (2023). GRAIN Algorithm Implementation for Lightweight Hardware-Based OTP Authentication. *2023 International Conference on Electrical Engineering and Informatics (ICEEI)*. IEEE. 10.1109/ICEEI59426.2023.10346638

Telo, J. (2017, January 17). *AI for Enhanced Healthcare Security: An Investigation of Anomaly Detection, Predictive Analytics, Access Control, Threat Intelligence, and Incident Response.* https://research.tensorgate.org/index.php/JAAHM/article/view/16

The most common entry points for a cyber attack. (n.d.). guptadeepak.com

Thomas, G., & Sule, M. (2022). A service lens on cybersecurity continuity and management for organizations' subsistence and growth. *Organizational Cybersecurity Journal*, *3*(1), 18–40. doi:10.1108/OCJ-09-2021-0025

Tiwari, S., Sharma, P., Choi, T., & Lim, A. (2023). Blockchain and third-party logistics for global supply chain operations: Stakeholders' perspectives and decision roadmap. *Transportation Research Part E, Logistics and Transportation Review*, *170*, 103012. doi:10.1016/j.tre.2022.103012

Tolossa, D. (2023). Importance of cybersecurity awareness training for employees in business. *VIDYA - a JOURNAL OF GUJARAT UNIVERSITY*, *2*(2), 104–107. doi:10.47413/vidya.v2i2.206

Tosh, D. K., Shetty, S., Liang, X., Kamhoua, C., & Njilla, L. (2017, October). Consensus protocols for blockchain-based data provenance: Challenges and opportunities. In *2017 IEEE 8th Annual Ubiquitous Computing, Electronics and Mobile Communication Conference (UEMCON)* (pp. 469-474). IEEE.

Tounsi, W., & Rais, H. (2018). A survey on technical threat intelligence in the age of sophisticated cyber attacks. *Computers & Security*, *72*, 212–233. doi:10.1016/j.cose.2017.09.001

Tran-Dang, H., Krommenacker, N., Charpentier, P., & Kim, D.-S. (2022). The Internet of Things for Logistics: Perspectives, Application Review, and Challenges. *IETE Technical Review*, *39*(1), 93–121. doi:10.1080/02564602.2020.1827308

Trappey, A., Trappey, C., Fan, C., Hsu, A., Li, X., & Lee, I. (2017, September). IoT patent roadmap for smart logistic service providers in the context of industry 4.0. *Zhongguo Gongcheng Xuekan*, *40*(7), 593–602. doi:10.1080/02533839.2017.1362325

Tripathi, B., Keil, S. J., Gulati, M., Cho, J. W., Machnicki, E. P., Herbeck, G. H., ... Dalal, A. (2019). *System on a chip with always-on processor which reconfigures SOC and supports memory-only communication mode*. Google Patents.

Tsang, Y. P., Yang, T., Chen, Z. S., Wu, C. H., & Tan, K. H. (2022). How is extended reality bridging human and cyber-physical systems in the IoT-empowered logistics and supply chain management? *Internet of Things : Engineering Cyber Physical Human Systems*, *20*, 100623. doi:10.1016/j.iot.2022.100623

Tsohou, A., Diamantopoulou, V., Gritzalis, S., & Lambrinoudakis, C. (2023). Cyber insurance: State of the art, trends and future directions. *International Journal of Information Security*, *22*(3), 737–748. Advance online publication. doi:10.1007/s10207-023-00660-8 PMID:36684688

Twizeyimana, J. D., & Andersson, A. (2019). The public value of E-Government–A literature review. *Government Information Quarterly*, *36*(2), 167–178. doi:10.1016/j.giq.2019.01.001

Ugochukwu, N. A., Goyal, S. B., Rajawat, A. S., Verma, C., & Illés, Z. (2023). Enhancing Logistics with The Internet of Things: A Secured and Efficient Distribution and Storage Model Utilizing Blockchain Innovations and Interplanetary File System. *IEEE Access : Practical Innovations, Open Solutions*, *1*. doi:10.1109/ACCESS.2023.3339754

Ujjan, R. M. A., Hussain, K., & Brohi, S. N. (2022). The impact of Blockchain technology on advanced security measures for E-Government. In *Cybersecurity Measures for E-Government Frameworks* (pp. 157–174). IGI Global. doi:10.4018/978-1-7998-9624-1.ch010

Ujjan, R. M. A., Khan, N. A., & Gaur, L. (2022). E-Government Privacy and Security Challenges in the Context of Internet of Things. In *Cybersecurity Measures for E-Government Frameworks* (pp. 22–42). IGI Global. doi:10.4018/978-1-7998-9624-1.ch002

Ujjan, R. M. A., Pervez, Z., Dahal, K., Bashir, A. K., Mumtaz, R., & González, J. (2020). Towards sFlow and adaptive polling sampling for deep learning based DDoS detection in SDN. *Future Generation Computer Systems*, *111*, 763–779. doi:10.1016/j.future.2019.10.015

Ujjan, R. M. A., Taj, I., & Brohi, S. N. (2022). E-Government Cybersecurity Modeling in the Context of Software-Defined Networks. In *Cybersecurity Measures for E-Government Frameworks* (pp. 1–21). IGI Global. doi:10.4018/978-1-7998-9624-1.ch001

Ujjan, R. M. A., Taj, I., & Brohi, S. N. (2022). *E-Government Cybersecurity Modeling in the Context of Software-Defined Networks. In Cybersecurity Measures for E-Government Frameworks*. IGI Global.

Ullah, A., Ishaq, N., Azeem, M., Ashraf, H., Jhanjhi, N., Humayun, M., . . . Almusaylim, Z. (2021). *A survey on continuous object tracking and boundary detection schemes in IoT assisted wireless sensor networks*. Academic Press.

Ullah, A., Pinglu, C., Ullah, S., Abbas, H. S. M., & Khan, S. (n.d.). *The Role of E-Governance in Combating COVID-19 and Promoting Sustainable Development: A Comparative Study of China and Pakistan*. https://link.springer.com/article/10.1007/s41111-020-00167-w

Ullo, S., Gallo, M., Palmieri, G., Amenta, P., Russo, M., Romano, G., . . . De Angelis, M. (2018). *Application of wireless sensor networks to environmental monitoring for sustainable mobility*. Paper presented at the 2018 IEEE International Conference on Environmental Engineering (EE). 10.1109/EE1.2018.8385263

Umrani, S., Rajper, S., Talpur, S. H., Shah, I. A., & Shujrah, A. (2020). -. *Indian Journal of Science and Technology*.

Umrani, S., Rajper, S., Talpur, S. H., Shah, I. A., & Shujrah, A. (2020). Games based learning: A case of learning Physics using Angry Birds. *Indian Journal of Science and Technology*, *13*(36), 3778–3784. doi:10.17485/IJST/v13i36.853

ur Rehman, S., Khaliq, M., Imtiaz, S. I., Rasool, A., Shafiq, M., Javed, A. R., ... Bashir, A. K. (2021). DIDDOS: An approach for detection and identification of Distributed Denial of Service (DDoS) cyberattacks using Gated Recurrent Units (GRU). *Future Generation Computer Systems*, *118*, 453-466.

Valashiya, M. C., & Luke, R. (2022). Enhancing supply chain information sharing with third party logistics service providers. *International Journal of Logistics Management*, *34*(6), 1523–1542. doi:10.1108/IJLM-11-2021-0522

Varshney, S., Kumar, C., Swaroop, A., Khanna, A., Gupta, D., Rodrigues, J. J., Pinheiro, P., & De Albuquerque, V. H. C. (2018). Energy efficient management of pipelines in buildings using linear wireless sensor networks. *Sensors (Basel)*, *18*(8), 2618. doi:10.3390/s18082618 PMID:30103372

Venkatesh, V., Thong, J. Y., Chan, F. K., & Hu, P. J. (2016). Managing citizens' uncertainty in e-government services: The mediating and moderating roles of transparency and trust. *Information Systems Research*, *27*(1), 87–111. doi:10.1287/isre.2015.0612

Venngage. (n.d.). Cyber Security Framework Mind Map. *Venngage*. https://venngage.com/templates/mind-maps/cyber-security-framework-mind-map-4f764669-28f5-411c-aa0b-6119d2c2acce

Verizon Business. (2022). *2022 Data Breach Investigations Report*. Verizon Business. Retrieved May 12, 2023, from https://www.verizon.com/business/resources/reports/dbir/

Verkada. (2021). *State of Physical Security 2021*. Genetec. Retrieved May 12, 2023, from https://resources.genetec.com/en-infographics/state-of-physical-security-2021

Vidhate, A. V., Saraf, C. R., Wani, M. A., Waghmare, S. S., & Edgar, T. (2022). Applying Blockchain Security for Agricultural Supply Chain Management. In *Research Anthology on Convergence of Blockchain, Internet of Things, and Security* (pp. 1229–1239). IGI Global. doi:10.4018/978-1-6684-7132-6.ch065

Wagner, E., Heye, D., Serror, M., Kunze, I., Wehrle, K., & Henze, M. (2023). *MADTLS: Fine-grained middlebox-aware end-to-end security for industrial communication. arXiv*. Cornell University., doi:10.1145/3634737.3637640

Walden, A., Cortelyou-Ward, K., Gabriel, M. H., & Noblin, A. (2020). To report or not to report health care data breaches. *The American Journal of Managed Care*, *26*(12), e395–e402. doi:10.37765/ajmc.2020.88546 PMID:33315333

Waller, L., & Genius, A. (2015). Barriers to transforming government in Jamaica: Challenges to implementing initiatives to enhance the efficiency, effectiveness and service delivery of government through ICTs (e-Government). *Transforming Government: People, Process and Policy*. https://www.emerald.com/insight/content/doi/10.1108/TG-12-2014-0067/full/html?fullSc=1

Wallis, T., & Dorey, P. (2023). Implementing partnerships in energy supply chain cybersecurity resilience. *Energies*, *16*(4), 1868. doi:10.3390/en16041868

Wang, Li, Liu, & Zhang. (n.d.). Real-time cyber-physical security solution leveraging an integrated learning-based approach: An integrated learningbased cyber-physical security solution. *ACM Transactions on Sensor Networks*.

Wang, Y., Jiang, D., Huo, L., & Zhao, Y. (2021). A new traffic prediction algorithm to software defined networking. *Mobile Networks and Applications*, *26*(2), 716–725. doi:10.1007/s11036-019-01423-3

Waters, D. (2016). *Supply Chain Risk Management: Vulnerability and Resilience in Logistics*. http://ci.nii.ac.jp/ncid/BB07882667

Wayne, T. (2014). *Benefits of Elliptic Curve Cryptography*. https://casecurity.org/2014/06/10/benefits-of-elliptic-curve-cryptography

Weil, T., & Murugesan, S. (2020). IT Risk and Resilience-Cybersecurity Response to COVID-19. *IT Professional*, *22*(3), 4–10. doi:10.1109/MITP.2020.2988330

Weippl, E., & Schrittwieser, S. (2023). Introduction to Security and Privacy. In SpringerLink (pp. 397–414). doi:10.1007/978-3-031-45304-5_26

Wen, H., Cao, Z., Zhang, Y., Cao, X., Fan, Z., Voigt, D., & Du, D. (2018, September). Joins: Meeting latency slo with integrated control for networked storage. In *2018 IEEE 26th International Symposium on Modeling, Analysis, and Simulation of Computer and Telecommunication Systems (MASCOTS)* (pp. 194-200). IEEE.

WensveenJ. G. (2023). *Air transportation*. doi:10.4324/9780429346156

Wiggen, J. (2020). *Impact of COVID-19 on cyber crime and state-sponsored cyber activities*. Konrad Adenauer Stiftung. https://www.jstor.org/stable/pdf/resrep25300.pdf?acceptTC=true&coverpage=false

Wijayanto, H., & Prabowo, I. A. (2020). Cybersecurity Vulnerability Behavior Scale in College During the Covid-19 Pandemic. *Jurnal Sisfokom (Sistem Informasi dan Komputer)*, *9*(3),395-399. https://www.aimspress.com/article/id/6087e948ba35de2200eea776

Williams, C. M., Chaturvedi, R., & Chakravarthy, K. (2020). Cybersecurity Risks in a Pandemic. *Journal of Medical Internet Research*, *22*(9), e23692. doi:10.2196/23692 PMID:32897869

Windapo, A., & Chiswanda, F. (2023). Perspectives of severity in the choice of risk management techniques. *E3S Web of Conferences*, *409*, 03016. doi:10.1051/e3sconf/202340903016

Wipro. (n.d.). *Importance of cybersecurity in the manufacturing industry*. WiPro. https://www.wipro.com/cybersecurity/cybersecurity-in-the-manufacturing-industry/

Wolak, Lysionok, Kosturek, Wi´sniewski, Wawryszuk, Kawa, Davidson, Ma´ckowiak, Starzyk, & Kulikowska-Wielgus. (2019). *Technological revolution. Directions in the development of the transport-forwarding-logistics (tfl) sector*. Academic Press.

Womack, J. E., & Jones, D. B. (1997). Lean Thinking—Banish Waste and Create Wealth in your Corporation. *The Journal of the Operational Research Society*, *48*(11), 1148. doi:10.1057/palgrave.jors.2600967

Wong, L., Lee, V., Tan, G. W., Ooi, K., & Sohal, A. S. (2022). The role of cybersecurity and policy awareness in shifting employee compliance attitudes: Building supply chain capabilities. *International Journal of Information Management*, *66*, 102520. doi:10.1016/j.ijinfomgt.2022.102520

World Health Organization. (2020). *WHO reports fivefold increase in cyber-attacks, urges vigilance*. WHO.

Wu, X., Du, Y., Fan, T., Guo, J., Ren, J., Wu, R., & Zheng, T. (2022a). Threat analysis for space information network based on network security attributes: A review. *Complex & Intelligent Systems*, *9*(3), 3429–3468. doi:10.1007/s40747-022-00899-z

Wu, Y., Wu, Y., Guerrero, J. M., & Vasquez, J. C. (2022). Decentralized transactive energy community in edge grid with positive buildings and interactive electric vehicles. *International Journal of Electrical Power & Energy Systems*, *135*, 107510. doi:10.1016/j.ijepes.2021.107510

Wylde, V., Prakash, E., Hewage, C., & Platts, J. (2023). Ethical challenges in the use of digital technologies: AI and big data. In Advanced sciences and technologies for security applications (pp. 33–58). Springer. doi:10.1007/978-3-031-09691-4_3

Wynn, M. G., & Jones, P. (2023). Corporate digital responsibility and the business implications of quantum computing. *Advances in Environmental and Engineering Research*, *04*(04), 1–15. doi:10.21926/aeer.2304053

Xiao, F., Zhang, J., Huang, J., Gu, G., Wu, D., & Liu, P. (2020). *Unexpected data dependency creation and chaining: a new attack to sdn. 2020 IEEE Symposium on Security and Privacy.*

Xiaojun, L., Ming, S., & Yuzhuo, L. (2023). Research on logistics service recommendation model and application under mobile cloud environment. *Optik (Stuttgart)*, *273*, 170446. doi:10.1016/j.ijleo.2022.170446

Xia, Q., Sifah, E. B., Smahi, A., Amofa, S., & Zhang, X. (2017). BBDS: Blockchain-based data sharing for electronic medical records in cloud environments. *Information (Basel)*, *8*(2), 44. doi:10.3390/info8020044

Xiong, Y., Lu, H., Li, G. D., Xia, S. M., Wang, Z. X., & Xu, Y. F. (2022). Game changer or threat: The impact of 3D printing on the logistics supplier circular supply chain. *Industrial Marketing Management*, *106*, 461–475. doi:10.1016/j.indmarman.2022.03.002

Xu, D., Wu, Y., & Duan, Y. (2017). *Sybil Attack Detection Scheme Based on Data Flow Monitoring and RSSI ranging in WSN*. doi:10.25236/icmit.2017.19

Xu, H., Zeng, M., Hu, W., & Wang, J. (2019). Authentication-Based Vehicle-to-Vehicle Secure Communication for VANETs. Mobile Information Systems. doi:10.1155/2019/7016460

XuanY. M.XuenM. T. Y.MuzafarS. (2023). *Cloud Computing Migration: A Thoughtful Decision.* doi:10.20944/preprints202311.0850.v1

Yaffe-Bellany, D. (2019, August 1). Equifax Data-Breach Settlement: Get Up to $20,000 If You Can Prove Harm. *The New York Times*. https://www.nytimes.com/2019/07/22/business/equifax-data-breach-claim.html

Yaga, D. J., Mell, P., Roby, N., & Scarfone, K. A. (2018). *Blockchain technology overview.* doi:10.6028/NIST.IR.8202

Yang, R., & Wibowo, S. (2020). *Risks and Uncertainties in Citizens' Trust and Adoption of E-Government: A Proposed Framework.* Academic Press.

Yang, R., & Wibowo, S. (2020). *Risks and Uncertainties in Citizens' Trust and Adoption of E-Government: A Proposed Framework.* https://aisel.aisnet.org/cgi/viewcontent.cgi?article=1073&context=acis2020

Yang, F., Wang, S., Li, J., Liu, Z., & Sun, Q. (2014, October). An overview of Internet of Vehicles. *China Communications*, *11*(10), 1–15. doi:10.1109/CC.2014.6969789

Yang, L., Elisa, N., & Eliot, N. (2019). Privacy and security aspects of E-government in smart cities. In *Smart cities cybersecurity and privacy* (pp. 89–102). Elsevier. doi:10.1016/B978-0-12-815032-0.00007-X

Yang, T., Guo, Q., Tai, X., Sun, H., Zhang, B., Zhao, W., & Lin, C. (2017, November). Applying blockchain technology to decentralized operation in future energy internet. In *2017 IEEE Conference on Energy Internet and Energy System Integration (EI2)* (pp. 1-5). IEEE. 10.1109/EI2.2017.8244418

Yang, W., Li, J., Zhang, Y., Li, Y., Shu, J., & Gu, D. (2014). APKLancet: tumor payload diagnosis and purification for android applications. *Proceedings of the 9th ACM symposium on Information, computer and communications security.* 10.1145/2590296.2590314

Yassein, M. B., Aljawarneh, S., Al-Rousan, M., Mardini, W., & Al-Rashdan, W. (2017, November). Combined software-defined network (SDN) and Internet of Things (IoT). In 2017 international conference on electrical and computing technologies and applications (ICECTA) (pp. 1-6). IEEE.

Yazdanmehr, A., Wang, J., & Yang, Z. (2020). Peers matter: The moderating role of social influence on information security policy compliance. *Information Systems Journal*, *30*(5), 791–844. doi:10.1111/isj.12271

Yeboah-Ofori, A., & Opoku-Boateng, F. A. (2023). Mitigating cybercrimes in an evolving organizational landscape. *Continuity & Resilience Review*, *5*(1), 53–78. doi:10.1108/CRR-09-2022-0017

Yli-Huumo, J., Ko, D., Choi, S., Park, S., & Smolander, K. (2016). Where is current research on blockchain technology?—A systematic review. *PLoS One*, *11*(10), e0163477. doi:10.1371/journal.pone.0163477 PMID:27695049

Yodo, N., & Wang, P. (2016). Engineering Resilience Quantification and System Design Implications: A Literature Survey. *Journal of Mechanical Design*, *138*(11), 111408. doi:10.1115/1.4034223

Yoo, C. W., Sanders, G. L., & Cerveny, R. P. (2018). Exploring the influence of flow and psychological ownership on security education, training and awareness effectiveness and security compliance. *Decision Support Systems*, *108*, 107–118. doi:10.1016/j.dss.2018.02.009

Yu, Y., Wang, X., Zhong, R. Y., & Huang, G. Q. (2016). E-commerce Logistics in Supply Chain Management: Practice Perspective. *Procedia CIRP*, *52*, 179–185. doi:10.1016/j.procir.2016.08.002

Zaenchkovski, A., Lazarev, A., & Masyutin, S. (2023). Multi-factor Authentication in Innovative Business Systems of Industrial Clusters. In Lecture notes in electrical engineering (pp. 271–281). Springer Science+Business Media. doi:10.1007/978-3-031-22311-2_27

Zanella, A., Bui, N., Castellani, A., Vangelista, L., & Zorzi, M. (2014). *Internet of things for smart cities*. Academic Press.

Zaripova, R., Kosulin, V., Shkinderov, M., & Rakhmatullin, I. (2023). Unlocking the potential of artificial intelligence for big data analytics. *E3S Web of Conferences, 460*, 04011. doi:10.1051/e3sconf/202346004011

Zawaideh, F., Abu-Ulbeh, W., Majdalawi, Y. I., Zakaria, M. D., Jusoh, J. A., & Das, S. (2023). E-Commerce Supply Chains with Considerations of Cyber-Security. *2023 International Conference on Computer Science and Emerging Technologies (CSET)*. IEEE. 10.1109/CSET58993.2023.10346738

Zhang, Y., Sóti, G., Hein, B., & Wurll, C. (2023). KI5GRob: Fusing Cloud Computing and AI for Scalable Robotic System in Production and Logistics. doi:10.1007/978-3-031-22216-0_47

Zhang, A., Luo, W., Shi, Y., Chia, S. H., & Sim, Z. H. X. (2016). Lean and Six Sigma in logistics: A pilot survey study in Singapore. *International Journal of Operations & Production Management*, *36*(11), 1625–1643. doi:10.1108/IJOPM-02-2015-0093

Zhang, H., Jia, F., & You, J. (2021). Striking a balance between supply chain resilience and supply chain vulnerability in the cross-border e-commerce supply chain. *International Journal of Logistics*, *26*(3), 320–344. doi:10.1080/13675567.2021.1948978

Zhang, Q., Shi, L., & Sun, S. (2023). Optimization of intelligent logistics system based on big data collection techniques. In *The International Conference on Cyber Security Intelligence and Analytics* (pp. 378–387). Springer. 10.1007/978-3-031-31860-3_40

Zhang, Y., Guo, Z., Lv, J., & Liu, Y. (2018, September). A framework for smart production-logistics systems based on CPS and industrial IoT. *IEEE Transactions on Industrial Informatics*, *14*(9), 4019–4032. doi:10.1109/TII.2018.2845683

Zhang, Z., Jin, J., Li, S., & Zhang, Y. (2023). Digital transformation of incumbent firms from the perspective of portfolios of innovation. *Technology in Society*, *72*, 102149. doi:10.1016/j.techsoc.2022.102149

Zhao, Z., Hao, Y., Chang, R., & Wang, Q. (2023). Assessing the vulnerability of energy supply chains: Influencing factors and countermeasures. *Sustainable Energy Technologies and Assessments*, *56*, 103018. doi:10.1016/j.seta.2023.103018

Zheng, Z., Xie, S., Dai, H. N., Chen, X., & Wang, H. (2018). Blockchain challenges and opportunities: A survey. *International Journal of Web and Grid Services, 14*(4), 352-375. https://www.inderscienceonline.com/doi/abs/10.1504/IJWGS.2018.095647

Zhu, J. (2018). Methods and System for Providing Software Defined Microcontroller Unit (MCU). Google Patents.

Zhu, K. J. (2017). A review of literature on the logistics and transportation service quality: A comprehensive analysis. *International Journal of Logistics Management*, *28*(4), 1118–1141. doi:10.1108/IJLM-08-2015-0136

Zhu, T., Kozuch, M. A., & Harchol-Balter, M. 2017. WorkloadCompactor: Reducing Datacenter Cost While Providing Tail Latency SLO Guarantees. In *8th ACM Symposium on Cloud Computing (SoCC 17).* ACM. 10.1145/3127479.3132245

Zong, S., Ritter, A., Mueller, G., & Wright, E. (2019). Analyzing the perceived severity of cybersecurity threats reported on social media. *arXiv preprint arXiv:1902.10680*. doi:10.18653/v1/N19-1140

About the Contributors

***

Humaira Ashraf is an accomplished Assistant Professor at the School of Computer Science, Faculty of Innovation & Technology, Taylors University, Malaysia. Boasting a rich experience of 18 years and 10 months, she has held significant leadership roles, including Head of Department for Computer Science at both the International Islamic University, Islamabad, and Sardar Bahadur Khan Women's University, Quetta. With a profound commitment to excellence, Dr. Ashraf has been recognized for her teaching prowess with the Teaching Excellence Award 2015-2016. Her contributions extend beyond teaching to impactful research work, featuring publications on diverse topics such as online reviews classification, deep learning-based question answering systems, and secure logistics monitoring systems. Dr. Ashraf's professional journey is marked by achievements, including the design and development of cutting-edge programs such as MS Data Science and Bachelor of Information Systems (Hons). Her expertise encompasses curriculum design, accreditation, and active participation in national and international research projects. Driven by a belief in trust-based performance, commitment, and dedication, Dr. Humaira Ashraf's work ethic and leadership make her a valuable asset to any academic institution.

Sumathi Balakrishnan holds a Master of Software Engineering from the University of Malaya, Malaysia, and a Bachelor of Computer Science from the University Putra Malaysia. She has taught various courses at Taylor's University, including Capstone Project, Internet of Things, Industrial Project, and Computer Architecture and Organization. Additionally, the author has authored several articles and book chapters related to smart city technologies, IoT, and user-centered design. She has been involved in multiple research projects focusing on IoT, smart city technologies, EEG signal processing and elderly care. She has also received several awards and recognition for their innovations and research efforts. Furthermore, the author holds professional memberships in Lembaga Teknologis Malaysia (MBOT) from 2022 to 2023, was also a member of IEEE from 2018 to 2019, and held a role of committee member in the IEEE Consumer Electronics Society Malaysia from 2018 to 2019.

Sarfraz Brohi is an educationist with extensive experience in curriculum development, programme audit and accreditation processes, UK-based higher education standards, assessment policies and analytical strategies to improve Teaching and Learning (T&L). He is the Programme Leader of MSc Information Technology and Senior Lecturer in Cyber Security in the Computer Science and Creative Technologies at UWE, Bristol. He has over ten years of computer science teaching, research and managerial experience at multiple universities, including Monash University Malaysia, Taylor's University and Asia Pacific University, where he served in various roles such as Senior Lecturer, Program Director and Coordinator of T&L. In his past administrative duties, he oversaw resource management, course coordination, staff recruitment, students support services and worked as a line manager. He provides consultancy to the universities and proudly participates in community engagement programs and outreach activities. His research domains include cyber security methods for connected places, unmanned aerial vehicles communication security, cloud security and machine learning techniques for malware detection. He supports journals as a reviewer/editorial board member and has presented research at international conferences organised in various countries such as New Zealand, Malaysia, United Arab Emirates, United Kingdom, Pakistan, Saudi Arabia, France, Singapore and Spain. He supervises undergraduate and postgraduate students on industry projects and dissertations. He has a reliable network of collaborators and secured funding from the British Council, Taylor's University and the Ministry of Higher Education Malaysia.

Sarfraz Brohi is an educationist with extensive experience in curriculum development, programme audit and accreditation processes, UK-based higher education standards, assessment policies and analytical strategies to improve Teaching and Learning (T&L). He is the Programme Leader of MSc Information Technology and Senior Lecturer in Cyber Security in the Computer Science and Creative Technologies at UWE, Bristol. He has over ten years of computer science teaching, research and managerial experience at multiple universities, including Monash University Malaysia, Taylor's University and Asia Pacific University, where he served in various roles such as Senior Lecturer, Program Director and Coordinator of T&L. In his past administrative duties, he oversaw resource management, course coordination, staff recruitment, students support services and worked as a line manager. He provides consultancy to the universities and proudly participates in community engagement programs and outreach activities. His research domains include cyber security methods for connected places, unmanned aerial vehicles communication security, cloud security and machine learning techniques for malware detection. He supports journals as a reviewer/editorial board member and has presented research at international conferences organised in various countries such as New Zealand,

Malaysia, United Arab Emirates, United Kingdom, Pakistan, Saudi Arabia, France, Singapore and Spain. He supervises undergraduate and postgraduate students on industry projects and dissertations. He has a reliable network of collaborators and secured funding from the British Council, Taylor's University and the Ministry of Higher Education Malaysia.

Sharon Goh Wei Wei is the Programme Director of the Dual Awards program in the School of Computing and IT, Faculty of Innovation and Technology in Taylor's University. Her expertise is in e-Learning Technologies. Her research interests includes E-Learning technologies, emerging web technologies, critical thinking skills, learning theories, MOOC, ontological based webpage segmentation, tools and applications, social media marketing and communications as well as persuasive messages and communications in social media. Some of her professional affiliations includes the International Association of Computer Science and Information Technology (IACSIT) and IEEE.

Kassim Kalinaki (MIEEE) is a passionate technologist, researcher, and educator with more than ten years of experience in industry and academia. He received his Diploma in Computer engineering from Kyambogo University, a BSc in computer science and engineering, and an MSc. Computer Science and Engineering from Bangladesh's Islamic University of Technology (IUT). Since 2014, He has been lecturing at the Islamic University in Uganda (IUIU), where he most recently served as the Head of Department Computer Science department (2019-2022). Currently, he's pursuing his Ph.D. in Computer Science at the School of Digital Science at Universiti Brunei Darussalam (UBD) since January 2022 and is slated to complete in August 2025. He's the founder and principal investigator of Borderline Research Laboratory (BRLab) and his areas of research include Ecological Informatics, Data Analytics, Computer Vision, ML/DL, Digital Image Processing, Cybersecurity, IoT/AIoMT, Remote Sensing, and Educational Technologies. He has authored and co-authored several published peer-reviewed articles in renowned journals and publishers, including in Springer, Elsevier, Taylor and Francis, Emerald and IEEE.

Amaranadha Reddy Manchuri, is a Research Professor at the environment and energy systems engineering laboratory, Department of Environment Engineering, Kyungpook National University, Daegu, South Korea. Currently, he is conducting research in a comprehensive discipline focused on engaging Machine learning in energy and environmental applications. His research and innovations lie in Sustainable Energy Technologies, Catalysis, Nanomaterials, Intelligent Systems, and Mathematical modeling. Dr. ANR is an alumnus of University Malaysia Sarawak, Malaysia where he obtained a Doctoral degree in Mechanical and Manufacturing Engineering and Undergraduate and Master's degrees from Jawaharlal Nehru Technological University, Hyderabad, India. He is a recipient of 'The Malaysian International Scholarship Govt. of Malaysia; 'Zamalah Graduate Scholarship UNIMAS, Malaysia; and Two Silver medals for his State-of-the-art research innovations in biofuels and nanocatalysts'. Since 2000, Dr Manchuri has been working in academic and research institutions and served in various responsible positions. He is a principal investigator of AICTE, Govt. of India, sponsored research project "Multi-Objective Optimization of Production Process Parameters using Evolutionary Algorithms". Dr ANR is a life member of ORSI, ISTAM, IndACM, ISTE, and EWB. He has active research collaborations with researchers in Japan, Korea, Malaysia, and India and Dr Manchuri has more than 37 research papers in national & international peer-reviewed journals, 01 patent to his credit, and served as an Editor for 04 conferences.

Sarah Namuwaya is highly accomplished procurement and logistics professional with a Bachelor of Procurement and Logistics from Islamic University in Uganda (IUIU) females' campus and an MSc in Procurement and Supply Chain Management from Kyambogo University. She has a passion for logistics operations and supply chain management with extensive experience in both the private and public sector. She is a certified Chartered Institute of Procurement and Supply (CIPS) member and regularly attends industry events and is actively involved in professional organizations, demonstrating her dedication to stay up-to-date in the field. She has previously worked as senior procurement officer at Wakiso District Local government and currently works as a senior officer Performance Monitoring – Regional offices at the Procurement and Disposal of Public Assets (PPDA), a government agency under the ministry of finance planning and economic development of Uganda. Sarah is known for her strong leadership skills, outstanding negotiation skills, strategic thinking, and expertise in managing complex procurement operations and supply chains as well as being passionate about the integration of digital technologies in procurement and supply chain operations.

Sumaya Namuwaya is a passionate accountant and customer care specialist with experience in the banking sector. She received her bachelor of accounting and finance from Kyambogo University in 2019 and works as a collections officer with Absa Bank Uganda Limited. She's pursuing her professional certification as a Certified Public Accountant (CPA) in Uganda. Her research interests include Finance and Accounts, Auditing, and Customer care excellence.

Wasswa Shafik (IEEE member, P.Eng) received a B.Sc. degree with honour rank in Mathematics and Computer Science in 2016 from Ndejje University, and an M.Sc. degree in Information Technology Engineering (MIT) in 2020, from the Computer

Engineering Department, Yazd University, Islamic Republic of Iran. He is an associate researcher at the Computer Science department, Network interconnectivity Lab at Yazd University, Islamic Republic of Iran, and at Information Sciences, Prince Sultan University, Saudi Arabia. He is the author and co-author of more than 80 papers in IEEE/ACM/IET/CRC press/IGI-Global/Wiley/Springer/Elsevier journals, conference papers, books and book chapters. He received many awards; the best M.Sc. student award from Yazd University, Iran, 2020, Young scientific research award. His areas of interest are Anomaly Detection, Drones (UAVs), Machine/ Deep Learning, AI-enabled IoT/IoMTs, IoT/IIoT/OT Security, Cyber Security and Privacy. Shafik is the chair/co-chair/program chair of some Scopus/EI conferences. Also, academic editor/ associate editor for set of indexed journals (Scopus journals' quartile ranking). He is the founder and lead investigator of Digital Connectivity Research Laboratory (DCR-Lab) since 2019.

Chong Eng Tan, an Associate Professor at Universiti Malaysia Sarawak (UNIMAS), has been a dedicated member of the Faculty of Computer Science and Information Technology since 1999. He earned his Ph.D. from the University of Cambridge in 2004, specializing in wireless networks and broadband access technology. With over 25 years of research experience, Dr. Tan has focused his research on connecting remote areas to the internet. Notably, he designed the pilot long-range wireless system in 2010 in Bario and played a pivotal role in establishing Telecentres in remote locations in Malaysia. Dr. Tan is a senior member of the IEEE and a graduate member of IEM, and he currently leads the 5G& Connectivity Keylab, contributing significantly to technology advancements in connectivity and rural ICT solutions. His notable research achievements include the development of the Virtual Telecentre concept and innovative solar power solutions for ICT systems.

Index

P

R

S

T

Milton Keynes UK
Ingram Content Group UK Ltd.
UKHW020842130324
439347UK00007BA/119